· **International Uniform Sunday School Series**

Editor
Wesley C. Reagan

Contributing Writers
Ron Durham, Ph.D.
Doug deGraffenried
David Dietzel
Phil Woodland, Ph.D.
William B. Wharton, Ph.D.
John Wright

Illustrator
Billy Ledet

The **Higley Commentary**, in this sixty-fifth year of its life, renews its commitment to careful and reverent scholarship, clear and understandable language, practical and insightful application, and interesting and readable writing. We send it to you with a prayer that it will be a powerful resource to you.

Higley Publishing Corporation
P. O. Box 5398
Jacksonville FL 32247-5398

Foreword

This is the sixty-fifth edition of **The Higley Commentary**. I have been involved in this ministry, either as a contributing writer or editor, since 1973. I continue to be impressed with the conscientious efforts that are made to make **The Higley Commentary** a truly helpful aid to the study of the Scriptures.

Without exception, the writers have . . .

* Good minds
* Tender hearts
* Excellent knowledge of the Bible
* Perceptive insight into human life
* Keen awareness of contemporary needs and problems
* Disciplined writing skills

These writers bring this significant collection of assets to bear on producing for you the finest of teaching and study resources. Our work and prayers have combined in hope of making this volume the best ever. We will try to improve on this one as we work on the sixty-sixth edition for next year.

May God bless your work and ours to bring hope, peace, and love to those who seek Him.

Wesley C. Reagan, Editor
The Higley Commentary

Lessons and/or readings are based on International Sunday School Lessons. The International Bible Lessons for Christian Training, copyright © 1991 by the Committee on the Uniform Series.

Preface

For fifteen years, working as a family law attorney, I have heard the following words on almost a daily basis, "My marriage is over." Just the notion of "no-fault" divorce says to us, "You are not responsible for breaking your marriage covenants and destroying your family. In fact, *no one* is responsible." We live in a sea of moral unaccountability and relational unfaithfulness. Even in the church, cultural Christianity often appears on the surface while chaos lurks just beneath.

By contrast, the old and new covenant Scriptures tell us this world is charged with God's grandeur, full of his gracious preserve and directed by His will. This Holy God of Biblical revelation calls us to the true humanity of love, moral accountability and covenant faithfulness.

The Higley Commentary, read in conjunction with Scripture, points us again and again to the authority, grace and truth of the Lord God. This commentary annually covers sizable portions of the Scripture witness. The verse by verse exposition of Scripture coupled with the keen life application sections challenge our worldliness.

Our minds must be renewed. God's Holy Spirit in us will re-shape our minds—not just by giving us spiritual highs, but through the day-to-day feeding on God and His will. I urge you to use **The Higley Commentary** to help you feed on, not just to analyze, God's word.

Use this great commentary tool to clear your mind and feed your soul. Prayerful use of this resource will help cause family attorneys, like myself, to go bankrupt! Praise God!

Jim Reynolds

Copyright © 1997
Higley Publishing Corporation
Available in
Softback ISBN 1-886763-07-0
Hardback ISBN 1-886763-08-9
Adult Student ISBN 1-886763-09-7

FALL QUARTER

God Leads A People Home

Unit I—The Opportunity to Return (Lessons 1–4)
Unit II—Daniel: A Call to Faithfulness (Lessons 5–8)
Unit III—Life After the Return (Lessons 9–13)

WINTER QUARTER

God's People in a Troubled World

Unit I—God's Love in a Troubled World (Lessons 1–4)
Unit II—God's People Living in Hope (Lessons 5–8)
Unit III—God's People Believing in Truth (Lessons 9–12)

SPRING QUARTER
The Gospel of Mark

Unit I—Early Ministry of Jesus (Lessons 1-5)
Unit II—From Praise to Resurrection (Lessons 6-7)
Unit III—The Meaning of Jesus' Death (Lessons 8-9)
Unit IV—The Teachings of Jesus (Lessons 10-14)

SUMMER QUARTER

Wisdom for Living (Ecclesiastes, Job, Proverbs)

Unit I—When Human Wisdom Fails (Lessons 1-4)
Unit II—Proverbs on Living a Disciplined Life (Lessons 5-8)
Unit III—The Way of Wisdom and the Way of Foolishness (Lessons 9-13)

Lesson 1

God Works for Good

Isaiah 44:24-26; 45:1, 4-7

24 Thus saith the Lord, thy redeemer, and he that formed thee from the womb, I am the LORD that maketh all things; that stretcheth forth the heavens alone; that spreadeth abroad the earth by myself;

25 That frustrateth the tokens of the liars, and maketh diviners mad; that turneth wise men backward, and maketh their knowledge foolish.

26 That confirmeth the word of his servant, and performeth the counsel of his messengers; that saith to Jerusalem, Thou shalt be inhabited; and to the cities of Judah, Ye shall be built, and I will raise up the decayed places thereof:

45:1 Thus saith the LORD to his anointed, to Cyrus anointed, to Cyrus, whose right hand I have holden, to subdue nations before him; and I will loose the loins of kings, to open before him the two leaved gates; and the gates shall not be shut;

4 For Jacob my servant's sake and Israel mine elect, I have even called thee by thy name: I have surnamed thee, though thou hast not known me.

5 I am the LORD, and there is none else, there is no God beside me: I girded thee, though thou hast not known me:

6 that they may know from the rising of the sun, and from the west, that there is none bgeside me. I am the LORD, and there is none else.

7 I form the light, and create darkness: I make peace, and create evil: I the Lord do all these things.

Memory Selection
Isaiah 44:22

Devotional Reading
Jeremiah 31:1-9

Background Scripture
Isaiah 44:21–45:8

Printed Scripture
Isaiah 44:24-26; 45:1, 4-7

1

Teacher's Target

Lesson Purpose: *To affirm, with the prophet Isaiah, the sovereignty of God over all of life, and to build trust that He can work in our lives through both the good times and the bad.*

For many believers, God's presence is easily affirmed when their health is good, the job is going well, the children aren't in trouble and the car hasn't broken down lately. When things go wrong, however, three questions spring easily to mind: *Why me? Why this? Why now?*

In other words, where is God in the hard times?

This lesson envisions God's people carried away from the Promised Land into Babylonia. Despite their discouragement, Isaiah insists that God is with them in that strange land. They are even able to see Him working through an alien king. Encourage class members to share experiences when they have felt the absence of God, and times when they eventually experienced Him—even in the hard times.

Lesson Introduction

The lessons in this quarter survey the gloomy days when God's people were led captive into Babylonia. In the first part of the book of Isaiah, the prophet warns the people, who had turned to other gods, that their unfaithfulness would bring on this exile. Sure enough, this occurred in 586 B.C., when Babylonia conquered the land and carried many of the people away into captivity.

Chapters 40–66 reflect this sad episode in Jewish history. We can hear the people's grief in the somber lament of Psalm 137:4: "How can we sing the Lord's song in a strange land?" (Ps. 137:4). In the present lesson, however, God reminds them that because He is the one true God, He was with them even in their exile.

The power of the Babylonians waned, and they in turn were conquered by the Persians. In His sovereign power, God called the Persian king Cyrus to be the deliverer of the Jews, and to allow them to return to their homeland.

Teaching Outline	Daily Bible Readings
I. The God Over All Creation–44:24-26	**Mon.** A Faithful God Deals with Rebellion *Isaiah 63:7-14*
A. Over nature, 24	**Tues.** See the Greatness of God *Isaiah 44:1-8*
B. Over people who defy Him, 25	**Wed.** Return with the Redeemed *Isaiah 44:21-28*
C. Over the people He loves, 26	**Thu.** God Defends the Servant People *Isaiah 41:1-10*
II. The God Over All People–45:1, 4-6	**Fri.** Water for the Poor *Isaiah 45:14-20*
A. The call of Cyrus, 45:1	**Sat.** Cyrus Serves God's People *Isaiah 45:1-8*
B. The witness to the nations, 4-6	**Sun.** River Gladdens the City of God *Psalm 46:1-11*
III. The God Over Good and Evil–45:7	

VERSE BY VERSE

I. God Over All Creation—44:24-26

A. Over nature, 44:24

24 Thus saith the Lord, thy redeemer, and he that formed thee from the womb, I am the Lord that maketh all things; that stretcheth forth the heavens alone; that spreadeth abroad the earth by myself;

The book of Isaiah emphasizes a basic biblical teaching that is capsuled in Deuteronomy 6:4— "Hear, O Israel: the Lord our God is one Lord." The other nations in the Middle East at this time worshipped many gods; but Israel was commanded to have "no other gods before me" (Exod. 20:3; see Isa. 45:5, below).

Why does Isaiah emphasize the doctrine of one God, or monotheism, at a time when Israel was in such distress? Their kings had been destroyed or deposed and their holy city, Jerusalem, was reduced to rubble. The people mourned their exile in a foreign land. Why does the prophet not just counsel the people to cheer up? Why preach what some might call an abstract doctrine at a time like this?

Recall that one reason God's people were in this predicament was that they had forgotten the doctrine of one God. They had lapsed into idolatry like the nations about them (Isa. 2:8). Since false gods had been their downfall, they could be restored only by reaffirming the one God.

In this verse, God speaks directly to His people, affirming to them that He is nature's Creator. While pagans often claimed their gods were "nature gods," and could control the elements, the true God created the elements. If the Jews could bring themselves to believe again that it was God who formed them in their mothers' wombs, and who made heaven and earth, perhaps they could also trust Him to redeem them from both their sin and their captivity.

B. Over people who defy Him, 25

25 That frustrateth the tokens of the liars, and maketh diviners mad; that turneth wise men backward, and maketh their knowledge foolish.

Isaiah uses both severe language and biting satire to describe God's sovereignty over the "shamans" or seers and magicians who served pagan gods. They have no real wisdom or knowledge, but perform their works by trickery. Here God's people are again subtly encouraged to trust the God who can so thoroughly expose these false prophets that they go mad.

This principle is illustrated in the apocryphal book, "Bel and the Dragon," which is set in this very period when the Jews were held captive in Babylonia. The pagan Babylonians believed an idol called Bel ate food that the priests placed there every evening. To expose the false priests, Daniel is supposed to have crept into Bel's temple and sprinkled ashes over the floor. The next morning, when the people showed Daniel that the food

3

offered to Bel was gone, he laughed and pointed to footprints in the ashes. Then he led the people to a trap door where the priests had crept out, retrieved the food, and returned to their quarters. By standing for the true God, Daniel frustrated the claims of the lying priests.

C. Over the people He loves, 26

26 That confirmeth the word of his servant, and performeth the counsel of his messengers; that saith to Jerusalem, Thou shalt be inhabited; and to the cities of Judah, Ye shall be built, and I will raise up the decayed places thereof:

In contrast to showing false prophets to be liars, the true God confirms the word of His servant—here probably referring to Isaiah himself. Here the word to be believed is that having served the term of their punishment in captivity, God's people will be returned to their homeland. They will rebuild that which their disobedience had caused to be destroyed.

Such a promise is to be heard also by modern believers in the grip of depression or in life circumstances that seem to hold us captive, too. Can we also trust that God, being the only true God, is able to raise us up?

II. The God Over All People—45:1, 4-6

A. The call of Cyrus, 45:1

45:1 Thus saith the Lord to his anointed, to Cyrus, whose right hand I have holden, to subdue nations before him; and I will loose the loins of kings, to open before him the two leaved gates; and the gates shall not be shut;

Now the prophet affirms that the one God is sovereign even over pagan peoples. He can even use the pagan Cyrus, king of Persia as His "anointed"—literally His "messiah," which here simply means a deliverer. It must have come as a shock to some Jews to know that the God they felt was exclusively theirs could use this non-Jew to accomplish His will (see also 44:28). Yet such far-reaching powers are a necessary part of the doctrine that there is only one God; there is no other real power for Cyrus to serve, even though he has not known the identity of the true God who rules over all.

God assures Cyrus that he has raised him up to defeat the Jews' captors, the Babylonians. "Loosing the loins" refers to undoing the sash that men who wore robes used to tie them up out of the way, "girding their loins" for battle. The Babylonian princes would be helpless before Cyrus. The "two leaves" apparently refer to the gates of Babylon. In his annals, Cyrus recorded that there was no resistance when he took the city. The people and their rulers were helpless before him.

B. The witness to the nations, 4-6

4 For Jacob my servant's sake and Israel mine elect, I have even called thee by thy name: I have surnamed thee, though thou hast not known me.

5 I am the Lord, and there is none else, there is no God beside me: I girded thee, though thou hast not known me:

6 That they may know from the rising of the sun, and from the west, that there is none beside me. I am the Lord, and there is none else.

Cyrus is to understand that he is being called for the sake of glorifying

God and delivering His people, not for the king's own glorification. A marvelous drama is about to be enacted on the stage of world history. God will use a king who does not know Him to defeat a people who do not know Him in order to lift up the nation who does know Him! This unheard-of event will be a witness or testimony to all other nations that there is only one God, and that He will care for those who love and serve Him.

Back home in Palestine, the Jews had turned to other nations such as Egypt for deliverance (see Isa. 31:1). Here God is careful to make both Cyrus and the Jews understand that He, no human power, is the only true source of ultimate deliverance.

III. The God Over Good and Evil — 45:7

7 I form the light, and create darknesss; I make peace, and create evil: I the Lord do all these things.

This last claim to sovereignty is the most awesome of all, and in some ways the greatest test of faith. Aren't we to assume that while God is light, Satan and his forces are darkness? Isn't it God who makes peace, while His opposition creates evil? How can we understand the God of goodness being the creator of evil?

The answer, while far from simple, lies in the basic thrust of this entire section: monotheism. If there is only one God, everything is ultimately traceable to Him. It is significant that this difficult teaching is given to Cyrus the Persian; for the Persian religion conveniently balanced the chief good god with a chief bad god. That option is not open to biblical people. If there is only one Sovereign God, the origin of everything—the evil as well as the good—is ultimately to be found in Him.

The doctrine of Satan does give us a way at least to speak about the origin of evil, if not to understand it fully. We can speak of Satan's having been created by God, then choosing evil and becoming a fallen angel. After that event, evil can be traced to Satan. We do not charge God with being evil in Himself, but understand Him only to have created beings with free will, and hence the awful capacity for evil.

Even at this point, as we struggle with the idea of the origin of evil, the truth that there is one God comes to our aid. If He is One, He is sovereign over evil itself. We can then trust Him, as Jesus taught us to pray, to "deliver us from evil."

5

Evangelistic Emphasis

American Christians have been long blessed by the privilege of personal involvement in the democratic processes of government. We campaign and vote for our favorite candidates. We speak out in behalf of governmental action that we perceive to be important. We aggressively oppose such proposals or policies that we think detrimental to the values we treasure. At times the voting power of Christians has been so significant that candidates from all of the primary parties have actively attempted to cast themselves as "the Christian's choice."

All that is as it should be, perhaps. Unfortunately, within the context of such political privilege, it is easy for the Christian to begin to think of God as dependent upon and bound by the democratic processes of politics. He is not simply attempting to place a Christian candidate in office, because he deems that to be beneficial. Rather, he has come to think that God is dependent on having a Christian in office in order to carry out his plan.

As strange as it may have seemed to the Israelites at the time, God worked mightily in the life and rule of the pagan ruler Cyrus in order to bring about the fulfillment of his will. More recently, many would say that God worked mightily through the life and rule of Mikhail Gorbachev in order to bring to an end the religious oppression that had reigned in the Soviet Union for so many years.

I wonder how God is working in the life and rule of present world leaders? Since God is who He is, we can be quite confident He is doing exactly that. As to *how* He is doing that, we will just have to wait to see how it all unfolds.

Memory Selection

I have blotted out, as a thick cloud, thy transgressions, and, as a cloud, thy sins: return unto me; for I have redeemed thee. —*Isaiah 44:22*

Jack and I visited through thick glass with only a telephone receiver connecting our voices. Each week our conversation was about the same things—his family, his church and his faith. Much of our conversation focused on Jack's faith in God. Tragically, Jack remained locked up behind steel bars. He had not been able to touch his wife's face in over a year as he awaited trial. The crime Jack had committed was a terrible one. He had sinned. This he acknowledged without reservation. Yet, he spoke confidently of God's forgiveness.

Forgiven, yet imprisoned? It is hard to make sense of, isn't it? Yet, wasn't that exactly the situation of God's people as Isaiah prophesied to them the words above. God said they were forgiven. Yet, they were still to be held prisoners, behind the bars of Babylonia's iron rule. The day would come when they would run free again. This, God promised, but *not immediately!* Yet, as far as "forgiveness" was concerned, they were already forgive—even as they served out their time.

Weekday Problems

It was a Texas school board election. One of the can-
ditates in pursuit of a position on the board focused his
campaign heavily toward the Christian constituency,
especially pastors. Being a local pastor in his district, I
received a weekly mailing from his campaign manager for
several months prior to the election. The thrust of the
propaganda targeted the task of alerting pastors to the

urgency of "reclaiming our public school for Christ." The appeal was for me as a
pastor to use my influence to make sure that "our Christian candidate" James
Anderson be elected to the board. The very strong implication of the campaign
material was that Mr. Anderson was *the only Christian candidate running* and
would become the only Christian voice to stand against the residing secular powers.
It just so happened, though, I knew personally three of the residing school board
members to be very fine Christians who were highly involved in their churches.

     * Should I have contacted Mr. Anderson to let him know of my knowledge of the
Christian character of those other candidates? Why? / Why not?

     * Ought I to have involved myself in the campaign efforts of Mr. Anderson's
opponent since his campaign material was misleading? Why?/ Why not?

     * Should I have used my pulpit as a force to support the candidate of my choice?
If so, how? If not, why?

This and That

The Bible shouldn't be viewed as a textbook old people use to cram for
their Finals, but as a series of daily quizzes and mid-terms that surprise us
with their truth.

Headline in the newspaper in Normal, Ill., which isn't far from the town
of Oblong: "Normal boy marries Oblong girl."

❖ ❖ ❖

Dad to Tad, when the boy brought his report card home from school:
"Why did you get marked down in Conduct?"

Tad to Dad: "Conduct is my worst subject."

❖ ❖ ❖

Keeping the Law perfectly is as impossible as that law said to have been
on the books for years in the state of Kansas: "When two trains approach
each other at a crossing, they shall both come to a full stop, and neither shall
start again until the other has passed."

This Lesson in Your Life

His name on the street was *Joker*. As I looked across the table at this fifteen-year-old inmate, I found myself almost overwhelmed with sadness for him and his good family. The charge on the arrest sheet was "murder" and the district attorney was boasting that he was certain to put Joker away for life with no provision for parole. The papers had already been filed to have Joker tried as an adult. The probability appeared strong that his case would be moved to the adult court.

I did not know him as "Joker," though. I knew him as Tommy, the nickname he had taken to substitute for his very long Laotian name. Tommy went to high school with one of the boys in our youth group. When invited to come to a youth event, he had eagerly accepted. For several months he had come regularly—and not only to "fun events" like outings and ski trips. Tommy was there regularly on Sunday morning for Sunday school and worship. It had been through Tommy's involvement that his parents had recently become Christians.

Unfortunately, Tommy was living two lives. One included active involvement in church. The other life embraced the loyalties and hostilities of an inner-city Asian gang. Had the church had more time to work with Tommy, it might have *won out over* his gang loyalties. But, as I visited with him across the table, I realized that we had to deal with life as it had come to be, instead of as it could have been.

Years after Isaiah wrote the words of this text, Judah was faced with the very same reality. Life as it *might have been* was no longer an issue. The people of God had to come to terms with life as it had come to be. Rather than living in the bounty of their homeland, they had to carve out a different life as servants in a foreign land. Instead of dancing in the freedom of their independence, their hearts would have to learn to dance, in spite of their shackled feet. Instead of celebrating the goodness of God within the splendor of the Temple built to his honor, they discovered the temple of their own hearts. From that private temple, they offered their sacrifices of praise. Life in Babylon was not what they would have wished, but it was the life that was.

Life is like that for many of us, isn't it? Rather than delighting in the bounty that God has chosen for us to enjoy in His holy presence, our foolish choices repeatedly alienate us from Him. Fearing that we might miss out on some of life's thrills if we get too close to God, we keep our distance and miss out on his treasures. Tragically, there are many different ways that the life we end up with is far less than what it could have been. Like Judah, however, comforted in the assurance that God has not forgotten us, we accept the life that we have and glean from it God's alternate blessings. In the process, we learn both that we can be forgiven for our shortcomings and that he finds ways to bless us in spite of our brokenness.

8

Seed Thoughts

1. As Isaiah brought the Word of the Lord to Judah, was it a threatening word or a comforting word?

Even though this prophesy brought awareness of consequences from their sins, its underlying message was one of reassurance of God's Love.

2. What term of relationship did God use of Israel?

"My servant." He said, "I have formed thee; thou art my servant."

3. What two surprising terms did God use of Cyrus, King of Persia?

First, Cyrus is referred to as "my shepherd." Then he is spoken of as the Lord's "anointed" (the same word from which came the term "messiah.")

4. About how long would it be before Cyrus would come to power?

Conservative dating holds that Cyrus did not come to power for 201 years after Isaiah delivered his message.

5. How could Isaiah have known about the rise of Cyrus to power years before he was to be born?

The message did not originate with Isaiah. It was a message from God, only being delivered by Isaiah.

---

1. As Isaiah brought the Word of the Lord to Judah, was it a threatening word or a comforting word?

2. What term of relationship did God use of Israel?

3. What two surprising terms did God use of Cyrus, King of Persia?

4. About how long would it be before Cyrus would come to power?

5. How could Isaiah have known about the rise of Cyrus to power years before he was to be born?

6. When the time came, did God choose Cyrus to carry out his mission because of his life of faith and worship?

7. What message did God give to Isaiah for Cyrus to receive personally?

8. What two reasons are given for God making Cyrus powerful and wealthy?

"frustrateth the tokens of the liars, and maketh diviners mad;" and *"turneth wise men backward"*?

9. What does it mean that the Lord

10. The Lord said, "I make peace, and create evil." What did He mean by that?

(Please turn page)

Even though this prophesy brought awareness of consequences from their sins, it's underlying message was one of reassurance of God's Love.

"My servant." He said, "I have formed thee; thou art my servant."

First, Cyrus is referred to as "my shepherd." Then he is spoken of as the Lord's "anointed" (the same word from which came the term "messiah.")

Conservative dating holds that Cyrus did not come to power for 201 years after Isaiah delivered this message.

The message did not originate with Isaiah. It was a message from God, only being delivered by Isaiah.

No. Cyrus was a foreign ruler. God chose him even though he did not know God.

God's message to Cyrus was that He would go with Cyrus, make him powerful and prosperous.

First, so that Cyrus would know that He is the God of Israel. Second, so that Cyrus could carry out his wishes for the freedom of Jacob.

NIV translates it: ". . . who foils the signs of false prophets and makes fools of diviners, who overthrows the learning of the wise and turns it into nonsense."

His primary message is that He is in control. NIV yields the translation, "I bring prosperity and create disaster."

6. When the time came, did God choose Cyrus to carry out his mission because of his life of faith and worship?

No. Cyrus was a foreign ruler. God chose him even though he did not know God.

7. What message did God give to Isaiah for Cyrus to receive personally?

God's message to Cyrus was that He would go with Cyrus, make him powerful and prosperous.

8. What two reasons are given for God making Cyrus powerful and wealthy?

First, so that Cyrus would know that He is the God of Israel. Second, so that Cyrus could carry out his wishes for the freedom of Jacob.

9. What does it mean that the Lord *"frustrateth the tokens of the liars, and maketh diviners mad;"* and *"turneth wise men backward"*?

NIV translates it: ". . . who foils the signs of false prophets and makes fools of diviners, who overthrows the learning of the wise and turns it into nonsense."

10. The Lord said, "I make peace, and create evil." What did He mean by that?

His primary message is that He is in control. NIV yields the translation, "I bring prosperity and create disaster."

Return to the Lord

Isaiah 55:1-11

1 Ho, every one that thirsteth, come ye to the waters, and he that hath no money; come ye, buy, and eat; yea, come, buy wine and milk without money and without price.

2 Wherefore do ye spend money for that which is not bread? And your labour for that which satisfieth not? Hearken diligently unto me, and eat ye that which is good, and let your soul delight itself in fatness.

3 Incline your ear, and come unto me: hear, and your soul shall live; and I will make an everlasting covenant with you, even the sure mercies of David.

4 Behold I have given him for a witness to the people, a leader and commander to the people.

5 Behold, thou shalt call a nation that thou knowest not, and a nation that knew not thee shall run unto thee because of the Lord thy God, and for the Holy One of Israel; for he hath glorified thee.

6 Seek ye the Lord while he may be found, call ye upon him while he is near:

7 Let the wicked forsake his way, and the unrighteous man his thoughts: and let him return unto the Lord, and he will have mercy upon him; and to our God, for he will abundantly pardon.

8 For my thoughts are not your thoughts, neither are your ways my ways, saith the Lord.

9 For as the heavens are higher than the earth, so are my ways higher than your ways, and my thoughts than your thoughts.

10 For as the rain cometh down, and the snow from heaven, and returneth not thither, but watereth the earth, and maketh it bring forth and bud, that it may give seed to the sower, and bread to the eater:

11 So shall my word be that goeth forth out of my mouth: it shall not return unto me void, but it shall accomplish that which I please, and it shall prosper in the thing whereto I sent it.

Memory Selection

Isaiah 55:6

Devotional Reading

Isaiah 49:8-13

Background Scripture

Isaiah 55

Printed Scripture

Isaiah 55: 1-11

11

Teacher's Target

Lesson purpose: *To build confidence in God's gracious, covenant-renewing love when, having strayed, we are willing to return to Him.*

This lesson calls for special sensitivity on the part of the teacher. You will have in your class some who know their imperfections all too well. Some may be struggling with sin even while seeking God by being present in your class. The teacher is faced with the special challenge of accepting the sinner while holding up God's standards of faithfulness—just as you accept yourself, with your own shortcomings.

Emphasize both "the goodness and the severity of God" (Rom. 11:22). Don't trivialize the guilty conscience by leaving the impression that God is such a softie He doesn't care how we live; but don't neglect this text's powerful promise of grace and pardon for those who return to Him.

Lesson Introduction

God's people have suffered long enough in Babylonia. Like the modern believer who has grieved for days or weeks over a loved one, there comes a time to get on with life. After 70 years in captivity, God judges that the people's suffering is sufficient; it is time to return to the Promised Land.

There must be more than a physical return. The people must also return to the Lord in their hearts. They must repent. They must recover proper priorities, and seek God instead of currying favor from the surrounding nations and their gods.

A historical note may indicate a special problem with priorities. Archeologists have uncovered evidence of a Jewish bank—the firm of Murashu—in what was ancient Babylonia. Were some Jews beginning to trust in riches even in exile? The people are also urged to accept with joy and confidence God's forgiving grace—something even Christians sometimes have difficulty doing.

Teaching Outline	Daily Bible Readings	
	Mon.	Salvation Is Coming Soon *Isaiah 1:18-27*
I. Return to Your Heritage—1-2	**Tues.**	Peace for Evermore *Isaiah 54:1-10*
II. Renew the Covenant—3-5	**Wed.**	Streams in the Desert *Isaiah 35:1-10*
III. Repent and Be Pardoned—6-7	**Thu.**	Chosen to Be Light *Isaiah 49:1-7*
IV. Rely on God's Promises—8-11	**Fri.**	Released from Bondage *Isaiah 49:8-12*
A. God beyond understanding—8-9	**Sat.**	You're Invited! *Jeremiah 31:1-6*
B. The certain Word, 10-11	**Sun.**	Homecoming *Jeremiah 31:7-13*

VERSE BY VERSE

I. Return to Your Heritage—1-2

1 Ho, every one that thirsteth, come ye to the waters, and he that hath no money; come ye, buy, and eat; yea, come, buy wine and milk without money and without price.

2 Wherefore do ye spend money for that which is not bread? And your labour for that which satisfieth not? Hearken diligently unto me, and eat ye that which is good, and let your soul delight itself in fatness.

As the modern hymn has it, God moves in mysterious ways. Many Jews had pondered His ways in allowing them to be punished so severely by the Babylonians. Now God invites them to believe in His grace in allowing them to return to Palestine. Although they will be commanded to repent, it was God's grace, not human reformation, that had moved God to stir Cyrus to allow them to return (see the previous lesson). They cannot buy God's favor. It has no price on it because it is priceless. It is sheer grace.

The chapter opens, however, with the reminder that it takes a certain attitude to accept grace. We have to thirst for it (vs. 1). The Jews are in the position of the infirm man Jesus healed at the pool of Bethesda. It was necessary to ask him, "Do you want to get well?" (John 5:6, NIV). Hence God questions His people sharply here to see whether they earnestly desire His unmerited favor.

Verse 2 broadens this line of questioning, requiring that the Jews examine their priorities. Like so many today, they had been making bad investments. They had sought political alliances instead of seeking the face of God (Isa. 31:1-3). As the Lesson Introduction indicated, perhaps they had even grown to trust in the wealth their captors had allowed them to accumulate. Instead of trusting for their sustenance in these false securities, they are urged to delight in the spiritual nourishment God has to offer.

II. Renew the Covenant—3-5

3 Incline your ear, and come unto me: hear, and your soul shall live; and I will make an everlasting covenant with you, even the sure mercies of David.

4 Behold I have given him for a witness to the people, a leader and commander to the people.

5 Behold, thou shalt call a nation that thou knowest not, and nations that knew not thee shall run unto thee because of the Lord thy God, and for the Holy One of Israel; for he hath glorified thee.

If God had based His relationship with His people on human standards, repaying their faithlessness in kind, He would never have renewed the promise He had made to King David: "I will set up thy seed after thee . . . and I will stablish the throne of his kingdom for ever" (2 Sam. 7:12). God had made David a witness, a leader, and a commander; and here David's descendants will benefit from that covenant. The "sure mercies of David" are taken by ome commentators to refer to Christ, since there is little evidence that the reestablished nation of Israel regained the influence with other nations mentioned here. Perhaps the prophecy is to be "spiritualized" and understood as a reference to the way Christ, the Jew of all Jews, has been sought after by people in all nations.

III. Repent and Be Pardoned—6-7

6 Seek ye the Lord while he may be found, call ye upon him while he is near:

7 Let the wicked forsake his way, and the unrighteous man his thoughts: and let him return unto the Lord, and he will have mercy upon him; and to our God, for he will abundantly pardon.

Now we are hearing not the voice of God but that of the prophet, calling his people to repentance. Although the door of deliverance has been opened by sheer grace, it will not remain open in the face of people whose hearts are too hardened to enter again into faithfulness. Yet God will abundantly pardon those who forsake their unrighteousness.

IV. Rely on God's Promise—8-11
A. The God beyond understanding, 9

8 For my thoughts are not your thoughts, neither are your ways my ways, saith the Lord.

9 For as the heavens are higher than the earth, so are my ways higher than your ways, and my thoughts than your thoughts.

This passage is often used to exalt God as being wiser than humans—which is certainly true. Its first application, however, is to be found in what has been affirmed about God's grace. Any serious Jew might well have concluded that Judah's idolatry had earned God's eternal rejection—since we humans often find it impossible to forgive those who reject us. God's unmerited favor in allowing Judah to return to Palestine is based on some system beyond human understanding. This truth has been capsuled in the familiar adage, "To err is human; to forgive is divine."

B. The certain Word, 10-11

10 For as the rain cometh down, and the snow from heaven, and returneth not thither, but watereth the earth, and maketh it bring forth and bud, that it may give seed to the sower, and bread to the eater:

11 So shall my word be that goeth forth out of my mouth: it shall not return unto me void, but it shall accomplish that which I please, and it shall prosper in the thing whereto I sent it.

Although verse 1 emphasized the fact that one must "thirst" for the healing waters of God's grace, verse 11 emphasizes that the healing flood will produce fruit. Here is the balance between God's sovereignty and man's free will. Someone—in biblical terminology, a "remnant"—will respond to God's grace. His Word will not be wasted. It is up to the individual to choose whether to allow God to place him in that body of the graced.

Still, we can well imagine the difficulty a captive Jew in Babylonia would have in accepting this sure Word. How could anyone really trust that God would shower such grace on His people as to use the Persian conquest of Babylonia as the means of returning the Jews to Palestine? Three basic reasons for such trust are implied here: *nature*, *God's Word* and *history*.

Any Jewish farmer or herdsman knew of God's grace through nature. It was God who sent the rain that watered the crops and flocks on which people depend for physical sustenance.

Even when the rains did not come on time by human reckoning, God had given His Word that He would care for the faithful. If not in a literal, physical sense, then through spiritual blessings, "The Lord thy God will make thee plenteous in every work of thine hand, in the fruit of thy body, and in the fruit of thy cattle, and in the fruit of thy land" (Deut. 30:9). More specifically, God gave His Word that He would rescue His people from captivity. In an amazingly direct prophecy, He promised that "the Lord thy God will turn thy captivity, and have compassion upon thee, and will return and gather thee from among all the nations, whither the Lord thy God hath scattered thee" (Deut. 30:3).

Finally, the people had their own history of deliverance on which to base their trust. The very nation of Israel had been founded on their miraculous rescue from Egypt, in the exodus—a theme repeated over and over to encourage them (and us) not to lose heart in times of darkness and despair (see, for example Ps. 68:7-11).

Evangelistic Emphasis

John and Bruce were "Bible salesmen." Both college students and novices, they had been assigned for the summer to live as roommates and fellow-encouragers in the beautiful Georgian town of Dawson. What they learned about God through the experience was far more important than what they learned about selling.

Bruce was from a white, upper middle-class family. He had grown up in a suburb known for its new brick homes and finely manicured lawns. As he looked about his assigned territory, discouragement overwhelmed him. So many of the homes seemed to him to be little more than shacks. He couldn't imagine that "those people" would actually be interested in buying a Bible—even if they could afford it.

John, on the other hand, had grown up in a "shack" much like those that discouraged Bruce. He had no trouble, at all, believing that the people inside them would be interested in the Bible. His own home had been one of love, faith and devotion. John's struggle was with the houses on the nicer side of town, reflecting comfort and financial success. It seemed to him that "these people" had made their choice. They had cast their lot with "this world" and its offerings. They could not be interested in the things of God!

By summer's end, both Bruce and John had learned that the call of God is not intimidated by economic factors. Both the rich and the poor are open to his call, and many have learned to call on Him while He is near.

Memory Selection

"Seek ye the LORD while He may be found, call ye upon Him while He is near"—*Isa 55:6*

It was definitely one of the most unusual weddings I ever performed. With the Intensive Care Unit of Houston's Hermann Hospital serving as the chapel, vows were hurriedly exchanged between Ted and Brenda. Word had come from the doctor that Ted was dying. Anxiously, he urged me to *"get on with it"* while time remained. It was Ted's most frantic wish to die as Brenda's husband. He did not want to face judgment as her "ex."

Is it possible that many of us are *not all that different from* Ted? Aren't we also suddenly concerned about our relationships (with family, friends and God) when we hear the word, "cancer" or "congestive heart failure" or "AIDS"? For weeks of counseling sessions before Ted had divorced Brenda, I had pleaded with him to reassess his priorities. Now, as he breathed his final breaths (*literally*), Ted was hurrying to do the right thing—for Brenda and in the sight of God. Unfortunately, not all of us will be blessed with such a forewarning.

Henrietta Jackson is not a scholar. During her 53 years of life, she has not ventured beyond three hundred miles from her Alabama home. The job she goes to each morning would not be the envy of many people. Yet, as a supervisor in a large Birmingham laundry, Henrietta lives each day with an extraordinary level of happiness. Faith saturates Henrietta "to the bone." She is a Christian.

Unfortunately, not all who share Henrietta's work day share either the song in her heart or her faith. Twyla, one of the new workers in Mrs. Jackson's crew, is of special concern to her. Never a day passes without some kind of a major acid spill from Twyla's bitter tongue. Any words of faith or praise from Henrietta are immediately countered with blasphemy or profanity from Twyla. Words of hope prompt answering words of doom. Love and affection yield derision and scorn. Testimony to the goodness of God guarantees a reply of angry claims of his hard and hostile ways.

* What do you suppose produced in Henrietta such a happy spirit of faith? Her childhood? Her call? Her awareness of forgiveness? Her life spent walking in faith?

* What do you suppose produced in Twyla her spirit of hostility against God?

* How can Henrietta most effectively communicate to Twyla the love of God so that it penetrates the hardness of her shell?

Roasts for Dinner

When I look at her, time stands still. (I mean her face would stop a clock.)

He has a face like a saint . . . a Saint Bernard.

Count to three. See if you can do it from memory.

You must be a twin. No one person could be that dumb.

He's a concrete thinker. His mind is all mixed up and permanently set.

She's a gross ignoramus—144 times worse than an ordinary ignoramus.

The Lord, through Isaiah, was telling the people that they were investing themselves in things of life that neither nourished nor satisfied.

He offered to sell them wine and milk without money. He offered to nourish them without price.

An everlasting covenant.

It's not that God hides Himself from us. We get lost from Him. Remember Jesus' parables of the lost coin, lost sheep and lost son (Luke 15).

To the wicked person who repents, the Lord promised mercy and abundant pardon.

The central message was that his Word is just as certain to produce harvest as people have come to expect of the heaven-sent rain.

The message was that *all of creation* will praise the Lord in celebration.

That application of this text might be abusive to its intended message. Nevertheless, it does point to the celebrative nature of worship.

This was a message of hope and joy. God presented Himself as a God of blessing—One who redeems.

It seems that way to us because we fail to understand His methods, and His reasoning is far superior to our comprehension.

6. What was the central message of the Lord's remarks about the rain and snow? Was He saying that they will no longer evaporate?

The central message was that his Word is just as certain to produce harvest as people have come to expect of the heaven-sent rain.

7. How do the trees of the field "clap their hands?" Was He referring to the rustling of the leaves?

The message was that *all of creation* will praise the Lord in celebration.

8. If the leaves "clap their hands," doesn't that prove that it is okay to clap during the Sunday morning worship?

That application of this text might be abusive to its intended message. Nevertheless, it does point to the celebrative nature of worship.

9. What exactly was the Lord, through Isaiah, promising to Israel?

This was a message of hope and joy. God presented Himself as a God of blessing—One who redeems.

10. Why does God sometimes seem to use "bad judgment" in the way He addresses problems in our lives?

It may seem that way to us because we fail to understand His methods, and His reasoning is far superior to our comprehension.

Lesson 3

A Time to Rebuild

Haggai 1:1-9; 2:1-5

1:1 In the second year of Darius the king, in the sixth month, in the first day of the month, came the word of the Lord by Haggai the prophet unto Zerubbabel, the son of Shealtiel, governor of Judah, and to Joshua the son of Josedech, the high priest, saying,

2 Thus speaketh the Lord of hosts, saying, This people say, The time is not come, the time that the Lord's house should be built.

3 Then came the word of the Lord by Haggai the prophet, saying,

4 Is it a time for you, O ye, to dwell in your cieled houses, and this house lie waste?

5 Now therefore thus saith the Lord of hosts; Consider your ways.

6 You have sown much, and bring in little; ye eat, but ye have not enough; ye drink, but ye are not filled with drink; ye clothe you, but there is none warm; and he that earneth wages earneth wages to put it into a bag with holes.

7 Thus saith the Lord of hosts; Consider your ways.

8 Go up to the mountain, and bring wood, and build the house; and I will take pleasure in it, and I will be glorified, saith the Lord.

9 Ye looked for much, and, lo, it came to little; and when ye brought it home, I did blow upon it. Why? Saith the Lord of hosts. Because of mine house that is waste, and ye run every man unto his own house.

2:1 In the seventh month, in the one and twentieth day of the month, came the word of the Lord by the prophet Haggai, saying,

2 Speak now to Zerubbabel the son of Shealtiel, governor of Judah, and to Joshua the son of Josedech, the high priest, and to the residue of the people, saying,

3 Who is left among you that saw this house in her first glory? And how do ye see it now? Is it not in your eyes in comparison of it as nothing?

4 Yet now be strong, O Zerubbabel, saith the Lord; and be strong, O Joshua, son of Josedech, the high priest; and be strong, all ye people of the land, saith the Lord, and work: for I am with you, saith the Lord of hosts:

5 According to the word that I covenanted with you when ye came out of Egypt, so my spirit remaineth among you: fear ye not.

Memory Selection
Haggai 2:

Devotional Reading
Psalm 132:1-14

Background Scripture
Haggai 1–2

Printed Scripture
Haggai 1:1-9; 2:1-5

Teacher's Target

Lesson purpose: *To focus on the importance of giving God first place in our priorities, and to develop faith in His intention to bless those who do so.*

Most people have had the experience of having "too much month left at the end of the money." We also know the meaning of "The tireder I work, the harder I get." We know what it's like to put money in a bag that turns out to be "holier" than safe (see Hag. 1:4).

Most people, however, are much slower to realize the point of this lesson: our resources go farther when we put God first. Somehow we think that God is only in charge of spiritual blessings, while we are in control of our time and our material resources. In this lesson, emphasize the truth that since God "owns" all the gold in the world, and "the cattle on a thousand hills" (Ps. 50:10), He doesn't really need our meager resources. We need to experience the blessing that comes from having a system of priorities that puts God first.

Lesson Introduction

Although its brevity classifies this little book among the "minor prophets," it has a major message—that a sovereign God is able to care for those who put Him first. The prophet Haggai proclaimed this message to fellow-Judeans who had returned from Babylonian captivity to rebuild the Temple. As time went by, the Persians had conquered Babylonia; and now the Persian king Darius was ruler. However, he honored his predecessor Cyrus' permission for work to proceed on the Temple (see Ezra 6).

Unfortunately, they had focused more on rebuilding their own homes and fortunes than on the Temple of God. It was during the reign of Darius, about 520 B.C., that Haggai took up his task (1:1, etc.).

His message was simple but profound. He called the people to take more seriously the testimony they could have before ungodly kingdoms if they would enthrone the Lord again not just in the Temple but in their hearts and lives as well.

Teaching Outline	Daily Bible Readings

I. Reconsider Your Priorities—1:1-4
  A. God's timing or ours? 1-2
  B. God's house or our own? 3-4
II. Reform Your Ways—1:5-9
  A. Bad investments, 5-6
  B. Attitudes and consequences, 7-9
III. Remember the Glory—2:1-5
  A. The commissioning, 1-2
  B. The charge, 3-4
  C. The covenant, 5
	Mon. Finding a Place for Worship
	   Psalm 132:1-10
	Tue. God has Chosen Zion
	   Psalm 132:11-18
	Wed. Rebuild Now!
	   Haggai 1:1-8
	Thu. Just Say Yes!
	   Haggai 1:9-15
	Fri. Vision of a Brighter Future
	   Haggai 2:1-9
	Sat. Blessing for the Obedient
	   Haggai 2:10-23
	Sun. God Builds the House
	   Psalm 127:1-5

VERSE BY VERSE

I. Reconsider Your Priorities—1:2-4

A. God's timing or ours? 1:1-2

1 In the second year of Darius the king, in the sixth month, in the first day of the month, came the word of the Lord by Haggai the prophet unto Zerubbabel, the son of Shealtiel, governor of Judah, and to Joshua the son of Josedech, the high priest, saying,

2 Thus speaketh the Lord of hosts, saying, This people say, The time is not come, the time that the Lord's house should be built.

Although it may be tempting to skim lightly over the difficult names in verse 1, each is an important member of the cast of characters in this brief book.

The prophet Haggai's name means "my feasts"—perhaps symbolic of the feast of good things awaiting those who put the prophet's word into practice. Darius, as the Lesson Introduction indicated, was king of the Persians, who conquered Babylon, and who honored King Cyrus' decree allowing the people to return to their homeland and rebuild the Temple (see Ezra 6). Darius may have appointed Zerubbabel to be governor; and Joshua (not, of course, the Joshua for whom the Bible book is named) was the high priest.

The significance of listing these players in the drama before us is that they give a concrete context to "the word of the Lord" that came to Haggai. This Word is from a King far greater than Darius, who is merely an instrument in God's hand to see that His Temple is rebuilt as a testimony to the nations that He is the true God. Furthermore, this Word is also to guide the actions of Governor Zerubbabel and the high priest Joshua. As the adage goes, few people can rise above the level of their leadership. When their leaders are godly leaders, respecting the Word of the Lord, the people have greater opportunity to live and worship as God desires.

Verse 2 lays out the reason the book of Haggai was written. Nearly two generations of Jews had been living in Judea since King Cyrus allowed them to return to rebuild the Temple (Ezra 1). Yet they had accomplished little or nothing, since they were preoccupied with other concerns (vs. 4). They had rationalized this dereliction of duty by presuming to see into God's mind and deciding His timing was off! The mere fact that He had moved the mighty kings of Persia to facilitate the people's return should have been sufficient evidence that it was time to rebuild the Temple.

B. God's house or our own? 3-4

3 Then came the word of the Lord by Haggai the prophet, saying,

4 Is it a time for you, O ye, to dwell in your cieled houses, and this house lie waste?

The people had presumed to discount God's timing; now the prophet challenges their own timing and priorities. He sees through their easy rationalization: "Where will we live while we rebuild the Temple? Shouldn't we establish ourselves in some trade, or develop farms and flocks in order to pay for the work on the Temple?"

Then after building a small house and establishing a business the self-justification could continue: "A person in my position should have a better house than this—one with paneling, yet." (See "paneled" for "cieled" houses in the NIV.) With the Temple continuing to lie in waste, how could the Jews who returned to Palestine show they were any different from the self-serving pagans who observed what was going on?

II. Reform Your Ways—1:5-9

A. Bad investments, 5-6

5 Now therefore thus saith the Lord of hosts; Consider your ways.

6 You have sown much, and bring in little; ye eat, but ye have not enough; ye drink, but ye are not filled with drink; ye clothe you, but there is none warm; and he that earneth wages earneth wages to put it into a bag with holes.

For all their self-serving ways, the people had little to show for their efforts. We know the feeling of "inverse return" on our time and efforts. Investors know what it's like to put their money in a project that loses principle instead of gaining interest. The prophet Haggai dares to suggest that this is because the people haven't put God and His House first.

Before rushing to apply this teaching to situations today when we may think we need a new church building, we should remember how the definition of God's House or Temple has changed. Under the Christian age, people are God's Temple—both individually (1 Cor. 6:15) and collectively (3:16). The parallel with Haggai, then, must seek a spiritual reference, leading us to ask questions such as, Am I tending to my physical needs to the detriment of the spiritual? and Am I

squandering my attention and resources on lesser causes than the Body of Christ?

B. Attitudes and consequences, 7-9

7 Thus saith the Lord of hosts; Consider your ways.

8 Go up to the mountain, and bring wood, and build the house; and I will take pleasure in it, and I will be glorified, saith the Lord.

9 Ye looked for much, and, lo, it came to little; and when ye brought it home, I did blow upon it. Why? Saith the Lord of hosts. Because of mine house that is waste, and ye run every man unto his own house.

Is it possible that putting God and His House first would result in an improvement in the people's own well-being? Many people who have put God to this very test—for example, "giving until it hurts"—report that He blesses them materially. Note, however, that the first result the prophet predicts will be the glorification of God, not of the people. We do not sacrifice in order to gain; but we always gain, either materially or spiritually, when we align our priorities with God's.

III. Remember the Glory—2:1-5

A. The consequence, 1-3

1 In the seventh month, in the one and twentieth day of the month, came the word of the Lord by the prophet Haggai, saying,

2 Speak now to Zerubbabel the son of Shealtiel, governor of Judah, and to Joshua the son of Josedech, the high priest, and to the residue of the people, saying,

3 Who is left among you that saw this house in her first glory? And how do ye see it now? Is it not in your eyes in comparison of it as nothing?

24

Now God exhorts the prophet to call the older people to celebrate their memory of the first Temple. By imaging its former grandeur they can resist discouragement and despair when they see it in ruins, and redouble their zeal to restore it. So today, it can be invigorating to envision the end result or consequence of our efforts instead of merely the task at hand.

B. The charge, 4

4 Yet now be strong, O Zerubbabel, saith the Lord; and be strong, O Joshua, son of Josedech, the high priest; and be strong, all ye people of the land, saith the Lord, and work: for I am with you, saith the Lord of hosts:

Note that this charge includes both "clergy" and "laity," leaders and followers. And what a powerful incentive to realize that God is our co-worker! There is additional encouragement in the names applied to God here. Not only is He called "Yahweh" (the self-existent One; kjv "the Lord," signified by a capital and small capitals—see Exod. 3:14-15); He is also "Lord of hosts" (Yahweh Sabaoth) or "Lord Almighty" (NIV). The people can take heart that the true God, mightier than the gods of the people round about them, is working side by side with them.

C. The covenant, 5

5 According to the word that I covenanted with you when ye came out of Egypt, so my spirit remaineth among you: fear ye not.

A final word of encouragement reminds the people that their temporary exile in Babylon did not mean that God had reneged on the covenant He made at the exodus.

Evangelistic Emphasis

Since the earliest days of the Protestant Reformation, the church has been divided over the importance that should be placed on the church building.

Reacting against extravagance of earlier eras, some taught that minimal expense should be spent on the physical plant. The primary emphasis was placed on building up the spiritual house—the congregation. Others, using passages such as these oracles of Haggai, maintain that the physical facilities reflect to the surrounding community the priority the church gives to God.

Though the basic winds of opinion on this subject have blown back and forth throughout the centuries, there has always remained a tension between the extremes—"extravagance" on the one hand and "shabby neglect" on the other. As one drives through town, he will find both cathedrals and store-front missions. Just as these are the products of two different "understandings" as to the importance of the physical, so also they effectively appeal to two different groups of unbelievers in evangelism. People who are reached by Christians working out of a store-front mission would likely not be drawn to an elaborate cathedral. Those who find themselves comfortable in a lavish cathedral would probably not be impressed by the same gospel being preached in a room with a make-shift pulpit and folding chairs. Rather than attempting to homogenize the church so as to arrive at a bland compromise, we would do better to thank God for working through the ministries of all.

Memory Selection

Yet now be strong, O Zerubbabel, saith the Lord; and be strong, O Joshua, son of Josedech, the high priest; and be strong, all ye people of the land, saith the LORD, and work for I am with you, saith the Lord.—*Haggai 2:4*

Do you remember the last time you got home from vacation and discovered that two weeks' laundry backlog was a task far more intimidating than you ever imagined? Remember the garage that was embarrassingly overdue for a thorough clearance and cleaning? Much worse by far was your neighbor's house that was damaged by the kitchen fire. What was not burned was badly smoked or ruined with water damage. Your neighbors just stood, staring for hours at the rubble, trying to decide *where to begin!*

All of those circumstances pale in comparison to what lay before that remnant of Israelites. Their beautiful temple, that had for centuries represented the presence of God among them, lay in ruins. The Babylonian military machine had leveled every stone. Some of the people wondered out loud whether the God of that temple was gone, too. God's word of encouragement was that He was not gone. He stood beside them as they challenged the task.

Weekday Problems

Winterdale Church could not have foreseen how the community would build up around it. Eighty years ago when her church building was erected, Winterdale was just a small country community that had developed at the crossroads of two rural highways, several miles from town. Today, that "town" is recognized as one of America's major southern cities, and Winterdale is the location of its most upscale housing development. The building housing Winterdale Church, however, has not changed. It remains "just a country church house" with a closet-size foyer and unpadded pews.

* Should Winterdale Church make plans to upgrade its facilities to more closely match the homes being constructed around it or should it remain "just a country church house" as it has always been? Why?

* What other factors (if any) ought to be considered in making such a decision?

* Suppose the situation were reversed. An elaborate church building suddenly finds itself surrounded by a low-income slum. Should the church downgrade to fit the surrounding community? Why?

In Response to Roasts

The famous 19th century Congregational preacher Henry Ward Beecher once found a letter awaiting him on the podium when he got up to preach. It had only one word on it: "Fool."

Beecher calmly announced to the congregation, "I have known many an instance of a man writing a letter and forgetting to sign his name, but this is the only instance I have ever known of a man signing his name and forgetting to write the letter."

Roasted good-naturedly at a banquet by his congregation, the minister stood up to reply. "I want you to know that in spite of the unkind things you've said, I know you'll be the first ones in heaven. For the Bible says, 'The dead in Christ shall rise first.'"

Blistered at a roast, the roastee complimented the roasters: "With wits like yours, no doubt you'll all become wealthy entertainers—your ignorance is comical."

Darius.

It was a time of economic depression. Drought caused the available food to be scarce and the prices to be high.

He was governor of Judah.

The comparison was not favorable. The former temple was much more elaborate and attractive than the one presently being built.

The Lord promised that in "a little while" He would "shake all nations, and the desire of all nations shall come" and fill that house.

"The glory of this latter house shall be greater than of the former."

Holy flesh is contaminated by coming in contact with something unclean.

Famine turned into plenty. Economic depression turned into a booming economy.

Four oracles of the Lord were delivered by Haggai during three months and twenty-three days.

All but one of the oracles were addressed specifically to Zerubbabel. The other one was addressed to the priests.

6. Once that promise has been fulfilled, what will be the state of the comparison between the two houses then?

"The glory of this latter house shall be greater than of the former."

7. What illustration did the Lord use to communicate the uncleanness of Judah and the sacrifices they offered?

Holy flesh is contaminated by coming into contact with something unclean.

8. What changed about the economy of the land once the people laid the foundation for the temple?

Famine turned into plenty. Economic depression turned into a booming economy.

9. How many oracles did Haggai bring to the people of Judah, and how long was it from the first to the last?

Four oracles of the Lord were delivered by Haggai during three months and twenty-three days.

10. To whom *specifically* were each of these oracles addressed?

All but one of the oracles were addressed specifically to Zerubbabel. The other one was addressed to the priests.

A Vision of Renewal

Zechariah 4

1 And the angel that talked with me came again, and waked me, as a man that is wakened out of his sleep.

2 And said unto me, What seest thou? And I said, I have looked, and behold a candlestick all of gold, with a bowl upon the top of it, and his seven lamps thereon, and seven pipes to the seven lamps, which are upon the top thereof;

3 And two olive trees by it, one upon the right side of the bowl, and the other upon the left side thereof.

4 So I answered and spake to the angel that talked with me, saying, What are these, my lord?

5 Then the angel that talked with me answered and said unto me, Knowest thou not what these be? And I said, No, my lord.

6 Then he answered and spake unto me, saying, This is the word of the Lord unto Zerubbabel, saying Not by might, nor by power, but by my spirit, saith the Lord of hosts.

7 Who art thou, O great mountain? Before Zerubbabel thou shalt become a plain: and he shall bring forth the head-stone thereof with shoutings, crying, Grace, grace unto it.

8 Moreover the word of the Lord came unto me, saying,

9 The hands of Zerubbabel have laid the foundation of this house; his hands shall also finish it; and thou shalt know that the Lord of hosts hath sent me unto you.

10 For who hath despised the day of small things? for they shall rejoice, and shall see the plummet in the hand of Zerubbabel with those seven; they are the eyes of the Lord, which run to and fro through the whole earth.

11 Then answered I, and said unto him, What are these two olive trees upon the right side of the candlestick and upon the left side thereof?

12 And I answered again, and said unto him, What be these two olive branches which through the two golden pipes empty the golden oil out of themselves?

13 And he answered me and said, Knowest thou not what these be? And I said, No, my lord.

14 Then said he, These are the two anointed ones, that stand by the Lord of the whole earth.

Memory Selection
Zechariah 4:6

Devotional Reading
Zechariah 7:1-10

Background Scripture
Zechariah 4

Printed Scripture
Zechariah 4

31

Teacher's Target

Lesson purpose: *To learn, through the vision of the prophet Zechariah, the importance of trusting the spirit over the flesh, and the will of God over the will of man.*

"Visionaries" are people who are possessed by a passionate picture of what can or should be done. At their best they are able to mobilize followers to accomplish their vision. At their worst they lack practical skills necessary to bring dreams to reality.

Zechariah was a visionary prophet whose dreams were given by God in order to muster the Jews to complete the restoration of the Temple in Jerusalem. Discuss with your class other projects—whether local or worldwide in scope—that might benefit from the leadership of visionary people. Emphasize Zechariah's insistence that godly dreams are accomplished by God's Spirit. (Zech. 4:6).

Lesson Introduction

Zechariah was contemporary with Haggai, whom we met in the preceding lesson. Both were sixth-century B.C. spiritual leaders in Judah who were allowed to return from Babylonian captivity to restore the Temple.

Zechariah confronted a people who had failed to bring to fruition the dream of rebuilding the Temple. They also seem to have been tempted to break away from the Persians and to make alliances with smaller Palestinian states. In attempting to set up an independent state, they had also neglected basic human justice.

Zechariah held up to the people a vision of the Kingdom of God as an earthly reality—but only when God's people follow God's ways. Late in his book, he also envisions an ultimate future when a divine Deliverer, whom Christians know to be Jesus, the Messiah, will extend this Kingdom throughout the earth.

Teaching Outline	Daily Bible Readings

I. The Elements of the Vision—1-3
  A. Candlestick and bowl, lamp
  and pipes, 1-2
  B. The two olive trees, 3
 	
II. The Energy of the Spirit—4-10
  A. The "smallness" of God, 4-6
  B. The election of Zerubbabel,
  7-10
 	
III. The Explanation of the
  Trees—1-14
	Mon. Call to Renewal
	  Zechariah 1:1-6
	Tue. God Will Live Among Us
	  Zechariah 2:6-13
	Wed. Empowered by God's Spirit
	  Zechariah 4:1-7
	Thu. No Day for Small Things
	  Zechariah 4:8-14
	Fri. Time for Kindness and Mercy
	  Zechariah 7:1-14
	Sat. Hearing God's Promise
	  Zechariah 8:1-13
	Sun. The Prince of Peace
	  Zechariah 9:9-13

VERSE BY VERSE

I. The Elements of the Vision—1-3
A. Candlestick and bowl, lamp and pipes, 1-2

1 And the angel that talked with me came again, and waked me, as a man that is wakened out of his sleep.

2 And said unto me, What seest thou? And I said, I have looked, and behold a candlestick all of gold, with a bowl upon the top of it, and his seven lamps thereon, and seven pipes to the seven lamps, which are upon the top thereof;

The prophet Zechariah is among those biblical seers who speak in symbols. Such language is often called "apocalyptic," meaning literally an "unveiling" or "revelation." In other words, symbolic language is often used in Scripture to unveil or portray otherwise hidden truth.

Just what truth, however, may be difficult to determine for those of us living so many years later and in such different times. Verses 4-5 show that even Zechariah could not understand the symbols God gave him apart from divine explanation. At times, New Testament authors also enlighten us with their own inspired interpretation of Old Testament symbols. For example, the apostle Peter explained that the astounding events on the first Day of Pentecost after the resurrection of Christ were a fulfillment of a vision of the prophet Joel (Acts 2:14-21).

This principle should be kept in mind as we try to assign meaning to the symbolic language in these verses—as well as elsewhere in the Bible. Unless we have other Bible passages to interpret such symbols, they can be made to mean virtually anything. In the absence of a "This is that which was spoken by the prophet . . . ," we can only speculate or give educated guesses.

Fortunately, a hint about how to interpret the lamps described in verse 2 will be given in verses 6 and 10. Our thinking about what they stand for will therefore be limited to suggestions actually found in Scripture.

What we have is an oil lamp, with its central candlestick apparently connected to a bowl of olive oil by wicks in small pipes. Each pipe is in turn connected to a lamp, making a light fixture with seven lights. Since this is similar to the lighting God prescribed for the Tabernacle (Exod. 25:31ff.), we may suppose that the lamp stands for the light God would shed on the Jews' predicament. They have been derelict in fulfilling the charge to rebuild the Temple. Perhaps Zechariah's vision is a sermon illustration saying that they should walk in the light of God's word to them about getting on with the rebuilding project.

B. The two olive trees, 3

3 And two olive trees by it, one upon

the right side of the bowl, and the other upon the left side thereof.

Fortunately, the light from the lamp isn't likely to go out because there is a permanent source of oil direct from two olive trees. As the trees produce oil, it flows through the pipes as a source of fuel for the candlestick and lamps. These trees will be assigned a specific interpretation at the end of the chapter.

II. The Energy of the Spirit—4-10
A. The "smallness" of God, 4-6

4 So I answered and spake to the angel that talked with me, saying, What are these, my lord?

5 Then the angel that talked with me answered and said unto me, Knowest thou not what these be? And I said, No, my lord.

6 Then he answered and spake unto me, saying, This is the word of the Lord unto Zerubbabel, saying Not by might, nor by power, but by my spirit, saith the Lord of hosts.

This is not the only place where a biblical prophet has to ask the meaning of a vision. The apostle John also confesses his ignorance of the meaning of the mysterious symbols in the book of Revelation (7:13-14). Perhaps this curious feature of some biblical prophecy is to remind us again that only God holds the ultimate key to penetrating its vivid but mysterious language.

If the word "these" in verse 4 refers to the lamps, then we are given to understand in verse 6 that they represent the Word of God—which is elsewhere called "a light unto my pathway" (Ps. 119:105). The people's efforts to rebuild the Temple have been hindered by enemies (Ezra 4:1-6), and by their own selfishness (Hag. 1:4). No doubt they were tempted to respond to the enemy opposition by marshaling an army. Here, however, God reminds them that the Temple's restora-tion—indeed any instance of obedience to God—is to be accomplished by following His Spirit-filled Word, not by human effort.

B. The election of Zerubbabel, 7-10

7 Who art thou, O great mountain? Before Zerubbabel thou shalt become a plain: and he shall bring forth the headstone thereof with shoutings, crying, Grace, grace unto it.

8 Moreover the word of the Lord came unto me, saying,

9 The hands of Zerubbabel have laid the foundation of this house; his hands shall also finish it; and thou shalt know that the Lord of hosts hath sent me unto you.

10 For who hath despised the day of small things? for they shall rejoice, and shall see the plummet in the hand of Zerubbabel with those seven; they are the eyes of the Lord, which run to and fro through the whole earth.

The "great mountain" in verse 7 may refer to the mountainous obstacles hindering the rebuilding of the Temple; or to an arrogant enemy who has challenged the leadership of Zerubbabel.

Verses 9-10 hint that this leadership was questioned. However, in one of the books of the Apocrypha—writings produced between the Old and New Testaments but not accepted by the Jews as authoritative—King Darius himself is said to have appointed Zerubbabel governor of Judah and ruler of those who returned. Zechariah therefore comes to Zerubbabel's defense, insisting that he both began the restoration of the Temple and will complete it.

The people may have thought that Zerubbabel's appointment was insignificant. Verse 10, however, affirms that it was not to be despised, for Zerubbabel has on his side "those seven" lamps that are now revealed specifically to represent the "the eyes of the Lord"—who Himself is the light that shines through His Word. Zerubbabel was God's man; woe to the people who resist his leadership.

III. The Explanation of the Trees—11-14

11 Then answered I, and said unto him, What are these two olive trees upon the right side of the candlestick and upon the left side thereof?

12 And I answered again, and said unto him, What be these two olive branches which through the two golden pipes empty the golden oil out of themselves?

13 And he answered me and said, Knowest thou not what these be? And I said, No, my lord.

14 Then said he, These are the two anointed ones, that stand by the Lord of the whole earth.

Now Zechariah asks about the meaning of the two olive trees described in verse 3. Trees often symbolize deep roots and stability (Ps. 1:3; Jer. 17:8). Like other fruit trees, olive trees are also sources of nourishment, providing here the oil for the lamps. Here they are said to represent two servants of God anointed to do His bidding.

Elsewhere we are told that the two people raised up for this situation are Zerubbabel, whose appointment has just been defended, and Joshua, the high priest (3:1; Hag. 1:1). This reminds the people again of the authority of their leaders. It stems not from any self-assertion but from the ordination of God Himself.

The restoration of the Temple cannot be accomplished without the organization Governor Zerubbabel has to offer and the spiritual leadership of Joshua the high priest. They are the authorized leaders though whom the fuel for God's light flows. Even today the energy needed to fire the furnace of faithfulness among the people of God often flows through people anointed or commissioned to minister to others in His name.

Evangelistic Emphasis

The building of the house of God is always evidence of the work of God in the world—in the days of Zerubbabel and today. As the temple served in Jerusalem and throughout Judah as testimony of the presence of the Lord, so also the church serves today. In each neighborhood where the church is found, a candlestick holds the light of his Truth. The church may be small and struggling or a mega-church with hundreds of ministries. It might be poor with tattered song books or wealthy with the latest computerized multimedia displays. But wherever the Word of God is proclaimed and the cross of Christ is held high, people will come to know, perhaps in spite of themselves, that God is near.

Since this is true, it is important that the church make an effort to be found in every place. It needs to stand strong in the suburbs where the growth and the vitality of the city's population of the future will be found. It also needs to be found in the inner-city where so much of the other evidences of God's presence is no longer found. Fleeing corruption, decay and poverty, it is easy for the church to abandon our cities and the people who live there, leaving them no reminder that God lives and cares.

Memory Selection

Then he answered and spake unto me, saying, This is the word of the Lord unto Zerubbabel, saying, Not by might, nor by power, but by my spirit, saith the Lord of hosts. —*Zechariah 4:6*

It would seem that those who profess faith in God as the creator and Lord of the universe would look to Him routinely for the answers to their needs. They would forge ahead, confident that He would provide whatever might be needed to meet success. On the one hand, there would be no thought of gloating over victories. How could they gloat for what God had provided. On the other hand, they would never be hesitant because of intimidation or fear of failure. Why should they doubt? Success does not rest on their abilities, but on God's!

Reality is, however, that even among those who are people of faith, there is to be found both hesitancy and boasting with oscillating regularity. We forget that it is by the Spirit of God that we live and accomplish and succeed. We must be reminded again and again. Each time, we must repent.

Weekday Problems

Eleven months ago Glenn and Marsha were introduced to Jesus Christ by one of Glenn's co-workers. Not only did this reorient their family goals and eternal pursuits, it also seemed to bring the stability to Marsha's life for which she had been hoping. A man of many talents, Glenn has spent most of the years of their marriage floating from one job to another. Each

change has come with excitement for Glenn. Though Marsha has been patient through all of this, after fifteen years, she has become concerned about the effects of this unsettled home on their children. Ever since Glenn found the Lord he has seemed to be *"finally settled"*—until this morning, that is.

This morning Glenn awoke full of excitement. He had had "this most amazing dream." A man was standing beside his work bench at his job beckoning him to leave everything and follow him. He promised to show Glenn a whole new world.

Waking suddenly, Glenn was convinced that the message had come from the Lord. He should quit his job, and the Lord would show him a better one!

* What should Marsha do? Should she accept this dream of Glenn's as a "message from the Lord"?

* What can Glenn do that would help provide a "reality check" to this dream or vision that he was given?

* How can one *know* whether a dream is "just a dream" or a "message from the Lord" to be followed?

Final Exam

Q: How do you avoid falling hair?
A. Jump out of the way.

Q: You load 16 tons, and whattaya get?
A: A hernia.

Q: Do you know what they got when they crossed a rattlesnake with a horse?
A: No, but if it bites you maybe you can ride it to the hospital.

Q: What do you get when you cross a cow with a porcupine?
A: A steak with built-in toothpicks.

Q: What is "practical nursing"?
A: Falling in love with a rich patient.

Q: What's the best way to drive a baby buggy?
A: Tickle its feet.

This Lesson in Your Life

"Vanity of vanities, saith the Preacher, vanity of vanities; all is vanity." Those are the words that begin Solomon's journal of his search for significance in life (Eccl. 1:2). Or as the NIV renders it, "Everything is meaningless." Neither translation really puts bounce in my step for beginning Monday morning. Yet, those painful words echo the gut-wrenching feelings with which a large percentage of people begin *every* Monday morning. Life seems to them to be so meaningless. They seem to themselves to be utterly insignificant. That is an agonizingly dismal way to live. No one lives very triumphantly under such a cloud of gloom.

Strange! Isn't it? We seem to gravitate toward one extreme or the other. Some of us want to see the universe with ourselves at the center. Others of us paint the world with ourselves added only as microscopic particles of dust that do little more than mar and obstruct the world's beauty. Most of us vacillate from one extreme to the other numerous times during our earthly sojourn.

It may be that Solomon's cry, *"Meaningless!"* echoes so hauntingly in our ears that we find ourselves perpetually on a treadmill attempting to convince ourselves that we do have worth—that we are significant. We use ego-stroking fantasies to bolster our sense of worth. We exaggerate! We envision ourselves, not simply in a place of importance, but in *the place* of importance. We, like Jesus' apostles, vie for the right-hand and left-hand positions in the Kingdom. Like Eve in the garden, we buy the serpent's lie that some forbidden fruit will even make us equal to God!

The discussion of psychologists throughout this century has argued the question of whether people really struggle with over-inflated egos or *precisely the opposite.* Some maintain that the vast majority struggle from egos so deflated that they gasp with all the strength within themselves just to breath. In desperate attempts to have some sense of notice, at all, people "act out" inappropriately and frantically trying not to disappear completely.

Whichever school of psychology is right, humanity has perpetually wrestled with the pursuit of an appropriate sense of worth. Into that arena of self-awareness for Judah came a dream that was experienced by the prophet Zechariah one night. Interestingly, the image of the dream depicted a place of importance that involved relationship *with* God. Instead of acting out His will separate from and independent of human involvement, God chose to *work through* His people in order to accomplish His will.

Notice, in the dream, the interconnection between the olive trees that provided oil for the lamps and the oil lamps that provided light for the trees. God worked through His servants to accomplish His will, and His servants carried out their roles of significance by the power and the working of God. Just as that was true in the days of Zechariah, so it is also true today. The church goes about the task of "doing the Lord's work" in the world. The individual task of each Christian is of no small importance. Yet, it is God's work. His power makes the accomplishment possible.

Seed Thoughts

1. In what condition was Zechariah to be found when the angel "came again" to speak to him?

Zechariah was asleep. The angel woke him.

2. What was the angel's first question to Zechariah?

The angel asked Zechariah, "What do you see?"

3. What answer did Zechariah give to the angel's first question?

He said he saw a candlestick of gold with a bowl on top, seven lampstands, seven pipes and two olive trees.

4. What message did the angel give to Zechariah about Zerubbabel and the temple?

The angel said that Zerubbabel had begun the temple by laying the foundation and that he would finish it.

5. What is a "plummet" that the angel said the people would see in the hand of Zerubbabel and what did it signify?

Contemporary translations have the word "plumb line." It signified that Zerubbabel held the role of a builder.

---

1. In what condition was Zechariah to be found when the angel "came again" to speak to him?

2. What was the angel's first question to Zechariah?

3. What was the answer that Zechariah gave to the angel's first question?

4. What message did the angel give to Zechariah about Zerubbabel and the temple?

5. What is a "plummet" that the angel said the people would see in the hand of Zerubbabel and what did it signify?

6. What would the mountain become before Zerubbabel?

7. What was Zerubbabel to shout as the headstone was brought forth?

8. What did the angel say that those who have "despised the day of small things" would do?

9. What did Zechariah want to know about the olive trees?

10. What answer did the angel give Zechariah about the trees?

(Please turn page)

Zechariah was asleep. The angel woke him.

The angel asked Zechariah, "What do you see?"

He said he saw a candlestick of gold with a bowl on top, seven lampstands, seven pipes and two olive trees.

The angel said that Zerubbabel had begun the temple by laying the foundation and that he would finish it.

Contemporary translations have the word "plumb line." It signified that Zerubbabel held the role of a builder.

The angel said that before Zerubbabel the mountain would become a plane.

"Grace! Grace unto it!"

The angel said that they would rejoice.

Zechariah wanted to know what they were (i.e. what they represented).

The angel said that the two olive trees were the two anointed ones who stand by the Lord of the whole earth.

6. What would the mountain become before Zerubbabel?

The angel said that before Zerubbabel the mountain would become a plain.

7. What was Zerubbabel to shout as the headstone was brought forth?

"Grace! Grace unto it!"

8. What did the angel say that those who have "despised the day of small things" would do?

The angel said that they would rejoice.

9. What did Zechariah want to know about the olive trees?

Zechariah wanted to know what they were (i.e. what they represented).

10. What answer did the angel give Zechariah about the trees?

The angel said that the two olive trees were the two anointed ones who stand by the Lord of the whole earth.

Lesson 5

Resisting Temptation

Daniel 1:3-16

3 And the king spake unto Ashpenaz the master of his eunuchs, that he should bring certain of the children of Israel, and of the king's seed, and of the princes;

4 Children in whom was no blemish, but well favoured, and skillful in all wisdom, and cunning in knowledge, and understanding science, and such as had ability in them to stand in the king's palace, and whom they might teach the learning and the tongue of the Chaldeans.

5 And the king appointed them a daily provision of the king's meat, and of the wine which he drank: so nourishing them three years, that at the end thereof they might stand before the king.

6 Now among these were of the children of Judah, Daniel, Hananiah, Mishael, and Azariah:

7 Unto whom the prince of the eunuchs gave names: for he gave unto Daniel the name of Belteshazzar; and to Hananiah, of Shadrach; and to Mishael, of Meshach; and to Arariah, of Abednego.

8 But Daniel purposed in his heart that he would not defile himself with the portion of the king's meat, nor with the wine which he drank: therefore he requested of the prince of the eunuchs that he might not defile himself.

9 Now God had brought Daniel into favour and tender love with the prince of the eunuchs.

10 And the prince of the eunuchs said unto Daniel, I fear my lord the king, who hath appointed your meat and your drink: for why should he see your faces worse liking than the children which are of your sort? Then shall ye make me endanger my head to the king.

11 Then Daniel said to Melzar, whom the prince of the eunuchs had set over Daniel, Hananiah, Mishael, and Azariah,

12 Prove thy servants, I beseech thee, ten days; and let them give us pulse to eat, and water to drink.

13 Then let our countenances be looked upon before thee, and the countenance of the children that eat of the portion of the king's meat: and as thou seest, deal with thy servants.

14 So he consented to them in this matter, and proved them ten days.

15 And at the end of ten days their countenances appeared fairer and fatter in flesh than all the children which did eat the portion of the king's meat.

16 Thus Melzar took away the portion of their meat, and the wine that they should drink; and gave them pulse.

October 5

Memory Selection
Daniel 1:8

Devotional Reading
Psalm 40:1-11

Background Scripture
Daniel 1

Printed Scripture
Daniel 1:3-16

Teacher's Target

Lesson purpose: *To emphasize, through the story of Daniel and his friends in Babylon, how resisting temptation is its own reward, rather than a "tool" to use to gain favor with God or others.*

Ours is an "instrumental" culture. That is, many people use moral choices as a "tool" that serves the chooser. If standing for God's way seems to be a way to gain acceptance or success or some other end, then Yes!—count them in. But when it ceases to be popular, or if it fails to deliver the desired outcome, then their behavior changes to fit the new situation.

On the other hand, Daniel was a "principled" person—the opposite of an instrumentalist. He marched to a different drum, regardless of whether it promised an immediate reward. He wanted to be God's person whether it "worked" or not. Although in Daniel's case resisting temptation brings a blessing after all, your challenge is to lead your class to the conclusion that Daniel would have been right even without such a reward.

Lesson Introduction

Like the previous books of Haggai and Zechariah, the book of Daniel reflects life in Babylon, where many of God's people have been led captive from Judah (vss. 1-2). This places its events in the sixth century B.C.

Conquering kings such as Nebuchadnezzar of Babylon (vs. 1) used several means of making sure the nations they conquered did not rise to power again. One means was sowing the fields with salt so it would be years before they could grow anything again. In this passage, Nebuchadnezzar tries also to pollute the minds of Judah's finest potential leaders. He has in mind re-acculturating them—fashioning them into Babylonians and realigning their loyalty.

However, the very character that made Daniel and his three friends attractive to the king strengthened their resolve to be God's people even in a foreign land. The text describes how God honored their heroic decision.

Teaching Outline	Daily Bible Readings	
	Mon.	Tempted to Taste *Daniel 1:1-7*
I. The Plot—3-4	**Tue.**	Refusing to Compromise *Daniel 1:8-13*
A. The candidates, 3		
B. The qualifications, 4	**Wed.**	Wisdom Comes from God *Daniel 1:14-21*
II. The Temptation—5-8		
A. Syncretism, 5-7	**Thu.**	God Rewarded Right Actions *1 Samuel 22:21-23*
B. Resistance, 8		
III. The Victory—9-16	**Fri.**	Amida Cloud of Witnesses *Hebrews 12:1-10*
A. The challenge, 9-13	**Sat.**	God's Law is a Lamp *Psalm 119:105-112*
B. The outcome, 14-16	**Sun.**	Proclaim the Bread and Cup *1 Corinthians 11:23-32*

VERSE BY VERSE

I. The Plot—3-4

A. The candidates, 3

3 And the king spake unto Ashpenaz the master of his eunuchs, that he should bring certain of the children of Israel, and of the king's seed, and of the princes;

Eunuchs, or castrated males, were commonly employed in the service of ancient Near Eastern kings because they were deemed safe around the kings' harems. The Hebrew word used here, however, can also simply mean "officer" or "official."

Having in mind remaking the most promising Judeans into imported Babylonians, King Nebuchadnezzar selects young men of the house of David and others of royal background. He must have been counting on their breeding making good "stock" from which to grow future leaders in his own country. Although many Jews of this period were idolaters, and adopted the customs of surrounding pagan nations, Daniel and his friends were exceptions, as we shall see.

B. The qualifications, 4

4 Children in whom was no blemish, but well favoured, and skillful in all wisdom, and cunning in knowledge, and understanding science, and such as had ability in them to stand in the king's palace, and whom they might teach the learning and the tongue of the Chaldeans.

Like fashion ads today, Nebuchadnezzar wanted only "beautiful people" to be model specicmens in his court. Even among the ancient Jews, the unblemished were prized. Only unblemished animals could be offered as sacrifice (Exod. 12:5), and physical imperfections disqualified a man from entering the Holy Place as a priest (Lev. 21:16-24). What a far cry from New Covenant religion, in which spiritual qualities are prized over physical (see 1 Pet. 3:3-4).

The shades of difference between the words for wisdom, knowledge, and scientific understanding show that the king valued learning of all kinds, and the wisdom to apply it. As everyone knows, however, mere "book-learning" doesn't always equip a person for effective leadership. Nebuchadnezzar also sought young men with poise, polish, and self-confidence. Perhaps he had in mind using them as ambassadors, which would require people who reflected well on his court. Finally, they must be able to learn the language of the Chaldeans (or Babylonians).

II. The Temptation—5-8

A. Syncretism, 5-7

5 And the king appointed them a daily provision of the king's meat, and of the wine which he drank: so nourishing them three years, that at the end thereof they might stand before the king.

6 Now among these were of the children of Judah, Daniel, Hananiah, Mishael, and Azariah:

7 Unto whom the prince of the eu-

nuchs gave names: for he gave unto Daniel the name of Belteshazzar; and to Hananiah, of Shadrach; and to Mishael, of Meshach; and to Arariah, of Abednego.

What young persons would not seize the opportunity to dine on the sumptuous fare of a pagan king? Those who perhaps had taken a religious vow not to eat meat or drink wine; or those whose loyalty to the true God made it impossible to join in pagan prayers of thanks for food. Eating was closely associated with worship in both Jewish and pagan religions. The temptation here is "syncretism"—the practice of blending elements of one faith with another.

Nebuchadnezzar is trying to assimilate the young Hebrews into his own culture, wooing them with high living in an attempt to win their hearts and loyalty, not just their bodies. More than one government official and employee have become "hooked" by a standard of living to which they became more loyal than to moral principle.

The final ploy is to give Daniel and the other Jews Babylonian names. After all, our name helps define ourselves to ourselves as well as others. Perhaps after hearing themselves called by Chaldean names long enough, the young men will come to think of themselves as Chaldeans instead of as Jews, the chosen people of God.

B. Resistance, 8

8 But Daniel purposed in his heart that he would not defile himself with the portion of the king's meat, nor with the wine which he drank: therefore he requested of the prince of the eunuchs that he might not defile himself.

Now Daniel emerges as the leader of the select group of Israelites. He has a strong sense of who he is—a part of the chosen race—so he is able to see in the king's proposal a threat to his identity and to his faithful service to the true God. His request not to eat meat from the king's table may be because it had first been offered as an animal sacrifice—as was the case among some Greeks even in New Testament times (see 1 Cor. 8).

III. The Victory—9-16

A. The challenge, 9-13

9 Now God had brought Daniel into favour and tender love with the prince of the eunuchs.

10 And the prince of the eunuchs said unto Daniel, I fear my lord the king, who hath appointed your meat and your drink: for why should he see your faces worse liking than the children which are of your sort? Then shall ye make me endanger my head to the king.

11 Then Daniel said to Melzar, whom the prince of the eunuchs had set over Daniel, Hananiah, Mishael, and Azariah,

12 Prove thy servants, I beseech thee, ten days; and let them give us pulse to eat, and water to drink.

13 Then let our countenances be looked upon before thee, and the countenance of the children that eat of the portion of the king's meat: and as thou seest, deal with thy servants.

Merely because Daniel was a servant of God did not mean he could not respect his pagan captors or be friends with the captain of the eunuchs. He had learned a lesson that isn't always easy: how to be "in the world but not of the world." Yet, friends or not, we can understand the captain's reluctance to risk his own head to protect Daniel's scruples.

Daniel is so confident that his own life-style will be blessed by God that he puts his plea in the form of a test. Instead of the king's wine, he and the other Hebrews will drink water. Instead of the king's meat, they will eat vegetables. ("Pulse" in the kjv is from an old English word for the seeds of various legumes, such as beans and peas. The Hebrew word could refer to various vegetables.) Daniel's diet of choice does not form a good argument for vegetarianism, but only indicates either a suspicion that he would need extra self-discipline to resist the gradual loss of his Hebrew identity, or something like a Nazirite vow that prohibited certain foods (see Num. 6:3).

B. The outcome, 14-16

14 So he consented to them in this matter, and proved them ten days.

15 And at the end of ten days their countenances appeared fairer and fatter in flesh than all the children which did eat the portion of the king's meat.

16 Thus Melzar took away the portion of their meat, and the wine that they should drink; and gave them pulse.

Daniel's challenge is accepted, and his faith is shown to be justified! The 10-day trial shows the Hebrews to be in such good condition that their regimen is apparently extended throughout the three years of training ordained by the king (vss. 5, 18).

Years ago, the publication of the book *None of These Diseases* showed the scientific and nutritional wisdom in following the diet prescribed in the Old Testament—for example, abstaining from birds of prey and other animals that feed on carrion. With no refrigeration, the Jewish ban on pork was also an obviously wise law. Daniel's experience, however, is testimony to the providence of God over those who choose His ways against the ways of competing cultures, rather than an argument for a particular diet.

What if Daniel's daring experiment had failed? The faith he expresses in our next lesson indicates that he would have still chosen God's ways. People of faith do right and resist temptation, as Martin Luther taught, *sola fide*i—by faith—not because they have something to prove, but because it's the right thing to do.

Evangelistic Emphasis

More than twenty years ago, Armad Abdy determined that *he would never* be a Christian. It wasn't that he had studied the Bible and had dismissed it as lacking credib-ility. Actually, before coming to America, he had been intrigued with the little he had heard of the Christian story. His initial fascination, however, turned to repug-nance fairly quickly after assuming his job as a restaurant manager in Houston. It seemed to Armad as though half the people he encountered were Christians— and a high percent-age of them were loud and discourteous. Armad was appalled.

The final blow to his openness to Christ came one Sunday evening. A large number of Christians came into Armad's restaurant after church services. The non-smoking section quickly filled to it's capacity. One more family came requesting to be seated in that section. When Armad told them that the section was full and offered to seat them in the "smoking section" where *no one was presently smoking*, the man of the family became aggressive and belligerent. He accused Armad of "not really trying" to find him a table and just trying to fill his "smoke stained tables" in his "ash heap, wreaking with tobacco."

It took Henry Jackson, Armad's next-door neighbor, more than 10 years even to get him to talk about faith. It was Henry's kind and honest life and his gracious family that broke through the barrier erected 20 years ago. Today, Armad Abdy and his family are Christians.

✳ ✳ ✳

Memory Selection

But Daniel purposed in his heart that he would not defile himself with the portion of the king's meat, nor with the wine which he drank: therefore he requested of the prince of the eunuchs that he might not defile himself. *—Daniel 1:8*

Integrity is an impressive quality in anyone. It is seen in the university student who behaves consistently with his professed values, *even though he is miles from home* with no parent to scold him for misbehavior. It is seen in the business woman who honors her vows of marriage, even when she is halfway around the world on an extended business trip. It is seen in the store keeper who alerts the wholesale dealer to the mistakenly large delivery, even when the paperwork recorded a correct amount, *and there would be no way to trace the discrepancy*. It was seen in Daniel when he rejected the king's choice morsels, even though he enjoyed privileged seclusion far from the eyes of his would-be critics.

Basically, integrity is being honest to who you are, even when no one is watching. George Buttrick is credited with having said, "A man's real religion is what he does with his aloneness—and afterwards what his aloneness does with him."

Weekday Problems

During the past year, both First Church and Saint Luke's Church have been petitioning the city to take action to keep pornography out of the hands of children. Though most communities have had such ordinances in effect for years, this town's leaders have not seen this as a priority issue. It was just last week that First and Saint Luke's learned about each other's efforts in this cause.

Unfortunately, they also learned that they are not approaching the issue quite the same way. Whereas the pastor at First Church has assumed the town council to be in an adversarial position regarding the matter and has addressed the council in absolute and adversarial terms, the pastor at Saint Luke's came to the council in a very different spirit. It has been his assumption that the council is interested in "doing what is right" and acting in behalf of the good of the town's people. All proposals that have been made, therefore, have been in "suggestive terms" with room for negotiation.

* Which of the approaches would work most effectively if addressing your community's leaders? Why?

* If you sat on the town council, which approach would you want its citizens to make when lobbying in behalf of an idea or an ordinance? Why?

* Is there ever a time when the other method might work more effectively and be more appropriate?

Getting to the Meat of It

Customer: "Those franks you sold me were meat at one end and corn meal at the other!"
Butcher: "Yep; these days it's hard to make both ends meat."

Diner: "Waitress, I can't eat this stuff! Call the manager!"
Waitress: "Won't do any good, sir. He can't eat it either."

Waiter: "And how did you find your steak, sir?"
Diner: "Why, I just lifted that little piece of lettuce and there it was."

Diner: "This food isn't fit for a pig!"
Waiter: "I'm sorry, sir. I'll bring you some that is."

Cook: "Want me to cut this pizza into six or eight pieces?"
Customer: "Six, I guess. I can't eat eight."

This Lesson in Your Life

It may not happen *every* day, but it certainly happens with near-predictable frequency. Because the Christian is called to live in a secular world, he often finds himself in a potentially compromising position. It may be a matter of *truthfulness*, where the circumstances of the moment entice the Christian to be something less than totally honest. It is sometimes a matter of *confidentiality*. Information is known that could be used for personal gain, professionally or financially.

Too often, the Christian finds himself or herself in a position where *sexual morality* is the arena of character testing. It may arise due to natural mutual attraction, emerging from many shared hours working together in matters of common interest. Sometimes, it emerges because of the desire of one in a superior position (male or female) to exploit the one in a lesser position (male or female). "Sexual harassment" is the term that has been applied to such practices. Joseph found himself to be a target of sexual harassment in Egypt (Gen. 39).

Perhaps, more common than any of these major assaults against the faith, the Christian is subjected to attacks that are more subtle and elusive. What is involved may not be a blatant enticement to be dishonest, unethical or promiscuous. Instead, it is the enticement to *betray himself*—to compromise who he is as a person. Financial incentives can blur one's vision and make the decision more enticing than it would be otherwise. Peer pressure may further add to the temptation.

One of the basic issues that must be faced by all Christians who find themselves *captives of* an unbelieving and secular world is the matter of "compromise." When is compromise a "dirty word," and when is it "quite appropriate"? How does one tell the difference? Is it arbitrary, or a matter of personal opinion? Is it simply a matter of *situation ethics,* or are there specific principles involved to provide some practical guidelines to such calls for decision?

The first chapter of Daniel can provide some insights for the Christian if he will pay attention. Though Daniel remained strong in his principles, he was approachable and willing to negotiate in the area of practicalities. He readily recognized that negotiation in the latter arena did not necessarily require compromise in the former. Maintaining his honor before God did not require that he make himself disagreeable in disposition. His loyalty to God did not require that he be ugly or belligerent in his behavior toward his Chaldean host.

Principle number one. Though character must never be compromised, circumstances and situations may be negotiable. Drafted "conscientious objectors" found it possible *both* to be true to their convictions (not to kill) *and* to be submissive, serving their country in military duty.

Principle number two. Though one's principles of faith and ethics may need to be firmly set, one's jaw does not. One can be firm without being defensive or mean-spirited.

Principle number three. Maintaining one's own standard of ethics and faith does not arrogantly insist on the same standard for everyone else. Daniel was faithful to his own dietary restrictions but did not insist that *everyone* in the king's palace must eat only vegetables.

Seed Thoughts

1. During what year of Jehoiakim's reign did Nebuchadnezzar besiege Jerusalem?

It was during Jehoiakim's third year of reign.

2. Who was Ashpenaz, and what was his role?

Ashpenaz was the servant of king Nebuchadnezzar in charge of the eunuchs.

3. What qualifications had to be met in order to be selected for service in the king's palace?

Servants were to have no blemish, be well-favored, wise, knowledgeable, understanding science, intelligent and able to learn the Chaldean tongue.

4. What "favor" did the king give immediately to the four chosen men?

He ordered for them a daily portion of the king's meat and wine during their preparation time.

5. What were the names of the four men selected for the palace service?

Their Hebrew names were Daniel, Hananiah, Mishael, and Azariah.

---

1. During what year of Jehoiakim's reign did Nebuchadnezzar besiege Jerusalem?

2. Who was Ashpenaz, and what was his role?

3. What qualifications had to be met in order to be selected for service in the king's palace?

4. What "favor" did the king give immediately to the four chosen men?

5. What were the names of the four men selected for the palace service?

6. Why did Daniel not want the king's meat and wine?

7. Why did the prince of the eunuchs fear Daniel's request not to be forced to eat of the king's fine food?

8. What agreement did Daniel make with the prince of the eunuchs?

9. How long did Daniel and the others spend in preparation and schooling for the kings service?

10. What names did the King assign to the four Hebrews serving in the palace?

(Please turn page)

It was during Jehoiakim's third year of reign.

Ashpenaz was the servant of king Nebuchadnezzar in charge of the eunuchs.

Servants were to have no blemish, be well-favored, wise, knowledgeable, understanding science, intelligent and able to learn the Chaldean tongue.

He ordered for them a daily portion of the king's meat and wine during their preparation time.

Their Hebrew names were Daniel, Hananiah, Mishael, and Azariah.

Daniel did not want to defile himself. Obviously, the food did not meet Jewish kosher standards.

The prince of the eunuchs was fearful that the king would be displeased with the men's physical health and he, the prince, would lose his head.

Daniel challenged the prince of the eunuchs to let the Hebrews try a vegetable diet for ten days, then judge how their condition.

Three years.

Daniel was named Belteshazzar. Hananiah was named Shadrach. Mishael was named Meshach. Azariah was named Abednego.

6. Why did Daniel not want the king's meat and wine?

Daniel did not want to defile himself. Obviously, the food did not meet Jewish kosher standards.

7. Why did the prince of the eunuchs fear Daniel's request not to be forced to eat of the king's fine food?

The prince of the eunuchs was fearful that the king would be displeased with the men's physical health and he, the prince, would lose his head.

8. What agreement did Daniel make with the prince of the eunuchs?

Daniel challenged the prince of the eunuchs to let the Hebrews try a vegetable diet for ten days, then judge how their condition.

9. How long did Daniel and the others spend in preparation and schooling for the kings service?

Three years.

10. What names did the King assign to the four Hebrews serving in the palace?

Daniel was named Belteshazzar. Hananiah was named Shadrach. Mishael was named Meshach. Azariah was named Abednego.

Unwavering Faith

Daniel 3:14-25

14 Nebuchadnezzar spake and said unto them, Is it true, O Shadrach, Meshach, and Abednego, do not ye serve my gods, nor worship the golden image which I have set up?

15 Now if ye be ready that at what time ye hear the sound of the cornet, flute, harp, sackbut, psaltery, and dulcimer, and all kinds of musick, ye fall down and worship the image which I have made; well: but if ye worship not, ye shall be cast the same hour into the midst of a burning fiery furnace; and who is that God that shall deliver you out of my hands?

16 Shadrach, Meshach, and Abednego, answered and said to the king, O Nebuchadnezzar, we are not careful to answer thee in this matter.

17 And if it be so, our God whom we serve is able to deliver us from the burning fiery furnace, and he will deliver us out of thine hand, O king.

18 But if not, be it known unto thee, O king, that we will not serve thy gods, nor worship the golden image which thou hast set up.

19 Then was Nebuchadnezzar full of fury, and the form of his visage was changed against Shadrach, Meshach, and Abednego: therefore he spake, and commanded that they should heat the furnace one seven times more than it was wont to be heated.

20 And he commanded the most mighty men that were in his army to bind Shadrach, Meshach, and Abednego, and to cast them into the burning fiery furnace.

21 Then these men were bound in their coats, their hosen, and their hats, and their other garments, and were cast into the midst of the burning fiery furnace.

22 Therefore because the king's commandment was urgent, and the furnace exceeding hot, the flame of the fire slew those men that took up Shadrach, Meshach, and Abednego.

23 And these three men, Shadrach, Meshach, and Abednego, fell down bound into the midst of the burning fiery furnace.

24 Then Nebuchadnezzar the king was astonied, and rose up in haste, and spake, and said unto his counsellers, Did not we cast three men bound into the midst of the fire? They answered and said unto the king, True, O king.

25 He answered and said, Lo, I see four men loose, walking in the midst of the fire, and they have no hurt; and the form of the fourth is like the Son of God.

October 12

Memory Selection
Daniel 3:18

Devotional Reading
Psalm 27:7-14

Background Scripture
Daniel 3

Printed Scripture
Daniel 3:14-25

Teacher's Target

Lesson Purpose: *To reflect on the call and the conse-quence of having the faith to live for God despite pressures to the contrary—especially from the state.*

Even non-Christians know the story of the three Hebrew "children" or young men who were cast into the "burning fiery furnace" for not worshiping a false god. Fewer, however, have examined seriously the implications of the story as they relate to the believer's relationship to non-Christian law. Since worshiping the golden image was a decree of the king, refusing to do so constituted what has been called in our day "civil disobedience." The incident therefore raises several questions that can be probed in your class. Could such an incident occur in our country, or does the fact that it is often considered a "Christian nation" make it difficult to draw a parallel with Daniel's story? On the other hand, are we really a "Christian nation"? Either way, what should Christians do when a nation's laws violate their conscience?

Lesson Introduction

In some ways, the setting of this lesson seems foreign to modern times. Especially in the U.S., distinctions between church and state, the sacred and the secular, have been sharply drawn.

To understand this lesson, it is necessary to recall that such distinctions were virtually unknown in the ancient world. A nation's identity was usually closely related to its gods. Hence, when the three Hebrews refused to bow down to Nebuchadnezzar's golden image, they were guilty of both theological heresy and treason. Hence the king's harsh sentence.

In another sense, however, the principle here applies universally and for all time. Not only may governments still make laws that conflict with God's; even believers sometimes pay allegiance to their own desires over the will of God. The lesson here recalls the defiant and courageous statement of Peter in Acts 5:29: "We ought to obey God rather than men."

Teaching Outline	Daily Bible Readings
	Mon. 'Bow to the Golden Shrine' *Daniel 3:1-7*
I. The Choice Between Gods—14-15	**Tue.** Stand Your Ground *Daniel 3:8-15*
A. The temptation, 14	
B. The consequence, 15	**Wed.** Into the Furnace *Daniel 3:16-23*
II. The Carefree Response—16-18	**Thu.** Four Unbound in the Fire *Daniel 3:24-30*
A. The possibility of deliverance, 16-17	
B. The uncompromising decision, 18	**Fri.** 'Rescue Me from the Lions' *Psalm 35:17-28*
III. The Cost of Discipleship—19-23	**Sat.** Save Me from My Foes *Psalm 27: 1-6*
IV. The Christ in the Furnace—24-25	
	Sun. Christ's Messengers Endure *Matthew 10:16-23*

VERSE BY VERSE

I. The Choice Between Gods—14-15

A. The temptation, 14

14 Nebuchadnezzar spake and said unto them, Is it true, O Shadrach, Meshach, and Abednego, do not ye serve my gods, nor worship the golden image which I have set up?

Chapter 3:1 records the erection of the golden idol by King Nebuchadnezzar (some ancient sources spell it Nebuchadrezzer) of Babylon. He should have known better, since Daniel had so impressed him with his dream interpretation that the king had confessed Yahweh as "a God of gods" (2:47). Perhaps the king was a henotheist—one who acknowledges a chief god among many.

The golden idol may have been a representation of the chief Babylonian god Marduk (also called Merodach, or Bel—Jer. 51:44). It was 90 feet high and nine feet wide (3:1). The fact that the king ordered everyone to worship the colossal idol he had made betrays his colossal ego. In worshiping the image, people were actually honoring its creator.

Daniel's three Hebrew companions (1:7) will not worship the image because they honor the first Commandment: "Thou shalt have no other gods before me." Their refusal had been reported to the king by others in his court who resented them—just as Jews in general have been "turned in" and/or persecuted by people in many other nations where they have lived.

B. The consequence, 15

15 Now if ye be ready that at what time ye hear the sound of the cornet, flute, harp, sackbut, psaltery, and dulcimer, and all kinds of musick, ye fall down and worship the image which I have made; well: but if ye worship not, ye shall be cast the same hour into the midst of a burning fiery furnace; and who is that God that shall deliver you out of my hands?

The KJV's names for the musical instruments used to sound the "call to worship" for the idol reflect those used during King James' day more than those in the sixth-century B.C. The NIV's terms are probably more accurate: "horn, flute, zither, lyre, harp and pipes."

The "furnace" with which the three Hebrews were threatened may have been a giant oven or kiln like those used to bake the bricks and tiles of the famed city of Babylon. Nebuchadnezzar was very familiar with such equipment, since it was he who constructed the "hanging gardens of Babylon"—one of the seven wonders of the ancient world.

II. The Carefree Response—16-18

A. The possibility of deliverance, 16-17

16 Shadrach, Meshach, and Abednego, answered and said to the king, O Nebuchadnezzar, we are not careful to answer thee in this matter.

17 And if it be so, our God whom we serve is able to deliver us from the burn-

ing fiery furnace, and he will deliver us out of thine hand, O king.

Saying they were "not careful" to answer the king indicates that the three Hebrews had already been very careful to make up their minds beforehand about such choices as the one they face here. Those whose very lives are spent practicing loyalty to God have no panic when they are put to the test. The NIV translates the phrase, "We do not need to defend ourselves before you in this matter."

Recall that the three had already found God faithful in giving them robust health on a diet that dedicated themselves to Him (chap. 1). So who was to say that He could not also rescue them from the new threat? Their nonchalance is testimony to their faith.

B. The uncompromising decision, 18

18 But if not, be it known unto thee, O king, that we will not serve thy gods, nor worship the golden image which thou hast set up.

But what if they weren't rescued? Amazingly, the three men clearly conceive this to be a possibility, but it doesn't affect their choice. Those who study Christian ethics speak of an "ethics of consequence." This term applies to making choices about right and wrong on the basis of what would happen if we choose one way or another. If the three Hebrews had had this philosophy, they would have said, "Now wait! If God doesn't rescue us the deal is off!" Instead, the consequence of their choice was beside the point. Their battle was already won when they made their decision to follow God. Those who have learned to live in the fear of the Lord need fear no earthly power. As someone has said, "A coward dies a thousand deaths, while a brave man dies only once."

What does their defiance of the king have to teach modern believers about disobeying our own rulers? The ideal, biblical answer was cited above, from Acts 5:29: "We ought to obey God rather than men." Unfortunately, our own choices between right and wrong are rarely as clear-cut as the three Hebrews'. Also, our nation is founded on laws hammered out by people who respected divine law. Still, as recently as the civil rights struggle in the '50s and '60s, we have become aware that justice is sometimes more a process than an event. Although faithful Christians will not compromise the clear teaching of God's Word even when the state asks them to, neither will they use conscience as an excuse to rebel against their government for self-interest.

III. The Cost of Discipleship—19-23

19 Then was Nebuchadnezzar full of fury, and the form of his visage was changed against Shadrach, Meshach, and Abednego: therefore he spake, and commanded that they should heat the furnace one seven times more than it was wont to be heated.

20 And he commanded the most mighty men that were in his army to bind Shadrach, Meshach, and Abednego, and to cast them into the burning fiery furnace.

21 Then these men were bound in their coats, their hosen, and their hats, and their other garments, and were cast into the midst of the burning fiery furnace.

22 Therefore because the king's commandment was urgent, and the furnace exceeding hot, the flame of the fire slew those men that took up Shadrach, Meshach, and Abednego.

23 And these three men, Shadrach, Meshach, and Abednego, fell down bound

into the midst of the burning fiery furnace.

Nebuchadnezzar carries through with his threat, although his scheme to heat the furnace seven times hotter than usual backfires, slaying his own men.

Unbelievers, or those who practice "consequential ethics," would say "All is lost!" In contrast, the three Hebrews know that whether they are burned up or rescued, they have won. The test is not whether God will release them but whether they remain faithful. The German Christian Dietrich Bonhoeffer said that he did not consider being put to death for his opposition to Adolph Hitler a loss; it was merely the cost of discipleship. Years after this incident in Babylon, early Christians would celebrate the anniversary of a martyr's death with a victory party, not a funeral! That is the power of faith.

IV. The Christ in the Furnace—24-25

24 Then Nebuchadnezzar the king was astonied, and rose up in haste, and spake, and said unto his counsellers, Did not we cast three men bound into the midst of the fire? They answered and said unto the king, True, O king.

25 He answered and said, Lo, I see four men loose, walking in the midst of the fire, and they have no hurt; and the form of the fourth is like the Son of God.

We know from verses 26-28 that God's servants were released unscathed from the furnace, but we do not know the specific identity of the fourth personage who rescued them. Our outline calls him "the Christ" because the figure functions as a savior, just as Christ Jesus walks with the faithful and delivers them from their own fiery trials today. Although the Babylonians say he is "like the Son of God," they of course have no knowledge of the Christ who would come five centuries later. The phrase is better rendered as in the NIV: "like a son of the gods." He is at least recognized as a divine figure.

Remembering that the real victory here is the decision to be faithful, we are not disillusioned when we recall that many Christian martyrs were burned at the stake instead of being delivered. Neither will we expect our own trials always to come out "right" in this life. What is certain is that God is with us "in the midst of the fire," whether the outcome is life or death.

Evangelistic Emphasis

It is not unusual for Christians to echo the idea that a whole lot more people would respond to the gospel if the price were not so high. If the demands were not so difficult, there would be many more "takers." If the morality regulations were loosened a bit.... If the church didn't stress *tithing* so strongly . . . . If the church would just lighten its doctrine a little . . . .

The testimony of history, however, clearly demonstrates that *watering down the gospel* has never served to advance the cause of the gospel in the world. People are rarely attracted to a diluted *anything!* Diluting the gospel doesn't merely reduce its cost, it destroys it value. It does not just become inexpensive, it takes on the gaudy look common to things that are cheap. There may be a sufficient market to support the liquidation of cheap wine, but nobody really wants to invest in a cheap gospel.

Nebuchadnezzar was not impressed because the three Hebrews were willing to forego every-fifth-Sabbath bonus so as to contribute to the king's refugee fund. The king was impressed because these three Hebrews were willing to forfeit their lives for what they believed, and because their God was powerful enough and personally involved enough to save them.

Memory Selection

There are certain Jews whom thou hast set over the affairs of the province of Babylon, Shadrach, Meshach, and Abednego; these men, O king, have not regarded thee: they serve not thy gods, nor worship the golden image which thou hast set up. —*Daniel 3:18*

The tattling syndrome is not limited to children. Anytime rules seem to be unequally applied or someone appears to be exempt, there awaits someone else in the wings to tattle. The foreman who is being pressured to meet his overdue quota is quick to point out some other foreman who is more overdue. The deaconess who has exceeded her budget casually mentions some other ministry leader who has exceeded the budget more. The student that was caught in the locker room with a can of spray paint in hand is easily forced to relay input of other students known to contribute their artful expressions on other occasions.

In Daniel 3, the issue is not a matter of the king's conscious priority *until* it was made a priority matter by the tattler. A contemporary equivalent often heard in religiously divided homes asks, "Mommy, why do I have to go to church when Daddy gets to stay home?"

Weekday Problems

Daniel Patterson was only 4 years old when he was first told "the story of the fiery furnace" and made aware that he was named after "Daniel in the lion's den." As a small boy, that was exciting to him, and he learned quickly to be proud of his name. At 14, though, Daniel sometimes feels haunted by his name. Whenever he feels squeezed by the pressures of his peers, he automatically remembers  the one after whom he was named. His name is like a second conscience, or at least a conscience of a higher order.

Last week, it all resurfaced during the quiet of his Anthropology exam. The period's material had not been presented from a believer's orientation. Darwinism saturated the lecture notes and his textbook material. As he sat reading his exam questions, Daniel realized that they were worded in such a way so as to elicit Darwinian answers. It seemed to Daniel that, if he gave the answers his teacher clearly wanted, he would be a traitor to his faith. Flashbacks of the "fiery furnace" story caused him to squirm uneasily in his seat.

   * Is Daniel's situation comparable to the story of Daniel chapter 3, or is he being melodramatic?

   * What ought to be Daniel Patterson's response to the questions? Should he provide the answers the teacher wants or give answers that are "true to faith"?

   * Should Daniel's parents intervene in his behalf or let him work it out on his own?

✠ ✠ ✠

Tidbits on Temptation

You can't see the flaw in a bridge until it falls down, or the flaw in a man's character until he meets with temptation.

Sometimes it's hard to tell who's knocking—opportunity or temptation.

When temptation calls, just drop the receiver.
Temptation sometimes tries to crash through our door—only to find that we've left it open.

Some people can hear the faintest whisper of temptation easier than the loudest call of duty.

We're supposed to flee temptation. Few people, however, set speed records doing so; and some even leave their forwarding address.

This Lesson in Your Life

The third chapter of Daniel presents us with a great children's story about the triumph of faith and how God rescues even in the most impossible circumstances. Children are awed at the idea that even the hair on the heads of these men was not singed. The fourth man witnessed in the fire along with the three sentenced to the flames only adds further intrigue and mystery to the story.

Having said all of that, though, how does one deal with the real-life circumstances when God does not bring such a dramatic rescue? How does one answer the heartbreak of the nine-year-old boy who stood by his principles, refusing to miss church for a special Wednesday evening school event, and got a "F" in Social Studies because of the absence? How does one give a satisfactory reply to the young, single mother who lost her job because she refused to compromise her morality to indulge her boss's lustful groping? How does one defend God to the fifty-five year old man who lost his medical insurance because of his tenacious insistence to be truthful? Now, he can't buy coverage for any price.

Each one of these seemed like perfect opportunities for God to ride in on his white horse and rescue the day. Nevertheless, Tommy still has an "F" in Social Studies. Janet is a single mother with two children and no source of income. Bill sees no prospects of being able to buy medical insurance for the remainder of his life. What is he going to do when the bills begin to stack up as the HIV virus takes it toll? What is his family going to do?

One of the most commendable parts of this whole story is often missed in the Sunday School presentation. After expressing confidence in their God's *ability* to save them from the fiery furnace and confidence that He *would indeed* deliver them, the three added an addendum to this statement of confidence. *"But if not . . . ,"* they proceeded to say, they would still remain loyal to their God and not worship the king's idol.

The faith of those men did not require that God jump to their assistance. They trusted Him, period. They would be loyal to Him, period. Theirs was not a conditional loyalty or a conditional faith. If it was God's choice to allow the flames to consume them, then they would accept that as their lot. It would not diminish their relationship to their God.

As two people stand at the altar to be married, they make vows to be loyal "for better or for worse." Marriage, by its very nature, requires that kind of *unconditional* commitment. A tenuous agreement between two people will never provide the same sense of security. Consequently, even in these times of high divorce statistics, the vows still echo sentiments of a "for better or for worse" pledge.

In much the same way, God pledges His unconditional commitment to His children. He does not say, *"I will love you if . . . ."* Instead, we are promised that nothing can separate us from the love of God in Christ Jesus (Rom. 831-39). It is not a legal contract that God made with us, filled with technicalities and loopholes for easy escape. God made with us *a covenant* that is based on His relationship to us as a Father to His children. Shouldn't I have that same kind of unconditional commit-ment to Him as His child?

Seed Thoughts

1. What did King Nebuchadnezzar have erected on the plain of Dura and what was its size?

He had built an image of gold 90 feet tall and nine feet wide (a cubit is approximately 18 inches).

2. To whom was the command given to bow down to the image?

The command was given to "peoples, nations and languages."

3. What was to be the cue for people to bow down before the image?

They were to bow down as soon as they heard the sound of the instruments of music.

4. What was to happen to those who did not comply with the kings decree to fall down and worship?

They were to be thrown into the midst of a burning fiery furnace.

5. What was Nebuchadnezzar's initial reaction when he learned that some were not following his edict to bow down before the idol?

He was outraged.

---

1. What did King Nebuchadnezzar have erected on the plain of Dura and what was its size?

2. To whom was the command given to bow down to the image?

3. What was to be the cue for people to bow down before the image?

4. What was to happen to those who did not comply with the kings decree to fall down and worship?

5. What was Nebuchadnezzar's initial reaction when he learned that some were not following his edict to bow down before the idol?

6. What was commendable about Nebuchadnezzar's handling of the initial report of the men's disobedience?

7. Did the three Hebrews believe God could deliver them from the fiery furnace? Did they believe He *would* deliver them?

8. What if God had not delivered them from the furnace? How would they have handled that disappointment?

9. What surprised Nebuchadnezzar after the men were cast into the furnace?

10. What decree did the king hand down after the men came out of the furnace?

(Please turn page)

He had built an image of gold ninety feet tall and nine feet wide (a cubit is approximately 18 inches).

The command was given to "peoples, nations and languages."

They were to bow down as soon as they heard the sound of the instruments of music.

They were to be thrown into the midst of a burning fiery furnace.

He was outraged.

Nebuchadnezzar asked the three personally if the report was true about their disobedience and gave them a second chance to comply.

They expressed confidence both that He was able to deliver them and that He would deliver them.

They seemed ready to die for their faith if that was their God's choice without feeling ill toward their God.

A. That they were not harmed. B. That there were four men in the furnace rather than three.

He made a decree that no one should speak against the God of Shadrach, Meshach and Abednego.

6. What was commendable about Nebuchadnezzar's handling of the initial report of the men's disobedience?

Nebuchadnezzar asked the three personally if the report was true about their disobedience and gave them a second chance to comply.

7. Did the Hebrews believe that God could deliver them from the fiery furnace? Did they believe He *would* deliver them?

They expressed confidence both that He was able to deliver them and that He would deliver them.

8. What if God had not delivered them from the furnace? How would they have handled that disappointment?

They seemed ready to die for their faith if that was their God's choice without feeling ill toward their God.

9. What surprised Nebuchadnezzar after the men were cast into the furnace?

A. That they were not harmed. B. That there were four men in the furnace rather than three.

10. What decree did the king hand down after the men came out from the furnace?

He made a decree that no one should speak against the God of Shadrach, Meshach and Abednego.

Lesson 7

Weighed and Found Wanting

Daniel 5:1-7, 25-28

1 Belshazzar the king made a great feast to a thousand of his lords, and drank wine before the thousand.

2 Belshazzar, whiles he tasted the wine, commanded to bring the golden and silver vessels which his father Nebuchadnezzar had taken out of the temple which was in Jerusalem; that the king, and his princes, his wives, and his concubines, might drink therein.

3 Then they brought the golden vessels that were taken out of the temple of the house of God which was at Jerusalem; and the king, and his princes, his wives, and his concubines, drank in them.

4 They drank wine, and praised the gods of gold, and of silver, of brass, of iron, of wood, and of stone.

5 In the same hour came forth fingers of a man's hand, and wrote over against the candlestick upon the plaister of the wall of the king's palace: and the king saw the part of the hand that wrote.

6 Then the king's countenance was changed, and his thoughts troubled him, so that the joints of his loins were loosed, and his knees smote one against another.

7 The king cried aloud to bring in the astrologers, the Chaldeans, and the soothsayers. And the king spake, and said to the wise men of Babylon, Whosoever shall read this writing, and shew me the interpretation thereof, shall be clothed with scarlet, and have a chain of gold about his neck, and shall be the third ruler in the kingdom.

25 And this is the writing that was written, MENE, MENE, TEKEL, UPHARSIN.

26 This is the interpretation of the thing: MENE; God hath numbered thy kingdom, and finished it.

27 TEKEL; Thou art weighed in the balances, and art found wanting.

28 PERES; Thy kingdom is divided and given to the Medes and Persians.

Memory Selection
Daniel 5:27

Devotional Reading
Daniel 7:1-3, 15-18

Background Scripture
Daniel 5

Printed Scripture
Daniel 5:1-7, 25-28

Teacher's Target

Lesson purpose: *To learn, through the experience of King Belshazzar, that God holds us accountable for the way we use His gifts and blessings.*

This lesson contains the origin of the phrase "the handwriting on the wall." We use it to speak of the predictable result or outcome of some action—as "He saw the handwriting on the wall in the company's inexperienced new management, and sold his stock in the firm."

You might also illustrate this lesson for your class by reminding them of Jesus' parable of the talents, in Matthew 25:14-30. (Remember that "talents" in the kjv refers to money, although the parable also applies to gifts or abilities.)

Like Belshazzar, and the servants in Jesus' parable, we too will be "weighed" in God's balance scales on the Day of Judgment. Even so, just as His gifts to us are out of His grace, we rely also on that grace to help us use our gifts responsibly.

Lesson Introduction

Nebuchadnezzar by driving him, apparently insane, into the fields to live as a beast (Dan. 4:29-33). The experience made him turn to the Lord (vss. 34-37). Evidently Belshazzar was a grandson (see the comment at 5:7) who was equally proud, but much more defiant.

Ancient non-biblical sources say that King Nabonidus, not Belshazzar, was ruler during Babylon's last days, and that he was overthrown by Cyrus the Persian rather than Darius the Mede (5:31). The present chapter apparently supplies additional insight into Babylonia's last kings and their downfall. Perhaps further research and discoveries in what is now Iraq will one day show how to harmonize the Bible's testimony with secular history.

At any rate, the booming judgment "Thou art weighed in the balance and found wanting" echoes down the centuries as a truth that overwhelms the quest for precise accuracy in historical detail.

Teaching Outline	Daily Bible Readings

I. Blasphemous Revelry—1-4
  A. Drunken pride, 1
  B. Disrespectful acts, 2-4
II. Mysterious Writing—5-7
  A. A hand of judgment, 5
  B. A hasty search for answers, 6-7
III. Disastrous Results—25-28
  A. Numbered, 25-26
  B. Weighed, 27
  C. Divided, 28
	Mon. Handwriting on the Wall
	    Daniel 5:1-9
	Tue. Daniel Can Read the Writing
	    Daniel 5:10-17
	Wed. Weighed and Found Wanting
	    Daniel 5:18-31
	Thu. A New Kingdom Coming
	    Daniel 7:1-3, 15-18
	Fri. Day of Judgment Fixed
	    Acts 17:22-31
	Sat. Judged by Careless Words
	    Matthew 12:33-37
	Sun. Be Patient Until the Coming
	    James 5:1-11

VERSE BY VERSE

I. Blasphemous Revelry—1-4

A. Drunken pride, 1

1 Belshazzar the king made a great feast to a thousand of his lords, and drank wine before the thousand.

Who was Belshazzar? His name means literally "May Bel (the chief Babylonian god) protect the king." Verses 2, 11, and 18 indicate that he was the son of Nebuchadnezzar. Ancient writings discovered in what is now Iraq, however, say that Nebuchadnezzar's son (and the last king of Babylonia) was Nabonidus, and that Belshazzar was his son rather than Nebuchadnezzar's. The puzzle is solved when we realize that the term translated "father" can also mean "grandfather" (see the footnote in many Bibles). Many scholars believe that Nabonidus placed his son Belshazzar on the throne as co-ruler while he left for a 10- to 12-year period.

Again, to the question Who was Belshazzar? verse 1 answers that he was a proud and vain man who reveled in his reputation as a "hard drinker." He was not content just to drink in excess; he wanted to do it before the thousand noblemen in his court. He was not the last person to take questionable pride in being able to "drink everyone else under the table." Both false pride and drunkenness are consistently condemned in Scripture, as in "Pride goeth before destruction" (Prov. 16:18) and "Be not drunk with wine" (Eph. 5:18).

B. Disrespectful acts, 2-4

2 Belshazzar, whiles he tasted the wine, commanded to bring the golden and silver vessels which his father Nebuchadnezzar had taken out of the temple which was in Jerusalem; that the king, and his princes, his wives, and his concubines, might drink therein.

3 Then they brought the golden vessels that were taken out of the temple of the house of God which was at Jerusalem; and the king, and his princes, his wives, and his concubines, drank in them.

4 They drank wine, and praised the gods of gold, and of silver, of brass, of iron, of wood, and of stone.

As the king began to feel the effects of the wine, his lowered inhibitions allow a blasphemous thought: Why not show my scorn for the God of these Hebrews we have captured by drinking from the holy vessels we confiscated from their Temple? Just as drinking or pouring out a "libation" was a common pagan way of honoring a god, drinking in mockery from the gold vessels from the Temple was calculated to abase Yahweh, the true God.

To double his blasphemy, Belshazzar dares even to toast his own gods from the Jews' sacred vessels. The "pantheons" or array of gods among pagan people included deities thought to be the governor of a wide variety of activities and things on earth. There were gods of the hearth and the harvest; of the sun, moon, and stars; of music and wine; and, here, of precious metals and even of stone. Belshazzar is not accidentally sinning here; he is deliberately scorning the true God. Verse 23 shows that Daniel correctly understood the king's action to be a gesture of pride "against the Lord of heaven."

II. Mysterious Writing—5-7

A. A hand of judgment, 5

5 In the same hour came forth fingers of a man's hand, and wrote over against the candlestick upon the plaister of the wall of the king's palace: and the king saw the part of the hand that wrote.

We may imagine that the sight of a man's fingers writing on the plaster of the wall could caused Belshazzar to wonder if the wine was causing delusions. Actually, his response indicates that the apparition jolted him sober!

Although it is actually the offended true God who is confronting the king with His message of judgment, He uses a man's hand to write it. This reminds us that God is a Spirit (John 4:24); apparently He uses a man's hand here as an "anthropomorphism"—a human form—because that's what men would recognize.

B. A hasty search for answers, 6-7

6 Then the king's countenance was changed, and his thoughts troubled him, so that the joints of his loins were loosed, and his knees smote one against another.

7 The king cried aloud to bring in the astrologers, the Chaldeans, and the soothsayers. And the king spake, and said to the wise men of Babylon, Whosoever shall read this writing, and shew me the interpretation thereof, shall be clothed with scarlet, and have a chain of gold about his neck, and shall be the third ruler in the kingdom.

If the writing on the wall might be taken as drunken delusions, Belshazzar's physical reaction may seem to be "delirium tremens"—the "DTs." He shakes and quakes for good reason—no one has ever seen such a sight

before.

Showing that he lacks the capacity for repentance which characterized his ancestor Nebuchadnezzar, the king sends for pagan advisors to interpret the language, promising them royal gifts and royal standing if they can do so. The fact that he promises the successful interpreter third place in the kingdom instead of second—as was the case with Joseph so many years earlier—may indicate that Belshazzar himself was second in command, under his father Nabonidus.

We are not told why the magicians and court seers could not read the writing (vs. 8), nor what language was used. Daniel's own report of it in verses 25-28 is in Hebrew, but he may have been translating it from the king's own Chaldean tongue. Even if the writing was in Hebrew, we would expect that some of the wise men at the king's feast could read it, since the Hebrews had been in Babylonia for many years. Perhaps, somehow, "their eyes were holden," as in the case of the risen Christ's followers in Luke 24:16.

III. Disastrous Results—25-28

A. Numbered, 25-26

25 And this is the writing that was written, MENE, MENE, TEKEL, UPHARSIN.

26 This is the interpretation of the thing: MENE; God hath numbered thy kingdom, and finished it.

As verses 9-12 have explained, Belshazzar's queen remembered Daniel's previous ability to interpret King Nebuchadnezzar's dreams (chaps. 2, 4)—reminding us of the way Pharaoh's chief butler had remembered Joseph (Gen. 41). Also in the intervening verses, Daniel has bluntly told the king that he must answer for his vanity and blasphemy. Now he is ready to give an explicit interpretation of the mysterious words on the wall.

"Mene," repeated for the sheer rhythm and ring of the phrasing, means to number or count, signifying that the king's days are numbered. The grandeur of Babylonia, with its famous hanging gardens, is ended. It did not use its wealth and power for God, but squandered it in power politics, oppression, and idolatrous worship.

B. Weighed, 27

27 TEKEL; Thou art weighed in the balances, and art found wanting.

The word "to weigh" is related to the concept of being found "too light." The imagery is of a set of balance scales, with God's standard on one side and King Belshazzar on the other. His vainglory and blasphemy have rendered him a lightweight. His misuse of God's blessings mean that he cannot measure up before the Judge of all the world.

C. Divided, 28

28 PERES; Thy kingdom is divided, and given to the Medes and Persians.

The word *peres* may be the same word that would later give the Jews the sectarian name "Pharisee," which apparently meant "separatist." Its use here is in the sense of dividing one part of a lump from another.

Scripture supplies a historical footnote not yet duplicated in the ancient records so far discovered. Those sources refer to the Persians, under King Cyrus, defeating the Babylonian king Nabonidus. Apparently the kingdom of the Medes, to the northeast, briefly intervened under Darius, whom God used to punish Belshazzar's pride and irresponsible use of his gifts (vs. 31).

Evangelistic Emphasis

Tuesday morning, I had breakfast with a young Christian about camp curriculum. He and I had been designated as cabin counselors for "Cabin #1." Mark became a Christians just a little over a year ago. During our breakfast, conversation strayed far away from anything having to do with curriculum.

Our concern for Peter, one of the campers assigned to us, resurrected some painful childhood memories for Mark. He identifies with some of the struggles Peter is presently going though. He understands the anger and frustration and self-destructive behavior that has taken over Peter's life. Mark followed that downward-spiraling road well into adulthood. "But one morning I woke up," he said, "and *I knew that the handwriting was on the wall.* If I didn't change my behavior, I would soon be dead."

It is interesting how prominent that phrase has come to be in our ordinary conversation, even among those who have no knowledge of Daniel. It is also interesting how often the phrase has to do with death (or at least, threatening possibilities). Fortunately, "handwriting on the wall" still appears to warn those whose doom is impending. It may assume any of a variety of forms in order to get across it's message of warning. The recipient may be a slave or a king, yet the message must always be received as coming from the Giver. The Giver writes the message that we might repent.

✳ ✳ ✳

Memory Selection

TEKEL; Thou art weighed in the balances, and art found wanting.—*Daniel 5:27*

As a child, I found myself intrigued by the court house at the center of downtown. Built of granite and marble, it always seemed to be cooler inside than just about any other building in town, even without air conditioning. At the top of the court house was a green dome—tarnished bronze, and on top of the dome stood a lady, wearing a blindfold with a balance in her hand.

I still remember my mother attempting to explain to me the symbolism of "blind justice" represented by the court house lady. It was not until years later that I comprehended why justice needed to be blind—to race, religion, economics and nationality.

It was this image of justice that Daniel conveys to Belshazzar as he interpreted the message of God written on the wall. The Lord had spoken, "Belshazzar has been weighed in the balance of ultimate judgment, and the verdict is not good."

Weekday Problems

It has been painful for Andrew's church friends to watch the change of attitude that has come to dominate his relationships. Though these changes are clear and appalling to his friends, they seem to be invisible to Andrew.

Andrew began his political involvement in the lowly arena of P.T.A. His motive was an honest one—to help make his children's school a better one. From the P.T.A., Andrew moved to the School Board, then into city politics. For the past five years, his clout has been growing. Last month, Andrew was elected mayor.

If Andrew's friends were to speak boldly their evaluation of this once servant-spirited man, they would use words like "arrogant," "big-headed," and "pompous."

* As fellow-Christians, what course of action might Andrew's friends take to communicate effectively their concern for him?

* What do you think causes humble, self-giving individuals like Andrew to change so dramatically?

* Have you known anyone like Andrew? What did you do in response to his change?

High-Flying Orators
(Brought Down to Earth)

The preacher got up to speak, only to find that someone had placed a card on the pulpit with these words: "If you don't strike oil within 20 minutes, stop boring."

Quiet, please, it's time to listen to our speaker. You can enjoy yourselves some other time.

In Bible times, it was considered a miracle when a donkey spoke. Listening to Senator Puffenblo, you can't help but realize how times have changed.

He holds people open-mouthed with his conversational skills. They can't stop yawning.

And now, ladies and gentleman, I'm going to say something in the public interest. Good night.

This Lesson in Your Life

It was Greg Foster's first time to be on his own. He left home to go to college, but it was a Christian college that his parents had required if they were to pay the tuition. At college, there were even more rules and closer supervision than at home. Chapel was required every day and at least one Bible class every semester. When summer came, Greg broke free.

It wasn't an impressive job (working in a Wisconsin cannery), but it was *away from* all the rules and regulations that Greg had come to find oppressive. And it was away from *all that religion!* For the past several years, it had been all Greg could do to tolerate it. Now, with a great sense of freedom, he put completely out of his mind anything that related to religion. *But then*, that package from his mother arrived.

Greg's mother had been worried that Greg would not have a break from his grueling work schedule to go to church. When she inquired about his church attendance, he had found her quickly gullible to his excuse for non-attendance in "the oppressive schedule" about which he cried. This concerned Greg's mother greatly. Immediately, she started thinking about how she could help her "poor little boy" nurture his spiritual life while away from the protective surroundings of home and in such a hostile climate. Before the next day ended, she had baked some "communion bread," carefully wrapped the bread and some individual servings of "fruit of the vine" and air-mailed them to her son.

I well remember the day that package arrived. I was there. Greg opened the package and called for the attention of all the fellows in the barracks. As the guys surrounded the table at the middle of the room, he announced to them all that he had received "communion bread" from his mother. In the few moments that followed the room was an uproar of raucous laughter as Greg conducted a mock communion ceremony. He spread peanut butter on the communion bread, popped the top on a canned beer and proceeded to reenact his own perverted version of the Last Supper.

From the message that was inscribed by the mysterious hand on the wall and from the words of Daniel subsequently spoken to the king, I'm led to wonder if such was not the spirit of Belshazzar that fateful evening as he arrogantly profaned the temple vessels. Didn't Babylon have any golden vessels of its own? Was there a dish shortage crisis in the land? Or was Belshazzar just "having a good laugh" at the expense of the religion of the Israelite people as he reveled with his friends that evening?

I've often wondered what happened to Greg Foster. Did he continue his irreverent disregard for the faith and tradition of his parents? Has his adult life demonstrated a perpetual contempt for religion, and if so, how has this nurtured his children? Or is it possible that Greg has come to regret those sacrilegious moments and words? Is it possible that he is, today, a man of faith and conviction?

I also wonder how many of the rest of us have been guilty of much the same kind of irreverence? Perhaps, it was exhibited in our "making light of" the horse and buggy of the Amish, the "turned around collar" of the priest, the "polyester suit" of the out-of-style pastor or the tattered robes of the choir. Anytime we mock the presence of some of God's servants, we stand in danger of mocking God. Jesus' words, *"Inasmuch as ye have done it unto one of the least of these my brethren, ye have done it unto me,"* may very well apply.

Seed Thoughts

1. Who was Belshazzar? How did he come to be the king? What happened to Nebuchadnezzar?

Nebuchadnezzar died in 562 B.C. This event was in 539. Belshazzar was Nebuchadnezzar's son (or grand-son—the word is not clear).

2. What was the nature of the event that caused the bringing out of the temple's vessels?

The king was celebrating a drunken feast with a host of his friends.

3. For what purpose did King Belshazzar use the temple vessels of the Israelites?

He used them to drink wine and to toast the various deities of the Babylonians.

4. What pagan gods did Belshazzar praise in this drunken toast?

He praised the gods of gold, silver, brass, iron, wood and stone.

5. What specifically was it that was seen writing upon the wall? Where on the wall did it write?

The fingers of a hand were seen writing. They wrote on the plaster near the candlestick.

1. Who was Belshazzar? How did he come to be the king? What happened to Nebuchadnezzar?

2. What was the nature of the event that caused the bringing out of the temple's vessels?

3. For what purpose did King Belshazzar use the temple vessels of the Israelites?

4. What pagan gods did Belshazzar praise in this drunken toast?

5. What *specifically* was seen writing upon the wall? Where on the wall did it write?

6. What was the king's initial response to this unusual sight?

7. What did the king promise to anyone who could read the message and tell him what it meant?

8. How did Belshazzar learn about Daniel and his gift for dispensing wisdom?

9. Upon being offered a reward by the king for his service, how did Daniel respond?

10. What was the message, and what did it mean?

(Please turn page)

Nebuchadnezzar died in 562 B.C. This event was 539. Belshazzar was Nebuchadnezzar's son (or grand-son—the word is not clear).

The king was celebrating a drunken feast with a host of his friends.

He used them to drink wine and to toast the various deities of the Babylonians.

He praised the gods of gold, silver, brass, iron, wood and stone.

The fingers of a hand were seen writing. They wrote on the plaster near the candlestick.

The king's countenance changed (NIV "His face turned pale"), his knees knocked and his legs became weak.

He promised that the person would be clothed in scarlet, have a gold chain put around his neck and be recognized as the third ruler of the kingdom.

He was told about Daniel by the queen.

Daniel told the king that he could keep his gifts and give the rewards to someone else, but that he would intepret the message.

"Mene, Mene, Tekel, Upharsin" meant the kingdom had come to an end. Belshazzar was found lacking, and his kingdom would be given to others.

6. What was the king's initial response to this unusual sight?

The king's countenance changed (NIV "His face turned pale"), his knees knocked and his legs became weak.

7. What did the king promise to anyone who could read the message and tell him what it meant?

He promised that the person would be clothed in scarlet, have a gold chain put around his neck and be recognized as the third ruler of the kingdom.

8. How did Belshazzar learn about Daniel and his gift for dispensing wisdom?

He was told about Daniel by the queen.

9. Upon being offered a reward by the king for his service, how did Daniel respond?

Daniel told the king that he could keep his gifts and give the rewards to someone else, but that he would interpret the message.

10. What was the message, and what did it mean?

"Mene, Mene, Tekel, Upharsin" meant that the kingdom had come to an end. Belshazzar was found lacking, and his kingdom would be given to others.

WISDOM = UNDERSTANDING

Lesson 8

A Prayer Is Answered

Daniel 9:1-6, 18-23

1 In the first year of Darius the son of Ahasuerus, of the seed of the Medes, which was made king over the realm of the Chaldeans;

2 In the first year of his reign I Daniel understood by books the number of the years, whereof the word of the Lord came to Jeremiah the prophet, that he would accomplish seventy years in he desolations of Jerusalem.

3 And I set my face unto the Lord God, to seek by prayer and supplications, with fasting, and sackcloth, and ashes:

4 And I prayed unto the Lord my God, and made my confession, and said, O Lord, the great and dreadful God, keeping the covenant and mercy to them that love him, and to them that keep his commandments;

5 We have sinned, and have committed iniquity, and have done wickedly, and have rebelled, even by departing from thy precepts and from thy judgments:

6 Neither have we hearkened unto thy servants the prophets, which spake in thy name to our kings, our princes, and our fathers, and to all the people of the land.

18 O my God, incline thine ear, and hear; open thine eyes, and behold our desolations, and the city which is called by thy name: for we do not present our supplications before thee for our righteousness, but for thy great mercies.

19 O Lord, hear; O Lord, forgive; O Lord, hearken and do; defer not, for thine own sake, O my God; for thy city and thy people are called by thy name.

20 And whiles I was speaking, and praying, and confessing my sin and the sin of my people Israel, and presenting my supplication before the Lord my God for the holy mountain of my God;

21 Yea, whiles I was speaking in prayer, even the man Gabriel, whom I had seen in the vision at the beginning, being caused to fly swiftly, touched me about the time of the evening oblation.

22 And he informed me, and talked with me, and said, O Daniel, I am now come forth to give thee skill and understanding.

23 At the beginning of thy supplications the commandment came forth, and I am come to shew thee; for thou art greatly beloved: therefore understand the matter, and consider the vision.

Memory Selection
Daniel 9:23

Devotional Reading
Daniel 7:7-14

Background Scripture
Daniel 9

Printed Scripture
Daniel 9:1-6, 18-23

Teacher's Target

Lesson purpose: *To delve into the mystery of prayer, especially prayers of confession and intercession as illustrated in the life of Daniel.*

Most members of your Bible class will be able to identify with the anguish that wrings from Daniel the prayer recorded in this passage. They have walked through the valley of the shadow of grief, if not death, and know what it's like to beg God for release. Many are aware of their need for forgiveness, and of the corporate sins of the nation.

Most Christians have also struggled with the question of unanswered prayer. Although we may affirm God's power to respond to our petitions, we also wonder why all of them are not answered. Use this time not only to lift up the power of prayer but to allow class members to share experiences in which they have found themselves saying "Lord, I believe; help thou mine unbelief" (Mark 9:24).

Lesson Introduction

Daniel was a young man—perhaps 15 or 16 years old—when the Babylonian (or Chaldean) king Nebuchadnezzar conquered Jerusalem. Although Daniel was among the captives carried away into Babylonian captivity, he did not go into exile alone. He had access at least to the scroll of the prophet Jeremiah, and perhaps to other portions of Scripture that were a part of the Hebrew heritage.

We can imagine both the anguish of being captive in a foreign land, and the comfort that God's Word must have brought to Daniel. The writings of Jeremiah had special relevance. Although Jeremiah had been one of the most stern critics of the spiritual decay among God's people, he had also foreseen God's gracious hand of deliverance. He predicted both the exile and the return of Israel (see for background Jer. 25:8-12; 29:10).

This blend of grief and hope provides the setting of Daniel's prayer and the focus of this lesson.

Teaching Outline	Daily Bible Readings
	Mon. No Fault Found in Daniel *Daniel 6:1-9*
	Tue. Prayers Break the King's Law *Daniel 6:10-18*
I. A Probe for Understanding—1-2	**Wed.** Protected from the Lions *Daniel 6:19-28*
II. A Prayer of Confession—3-6	
A. Praise, 3-4	**Thu.** Open Shame for Disobedience *Daniel 9:1-10*
B. Contrition, 5-6	**Fri.** Claiming the Mercies of God *Daniel 9:11-19*
III. A Petition of Intercession—18-19	**Sat.** Wisdom and Mystery in Reply *Daniel 9:20-27*
IV. A Promise of Hope—20-23	**Sun.** The Lord Is Our Saving God *Habakkuk 3:13-19a*

VERSE BY VERSE

I. A Probe for Understanding—1-2

1 In the first year of Darius the son of Ahasuerus, of the seed of the Medes, which was made king over the realm of the Chaldeans;

2 In the first year of his reign I Daniel understood by books the number of the years, whereof the word of the Lord came to Jeremiah the prophet, that he would accomplish seventy years in he desolations of Jerusalem.

Some scholars think Darius the Mede received his commission from Cyrus the Persian, and that Babylonia was conquered by a "Medo-Persian" alliance. It was in King Darius' first year that Daniel, now a grown man, began to search the "books" (literally "writings," which would have been in the form of scrolls since bound books with pages as we know them weren't invented until early in the Christian era).

Why did Daniel study Jeremiah's writings instead of some of the many wise writings of the Chaldeans? Because already in Jewish history the writings of their prophets were being elevated to the status of Scripture—holy writings. Note that while Daniel will rely on prayer, it is combined with serious study of Scripture. Even today, as essential as prayer is, it is no substitute for being informed of God's overall will as revealed through His Word.

What Daniel found predicted in Jeremiah was that after 70 years of captivity, God would enable the Jews to be restored to their homeland (see Jer. 25:8-12; 29:10). Yet this sovereign decree does not cause Daniel to sit idly by and do nothing. His fervent prayer is prompted by God's preordained plan, as the means God can use to accomplish what He promised. Here is a subtle but profound glimpse of how the oft-debated topic of predestination is worked out in history. God's overall plan may be set from before the worlds were made; but He grants humans the power to involve themselves in being a part of that plan.

II. A Prayer of Confession—3-6

A. Praise, 3-4

3 And I set my face unto the Lord God, to seek by prayer and supplications, with fasting, and sackcloth, and ashes:

4 And I prayed unto the Lord my God, and made my confession, and said, O Lord, the great and dreadful God, keeping the covenant and mercy to them that love him, and to them that keep his commandments;

Daniel prepares for prayer with symbols of humility and contrition. Wearing "sackcloth" was such a symbol because it was a rough, scratchy material woven from camel or goat hair. (The English word "sack" comes from the Hebrew saq.) Heaping ashes on one's head symbolized a "burning" sense of unworthiness or sadness. Even today, many Christians find that such self-denial, especially in the form of fasting, helps them draw closer to God (see Elmer Towns, *Fasting for Spiritual Breakthrough* [Ventura, Calif.: Regal Books, 1996]).

In the latter part of verse 4, Daniel praises God as "dreadful" (niv "awesome"), covenant-keeping, and merciful. Even in prayers confessing our sin, praise is appropriate because it makes us more aware of how far different we are from the praiseworthy God. After the people were allowed to return to Palestine, Nehemiah prayed a similar prayer with the same pattern—praise first, then confession (see Neh. 9).

B. Contrition, 5-6

5 We have sinned, and have committed iniquity, and have done wickedly, and have rebelled, even by departing from thy precepts and from thy judgments:

6 Neither have we hearkened unto thy servants the prophets, which spake in thy name to our kings, our princes, and our fathers, and to all the people of the land.

What a remarkably accurate condensation of Israel's history under her kings! The books of Kings and Chronicles record cycle after cycle when God raised up a king only to have him rule unjustly, and establish idol worship in the land. Then God would raise up a prophet such as Elijah or Jeremiah who rebukes the wickedness of the ruler, and predicts judgment at the hand of God, through its behalf. Do modern believers serve this function in our own land?

III. A Petition of Intercession—18-19

18 O my God, incline thine ear, and hear; open thine eyes, and behold our desolations, and the city which is called by thy name: for we do not present our supplications before thee for our righteousness, but for thy great mercies.

19 O Lord, hear; O Lord, forgive; O Lord, hearken and do; defer not, for thine own sake, O my God; for thy city and thy people are called by thy name.

Fully aware that he and his people do not deserve to be delivered from Babylonian captivity, Daniel can only throw himself on God's mercy. He also appeals to God's reputation. Jerusalem, the holy city, and the people of God themselves are being observed by other nations. Perhaps God will deliver His people as a witness to the nations that He is in fact a loving and forgiving and all-powerful God, unlike the gods of the nations.

Verse 19 is a powerful pattern for prayers of contrition even today: "Hear and forgive, listen and act!"

IV. A Promise of Hope—20-23

20 And whiles I was speaking, and praying, and confessing my sin and the sin of my people Israel, and presenting my supplication before the Lord my God for the holy mountain of my God;

21 Yea, whiles I was speaking in prayer, even the man Gabriel, whom I had seen in the vision at the beginning, being caused to fly swiftly, touched me about the time of the evening oblation.

22 And he informed me, and talked with me, and said, O Daniel, I am now come forth to give thee skill and understanding.

23 At the beginning of thy supplications the commandment came forth, and I am come to shew thee; for thou art greatly beloved: therefore understand the matter, and consider the vision.

Although Daniel is portrayed as a model of Hebrew manhood, he is not perfect; and he appropriately confesses his own sin as well as that of the nation. The text now moves swiftly from narrative to "apocalyptic"—the unveiling of the future in symbolic terms. The angel Gabriel, who had helped Daniel understand a vision in chapter 8, returns with another, at the time of the evening sacrifice. This time Gabriel apparently foretells in mysterious terms what would happen after the 70 years' captivity Daniel had learned from Jeremiah.

Although Gabriel gives Daniel the skill to understand the vision (vs. 22), other interpreters ever since who lack this direct divine touch have also claimed to understand it. In fact, the rest of chapter 9 has been the subject of more speculation than the rest of the book

altogether. Although not included in the scope of this lesson, the main interpretations of verses 24-27 are:

1. The commandment to restore Jerusalem refers to Cyrus' decree in Ezra 1:1; and since "messiah" means "anointed," verse 25 refers to some leader such as one of the Maccabean princes who would arise to throw off the yoke of Rome many years later.

2. The picture refers to the first coming of Christ, and the time shortly thereafter when Jewish sacrifices at the Temple in Jerusalem would cease (vs. 27) after it was destroyed by the Romans.

3. The language predicts the second coming of Christ and the tribulation before the final Judgment.

In keeping with the position taken in this commentary (see Lesson 4), we conclude that it is best to leave the precise application of this prophecy in the arena of discussion rather than dogmatics, since the New Testament itself does not interpret it for us.

Evangelistic Emphasis

Perhaps the greatest single obstacle to communicating effectively the message of salvation is getting past the various illusive images of a hostile God. Though these images are rarely verbalized, they may still hide unnoticed at the depth of the  unbeliever's soul. "God, the frowning tyrant" is possibly the most common conception. He is depicted as a "spoiler of fun," "insidiously conspiring," "relentlessly watching" so as to catch one in even the tiniest mistake and so "get his jollies by torturing them for eternity".

It is no wonder that someone envisioning God in such terms refuses to accept Him as Savior and Lord. No amount or quality of logical argument is likely to convince one to "believe" until the resident *image* of God that is held within one's mind is significantly changed. Rather than perceiving God as *his opponent attempting to pin his shoulders to the mat, boasting another victory*, the unbeliever must come to see God as an ally. He must come to think of God as *on his side,* working in his behalf, waiting for his permission to rescue his life from waste and ruin. Gabriel brought to Daniel this image and more.

✳ ✳ ✳

Memory Selection

At the beginning of thy supplications the commandment came forth, and I am come to shew thee; for thou art greatly beloved therefore understand the matter, and consider the vision. —*Daniel 9:23*

"Touched By An Angel" has come to be a *must see* at our house. Though it surely could not be described as "Bible-sanctioned" programming, it certainly is overtly spiritual. Unabashedly, it proclaims, week after week, that God is good and loves his people unconditionally. Repeatedly the message of Gabriel to Daniel echoes from the lips of Monica to someone placed in her care. *"God has been there all along,"* she says. *"He has just been waiting for you to pray and give Him permission to intercede."*

All of this fits well with the message that Jesus, Himself, proclaimed when He ministered on earth in human flesh. "Ask!" He encouraged. "Seek!" He challenged. "Knock!" He invited. Always, He promised that His Father would respond with welcome grace. Yet, He will not intrude into our lives unless we first invite Him in.

Weekday Problems

Alicia learned to pray when she was just a little girl. Her first prayers were very elementary, a litany of "thank you" and "give me" recitations. Over the years, however, she has cultivated a very personal prayer life that involves relaxed conversation, reverent silence and a listening ear conditioned by a sense of awe.

It really shocked Alicia last week when her very best friend confessed to her that she did not pray. For years they have gone to church together. They have taught Sunday School together, laughed together, cried together and *prayed together*. Yes, they have prayed together many times over the years. How could Ruth say she did not pray? What Ruth went on to explain was that she prayed *only as a matter of accommodation* to her Christian friends who did pray. She respected their belief in prayer, so went along with their wish or need to pray. Yet, Ruth did not pray. Neither did she believe that prayer accomplished anything beyond comforting the person praying, like giving a placebo to a hypochondriac.

* What kind of impact do you think Alicia's new knowledge of Ruth will have on their friendship and their Christian relationship?

* What are some of the things Alicia might do better to understand Ruth's absence of a prayer life and to minister effectively to her as a fellow Christian?

* What can Ruth do to help Alicia understand her struggle with prayer and to nurture their sharing of faith?

Perspectives on Prayer

Prayer is not overcoming God's reluctance; it is laying hold of His highest willingness.—*Trench*

Heaven is never deaf but when man's heart is dumb.—*Quarles*

Certain thoughts are prayers. There are moments when, whatever be the attitude of the body, the soul is on its knees.—*Hugo*

Prayer is not eloquence, but earnestness; not the definition of helplessness, but the feeling of it; not figures of speech, but earnestness of soul.—*More*

God's way of answering the Christian's prayer for more patience, experience, hope, and love, often is to put him into the furnace of affliction.—*Cecil*

This Lesson in Your Life

Tom Watson once said, commenting on Peter's angelic release from prison (Acts 12), "The angel fetched Peter out of prison, but it was prayer that fetched the angel." This was precisely the case with Daniel. It was prayer that dispatched the angel Gabriel.

Too many are confused as to what ought to happen when they pray. Some Christians don't really expect anything to happen. It may be that they don't believe they are *important enough to have any clout with God.* They go through the motions of praying as a matter of "spiritual duty," but they really think one has to be "in the big league" to have much effect. Their *pastor* might successfully get through to Heaven's ear, but they would really prefer someone like Billy Graham pray for them.

Some Christians do not pray because they are not really convinced that Almighty God in Heaven really cares about the trivial whims and concerns of people. *"Surely, He has more important things to worry about than my prayers!"* They don't want to bother God with their petty concerns.

Others have difficulty believing that prayer really makes a difference. They have prayed diligently in the past, and did not receive the answer they had expected. Since they did not receive immediately what they had requested, they came to believe that God does not listen to their prayer.

Alexander Solzhenitsyn tells of the experiences of Ivan Denisovich enduring the horrors of a Soviet prison camp. One day he was praying with his eyes closed when a fellow prisoner noticed him and said with ridicule, "Prayers won't help you get out of here any faster." Opening his eyes, Ivan answered, "I do not pray to get out of prison but to do the will of God."

So often we pray, attempting to sell God on the idea of *doing something for us.* Less often, our prayers are offerings of ourselves to God, surrendering ourselves into His will. Daniel's prayer was clearly one of submission. He recognized the reality of Israel's guilt. It was only in the context of decisive surrender and confession that Daniel placed petition before the throne of God.

What is the attitude of your prayer? Is it characterized by one of the following expressions?

—*"You've got to give me this, because You promised!"*
—*"I've lived a pretty good life. You owe me!"*
—*"Super Santa, I want you to bring me a . . . and some . . . and . . . ."*
—*"I know this doesn't really do any good, but since I have to . . . ."*
—*"Hello. God? Is any one up there? Yoo Hoo! Hello. It's me. Remember me? You don't?"*

Though all of these are common among Christians, none of them really capture the nature of prayer. Instead, think of prayer as the cultivation of *a relationship.* As in other close relationships, in prayer you have to find out by trial and error what is right for you. In the words of James Packer, "You learn to pray by praying."

Some of us talk on endlessly. Others say few words, but they are words from the depth of the soul. Some cultivate eloquent precision in their wording. Others develop a reverent silence before God which is very real prayer. Beyond our concern for our prayer life to be Biblical, perhaps only one rule is needed. In the words of John Chapman, "Pray as you can, and don't try to pray as you can't."

Seed Thoughts

1. What writings of books (NIV) "from the Scriptures") had Daniel read that caught his attention?

He had read the writings of the word of the Lord given to Jeremiah.

2. From his reading, what did Daniel come to understand that he had not realized before?

Daniel came to understand the "desolation of Jerusalem" would last 70 years.

3. Where *specifically* (chapter and verse) in this book of Scripture might Daniel have been reading?

It could have been either Jeremiah 25:11-12 or Jeremiah 2910. The "70 years" are mentioned both places.

4. What did most of Daniel's prayer emphasize?

The majority of Daniel's prayer involved confession of Israel's sin.

5. What was the obvious purpose and goal of Daniel's prayer?

The objective of Daniel's prayer was to seek God's mercy in behalf of Israel (see vs. 18).

(Please turn page)

1. What writings of books (NIV "from the Scriptures") had Daniel read that caught his attention?

2. From his reading, what did Daniel come to understand that he had not realized before?

3. Where *specifically* (chapter and verse) in this book of Scripture might Daniel have been reading?

4. What did most of Daniel's prayer emphasize?

5. What was the obvious purpose and goal of Daniel's prayer?

6. Who came to Daniel while he was praying? About what time of the day did he appear?

7. For what purpose did this messenger appear to Daniel?

8. In addition to the technical information, what personal message did the messenger give Daniel?

9. About whom did the messenger speak to Daniel? What was the nature of the information?

10. In Daniel's prayer for forgiveness for the nation of Israel, what was the basis of his request?

He had read the writings of the word of the Lord given to Jeremiah.

Daniel came to understand the "desolation of Jerusalem" would last 70 years.

It could have been either Jeremiah 2511-12 or Jeremiah 2910. The "70 years" are mentioned both places.

The majority of Daniel's prayer involved confession of Israel's sin.

The objective of Daniel's prayer was to seek God's mercy in behalf of Israel (see vs. 18).

Gabriel appeared to Daniel about the time of the evening oblation (sacrifice).

By the messenger's own testimony, he came to give Daniel skill and understanding.

The personal message given to Daniel was that he was "greatly loved."

The messenger spoke to Daniel about the Messiah who was to come. He provided Daniel with numbers related to *the time until his coming.*

His request was made on the basis of God's mercy, not on the basis of Israel's righteousness.

6. Who came to Daniel while he was praying? About what time of the day did he appear?

Gabriel appeared to Daniel about the time of the evening oblation (sacrifice).

7. For what purpose did this messenger appear to Daniel?

By the messenger's own testimony, he came to give Daniel skill and understanding.

8. In addition to the technical information, what personal message did the messenger give Daniel?

The personal message given to Daniel was that he was "greatly loved."

9. About whom did the messenger speak to Daniel? What was the nature of the information?

The messenger spoke to Daniel about the Messiah who was to come. He provided Daniel with numbers related to *the time until his coming.*

10. In Daniel's prayer for forgiveness for the nation of Israel, what was the basis of his request?

His request was made on the basis of God's mercy, not on the basis of Israel's righteousness.

Lesson 9

The Temple Completed

Ezra 6:14-22

14 And the elders of the Jews builded, and they prospered through the prophesying of Haggai the prophet and Zechariah the son of Iddo. And they builded, and finished it, according to the commandment of the God of Israel, and according to the commandment of Cyrus, and Darius, and Artaxerxes king of Persia.

15 And this house was finished on the third day of the month Adar, which was in the sixth year of the reign of Darius the king.

16 And the children of Israel, the priests, and the Levites, and the rest of the children of the captivity, kept the dedication of this house of God with joy,

17 And offered at the dedication of this house of God an hundred bullocks, two hundred rams, four hundred lambs; and for a sin offering for all Israel, twelve he goats, according to the number of the tribes of Israel.

18 And they set the priests in their divisions, and the Levites in their courses, for the service of God, which is at Jerusalem; as it is written in the book of Moses.

19 And the children of the captivity kept the passover upon the fourteenth day of the first month.

20 For the priests and the Levites were purified together, all of them were pure, and killed the passover for all the children of the captivity, and for their brethren the priests, and for themselves.

21 And the children of Israel, which were come again out of captivity, and all such as had separated themselves unto them from the filthiness of the heathen of the land, to seek the Lord God of Israel, did eat,

22 And kept the feast of unleavened bread seven days with joy: for the Lord had made them joyful, and turned the heart of the king of Assyria unto them, to strengthen their hands in the work of the house of God, the God of Israel.

November 2

Memory Selection
Ezra 6:16

Devotional Reading
Psalm 126:1-6

Background Scripture
Ezra 6

Printed Scripture
Ezra 6:14-22

Teacher's Target

Lesson purpose: *To learn, from the experience of the Jews who rebuilt the Temple, the importance of celebrating important milestones with religious observances.*

There seems to be no end to the challenge to do more, be more, work harder, work smarter—life can become one supreme effort after another. This pace isn't all bad; great accomplishments are usually achieved only by great effort.

Yet those who best manage the challenge to achieve know also the wisdom of pacing themselves. They give themselves permission to pause occasionally to celebrate landmarks along the way.

Invite class members to share events in their family, their Christian pilgrimage, or their work that are worth a party! Share also the nature of the celebration—especially those that mark events such as a baptism or a wedding, in which God is especially present.

Lesson Introduction

The setting of the books of Ezra and Nehemiah reflect the situation immediately after the time of Daniel. The setting is about 500 years before the birth of Christ. After some 70 years of captivity in Babylon, the Jews are allowed to return and rebuild the holy city, Jerusalem, as well as the Temple of the Lord.

We noticed in Lesson 3 that the work progressed slowly at first because of self-interest among the people. In the earlier chapters of Ezra we learn that Israel's enemies opposed the work as well. Finally, however, the Temple was completed, as described in this lesson.

The Restoration God had promised through prophets such as Jeremiah and Isaiah had been accomplished. The people engaged in an outburst of praise and worship that included the reinstitution of the Passover, the annual observance that had been interrupted by the captivity. It was time to celebrate!

Teaching Outline	Daily Bible Readings	
	Mon.	Altar Set in Place *Ezra 3:1-7*
I. Completing the Temple—14-15	**Tue.**	Cheers and Tears at the Start *Ezra 3:8-13*
II. Celebrating the Event—16-18	**Wed.**	Darius Backs the Temple Project *Ezra 6:1-12*
III. Commemorating the Passover —19-22	**Thu.**	They Built and Prospered *Ezra 6:13-22*
	Fri.	God Dwells with the Contrite *Isaiah 57:14-21*
	Sat.	No Earthly Temple Large Enough *Isaiah 66:1-5*
	Sun.	Zion Restored Once More *Psalm 126:1-6*

VERSE BY VERSE

I. Completing the Temple—14-15

14 And the elders of the Jews builded, and they prospered through the prophesying of Haggai the prophet and Zechariah the son of Iddo. And they builded, and finished it, according to the commandment of the God of Israel, and according to the commandment of Cyrus, and Darius, and Artaxerxes king of Persia.

15 And this house was finished on the third day of the month Adar, which was in the sixth year of the reign of Darius the king.

Although verse 14 does not mention everyone involved in the restoration of the Temple at Jerusalem, it is remarkably inclusive. Perhaps we are to understand the word "elders" to include the high priest Joshua and the governor Zerubbabel, who also played important roles (Zech. 2-3).

It was leadership like that which inspired the hosts of other workers that also participated. Masons and carpenters helped with the construction, and even sailors served by bringing cedar wood from Lebanon (Ezra 3:7). The scene is of a beehive of activity requiring the hearty cooperation and participation of both leaders and the people—just as any worthwhile project among believers today requires all-inclusive participation. People need leaders who work, and leaders need people who serve.

Note also that the prophets Haggai and Zechariah, whose writings were studied in Lessons 3 and 4, are also included. The people needed spiritual inspiration to resist the opposition of Israel's adversaries (Ezra 4). As we have seen, these prophets reminded the people that the Temple would never be rebuilt as long as everyone tended selfishly to their own affairs. The prophets insisted that God's work has its own priority (Hag. 1:3).

This passage also reminds us that the people of God have the privilege of being God's co-workers in helping to implement His will. How can the work of the church become commonplace and boring if we keep in mind that our work is God's work?

Note also that the author gives credit not only to God for commanding the kings of the captivity to authorize the Jews' return, but to the kings themselves. God can use national leaders to accomplish His will even when those leaders do not honor Him. He is sovereign over all nations.

II. Celebrating the Event—16-18

16 And the children of Israel, the priests, and the Levites, and the rest of the children of the captivity, kept the dedication of this house of God with joy,

17 And offered at the dedication of this house of God an hundred bullocks, two hundred rams four hundred lambs; and for a sin offering for all Israel, twelve he goats, according to the number of the tribes of Israel.

18 And they set the priests in their divisions, and the Levites in their

courses, for the service of God, which is at Jerusalem; as it is written in the book of Moses.

The phrase "the children of the captivity" appears several times in this section, reminding us that the Jews' long years in Babylon are over. It is time for the captives—from the least-gifted person among them to their leaders—to celebrate!

Both "priests" and "Levites" are mentioned because by this time not all Levites were priests who served formally in offering sacrifices. Originally the two groups were apparently the same (Deut. 17:18). They consisted of descendants of the tribe of Levi, one of Jacob's 12 sons. Aaron, Moses' brother, was the first high priest or chief Levite, heading the entire priestly service (Num. 3:1-6). Eventually, perhaps because some priests became unfaithful (2 Kings 23:8-9), differences developed between priests and Levites and their respective duties. The terms "divisions" and "courses" (NIV "groups") in verse 18 indicate these distinctions.

The important point here is the sacrifices that accompanied the celebration. Although the numbers of animals slaughtered were tiny compared to the first dedication of the Temple (1 Kings 8:63), they represented all the small and no doubt impoverished community of worshipers could afford.

To Christians it might seem strange to include taking the life of these animals in the midst of the great celebration. Why is death placed alongside the new life and the joy of seeing Temple worship restored? Because the celebrants are confessing the sin for which Daniel prayed in our last lesson, and "without shedding of blood is no remission" (Heb. 9:22). Of course animal sacrifice was also integral to Temple worship.

Even today, Christian celebrations at such events as baptism and Communion contain a similar element—the remembrance of the sacrifice of Christ on the Cross.

III. Commemorating the Passover —19-22

19 And the children of the captivity kept the passover upon the fourteenth day of the first month.

20 For the priests and the Levites were purified together, all of them were pure, and killed the passover for all the children of the captivity, and for their brethren the priests,

21 And the children of Israel, which were come again out of captivity, and all such as had separated themselves unto them from the filthiness of the heathen of the land, to seek the Lord God of Israel, did eat,

22 And kept the feast of unleavened bread seven days with joy: for the Lord had made them joyful, and turned the heart of the king of Assyria unto them, to strengthen their hands in the work of the house of God, the God of Israel.

With highly appropriate timing, the people also celebrate the Passover on the anniversary of the very day it had been instituted as their ancestors prepared to leave Egypt (Exod. 12:6). The Passover celebrated the passing over or sparing of the Jewish children when the angel of death took vengeance on the Egyptians for abusing God's people. The great feast marked the formal beginning of Abraham's descendants as a nation as Israel—hence the month in which it was instituted is called "the beginning" (Exod. 12:2). In a similar way, Israel is starting over with the rebuilding of the Temple. God has "passed over" their sin. The "children of captivity" are

84

now the children of the New Israel.

Notice that verse 21 indicates that the great celebration also included people who had been spared the captivity. Nebuchadnezzar, the Babylonian king who conquered Judah more than 70 years earlier, had left some of the Jews in Palestine. Many had blended in with the pagan cultures about them, worshipping the Baals and other false gods that are called "filthiness." Others, however, had remembered their roots and remained faithful to Yahweh worship. It is this remnant that is included in the Passover, which by this time had been combined with the feast of unleavened bread.

Not only did the great Passover celebration build up the people of God as they worshipped Him; it also made an impact on "the king of Assyria." This term may seem odd, since Assyria had been conquered by the very Chaldeans that had captured the Jews. Perhaps it is a reference to Darius not only as king of Medea, or Artaxerxes, king of Persia (vs. 14), but also of the now-conquered kingdom of Assyria.

At any rate, the sheer joy of the people as they celebrated the restoration of the Temple of God made its impact on the king. Often we think of evangelism as occurring only when we explicitly reach out to unbelievers with the Good News. This passage, however, reminds us that worship can also have an evangelistic impact. The Jewish concepts of corporate personality and remembering included more than merely honoring the past. They implied also being caught up in the spirit of the past event as though it were happening to them again. God had not just delivered their forefathers; He was in the process of delivering them as well.

Cannot Christian worship also partake of this fervency? The sacrifice of Christ that we remember in the Communion, for example, is more than an historical event. The blood that flowed so long ago still cleanses us (1 John 1:7). As we worship with that concept, our commitment has its own attraction, often appealing to others who feel the need for commitment and devotion in their own lives.

Evangelistic Emphasis

Who would have ever believed that the Persian king's treasury would pay for the construction of the Jewish temple? That was as unlikely among the Jewish culture in that day as it would be for the Mississippi state treasury to fund the construction of a Buddhist temple in Jackson today. Those who watched from the sidelines must have been amazed as they watched the construction. As testimony went out that it was because of the sovereignty of God that the king had given such an order, those who had begun to doubt their God's power found their faith rekindled.

Even today, it is impressive to witness the sovereign hand of God at work in the world's political arena. Not always is it easy to see, just as it was not easy for the citizens of Judah to grasp the work of God a few years earlier as their city fell to a pagan nation. As Eastern Europe was being devoured by the seemingly relentless control of Atheistic Communism, it was not easy to understand where God was and what he was doing. Yet, in recent years the crumbling of the Communist regime, the tearing down of the Berlin Wall and the opening of Red Square testified quite clearly that God had been at work in the affairs of Communist U.S.S.R. all along. Though we did not understand his involvement as Communism reigned strongly, it is now clear that He has been *in control* all along.

Memory Selection

And the children of Israel, the priests, and the Levites, and the rest of the children of the captivity, kept the dedication of this house of God with joy.—*Ezra 6:16*

One of the great illusions of contemporary American life is that nothing excels *getting*. Routinely, we indulge in fantasies of being given riches unlimited to pamper our self-pitied souls. *"One of these days, my ship is going to come in!"* promises the perpetual dreamer. He chases one get-rich-quick gimmick after another, but only ends further in debt than before.

Lottery cash drawers bulge with profits, while the would-be winners shell out ever more dollars for one more ticket than was bought last week. Any signs of discouragement among buyers prompts the pot to be fattened a bit or the profile of the last winner raised to generate more tangible dreams.

In spite of our illusions, though, easy riches rarely bring lasting joy. What we have not invested in comes to us with a hollow core. The true fuel for celebration is not actually found in getting, but in *accomplishing*. The prize claimed has meaning primarily because of the victory accomplished in the pursuit.

Weekday Problems

In matters pertaining to church Velma and Erasmus Hamboldt certainly come from different cultural backgrounds. Velma grew up as a member of the Jackson family of Mobile, Alabama. The Jacksons are a family of singers. One of Velma's earliest memories is that of singing with her family at the Missionary Baptist Church in celebration of the new pastor who had been called. Erasmus, growing up in  a very conservative Lutheran home in La Cross, Wisconsin, thinks of church in more somber tones. What Velma calls "Christian celebration," Erasmus regards as *holy hollering*. What Erasmus regards to be "proper worship demeanor," Velma denounces as *death warmed over*. In spite of their love for each other, this matter of church, and how it ought to be conducted, has brought many major stresses to their marriage.

* Who is right in this contest of values over the appropriate spirit and conduct of the worship hour? Why is he or she more correct in this matter?

* What about Erasmus's background could provide needed instruction to Velma's religious training? What about Velma's could instruct Erasmus?

* Considering the fact that both Erasmus and Velma are heavily conditioned in their own church culture and unlikely to be persuaded differently, how can they handle these differences so that their relationship with one another is not destroyed?

Tall Talk from Texas

Did you hear about the Texan who was trying to call New York? "Operator!" he demanded, "How much does it cost to call New York?"

"It costs $3.75, the operator said.

"Why, I can call hell and back for that much!" the Texan exploded.

"Yes, sir," said the operator, "but that's a local call."

An ardent fisherman from Dallas made a trip to Bull Shoals Lake, Ark. He landed a 6°-pound bass, but boasted to his native guide, "That ain't nothin'. Why, in Texas we use that size for bait."

The Arkansan nodded appreciatively—and dropped the fish back into the lake.

What do you have when you see a pair of boots with a 10-gallon hat on them? A Texan with all the hot air let out.

This Lesson in Your Life

Bruce Larson tells about a conference at a Presbyterian church in Omaha. As a tangible enhancement to one presentation's theme, "Celebration," people were given helium filled balloons. Since most of those at the conference were Presbyterians, they really were not free to say *"Hallelujah, Praise the Lord!"* as some Christians might have done. Attempting to accommodate the inhibitions of their especially reserved church culture, the speaker told the people to *release the balloons* at some point in the service when they felt like expressing the joy in their hearts. This, the speaker thought, was well within the comfort zones of the conference attendees. All through the service balloons, one by one, ascended. It was exciting to see this tangible declaration of the people's joy. Unfortunately, according to Larson, when it was over one third of the balloons remained unreleased.

Uncomfortably, I empathize with those people at that Omaha conference. I understand that the absence of celebration does not necessarily indicate the absence of joy. While some were reared from infancy in an atmosphere of ready celebration of the smallest victory, other were not. Instead, there was caution placed on the urge to celebrate. "One must not be given to frivolity or emotionalism, *especially in the realm of religion.*" To do so, it was said, cheapens our faith and turns quality conviction into little more than a faddish frenzy.

As wise as such cautions might have been, excessive emphasis on restraining our joy has sometimes terribly inhibited our ability to celebrate, even when celebration is most appropriate. As a result, we potentially end up appearing to the nonbelieving world as people devoid of joy or anything else evident of "real living."

Ezra 6 portrays people who knew well how to celebrate. It was not just a Friday night event that lasted a couple of hours, either. Not only did the people celebrate when the temple was dedicated. The first Passover to arrive also rekindled their outpouring of joy. Another week was spent in joyful celebration.

This occasion of celebration was certainly special in its circumstance, yet the people of Judah were no strangers to celebration. God had built into His Law multiple feast days and festivals throughout the calendar. These feast days and festivals called the people together regularly to celebrate in the presence of God. They were to feast at His table and remember his blessings. They were to dance in His honor and be thankful for His goodness.

Unfortunately, in our earnest attempt to "do things decently and in order," we sometimes forget how to celebrate. Our joy is so suppressed that it fails to become contagious. Isolated for too long, it dies. Rather than being a church full of joyful people, celebrating the goodness of our God, we find that we have become a cathedral of bored people who cannot remember any reason that would prompt celebration.

Though I identify thoroughly with Omaha's inhibitions, I have come to recognize keenly our need to release our balloons. It is only when we allow our joy to be witnessed by others that it becomes contagious. It is only in sharing it that it is enabled to live and grow. Perhaps, it is for that reason that the Apostle said, "Rejoice evermore."

Seed Thoughts

1. From where did the money come to pay for the rebuilding of the temple in Jerusalem?

It came from the royal treasury of the king of Persia.

2. Why would the king of Persia pay for the rebuilding of a temple for the Israelites?

So the people would offer sacrifices and prayers for the well-being of his reign.

3. Who were the prophets of the Lord living in the land during this time of reconstruction?

Haggai and Zechariah were the prophets encouraging the people then.

4. What national (or racial) designation emerges in Ezra that has not been found earlier in Scripture?

The term "Jew" or "Jews" is not found in Scripture before the book of Ezra. It first appeared in 4:12.

5. When was the temple construction completed?

It was completed on the third day of the month of Adar in the third year of the reign of Darius. March 12, 516 B.C. according to our dating system.

1. From where did the money come to pay for the rebuilding of the temple in Jerusalem?

2. Why would the king of Persia pay for the rebuilding of a temple for the Israelites?

3. Who were the prophets of the Lord living in the land during this time of reconstruction?

4. What national (or racial) designation emerges in Ezra that has not been found earlier in Scripture?

5. When was the temple construction completed?

6. How long did the reconstruction of the temple take?

7. How many animals were killed to accommodate the celebration of the temple's completion?

8. When was the first Passover celebrated after the completion of the temple?

9. How long did the celebration of the Passover last?

10. What was the mood of the people as they celebrated this Passover? Why?

(Please turn page)

It came from the royal treasury of the king of Persia.

So the peopleth would offer sacrifices and prayers for the well-being of his reign.

Haggai and Zechariah were the prophets encouraging the people during that period.

The term "Jew" or "Jews" is not found in Scripture before the book of Ezra. It first appeared in 4:12.

It was completed on the third day of the month of Adar in the third year of the reign of Darius, or March 12, 516 B.C.

Three and one-half years.According to Haggai 1:15 the work was begun on the 24th day of the seventh month of Darius second year of reign.

One hundred bulls, two hundred rams, four hundred male lambs and twelve male goats. A total of seven hundred

On the 14th day of the first month (April 21, 516 B.C.), more than a month later.

The Passover celebration lasted seven days.

The people's celebration was filled with joy, because God had changed the attitude of the king to make the completion of the temple possible.

6. How long did the reconstruction of the temple take?

Three and one-half years. According to Haggai 1:15 the work was begun on the 24th day of the seventh month of Darius second year of reign.

7. How many animals were killed to accommodate the celebration of the temple's completion?

Totals were 100 bulls, 200 rams, 400 male lambs and 12 male goats. A total of seven hundred twelve.

8. When was the first Passover celebrated after the completion of the temple?

On the 14th day of the first month (April 21, 516 B.C.), more than a month later.

9. How long did the celebration of the Passover last?

The Passover celebration lasted seven days.

10. What was the mood of the people as they celebrated this Passover? Why?

The people's celebration was filled with joy, because God had changed the attitude of the king to make the completion

Lesson 10

Preserving the Faith

Ezra 9:1-3; 10:2-4, 9-14

1 Now when these things were done, the princes came to me, saying, The people of Israel, and the priests, and the Levites, have not separated themselves from the people of the lands, doing according to their abominations, even of the Canaanites, the Hittites, the Perizzites, the Jebusites, the Ammonites, the Moabites, the Egyptians, and the Amorites.

2 For they have taken of their daughters for themselves, and for their sons: so that the holy seed have mingled themselves with the people of those lands: yea, the hand of the princes and rulers hath been chief in this trespass.

3 And when I heard this thing, I rent my garment and my mantle, and plucked off the hair of my head and of my beard, and sat down astonied.

10:2 And Shechaniah the son of Jehiel, one of the sons of Elam, answered and said unto Ezra, We have trespassed against our God, and have taken strange wives of the people of the land: yet now there is hope in Israel concerning this thing.

3 Now let us make a covenant with our God to put away all the wives, and such as are born of them, according to the counsel of my lord, and of those that tremble at the commandment of our God; and let it be done according to the law.

4 Arise; for this matter belongeth unto

thee: we also will be with thee: be of good courage, and do it.

9 Then all the men of Judah and Benjamin gathered themselves together unto Jerusalem within three days. It was the ninth month, on the twentieth day of the month; and all the people sat in the street of the house of God, trembling because of this matter, and for the great rain.

10 And Ezra the priest stood up, and said unto them, Ye have transgressed, and have taken strange wives, to increase the trespass of Israel.

11 Now therefore make confession unto the Lord God of your fathers, and do his pleasure: and separate yourselves from the people of the land, and from the strange wives.

12 Then all the congregation answered and said with a loud voice, As thou hast said, so must we do.

13 But the people are many, and it is a time of much rain, and we are not able to stand without, neither is this a work of one day or two: for we are many that have transgressed in this thing.

14 Let now our rulers of all the congregation stand, and let all them which have taken strange wives in our cities come at appointed times, and with them the elders of every city, and the judges thereof, until the fierce wrath of our God for this matter be turned from us.

Memory Selection
Ezra 10:11

Devotional Reading
Deuteronomy 6:1-9

Background Scripture
Ezra 9:1–10:17

Printed Scripture
Ezra 9:1-3; 10:2-4, 9-14

Teacher's Target

Lesson purpose: *To inspire class members to be willing to make life-style decisions not only on the basis of self-interest but also in the light of their impact on the community of faith.*

This lesson is likely to be taken as a "hard saying" by many people today. Would we really be expected to separate from an unbelieving spouse, as Ezra the priest called for God's people to do in this text?

The effective teacher will try to walk between two extremes in presenting this lesson. On the one hand it should be pointed out that the historical context (see Lesson Introduction) is far different from our own. On the other hand Scripture is given "for our example" (1 Cor. 10:11), and we should be cautious about dismissing any of it as having nothing to say to us today.

What the passage says to us today is that some decisions we may think are personal affect others so directly that living in community with them requires that we make life-style decisions on a broader base than mere personal preference.

Lesson Introduction

A "mixed multitude" of nationalities came out of Egypt with the Israelites (Exod. 12:38), and Joseph and Moses married foreign women. Why, then, does the book of Ezra close with the harsh commandment in this lesson for Jews who had married foreign spouses to put them away?

Because God's plan of salvation called for a Messiah to come through a people who knew His ways. Only by seeing those ways lived out in the lives of a particular people could others learn what following Him really meant. Earlier, intermarriage with other people had polluted that stream of faithfulness. Now that the Jews have returned from captivity, it is more important than ever to re-establish themselves as a people who can resist paganism. Without this radical separation from foreign faiths, there could not have existed a people of faith through whom Messiah would come.

Teaching Outline	Daily Bible Readings
	Mon. A Scribe Skilled in the Law *Ezra 7:6-1*
	Tue. Courage from the Hand of God *Ezra 7:21-28*
I. A Compromised Covenant–9:1-3	**Wed.** Guilt Mounting up to Heaven *Ezra 9:1-9*
II. A Courageous Confession–10:9-12	**Thu.** Fear a Just God's Anger *Ezra 9:10-15*
III. An Encouraging Word–10:2-4	**Fri.** Hope for the Returned Exiles *Ezra 10:1-8*
IV. A Common-sense Solution–13-14	**Sat.** Confess and Separate Yourselves *Ezra 10:9-17*
	Sun. House of Prayer for All Peoples *Isaiah 56:1-8*

VERSE BY VERSE

I. A Compromised Covenant—9:1-3

1 Now when these things were done, the princes came to me, saying, The people of Israel, and the priests, and the Levites, have not separated themselves from the people of the lands, doing according to their abominations, even of the Canaanites, the Hittites, the Perizzites, the Jebusites, the Ammonites, the Moabites, the Egyptians, and the Amorites.

2 For they have taken of their daughters for themselves, and for their sons: so that the holy seed have mingled themselves with the people of those lands: yea, the hand of the princes and rulers hath been chief in this trespass.

3 And when I heard this thing, I rent my garment and my mantle, and plucked off the hair of my head and of my beard, and sat down astonied.

Many years earlier, as Moses led Israel toward the Promised Land, God had expressly commanded them not to marry the pagan peoples in verse 1 (Deut. 7:1-3). There was no racism involved in this rule. Moses himself had married a Midianite (Exod. 2:16-22). The ban against foreign marriages was for theological, not racial reasons: "For they (pagan spouses) will turn away thy son from following me, that they may serve other gods" (Deut. 7:4).

The Israelites who had been taken away captive to Babylon had naturally huddled together in a Jewish enclave and protected their identity. So when Ezra the priestly scribe found that the people who had been left in Palestine had freely intermarried with the surrounding pagans, he was almost struck dumb with astonishment (KJV "astonied").

It must have been especially shocking to realize that the priests, Levites and others charged with protecting the worship of Yahweh among the Jews had led in this wholesale flaunting of God's express command: "They have been chief in this trespass." No wonder Ezra adopted the posture of mourn-ing—tearing his garments and shaving his head. Ezra had gone to great lengths to re-establish God's covenant people in their homeland. Now he saw that they themselves had violated the covenant.

II. An Encouraging Word—10:2-4

2 And Shechaniah the son of Jehiel, one of the sons of Elam, answered and said unto Ezra, We have trespassed against our God, and have taken strange wives of the people of the land: yet now there is hope in Israel concerning this thing.

3 Now let us make a covenant with our God to put away all the wives, and such as are born of them, according to the counsel of my lord, and of those that tremble at the commandment of our God; and let it be done according to the law.

4 Arise; for this matter belongeth unto thee: we also will be with thee: be of good courage, and do it.

Shechaniah makes only this appearance in all of Scripture, but he makes an impact. Seeing Ezra's paralyzing grief and hearing his agonizing prayer, he comes to the aid of the priest. We are reminded of how Barnabas, in the New Testament, came to the aid of the newly-commissioned apostle Paul who needed that word of encouragement from one among the people.

This "layman" is willing to renew the covenant that the people had broken by intermarriage. While admitting that the matter was of special concern to Ezra, as the priestly scribe commissioned to see that the Temple is rebuilt, Shechaniah also insists that it a matter for the people themselves to solve: "We also will be with thee." Many a minister feels the pressure of leading a people into deeper commitment, and needs just such a word from those who are lead.

III. A Courageous Confession–10:9-12

9 Then all the men of Judah and Benjamin gathered themselves together unto Jerusalem within three days. It was the ninth month, on the twentieth day of the month; and all the people sat in the street of the house of God, trembling because of this matter, and for the great rain.

10 And Ezra the priest stood up, and said unto them, Ye have transgressed, and have taken strange wives, to increase the trespass of Israel.

11 Now therefore make confession unto the Lord God of your fathers, and do his pleasure: and separate yourselves from the people of the land, and from the strange wives.

12 Then all the congregation answered and said with a loud voice, As

thou hast said, so must we do.

Ezra must have been a person of towering integrity. His obvious grief pricked the consciences of the offenders more than any terroristic threat could have done. Their gathering sadly in the rain before the Temple is testimony to the power of moral persuasion over force in calling a people to upright living.

Ezra speaks forthrightly to the people. He charges them with direct violation of the Law, calls them to confess their sin, and commands them to separate themselves from their idolatrous entanglements. Had the foreign wives converted to Judaism and supported the instruction of their children in the ways of God, this appalling order might not have been issued. The marriages, however, had not merely tested interracial social customs. The foreign spouses were worshippers of Baal, Marduk, Astarte, and a host of other pagan gods. The marriages therefore threatened to import child sacrifice, cult prostitution, and other practices that would have thwarted God's plan to keep a people for Himself through whom to bring the Messiah.

Instead of protesting that who they married was their own business, the people are remarkably penitent. They affirm their willingness to pay a cost most of us can scarcely imagine — separating from their foreign wives and children.

IV. A Commonsense Request–13-14

13 But the people are many, and it is a time of much rain, and we are not able to stand without, neither is this a work of one day or two: for we are many that have transgressed in this thing.

14 Let now our rulers of all the congregation stand, and let all them

which have taken strange wives in our cities come at appointed times, and with them the elders of every city, and the judges thereof, until the fierce wrath of our God for this matter be turned from us.

Willing though they are to follow Ezra's (actually God's) edict, the people ask for time to carry it out. The heavy rains, unusual in Palestine, would mean severe hardship for women and children without housing.

They also apparently appeal for the elders and leaders of each city whose marriages are also an offense to God to take the lead in separating from their foreign attachments. Both requests make sense; if it is necessary to endure the trauma of breaking up whole families, it is not unreasonable to ask for time to make provision for those that would be losing their homes and means of support.

We are not told what provisions were made. We can only hope that enough justice and compassion were extended to them to balance the people's willingness to conform with God's will.

Applying the intent of Ezra's decree in the life of believers today is a delicate matter. Since God's mission of keeping a "holy seed" (Ezra 9:2) was completed in the coming of Christ, marrying across social, racial, and religious barriers would now seem to be more a matter of individual choice. Although the apostle Paul taught Christians not to be "unequally yoked together with unbelievers" (2 Cor. 6:14), he also said that an unbelieving spouse is not to be divorced for that reason (1 Cor. 7:12ff.).

In any case, this tragic chapter in Israel's history is a sober reminder that what we do individually can have vast consequences for fellow-believers. The attitude that ethical behavior is purely a matter of personal choice does not grow out of the Bible's concept of the oneness of the people of God. Fellow-believers are not to be busy-bodies or try to force their opinion on others. Much less are they to go about pinning "scarlet letters" on fellow-sinners. They are, however, to care for each other's spiritual welfare; and their concern should be seriously considered as we consider any action that might affect our faith, or that of the larger circle of faith.

Evangelistic Emphasis

I'm reminded of the comic I once saw that was advertising the "cut-rate church." In this church, everything was marked down. The "tithe" had been reduced to 8 percent, the Ten Commandments had become the "five suggestions," and so on the comic went, driving home its point. Unhappily, there was far too much truth in that comic for it to be funny.

Strange, isn't it! We easily buy into the idea that Christianity can be made more attractive to those on the outside if we make it easier—by removing the hard choices. But, it never works that way. The words of Eleanor Roosevelt ring true, "One's philosophy is not best expressed in words. It is expressed in the choices one makes. In the long run, we shape our lives and we shape ourselves. The process never ends until we die. And the choices we make are ultimately our responsibility."

If our faith is ever to be compelling to those who long for something substantially better than the superficiality they know, it must have character that runs deeper than words. It must have a value worth dying for. It must have substance that requires us to choose. Only then, does this Christianity have something of value to offer life.

Memory Selection

Now therefore make confession unto the LORD God of your fathers, and do his pleasure and separate yourselves from the people of the land, and from the strange wives. — *Ezra 10:11*

This is one of the most difficult of all Biblical passages for some to understand. Ezra's demand that all these men separate from their wives and children seems so harsh. Certainly, there are Scriptures where a much more gracious approach is taken. David was clearly wrong in taking Bathsheba, yet God came to bless that union, in spite of it's ungodly origin. The woman caught in the act of adultery was simply told to go and sin no more. Why is the word of God spoken through Ezra so harsh?

It is important to understand the crisis state of Israel at that time. Only a remnant of the people of God remained as the "children of the captivity" returned to their homeland. Of this remnant at least 110 of the men (including several leaders) had compromised their integrity by marrying women of foreign gods. The faith and race of Israel stood severely endangered of being lost. These were not *ordinary circumstances*. They were drastic times of crisis. Drastic measures were required for survival.

Bill and Ann Stuttgart fear for their children. They wonder whether they will follow in their steps of faith or not. So many of their friends' children have not. Even their pastor's son, Jim, married a young woman who is not a believer, and Jim has discontinued all Christian involvement and relationships. Several other of their church friends have had similarly disappointing experiences with one or more of their children. It seems to Bill and Ann that almost always the believer is lost to the faith if he or she marries an unbeliever. They find themselves puzzled as to why this is true.

As the Stuttgarts contemplate this rejection of the faith by their friends' children, they wonder how they can assure that their own children will marry "in the faith." If they marry nonbelievers, how can they help that to be a situation that wins one to Christ, instead of one that loses one to secularism?

* What are some things Bill and Ann can do to instill an early longing in their children to marry Christians?

* What can they do to help their Children find a suitable Christian mate? Or, is there really anything that they can do?

* Should the Stuttgarts' children marry unbelievers, how can they use the situation effectively to convert the unbelieving mates?

Memos on Marriage

Keep your eyes wide open before marriage—and half-shut afterward.

Kay: Our minister said we can have 16 husbands.
May: You can't be serious!
Kay: No, really. At the last wedding I attended I distinctly heard him say, "Four better, four worse, four richer, and four poorer."

Old Aunt Emma had lived with Bob and Betty for seven years—demanding, grouchy, and selfish. Finally she died. Said Bob, on the way back from the funeral, "Honey, I'd never have tolerated your Aunt Emma living with us if I didn't love you so much."
"My Aunt Emma!" his wife said. "I thought she was your Aunt Emma!"

A good marriage is like a good violin. After the music stops, the strings are still attached.

This Lesson in Your Life

Brothers Paul and Ed Kartic spent their childhood years in "the big valley" just outside of Fresno, California. Their dad was a supplier of grapes to the producers of California raisins. After college, both Paul and Ed returned to their family business to be trained to take over their dad's work. For 15 years, their efforts joined with the work of their dad, enabling the vineyards to be multiplied and expanded. New methods were tried. Irrigation was improved. Additional land was purchased. Within those 15 years, the Kartic vineyard went from being *one of* the suppliers to "the chief" supplier of California grapes. As their dad retired from the business, he did so with great pride, handing over the work to his two capable sons.

The first year to have the family business on their own, Ed and Paul decided it was time to diversify their holdings. During the previous 10 years the business had been so profitable that their books showed a rather sizable surplus of capital in the bank. The brothers thought it better to put that money to work in some aggressive business stock than to allow it to lie idly in the bank drawing minimal interest. So they began looking around for something promising in which to invest their funds.

Six months later, Paul announced to Ed that he had found their gold mine. It was a computer-related industry that was just waiting to be born. A new hardware/software company promised to place Fresno on the map for something other than "shriveled grapes." Though neither Paul nor Ed knew much about computers, they were more than aware that they represented the way of the future. And it so happened that one of Paul's high school friends was the mind behind this incredible idea.

Big ideas, though, require big capital to underwrite them. At first, Paul and Ed committed only $50,000 dollars. But 50 turned into 100, then 200. Their surplus was finally exhausted when they gave Paul's friend the last of their $375,000.

It should not have surprised the Kartic brothers that their years of bountiful harvests did not go on forever. About the time their surplus account was depleted, their crop was attacked by a new and unexpected virus. Though they spotted it early, they were unable to remedy it before it had ruined most of their crop. As luck would have it, a week later Paul's friend showed up on their door step begging for another hundred thousand dollars to keep the computer venture from dying a certain death. Could they borrow the money and get it to him by Monday? he wanted to know.

Ed and Paul were forced to make some very hard choices. They had invested a considerable sum in this computer brainstorm. A few more dollars might make the difference as to whether the idea lived or died. Yet, even more of themselves were invested in their "shriveled grapes." Ought they to jeopardize the family business their dad had built to save a fascinating idea?

As difficult as it was for them to choose with such finality, their choice was unmistakably clear. They were in the raisin business. It wasn't just "a job." Raisins represented who they were as a family. As Kartics, there was no way that they could jeopardize that. It was an expensive lesson they would later be glad that they had learned.

Seed Thoughts

1. What distressing news did some of the leaders bring to Ezra upon his arrival in Jerusalem?

Ezra was told that many of the people, even some of the leaders and Levites, had disobeyed God by taking wives from their pagan neighbors.

2. What does the Bible say was Ezra's response to this unfortunate news?

When Ezra heard this news, he rent his garment and mantle, pulled out hair from his head and beard and sat down astonished (NIV "appalled").

3. At the evening sacrifice, how did Ezra say that he felt?

He said that he felt ashamed and that he blushed to lift his face heavenward.

4. Why was Ezra ashamed? Was this transgression the only reason?

Ezra was ashamed because his people had once again proved disobedient, even though God had been repeatedly gracious with their disobedience.

5. Where were the "children of the captivity" to gather? What would happen to those who didn't show?

Those who did not appear in Jerusalem within three days for a meeting with Ezra would lose their land and be expelled from the assembly.

(Please turn page)

---

1. What distressing news did some of the leaders bring to Ezra upon his arrival in Jerusalem?

2. What does the Bible say was Ezra's response to this unfortunate news?

3. At the evening sacrifice, how did Ezra say that he felt?

4. Why was Ezra ashamed? Was this transgression the only reason?

5. Where were the "children of the captivity" to gather? What would happen to those who didn't show?

6. How many of those who had been summoned to the meeting came?

7. What did Ezra tell the men who came to Jerusalem for the meeting that he had requested?

8. What initial response did the people give to this call of Ezra?

9. Was the response to Ezra's call unanimous?

10. How long did it take to carry out this radical discipline?

Ezra was told that many of the people, even some of the leaders and Levites, had disobeyed God by taking wives from their pagan neighbors.

When Ezra heard this news, he rent his garment and mantle, pulled out hair from his head and beard and sat down astonished (NIV "appalled").

He said that he felt ashamed and that he blushed to lift his face heavenward.

Ezra was ashamed because his people *had once again* proved disobedient, even though God had been repeatedly gracious with their disobedience.

Those who did not appear in Jerusalem within three days for a meeting with Ezra would lose their land and be expelled from the assembly.

The Bible says that *all* the men of Judah and Benjamin came to the meeting.

Ezra said that they (1) had sinned by taking foreign women as wives, (2) must confess their guilt and (3) must separate from their foreign wives.

They said that he was right; they must do as he said.

No. Four men opposed Ezra—Jonathan, Jehazia, Meshullam and Shabbethai the Levite.

From the time Ezra began his investigation of individual cases, the process took three months.

(Seed Thoughts, continued)

6. How many of those who had been summoned to the meeting came?

The Bible says that *all* the men of Judah and Benjamin came to the meeting.

7. What did Ezra tell the men who came to Jerusalem for the meeting that he had requested?

Ezra said that they (1) had sinned by taking foreign women as wives, (2) must confess their guilt and (3) must separate from their foreign wives.

8. What initial response did the people give to this call of Ezra?

They said that he was right; they must do as he said.

9. Was the response to Ezra's call unanimous?

No. Four men opposed Ezra— Jonathan, Jehazia, Meshullam and Shabbethai the Levite.

10. How long did it take to carry out this radical discipline?

From the time Ezra began his investigation of individual cases, the process took three months.

LET US REBUILD THE WALL OF JERUSALEM...

Lesson 11

A Leader Appears

Nehemiah 2:4-8, 12-18

4 Then the king said unto me, For what dost thou make request? So I prayed to the God of heaven.

5 And I said unto the king, If it please the king, and if thy servant have found favour in thy sight, that thou wouldest send me unto Judah, unto the city of my fathers' sepulchres, that I may build it.

6 And the king said unto me, (the queen also sitting by him,) For how long shall thy journey be? And when wilt thou return? So it pleased the king to send me; and I set him a time.

7 Moreover I said unto the king, If it please the king, let letters be given me to the governors beyond the river, that they may convey me over till I come into Judah;

8 And a letter unto Asaph the keeper of the king's forest, that he may give me timber to make beams for the gates of the palace which appertained to the house, and for the wall of the city, and for the house that I shall enter into. And the king granted me, according to the good hand of my God upon me.

12 And I arose in the night, I and some few men with me; neither told I any man what my God had put in my heart to do at Jerusalem: neither was there any beast with me, save the beast that I rode upon.

13 And I went out by night by the gate of the valley, even before the dragon well, and to the dung port, and viewed the walls of Jerusalem, which were broken down, and the gates thereof were consumed with fire.

14 Then I went on to the gate of the fountain, and to the king's pool: but there was no place for the beast that was under me to pass.

15 Then went I up in the night by the brook, and viewed the wall, and turned back, and entered by the gate of the valley, and so returned.

16 And the rulers knew not whither I went, or what I did; neither had I as yet told it to the Jews, nor to the priests, nor to the nobles, nor to the rulers, nor to the rest that did the work.

17 Then said I unto them, Ye see the distress that we are in, how Jerusalem lieth waste, and the gates thereof are burned with fire: come, and let us build up the wall of Jerusalem, that we be no more a reproach.

18 Then I told them of the hand of my God which was good upon me; as also the king's words that he had spoken unto me. And they said, Let us rise up and build. So they strengthened their hands for this good work.

November 16

Memory Selection
Nehemiah 2:17

Devotional Reading
Psalm 146:1-10

Background Scripture
Nehemiah 1–2

Printed Scripture
Nehemiah 2:4-8, 12-18

101

Teacher's Target

Lesson purpose: *To review the work of Nehemiah in marshaling efforts to rebuild the wall of Jerusalem, with an eye to applying his strategy to our own situation.*

The Hebrews' task of rebuilding the city of Jerusalem after 70 years of captivity in Babylon was a massive undertaking. The work progressed only in fits and starts, interrupted by self-centered preoccupation with the builders' own concerns, and by opposition from surrounding nations. It required more than one kind of leader, from those who could offer spiritual encouragement to those who had management expertise and the ear of the Persian kings.

Nehemiah was the latter kind of leader. He was sent as a "layman" to superintend the work as Jerusalem's governor. In this lesson we shall see Nehemiah at prayer, at work in the court of the king, in the work of surveyor and appraiser, and in the task of inspiring the people to work.

What tasks facing God's people where you work could benefit from such a multi-faceted approach to "making a difference"?

Lesson Introduction

The books of Ezra and Nehemiah reflect the same period of the Jewish "Restoration"—the time when they were allowed to return from captivity and rebuild the Temple and the city of Jerusalem. The Persian king Cyrus authorized the first return under Ezra the priest (Ezra 1:1).

In this lesson, Persia has a new king—Artaxerxes. Ezra is still at work in Jerusalem, as we can see from Nehemiah 8:1ff. Now the priest is joined by a government official, Nehemiah, who wins permission from Artaxerxes to continue the work that had been started several years earlier.

Other Persian subjects near Jerusalem take a dim view of the activities; but Nehemiah and others persist until, as Lesson 9 recounted, the Temple is rebuilt.

Teaching Outline	Daily Bible Readings
	Mon. Jerusalem Is Destroyed *2 Chronicles 36:1-9*

I. Asking for Assistance—4-8
  A. Praying to God, 4
  B. Petitioning the king, 5
  C. Planning the work, 6-8
	Tue. Claiming God's Promise
	Nehemiah 1:1-11
	Wed. Enlisting Help from the King
	Nehemiah 2:1-10

II. Appraising the Task—12-16
  A. A lonely decision, 12
  B. A night-time ride, 13-16
	Thu. Let's Work Together
	Nehemiah 2:11-20
	Fri. Peace Within the Walls
	Psalm 122:1-9

III. Activating a Response—17-18
  A. Stating the case, 17a
  B. Making a direct appeal, 17b-18
	Sat. Happy Are Those Who Trust God
	Psalm 146:1-10
	Sun. Peace for Lovers of God's Law
	Psalm 119:162-176

VERSE BY VERSE

I. Asking for Assistance—4-8

A. Praying to God, 4

4 Then the king said unto me, For what dost thou make request? So I prayed to the God of heaven.

The king here, as verse 1 has said, is Artaxerxes, ruler of Persia. He is one of perhaps three kings by this name. Ironically, another king Artaxerxes had stopped work on the Temple (Ezra 4). The Artaxerxes to whom Nehemiah will appeal to rescind the order was nicknamed "Longimanus," which meant "long-handed," because his right hand was deformed. Yet his mind was open to the guidance of God. He had already given Ezra similar permission (Ezra 7).

As a Hebrew captive, Nehemiah was cup-bearer to the king (2:1). Hearing about the work stoppage in Jerusalem, Nehemiah (whose name means "Yah [or Yahweh] comforts") had been deeply moved, and had prayed fervently about the problem (chap. 1). When the king asks about his sad countenance, it is to God that Nehemiah first turns—always a wise move when we face a crucial moment.

B. Petitioning the king, 5

5 And I said unto the king, If it please the king, and if thy servant have found favour in thy sight, that thou wouldest send me unto Judah, unto the city of my fathers' sepulchres, that I may build it.

It must have taken courage to make this request, in light of the previous Artaxerxes' negative ruling on the restoration of Jerusalem. Yet Nehemiah, like Esther, apparently felt that God had placed him in a potentially influential position, and he was determined to marshal the resources of the mighty kingdom of Persia in order to do God's work.

C. Planning the work, 6-8

6 And the king said unto me, (the queen also sitting by him,) For how long shall thy journey be? And when wilt thou return? So it pleased the king to send me; and I set him a time.

7 Moreover I said unto the king, If it please the king, let letters be given me to the governors beyond the river, that they may convey me over till I come into Judah;

8 And a letter unto Asaph the keeper of the king's forest, that he may give me timber to make beams for the gates of the palace which appertained to the house, and for the wall of the city, and for the house that I shall enter into. And the king granted me, according to the good hand of my God upon me.

The king—apparently with no objection from the queen—grants Nehemiah's request. This is testimony to the Hebrew servant's faithful service. Like Daniel, he had been faithful to his duties even to a foreign ruler. Making the best of his situation, he had apparently worked "heartily, as to the Lord, and not unto men" (Col. 3:23). Who knows what kind of "break" awaits the person who tends to even an obscure task faithfully?

Taking advantage of the king's positive response, Nehemiah asks for a kind of "visa" or travel authorization from Persian-held kingdoms along the way. He may also have in mind impressing them with the king's permission for the work in Jerusalem to resume (contrast the opponents' success in stopping it in Ezra 4). Nehemiah also succeeds in requisitioning lumber from royal forests nearby to use in the great rebuilding project.

II. Appraising the Task—12-16
A. A lonely decision, 12

12 And I arose in the night, I and some few men with me; neither told I any man what my God had put in my heart to do at Jerusalem: neither was there any beast with me, save the beast that I rode upon.

In contrast to his openness in confiding his dream to the king, Nehemiah at first shares with no one in Jerusalem. Perhaps he does not want word of the new plan to leak to Israel's enemies. As verse 10 has said, they were upset that Nehemiah had been given permission to "seek the welfare of the children of Israel."

B. A night-time ride, 13-16

13 And I went out by night by the gate of the valley, even before the dragon well, and to the dung port, and viewed the walls of Jerusalem, which were broken down, and the gates thereof were consumed with fire.

14 Then I went on to the gate of the fountain, and to the king's pool: but there was no place for the beast that was under me to pass.

15 Then went I up in the night by the brook, and viewed the wall, and turned back, and entered by the gate of the valley, and so returned.

16 And the rulers knew not whither I went, or what I did; neither had I as yet told it to the Jews, nor to the priests, nor to the nobles, nor to the rulers, nor to the rest that did the work.

The "gate of the valley" is said by some to be the modern gate into the Old City of Jerusalem that leads to the Gihon Valley; but the many destructive battles in the city since these words were written may make it impossible to identify these landmarks. Some would also translate "the dung port" instead of "gate," identifying it as merely a conduit through which the city's refuse was passed. Part of the wall was in such bad repair that the donkey or horse Nehemiah rode could not pass. Again it is repeated that the new governor of the city did not yet report the sad results of his survey. Yet he had to confirm for himself what he had heard back in Sushan.

III. Activating a Response—17-18
A. Stating the case, 17a

17 Then said I unto them, Ye see the distress that we are in, how Jerusalem lieth waste, and the gates thereof are burned with fire:

Now it is time for Nehemiah to state clearly that Jerusalem's razed walls subject the city and what few inhabitants are left to raids from their enemies, and make their faith a laughing-stock among the pagans. As in any crisis, it is important that the both leaders and people have the facts. The project is too urgent to try to put a "positive spin" on the situation, or to keep the people uninformed.

B. Making a direct appeal, 17b-18

17b come, and let us build up the wall of Jerusalem, that we be no more a reproach.

18 Then I told them of the hand of my God which was good upon me; as also the king's words that he had spoken unto me. And they said, Let us rise up and build. So they strengthened their hands for this good work.

As the first phase of Nehemiah's task nears an end, it is interesting to survey his strategy. First he made sure he had the resources to complete the project. He had won from the king both permission to return and resources with which to rebuild the city. He was not going to be like the man in Jesus' parable who started to build a tower without counting the cost (Luke 14:28-30).

Second, Nehemiah surveyed the job to be done personally and in great detail. He would not be guilty of making an appeal for help based on claims he could not back up. Third, he was fully convinced in his own mind of the need before sharing it with others. The leader who can be argued out of his vision will not be able to marshal the necessary resources to carry it through.

Fourth, here in the latter part of verse 17, Nehemiah makes a direct appeal to those who can do something about the need. He gathers others who will be able in turn to enlist still others. Fifth and finally, he inspires them with the vision. If the walls are to be rebuilt, the leaders and the people must have more than the facts. They must also be inspired by hearing of the king's backing; they must be emotionally convinced of the critical need to rebuild the holy city, and they must have the positive conviction that God is with them, and will strengthen their hands to accomplish the work before them.

Would these strategies help accomplish some good work where you worship?

Evangelistic Emphasis

Jesus' disciples asked Him to teach them to pray. The instruction He gave to them consisted of a model prayer of only sixty words—just over three lines of a typical business letter. Yet, churchmen often make prayer so complex and  word-laden that laymen are too intimidated to pray. How can they possibly measure up to what they have heard all their lives from "prayer professionals." Surely, their attempts would only insult God.

When we read between the lines of Nehemiah 24, however, we learn of a different kind of prayer. Somewhere between the king's question, "What is your request?" and Nehemiah's response, "If it please the king...." this great leader offered up a prayer. It was not received by God as "irreverent" or "amateurish." Instead, it found a welcome and speedy reply.

Perhaps, if religionists did not serve up religion in such polished wineskins, the nonreligious would more readily taste the wine. It is not that we ought to be careless with our words that we offer to God or shoddy in our presentation of the Gospel. Instead, we ought to be down-to-earth. Simple. Real. Most important, at all costs, we must avoid presenting faith and godliness as "stuffy."

Memory Selection

Then said I unto them, Ye see the distress that we are in, how Jerusalem lieth waste, and the gates thereof are burned with fire come, and let us build up the wall of Jerusalem, that we be no more a reproach.— *Nehemiah 2:17*

To what can one compare the torn down walls of Jerusalem? Our cities have no walls, so there is no urgency to rebuild them. Nor is there any shame to be found in their absence. At the city level, perhaps the ghetto, standing out as an eyesore near the business district, provides a close parallel. Ghettos reflect the shame of a city that has lost its pride. It is evident that the needs of some of the city's people have been neglected, and those people themselves have lost hope.

At the home level, a house in dire need of maintenance reflects much the same kind of shame. Unfortunately, the people living in the house may be oblivious as to how shameful their home has become. The deterioration did not happen overnight. It came so gradually that those who live there did not notice. Those who see the house from a distance (like Nehemiah) notice and feel the shame that the house owners do not see.

Weekday Problems

Kay Morgan and Kevin Adams are the middle-aged children of Bill and Gloria Adams. They both remember fondly their days running free in the open fields and orchards of their Tennessee home near Humboldt. Those were carefree days, so unlike what they know in the gang-infested cities they now call "home." The vegetable garden provided plenty of memories involving both their labors and their palates. Now, that vegetable garden is little more than a snake-infested weed patch. The orchard is overwhelmed with underbrush. The field that once provided hay for the livestock no longer bears any resemblance to a hayfield. The paint on the farm house has been peeling for years.

Kevin and Kay are pained with the sad deterioration of their childhood home. They do not understand why their parents have allowed it to become such an eyesore. That in which they once had great pride has come to be a source of embarrassment and shame.

* How ought Kay and Kevin approach their parents about the condition of their home? Should they say nothing?

* What factors might have contributed to the decline of the Adams home?

* What might the Adams children do (or offer to do) that would make possible a restoration of their childhood home?

Working Wisdom

Half the people like to work and the other half don't. Or is it the other way around?

Lady to man asking for a hand-out: Why don't you work? Hard work never killed anyone.
Man with hand out: You're wrong, ma'am. I lost both my wives that way.

Work is the yeast that raises the dough.

Some people are like blisters. They don't show up until the work is finished.

Teach your son to cut his own wood. It will warm him twice.

Flo: I lost my job from illness and fatigue.
Jo: Too bad.
Flo: Yeah—the boss got sick and tired of me.

This Lesson in Your Life

Sometimes, going home is a *totally positive* experience, filled with nothing but love, joy, laughter, hugs, good food and fun memories. For some, going home is *totally negative*. They do not have good memories of home. For them, it was not a place of love and joy. Instead, drunkenness, fighting, bickering, bitterness, and abuse ruled the day—every day.

For most, going home is a mixture of *positive* and *negative*—joy and pain. Even under the best circumstances, there is at least the *joy* of arriving accompanied by the *pain* of leaving. Usually, there is much more.

There are the joys of seeing and being with loved ones—retreating momentarily into the womb of childhood innocence. There are the joys of digging through the attic with its old toys, clothes, and memorabilia. There is the joy of sitting up late, retelling stories about days-gone-by. There are the joys of watching home movies and eating together—lots of eating. There are the joys to be found in exploring again the old neighborhood (or the woods out back) and catching up on what has been happening in everyone's life.

But, there is also the pain of noticing the deterioration that has taken its toll on the old house and neighborhood. There is the pain of learning that your childhood friends, who married right out of high school, have gone their separate ways. You learn that your best friend just received treatment for alcoholism—his third round. The next-door neighbor lady who gave you brownies died last month. The church in which you grew up split last year, and people you've known and loved all your life don't speak to each other any more. Your high school has been torn down — consolidated into one of those massive, generic, assembly-line schools that is devoid of personality. Perhaps, Dad is no longer around. Mom's health is noticeably worse. Or maybe Mom and Dad have split up, and relationships have become awkward.

Going home can be painful because your own brokenness travels back home with you. Your failures, lost innocence, and compromised dreams are all too obvious. There is this incredible pain that comes with being reminded that you are no longer who you used to be. Neither are you who you aspired to become. Both the *joy* and the *pain* are blended together in this adventure of going home.

Though the circumstances are somewhat different, the mixture of emotions was much the same for Nehemiah as he traveled home. Going home, he was touching base with his roots—his identity. He was facing the brokenness of his homeland. At the same time, he was taking home with him his own brokenness, even as he set out to administer repair.

There is a sense in which every Sunday is an experience of *"going home."* As described above, it is an experience filled with a mixture of *joy* and *pain*. It is there, at church, where we touch our roots, reminding ourselves again *who* we are and *whose* we are. Yet, even as we do, we are reminded of where we have been, how we have failed, and the dreams that have been lost (or sold) during the past week. Of course, we see the brokenness of others also—perhaps even better than we see our own. Disappointment flutters at the edges of our minds, but as we embrace and laugh and sing and cry, we notice that all those flutterings are than drowned out by the renewal of our joy and dreams and determination to try again.

1. What made Nehemiah so sad?

Nehemiah was sad because he had received word from his homeland that his city's walls still lay in ruins.

2. When the king asked Nehemiah the reason for his sadness, what did he do before he answered the king?

Before Nehemiah answered the king's inquiry, he first prayed.

3. What request did Nehemiah make of the king?

Nehemiah asked the king to send him back to the city of his fathers to rebuild it.

4. What questions did the king have regarding this request?

The king asked Nehemiah how long the journey would take and when he would get back.

5. What kind of letters to governors did Nehemiah request from the king?

Nehemiah asked for letters to the governors beyond the river (Trans-Euphrates) requesting them to provide him safe passage to Judah.

(Please turn page)

1. What made Nehemiah so sad?

2. When the king asked Nehemiah the reason for his sadness, what did he do before he answered the king?

3. What request did Nehemiah make of the king?

4. What questions did the king have regarding this request?

5. What kind of letters to governors did Nehemiah request from the king?

6. What other letter did Nehemiah request?

7. To whom did Nehemiah credit the king's generosity to grant his requests?

8. What did Nehemiah first do before approaching the city officials with the challenge to rebuild Jerusalem's walls?

9. What did Nehemiah tell the city officials that prompted them to agree to the rebuilding?

10. What was the response of the city officials?

109

Nehemiah was sad because he had received word from his homeland that his city's walls still lay in ruins.

Before Nehemiah answered the king's inquiry, he first prayed.

Nehemiah asked the king to send him back to the city of his fathers to rebuild it.

The king asked Nehemiah how long the journey would take and when he would get back.

Nehemiah asked for letters to the governors beyond the river (Trans-Euphrates) requesting them to provide him safe passage to Judah.

Nehemiah requested a letter to Asaph, the keeper of the kings forests to provide timber for the rebuilding process.

He credited God with prompting the king's generosity.

Before approaching the city officials with the challenge to rebuild the city's walls, he first inspected them to estimate the size of the job.

Nehemiah told them how the Lord had been with him and of the blessings of the king upon the project.

They said, "Let's rise up and build."

6. What other letter did Nehemiah request?

Nehemiah requested a letter to Asaph, the keeper of the kings forests to provide timber for the rebuilding process.

7. To whom did Nehemiah credit the king's generosity to grant his requests?

He credited God with prompting the king's generosity.

8. What did Nehemiah first do before approaching the city officials with the challenge to rebuild Jerusalem's walls?

Before approaching the city officials with the challenge to rebuild the city's walls, he first inspected them to estimate the size of the job.

9. What did Nehemiah tell the city officials that prompted them to agree to the rebuilding?

Nehemiah told them how the Lord had been with him and of the blessings of the king upon the project.

10. What was the response of the city officials?

They said, "Let's rise up and build."

Lesson 12

The Courage to Continue

Nehemiah 4:6-8, 15-23

6 So we built the wall; and all the wall was joined together unto the half thereof: for the people had a mind to work.

7 But it came to pass that Sanballat, and Tobiah, and the Arabians, and the Ammonites, and the Ashdodites, heard that the walls of Jerusalem were made up, and that the breaches began to be stopped, then they were very wroth,

8 And conspired all of them together to come and to fight against Jerusalem, and to hinder it.

15 And it came to pass, when our enemies heard that it was known unto us, and God had brought their counsel to nought, that we returned all of us to the wall, every one unto his work.

16 And it came to pass, from that time forth, that the half of my servants wrought in the work, and the other half of them held both the spears, the shields, and the bows, and the habergeons; and the rulers were behind all the house of Judah.

17 They which builded on the wall, and they that bare burdens, with those that laded, every one with one of his hands wrought in the work, and with the other hand held a weapon.

18 For the builders, every one had his sword girded by his side, and so builded. And he that sounded the trumpet was by me.

19 And I said unto the nobles, and to the rulers, and to the rest of the people, The work is great and large, and we are separated upon the wall, one far from another.

20 In what place therefore ye hear the sound of the trumpet, resort ye thither unto us: our God shall fight for us.

21 So we laboured in the work: and half of them held the spears from the rising of the morning till the stars appeared.

22 Likewise at the same time said I unto the people, Let every one with his servant lodge within Jerusalem, that in the night they may be a guard to us, and labour on the day.

23 So neither I, nor my brethren, nor my servants, nor the men of the guard which followed me, none of us put off our clothes, saving that every one put them off for washing.

Memory Selection
Nehemiah 4:20

Devotional Reading
Nehemiah 9:6-15

Background Scripture
Nehemiah 4

Printed Scripture
Nehemiah 4:6-8,15-23

Teacher's Target

Lesson purpose: *To gain inspiration and courage to stand steadfastly at our posts, from the example of the Israelites who worked to rebuild the walls of Jerusalem.*

The people in any group you work with will know something about discouragement. They may be running low on spiritual energy, as in "burn-out." They may have experienced active opposition in their attempt to live the Christian life. They may be so burdened with a sense of failure that they have lost heart for the battle.

Use this lesson as a means of saying "Take heart!" The Israelites faced with the task of rebuilding the wall surely had as many reasons to become discouraged and to give up as we do today. How did they gain the courage to continue? And how can we borrow that can-do attitude in facing discouragement in our lives?

Lesson Introduction

Nehemiah, the former cup-bearer to Artaxerxes, king of Persia, had succeeded in winning the favor of the king, along with permission and resources to rebuild the walls of Jerusalem. After surveying the walls and marshaling the Israelites to tackle the immense task, Nehemiah faces a new problem: opposition from the pagan forces in the land.

God had given Canaan, the Land of Promise, to His chosen people, the Jews. Although they were commanded to drive out the pagans, they had never done a thorough job of doing so. Now they experience the consequences. Their attempt to rebuilt the holy city of Jerusalem, the center of Jewish worship, is taken to be another threat to the various peoples of Canaan. It is Governor Nehemiah's task to defy them courageously, and to inspire the people to protect themselves as they work on the walls.

Teaching Outline	Daily Bible Readings
	Mon. They Had a Mind to Work *Nehemiah 4:1-9*
I. The Threat of Opposition—6-8	**Tue.** "Our God Will Fight for Us" *Nehemiah 4:10-20*
II. The Power of Focusing—15	**Wed.** God's Sentinels on the Wall *Isaiah 62:6-12*
	Thu. The Prophet as Sentinel *Ezekiel 33:1-9*
III. The Wisdom of Watchful ness—16-18,21-23	**Fri.** God as Refuge and Fortress *Psalm 91:1-16*
IV. The Strength of Unity—19-20	**Sat.** All Nations Worship in Jerusalem *Zechariah 14:16-21*
	Sun. Heaven's Bread for Their Hunger *Nehemiah 9:6-15*

VERSE BY VERSE

I. The Threat of Opposition—6-8

6 So we built the wall; and all the wall was joined together unto the half thereof: for the people had a mind to work.

7 But it came to pass that Sanballat, and Tobiah, and the Arabians, and the Ammonites, and the Ashdodites, heard that the walls of Jerusalem were made up, and that the breaches began to be stopped, then they were very wroth,

8 And conspired all of them together to come and to fight against Jerusalem, and to hinder it.

Verse 6 probably means that the Israelites had succeeded in rebuilding the wall around Jerusalem up to half its height (see the NIV). This was done only with great effort and perseverance. We can imagine that the spirits of the workers rose as they looked back at their work and saw that the rising height of the wall promised new protection from their enemies.

Unfortunately the workers were not the only ones who observed the renewed fortifications about the city. Sanballat and Tobiah were probably Samaritan princes who themselves were vassals of Persia (hence "Tobias the servant [of Artaxerxes]"; see also 2:10). They probably were already acquainted with many of the people who been left behind during the Captivity and had risen to positions of influence among their fellow Hebrews. They knew, therefore, who to conspire with in an attempt to halt the rebuilding of the walls, and sent messages more than once—no doubt with offers of bribes and/or threats of war (see 6:17; 13:4, 28). It is bad enough to have opposition to a worthy cause from without. It is especially disheartening to have nay-sayers from within; but these are the personalities that Israel's enemies sought out in order to foment fear and rebellion among the very people charged with rebuilding the walls.

The Arabians and the Ammonites, from the southeast, were ancient enemies of Israel, and they also viewed the rebuilding of Jerusalem as a threat. Ashdod was a chief city of the Philistines.

II. The Power of Focusing—15

15 And it came to pass, when our enemies heard that it was known unto us, and God had brought their counsel to nought, that we returned all of us to the wall, every one unto his work.

The conspirators are found out, and their attempts to create dissension and doubt among the people are cut short. Their exposure enabled the faithful to focus on their work—which is always an antidote worth trying when we face discouragement. Some problems in everyday life resist immediate solutions; some reasons for being "down" and despairing can't always be named. At such times the advice of the old janitor is worth hearing: "Just pick up the broom and sweep."

III. The Wisdom of Watchfulness—16-18, 21-23

16 And it came to pass, from that time forth, that the half of my servants wrought in the work, and the other half of them held both the spears, the shields, and the bows, and the habergeons; and the rulers were behind all the house of Judah.

17 They which builded on the wall, and they that bare burdens, with those that laded, every one with one of his hands wrought in the work, and with the other hand held a weapon.

18 For the builders, every one had his sword girded by his side, and so builded. And he that sounded the trumpet was by me.

21 So we laboured in the work: and half of them held the spears from the rising of the morning till the stars appeared.

22 Likewise at the same time said I unto the people, Let every one with his servant lodge within Jerusalem, that in the night they may be a guard to us, and labour on the day.

23 So neither I, nor my brethren, nor my servants, nor the men of the guard which followed me, none of us put off our clothes, saving that every one put them off for washing.

At least four distinct strategies of watchfulness seem to be described here. At some sections of the rebuilding project—perhaps where archeologists have found huge stones that would have required several men to heave into place—some workers apparently had to use both hands in the work. At such sites fellow-Israelites were posted with the sole duty of bearing arms to protect the workers. They not only had spears, swords, bows, and shields, but metal jackets or coats of mail known in the time of the King James translators as "habergeons" (NIV "armor").

At other places—perhaps where the workers were applying mortar to the seams of the stones in the wall—the workmen could wield a tool in one hand and a sword or spear in the other. The picture is like that of a mother cow and calf beseiged by wolves. The enemy is ever-present, seeking an opening to attack; but the mother uses horns and heels, now whirling now charging, to keep them at bay.

A third member of the workforce stood by the governor ready to sound the trumpet of alarm upon seeing attackers try to scale the half-completed wall. We are reminded of the word of the Lord to Ezekiel, commanding a watchman to blow the trumpet of warning when the enemy approaches (Ezek. 33:1-6).

Skipping down to verses 21-23 we find a fourth component of Nehemiah's defense that may more aptly be considered here. The arms-bearing workers labored in shifts, serving as fighting men during the day and laboring at night—surely snatching a few hours' sleep sometime during their 24-hour watch.

Other workers slept inside the walls while the watchmen stood guard. They were so beseiged that they could not afford to take off their clothes to sleep, but only, occasionally, to wash them. (Or, see the NIV reading that portrays workers wearing their clothes even when they "went for water.")

Armor is first mentioned among the Israelites when David fought Goliath (1 Sam. 17:5-7). Archeologists and historians describe the armor of his day as consisting of bronze and leather protective clothing.

On the other hand, the swords used by the Israelites would have been made of iron, which, since it is harder than bronze, could keep a sharper edge. Iron had been known since about 1200 B.C. (the beginning of "the Iron Age"). The Philistines were more advanced than the Jews in the use of iron in warfare during the early days of the Jews' conquest of Canaan, and for awhile had a monopoly on its use and prevented the Israelites from making many iron swords and spears (see 1 Sam. 13:19-22).

IV. The Strength of Unity—19-20

19 And I said unto the nobles, and to the rulers, and to the rest of the people, The work is great and large, and we are separated upon the wall, one far from another.

20 In what place therefore ye hear the sound of the trumpet, resort ye thither unto us: our God shall fight for us.

Governor Nehemiah's brief word of encouragement to the workers and their leaders must have been one of several rallying calls he found necessary to boost morale. His point is that despite all their precautions and strategies, weapons and armor, they are too few to stand shoulder-to-shoulder along the wall. They must do all they can do, but they must also count on Another standing in the gaps between them. In other words, they are not in the battle alone. When they hear the warning trumpet they are to unify their forces at the threatened site. They are also to fight not merely in their own strength, but in the knowledge that "the battle is the Lord's" (1 Sam. 17:47; 2 Chron. 32:8).

Evangelistic Emphasis

Dr. Alfred Adler tells of a painful childhood, academically. He got off to a poor start in arithmetic. His teacher became convinced that he was "dumb in mathematics" (to use her words), advising his parents of this "fact." She told them not to expect too much of him in any area of academics.

Subtly, silently, Adler's parents passed on to him these disappointed expectations. He in turn, then, passively accepted the evaluation and proceeded to *live down to* it. Predictably, his grades on his report card proved that his teacher was correct in his analysis.

Then one particular day, that he still remembers with pain, Adler had a sudden flash of insight into a problem that had the other students stumped. Announcing to his teacher his solution to the problem, she and the whole class laughed.

That's what Sanballat and the other discouragers did when Nehemiah and the Jews decided to rebuild Jerusalem's walls. They laughed. They mocked. They jeered. In much the same way, discouragers will sometimes laugh, mock and jeer when they hear of a sinner's decision to *surrender his life to be rebuilt.*

It is reassuring to know that God does not laugh. While others scoff, He washes us clean. While others sneer, He enables us to be *born anew.* So completely is our life rebuilt, it is almost as though our life had never been broken, at all.

Memory Selection

In what place therefore ye hear the sound of the trumpet, resort ye thither unto us our God shall fight for us. —*Nehemiah 4:20*

Every soldier going into battle, if he is a believer, covets the alliance of God as he approaches the foe. It may be that he realizes all too well the fragility of life because of watching his comrades come back from the front lines in body bags. But even if the soldier is a rookie and this is his first engagement, his pre-battle jitters are enough to bring somber tones to his morning prayers.

Surely these words spoken by Nehemiah were words of comfort for those people. It was no longer merely a wistful hope of theirs that their God would go with them into battle. Nehemiah delivered to them a direct message from their God that He promised He would fight for them against their foe.

Isn't that what our God promised us when He sent his Son to the cross? If God is on our side, who would *dare* to raise a finger against us!

Weekday Problems

For Linda Rankel, last week was the worst she can remember. It all began when she announced to the news reporter that she had decided to rebuild the family hardware business that her dad had owned and operated until his untimely death. One night as he was closing the store, a robber hit him over the back of the head, taking the day's

cash receipts. Linda's dad remained in a coma for weeks before his death. He never regained consciousness. The killer was never caught. During the weeks that followed, just about every window in the "mom 'n pop hardware" was broken and most of the store's products were either stolen or destroyed.

Since announcing her plans to rebuild, no word of encouragement has been heard by Linda. The rest of her family thinks she is insane. Several police officers have warned her of the dangers of her plan. Some discouragers from the community have responded with more broken windows and an endless maze of spray paint graffiti.

    * Is Linda being unreasonable to think of rebuilding a hardware business where her father was murdered? If so, what are some alternative options?

    * If Linda should decide to proceed with her plan to rebuild, what instruction could she glean from Nehemiah for the task?

    * How is what Linda is trying to do different from what Nehemiah attempted? How is it the same?

Tales from the Trenches

The soldiers in the war games were not allowed to use live ammunition. Instead of shooting a rifle they were supposed to shout, "Bang, bang!" Instead of using bayonets they were told to say "Stab, stab!" And for grenades they were to say "Lob, Lob." In each case the person addressed was to fall down and play dead.

As the "battle" progressed, one soldier ran up to the "enemy" and said "Bang, bang!" but his target refused to fall. "Stab, stab!" and finally "Lob, lob!" came the cries, but the enemy stood unharmed. "Look," the frustrated attacker said, "You're supposed to fall dead."

"Rumble, rumble," his enemy replied. "I'm a tank."

The soldiers had been at the front for three weeks when the sergeant said, "Men I have good news and bad news. The good news is that everyone gets a change of socks. The bad news is: Walters, you change with Jones, Jones changes with Brown, Douglas with Dickson...."

This Lesson in Your Life

In our battle against evil, it is easy for us to fall into the delusion that *the enemy is working hardest where we see his handiwork*. We tell ourselves that the greatest danger is "out there" in the world—in the enemy's territory. We think that we can tell when danger arrives at our house by watching out the window. *"We will be able to see him approaching our door.* At that time, we will be able to arm ourselves. There is no need to worry about all that now!" Periodically, we even convince ourselves that we've beaten the enemy, so he has gone to pick on someone else for a while.

Nehemiah and the Jews were more alert to the enemy's wiles than that. It is obvious that they did not let down their guard even during the most peaceful moments of the day. When an attack *was least expected*, they waited with weapons in hand, expecting the worst. Whether working on the wall or carrying supplies, whether nobleman or laborer, whether by night or by day, every person remained alert and prepared for battle. It cost them heavily in production time. But what good would there have been in faster production time, if death and destruction only awaited them at the end of the work day?

Satan would not gain nearly so many victories if we were as vigilant. His obvious assaults on our life are often merely distractions, drawing our eyes away from the area of our life where he plans his *real* attack.

More than once, Christians have rallied to fight some "evil" in the community or church, only to find later that *an evil spirit* had taken over the rally itself. Righteous indignation becomes self-righteous hatred. A march against evil becomes an advertisement for it. Fighting against liberalism, we become enslaved by legalism. Warring against legalism, we are seduced by lawlessness. Pursuing love for humankind, we demonstrate hatred toward individuals. Attempting to defend some "truth," we ignore another truth. Trying to keep out the enemy, we wall in the children. Attempting to protect the faithful, we imprison them. Fighting bitterly for a cause, bitterness comes to be our cause. The list could go on endlessly!

How then do we defend ourselves against such a relentless enemy? Nehemiah offers a model worth imitating.First, Nehemiah and the people prayed, petitioning God's involvement. Second, they took appropriate precautions to defend themselves against attack, posting a guard day and night to meet this threat. Third, they remembered the Lord. That is, they remembered that he was with them, fighting for them. In remembering, they found courage. Fourth, Nehemiah and his people refused to let down their guard. All the way to the completion of the wall, they stayed alert. Every attack that the enemy tried proved unsuccessful, because the people of God never forsook their guard.

This is certainly the strategy that we need to win our battles against the evil one. Passive faith and cocky self-assurance will inevitably fail us when we least expect it. Constant vigilance with prayer faithfulness is sure to win.

Seed Thoughts

1. Who was Sanballat and what was the nature of his reception of the news that the Jews planned to rebuild their walls?

Sanballat seems to have been the governor of Samaria. The news of the Jews' plan to rebuild was received with anger and mockery.

2. What did Tobiah the Ammonite say would cause the wall that the Jews were building to break?

Tobiah said that if a fox climbed upon the wall that the Jews were building, it would fall down.

3. What was the first response that the Nehemiah and the Jews made in reply to Sanballat's and Tobiah's mockery?

They prayed.

4. How much of the wall was completed before the next problems arose?

The wall was built to half its height before the next problems arose.

5. When Sanballat and Tobiah again caused trouble with their schemes to sabotage the work, how did Nehemiah and the people respond?

Again, they prayed. Then they posted guard day and night to meet the threat.

1. Who was Sanballat and what was the nature of his reception of the news that the Jews planned to rebuild their walls?

2. What did Tobiah the Ammonite say would cause the wall that the Jews were building to break?

3. What was Nehemiah's and the people's first response to Sanballat's and Tobiah's mockery?

4. How much of the wall was completed before the next problems arose?

5. When Sanballat and Tobiah again caused trouble with their schemes to sabotage the work, how did Nehemiah and the people respond?

6. From which direction was the en-emy expected to attack?

7. Whom did Nehemiah have armed and ready to do battle?

8. How were the laborers divided for work and for battle?

9. Whom did Nehemiah tell the people would battle for them?

10. What comment was made about their clothes to indicate how prepared for battle they remained?

Sanballat seems to have been the governor of Samaria. The news of the Jews' plan to rebuild was received with anger and mockery.

Tobiah said that if a fox climbed upon the wall that the Jews were building, it would fall down.

They prayed.

The wall was built to half its height before the next problems arose.

Again, they prayed. Then they posted guard day and night to meet the threat.

From every direction.

Nehemiah made sure that *everybody* was either armed for battle or being guarded by someone who was armed.

One half of the people did work on the wall. The other half of the people stood guard, armed for battle.

Nehemiah told the people that God would fight for them.

It is said that they did not take off their clothes for any reason (with the possible exception of for washing—KJV).

(Seed Thoughts, continued)

6. From which direction was the enemy expected to attack?

From every direction.

7. Whom did Nehemiah have armed and ready to do battle?

Nehemiah made sure that *everybody* was either armed for battle or being guarded by someone who was armed.

8. How were the laborers divided for work and for battle?

One half of the people did work on the wall. The other half of the people stood guard, armed for battle.

9. Whom did Nehemiah tell the people would battle for them?

Nehemiah told the people that God would fight for them.

10. What comment was made about their clothes to indicate how prepared for battle they remained?

It is said that they did not take off their clothes for any reason (with the possible exception of for washing—KJV).

Lesson 13

Reward of the Faithful

Malachi 3:6-18

6 For I am the Lord, I change not; therefore ye son of Jacob are not consumed.

7 Even from the days of your fathers ye are gone away from mine ordinances, and have not kept them. Return unto me, and I will return unto you, saith the Lord of hosts. But ye said, Wherein shall we return?

8 Will a man rob God? Yet ye have robbed me. But ye say, Wherein have we robbed thee? In tithes and offerings.

9 Ye are cursed with a curse: for ye have robbed me, even this whole nation.

10 Bring ye all the tithes into the storehouse, that there may be meat in mine house, and prove me now herewith, saith the Lord of hosts, if I will not open you the windows of heaven, and pour you out a blessing, that there shall not be room enough to receive it.

11 And I will rebuke the devourer for your sakes, and he shall not destroy the fruits of your ground; neither shall your vine cast her fruit before the time in the field, saith the Lord of hosts.

12 And all nations shall call you blessed: for ye shall be a delightsome land, saith the Lord of hosts.

13 Your words have been stout against me, saith the Lord. Yet ye say, What have we spoken so much against thee?

14 Ye have said, It is vain to serve God: and what profit is it that we have kept his ordinance, and that we have walked mournfully before the Lord of hosts?

15 And now we call the proud happy; yea, they that work wickedness are set up; yea they that tempt God are even delivered.

16 Then they that feared the Lord spake often one to another: and the Lord hearkened, and heard it, and a book of remembrance was written before him for them that feared the Lord, and that thought upon his name.

17 And they shall be mine, saith the Lord of hosts, in that day when I make up my jewels; and I will spare them, as a man spareth his own son that serveth him.

18 Then shall ye return, and discern between the righteous and the wicked, between him that serveth God and him that serveth him not.

Memory Selection
Malachi 3:7

Devotional Reading
Malachi 2:17–3:5

Background Scripture
Malachi 2:17–3:18

Printed Scripture
Malachi 3:6-18

November 30

121

Teacher's Target

Lesson purpose: *To weigh our own practice of contributing to the work of the Lord with those required under the Law, through an understanding of the prophet Malachi's teaching.*

Every worthwhile work and every useful institution requires money. Although some people accuse churches of "always harping on money," such charges must not make us apologize for examining what the Bible has to say about giving.

Your class members may disagree on how to apply to their own life the principle of tithing. Is it just that—a principle—or is it a requirement? Instead of allowing the class to degenerate into arguments, lead members to assess the level of their support of the work of the church at a deeper level. As someone wisely said, the Old Law set apart one day to be holy, while the New says that all days are holy. The Old set apart one tribe as priests, the New says we are all priests. The Old set apart a tithe for God's work; the New insists that all we have belongs to Him. This, of course, does not relieve us of the choosing responsible what portion of our income to foster the work of the church.

Lesson Introduction

The book of Malachi, standing as it does at the end of the Old Testament, was considered by ancient Jews as "the last word" of prophecy. Just as the last words of a person are often significant, so this book's call to return to God's Covenant is important.

Part of the Covenant involved tithing. During the long years when the Temple lay in ruins, many religious practices—including tithing—were discontinued. Now their financial contributions were urgently needed, and it was Malachi's task to remind them of their duty.

He found, however, that the Captivity's crushing judgment on Israel had caused many to doubt whether the Covenant, on which tithing was based, was valid. Would God really bless them materially if they were faithful in returning a portion to Him? Malachi not only dares them to put God to the test, but to rebuild the kind of fellowship with Him and with each other that encourages giving their all in His service.

Teaching Outline	Daily Bible Readings	
I. Contrast—6-7	**Mon.**	Bring an Acceptable Offering *Malachi 1:6-14*
A. God's constancy, 6	**Tue.**	Priests Neglected Their Calling *Malachi 2:4-9*
B. The people's fickleness, 7		
II. Covenant—8-12	**Wed.**	God of Justice Coming *Malachi 2:17–3:5*
A. Punishment for rebellion, 8-9		
B. Blessings in obedience, 10-12	**Thu.**	Doing What God Asks *Malachi 3:6-18*
III. Questions—13-15		
A. Do the good really profit?, 13-14	**Fri.**	Faithfulness Remembered *Malachi 4:1-6*
B. Do the wicked go free? 15		
IV. Consolation—16-18	**Sat.**	Renewing the Covenant *Exodus 24:1-11*
A. The fellowship of encouragement, 16		
B. God's precious treasure, 17-18	**Sun.**	God's Promises Can Be Trusted *Jeremiah 33:14-22*

VERSE BY VERSE

I. Contrast—6-7

A. God's constancy, 6

6 For I am the Lord, I change not; therefore ye son of Jacob are not consumed.

The captivity and exile of Israel shook the faith of some Israelites. Had God abandoned them? Was the historic teaching that they were His chosen people a fiction? The prophet Malachi prefaces his teaching on tithing with the affirmation that if God had really abandoned the Jews, the sons of Jacob, then none would remain. The fact that a "remnant" had returned from exile with permission to rebuild the Temple was evidence that He still longed for an intimate relationship with His people.

B. The people's fickleness, 7

7 Even from the days of your fathers ye are gone away from mine ordinances, and have not kept them. Return unto me, and I will return unto you, saith the Lord of hosts. But ye said, Wherein shall we return?

The problem was not with God, but with the people. They had not only forsaken His "ordinances" or laws; the had forgotten their part of the Covenant relationship. Malachi's entire teaching on tithing is based on the Covenant, in which God promised to bless them if they would serve Him (see Gen. 28:1-14, for example).

Malachi's favorite style of writing is

the dialog, in which he makes a statement and poses a question that might naturally follow. Here the question he puts in the mouth of the people is "Just how do we need to return?"

II. Covenant—8-12

A. Punishment for rebellion, 8-9

8 Will a man rob God? Yet ye have robbed me. But ye say, Wherein have we robbed thee? In tithes and offerings.

9 Ye are cursed with a curse: for ye have robbed me, even this whole nation.

A rhetorical question continues the dialogue, is answered, then followed by another posed question. It is asked as though the prophet is astounded at anyone having the audacity to suppose they could rob the One who created it all.

The ancestors of these Jews had specifically committed themselves to keep the Covenant (cf. Josh. 24:16-25). Furthermore, they had only recently renewed this commitment (Neh. 10:28ff,). That Covenant specifically included tithing (Deut. 14:22-23). Since they had failed to make good their promise, Malachi says they would incur the "curses" Moses had clearly laid out before their forefathers (28:15ff.)

Tithing—giving a tenth of one's income—had been practiced hundreds of years before it was included in the Law of Moses. Historians say it existed in ancient Egypt, and in China. Abraham gave a tithe to King Melchizedek (Gen. 14:17-20). In addition to the continuous practice of tithing, there may have been an extra tithe every three years. Like any religious observance, it was subject to abuse both by those who withheld some of what properly belonged to the Lord, and by those who boasted of how well

Evangelistic Emphasis

What is it about the promised reward that entices the Christians to a life-long walk of faithfulness? Is it *merely* life that goes on forever? Streets of gold? A mansion over the hilltop? Or, is it something more significant but less terrestrial?

It is said that one of the most grueling of all bicycle races is the Tour De France. It is a race that covers about 2000 miles, including some of France's most difficult, mountainous terrain. Eating and drinking are done on the run. The variations in temperature accompanying the course are extreme. To train for the event, a contestant will commonly ride his bike as much as 20,000 or more miles per year.

What kind of prize makes people endure so much hardship and pain! Ten thousand dollars? One hundred thousand dollars? No. The race is not really about prize money. The prize is just a special winner's jersey. What then motivates the contestants? They are motivated by the wish to sweep through the Arc de Triomphe on the last day and to be able to say that they finished the Tour de France.

Yes, the Christian looks forward expectantly to the reward that he is to claim. Nevertheless, the real drive behind the holy life is to hear the approving word from his Lord, *"Well done, my good and faithful servant."* The disciple's desire is to please his Master.

Memory Selection

Even from the days of your fathers ye are gone away from mine ordinances, and have not kept them. Return unto me, and I will return unto you, saith the LORD of hosts. But ye said, Wherein shall we return?— *Malachi 3:7*

The day after Thanksgiving Mary Sue tagged along with her mother on a shopping spree at the mall. Before leaving the house, Mary Sue's mother had made her promise to *stay close by her side at all times* so as not to become lost in the large crowd of Christmas shoppers.

Promises, however, are easier made than kept—especially when surrounded by so many interesting things being displayed for early Christmas shoppers. At some point during the morning, Mary Sue left her mother's side *for only a moment* to get a closer look at a new doll like the one she had seen on television. It wasn't long before the department store's speaker system sounded out the call for "the lost mother of a little girl, named Mary Sue."

Isn't it amazing how, when we wander away from God's presence, we also usually accuse Him of deserting us!

Weekday Problems

Mark Cougan is a new Christian. After leaving behind all religious ties during his teens and living in rebellion to the values that his parents had tried to instill, Mark *came home* just over a year ago. Like the prodigal that Jesus told about in Luke 15, Mark returned to claim the Father's abundant love. It wasn't a token repentance. His life became suddenly  so changed that his old cronies at first did not believe that it was real. They had known him too long. Yet, it was real!

What Mark is trying to understand right now is why he has so painfully struggled with his family's finances since becoming a Christian. His wall paper business was doing so well for a while. Recently, however, *in spite of his faithful tithing and eager church involvement*, he has been scrambling feverishly just to keep from filing bankruptcy. Mark's question is, "Where is God? Why isn't He keeping his promise to open the windows of heaven in response to the faithful tither"?

* Mark's question is a fair one, where is God? Why have Mark's finances worsened since his tithing began, rather than improving?

* Since this promise seems to be so *unqualified*, how is it that there are poor Christians in the world?

* If a Christian family is struggling financially, is that a clear indication that the family is not tithing? Why?

Passing the Plate

An artist was asked to contribute to the church's fund-raising campaign. "I'm broke," he said, "but I'll donate a $300 painting."

When the drive was over the minister announced that the campaign was just $100 short of its goal. "No problem!" said the artist. "I'll just increase the price of my painting to $400."

Doctor to his minister: Sorry it's been three months since I've tithed.
Minister: Hmm. Seems to be a lot of that going around.

Slick Sam: What's the most sensitive nerve in the human body?
Minister Mike: The one to the pocketbook.

Mom: Quick, Henry, call the doctor. Johnny just swallowed a coin.
Dad: We ought to call the minister. He can get money out of anybody.

127

This Lesson in Your Life

It was an exciting day for Jane Hendrix when Shirley King came to work at Big Valley Motors. Jane had worked at Big Valley three years and had often grown weary of the idle talk and coarse joking that seemed to flourish when the showrooms were not active with prospective buyers. Shirley, Jane had been told, is a Christian. With child-like eagerness, Jane watched the showroom entrance the next morning, anxious to meet her.

At first, the working atmosphere seemed to become suddenly delightful. Jane and Shirley talked about their faith and families every chance they got. Though the idle showroom scuttlebutt continued, it faded into the background as far as the two of them were concerned. Their minds and conversations were *otherwise occupied*. In all of Jane's employment years, she could not remember a time when she so enthusiastically looked forward to going to work. It was so much better having another Christian there, with whom she could visit when business was slow.

As time gradually passed, however, Jane began to began to feel uneasy about the nature of their conversations. More and more, critical remarks were whispered about people—people at church, other salespersons in the showroom and family members of Shirley that Jane did not even know. At first, Jane did not realize what was happening. Though her guard usually erected immediately anytime gossip was voiced, she sensed no ready arousal of her defenses in her chats with Shirley. This was not gossip that was disturbing Jane. It was something else. The feeling was eerie.

One evening, her conscience haunting her as she readied herself for bed, Jane carefully replayed in her mind the day's conversations with Shirley in an effort to determine what exactly was bothering her. Not until well after midnight did Jane finally satisfy her search. The focus of Shirley's negative remarks was not people, at all. It was God. Her criticisms were always criticisms of God. That's why Jane's defenses against gossip had not sounded their alert. People were mentioned in these negative complaints of Shirley, but her real complaints were attacks against the injustice of God.

"Can you believe that Bill Jordan is the salesperson of the month *again!* He's not even a believer!" Jane remembered Shirley having complained more than once.

"I don't understand why God does not send a lightning bolt to zap my brother-in-law. He's got the morals of a dog and lives like a pig. But no! He's raking in the dough and living like a king!" she said with annoyance.

One by one, Jane replayed the tapes of their conversations in her mind. The people of the conversations varied, but the theme always seemed to be the same. Shirley was angry at God for allowing others to prosper financially more than her. She resented especially the generosity He bestowed on the unbelieving and the mercy He extended to the wayward. Shirley was anxious for God to send swift justice on the world. She was eager to be vindicated for her faith.

Shirley, of course, is not alone in her cry for vindication. Like Shirley, we are sometimes quick to think God's mercy is "injustice" and see his patience as being somehow "unfair" to us. What we all-too-easily forget is how many times He has been merciful and patient with us. Were it not for His kindness to us, we would have no relationship with Him to enjoy.

Seed Thoughts

1. What did the Lord, speaking through Malachi, tell the people that He *does not* do?

The Lord declared that He does not change.

2. How long did the Lord say the people had been disobeying Him?

From the time of their fathers they had been turning away from His statutes and not keeping them.

3. What image did the word of the Lord use to describe the impact of His people withholding their tithes?

The term the Lord used was, "rob." The people were depicted as robbers of God.

4. What did the Lord tell the people to do with their tithes?

He told them to bring their tithes into the storehouse.

5. What did God promise to do when the people began to tithe again as they ought to be doing?

He promised to open the windows of heaven and to pour out a blessing so big they would not have room to receive it.

---

1. What did the Lord, speaking through Malachi, tell the people that He *does not do*?

---

2. How long did the Lord say the people had been disobeying Him?

---

3. What image did the word of the Lord use to describe the impact of His people withholding their tithes?

---

4. What did the Lord tell the people to do with their tithes?

---

5. What did God promise to do when the people began to tithe again as they ought to be doing?

---

6. What else did God promise to do?

---

7. What did the Lord say would be the response of the other nations to Judah's good fortune?

---

8. What had the people been saying about God that had disappointed Him?

---

9. How did the people respond to this rebuke of their attitude toward God?

---

10. What did the Lord promise that the people would again be able to do?

(Please turn page)

The Lord declared that He does not change.

From the time of their fathers they had been turning away from His statutes and not keeping them.

The term the Lord used was, "rob." The people were depicted as robbers of God.

He told them to bring their tithes into the storehouse.

He promised to open the windows of heaven and to pour out a blessing so big they would not have room to receive it.

He promised to "rebuke the devourer" so that he would no longer destroy the fruit of their ground.

He said that the other nations would call them blessed.

The people had been saying they were serving God in vain, since the wicked were more blessed than they.

They talked it over and the Lord listened to them and heard them.

That they would again discern between the righteous and the wicked, those who serve God and those who do not.

6. What else did God promise to do?

He promised to "rebuke the devourer" so that he would no longer destroy the fruit of their ground.

7. What did the Lord say would be the response of the other nations to Judah's good fortune?

He said that the other nations would call them blessed.

8. What had the people been saying about God that had disappointed Him?

The people had been saying they were serving God in vain, since the wicked were more blessed than they.

9. How did the people respond to this rebuke of their attitude toward God?

They talked it over and the Lord listened to them and heard them.

10. What did the Lord promise that the people would again be able to do?

That they would again discern between the righteous and the wicked, those who serve God and those who do not.

Lesson 1

Living in God's Light

1 John 1:5-10; 2:3-11

5 This then is the message which we have heard of him, and declare unto you, that God is light, and in him is no darkness at all.

6 If we say that we have fellowship with him, and walk in darkness, we lie, and do not the truth:

7 But if we walk in the light, as he is in the light, we have fellowship one with another, and the blood of Jesus Christ his Son cleanseth us from all sin.

8 If we say that we have no sin, we deceive ourselves, and the truth is not in us.

9 If we confess our sins, he is faithful and just to forgive us our sins, and to cleanse us from all unrighteousness.

10 If we say that we have not sinned, we make him a liar, and his word is not in us.

2:3 And hereby we do know that we know him, if we keep his commandments.

4 He that saith, I know him, and keepeth not his commandments, is a liar, and the truth is not in him.

5 But whoso keepeth his word, in him verily is the love of God perfected: hereby know we that we are in him.

6 He that saith he abideth in him ought himself to walk, even as he walked.

7 Brethren, I write no new commandment unto you: but an old commandment which ye have heard from the beginning.

8 Again, a new commandment I write unto you, which thing is true in him and in you: because the darkness is past, and the true light now shineth.

9 He that saith he is in the light, and hateth his brother, is in darkness even until now.

10 He that loveth his brother abideth in the light, and there is none occasion of stumbling in him.

11 But he that hateth his brother is in darkness, and walketh in darkness, and knoweth not whither he goeth, because that darkness hath blinded his eyes.

Memory Selection
1 John 1:7

Background Scripture
1 John 1:1–2:11

Devotional Reading
1 John 1:1-141

Printed Scripture
1 John 1:5-10; 2:3-11

Teacher's Target

Lesson purpose: *To learn the apostle John's definition of love: openness and obedience to God's Word, and right attitudes and behavior toward others.*

"Love makes the world go 'round," we sing. Even in the midst of a violent society, pop singers croon about love, psychologists speak of love, and lovers either revel at being in love or complain about lost love.

What is this psychological and social commodity called love? You might introduce this lesson by inviting class members to share some of the definitions of love offered by popular culture. Then note that Christ's followers should seek biblical definitions such as those offered by John.

The Bible insists that love is more than a feeling. For John, love—*agape*—is *an enfleshed attitude* that shows selfless concern for others by deeds. As the lesson unfolds, encourage class members to share experiences where this extra dimension of love has enriched their lives.

Lesson Introduction

Reliable tradition holds that 1, 2, and 3 John were written by the apostle John, the son of Zebedee, who also wrote the first Gospel and the Revelation. The similarity of language and the stately, "simply profound" style in these writings uphold this view.

Some traditions hold that John lived to such an advanced age that he had to be carried to church, where he was accustomed to repeating over and over, "Little children, love one another." This, he said, is an adequate summary of Jesus' teachings. If the portrait is true, it shows the power of Christ in transforming a man who was at first known as a "son of thunder" (Mark 3:17)—one who was ready to call down fire from heaven on his adversaries (Luke 9:54)—into "the apostle of love."

The Epistles of John are known for their use of contrasting images such as light and darkness, love and hate, knowing and doing.

Teaching Outline	Daily Bible Readings

I. Darkness and Light—1:5-7
  A. The nature of God, 5
  B. The walk of His followers, 6-7
II. Sin and Salvation—8-10
  A. The fact of sin, 8
  B. The way of salvation, 9-10
III. Knowing and Doing—2:3-5
  A. To know is to obey, 3
  B. To love is to be "perfected," 4-5
IV. Walking and Stumbling—6-11
  A. The old path, 6-7
  B. The new light, 8
  C. The true sign, 9-11
	Mon. Living in the Light
	  1 John 1:1-10
	Tue. To Love God Is to Obey Him
	  John 14:15-21
	Wed. True Light Already Is Shining
	  1 John 2:7-11
	Thu. Be Merciful as God Is Merciful
	  Luke 6:32-38
	Fri. A Child to Be Called God's Son
	  Luke 1:26-28
	Sat. Christ Shines in the Darkness
	  John 1:1-13
	Sun. See the Salvation of God
	  Luke 3:1-6

VERSE BY VERSE

I. Darkness and Light—1:5-7
A. The nature of God, 5

5 This then is the message which we have heard of him, and declare unto you, that God is light, and in him is no darkness at all.

In the preceding verses, the author has emphasized his first-hand knowledge of both Jesus and His teachings. John has heard, seen, and even handled "the Word of life" (vs. 1)! To us it may be startling to think of "handling the Word." The language blends the material with the spiritual, actions with ideas. Such expressions, however, were typical among the Jews, and they remind us of John's Jewish heritage.

John also typically summarizes massive ideas into simple, one-word definitions: God is light (and love, the door, the way, truth, and life, etc.). By the time he wrote, some false teachers questioned whether the "creator God" was totally good, since they assumed that matter is evil. John insists that the true God is total light. This figure, of course, cuts both ways: we can see to walk when we are near God, but the Light also glaringly exposes our flaws.

B. The walk of His followers, 6-7

6 If we say that we have fellowship with him, and walk in darkness, we lie, and do not the truth:

7 But if we walk in the light, as he is in the light, we have fellowship one with another, and the blood of Jesus Christ his Son cleanseth us from all sin.

John is impatient with hypocrisy. He draws such sharp contrasts between right and wrong that some have charged him with being legalistic—for no one's behavior is all right or all wrong. Actually, however, he does not speak out against human frailty but an overall pattern of behavior—false "walks" that betray a pretension to love the lighted pathway while consistently choosing to go down the unlit byways so one's evil deeds can't be seen.

Verse 7 assures us that John is no legalist, but relies on grace for salvation. The psalmist sang, "Thy word is a light unto my feet and a light to my path" (Ps. 119:105). Walking in the light does not mean being perfect, but being willing for all our deeds to be compared to, and exposed by, the Word of God. When this spirit characterizes our walk, the blood of Jesus—not our sinlessness—guarantees our "cleansing." (The original word also gives us the word "catharsis.")

What a reassuring truth! Christ's blood did not just flow *at* the Cross; it flows *from* the Cross in a continuously healing stream down through the ages, for those who walk in the light.

II. Sin and Salvation—8-10
A. The fact of sin, 8

8 If we say that we have no sin, we deceive ourselves, and the truth is not in us.

A man once said to a minister, "It's been, oh, eight or 10 years since I sinned." The early church faced just such perfectionist views in some quarters, especially from those later called "gnostics."Such views are hard to square with verse 8—and with the apostle Paul's own experience when he cried out in agony over his continual battle with sin (Rom. 7:15-24). Even if we are not conscious of doing something overtly wrong, we have left undone good things we could have done. Even if we have not done wrong deeds, we have thought wrong thoughts. John says the very claim of sinlessness even constitutes a sin—it's a lie, and we are self-deceived.

B. The way of salvation, 9-10

9 If we confess our sins, he is faithful and just to forgive us our sins, and to cleanse us from all unrighteousness.

10 If we say that we have not sinned, we make him a liar, and his word is not in us.

Although sin is everywhere-present, so is God's grace—for those who are willing to admit their sinfulness. The word translated "confess" means to "agree with." Confessing our shortcomings to God is therefore a way of agreeing with His judgment against a sinful way of life—and it implies our rejection of sin as a life-style. On the other hand, to maintain the fiction of sinlessness is to make Christ a liar. First, this is because He says the opposite in His Word, which cannot be "in" us if we deny its truth. Second, claiming to be sinless "puts the lie" to the need for the Cross. In short, claiming to be perfect is blasphemy.

III. Knowing and Doing—2:3-5
A. To know is to obey, 3
2:3 And hereby we do know that we know him, if we keep his commandments.

Again John addresses a typically "gnostic" notion—and an error commonly held in our own day. It stems from the Greek view of persons. The mind and soul were thought to be totally foreign and separate from the body. One could therefore "know" a truth, while living in a totally opposite direction. Out of his Jewish background, John knows that we are whole persons. At the creation of the body, "man became a *living soul*" (Gen. 2:7). Modern science confirms this interrelationship between mind and body when it speaks of "psychosomatic" diseases." It is out of this understanding of people as whole persons that John can affirm that the proof of *knowing* God is *doing* what He commands.

B. To love is to be "perfected,' 4-5

4 He that saith, I know him, and keepeth not his commandments, is a liar, and the truth is not in him.

5 But whoso keepeth his word, in him verily is the love of God perfected: hereby know we that we are in him.

Verse 4 simply states negatively what verse 3 affirmed positively—with the added bluntness of a warning that deliberately living in opposition to what we know as God's will makes us liars.

Obviously, in view of what John has said about no one being perfect, we should not read verse 5 as expecting us to be totally sinless. In fact, the verb is in the passive voice, referring not to something we do, but to something done for us. It is the love of God that is perfected, not people.

A second understanding is equally important. The King James word "perfect" often means "complete." As the niv reads, "God's love is truly made complete." That is, the true goal of God's love as shown in the sending of His Son is met when we are willing to have the light of His Word illuminate our path.

IV. Walking and Stumbling—6-11

A. The old path, 6-7

6 He that saith he abideth in him ought himself to walk, even as he walked.

7 Brethren, I write no new commandment unto you: but an old commandment which ye have heard from the beginning.

John writes in the style of the "Wisdom" literature of the Old Testament, especially the book of Proverbs. Just as a proverb states a truth in one way, then restates it slightly differently (parallelism), so John repeats in verse 6 what he has said about the need to do what we know is right.

Verse 7 assures us that this is consistent with what John's hearers already knew. This probably refers to what they had long known from the Old Testament: "Thou shalt love thy neighbor as thyself" (Lev. 19:18). As Paul had taught, "Love is the fulfilling of the law" (Rom. 13:10).

B. The new light, 8

8 Again, a new commandment I write unto you, which thing is true in him and in you: because the darkness is past, and the true light now shineth.

In another sense, however, John *is* giving a new commandment, for the Old Covenant was given before the supreme act of love, the death of God's Son on the Cross, finally ratified the principle of love for all time. Formerly, love had been a concept; in the sacrifice of Jesus, the *enfleshed* nature of love was made known in the darkness.

C. The true sign, 9-11

9 He that saith he is in the light, and hateth his brother, is in darkness even until now.

10 He that loveth his brother abideth in the light, and there is none occasion of stumbling in him.

11 But he that hateth his brother is in darkness, and walketh in darkness, and knoweth not whither he goeth, because that darkness hath blinded his eyes.

Finally John insists that love is not only shown by obeying God but by loving others. We must not be like the philosopher who loved mankind but hated people. That pathway is shrouded in darkness.

Evangelistic Emphasis

The evangelist Vance Havner drew a word picture about turning over a rock. He said, "When you kick over a stone that's been sitting for a while, all kinds of varmints will scurry to the cover of darkness." If you've ever kicked over a rock, sure enough the creatures under it all run toward darkness.

Our world never sleeps. If you live in a city or town no matter what time of night, you can look out a window and see light. Even in the country the darkness is so feared that "security lights" now dot the landscape. All the numbers indicate that burglars do not like light. Light brings safety and security. The elements of darkness in our world, do not like the light either.

The point that John made to the early church was that God, in Jesus Christ had brought light into the world. The light that Christ brought drove the darkness away. We are preparing again to celebrate the birth of the Messiah. As we do so, we light our homes, our offices and our trees with Christmas lights. These lights also drive away darkness. They do so in ways that bring joy to all who see them.

Whatever the darkness in your life, Jesus the light of the World, has come to drive that darkness away. We no longer have to fear the darkness, because the light of the world has come. Truly, that is the good news.

Memory Selection

If we walk in the light as he is in the light, we have fellowship with one another, and the blood of Jesus his Son cleanses us from all sin.—*1 John 1:7*

My body parts often have conversation with each other late at night. The stomach will cause the eyes to pop open. The eyes look at the clock and see that it is the wee hours of the morning. The stomach tells any body part that will listen, "Hey, if you want to go back to sleep, you'd better take me to the refrigerator for a glass of milk." My body parts lack dietary discipline, so they all agree on a nocturnal excursion to the refrigerator for a glass of milk. Everyone agrees to this trip, except for the toes. The toes always have a question. They want to know if the stomach and the eyes are planning to turn on any lights.

Being sneaky and not wanting to wake my wife, the stomach and eyes agree that no lights will be turned on to light our refrigerator-raiding trip. My toes usually don't like this. "Remember what we ran into last time," they warn. Because my eyes can't clearly see in the darkness, the toes usually get "stubbed." The noise I make as a result wakes the whole house. The pain from that experience affects all the body parts.

We are commanded to walk in the light as Jesus is in the light. It keeps all of those parts "in fellowship."

Weekday Problems

Do you see the fellow in the illustration in this section? He is sitting there with his hands folded behind his head. He is wondering something. He is wondering if God will forgive him for what he has just done. You can look at the picture and imagine for yourself what sin he might have committed. I wouldn't mention those sins to anyone in the class, because you are probably wondering if he has done the same thing you have. You might be wondering if he doesn'tlook like the person who has recently victimized you.

Whatever the sin he has committed, he's wondering if God will forgive him. I wonder. Will God forgive him?

This is more than a "weekday problem." That question and its ramifications are a daily problem. John wrote the early church, "If we confess our sins, he is faithful and just to forgive us our sins, and to cleanse us from all unrighteousness" (1 John 1:9). He would have other things to say about sin as well. This sentence stands out as good news. The good news is that God will forgive all of our sins. In searching the Scriptures, I have found only one sin that God will not forgive, and that is blasphemy against the Holy Spirit (Matthew 12:31).

If the fellow in the picture will confess his sins. God will be faithful and just and forgive those sins. The other thing you might be wondering about him, is whether he will forgive himself for his transgression.

* What sin do you think the fellow in the illustration has committed?

* If God has forgiven us, why is it hard to forgive ourselves?

Love Notes

Many a man in love with a dimple makes the mistake of marrying the whole girl.—*Stephen Leacock*

Tell me what you love, and I will tell you what you are. The man who loves right and righteousness will do right, law or no law, while the man who loves wrong will do wrong in spite of all law.—*Home Missions*

Money can buy a fine dog; but only love can make him wag his tail.

Hate cannot destroy hate, but love can and does. Not the soft and negative thing that has carried the name and misrepresented the emotion, but love that suffers all things and is kind, love that accepts responsibility, love that marches, love that suffers, love that bleeds and dies for a great cause—but to rise again.—*Daniel A. Poling*

This Lesson in Your Life

The Christmas lights have been up in the malls for some time. By now, most of you have untangled the strings of lights from last year. You looked patiently for the one nefarious bulb that was causing the whole string to be dark, and you replaced it. The lights now hang on your tree. Light is a part of the Christmas celebration and festivities. Perhaps all this Christmas lighting will remind us that light is necessary for the functioning of life.

Before God even created the world, He created light (Genesis 1:3). The Psalmist proclaimed, "The Lord is my light and my salvation, whom shall I fear?" (Psalm 27:1). Jesus claimed to be the light of the world. Light is a symbol for the divine in our world. Light is a symbol for all that is good and pure.

Light brings comfort to us. Do you remember your childhood or when your children were younger? Frightened children will often ask for a light to be turned on. The smallest light was enough to calm that child. Fear and darkness seem to travel in tandem just as powerfully as do light and security. There is nothing that gives us a feeling of security quite like going into a dark room and turning on a light.

As powerful as light is, we still struggle with darkness. Even at Christmas time there will be at least one story of someone stealing a child's Christmas joy. There will still be stories of death and tragedy even as we celebrate the majesty and mystery of the Incarnation.

Darkness will always be with us. The good news of Jesus Christ is that darkness cannot overcome light. Light a small birthday candle in the darkest room and soon you can see everything in the room. That is the power of light over darkness. John said, "And the light shineth in the darkness; and the darkness comprehended it not" (John 1:5). We might say that the "darkness has not overcome the light." The good news is that the bad news is not true! As Jesus brings his light into the world, He overcomes all of the evil. Each ray of light may only drive out a small piece of darkness. Still, piece by piece, Jesus is constantly chipping away at the darkness we face.

Just as light drives out darkness, forgiveness drives out sin. Sin is the personal darkness that hides in our soul. Sin drives a wedge into all of our meaningful relationships. It keeps us from experiencing God's perfect will in our lives.

John's advice to us is that confession is good for the soul. Confession brings our sins to "light." Once those sins are exposed to the light of God's law and love, they can be eradicated. John was echoing the Psalmist. The thirty-second Psalm illustrates the dangers of hiding sin, and the relief of confessing them. There is another side to the sin issue as John presented it. Those who claim they have no sin are deceiving themselves. They are walking in darkness. They are deceiving themselves.

Deception and darkness occur when a believer refuses to be obedient to the Light. Obedience means that we submit ourselves to God's light. He opens our souls and looks into the motivations behind our actions. Obedience requires that our words and our actions be congruent. "He that saith he is in the light, and hateth his brother, is in darkness even until now" (1 John 2:9). Too many children of God have darkened their witness by claiming one set of beliefs and living another.

The walk of a Christian is to be the walk of light. Light shines in our souls when we are honest about our sins. When we confess the darkness that sin has caused, God will forgive that sin and remove the darkness. Walking in the light is the walk of obedience. We are called to be obedient to God. We are called in Christian fellowship to be obedient to one another.

Seed Thoughts

1. What was the message that was proclaimed in the first two chapters of 1 John?

That "God is light and in Him there is no darkness at all."

2. There were three different claims that were not true. John pointed them out by the phrase, "If we say." What were they?

If we say we have fellowship and walk in darkness . . . we have no sin . . . and we have not sinned.

3. In the three "If we say" passages, what was indicated about the personality of those making the claims to fellowship, no sin, and not sinning?

These three groups of people were not keeping truth. They were lying and the word of God did not dwell in them.

4. If light and darkness were primary themes of 1 John 1-2, what is a secondary theme?

The issue of sin was dealt with in the first and second chapter. John is bold in his proclamation of God's forgiveness.

5. John shared a promise about those persons who are willing to confess their sins. What was that promise?

"If we confess our sins, he is faithful and just to forgive us our sins, and cleanse us from all unrighteousness" (1 John 1:9).

1. What was the message that was proclaimed in the first two chapters of 1 John?

2. There were three different claims that were not true. John pointed them out by the phrase, "If we say." What were they?

3. In the three "If we say" passages, what was indicated about the personality of those making the claims to fellowship, no sin, and not sinning?

4. If light and darkness were primary themes of 1 John 1-2, what might be a secondary theme?

5. John shared a promise about those persons who are willing to confess their sins. What was that promise?

6. It can be implied that persons in John's faith community were making a bold claim. What was that claim?

7. What is your church's position on sin that is committed by a Christian?

8. What made a person a liar according to 1 John 2:4?

9. How can one have the assurance that his relationship with Christ is on the right track?

10. According to 1 John . what was the definition of hypocrisy?

That "God is light and in Him there is no darkness at all."

If we say we have fellowship and walk in darkness . . . we have no sin . . . and we have not sinned.

These three groups of people were not keeping truth. They were lying and the word of God did not dwell in them.

The issue of sin was dealt with in the first and second chapter. John is bold in his proclamation of God's forgiveness.

"If we confess our sins, he is faithful and just to forgive us our sins, and cleanse us from all unrighteousness" (1 John 1:9).

Certain people were claiming they were living without any sin in their lives.

You will need to seek out your minister to ask about your church's position on sin after a person is baptized.

A person was a liar if he claims to have a personal knowledge of Jesus Christ, yet refuses to obey His commandments.

"And hereby we do know that we know Him, if we keep His commandments" (1 John 2:3).

John would define hypocrisy as claiming to love the Lord and at the same time hating one's brother.

6. It can be implied that persons in John's faith community were making a bold claim. What was that claim?

Certain people were claiming they were living without any sin in their lives.

7. What is your church's position on sin that is committed by a Christian?

You will need to seek out your minister to ask about your church's position on sin after a person is baptized.

8. What made a person a liar according to 1 John 2:4?

A person was a liar if he claims to have a personal knowledge of Jesus Christ, yet refuses to obey His commandments.

9. How can one have the assurance that his relationship with Christ is on the right track?

"And hereby we do know that we know Him, if we keep His commandments" (1 John 2:3).

10. According to 1 John . what was the definition of hypocrisy?

John would define hypocrisy as claiming to love the Lord and at the same time hating one's brother.

Living in God's Love

1 John 3:1-5, 9-18

1 Behold, what manner of love the Father hath bestowed upon us, that we should be called the sons of God: therefore the world knoweth us not, because it knew him not.

2 Beloved, now are we the sons of God, and it doth not yet appear what we shall be: but we know that, when he shall appear, we shall see him as he is.

3 And every man that hath this hope in him purifieth himself, even as he is pure.

4 Whosoever committeth sin transgresseth also the law: for sin is the transgression of the law.

5 And ye know that he was manifested to take away our sins; and in him is no sin.

9 Whosoever is born of God doth not commit sin; for his seed remaineth in him: and he cannot sin, because he is born of God.

10 In this the children of God are manifest, and the children of the devil: whosoever doeth not righteousness is not of God, neither he that loveth not his brother.

11 For this is the message that ye heard from the beginning, that we should love one another.

12 Not as Cain, who was of that wicked one, and slew his brother. And wherefore slew he him? Because his own works were evil, and his brother's righteous.

13 Marvel not, my brethren, if the world hate you.

14 We know that we have passed from death unto life, because we love the brethren. He that loveth not his brother abideth in death.

15 Whosoever hateth his brother is a murderer: and ye know that no murderer hath eternal life abiding in him.

16 Hereby perceive we the love of God, because he laid down his life for us: and we ought to lay down our lives for the brethren.

17 But whoso hath this world's good, and seeth his brother have need, and shutteth up his bowels of compassion from him, how dwelleth the love of God in him?

18 My little children, let us not love in word, neither in tongue; but in deed and in truth.

Memory Selection
1 John 3:11

Devotional Reading
Micah 4:1-7; 5:2-41

Background Scripture
1 John 3

Printed Scripture
1 John 3:1-5, 9-18

Teacher's Target

Lesson purpose: *To focus on the moral and ethical standards inherent in accepting the love of God and becoming His child.*

God loves us unconditionally. He did not wait for people to reform before sending His Son Jesus Christ. Instead, "God commended his love toward us, in that, while we were yet sinners, Christ died for us" (Rom. 5:8).

Yet those who respond to this great love, becoming children of God, are expected to reflect that status in the way they live. We do not continue to behave as though God were not our Father. Believers are citizens in His kingdom. We do not play the traitor in the courts of the Lord and actually serve His enemies.

Inherent in becoming a child of God is the calling to live in joyful obedience to the Father—which, as John teaches in this lesson, also entails loving others.

Lesson Introduction

Sometimes it surprises new Christians to discover that believers need to be urged to love each other. However, even a glance at the church at Corinth, for example, reminds us that dissent and discord are no strangers to the faith. Christians do not lose their humanity just by partaking of Christ's divinity.

John had special reasons for urging his readers to practice God's love. He will teach in 1 John 4:16 that "as he is, so are we in this world." This implies that the way believers behave is a reflection of the nature of the One they claim to serve. If Christians act hatefully to each other, unbelievers may well assume that God is hate, not love.

This lesson affirms the power of love as an antidote for sin, as inspiration for moral behavior, and as a testimony to unbelievers.

Teaching Outline	Daily Bible Readings

I. The Status of Sons—3:1-2
  A. Beloved strangers, 1
  B. Like Father, like sons, 2
II. The State of Purity—3-5
  A. Purity and hope, 3
  B. Sin and salvation, 4-5
III. The Seed of Holiness—9-10
  A. The impossible possibility, 9
  B. The basic difference, 10
IV. The Summons to Love—11-18
  A. Hatred's root, 11-15
  B. Love's reason, 16-18
	Mon. Living in God's Love
	  1 John 2:18-28
	Tue. We Are God's Children Now
	  1 John 2:29–3:8
	Wed. Give Our Lives for One Another
	  1 John 3:9-17
	Thu. Love in Truth and Action
	  1 John 3:18-24
	Fri. The Way of Peace
	  Micah 4:1-7; 5:2-5a
	Sat. Fruits Worthy of Repentance
	  Luke 3:17-18
	Sun. God's Peace Goes with Us
	  Philippians 4:4-9

VERSE BY VERSE

I. The Status of Sons—3:1-2

A. Beloved strangers, 1

1 Behold, what manner of love the Father hath bestowed upon us, that we should be called the sons of God: therefore the world knoweth us not, because it knew him not.

The word "behold," which John chooses from among several Greek words for "see," is a remarkable "flag" used to alert the reader to something about to be said that is especially noteworthy. It serves something like the upside-down exclamation point in Spanish before an exclamatory sentence. The sentence would have been taken something like "Hey—look how much God loves us!" Other translations reflect this emotional quality: "Consider the incredible love..." (Phillips); and "How great is the love...!" (NIV).

The "manner" or type of love that elicits such awe is *agape*—the selfless kind of love exhibited in the giving of God's Son, which in turns gives us the right to become God's children, too (the KJV "sons" is actually "children"). As has often been said, *agape* is to be distinguished from other Greek words for love such as *eros*, attraction (including sexual attraction); *philia*, friendship; and *storge*, family love. Each of these other loves has "something in it" for the lover. In contrast, God has nothing to gain from loving us into His family.

Twice in this section on God's love John notes how being a recipient and a reflector of God's love may cause unbelievers to respond negatively. Here we are warned that taking God's love seriously causes loving behavior that the world often rejects because it is deemed unnatural. (See also the comment at verse 13, below.)

B. Like Father, like sons, 2

2 Beloved, now are we the sons of God, and it doth not yet appear what we shall be: but we know that, when he shall appear, we shall see him as he is.

Again, "sons" in the original means "children"; but John means for us to understand the term as describing the royal state of a son in the court of his father the King. "We shall all be changed" at the second coming (1 Cor. 15:51), and we have no way of knowing what our "spiritual bodies" will be like. Yet, what we do know is that even now we bear the image of our Father! As we shall see, this implies not only royal status, but sobering responsibility.

II. The State of Purity—3-5

A. Purity and hope, 3

3 And every man that hath this hope in him purifieth himself, even as he is pure.

Since we hope to see the holy One at the Second Coming, we prepare for the great event by aiming at holiness ourselves. Paul was so concerned that Christians keep themselves pure for this event that he compared us to a bride who keeps herself "a chaste virgin" in preparation for her wedding (2 Cor. 11:2).

B. Sin and salvation, 4-5

4 Whosoever committeth sin

transgresseth also the law: for sin is the transgression of the law.

5 And ye know that he was manifested to take away our sins; and in him is no sin.

The opposite of purity (vs. 3) is sinfulness; and John bluntly reminds us of the folly of thinking we can dally with habitual sin while supposedly being "chaste" or pure. Yet, fortunately, the source of salvation is not our own sinlessness but the sinless Savior, Christ Jesus.

III. The Seed of Holiness—9-10

A. The impossible possibility, 9

9 Whosoever is born of God doth not commit sin; for his seed remaineth in him: and he cannot sin, because he is born of God.

This verse sometimes raises questions because it seems at first glance to say that it's impossible for the born-again person to sin. Obviously this would contradict what John said in our last lesson: "If we say that we have no sin, we deceive ourselves (1: 8). The questions are resolved when we note the "continuous" tense of the verb in the original. As the niv translates, "No one who is born of God will *continue* to sin."

B. The basic difference, 10

10 In this the children of God are manifest, and the children of the devil: whosoever doeth not righteousness is not of God, neither he that loveth not his brother.

Lest we mistake verse 9 to imply that in some mystical way believers are sinless even though they habitually sin without a penitent attitude, John lays it on the line: a person like that is not "of God." This is like saying that pretending to be "of Jones," or a member of the godly Jones family, is foolish if in fact

we habitually act like a member of the ungodly Mafia clan.

IV. The Summons to Love—11-18

A. Hatred's root, 11-15

11 For this is the message that ye heard from the beginning, that we should love one another.

12 Not as Cain, who was of that wicked one, and slew his brother. And wherefore slew he him? Because his own works were evil, and his brother's righteous.

13 Marvel not, my brethren, if the world hate you.

14 We know that we have passed from death unto life, because we love the brethren. He that loveth not his brother abideth in death.

15 Whosoever hateth his brother is a murderer: and ye know that no murderer hath eternal life abiding in him.

John probably uses the term "brother" here to refer to all people, who are brothers and sisters by virtue of having a common Creator, rather than only to brethren in Christ or fellow-Christians. Yet it is remarkable that love is so often absent in relationships within the family of God!

The illustration John uses to call attention to this sad state of affairs is the original murder, when Cain killed Abel. John's answer to the rhetorical question, Why did he do it?, illuminates a root of hatred by showing that jealousy is often involved. Cain offered a sacrifice from the field, not the flock, and God did not look on it with favor as He did Abel's (Gen. 4:3-5). We are not told exactly why, only that Cain's sacrifice was not "by faith" (Heb. 11: 4)—implying either that his heart was not in it or that God had commanded an offering from the flock, not the field (since "faith comes by hearing...the word of God," Rom. 10:17).

In verse 13, John again warns that the pure and loving life of the believer may alienate unbelievers. The world asks, What kind of person would love his enemies? and often recoils from such a lofty ethic.

Verses 14-15 "collapse" the heavenly future into the earthly present. Living the challenging life of love is tantamount to having eternal life (see John 3:16). Eternal life is the quality (not just the length) of life Christ has; and those who love have Christ within.

John, however, adds the blunt warning that the person who hates others also "collapses" the emotion of hatred into the judgment of murder! We say something like this when we comment that "She 'killed him off' by a hateful remark." This is a severe reminder of the moral importance of *thinking* in the Christian ethic. It is not simply an ethic of *doing*. (Of course this verse doesn't say that the *consequence* of hating is as drastic as murder, but only that hatred and murder have the same ungodly motivation.)

B. Love's reason, 16-18

16 Hereby perceive we the love of God, because he laid down his life for us: and we ought to lay down our lives for the brethren.

17 But whoso hath this world's good, and seeth his brother have need, and shutteth up his bowels of compassion from him, how dwelleth the love of God in him?

18 My little children, let us not love in word, neither in tongue; but in deed and in truth.

John concludes the section by revealing the motive both for not hating and for ministering to the needy: the love of Christ that we ourselves have experienced in His sacrifice on the Cross. "Humanism" also teaches the love of others; but when others prove unlovable, this motive proves shallow. Loving others because we know Christ died for them as He did for us is a more powerful motivation. It should impel us to love in deed, not just in theory or stated claim.

Evangelistic Emphasis

As Christmas nears you are discovering that all kinds of people love you. Perhaps you have received Christmas cards from your car dealer, your plumber, your doctor and your insurance agent. Each card had something to say about experiencing "the joy of this season." Strange isn't it, that all those people suddenly need to tell you about the joy of this holiday season. Your minister has told you several times from the pulpit during this Christmas season that you are loved. The whole point of Christmas was God coming into the world to make His love flesh and blood.

Do you feel loved? With all these expressions of loving care many persons simply don't feel loved. These same people look for that feeling in all sorts of self-diminishing ways.

You don't have to feel loved to understand that you are loved. With mushy words and maudlin sentiments, all sorts of strangers are telling you of their love especially at this "holiday time of the year." This season is the celebration of a historical act of love. The coming of Jesus means you are loved.

Jesus Christ is the incarnation of God's love. Jesus is a greater proof of God's love than mere words. His loving sacrifice on Calvary proved His love for us. Beyond the sentiment of this season, there stands a resurrected Lord. His nail scarred hands are reaching out to you, in love. The good news of Jesus is that you don't have to feel loved to know that you are loved. The cross of Christ is objective proof that the God of the universe loves you.

Memory Selection

For this is the message that ye heard from the beginning, that we should love one another.—*1 John 3:11*

Back in the "good old days" before fathers went into the delivery room, one of their first questions about their child was, "What does he look like?" We have another saying, "The nut doesn't fall far from the tree."

Loving another person is a hard task. Loving strangers is a daunting task. Loving all those persons that Jesus commanded us to love is nearly impossible. Yet, we are commanded in the Bible to love, even our enemies, with a Christ-like love. When we do so, we are reflecting not what is in our hearts, so much as Who is in our hearts. When we love one another we are living as sons and daughters of God.

Loving the unlovely can only be done with Christ in our hearts. When He abides in us and we show His presence through our love for each other, we reflect Him to our world. "What do Christians look like?" If we are reflecting God's love we begin to look like Jesus. Because as we love each other people begin to see the Jesus in us.

Weekday Problems

Earl and Irene Myer had been members of First Church for as long as anyone could remember. Earl was the church historian and a pillar of the church and community. Irene had the gift of being the perfect wife. She had become the matriarch of First Church. They were a loving, kind couple.

Earl reached his eightieth birthday and it seemed like he fell apart all at once. His hearing was the first thing to go. He became stooped and bent. The most frustrating thing for the members of First Church was that his disposition, once cheery, was now sullen and sour. Irene continued to be a good wife. She also became astute at covering for Earl.

One Sunday the ushers at First Church made an egregious error. They allowed the Young family, newcomers in the community, to sit in Earl's seat. When Earl saw it he was more than upset. Irene attempted to calm him by trying to seat him in the pew directly behind the Young family.

Earl sat there, wiggling for most of the service. At the time when there was silence in the church service, Earl said, "I want to go home, I can't enjoy church with someone in my pew." Not only did the Almighty hear Earl, the Young family heard him too.

From the pulpit the pastor could see it all unfolding. Mr. and Mrs. Young were obviously embarrassed. Their children were wondering what was happening. Irene turned and gave a apologetic look back at the preacher as they left in mid-service.

* If you were the pastor of First Church, how would you deal with this new family?

* John admonished the early Christians to love one another, did Mr. Myer show love? Do you think he is guilty of anything?

Reflections

The real problem is in the hearts and minds of men. It is not a problem of physics but of ethics. It is easier to denature plutonium than to denature the evil spirit of man.—*Albert Einstein*

"Resist not evil" means "Do not resist the evil man," which is to say: "Never offer violence to another," which is to say, "Never commit an act that is contrary to love."— *Leo Tolstoy*

Purity of soul cannot be lost without consent."—*Augustine*

> Still to the lowly soul
> He doth himself impart,
> And for His cradle and His throne
> Chooseth the pure in heart.
> —John Keble

This Lesson in Your Life

The origin of the family names of class members would make a good discussion. Some may want to share stories about heroes and villains nesting in their family tree.

This could lead to a discussion of 1 John 3:1. We are told "that we should be called the sons of God." This is a family relationship with which some might not be familiar. As Christians we are the children of God.

This means that God is our Father—one of the more easily understood descriptions of God. Yet I wonder how many members of your class are living with God as their father? As the children of God we have "rights before the throne." Most children learn early that their parents can be trusted to protect them. When a child is frightened and calls out for a parent, that parent comes running. Jesus said, "If you then, who are evil, know how to give good gifts to your children, how much more will your Father in heaven give good things to those who ask him!" (Matt. 7:17). When we are frightened, our Heavenly Father "comes running." When we call out to Him in prayer.

Parents not only love children, they guide and protect children. How much more is God able to answer our needs. As children of God we have access to the Father. We can know His will as we face the forks in life's road

We are part of a larger family as children of God. Ministers love to participate in family reunions. We love listening to the family stories as much as we love eating the ever-present food. Many churches have the blessing of having large powerful families within their membership. These families can do wondrous things for the church and the kingdom of God. We are all part of a larger spiritual family with God as the Father. We are all brothers and sisters together with Christ in ministry to our world.

My little brother was lucky because he had me around. Older brothers tend to keep their younger brothers out of trouble. More than once I have "covered for" my little brother. We, as brothers and sisters in Christ, have a big family watching out for us. Discuss with the class the benefits of this watchfulness. Are there any disadvantages?

My mother used to have a saying before I would go out on a date. She would say, "Remember who you are." I knew what that meant. She wanted me to remember that my actions reflected directly on the way I was raised. John wrote to the early church that their actions reflected on their Father and the other members of their Christian family. Sin was something that tarnished the reputation of everyone connected with the church. John was adamant that sin and the Christian faith were diametrically opposed to one other.

As children of God we are called to live in the light, not walk in darkness. When sin enters our lives, we are in small ways diminishing the light of God's love in our lives. The sins John referred to in the third chapter were lifestyle choices. He was not talking about errors or mistakes. John was addressing persons who had made a knowing decision to live in sin.

Living in sin takes many forms in our society. The calamity for the church is that we have accepted so many of these things as "lifestyle decisions." A careful discussion of these "lifestyle decisions" could very well consume the rest of the class time.

The lesson for us is simple. If God is our father we will act like His children. He demands certain behaviors from us. He is not capricious. He does not wish to deny us anything we need. God simply understands the natural consequences of our sins. He, as a loving Father, doesn't wish to see us hurt.

That is why, at Christmas, we celebrate God coming as one of us to show us how to live in the light.

Seed Thoughts

1. What was the immediate benefit of the great love that God had given to the Christians?

The benefit of God's love was that the Christians were called the sons of God.

2. Why didn't the world know or acknowledge the Christians as the sons of God?

The world did not acknowledge the Christians because the world did not acknowledge Christ.

3. What was the future promise attached to the claim of being the sons of God?

The benefits of being the sons of God will not be completely known until Christ appears. Then the sons of God will be like Him.

4. What was the responsibility of the person who had this hope of being like Christ?

These persons would purify themselves even as Christ Himself is pure.

5. According to John, why did Christ appear?

He came to take away our sin. That was possible because Jesus was without sin (see vs. 5.)

1. What was the immediate benefit of the great love that God had given to the Christians?

2. Why didn't the world know or acknowledge the Christians as the sons of God?

3. What was the future promise attached to the claim of being the sons of God?

4. What was the responsibility of the person who had this hope of being like Christ?

5. According to John, why did Christ appear?

6. What did John say about the nature of sin?

7. What startling statement and promise was made to the Christian concerning sin?

8. What was the message that the Christians had heard "from the beginning?"

9. Which characters from the book of Genesis were used as an example of what happens when we don't love each other?

10. If we are sons of God, how should we be showing our love to the world?

(Please turn page)

The benefit of God's love was that the Christians were called the sons of God.

The world did not acknowledge the Christians because the world did not acknowledge Christ.

The benefits of being the sons of God will not be completely known until Christ appears. Then they will be like Him.

These persons would purify themselves even as Christ Himself is pure.

He came to take away our sin. That was possible because Jesus was without sin. (See vs. 5.)

Persons who commit sin had transgressed the law of God. Sin, according to John, was lawlessness.

Those persons born of God "do not commit sin" and "cannot sin" because the seed of God is in them (vs. 9).

The message heard from the beginning was "that we should love one another."

John made reference to the story of Cain and Abel. He warned against allowing evil a foothold.

"My little children, let us not love in word, neither in tongue, but in deed and truth" (1 John 3: 18).

6. What did John say about the nature of sin?

Persons who commit sin had transgressed the law of God. Sin, according to John, was lawlessness.

7. What startling statement and promise was made to the Christian concerning sin?

Those persons born of God "do not commit sin" and "cannot sin" because the seed of God is in them (vs. 9).

8. What was the message that the Christians had heard "from the beginning?"

The message heard from the beginning was "that we should love one another."

9. Which characters from the book of Genesis were used as an example of what happens when we don't love each other?

John made reference to the story of Cain and Abel. He warned against allowing evil a foothold.

10. If we are sons of God, how should we be showing our love to the world?

"My little children, let us not love in word, neither in tongue, but in deed and truth" (1 John 3: 18).

Lesson 3

Celebrating God's Love

December 21

Matthew 1:20-21; 1 John 4:7-17

20 But while he thought on these things, behold, the angel of the Lord appeared unto him in a dream, saying, Joseph, thou son of David, fear not to take unto thee Mary thy wife: for that which is conceived in her is of the Holy Ghost.

21 And she shall bring forth a son, and thou shalt call his name JESUS: for he shall save his people from their sins.

7 Beloved, let us love one another: for love is of God; and every one that loveth is born of God, and knoweth God.

8 He that loveth not knoweth not God; for God is love.

9 In this was manifested the love of God toward us, because that God sent his only begotten Son into the world, that we might live through him.

10 Herein is love, not that we loved God, but that he loved us, and sent his Son to be the propitiation for our sins.

11 Beloved, if God so loved us, we ought also to love one another.

12 No man hath seen God at any time. If we love one another, God dwelleth in us, and his love is perfected in us.

13 Hereby know we that we dwell in him, and he in us, because he hath given us of his Spirit.

14 And we have seen and do testify that the Father sent the Son to be the Saviour of the world.

15 Whosoever shall confess that Jesus is the Son of God, God dwelleth in him, and he in God.

16 And we have known and believed the love that God hath to us. God is love; and he that dwelleth in love dwelleth in God, and God in him.

17 Herein is our love made perfect, that we may have boldness in the day of judgment: because as he is, so are we in this world.

Memory Selection
1 John 4:9

Devotional Reading
Isaiah 9:2-7

Background Scripture
Matthew 1:18-25; 1 John 4

Printed Scripture
Matthew 1:20-21; 1 John 4:7-17

151

Teacher's Target

Lesson purpose: *To celebrate the love of God as revealed in the sending of His Son Jesus, and to renew our commitment to reflect that love in our interaction with Him and with each other.*

This lesson focuses first on the timeless story of the birth of Jesus, then moves to the apostle John's commentary on how that event should impact our own lives. Ask class members to share stories of some of the most joyous Christmas gifts they've experienced. What made them meaningful? Were they costly or common? Most important, what did the gift say about the giver, and his or her relationship with the gifted?

Then shift the focus to gifts class members have given to children. Were they always appreciated? Point out that while giving gifts should not be for the purpose of "purchasing" love, the giver is gratified by gratitude. Ideally, Christians accept the loving gift of God's Son with thanksgiving that runs so deep that their own lives become characterized by loving and giving, too.

Lesson Introduction

Despite the many ways God is described in Scripture, "God is love" remains the most basic. Despite the many times the story of Christ's birth has been told, it remains the ultimate expression of what God's love means. God is by nature "love," and love by nature involves giving. It is therefore impossible to imagine God as the only Being in the universe. If He is by nature love, He must love someone or something; and if He loves something, He must *give* as an expression of that love.

This is why the most fundamental truth in all of Scripture is that "God so loved the world that he gave his only begotten Son." Furthermore, as the apostle Paul said, this love has been "shed abroad in our hearts."

Matthew 1:20-21 records the origin of the process of "cosmic loving." The passage from 1 John then describes the "ripple effect" that occurs when Christians have been so grasped by the gift of God's Son that they in turn become givers themselves.

Teaching Outline	Daily Bible Readings
	Mon. Christ Has Come in the Flesh *John 1:14-18*
I. Annunciation—Matt. 1:20-21	**Tue.** Emmanuel: God Is with Us! *Matthew 1:18-25*
A. The word to Joseph, 20	
B. The word to the world, 21	**Wed.** God's Love for Us *1 John 4:7-16a*
II. Realization—1 John 4:7-10	
A. The result of love, 7-8	**Thu.** Our Love for Others *1 John 4:16b-21*
B. The order of love, 9-10	
III. Manifestation—1 John 4:11-17	**Fri.** Living in Love *Psalm 133:1–134:3*
A. The evidence of love, 11-15	**Sat.** Clothing Ourselves with Love *Colossians 3:12-17*
B. The testimony of love, 16-17	**Sun.** Light and Love Are Coming! *Isaiah 9:2-7*

VERSE BY VERSE

I. Annunciation—Matt. 1:20-21
A. The word to Joseph, 20

20 But while he thought on these things, behold, the angel of the Lord appeared unto him in a dream, saying, Joseph, thou son of David, fear not to take unto thee Mary thy wife: for that which is conceived in her is of the Holy Ghost.

Joseph, the human father of Jesus, is first mentioned in verse 16 at the end of the "genealogy" or family tree of Christ (vss. 2-17). Matthew says Joseph was the son of Jacob, while Christ's genealogy as given by Luke says Joseph's father was Heli (Luke 3:23). The many other differences between these two lists lead many scholars to say that Matthew's account gives Joseph's family tree, while Luke's is of Mary's lineage. Perhaps Heli was actually Joseph's father-in-law, and is said here to be his father in accordance with the Jewish custom of emphasizing the male as head of the household.

A more important point is the fact that both Matthew and Luke show that Joseph and Mary were of the tribe of Judah and descendants of King David (Matt. 1:6, 20; Luke 3:31). Thus Jesus' fulfills through both his mother and father the Old Testament prophecies that Messiah would be of the tribe of Judah (see Gen. 49:10).

Verse 18 indicates that Mary was found to be pregnant during the engagement period of Jewish marriages. Engaged couples were expected not to have sexual relations during this period, so being found with child was equivalent to having been unfaithful—and therefore grounds for a kind of premarital "divorce" (a "putting away," vs. 19). The angel, however, reassures Joseph that Mary's womb has been mysteriously filled by the Holy Spirit—the basis for the doctrine of the virgin birth.

If modern people have difficulty accepting this truth, think of how poor Joseph must have struggled with it! It must have required colossal humility, trust in his betrothed virgin, Mary, and faith in God for Joseph to enter into this monumental plan to bring the Son of God into the world.

The significance of the virgin birth is not simply that it was a biological miracle, but that God chose it as the means of "incarnating" (enfleshing) Himself. Jesus becomes both the "son of man" (through Mary) and the son of God (through the Holy Spirit). The basis of our trust in Jesus as Savior is that He partakes both of human nature, knowing our weakness, and the divine nature, knowing our destiny.

B. The word to the world, 21

21 And she shall bring forth a son, and thou shalt call his name JESUS: for he shall save his people from their sins.

With understated drama, the angel quietly announces the event to which the entire Old Testament points. Salvation—the reconciliation of persons to God, which persons cannot accomplish of themselves—has come in the form of a divine Child! His very name—*Iesous* in Greek, *Yeshua* (Joshua) in Hebrew—means "salvation." While the reference to "his people" may refer in the first instance to His fellow-Jews, it is a promise that will be expanded to "all people" (Luke 2:10).

II. Realization—1 John 4:7-10

A. The result of love, 7-8

7 Beloved, let us love one another: for love is of God; and every one that loveth is born of God, and knoweth God.

8 He that loveth not knoweth not God; for God is love.

Now the "second movement" in the great symphony of the Christian faith begins. The love shown in the giving of God's Son takes root in the hearts of those who respond to God's unfathomable grace. The realization of how love has been extended to them becomes the seed of the new birth. This new life is not available to those who merely give intellectual assent to the fact that "God so loved"; unless accepting God's love in turn results in *loving*, we are not "of" Him—we are not His children.

B. The order of love, 9-10

9 In this was manifested the love of God toward us, because that God sent his only begotten Son into the world, that we might live through him.

10 Herein is love, not that we loved God, but that he loved us, and sent his Son to be the propitiation for our sins.

Now John counters a universal urge to make ourselves right with God. He insists on a sequence of love that forever prevents our presuming to live such a self-sacrificing life that we prove by our love that we are worthy of salvation. Saving love does not begin with persons, but with God. As John put it in his Gospel, "You have not chosen me, but I have chosen you" (John 15:16).

The meaning of the word "propitiation" (Greek *hilasmos*) is expressed by two words in the niv, which affirms that Christ is our "atoning sacrifice." This language is often taken to imply that God is an angry and blood-thirsty tyrant whose wrath had to be appeased by the blood of Christ. That this cannot be the meaning, however, is apparent from the doctrine of the Incarnation in the first part of this lesson. God gave *Himself* for our sins, in the form of His Son. It is better to understand the atonement on the basis of the Old Testament "scapegoat," rather than using the imagery of a medieval king who requires blood-vengeance. Jesus bears our sins into the wilderness—into nothingness—leaving us cleansed and whole (see Lev. 16).

III. Manifestation—1 John 4:11-17

A. The evidence of love, 11-15

11 Beloved, if God so loved us, we ought also to love one another.

12 No man hath seen God at any time. If we love one another, God dwelleth in us, and his love is perfected in us.

13 Hereby know we that we dwell in him, and he in us, because he hath given us of his Spirit.

14 And we have seen and do testify that the Father sent the Son to be the Saviour of the world.

15 Whosoever shall confess that Jesus is the Son of God, God dwelleth in him, and he in God.

Proclaiming the *evangel* or Good News is only one way to affirm that "God so loved that He gave." Another way is give as He did—to evangelize by gladly serving others in His name. John would encourage us to bypass the endless philosophical task of "seeing" or fathoming the nature of God by mere thought. In typical Jewish fashion he "cuts to the chase" and suggests that loving service, not philosophy, is the road to knowing God and dwelling with Him. "Perfected" means "fulfilled" or "made complete." God's love in the giving of His Son began an eternal trajectory that flies off into space unless we in turn love others, bringing it full circle.

In verses 13-14 John defends himself against questions some might ask about his authority to speak like this. "We" probably refers to himself and the other apostles, whose testimony both about God's love through Christ and the necessity of "passing it on" are guaranteed by the Holy Spirit. This guarantee was often displayed explicitly through miracles that resulted from the Spirit's power (see Mark 16:20).

While verse 12 affirmed that *loving* ensures that God dwells within the believer, verse 15 states that *confessing the truth of the Incarnation* is another kind of guarantee. The Bible view of persons implies that both saying and doing are important.

B. The testimony of love, 16-17

16 And we have known and believed the love that God hath to us. God is love; and he that dwelleth in love dwelleth in God, and God in him.

17 Herein is our love made perfect, that we may have boldness in the day of judgment: because as he is, so are we in this world.

Now John summarizes his teaching by affirming that loving God and others is important in two profound ways. First, it will be a means of boldness at judgment (vs. 17a). Of course we will have no grounds for boasting on the day of judgment; if we have loved it will only be because we were responding to God's love (vs. 10).

Second, loving others testifies to the nature of God (17b). To say that "as he is, so are we" reminds us that "like father, like sons." Children of God have His spiritual genes; we partake of His nature. When we fail to show love for each other, we portray Him as an unloving Father. When we love each other, we testify that the One whose nature we bear is a God of love.

Evangelistic Emphasis

Christmas is almost here again. I wish we could capture the warmth and the love that seems to be compressed into the season between Thanksgiving and New Year's. People actually are courteous to one another, even maneuvering for the last parking place in front of the mall. Stories of love and kindness seem to find their way into the news. Smiling strangers and gracious store clerks herald the arrival of the Christmas season.

The irony is that all this goodness will disappear on January second. God did not intend it to be so. We are called to love one another all the time. Our mandate is to show the love of God each and every moment of life. The good news is that this is possible.

John writes that "God is love." God is love and those who dwell in Him have that love dwelling in them. If Jesus is in your heart, the love you have to share is boundless. The love that you have to give is rooted in eternity. Each day as you open your life to God's love, you can experience the excitement, enthusiasm and joy that you are feeling in this holiday season.

The greater news is that as we show love to others, God's love is perfected in us. With each loving act we will experience in a deeper way God's love for us. As we love others, we are loved by God. It is a wonderful eternal circle of love. The more love we give others, the more we experience God's love for us.

Memory Selection

God's love was revealed among us in this way; God sent his only Son into the world so that we might live through him.—*1 John 4:9*

Are you a package shaker? If you are, those gifts under the tree are providing you with hours of entertainment. I love my package shakers. I like putting marbles and other noisy items in boxes to frustrate my package-shaking wife and children. It is fun on Christmas morning to see how wrong they were when they thought they'd figured out the noisy contents of their gifts.

God didn't want us guessing about His love. He wanted us to be certain that we were being loved from the foundations of time. God removed all doubt about His love in sending Jesus. Our Lord spent His ministry showing us what God's love is all about. Jesus taught that God is accessible, forgiving, loving and powerful to keep His own. Dying for us on the cross, He showed that God's love will go to any lengths to save.

God's gift came wrapped in swaddling clothes and was worshiped by the shepherds in a humble manger. Is there any doubt now about the contents of God's gift to all of us?

Weekday Problems

The holiday season is particularly difficult on persons who have experienced loss in their lives. Those who have recently endured the death of a spouse or parent, divorced persons and persons who have recently moved or changed jobs are vulnerable to the "holiday blues." Christmas is especially hard for persons who are away from their families. The message  of Christmas is an unabashed message of love. This is the time of year when even the meanest Scrooge suddenly becomes generous.

Trying to minister to people who are dealing with loss can be challenging at this time of year. Those going through loss, often don't feel that "God is love." When they are honest, many will admit they feel just the opposite about God. Their loss is compounded by the awful sense that God could have prevented the pain. Holidays remind them that their lives have changed drastically.

It is more than a holiday phenomena or a week day problem when people feel that God has disappointed them. Sometimes we can't relate to their feelings of betrayal and bitterness, especially those directed to God.

* In what ways do the holidays remind persons of their losses?

* In what ways might you share the message that "God is love" with a person struggling with a personal loss.

* Have you ever wondered why, if "God is love," bad things seem to happen to His people?

Holiday Highlights

Christmas began in the heart of God. It is complete only when it issues from the heart of people.

I love Christmas. I receive a lot of wonderful presents I can't wait to exchange.

There's nothing like the Christmas season to put a little bounce in your checks.

Tom: Guess what! I have a part in the Christmas play!
Mom: Wonderful! Who do you play?
Tom: I'm one of the three wise guys!

Kay: Guess what! At Christmas I was visited by a jolly, bearded fellow with a big bag over his shoulder.
May: I know—*my* son came home from college, too.

This Lesson in Your Life

We are most familiar with the Christmas saga. We know well the story of a simple carpenter named Joseph and his betrothed Mary, the angels' announcement, the journey to Bethlehem, the visit of the shepherds and magi and the flight into Egypt. What we might miss amidst all the Biblical activity is the purpose behind all of this. Why would God go to such extraordinary lengths to provide humanity with a Savior? The answer is found in the second affirmation of the lesson, "God is love." In the late 1960s the hippies read a part of Scripture and began to remind the church of this truth. These flower children preached love and peace to all who would listen. Yet the God they pictured as love was much less than the Bible proclaims Him.

Some Christians are uncomfortable with the idea that God is love. They want Him to be sovereign. A God who rules heaven and earth with unbridled justice makes them more comfortable than a God who is love. Some who like the image of God as love have also weakened many of the moral demands of the gospel.

We live in a world in which moral norms hardly exist. Persons no longer have to be responsible for their actions, they simply have to profess some sort of syndrome. To hold people accountable for their actions, is to be closed-minded and narrow. To demand excellence is to violate a person's individual right of expression and self-mastery. Those who don't want to excel who need excuses, are glad to hear that "God is love." They feel He might overlook their ineptitude.

"God is love," however, *is* an affirmation that God is sovereign. It is an affirmation that God is in control. It is our assurance that God will hold everyone accountable for actions and deeds. The love that God reveals is not some ethereal "I'm okay, you're okay" warm fuzzy feeling. The love of God is bold in its activity and universal in its quest. One preacher has said that God's love is unscrupulous in naming and claiming its own. God had to come to earth in the person of Jesus the Messiah. It was totally in character with His great love for us.

In the person of Jesus, God showed what His love was about. It was a love that called persons from a life of sin to a life of righteousness. In living a sinless life, Jesus modeled what joy is found in righteous living. One is struck by the fact that most of the gospel stories take place with Jesus at some kind of party or dinner. Even when He was "on the road," impromptu parties were thrown with only loaves and fishes. Somehow the church has skewed the message of righteousness to mean that we all should look like we have been dipped in alum and sprinkled with persimmon. We have not been faithful in proclaiming righteous living yields a joyous life. Jesus called sinners to repent, but he did it by showing what fun could be found in righteous living. His harshest words were saved for those who would make a burden out of faith.

Jesus showed that God's love meant forgiveness. His story about the Waiting Father in Luke 15 revealed His understanding of grace. Love allows for mistakes, and freely forgives when mistakes are confessed. Simon Peter is an example of a life changed by forgiveness. This disciple fled before the crucifixion and was the same one boldly preaching on Pentecost. Forgiveness is a powerful component of God's love.

"God is love" is not a simple theological proposition. It is a way of life. When we love like God loved us, we hold others accountable. We allow for second chances. We receive acts of love as well as give love to others.

Seed Thoughts

1. What was the relationship between Mary and Joseph when the angel appeared to Joseph?

Mary and Joseph were engaged but had not yet married. Because Mary was "with child," Joseph was planning to divorce her.

2. What was the three-part message the angel gave to Joseph?

He was told not to be afraid to marry Mary. The child was conceived by the Holy Spirit. The child was to be named Jesus.

3. What was the translation of the name given to this promised Messiah?

His name was to be called Jesus, because "He would save His people from their sin."

4. If a person is faithful to the admonition to love others, what does that communicate about his relationship with God?

That person is born of God and knows God.

5. What is said about a person who is not able to love others?

That person does not know God, because God is love.

---

1. What was the relationship between Mary and Joseph when the angel appeared to Joseph?

2. What was the three part message the angel gave to Joseph?

3. What was the translation of the name given to this promised Messiah?

4. If a person is faithful to the admonition to love others, what does that communicate about his relationship with God?

5. What is said about a person who is not able to love others?

6. According to John, how was God's love revealed to humanity?

7. What is the proof that God is abiding in us and we are abiding in Him?

8. What is the motivation for persons to live out the challenge to "love one another?"

9. What must happen before Jesus will abide with a person?

10. What does this passage from 1 John say about those who abide in love?

(Please turn page)

Mary and Joseph were engaged but not yet married. Since Mary was with child, Joseph was planning to divorce her.

He was told not to be afraid to marry Mary. The child was conceived by the Holy Spirit, and was to be named Jesus.

His name was to be called Jesus, because "He would save His people from their sin."

That person is born of God and knows God.

That person does not know God. Because God is love.

"God sent his only begotten Son into the world that we might live through Him" (1 John 4:9).

The proof of God's abiding presence is the Spirit which dwells with us.

"If God so loved us, we ought also to love one another" (1 John 4: 11).

People must confess that Jesus is the Son of God. Then they abide in Him.

"He that dwelleth in love dwelleth in God, and God in him" (I John 4:16).

6. According to John, how was God's love revealed to humanity?

"God sent his only begotten Son into the world that we might live through Him" (1 John 4:9).

7. What is the proof that God is abiding in us and we are abiding in Him?

The proof of God's abiding presence is the Spirit which dwells with us.

8. What is the motivation for persons to live out the challenge to "love one another?"

"If God so loved us, we ought also to love one another" (1 John 4: 11).

9. What must happen before Jesus will abide with a person?

People must confess that Jesus is the Son of God. Then they abide in Him.

10. What does this passage from 1 John say about those who abide in love?

"He that dwelleth in love dwelleth in God, and God in him" (I John 4:16).

Conquering Through Faith in Christ

1 John 5:1-12

1 Whosoever believeth that Jesus is the Christ is born of God: and every one that loveth him that begat loveth him also that is begotten of him.

2 By this we know that we love the children of God, when we love God, and keep his commandments.

3 For this is the love of God, that we keep his commandments: and his commandments are not grievous.

4 For whatsoever is born of God overcometh the world: and this is the victory that overcometh the world, even our faith.

5 Who is he that overcometh the world, but he that believeth that Jesus is the Son of God?

6 This is he that came by water and blood, even Jesus Christ; not by water only, but by water and blood. And it is the Spirit that beareth witness, because the Spirit is truth.

7 For there are three that bear record in heaven, the Father, the Word, and the Holy Ghost: and these three are one.

8 And there are three that bear witness in earth, the spirit, and the water, and the blood: and these three agree in one.

9 If we receive the witness of men, the witness of God is greater: for this is the witness of God which he hath testified of his Son.

10 He that believeth on the Son of God hath the witness in himself: he that believeth not God hath made him a liar; because he believeth not the record that God gave of his Son.

11 And this is the record, that God hath given to us eternal life, and this life is in his Son.

12 He that hath the Son hath life; and he that hath not the Son of God hath not life.

Memory Selection
1 John 5:4-5

Devotional Reading
Romans 8:31-39

Background Scripture
1 John 5:1-12

Printed Scripture
1 John 5:1-12

Teacher's Target

Lesson purpose: *To understand John's portrayal of obedient faith as the key to victory in this life, and the means of accessing Christ's gift of eternal life.*

We have noted that John's writings are "simply profound." This lesson illustrates the point. On the one hand, it is with supreme simplicity that John says that the new birth, and eternal life, are accessed through *belief.* On the other hand, since John links loving God with "keeping the commandments," we suspect that the kind of faith he has in mind isn't so simple after all—for we know our inability to keep all the commandments perfectly.

The class can be introduced by asking members to do a "free association" exercise with the word "belief." What synonyms can they think of? What Bible definitions of faith can they recall? (see Heb. 11:1). What examples—from the Bible or from life—illuminate and illustrate genuine faith?

Invite the group to a deeper understanding of "belief" as we sit at the feet of this aged apostle.

Lesson Introduction

This section of John's letter calls us to balance two facts of biblical teaching that have caused deep historical divisions among Christians. On the one hand, remaining faithful is possible because of what God does for us, in the new birth. On the other, we are to exert our own efforts, endeavoring to keep His commandments.

This dual emphasis knifes through mountains of later debate in important Church councils. John seems to anticipate the division between John Calvin, who emphasized God's sovereign work in calling and keeping the faithful; and Arminius, who emphasized the "whosoever *will*" teaching of Scripture.

John refuses to take sides. Just as Jesus is both "very God and very man," John seems to say that we are both saved by grace, and able to respond out of our own will.

Teaching Outline	Daily Bible Readings

I. The Power of Faith—1-2
  A. Being born again, 1
  B. The proof of birth, 2
II. The Promise of Obedience—3-5
  A. To love is to obey, 3
  B. To believe is to overcome, 4-5
III. The Proof of the Witnesses—6-12
  A. The reality of the Christ event, 6-8
  B. The assurance of God, 9-12
	Mon. Living Victoriously
	    1 John 5:1-12
	Tue. Love Poured into Our Hearts
	    Romans 5:1-11
	Wed. Peace Among Those God Favors
	    Luke 2:1-15
	Thu. Shepherd for the People of God
	    Matthew 2:1-12
	Fri. God Has Spoken by the Son
	    Hebrews 1:1-6
	Sat. See the Salvation of Our God
	    Isaiah 52:7-10
	Sun. Victory Through Jesus Christ
	    1 Corinthians 15:50-58

VERSE BY VERSE

I. The Power of Faith—1-2
A. Being born again, 1
1 Whosoever believeth that Jesus is the Christ is born of God: and every one that loveth him that begat loveth him also that is begotten of him.

What power is packed into this one brief verse! Modern discussions sometimes draw a distinction between "belief" and "faith," to distinguish between *belief* as mere "mental assent" and *faith* as trust, or "saving faith." Actually, the same Greek word is translated both "faith" and "belief." Yet, there is a difference between effective and ineffective faith (or belief). As essential as belief is here in our text, we recall that James warned that "the devils also believe, and tremble" (Jas. 2:19). Devils, however, lack the *personal trust that leads to obedience*—which is how John will define saving faith.

The primary point here is that genuine faith makes it possible for mere humans to have within them the "seed" of divinity. This is the significance of being "born of God." In verses 11-12 John refers to this quality of life as "eternal life"; and in his Gospel, he calls it being "born again" (John 3:3-5). Here in the latter part of verse 1, John quickly adds that the person who is really born by Him who "begat," or originated the new birth, loves everyone else who has also been born again. He is questioning whether those who cannot bring themselves to love their spiritual brothers and sisters really have the divine life within them—a point made even more sharply in the next verse.

B. The proof of birth, 2
2 By this we know that we love the children of God, when we love God, and keep his commandments.

In writing that is similar to that in the book of Proverbs, John restates what he said in verse 1b, in slightly different terms, and with a different twist. Just as loving others is proof that we love God, so loving God entails loving others. In turn, loving God entails keeping His commandments. But which commandments? Is John saying that keeping the 613 laws the Jews had catalogued under the Old Covenant is the only way to prove our love for God? No, he is probably referring to the one law that sums up God's will: the law that we love each other (see 2:7-11, as explained in Lesson 1 of this Quarter).

II. The Promise of Obedience—3-5
A. To love is to obey, 3
3 For this is the love of God, that we keep his commandments: and his commandments are not grievous.

Certainly it would be a "grievous" burden to think that we could earn God's favor only by keeping the Law in all its bewildering detail. Instead, we keep the law of love, as verses 1b-2 implied; and when we love God and others, all the other commandments fall into place.

B. To believe is to overcome, 4-5
4 For whatsoever is born of God overcometh the world: and this is the victory that overcometh the world, even our faith.

5 Who is he that overcometh the world, but he that believeth that Jesus is the Son of God?

"Whatsoever" is used for "whosoever" because it is more sweeping and inclusive. It means that *nothing* escapes this maxim: having God's life is the universally potent way to overcome all the forces that oppose Him—said here to be "the world." The Bible often characterizes anti-God forces as "the world"—not because the world itself is evil but because those whose life-styles conform *only* to this-worldly concerns exclude spiritual concerns. Ironically, those who lack faith—who say No to God and His will—bar themselves from the very power that overcomes the world. This is because that power—which John calls "eternal life"—resides in Jesus, whom we must accept by faith in order to be "born again" or access the divine life. The ultimate "worldly" power is death—which can only be conquered by the eternal life promised to believers.

III. The Proof of the Witnesses—6-12

A. The reality of the Christ event, 6-8

6 This is he that came by water and blood, even Jesus Christ; not by water only, but by water and blood. And it is the Spirit that beareth witness, because the Spirit is truth.

7 For there are three that bear record in heaven, the Father, the Word, and the Holy Ghost: and these three are one.

8 And there are three that bear witness in earth, the spirit, and the water, and the blood: and these three agree in one.

Having noted that overcoming faith resides in Christ, John now describes Him—but in terms that are not easily understood. His meaning may be clearer if we assume that these verses are a parenthesis in which John wants to counter the false teaching that Jesus was only a spirit. This notion was a part of a line of thought that would flower in the second century, when "gnostics" would hold that the flesh is evil. Some held that for Christ to be divine His spirit—the real saving power—would have to be totally separate from His fleshly body. John, however, insists that Jesus came with the this-worldly traits of water and blood—a blunt denial of any "pre-gnostic" view of matter as evil. John may be referring to Christ's human birth, which was accompanied by both water and blood; or to the event of the Cross, when both water and blood flowed from His pierced side. Connecting this with John 19:34 makes the latter more likely, since John's Gospel is the only one to record this footnote to the Crucifixion.

In the latter part of verse 6, John again echoes a statement from his Gospel: the Holy Spirit, "the spirit of truth," testifies to the fact that Jesus is the Christ (John 15:26).

The Spirit uses the Word to communicate this truth (Rom. 10:9-10) — which, just as we back up our testimony in a court of law by "swearing on the Bible," is backed up by divine witnesses. In the kjv these witnesses are said to be the Father, the Word, and the Holy Ghost—three heavenly witnesses—and the spirit, the water and the blood—three earthly witnesses. Manuscripts older than those used by the kjv translators omit verse 7b-8a, which is why later translations have only the three witness in 8b. The overall point is that our faith that Jesus is the Christ is not an empty claim; it has "substance" to it (see the definition of faith in Heb. 11:1). Eye-witnesses saw not only blood and water come from Jesus' side at the Cross, but they viewed Him in His resurrection body as well.

B. The assurance of God, 9-12

9 If we receive the witness of men, the witness of God is greater: for this is the witness of God which he hath testified of his Son.

10 He that believeth on the Son of God hath the witness in himself: he that believeth not God hath made him a liar; because he believeth not the record that God gave of his Son.

11 And this is the record, that God hath given to us eternal life, and this life is in his Son.

12 He that hath the Son hath life; and he that hath not the Son of God hath not life.

We can trust the testimony of those who first beheld the risen Lord because it was authorized by the Father and inspired by the Spirit. Eventually, however, the true believer grows past the need for ordinary evidence reassuring them that Jesus is Savior and Lord— the evidence has sunk deeply into their soul and become a part of them.

"Record" in verse 11 is from the same word which gives us the word "martyr." It is often translated "witness" or "testimony"; and came to mean "martyr" because so many early believers paid for their testimony about Jesus with their lives. The Word about Jesus as Savior is a "record" in another sense as well. Some religions teach "saving ideas." Christianity is based on the historical record of a Man who lived at a specific place and time.

"Eternal life" in verses 11-12 means "the life of the Eternal One." Believers have not only the promise of life unending after death, but of life that overcomes the world, even in this life.

Evangelistic Emphasis

Overcoming the world is no small feat. Think about that list of New Year's resolutions that you are making. You are thinking about conquering the waistline, overcoming debt and being victorious with time management. You are confident that your resolutions will change your life, this year. You have learned from all those past resolutions what went wrong and why your resolve lagged. Perhaps you have learned that many of the changes you wish to make in your life you can't do alone.

John wrote to an early church that was struggling with faith and world issues. His message from God was simple. ". . .and this is the victory that overcometh the world, even our faith" (1 John 5: 4).

Victory is a word rarely used in most churches. "Victory Sunday" is a day reserved most often for the culmination of the Stewardship Campaign. The only other time we use the word is in describing what our church athletic programs have achieved against another team. Victory as a word for Christians in their relationship with the world is rarely used.

The promise of God is that our faith has overcome the world. When history is concluded and the books opened, we will then understand the scope of our victory. Right now, be confident that whatever you face, your faith will make you victorious.

Memory Selection

This is the victory that conquers the world, our faith. Who is it that conquers the world but the one who believes that Jesus is the Son of God?— *1 John 5:4-5*

My son Andrew plays baseball. He is getting old enough now that winning has become important. One night they were playing a team that earlier in the season had won a huge victory over Andrew's team. This other team was in first place and now the two teams were playing the last game of the season. Andrew's team, soundly defeated earlier, didn't hold out much hope for victory.

When Andrew got home that night, I asked how they did. Andrew got a big smile on his face and said, "We won!" It was one of those miraculous victories that takes place in boy's baseball leagues.

There is no feeling in the world like winning. With all the management styles that affirm a "win-win" attitude, we have lost our competitive edge. It is wrong now to have losers. Pop psychology teaches that to win is to create a loser and thus make the winner a loser. (Go figure!)

According to Jesus, we win! The devil and the world lose!

Weekday Problems

Harlan Waters was worse than the villain in the old Westerns. He had managed to buy up all the property in downtown Littlefield. The property he didn't own, he held the insurance contracts on. Harlan had managed in his thirty years in business to cheat almost everyone in town. He had even over-charged the local Baptist and Methodist churches for their insurance policies. Harlan was unapologetic about  his business practices. He said, "There are winners and there are losers, and I don't plan to be a loser." He bragged about over- bidding people for property and underbidding on insurance. He was proud that he'd driven all other insurance agents out of Littlefield.

Harlan had never counted on Mike Morgan being elected mayor of Littlefield. Mike had been an all-American boy and had come back to his town. He had opened a pharmacy in town. Mike had grown tired of Harlan's business practices and the damage he was doing. The only reason that Mike had run for mayor was to put Harlan Waters in his place.

Mike liked to quote from 1 John. He said that his faith would make him victorious. He believed that his faith would also help him overcome the town's villain. The interesting situation for one of the local pastors was that Mike Morgan and Harlan Waters were both members of the same church. They were both in church each and every time the doors were opened. Mike had never questioned Harlan's faith in the open. It was no secret around Littlefield that many persons wondered what kind of faith Harlan had that would allow such devious business practices.

* If Mike Morgan were to be victorious over Harlan Waters, what role do you think faith played?

* Does God "fight our battles for us"?

Animal Antics

A family of polar bears sat on an iceberg. "I have a tale to tell," said the papa bear.

"I have a tale to tell, too," mama bear said.

The baby polar bear got up to leave. "My tale is told," he said.

Did you hear about the gorilla that walked into the ice cream shop and ordered a sundae? When he paid for it with a $10 bill the clerk thought, "What can an ape know about money?"—and gave the gorilla only a dollar back in change.

Trying to cover his dishonesty with small talk the clerk said, "You know, we don't get many gorillas in here."

"No wonder," the gorilla said—"at $9 a sundae."

This Lesson in Your Life

It is appropriate at the end of one year and the beginning of another to think about victory and defeat. The message of this lesson is ". . . this is the victory that overcometh the world, even our faith" (1 John 5:4). As we look at our lives we wonder if this promise might be a bit optimistic. Think back over this past year. Can you remember people who defeated you? They lured you into situations or conversations that left you in a bind. Maybe you made a promise to act and react in new ways and you found yourself breaking that promise. Defeat comes in all shapes, sizes and volumes. Defeat most often comes in the form of little discouragements. Then there is the voice inside that whispers to our souls that we are failures.

Many persons make resolutions this time of year. They promise themselves they will or will not do certain things. Most resolutions never last more than the first 24 hours of a year. However, in Christ we have the power to make life changes.

First, we need to name that habit, attitude or response pattern that defeats us. We need to be in honest prayer that the Lord will show us what needs to be changed. Honesty is important in having a victory. We often pray for help with another person, when in fact it is our response to that person that is causing the problem. The truth is, we can do little to change others. We can do everything to change our response to others. A bad habit might be the result of our attitude toward something in our past. So honesty is necessary if we are to ferret out what needs to be changed.

For example if our problem is debt, our prayers should be two-fold. We should pray that the Lord would help us to get a handle on the debt problem. Before we can do that we have to determine what inside of us is pressuring us to spend beyond our means. We should also pray that the Lord would help us to live his will in the area of stewardship. Haven't you noticed that most of our problems are rooted in our ignorance of God's purposes? Understanding God's ownership of all our resources makes us better managers of those resources.

Second, pray for victory over that situation or attitude in your life. Pray not that you would defeat the problem, but that the Lord would defeat the problem for you. This is where our independence becomes a foe. Paul said, "I can do all things through Christ Jesus who strengthens me" (Philip. 4: 13). When we learn to lean on Him for our strength and insight we find our problems less able to defeat us. It is when we try to tackle them alone that they get the upper hand.

Third, trust His resources for your life. "There are three that bear record in heaven, the Father, the Word, and the Holy Ghost and these three are one" (1 John 5:7). The Trinity is ministering on your behalf. There are situations in your life you can't overcome alone. Trust the Father, Son and Holy Spirit to come to your aid.

Fourth, claim that which is your own. The victory in Christ Jesus is already won. We have eternal life. The life we know now is only fleeting. We are pilgrims passing through on our way to the Promised Land. When we live with our eternal goal in mind, problems fall into proper perspective. The things we thought were problems suddenly we see as the training ground for deeper discipleship.

Our inheritance is not only *eternal* life but *abundant* life as well. The life of the Spirit should be a life of joy and power. When we listen to those voices of discouragement we open the door to defeat. When we claim God's victory and live like winners, we experience that kind of life. Preachers and popular motivators are in agreement about one thing. If you live and act like a winner you will become a winner. Christ Jesus has given you the victory. Live this next year in the power of that victory.

Seed Thoughts

1. Is there a restriction on who might become a Christian? To whom is the kingdom of God open?

John wrote, "Whosoever believeth. . ." and "every one that loveth him. . ." All who accept Christ are members of the kingdom.

2. How can we be certain that we love the children of God?

We are certain of our love for the children of God when we love God and when we keep God's commandments.

3. How does one properly express his love for God the Father?

He shows his love for God by obediently keeping His commandments.

4. Who are those persons who have overcome the world?

Those persons who are born of God, who believe on His Son Jesus and who apply their faith are the ones who overcome the world (1 John 5: 4-5).

5. What does 1 John 5:6 reveal about the nature of Jesus Christ?

He was a human being as well as being God. "He came by the water and the blood."

(Please turn page)

---

1. Is there a restriction on who might become a Christian? To whom is the kingdom of God open?

2. How can we be certain that we love the children of God?

3. How does one properly express his love for God the Father?

4. Who are those persons who have overcome the world?

5. What does 1 John 5:6 reveal about the nature of Jesus Christ?

6. How do we know we can trust what Jesus said about himself?

7. There are three that bear witness to the truthfulness of Jesus on earth, who are they?

8. What theological concept might be implied by 1 John 5: 7-8?

9. What description is given of a person who refuses to believe the witness?

10. What is the nature of the record that we are to believe?

John wrote, "Whosoever believeth. . ." and "every one that loveth him. . ." All who accept Christ are members of the kingdom.

We are certain of our love for the children of God when we love God and when we keep God's commandments.

He shows his love for God by obediently keeping His commandments.

Those persons who are born of God, who believe on His Son Jesus and who apply their faith are the ones who overcome the world (1 John 5: 4-5).

He was a human being as well as being God. "He came by the water and the blood."

The three witnesses to the record are in heaven. These three are the Father, the Word and the Holy Ghost.

The Spirit, the water and the blood bear witness on earth.

There are a couple of concepts you might discuss. The first is the unity of God. The second is the Trinity.

That person is described as making God out to be a liar because he refuses to believe His witness.

God has given to His people eternal life and has done so through the person of Jesus Christ

6. How do we know we can trust what Jesus said about himself?

The three witnesses to the record are in heaven. These three are the Father, the Word and the Holy Ghost.

7. There are three that bear witness to the truthfulness of Jesus on earth, who are they?

The Spirit, the water and the blood bear witness on earth.

8. What theological concept might be implied by 1 John 5: 7-8?

There are a couple of concepts you might discuss. The first is the unity of God. The second is the Trinity.

9. What description is given to a person who refuses to believe the witness?

That person is described as making God out to be a liar because he refuses to believe His witness.

10. What is the nature of the record that we are to believe?

God has given to His people eternal life and has done so through the person of Jesus Christ.

Lesson 5

God Provides Hope

January 4

1 Peter 1:3-12

3 Blessed be the God and Father of our Lord Jesus Christ, which according to his abundant mercy hath begotten us again unto a lively hope by the resurrection of Jesus Christ from the dead.

4 To an inheritance incorruptible, and undefiled, and that fadeth not away, reserved in heaven for you,

5 Who are kept by the power of God through faith unto salvation ready to be revealed in the last time.

6 Wherein ye greatly rejoice, though now for a season, if need be, ye are in heaviness through manifold temptations:

7 That the trial of your faith, being much more precious than of gold that perisheth, though it be tried with fire, might be found unto praise and honour and glory at the appearing of Jesus Christ:

8 Whom having not seen, ye love; in whom, though now ye see him not, yet believing, ye rejoice with joy unspeakable and full of glory:

9 Receiving the end of your faith, even the salvation of your souls.

10 Of which salvation the prophets have inquired and searched diligently, who prophesied of the grace that should come unto you:

11 Searching what, or what manner of time the Spirit of Christ which was in them did signify, when it testified beforehand the sufferings of Christ, and the glory that should follow.

12 Unto whom it was revealed that not unto themselves, but unto us they did minister the things, which are now reported unto you by them that have preached the gospel unto you with the Holy Ghost sent down from heaven; which things the angels desire to look into.

Memory Selection
1 Peter 1:3

Devotional Reading
Hebrews 11:1-12

Background Scripture
1 Peter 1:3-25

Printed Scripture
1 Peter 1:3-12

171

Teacher's Target

Lesson purpose: *To learn from the apostle Peter the unique basis of Christian hope, and his perspective on meaning in the midst of trials.*

The positive effects of living with a sense of meaning and hope have been documented in many situations. One of the most famous examples was described by Dr. Victor Frankl, who told of life and death among his fellow-prisoners in a German concentration camp during World War II. Those who lived with a sense that their suffering could have some kind of meaning or purpose—those who lived with hope—were more likely to survive than those who despaired. Frankl titled his book *Man's Search for Meaning.*

Ask class members to share personal definitions of hope, and situations when they struggled to maintain a sense of meaning during otherwise hopeless times. Point out that Peter affirms that for Christians hope is more then a mind-set. It is based on the historical event of the resurrection of Christ.

Lesson Introduction

The letters of 1 and 2 Peter were probably written toward the end of the first century. The immediate return of Christ that some had expected turned out to be postponed. Persecution had arisen in some parts of the Roman-dominated world. Believers found themselves "strangers" in an alien world (1:1). Not surprisingly, some found their faith wilting and their hope waning.

The apostle Peter does more than just advise people to "cheer up," or to keep a positive attitude. As important as such an attitude can be, we eventually must ask about the *basis* for good cheer. Peter, a Jew, worships a God who has long been active in history. Since the exodus, He has revealed Himself through real events, not just happy human attitudes. The resurrection of Christ was a new "exodus"—Jesus escaped from the tomb. Here Peter writes to connect that event to hope and meaning in the midst of suffering.

Teaching Outline	Daily Bible Readings
	Mon. News Angels Want to Know *1 Peter 1:10-16*
	Tue. Faith and Hope Set on God *1 Peter 1:17-21*
I. Hope that Lives—3-5	**Wed.** Hope Overcomes Death *1 Corinthians 15:12-20*
II. Trials that Testify—6-7	**Thu.** Faith Makes Hope Sure *Hebrews 10:39—11:7*
III. Faith that Perseveres—8-9	**Fri.** The Spirit Gives Power *Acts 1:6-11*
IV. Salvation that Sustains—10-12	**Sat.** Filled with the Spirit *Acts 2:1-4, 14-21*
	Sun. God Gives Us Hope *Acts 2:37-47*

VERSE BY VERSE

I. Hope that Lives—3-5

3 Blessed be the God and Father of our Lord Jesus Christ, which according to his abundant mercy hath begotten us again unto a lively hope by the resurrection of Jesus Christ from the dead.

4 To an inheritance incorruptible, and undefiled, and that fadeth not away, reserved in heaven for you,

5 Who are kept by the power of God through faith unto salvation ready to be revealed in the last time.

Immediately after addressing those to whom he writes, Peter launches into his main theme: *hope*. By first praising God and His Son, Peter serves notice that the Christian's hope is rooted in a divine blessing—not in the subjective recesses of our minds. When we become depressed by trials, it is helpful to remember that depression is subjective, while God's action through Jesus is an objective event in the full light of history. That is the fundamental difference between Christian hope and mere "positive thinking"—which can come or go depending on how we feel.

In verse 3b Peter affirms that this historical event on which Christian hope is based is the resurrection of Christ. This is what makes Christian hope "living"—which is from a word with the same root as our word "zoology," the study of living animals. As a Jew, Peter knows that past events such as the

exodus from Egypt give plenty of reason to hope for better times. Christian hope, however, goes a step further. Christ was not only resurrected; He ascended into heaven where He now lives. This makes Christian hope "deathless" or incorruptible (vs. 4). The suffering Christian can have confidence that he too will live—if not through the immediate distress then in heaven with his Lord.

How certain is this promise? Verse 5 notes again that it doesn't just depend on our being "upbeat." Christians are "kept" safe by God's power, not our own. Certainly this should ordinarily *produce* an upbeat spirit of confidence; but whether we can muster such an attitude or not we can *believe* that our spirits are secure with God regardless of what happens to our bodies and minds.

II. Trials that Testify—6-7

6 Wherein ye greatly rejoice, though now for a season, if need be, ye are in heaviness through manifold temptations:

7 That the trial of your faith, being much more precious than of gold that perisheth, though it be tried with fire, might be found unto praise and honour and glory at the appearing of Jesus Christ:

The Christians Peter addressed were living in a season of manifold temptations. Persecution even to the death had broken out here and there throughout the Empire. As verse 1 implies, their enemies had scattered them throughout Asia Minor, and even farther. Acts

8:1 describes one of these instances of "scattering."

The KJV word "heaviness" means "sadness." Many Christians can testify to the way grief can produce a heaviness of spirit that is as real as a weight on the chest. How can Peter expect them to be "light-hearted," or to rejoice? Because, once more, there is an outer, objective dimension to their suffering: remaining faithful in suffering testifies to the truth of Jesus. People do not willingly endure trials for a cause they know to be false. All people suffer; but Christians who suffer while continuing to affirm their faith give the unique testimony that *Jesus cares*.

People who have come through suffering with their faith intact know how precious it is; but the reason Peter says such faith is more precious than gold is that it honors the *object* of faith, Jesus Himself. So many Christians in the ancient world responded positively to Peter's challenge that *patience in suffering* came to have a worldwide evangelistic influence.

III. Faith that Perseveres—8-9

8 Whom having not seen, ye love; in whom, though now ye see him not, yet believing, ye rejoice with joy unspeakable and full of glory:

9 Receiving the end of your faith, even the salvation of your souls.

Now Peter addresses the very nature of Christian faith. People of faith insist on believing and persist in hoping even though they never laid eyes on their risen Lord. In one sense this is simply the essence of faith, which is "the evidence of things not seen" (Heb. 11:1). In another sense it is a rare and precious thing, again like gold, since so many people can believe only in what they can see, or test with their other senses.

Verse 9 is both an encouragement and a warning. Persistent faith results ("ends" in) salvation; but it may not be evident under the immediate pressure of suffering. It may not be revealed until "the appearing of Jesus Christ" (vs. 7b). Again, however, this is the nature of faith and hope: "hope that is seen is not hope" (Rom. 8:24).

IV. Salvation that Sustains—10-12

10 Of which salvation the prophets have inquired and searched diligently, who prophesied of the grace that should come unto you:

11 Searching what, or what manner of time the Spirit of Christ which was in them did signify, when it testified beforehand the sufferings of Christ, and the glory that should follow.

12 Unto whom it was revealed that not unto themselves, but unto us they did minister the things, which are now reported unto you by them that have preached the gospel unto you with the Holy Ghost sent down from heaven; which things the angels desire to look into.

The final verses of the passage are an interesting side-light on the nature of Old Testament prophecy. It is prompted by Peter's reference to salvation—the central subject of the prophetic material in our Bibles. God's people are saved from Egypt; then from the wilderness; then from the Philistines and other Canaanite enemies; then from Assyria and Babylon.

This recurring theme was both a blessing and problem for the prophets. Why were God's people so often in need of salvation? Obviously because they so often sinned and came under God's judgment. While the Old Testament rings with the triumph of God's

174

power to save, it also testifies to the consistent inability of persons to save themselves. A part of the prophetic message, therefore, was that a dimension of salvation lay beyond the relief God's people sought from their enemies. Their *primary* enemy was sin; and only God himself could conquer that foe.

All this gave rise to the messianic theme in the prophetic writings. While just judges and righteous kings and even foreign rulers such as Cyrus king of Persia were temporary "saviors," one day *the* Savior would appear to do for people what they could not do for themselves—accomplish salvation. This One is often called "the anointed" (Messiah)—so Peter calls the prophetic spirit predicting His coming "the Spirit of Christ," since "Christ" means "anointed."

The prophets wondered when this Coming One would appear, and what He could accomplish that preceding, lesser "saviors" not effect. The Spirit of the Anointed gave the prophets partial answers. Isaiah, for example, foresaw the mystery of "vicarious suffering" —that Messiah would bear our griefs and carry our sorrows (Isa. 53). Yet, as verses 11 and 12 show, all this was a mystery both to the prophets themselves and to angels. After all, should not we all pay for our own sins?

The prophets were told that the answer to this mystery was reserved for those who heard the gospel of Christ (vs. 12). It is only in that message that we learn that salvation comes not from the reformations the prophets demanded, nor through the sacrifices under the Old Law. Salvation is possible only because God Himself became the sacrifice in the form of His Son Jesus; and the effectiveness of this event is seen in the resurrection of Christ. It is this message that forms the kind of faith and hope that brings His followers through suffering.

Evangelistic Emphasis

There was a nuclear power plant up river from my boyhood home. The workers in certain parts of the plant had disposable clothing. Each day after work, their big yellow suits were thrown in the trash. The reason for the care was the desire to avoid contaminating anything outside the plant. The clothes also served as a protection to the workers.

Do you remember the story of Adam and Eve in the Garden of Eden? After the fall they sewed together fig leaves for themselves. Then they hid from God. I am told that the underside of a fig leaf is an irritant to the skin. If you rub the leaf against you, you will itch. So Adam and Eve were hiding from God in the bushes, itching and scratching. They made clothing from fig leaves because they knew that they were naked.

In giving us the new birth, Jesus has given us new spiritual clothing. The old has passed away and the new has been presented. We no longer need to try to make our own garment to hide our sinfulness. God has clothed us in love.

Just as those power plant workers wouldn't dream of putting on yesterday's contaminated coveralls, we shouldn't dream of returning to our old ways.

Memory Selection

God . . . has given us a new birth into a living hope through the resurrection of Jesus Christ from the dead.—*1 Peter 1:3*

In the middle of a cemetery in North Louisiana there is a mailbox. I have often wondered which one of the occupants of cemetery was waiting for mail. The only people with the nerve to send mail to a cemetery would be the IRS. I have often thought that the mailbox was some person's testimony to his faith, or lack of it, in resurrection. He must have thought that his physical address was the ground of that cemetery. If he died with such a thought, he died without hope.

Hope sustains us in the hard times. Once a person has "given up hope" you can almost watch them waste away. Our hope is that life goes on beyond the grave. The empty tomb of Jesus Christ was the harbinger of what our resurrection will be like. Christ has pioneered the way through the valley of the shadow of death. We need no longer fear death, because Jesus has gone before us. He has made a way through to the other side.

Peter wrote to a persecuted church. Many had died for their faith. He promised that church, and us, that our hope is in Jesus, whom God raised from the dead.

Our hope is that mail can't be delivered to the Christian at a cemetery, because his address will be in Heaven.

Weekday Problems

There are three classic answers to the rhetorical question, "Why are these bad things happening?"

The first classic answer is found in 1 Peter. We learned somewhere that when bad things are happening to Christians there must be some kind of lesson involved. After all Simon Peter wrote, "That the trial of your faith, being much more precious than of gold that perisheth, though it be tried with fire, might be found unto the praise and honour and glory at the appearing of Jesus Christ" (1 Peter 1:7). The implication of this verse is that our faith will be put to the test. The result of the testing is that all the impurities will be "burned away."

The second image comes from our Lord. Jesus told His disciples to take up their crosses and follow Him. He was clear about self-denial and self-sacrifice. You have heard many persons refer to some hardship in their lives as "the cross they must bear." Yet, from the Jesus' words, it is evident that the cross is something that is willingly taken up. It is not something thrust on an unwilling victim.

The third image is that of the violation of God's covenant. When we break faith with God the consequences of our actions often come to bear on our souls. If you walk too close to the edge of a cliff, you might slip. If you slip you don't break the law of gravity, you prove it true. It might happen that a person who smokes heavily will develop lung cancer. It might happen that a sedentary person, who eats high fat food develops heart disease.

So with these three things in mind ask yourself the following question:

* Are my trials a result of God's testing, a sin or is it my cross to bear?

Alternatives to Faith?

Did you hear about the new dial-a-prayer service for atheists? You call a number and nobody answers.

An atheist is a person with no invisible means of support.

Billy to his atheist father: Who's "Hmmm," Dad?
Father: What do you mean, "Hmmm"?
Billy: You know—like when you sing, "Hmmm, bless America."

Did you hear about the village atheist who gave up his views because it meant there were no holidays?

Doubting Thomas: Come on—you surely don't believe in heaven. How will you get your coat on over your wings?
Believing Bill: The same way you'll be able to get your pants on over your tail.

This Lesson in Your Life

Arnold Palmer was once asked what made a great golfer. The interviewer expected some of the usual trite answers. A great golfer is a great putter. A great golfer can drive the ball straight. Arnold Palmer said something the interviewer didn't expect. "A great golfer knows how to handle the sandtraps."

Sandtraps are placed on every golf course as hazards. They are a source of great consternation to us weekend hackers. To the skilled golfer, a sandtrap affords an opportunity to make a great shot.

As Christians we need to learn to live with the sandtraps in our lives. Simon Peter wrote to a church undergoing troubling times. They were suffering persecution as a result of their faith in Jesus Christ. Peter wrote to encourage their faith and to comfort them in their trials. His words are important for life in the church at the end of the twentieth century. When Christians are starting to ask about struggles of life and of faith. Sandtraps, or obstacles, are a part of life. At one time or another, you will find yourself in the middle of a trial.

The trials of faith come to those who are walking daily with the Lord and those are only nominally following Jesus. In both cases, the trial comes as an opportunity to deepen the faith commitment to Jesus Christ. The goodness of your life does not exempt you from trials. There is a vain of thought among Christians that teaches that goodness is an insulator against pain and suffering. The Bible assumes that suffering will be a part of each and every life. The key is how one handles the hardship when it comes. Persons of deep faith, who are practiced in prayer, know what to do when a trial befalls them. Others, not so experienced, are like weekend golfers in a sandtrap. Something worse is about to happen!

Trials don't last forever. They come to be sure, but they are fleeting. I think that is how many of us endured school. We knew the end was coming. Graduation was on the horizon. When trials come, you have the assurance that trials last "though now for a season" (1 Peter 1:6). In terms of the length we are on earth our trials are relatively short. In terms of eternity, these trials are brief glimpses of anguish. When we learn to look at them as short periods, our faith is bolstered by hope.

Trials purify our faith. This is a personal issue for most Christians. Some persons, when faced with suffering, immediately start asking, "I wonder what I have done to deserve this?" Perhaps that is the wrong question to ask. A more appropriate question might be, "What can I learn as a result of this?"

Two universal lessons come to mind when thinking about trials. In every occasion we can learn patience. We are an impatient lot. If you don't believe it, try standing in the express lane at the grocery store. Listen to all the comments about the slow service. We want everything right now. With the advent of computer technology, our patience is growing thinner. We want things instantly. When we are facing a trial, we want answers and a corrective right now! Patience is often one of the lessons we learn when facing a trial.

The other lesson is that of trusting. As we face struggles, we learn to put our faith and trust in the Lord. So often these trials come as a way of removing the artificial props we have placed around our lives. When all that is false and pretense is gone the purity of our faith grows. It is sometimes hard to admit we can't handle a problem on our own. It is at that moment that God opens a window for our escape. When we learn to trust Him we find He is never late, and always prepared for our need.

Our faith grows as we learn to face the sandtraps that are a part of every life.

Seed Thoughts

1. According to 1 Peter what is the new birth?

The new birth is the "lively hope by the resurrection of Jesus Christ from the dead" (1 Pet. 1:3).

2. The inheritance kept for us in heaven—how is it described?

It is said to be "incorruptible, and undefiled and that fadeth not away" (1 Pet. 1:4).

3. How is this inheritance being kept "incorruptible, and undefiled and that fadeth not away?"

It is being kept by the power of God through faith.

4. When will the church see its inheritance now being kept in heaven?

The inheritance will be revealed in the last time.

5. Peter acknowledged the believers joy over the inheritance. But how was their joy was tempered?

Their joy was tempered by the fact they are enduring various trials associated with their faith.

1. According to 1 Peter, what is the new birth?

2. The inheritance kept for us in heaven—how is it described?

3. How is this inheritance being kept "incorruptible, and undefiled and that fadeth not away?"

4. When will the church see its inheritance which is being kept in heaven?

5. Peter acknowledged the believers' joy over the inheritance. But how was their joy was tempered?

6. What was the image used in verse seven to describe to results of their trial?

7. When will the Christian receive his reward for being faithful through these trials?

8. Peter wrote to these Christians about the person of Jesus. What did Peter write?

9. What was the goal or end of their faith in Jesus Christ?

10. What is the difference between the Christians and the prophets of old?

(Please turn page)

The new birth is the "lively hope by the resurrection of Jesus Christ from the dead" (1 Pet. 1:3).

It is said to be "incorruptible, and undefiled and that fadeth not away" (1 Pet. 1:4).

It is being kept by the power of God through faith.

The inheritance will be revealed in the last time.

Their joy was tempered by the fact they are enduring various trials associated with their faith.

Their trials were like fire that burns off the impurities in gold. After the trial is over their faith will be "more pure."

The reward will come at the "appearing of Jesus Christ."

They are blessed because even though they had not seen Jesus (like Peter) they still believe in Him.

"Receiving the end of your faith, even the salvation of your souls." (1 Peter 1:9)

The prophets predicted the coming of the Messiah. The Christians have personally experienced that Messiah.

6. What was the image used in verse seven to describe to results of their trial?

Their trials were like fire that burns off the impurities in gold. After the trial is over their faith will be "more pure."

7. When will the Christian receive his reward for being faithful through these trials?

The reward will come at the "appearing of Jesus Christ."

8. Peter wrote to these Christians about the person of Jesus? What did Peter write?

They are blessed because even though they had not seen Jesus (like Peter) they still believe in Him.

9. What was the goal or end of their faith in Jesus Christ?

"Receiving the end of your faith, even the salvation of your souls." (1 Peter 1:9)

10. What is the difference between the Christians and the prophets of old?

The prophets predicted the coming of the Messiah. The Christians have personally experienced that Messiah.

Lesson 6

Becoming God's People

1 Peter 2:1-10

1 Wherefore laying aside all malice, and all guile, and hypocrisies, and envies, and all evil speakings,

2 As newborn babes, desire the sincere milk of the word, that ye may grow thereby:

3 If so be ye have tasted that the Lord is gracious.

4 To whom coming, as unto a living stone, disallowed indeed of men, but chosen of God, and precious,

5 Ye also, as lively stones, are built up a spiritual house, an holy priesthood, to offer up spiritual sacrifices, acceptable to God by Jesus Christ.

6 Wherefore also it is contained in the scripture, Behold, I lay in Sion a chief corner stone, elect, precious: and he that believeth on him shall not be confounded.

7 Unto you therefore which believe he is precious: but unto them which be disobedient, the stone which the builders disallowed, the same is made the head of the corner.

8 And a stone of stumbling, and a rock of offence, even to them, which stumble at the word, being disobedient: whereunto also they were appointed.

9 But ye are a chosen generation, a royal priesthood, an holy nation, a peculiar people; that ye should shew forth the praises of him who hath called you out of darkness into his marvellous light:

10 Which in time past were not a people, but are now the people of God: which had not obtained mercy, but now have obtained mercy.

Memory Selection
1 Peter 2:10

Devotional Reading
2 Corinthians 1:3-14

Background Scripture
1 Peter 2:1-10

Printed Scripture
1 Peter 2:1-10

181

Teacher's Target

Lesson purpose: *To catch Peter's inspired vision of peoplehood or community as a means of growth, strength, and hope.*

In the preceding lesson we noted the role of resurrection faith in withstanding trials. Now Peter moves from the personal to the corporate, from the individual to the community.

A good way to introduce this lesson is to ask members of the group to reflect on positive aspects of the church—both in a congregational sense and in the world-wide fellowship of believers. Since the church is not lacking in critics, let this be a time for "the rest of the story"—for unapologetic appreciation for the people of God. Ask for specifics: "In what ways is the church a source of inspiration to you?"

Then point out that Christians in the first century faced special threats and had special needs that the church met. Several of these needs are addressed in the passage for today.

Lesson Introduction

The apostle Peter has shown that the resurrection of Christ offers a solid, historical basis for hope in the midst of trials and suffering (1:3-12). He has spoken of being redeemed by Christ's blood, and of being "born again" (1:18-25).

Now what? Newborns need to grow. As they mature, they need to learn social skills—to interact with others in wholesome ways. They need to contribute to being a family—with both the privileges and responsibilities this entails.

In the present lesson, Peter urges precisely this sort of growth on a spiritual plane. He doesn't anticipate that anyone will remain a child in the Kingdom of God. Although our hope rests on the resurrection of Jesus, our growth in faith depends partly on our *diet*, and on how we interact with other children in God's family, the church.

Teaching Outline	Daily Bible Readings

I. Diet for Growth—1-3
  A. Declining unhealthy food, 1
  B. Desiring the milk of the Word, 2-3
II. Design for a Temple—4-5
  A. Christ as the foundation, 4
  B. Christians as building blocks, 5
III. Decision about Jesus—6-8
  A. A cornerstone, 6-7
  B. A stumblingstone, 8
IV. Delight in Peoplehood—9-10
	Mon. Now We Are God's People
	Psalm 100:1-5
	Tue. Glory of the Lord Appears
	Isaiah 60:1-6
	Wed. First Fruits of the Spirit
	Romans 8:18-27
	Thu. Comfort in Time of Suffering
	2 Corinthians 1:3-14
	Fri. Be a Holy Priesthood
	Deuteronomy 6:1-9
	Sat. Proclaim God's Mighty Acts
	Psalm 145:8-13
	Sun. Love God and Your Neighbor
	Matthew 22:34-40

VERSE BY VERSE

I. Diet for Growth—1-3

A. Declining unhealthy food, 1

1 Wherefore laying aside all malice, and all guile, and hypocrisies, and envies, and all evil speakings,

Note that Peter introduces a classic passage on individual spiritual growth by listing negatives to avoid in our relationships with others. Growing spiritually involves avoiding these relational sins as well as taking in healthy spiritual food. "For no man liveth to himself" (Rom. 14:7). As has been said, Christianity is personal, but never private.

To say that we are to eliminate *malice* from our lives does not mean that we should never be *angry*, as some Christians assume. It is sometimes healthful to be angry; but we are not to let that lead us to the sin of committing evil (Eph. 4:26). *Guile* means deceit, the opposite of pure-hearted openness and sincerity. Jesus once saw into the pure heart of a Jew named Nathaniel and said he was "an Israelite without guile" (John 1:47). Here Peter anticipates the next verse when he will recommend the opposite of guile, *sincerity*.

Hypocrisy is straight from the Greek word for "play-acting." It was often used in connection with the famous masks, one unhappy and the other smiling, that even today may illustrate a playbill. Peter is warning against "mask-

ing" our true feelings by lying pretensions. *Evil speakings* refers literally to "talking down" someone, or making false accusations.

B. Desiring the milk of the Word, 2-3

2 As newborn babes, desire the sincere milk of the word, that ye may grow thereby:
3 If so be ye have tasted that the Lord is gracious.

With major harmful "foods" described, Peter now gives the one essential in a healthful spiritual diet: God's Word. The term "newborn babes" is not intended to label all Christians as babies; many to whom Peter wrote had been Christians for years. Instead, the term is to be related to the word "desire." We are to desire the Word just as instinctively and intensely as an infant desires its mother's milk.

The KJV word "sincere" means literally "unbad," in a play on the word "malice" (bad) in verse 1. The NIV's "pure spiritual milk" is closer to the original. The word for "spiritual" does not relate the Word to the Holy Spirit, but in this context probably means "figurative." It is Peter's way of saying "I refer to 'milk' in a figurative sense, of course." He is repeating his reference to the gospel in 1:25; and his point is that "drinking in" the message about Jesus is the only way we can grow up to be strong enough in the faith to endure the trials the author spoke of in chapter 1.

In a quotation of Psalm 34:8a, verse 3 adds the expectation that Christians who have "tasted" God's goodness and grace in initial salvation will surely want to go on to maturity.

II. Design for a Temple—4-5

A. Christ as the foundation, 4

4 To whom coming, as unto a living stone, disallowed indeed of men, but chosen of God, and precious,

Peter now changes his vivid pictorial language from a spiritual diet to a spiritual building. The relationship is that both involve "growth." Verses 4-10 are built around Isaiah 28:16: "Behold I lay in Zion for a foundation a stone, a tried stone, a precious corner stone, a sure foundation." Isaiah is referring to the Messiah, the Chosen One who was to come. Peter reaffirms that indeed Messiah not only came, but provided a solid foundation on which Christians can build their lives. Unbelievers, of course, "disallow" that Jesus is the Messiah; and Peter will have more to say about that later.

B. Christians as building blocks, 5

5 Ye also, as lively stones, are built up a spiritual house, an holy priesthood, to offer up spiritual sacrifices, acceptable to God by Jesus Christ.

Focusing again on the *corporate* nature of the faith, Peter moves from speaking of Christ as the cornerstone to Christians as building blocks laid atop the foundation. Individual, scattered, self-sufficient stones don't comprise a temple. The author reminds us again that he is speaking figuratively: we are "lively" (living) stones, not chunks of literal granite (hopefully!). He may also be comparing Christians to stones such as limestone, which can be shaped and fitted as "live rock" when first taken from the quarry.

Again the imagery shifts, this time from Christians as stones fitted together to form a temple to the priests in the temple. Once more, we offer "spiritual" sacrifices—not literal animals. Good works, songs of praise, acts of building each other up—not bulls and goats—become the "sacrifices" in the new temple Peter describes. Even these gifts to Christ are perfected only by Christ's own sacrifice.

III. Decision about Jesus—6-8

A. A cornerstone, 6-7

6 Wherefore also it is contained in the scripture, Behold, I lay in Sion a chief corner stone, elect, precious: and he that believeth on him shall not be confounded.

7 Unto you therefore which believe he is precious: but unto them which be disobedient, the stone which the builders disallowed, the same is made the head of the corner.

Here Peter quotes directly from Isaiah 24:18, reminding us of the two basic ways Jesus has been received—either as Messiah, the foundation stone of God's new "temple" of believers, or as an imposter. Accepting or rejecting Christ is of eternal significance, for the decision determines whether He plays the role of foundation or stumblingblock in our lives (vs. 8). If we choose to build our lives on Him, we will not be "confounded" (literally, ashamed or disgraced).

B. A stumblingstone, 8

8 And a stone of stumbling, and a rock of offence, even to them, which stumble at the word, being disobedient: whereunto also they were appointed.

Elaborating on the negative effects of a negative view of Jesus, Peter paints a vivid picture of a construction site. A huge foundation stone lies on the ground, ready to be moved into its place at the corner of the foundation. It has been cut and shaped in the quarry to fit the architect's blueprint. Some workmen, however, decline to use it, and turn to other possibilities—only to stumble over the stone they rejected. Adding that such people were "appointed" to reject Jesus does not imply that they were fatally doomed to do so, but that God knew in advance that some would reject His Son.

IV. Delight in Peoplehood—9-10

9 But ye are a chosen generation, a royal priesthood, an holy nation, a peculiar people; that ye should shew forth the praises of him who hath called you out of darkness into his marvellous light:

10 Which in time past were not a people, but are now the people of God: which had not obtained mercy, but now have obtained mercy.

In a ringing affirmation of his confidence that his readers would not be among the "stumblers," Peter freely mixes the preceding figures of speech with others that describe how people of faith depend on each other. His words

form an exhilarating rout of all hang-dog, poor-me, lonely attitudes of defeatism and despair.

Many of Peter's readers would have been Gentiles. They were from many tongues and countries, people without a proud national heritage—until they became Christians. In Christ, however, they are part of the "chosen people." Followers of the Messiah, not just members of His ethnic heritage, are the chosen race and the holy nation! Brothers and sisters in Christ, not just an exclusive tribe, are "priests to each other." The KJV "peculiar" is used as we might say "Light is a peculiar trait of the sun," meaning a special possession. How could Peter's readers—or ourselves—allow discouragement to defeat us? We are God's special possession!

All this carries with it a commission, not just a static blessing. As chosen people, believers are to announce to others that they can be chosen, too—"showing forth" praise for our having been included in the spiritual house God is building.

Evangelistic Emphasis

We are social creatures. We all have the need to belong to a group. The family is one group that fulfills this need for belonging. Other social groups and clubs can fulfill our need to belong to a group.

First Peter has an interesting image for belonging. Peter wrote, "Ye also, as lively stones, are built up a spiritual house, a holy priesthood . . ." (1 Pet. 2:5). Jesus Christ is the rock upon which the church foundation rests. You and I are the stones that make up the household of God. The church is more than a club or an organization. It is a living organism. We are the living parts of that organism called the church.

Not only are we the stones that make up the edifice, we are also the priests who function before God. Each one of us has been called into ministry by virtue of our baptism. We are all ministers of the gospel of Jesus Christ. Not only do you belong to an eternal organization. You have a purpose for belonging to that organization.

The good news of Jesus Christ is that you belong. Your gifts and talents are needed in the church. You are the stone, resting on others like you and supporting still others. The church is diminished without you and blessed because of you. It is nice to be needed. It is even better to belong.

✳ ✳ ✳

Memory Selection

Which in time past were not a people, but are now the people of God: which had not obtained mercy, but how have obtained mercy.— *1 Peter 2: 10*

"I'm not good enough to go to church."

"I'm not good enough to go to church." This is excuse number 18 in the layperson's excuse book for not coming to church. Ministers have heard it over and over again. The whole point of the gospel is that the love of God is not predicated on your goodness. We may come to the Father as we are right now. When we come to God we find love, mercy and grace.

Peter captured that essence as he wrote to the early church. They were no people, who had become God's people. He was saying they had no identity. Previously they did not belong. Their sins were unforgiven. Now, in coming to God, they are His people. They belong to a spiritual family. They have received God's mercy in their lives.

The movement of this verse is from loneliness and estrangement to belonging and reconciliation. This verse is also an invitation, an invitation for you to experience God's mercy.

Weekday Problems

Sally Martin almost skipped this lesson in the **Higley Sunday School Commentary**. She feared the heated discussion that would result as Mark Spiller and Rhonda Weber tied into each other on the matter of spiritual maturity. Mark had only been a member of New Harmony Church for three years. Rhonda had been in that same church all her life. Mark and Rhonda also came from different spiritual backgrounds. Mark was, until four years previous, a non-believer. Rhonda had been baptized as a child.

Sally read, "Like newborn infants, long for the pure spiritual milk, so that you may grow into salvation" (1 Pet. 2:2.) Mark didn't let Sally take a good breath before he jumped in.

"That's the problem with this church, too many babies still taking the bottle." He opened his Bible to Hebrews 5:13: "For everyone who lives on milk, being still an infant, is unskilled in the word of righteousness." He sat back with his arms folded, waiting for Rhonda's response.

"Well, Mark," she said, "you've got to begin somewhere. I guess we're just not spiritual enough for you. Why don't you find a church that believes like you do?"

With that the debate of the century had begun in Sally Martin's Sunday School class aptly called, "The Seekers Class."

* How do you reconcile 1 Peter 2:2 with Hebrews 5: 13?

* How are both Mark and Rhonda showing the childishness of their understanding of the Bible?

* What is the difference between the "milk of the Word" and the "meat of the Word?"

These People!

A minister was faced with the task of telling a church member with a heart condition that he had inherited $1 million. He was afraid the shock might kill him, so he said gently, "Jim, what would you do if you inherited $1 million?
"Why, I'd give it all to the church," Jim said.
The minister fell over dead.

Did you hear about the church that had a membership drive? It drove off 50 people.

"We need a new song leader," the minister complained to an elder.
"What's wrong with this one?" the elder asked.
"When I preached against gossip he lead the hymn, "I Love to Tell the Story"!

Church sign warning against driving while drinking: "Jug not that ye be not jugged."

This Lesson in Your Life

I once lived in a house that had a "doggy door" installed in it. That allowed our two little dachshunds and one obnoxious cat access to the outside world. It was a convenience for the pet owners not to have to awaken at all hours to let the animals "go out." The problem with the door was the cat. This cat was a hunter. As cats will do, it wanted all the humans in the house to know what had been captured. In the year the "doggy door" existed, the cat brought into the house three snakes, three live squirrels, one live bird, three dead birds and assorted rodents. The door that should have made it convenient to care for our pets became a "Wild Kingdom" nightmare. We decided that the cat or the "doggy door" had to go. The kids loved the cat too much to hear of my suggestion.

That door opened our home to all sorts of pests. In your life you have a door. Through this door, malice, guile, insincerity, envy and all slander come through. It is a door that only you know about. It is a door that only you can allow God to close. The door is built when you have two different characters, one for Sunday and one for the rest of the week. When you have that situation in our lives, you open yourself to having these spiritual varmints running around in your soul. When you close off the door to negative feelings and seek God, you experience the salvation of your soul. All that is dark and evil is melted away in the light of God's love.

Peter admonished the early church to put all of this aside and seek the "pure, spiritual milk." His advice is sound today. Substitute the thoughts of God for all of those negative thoughts in your life. Your actions are a result of your thoughts, so the process begins in your mind. "As a person thinks in his heart, so he is," the Bible says.

Malice, guile, insincerity, envy and slander are eventually driven out of your life as you substitute God's Word for these negative emotions. The process of change might take a lifetime. Even in beginning you will notice an immediate change in your outlook.

The need for persons to grow into their salvation is made clear later in this same chapter. We are all called to be a "chosen race, a royal priesthood, a holy nation, God's own people, in order that we may proclaim the mighty acts of him who called us out of darkness into his marvelous light" (1 Pet. 2: 9). Peter is clear about the ministry of all believers. We are more than priests before God. We are ministers to the congregation and to the world.

The call of God is not to privilege. It is a call to sacrificial service in His kingdom. The need for the pure milk arises out of our function within the plan of God. The priests were called to be pure, without blemish, in order to come into the presence of God. Once the sacrifice was made, the priests were to carry the message of God back to the people.

As members of the Body of Christ you are called to proclaim His praises (1 Pet. 2:9). This includes sharing the story of how God called you out of darkness into his light. You are the only sermon that many people will ever hear. You are the only church with which many people will have contact. You are the only Bible that many people will ever read. You are the only Christian that many people will ever know. Do you see why, with the world watching, our witness for Jesus Christ must be so consistent?

We have a marvelous message to proclaim to a lost world. The message is that "God is love," that sinners are welcomed into the fold of God. Our message is of a God who brings mercy to those who are longing for mercy.

Seed Thoughts

1. What personality characteristics are Christians to rid themselves of?

We are to rid ourselves of all malice, guile, insincerity, envy and slander.

2. Rather than the negative traits listed above, what were the Christians to long for?

They were to long for the pure, spiritual milk that would cause them to grow into salvation.

3. From your reading of the second verse, how would you describe salvation?

Salvation is a process. The newborn infants feed on spiritual milk to "grow into salvation."

4. To whom are we invited to come for our salvation?

We are invited to come to Him, a "living stone, rejected by mortals but precious in God's sight."

5. What image is begun in the fourth verse and continued through the eighth verse?

The image of Jesus as a rock. The secondary image is of Christians as the stones that build the Body.

(Please turn page)

1. What personality characteristics are Christians to rid themselves of?

2. Rather than the negative traits above, what were the Christians to long for?

3. From your reading of the second verse, how would you describe salvation?

4. To whom are we invited to come for our salvation?

5. What image is begun in the fourth verse and continued through the eighth verse?

6. Why would you suspect this image would have been used by Peter?

7. What relationship do those who do not believe have with the stone?

8. In terms of function, how are the early Christians described by Simon Peter?

9. What tasks are the Christians given?

10. How does Peter continue to describe the process of being called out of darkness into light?

We are to rid ourselves of all malice, guile, insincerity, envy and slander.

They were to long for the pure, spiritual milk that would cause them to grow unto salvation.

Salvation is a process. The newborn infants feed on spiritual milk to "grow into salvation."

We are invited to come to Him, a "living stone, rejected by mortals but precious in God's sight."

The image of Jesus as a rock. The secondary image is of Christians as the stones that build the Body.

In Matthew 16:16-20 these same images are used by Jesus in speaking of himself and Simon Peter.

The rejected stone becomes the cornerstone. This stone makes them stumble and this rock makes them fall.

They are a chosen race, a royal priesthood, a holy nation and God's own people.

"They are to proclaim the mighty acts of Him who called you out of darkness into His marvelous light."

The Christians were once "not a people but are now God's people." They once had not received mercy but have received mercy."

6. Why would you suspect this image would have been used by Peter?

In Matthew 16:16-20 these same images are used by Jesus in speaking of himself and Simon Peter.

7. What relationship do those who do not believe have with the stone?

The rejected stone becomes the cornerstone. This stone makes them stumble and this rock makes them fall.

8. In terms of function, how are the early Christians described by Simon Peter?

They are a chosen race, a royal priesthood, a holy nation and God's own people.

9. What tasks are the Christians given?

"They are to proclaim the mighty acts of Him who called you out of darkness into His marvelous light."

10. How does Peter continue to describe the process of being called out of darkness into light?

The Christians were once "not a people but are now God's people." They once had not received mercy but have received mercy."

Lesson 7

Hope in Suffering with Christ

1 Peter 3:13-21; 4:12-16

13 And who is he that will harm you, if ye be followers of that which is good?

14 But and if ye suffer for righteousness' sake, happy are ye: and be not afraid of their terror, neither be troubled;

15 But sanctify the Lord God in your hearts: and be ready always to give an answer to every man that asketh you a reason of the hope that is in you with meekness and fear:

16 Having a good conscience; that, whereas they speak evil of you, as evildoers, they may be ashamed that falsely accuse your good conversation in Christ.

17 For it is better, if the will of God be so, that ye suffer for well doing, than for evil doing.

18 For Christ also hath once suffered for sins, the just for the unjust, that he might bring us to God, being put to death in the flesh, but quickened by the Spirit:

19 By which also he went and preached unto the spirits in prison;

20 Which sometime were disobedient, when once the longsuffering of God waited in the days of Noah, while the ark was a preparing, wherein few, that is, eight souls were saved by water.

21 The like figure whereunto even baptism doth also now save us (not the putting away of the filth of the flesh, but the answer of a good conscience toward God,) by the resurrection of Jesus Christ:

4:12 Beloved, think it not strange concerning the fiery trial which is to try you, as though some strange thing happened unto you:

13 But rejoice, inasmuch as ye are partakers of Christ's sufferings; that, when his glory shall be revealed, ye may be glad also with exceeding joy.

14 If ye be reproached for the name of Christ, happy are ye; for the spirit of glory and of God resteth on you: on their part he is evil spoken of, but on your part he is glorified.

15 But let none of you suffer as a murderer, or as a thief, or as an evildoer, or as a busybody in other men's matters.

16 Yet if any man suffer as a Christian, let him not be ashamed; but let him glorify God on this behalf.

Memory Selection
1 Peter 4:16

Devotional Reading
1 Peter 2:18-25

Background Scripture
1 Peter 3:8-22; 4:12-16

Printed Scripture
1 Peter 3:13-21; 4:12-16

Teacher's Target

Lesson purpose: *To gain a biblical perspective on the Christian's attitude toward suffering and those who oppose the faith.*

Religious persecution was so common in ancient times that the apostle Peter assumes in this lesson that Christians will suffer for their faith. Today such persecution is the exception rather than the rule, especially in civilized nations. Although some of your class members may be able to recount times when they were made fun of for their faith, there may be few real parallels between their experience with pain and suffering and the persecutions endured by the early Christians.

Still, as Lesson 5 emphasized, all who suffer have the need to find meaning in it. Lead your class to see that "suffering for Christ" in our day may mean "bearing pain and suffering while remaining faithful and testifying to God's goodness."

Lesson Introduction

No one escapes suffering. Most religions and many schools of philosophy were born in the struggle to make sense of this universal fact of life. They attempt to answer the question of why or how undeserved pain and suffering can co-exist with a benevolent God.

The Bible does not offer a systematic or philosophical answer to this great question. Its anwswer requires not philosophical reason but faith. That answer centers on the proclamation that Christ conquered the ultimate evil—death— in His crucifixion-resurrection. It follows that the disciples of Christ would seek to relate their own suffering to that event. Peter therefore deals with the question of suffering not in philosophical terms, but by describing how believers can transform their suffering to a testimony about Jesus.

Teaching Outline	Daily Bible Readings	
I. Responding to Persecution—3:13-17	**Mon.**	Living with Persecution *1 Peter 2:18-25*
A. Suffering for the right reason, 13, 17	**Tue.**	Follow Christ's Example *1 Peter 3:8-22*
B. Giving the real reason, 14-16	**Wed.**	Sufferers for Christ Are Blessed *1 Peter 4:12-19*
II. Remembering Christ's Suffering —18-22	**Thu.**	Peter Defends the Gospel *Acts 4:1-3*
A. The testimony of Jesus, 18-20	**Fri.**	Be Glorified with Christ *Romans 8:16-17*
B. A parallel in baptism, 21		
III. Reacting with joy—4:12-16	**Sat.**	Crown of Life for Enduring *Revelation 2:8-11*
A. The fellowship of suffering, 12	**Sun.**	A Privilege to Suffer for Christ *Philippians 1:25-30*
B. Reflected glory, 13-16		

VERSE BY VERSE

I. Responding to Persecution—3:13-17

A. Suffering for the right reason, 13, 17

13 And who is he that will harm you, if ye be followers of that which is good?

17 For it is better, if the will of God be so, that ye suffer for well doing, than for evil doing.

Peter first assumes that those in authority will punish only wrong-doers, and not harm those who do good. It is to be hoped that corrupt government officials who punish people without just cause are exceptions rather than the rule.

Although doing right is always "in season" for Christians, it was of special importance to early Christian leaders. The reputation of the new-born Christian faith was at stake. Since the Empire and the Jews scrutinized believers' every act, it was especially important that Christians not give any excuse for just punishment by being criminals, thus bringing reproach on the whole Christian movement.

The word translated "followers" gives us our word "zealots"—showing the intensity with which we are to seek the good instead of the evil. It may be God's will for us to suffer, but only for following Him, not for wrong-doing. Why would God will suffering upon us? The next verses will reveal one reason.

B. Giving the real reason, 14-16

14 But and if ye suffer for righteousness' sake, happy are ye: and be not afraid of their terror, neither be troubled;

15 But sanctify the Lord God in your hearts: and be ready always to give an answer to every man that asketh you a reason of the hope that is in you with meekness and fear:

16 Having a good conscience; that, whereas they speak evil of you, as evildoers, they may be ashamed that falsely accuse your good conversation in Christ.

"Happy" in verse 14 is the same word translated "blessed" in the Beatitudes (Matt. 5:1-12). We should note that twisted notions of suffering as a sadistic kind of "good" are totally foreign to the Christian faith. Christians do not intentionally bring suffering on themselves. There is no more sadly misguided person that one who thinks he can win salvation by hurting. The happiness of which Peter speaks stems from being persecuted for doing right, or for standing for the Righteous One, not from simply experiencing pain.

Suffering for the faith is a "blessing" because it enables us to identify with Jesus in His greater suffering; and because it often provides an opportunity to explain why the faith is a cause worth remaining faithful even through suffering. Many unbelievers, including judges who presided at the trials of early Christians, have been converted by the courage and faith of someone willing to endure suffering for the Cause.

The word "sanctify" basically means *to set apart for holy use.* Of course we do not make the Lord holy; we set Him apart as One for whom we are ready to suffer—or to defend by explaining why we believe in Him.

The word translated "answer" gives us our word "apology," but it originally meant "reason" or "answer." Thus, the discipline of providing reasons for faith is called Christian *apologetics.* Although apologetics can occupy the greatest minds for a lifetime, every Christian can pause to ask himself why he believes, and be ready to pass along the reason to an unbeliever who challenges his faith.

Verses 15b-16 describe three character traits we are to have when we give such reasons for faith: humility, respect (one meaning of the KJV word "fear"), and integrity. Of what value is it when a boastful, disrespectful, or unrighteous Christian gives a brilliant defense of the faith with a belligerent or arrogant attitude? Only when we answer with integrity will anyone be ashamed of falsely charging us with evil. ("Conversation" meant "lifestyle" when the KJV was translated.)

II. Remembering Christ's Suffering—18-22

A. The testimony of Jesus, 18-20

18 For Christ also hath once suffered for sins, the just for the unjust, that he might bring us to God, being put to death in the flesh, but quickened by the Spirit:

19 By which also he went and preached unto the spirits in prison;

20 Which sometime were disobedient, when once the longsuffering of God waited in the days of Noah, while the ark was a preparing, wherein few, that is, eight souls were saved by water.

Suffering for the sake of righteousness naturally brings up the subject of Jesus' own suffering. Just as Christians might testify to the faith by being persecuted, so Christ testified to "the spirits in prison"—a passage that has prompted a variety of interpretations.

First, we should note that the suffering that effected the forgiveness of sins was done "once," by Christ—again focusing on the futility of anyone thinking to gain salvation by their own suffering. Second, although Christ was slain on the Cross, His murder did not put His Spirit to death. And in that spiritual form, Christ apparently proclaimed the Good News to those imprisoned by time, awaiting the eventual proclamation of the gospel of Christ.

A common interpretation of this passage is that while Christ's body experienced death on the Cross His spirit went to the unseen realm of the dead awaiting judgment and gave an opportunity to those under the Old Covenant to accept or reject His sacrifice. Hence, believers who accepted God's grace under the Covenant with Noah (and, presumably, with Moses) have equal standing with believers today; and those who were disobedient to God's call in those days receive the same judgment as people today who reject Christ.

B. A parallel in baptism, 21

21 The like figure whereunto even baptism doth also now save us (not the putting away of the filth of the flesh, but the answer of a good conscience toward God,) by the resurrection of Jesus Christ:

Peter draws an analogy between the waters of the flood in Genesis 3 and the waters of baptism. The surging waters in Noah's day were more than a flood;

they buoyed up Noah's ark. Similarly, baptism is more than a bath; it is the "answer"—or the *request* of the believer or the *pledge* (NIV) of God for a conscience washed clean of all sin. Note that Peter links this request to the resurrection of Christ—the final proof that He was God's Son, and qualified to take away our sins (Rom. 1:4).

III. Reacting with Joy—4:12-16

A. The fellowship of suffering, 12

12 Beloved, think it not strange concerning the fiery trial which is to try you, as though some strange thing happened unto you:

Since suffering is subjective, we tend to think that our trials are uniquely traumatic. Job said that his suffering would weigh more than the sand of the sea (Job 6:3). Peter, however, calls for a more objective view: our suffering is not unique or "strange"—as Paul said, "it is common to man" (1 Cor. 10:13).

B. Reflected glory, 13-16

13 But rejoice, inasmuch as ye are partakers of Christ's sufferings; that, when his glory shall be revealed, ye may be glad also with exceeding joy.

14 If ye be reproached for the name of Christ, happy are ye; for the spirit of glory and of God resteth on you: on their part he is evil spoken of, but on your part he is glorified.

15 But let none of you suffer as a murderer, or as a thief, or as an evildoer, or as a busybody in other men's matters.

16 Yet if any man suffer as a Christian, let him not be ashamed; but let him glorify God on this behalf.

Again Peter affirms that there is no glory in suffering for wrong-doing. The reason Christians can glory in suffering is that it brings them into fellowship with their Lord, who suffered even more, bearing the sins of the world on the Cross. Peter has in mind first those who suffer for the faith. Secondarily, all believers who suffer can take heart in that they enter into a sacred partnership with their Lord, who suffered for them. They find a purpose in suffering by continuing to believe, thus testifying to their confidence that clinging to the name "Christian" will eventually be rewarded.

Evangelistic Emphasis

"Don't rock the boat." That is a polite way of saying don't make anyone uncomfortable. When you rock a boat, people in the boat become nervous and afraid. So to keep everyone calm, we "don't rock the boat."

"Now who will harm you if you are eager to do what is good?" (1 Pet. 3:13). This is a rhetorical question that Simon Peter asked the church. The answer is, almost everyone. By doing what is good and what is right one is almost guaranteed to "rock the boat." In an age of self-expression, it seems that righteous self-expression is taboo. When you and I live out our goodness, we make those persons living in "darkness" uncomfortable. Ministers love to come upon an "inactive" church member. He will give every excuse in the book for missing church. He will make every promise that he will be there next Sunday. He never comes. What has happened is that he has been made to feel uncomfortable. He knows his behavior is inconsistent with his profession (supposed) of the faith.

By your goodness you will make sinners uncomfortable. Jesus did in His day. Even as He saw them uncomfortable, He offered them salvation. The good news is that the uncomfortable feeling in the presence of goodness is the Holy Spirit convicting of sin.

Never apologize for your goodness. God will use it to lead others to His grace. Don't feel bad that you make others uncomfortable. God will use that to bring persons back into the fold.

Memory Selection

If any man suffer as a Christian, let him not be ashamed; but let him glorify God on this behalf.— *1 Peter 4:16*

There is a cartoon of a lady speaking to a rather disheveled man. They are traveling on a subway together. The lady looks at the man and asks, "Are you a minister?" He retorts, "No ma'am, I've just been sick for a few days." I'm not sure of all the implications of that cartoon, but I am certain of one. Some persons assume that ministers are battered and bruised from being good all the time. The bruising comes from those who are not quite so good themselves.

The same is true for other children of God. In these troubled days, you will begin to experience suffering as a result of your faith. Our world does not want to hear the message of Jesus Christ. The call of moral righteousness is particularly odious to the world. As the Sabbath becomes less sacred, you will find yourself being asked to work, or else. You will be asked to conform to societal norms, or else. You will be asked to subscribe to some political agenda, or else.

It seems to me that these things are already happening. But we rejoice, because we bear the image of the Christ. You remember, they crucified Jesus for living a righteous life in the midst of a sinful generation.

Weekday Problems

Ray Reed was the vice president of the major engineering firm in town. The president of the firm had purchased new computer software that would greatly reduce the time the engineers would have to spend drawing plans for various projects. He had also arranged for Ray to take several of the junior engineers off to a software training seminar.

Ray and five of the junior engineers went off for the weekend seminar. The night they arrived, Ray decided to take the engineers out on the town. Leagh Ann and Martha decided to stay in the room. They said they didn't want to inhibit the "boy's night out." It was quite a tour Ray gave. They stopped in every bar, went into most of the clubs. They consumed several gallons of spirits between them. Everyone had a great time.

Ray and the fellows returned quite inebriated. The next morning they all gathered for breakfast. Ray had a funny look on his face. He told the group that after they had all come in, he had decided to go back out to one of the all night bars. In the process of walking to the bar, he was mugged. The robbers took all of his money. It was money which the firm had provided for the group's expenses for the seminar. Ray did note for the group that the robbers didn't take his wallet or credit cards, just his money. He asked the group not to say anything about the mugging, and that he would still take care of the expenses.

* If you were "one of the guys" what would be right thing to do?

* How do you think Martha and Leagh Ann should respond to this situation?

* What would happen if the group "covered" for Ray?

Insights on Suffering

God washes the eyes by tears until they can behold the invisible land where tears shall come no more—*Henry Ward Beecher*

Night brings out stars, as sorrow shows us truths.—*G. Bailey*

We need to suffer that we may learn to pity.—*Lititia Elizabeth Landon*

Forgiveness is rarely perfect except in the breasts of those who have suffered.—*Anon.*

It is only the strong who are strengthened by suffering; the weak are made weaker.—*Feucthwanger*

It is by those who have suffered that the world has been advanced. —*Tolstoy*

This Lesson in Your Life

First Peter 3:18-22 is one of the hardest passages to interpret in the Bible. Perhaps in preparing for this lesson you might talk to your minister about the meaning of these verses. Contained within the passage are some ideas worth consideration in your life and discussion for your class.

"For Christ also suffered for sins once for all, the righteous for the unrighteous, in order to bring you to God" (1 Pet. 3:18). In the midst of suffering, the Christians in Asia Minor are reminded by Peter of the suffering of Christ. His suffering was at the hands of the unrighteous of that day. His suffering was for the sins of humanity. Paul wrote the church in his day, "I want to know Christ and the power of his resurrection and the sharing of his sufferings by becoming like him in his death" Phil. 3:10 One early theme that develops in the New Testament is the idea of suffering. In their suffering, the early disciples were "participating in the suffering of Jesus."

This kind of thought is foreign to our culture. Ask the members of your class to define sacrifice. Ask them if they have ever made a sacrifice on behalf of Christ or His church. After they have struggled with sacrifice, ask if any of them have suffered for the cause of Jesus Christ. The silence in the class is indicative of a society and a church that has downplayed the importance of sacrifice. Jesus' sacrifice of His life was for our sins.

The second image in this passage has to do with baptism. Baptism is likened to the ark which saved Noah and his family during the flood. Peter wrote that "baptism. . . now saves you." If you have persons in your church who have come from other faith traditions they are going to have various views on what this means. If baptism is the initiation into the church, then Peter was offering the image of the church as the Ark. Truly one of the pictures of the church is that of the Ark.

The church can be a saving station in times of turmoil. At the end of this century, we have become good in the church at offering people a committee rather than a community. We have downplayed the idea of the church as a safe place. Saints of God need a place to come to be protected from the storms of life. The children of God need a home where they can be nurtured in the faith. Tragically more of our programming is based on the financial bottom line than on reaching our world with the gospel.

As we struggle with what the church will be in the next century, we need to cling to the image of the Ark. As persons suffer more for their faith, the church should offer a safe harbor and way through their storms. Even as we are doing that, we must interpret their suffering.

The day is upon us where Christians in America are beginning to be made uncomfortable because of their beliefs. It is not long before suffering will take place. The church should be ready to interpret that suffering in the light of the Bible. Peter wrote, "Beloved, do not be surprised at the fiery ordeal that is taking place among you to test you, as though something strange were happening to you" (1 Pet. 4: 12). We will suffer for doing good. Our high moral standards will make the church the butt of jokes and the object of ridicule. The good news is that we are not the first, nor the last to suffer this indignity. The Apostle promised our suffering will bring blessing into our lives.

The image of the Ark is that God will carry us through to our destination. If our home is Heaven and we are just passing through, He will make sure we arrive home safely. Our glory and our joy are not associated with this world. They both are kept for us in Heaven.

Seed Thoughts

1. From your reading of 1 Peter 3:13-14, what might you assume was happening to the early Christians?

It would appear that the Christians were suffering because of their faith.

2. In light of their suffering, what was the admonition Peter made to the early church?

They were to be ready to give a defense to anyone who asked about the hope that was in them.

3. If Christians continue living righteously even with persecution, what will happen to their accusers?

The persons who are making accusations against the Christians will be put to shame.

4. Which is the better kind of suffering—suffering for good or suffering for evil?

It is better to suffer for doing good, if it be God's will, than to suffer for doing evil.

5. How was Christ's suffering described in this passage?

He suffered for all, the righteous for the unrighteous. He was put to death in the flesh and made alive in the spirit.

(Please turn page)

1. From your reading of 1 Peter 3:13-14, what might you assume was happening to the early Christians?

2. In light of their suffering, what was the admonition Peter made to the early church?

3. If the Christians continue living righteously even with persecution, what will happen to their accusers?

4. Which is the better kind of suffering, suffering for good or suffering for evil?

5. How was Christ's suffering described in this passage?

6. What happened between the time Christ died and Christ rose from the dead?

7. How many people were on the Ark and thus saved with Noah through the flood?

8. What is the significance of Christ sitting at the right hand of God?

9. According to Peter why is the fiery ordeal happening in the lives of these Christians?

10. What blessing is promised to those who are reviled for the sake of Christ?

It would appear that the Christians were suffering because of their faith.

They were to be ready to give a defense to anyone who asked about the hope that was in them.

The persons who are making accusations against the Christians will be put to shame.

It is better to suffer for doing good, if it be God's will, than to suffer for doing evil.

He suffered for all, the righteous for the unrighteous. He was put to death in the flesh and made alive in the spirit.

He was preaching to the spirits in prison, those spirits who were disobedient in the time of Noah.

There were eight persons which were saved through water.

He has authority over angels, authorities and powers—which the early church believed brought suffering.

Their faith is being tested by this time of suffering. See also 1 Peter 1:6-7.

The spirit of glory, which is the Spirit of God, is resting on them.

6. What happened between the time Christ died and Christ rose from the dead?

He was preaching to the spirits in prison, those spirits who were disobedient in the time of Noah.

7. How many people were on the Ark and thus saved with Noah through the flood?

There were eight persons which were saved through water.

8. What is the significance of Christ sitting at the right hand of God?

He has authority over angels, authorities and powers. These were some of the beings that the early church believed brought suffering.

9. According to Peter why is the fiery ordeal happening in the lives of these Christians?

Their faith is being tested by this time of suffering. See also 1 Peter 1:6-7.

10. What blessing is promised to those who are reviled for the sake of Christ?

The spirit of glory, which is the Spirit of God, is resting on them.

God's People Living in Humility

1 Peter 5:1-11

1 The elders which are among you I exhort, who am also an elder, and a witness of the sufferings of Christ, and also a partaker of the glory that shall be revealed:

2 Feed the flock of God which is among you, taking the oversight thereof, not by constraint but willingly; not for filthy lucre, but of a ready mind.

3 Neither as being lords over God's heritage, but being ensamples to the flock.

4 And when the chief Shepherd shall appear, ye shall receive a crown of glory that fadeth not away.

5 Likewise ye younger, submit yourselves unto the elder. Yea, all of you be subject one to another, and be clothed with humility: for God resisteth the proud, and giveth grace to the humble.

6 Humble yourselves therefore under the mighty hand of God, that he may exalt you in due time:

7 Casting all your care upon him; for he careth for you.

8 Be sober, be vigilant; because your adversary the devil, as a roaring lion, walketh about, seeking whom he may devour:

9 Whom resist stedfast in the faith, knowing that the same afflictions are accomplished in your brethren that are in the world.

10 But the God of all grace, who hath called us unto his eternal glory by Christ Jesus, after that ye have suffered a while, make you perfect, stablish, strengthen, settle you.

11 To him be glory and dominion for ever and ever. Amen.

January 25

Memory Selection
1 Peter 5:51

Devotional Reading
Romans 12:9-21

Background Scripture
1 Peter 5:1-11

Printed Scripture
1 Peter 5:1-11

Teacher's Target

Lesson purpose: *To learn the implications of Peter's counsel to humility, and to distinguish between true and false humility.*

A few years ago, U. S. School children scored worse than those from any other nation on a standardized math test, Yet they scored highest in their estimate of how good they were in math!

The incident illustrates the fact that humility is not a highly valued trait in modern times. We are counseled to strive to be "Number One," to be assertive, to think of ourselves as winners. Americans in general have learned such lessons well. While there is much to be said in their favor, how do we square this mind-set with Peter's counsel of humility?

One way to begin this study is to ask group members to give synonyms that come to mind when they think of the word "humility." As we will discover, humility isn't necessarily the opposite of thinking well of ourselves. Yet, the teacher should accept each suggestion, filing all of them away for later reference as the lesson unfolds.

Lesson Introduction

The ancient world had some powerful models of how to govern people. Kings of Persia and Assyria, pharaohs of Egypt, Alexander the Great, Hebrew kings— all had marched heavily across the pages of history, ruling by might.

Now comes Peter, telling early Christians about governance in their own community, the church. Suddenly a new model is revealed. Rulers are to be characterized by humility. Their authority is to be patterned after the moral and spiritual leadership of the Servant Shepherd—Christ Himself.

Although followers in such a community are counseled to submit to this "unpower," leaders are also told to submit to their followers. How could this be? What is the nature of this kind of humility? Can the modern church recover it?

Teaching Outline	Daily Bible Readings
I. Humility in Leading—1-4	**Mon.** Living in Humility *1 Peter 5:1-11*
A. Pastoring, 1-2	**Tue.** Living in Harmony *Romans 12:9-21*
B. Serving, 3-4	**Wed.** Be Wary of Human Wisdom *1 Corinthians 1:18-25*
II. Honor in Following—5-7	**Thu.** Delighting in God's Law *Psalm 119:33-48*
A. Submitting, 5-6	**Fri.** More Blessed to Give *Acts 20:28-35*
B. Trusting, 7	**Sat.** Fools for the Sake of Christ *1 Corinthians 4:8-13*
III. Help in Overcoming—8-11	**Sun.** Take the Cross and Follow Christ *Matthew 16:21-28*
A. Resisting, 8-9	
B. Glorifying, 10-11	

VERSE BY VERSE

I. Humility in Leading—5:1-4
A. Pastoring, 1-2

1 The elders which are among you I exhort, who am also an elder, and a witness of the sufferings of Christ, and also a partaker of the glory that shall be revealed:

2 Feed the flock of God which is among you, taking the oversight thereof, not by constraint but willingly; not for filthy lucre, but of a ready mind.

Three significant terms for early church leaders, each with important implications for their qualifications, are packed into these two verses.

The first term, *presbyteros*, translated "elder," is still preserved in the leadership of Presbyterian churches. Informally, this word simply meant an older person. In the context of church leadership, it implies that a church leader should have the wisdom and experience of years. It is rooted in the respect typically given older people in the ancient middle east—even the pharaohs of Egypt had "middle management" leaders called elders (Gen. 50:7). A more immediate pattern for the early Christian leaders Peter addresses were the elders in the Jewish community, whose role is noted as far back as the Egyptian captivity (Exod. 3:16ff.).

Peter's exhortation models the humility he will counsel. Although he is an apostle, he addresses these leaders as fellow elders. They are also in a fellowship of suffering, since being a "point man" in the early church often meant being singled out by Rome to bear the brunt of persecution. In one brief sentence Peter encourages them to view such suffering positively—it enables them to share the treatment given Christ, and it ensures that they will also partake of His glory when He returns (vs. 1b).

The second leadership term, in verse 2, is from *poimaino*, translated "feed." The noun form refers to a shepherd or "pasturer" (pastor), who was responsible for seeing that a flock of sheep had adequate food. Church leaders, therefore, are to be equipped to feed God's Word to His flock (1 Pet. 2:2).

It is this capacity that gives a church leader the authority of "oversight," the third word in verses 1-2 that describes church leaders. This term is from the word *episcopos*, meaning "overseer" (or, from the Latin, "bishop") Note that this role is to be assumed without "constraint" or pressure, but gladly. Also, while it is right for such overseers to be paid for their service (Luke 10:7), this is not to be their chief motive for serving.

B. Serving, 3-4

3 Neither as being lords over God's heritage, but being ensamples to the flock.

4 And when the chief Shepherd shall appear, ye shall receive a crown of glory that fadeth not away.

A shepherd who spends his time boasting of his authority or "lording it over the flock" instead of feeding the sheep would soon lose them. So Peter begins his emphasis with a distinction between church leaders and worldly leaders. Church leaders are to rule by example, with the authority of moral and spiritual persuasion, rather than by raw power. One reason for this is that Jesus Himself has "all power" (Matt. 28:18). Church shepherds need not expect to wear the crown of authority in this life; it is reserved for the Second Coming.

II. Honor in Following—5-7

A. Submitting, 5-6

5 Likewise ye younger, submit yourselves unto the elder. Yea, all of you be subject one to another, and be clothed with humility: for God resisteth the proud, and giveth grace to the humble.

6 Humble yourselves therefore under the mighty hand of God, that he may exalt you in due time:

Effective leadership depends on faithful followership. The first "qualification" of followers is said here to be the capacity to submit to their leaders. The term does not imply a subservient position but the ability to "arrange oneself under" leadership in order to complete a task. Submission in the church, therefore, is functional, and does not imply inferiority. In fact, Peter is quick to follow this admonition with the counsel that both leaders and their followers are to don the garments of humility.

This word, so central to this entire lesson, deserves careful notice. We are instructed more from its English derivation than from the Greek. The root word for humility is related to humus—which is simply good, rich dirt. The humble person realizes that he both came from the dust of the earth and will eventually wind up there as well (Gen. 3:19). Since both leaders and followers share this

nature, there is no ground for boasting over each other.

Yet what would we do without good, rich humus? Life and growth depend on its nutrients. The truly humble person, therefore, will not waste time putting himself down, or consider herself mere dirt! There are others to be nourished, and God has placed in our nature the capacity to feed them, not just the doom of decay. The Christian who declines to be put in positions of service out of humility has a false sense of the term. Such an attitude, in fact, cuts one off from the grace Peter says God gives to the truly humble, equipping them to serve.

B. Trusting, 7

7 Casting all your care upon him; for he careth for you.

While this admonition certainly applies to all Christians, it is probably prompted by what Peter has just said about the grace God gives to disciples who qualify for leadership by their humility. They are not to be worried about their inadequacies, but buoyed up by the confidence that "underneath are the everlasting arms" (Deut. 33:27).

III. Help in Overcoming—8-11

A. Resisting, 8-9

8 Be sober, be vigilant; because your adversary the devil, as a roaring lion, walketh about, seeking whom he may devour:

9 Whom resist stedfast in the faith, knowing that the same afflictions are accomplished in your brethren that are in the world.

Referring to the grace God provides the humble leads Peter to turn to the grace needed by everyone who dares champion the cause of Christ in a hostile world. Alertness is required, since the voracious appetite of our great en- my,

Satan, is never sated.

The precarious position of these early Christians under the heel of Rome made it doubly necessary for them to resist the temptation to deny the faith. Scattered throughout the Mediterranean world (1:1), it would have been easy for Christ's followers to become discouraged, and to think they were being singled out for Rome's special wrath. Letters such as this one from the apostles and other Christian leaders tied them together, making them aware that their suffering was not unique.

B. Glorifying, 10-11

10 But the God of all grace, who hath called us unto his eternal glory by Christ Jesus, after that ye have suffered a while, make you perfect, stablish, strengthen, settle you.

11 To him be glory and dominion for ever and ever. Amen.

Anticipating the close of the body of his letter, Peter pronounces a remarkable benediction on the readers of his letter. He does not paint a sentimental "happy face" on their critical situation. He does say that it is a state to which God has called them, implying that "where God guides, God provides." The suffering to which they are called has a purpose—testifying that there is a cause worth suffering and even dying for. It is a temporary state, having the further purpose of "perfecting" them by making them strong (not implying that suffering would make them sinless). Remaining faithful under trials enables us eventually to share the eternal glory and reign of Christ Himself.

Evangelistic Emphasis

Right now I'll bet you can think about something that is worrying you. Go ahead, I am giving you permission to worry. You thought by reading your Sunday School lesson material it would take your mind off of your troubles. Now the author is asking you to worry. Go ahead, worry!

Sometimes I have even worried because I wasn't worried about anything. I think that is just the time in which you and I live. "If it is not one thing, it is a hundred more," we lament. Our day planners, beepers, car phones, fax machines and computers give us a new set of problems each day.

Simon Peter wrote, "Cast all of your anxiety on Him, for He cares for you" (1 Pet. 5:7). When we truly learn to lean on Him we find that indeed His care is more than sufficient for our every day needs. Discipleship is diminished when we spend valuable time worrying about all those things which will never happen anyway. When we worry we take our minds off of the Lord and His power to intervene. We find ourselves plotting and planning our own strategies and solutions. This not only saps our spiritual strength, it takes a toll on our bodies too. Worry is a sin because it is failure to acknowledge God's power in that area of our life.

Jesus has invited us to cast all of our cares on him. So whatever you are worried about, give it to Jesus right now. There don't you feel better?

Memory Selection

Likewise, ye younger, submit yourselves unto the elder. Yea, all of you be subject one to another, and be clothed with humility; for God resisteth the proud, and giveth grace to the humble.—*1 Peter 5:5*

"Pride goeth before a fall." Do you know why that is so? Peter has given us the answer. "God opposes the proud." (1 Pet. 5:5 NRSV) Pride is a sin because it fails to acknowledge God. Pride claims for itself the rights and abilities of sovereignty. It is the attitude that so many of us have used when we say, "Leave me alone, I can do this myself."

The book of Genesis begins with the Hebrew letter "Beth." It could be translated as "Together, in the beginning." The created order is a result of God's work. Subduing and being a steward of creation is our work. Together, the Creator and the created, watch over and care for the earth. The incident in the Garden of Eden was about pride. Adam and Eve wanted to be on equal footing with God. Their pride was to think they didn't have to obey God's right to say, No.

Together, with God we can live victorious lives. When we try to go it alone, we learn, "Pride goeth before a fall."

Weekday Problems

Joe was furious with his pastor. Joe was the president of the largest construction firm in the state. He had started out of college and now, in his mid-50s, was on top of the world. Joe attributed his success to hard work, clean living and the good Lord. He meant it all. Joe was also a faithful member of First Church. He served in every capacity in the church. Currently Joe was serving as the chairman of the Personnel Committee. It was in this capacity that he was having a heated discussion with his pastor.

Brother Briggs had been at First Church for less than two years. Most people seem to like his preaching. Everyone bragged about his visitation skills. He never missed a hospital visit. He never kept a shut-in waiting. Brother Briggs saw himself as the humble servant of First Church. What caused Joe's ire was the way that Brother Briggs attended to the temporal affairs of the church.

It seemed that Brother Briggs was not too interested in going to Finance Committee Meetings. He was not interested in dictating to the Worship Committee what kind of hymns would be sung each Sunday. He didn't demand his ideas be passed by the Building Committee. This made Joe mad.

Joe demanded a meeting with Brother Briggs and wanted to know why he wasn't acting more like a CEO than a pastor. "All that visiting is great, preacher," Joe said, "but if you don't keep up better with the finances, the church is going to shut down." You need to run this church like I run my business."

* How is Brother Briggs doing in being faithful to his call?

* Would you say Joe has a pride problem?

* Are decisions in your church made on the basis of what is best for the bottom line?

Lines on Leadership

People, like sheep, tend to follow a leader—occasionally in the right direction.— *Alexander Chase*

There is a kind of leader who out of the very certainty of his purpose, right or wrong, both assumes leadership and is conceded leadership. No quality so assures public success.—*John Kenneth Galbraith*

I never came to this through driving personal ambition. A combined opportunity and duty presented itself and I took it.—*Margaret Thatcher, on becoming leader of England's Conservative Party.*

I must follow them. I am their leader.—*Lord Longford*

The leader of genius must have the ability to make different opponents appear as if they belonged to one category.—*Adolf Hitler*

This Lesson in Your Life

In preaching I often tell my church, "My job is to get you to do your job." In previous lessons I reminded you that all Christians are called by virtue of their baptism into ministry. The clergy are shepherds of the sheep. Unfortunately we spend a great deal of time being veterinarians and officiating at fights between warring factions. We administer booster shots to those persons whose faith has lagged. We round up the sheep for corrective behavioral training. We seem, as ministers, to do precious little shepherding of the flock of God. A good class discussion might ensue on the role of the minister in the modern church.

Both church leaders and followers are called to be humble. This is not a trait widely spoken of in our day. Humility and meekness are not traits that get one ahead in the world. Yet, both are important in the life of the believer. Humility recognizes our place before the Father. When we understand that He is the Creator and we are the creatures, we stand in humbling awe. The humility Peter wrote about is not weakness that allows us to be stepped on by everyone. It is a quiet power that recognizes that God sustains our daily lives and is the source of our hopes and our dreams. If we humble ourselves in our daily living, God promises to exalt us.

Christians are called to cast our anxieties on God. This goes hand in hand with humility. As we acknowledge His Lordship, we trust in His supplying our needs. Only those with old fashioned pride believe they can deal with all the challenges life offers. Casting our cares on Him, is an affirmation of our inability to control our situation. We can neither control nor predict outcomes of situations. We have to trust God with today as well as with tomorrow. Only human pride says we can manipulate tomorrow.

Christians are challenged to be disciplined. This is another word that has faded from the church's vocabulary. Some persons in your congregation may actually remember a time when members were disciplined. Some persons were actually "churched" for going to the movies, dancing or playing cards. In today's world that would never happen. That is one form of the idea of discipline. The other is related to the word *discipleship*. Bible study on a daily basis won't happen without discipline. Daily prayer and meditation can't happen without discipline. Some people claim not to have the time to give themselves to these areas. I have suggested to them they discipline themselves to set the alarm clock thirty minutes earlier than usual.

A disciplined Christian walk is necessary because we are being pursued. The devil is on our heels looking for persons to victimize. If he can ruin your witness by having you slip, that is one less evangelist he has to worry about. If he can get you to quit the faith by bringing a trial in your life, that is one less Christian to be concerned about. He is prowling around looking for victims. We need to stay alert to his old tricks and his new tactics.

Christians are admonished to remember the sufferings of others in the world. When we remember our brothers and sisters in Christ through prayer and ministry we have little time for those diversions which the devil uses. We are all bound together across the globe through the blood of Jesus Christ. Some of our brothers and sisters are dying as a direct result of their faith. As we pray for their protection and for their lives, it helps us to remember what is really important.

Simon Peter mentions the call that we all share and promises us that Jesus Christ will give us the strength necessary to carry out our calling faithfully.

Seed Thoughts

1. How did Simon Peter identify himself in the first verse of this chapter?

He identified himself as a fellow elder and as a person who was an eyewitness to the suffering of Christ.

2. What were the duties that Simon Peter gave to the elders of the church?

They were to tend the flock of God. They were to exercise oversight, and do this willingly.

3. What attitude should an elder have in relationship to his calling and his flock?

He should minister not out of compulsion but willingly. He should not minister for financial gain but willingly.

4. How should the elder practice his faith and ministry before the flock?

He should not lord it over those in his charge, but be an example to the flock.

5. What was the advice that Simon Peter gave to the younger elders in the church?

They were to accept the authority of the other elders. They were to minister with a spirit of humility.

(Please turn page)

---

1. How did Simon Peter identify himself in the first verse of this chapter?

2. What were the duties that Simon Peter gave to the elders of the church?

3. What attitude should an elder have in relationship to his calling and his flock?

4. How should the elder practice his faith and ministry before the flock?

5. What advice did Simon Peter give to the younger elders in the church?

6. What three pieces of advice did Simon Peter give to the Christian in terms of practicing their faith?

7. Why were the Christians called to be humble, not to be anxious and to be disciplined?

8. What was the devil trying to do to the church in Simon Peter's day?

9. What did Simon Peter again emphasize about the nature of suffering in the life of a Christian?

10. What was the promise for those who remained faithful in the midst of suffering?

He identified himself as a fellow elder and as a person who was an eyewitness to the suffering of Christ.

They were to tend the flock of God. They were to exercise oversight, and do this willingly.

He should minister not out of compulsion but willingly. He should not minister for financial gain but willingly.

He should not lord it over those in his charge, but be an example to the flock.

They were to accept the authority of the other elders. They were to minister with a spirit of humility.

They were to humble themselves. They were to cast their anxieties on Jesus. They were to practice discipline.

They were to practice these things so they would be prepared to resist the devil.

He was looking for someone to devour. He was doing this by bringing suffering into the lives of the Christians.

This suffering will last only for a short time. This has been a theme throughout these lessons from 1 Peter.

God will Himself restore, support, strengthen and establish them.

6. What three pieces of advice did Simon Peter give to the Christian in terms of practicing their faith?

They were to humble themselves. They were to cast their anxieties on Jesus. They were to practice discipline.

7. Why were the Christians called to be humble, not to be anxious and to be disciplined?

They were to practice these things so they would be prepared to resist the devil.

8. What was the devil trying to do to the church in Simon Peter's day?

He was looking for someone to devour. He was doing this by bringing suffering into the lives of the Christians.

9. What did Simon Peter again emphasize about the nature of suffering in the life of a Christian?

This suffering will last only for a short time. This has been a theme throughout these lessons from 1 Peter.

10. What was the promise for those who remained faithful in the midst of suffering?

God will Himself restore, support, strengthen and establish them.

Confirming Our Calling

2 Peter 1:3-15

3 According as his divine power hath given unto us all things that pertain unto life and godliness, through the knowledge of him that hath called us to glory and virtue.

4 Whereby are given unto us exceeding great and precious promises: that by these ye might be partakers of the divine nature, having escaped the corruption that is in the world through lust.

5 And beside this, giving all diligence, add to your faith virtue; and to virtue knowledge;

6 And to knowledge temperance; and to temperance patience; and to patience godliness;

7 And to godliness brotherly kindness; and to brotherly kindness charity.

8 For if these things be in you, and abound, they make you that ye shall neither be barren nor unfruitful in the knowledge of our Lord Jesus Christ.

9 But he that lacketh these things is blind, and cannot see afar off, and hath forgotten that he was purged from his old sins.

10 Wherefore the rather, brethren, give diligence to make your calling and election sure: for it ye do these things, ye shall never fall:

11 For so an entrance shall be ministered unto you abundantly into the everlasting kingdom of our Lord and Saviour Jesus Christ.

12 Wherefore I will not be negligent to put you always in remembrance of these things, through ye know them, and be established in the present truth.

13 Yea, I think it meet, as long as I am in this tabernacle, to stir you up by putting you in remembrance;

14 Knowing that shortly I must put off this my tabernacle, even as our Lord Jesus Christ hath shewed me.

15 Moreover I will endeavour that ye may be able after my decease to have these things always in remembrance.

Memory Selection
2 Peter 1:10

Devotional Reading
2 Peter 1:16-21

Background Scripture
2 Peter 1

Printed Scripture
2 Peter 1:3-15

Teacher's Target

Lesson purpose: *To elaborate on Peter's recipe for spiritual growth toward maturity, to confirm our election in Christ.*

A favorite story concerns the little boy who came crying from his bedroom late one night, having fallen out of bed. When his parents consoled him and asked what happened, the lad replied, "I stayed too close to where I got in."

Likewise, many Christians stay too close to their point of entry into the Christian walk. Failing to add the Christian graces and to grow spiritually, they miss out on many of the joys of being a child of God.

In this lesson, Peter affirms that fruit-bearing and confidence in our salvation are some of these joys. Invite your class to experience the full benefits of salvation by growing beyond the place "where they got in."

Lesson Introduction

The apostle Peter's "second epistle" (3:1) was probably written to the same audience as 1 Peter, about A.D. 66. Although it pronounces severe judgment on the disobedient, it also offers positive encouragement for living the Christian life.

The present passage contains a list of ideal traits and qualities necessary for such a life. It is similar to Paul's "fruits of the spirit" in Galatians 5:22-23. The Greeks also wrote about such virtues as "charms that eagle-plume men's souls." The Christian "charms" or graces given here, however, are attainable not through noble striving, as the Greeks taught, but through the grace of Christ.

In fact, the virtues Peter lists are none other than the characteristics of Christ. We do not strive to decorate or "eagle-plume" our souls so much as simply to follow the pattern set by Jesus. We do not achieve these virtues out of our own virtue, but out of His indwelling Spirit and bountiful grace.

Teaching Outline	Daily Bible Readings

I. The Summons to Virtue—3-7
  A. The sufficiency of Him who calls, 3-4
  B. The Christian graces, 5-7
II. The Serious Consequences —8-11
  A. Fruitfulness and sight, 8-9
  B. Confirmation and certainty, 10-11
III. The Stirring of the Memory —12-15
	Mon. Support Your Faith with Goodness
	  2 Peter 1:1-11
	Tue. Make the Good Confession
	  1 Timothy 6:12-16
	Wed. Transformed by a Renewed Mind
	  Romans 12:1-8
	Thu. Living by Christ's Teaching
	  Matthew 5:1-12
	Fri. Share Bread with the Hungry
	  Isaiah 58:6-12
	Sat. Seek Peace and Pursue It
	  Psalm 34:4-14
	Sun. Doing the Works of God
	  John 14:8-17

VERSE BY VERSE

I. The Summons to Virtue—3-7
A. The sufficiency of Him who calls, 3-4

3 According as his divine power hath given unto us all things that pertain unto life and godliness, through the knowledge of him that hath called us to glory and virtue.

4 Whereby are given unto us exceeding great and precious promises: that by these ye might be partakers of the divine nature, having escaped the corruption that is in the world through lust.

Before listing the "Christian graces" or virtues, Peter asserts that grace, not works, is the foundation of the faith. He even makes the sweeping claim that the knowledge of Christ is all-sufficient for "godliness" or spiritual life. As important as it is to grow as a Christian and to add the qualities Peter will mention, this does not make us "more saved" than when we first came to Christ. It is the knowledge of Him, not the process of honing virtues, that makes us "sons"—part of the divine family with His nature within (see John 1:12-13). Still, the fact that He calls us to virtue (vs. 3b) makes growing in the virtues Peter will list a natural response of every believer.

B. The Christian graces, 5-7

5 And beside this, giving all diligence, add to your faith virtue; and to virtue knowledge;

6 And to knowledge temperance; and to temperance patience; and to patience godliness;

7 And to godliness brotherly kindness; and to brotherly kindness charity.

Christian growth is a process of addition. Some commentators try to show that the qualities the author lists are cumulative and progressive, with each new trait depending on the one preceding it. If this were true, it would be impossible to truly have love (KJV "charity,") until we are first kind (vs. 7b). The fact is, love is a trait underlying all these qualities; and it seems artificial to view the list as a series of stepping-stones culminating in love.

Peter mentions *faith* first because that is the way we became Christians; yet faith, like love, is a continuing necessity rather than a quality we obtain and then leave by the wayside. Faith or belief usually means "responsive trust" in the New Testament. It means "mental assent" only when describing vain or inadequate recognition of the mere fact that Jesus is who He claims to be— as in "the devils also believe (or "have faith"), and tremble" (Jas. 2:19).

Although *virtue* is a word commonly used to describe all these qualities, it can also mean "moral excellence" (or "goodness," NIV). New Christians are given the righteousness of Christ by faith (Rom. 4:5, etc.), but Peter suggests that Christian effort is required to become morally mature. This does not mean that we are saved by grace but kept saved by works. It was to saved people that the apostle Paul wrote, "it is God who works in you to will and to act according to his good purpose" (Philip. 2:13, NIV).

Knowledge also has a double meaning in the passage. Saving knowledge enabled us to escape the confines of lust and become Christians (vs. 3). Growth-knowledge is what we learn day by day through studying God's Word and through the rough and tumble of human experience. In our spiritual infancy we had limited knowledge of good and evil, but we are expected to sharpen our moral discernment through growth (see Heb. 5:14).

Temperance is commonly translated "self-control" (see the NIV). The original word contains a Greek term for power, authority, or control. It therefore refers to a person who can exert power over himself, as when Paul said he brought his bodily impulses into subjection (1 Cor. 9:27). This quality is also a matter of growth rather than being present full-grown at the moment of our spiritual birth.

Patience means literally "remaining under," and refers to the quality of "hanging in" under pressure. Ironically, some people grow less patient with time—as with their spouse and family—instead of developing more patience as they grow older.

Godliness means genuine piety or reverence toward God. Once more, this is a quality that is both a requirement for submitting our will to God in becoming a Christian (vs. 3), and a matter of long-term growth. The ways in which this reverential attitude is expressed may vary from culture to culture. We do not serve the Cause well, therefore, when we judge other Christians by our own external standards of piety.

To godliness we are to add *brotherly kindness* (lit. *philadelphia*, as in "the city of brother love"). This virtue is both vital for internal harmony among Christians, and as a factor in evangelism. A watching world might be won by noting Christians' love for other members of "the family."

This trait leads naturally to the quality of another form of *love—agape*, the capstone of all Christian virtues. This is the kind of love that seeks the good of the other, as distinguished from mere eros, attraction because of self-interest; philia, the attraction between friends; and storge, love for relatives. Agape is the kind of love God extended to us, even when we were unlovable (John 3:16; Rom. 5:8).

II. The Serious Consequences—8-11

A. Fruitfulness and sight, 8-9

8 For if these things be in you, and abound, they make you that ye shall neither be barren nor unfruitful in the knowledge of our Lord Jesus Christ.

9 But he that lacketh these things is blind, and cannot see afar off, and hath forgotten that he was purged from his old sins.

Although Peter has emphasized that salvation is distinct from Christian growth, he also affirms its urgency. People who do not add the Christian graces to their lives are barren of fruit. They forfeit opportunities to bear witness to others who are observing the way they live.

Failure to grow spiritually also blocks our vision of where we are going, causing us to settle for yesterday's standards when we should be stretching toward new areas of service (see Heb. 5:12-13). Finally, failure to add these graces is a sign that we have forgotten the alternative to living in the freedom bought by Christ—living in our former prison of sin.

B. Confirmation and certainty, 10-11

10 Wherefore the rather, brethren, give diligence to make your calling and election sure: for it ye do these things, ye shall never fall:

11 For so an entrance shall be ministered unto you abundantly into the everlasting kingdom of our Lord and Saviour Jesus Christ.

Christian growth, Peter says, confirms the fact that we have been called or "elected" to be a part of God's family. Just as we know that something is wrong with a child who does not develop normally in body or mind, so Christians who do not mature spiritually give no testimony to the fact that they were born into God's family, and no signal that they are bound for heaven.

III. The Stirring of the Memory—12-15

12 Wherefore I will not be negligent to put you always in remembrance of these things, through ye know them, and be established in the present truth.

13 Yea, I think it meet, as long as I am in this tabernacle, to stir you up by putting you in remembrance;

14 Knowing that shortly I must put off this my tabernacle, even as our Lord Jesus Christ hath shewed me.

15 Moreover I will endeavour that ye may be able after my decease to have these things always in remembrance.

The Greek philosopher Plato believed that learning is a process that taps into what we already know subconsciously. Likewise, Peter knows that anyone who becomes a child of God instinctively knows that he is to grow. Yet he also knows that we need this instinct "stirred up." As long as he is numbered among the living, or dwells in the tabernacle or tent of his flesh, he will dedicate himself to "pasturing" the flock (5:1) by reminding us of the urgency of adding the Christian graces. Indeed, our very study of this passage testifies to the fact that Peter left a living legacy after his "decease" (in Grk., his *"exodus"* from this life).

215

Evangelistic Emphasis

If you have rented an apartment recently you know about the disappearing deposit you have to pay. It is called a "security deposit" or a "maintenance deposit." There is fine print in both that gives the landlord power to keep part of your deposit for almost any reason. I have often wondered why insurance companies make you pay twenty percent of every medical claim. By the same logic you and I should only be paying eighty percent of our premium. Have you also noticed organizations that claim to be "full service" are anything but.

Simon Peter in writing to the early Christians said, "His divine power has given us everything we need for life and godliness . . ." (2 Pet. 1:3). Unlike renters, car dealers or even our insurance people, there is no fine print allowing God to "hold back a portion." In His abundant mercy He has provided everything we need to have a good, godly life.

Think about all the blessings in your life. Thank God for your home and family. Thank Him for your education and career. Thank Him for your church and pastor. Most of all thank Him that He gave you everything you needed to get through life to this point.

The great promise of our faith is that as He has provided for us today, He will take care of us tomorrow. That was the hope that allowed the early church to endure the persecutions of the Roman government. It was their unswerving confidence in God's provision that eventually allowed them to overcome the Roman Empire.

If God could do that, imagine what He can do in your life. The possibilities themselves are good news.

Memory Selection

Wherefore the rather, brethren, give diligence to make your calling and election sure; for if ye do these things, ye shall never fall.— *2 Peter 1:10*

Faithful discipleship means never looking over your shoulder to see who might be gaining on you. When we try to cut corners, personally and spiritually, we have this sense that the next phone call will reveal our foible. So we live always looking over our shoulder and covering our tracks. A much simpler way to live is faithfully.

All kinds of things can happen if you are moving forward while looking backward. You have had the experience merging on an interstate and having the car merging in front of you stop, haven't you? Or you have run over someone in a hall because you were looking backward toward someone.

Sin causes us to look backwards. We can't walk faithfully looking behind us. It is too easy to stumble that way. If we are looking to God, confirming our call and election, we keep our eyes on our spiritual goal.

When we walk in that attitude there will be no stumbling.

Weekday Problems

How many obituaries have you read that contained the phrase "an active member of the church"? I have often wondered if there is another kind of church member. Honestly, we know that there are. There are members of your church who are "ineffective and unfruitful." They occupy a pew on Sunday morning. They might come to a special service if the choir is singing. They give a fraction of a percentage of their incomes to God's work. Why is it that nothing is done for them or about them?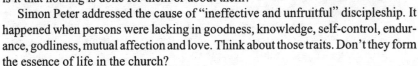

Simon Peter addressed the cause of "ineffective and unfruitful" discipleship. It happened when persons were lacking in goodness, knowledge, self-control, endurance, godliness, mutual affection and love. Think about those traits. Don't they form the essence of life in the church?

We are supposed to be good. Our Bible reading, Sunday School attendance, Bible study participation and sermon hearing should lead to some knowledge. As we understand what God wants us to do, we can practice self-control. That self-control allows us to endure life's hard times. When we do that, and see others doing it, we develop mutual affection and love. These are the basic ideas behind faithful discipleship. These are the tangibles that bear witness to what is happening, or not happening in a person's soul.

* How are you ministering to the marginally active members of your church?

* Have you always been dedicated in your discipleship?

Excuses, Excuses...

The excuses some Christians give for failing to grow are like these comments motorists wrote on their accident claim forms, as recorded by a Toronto newspaper.

"I misjudged a lady crossing the street."

"I thought my window was down, but found it was up when I put my hand through it."

"My car was stolen, and I sent up a human cry but it has not been recovered."

"A pedestrian hit me and went under my car."

"The guy was all over the road. I had to swerve a number of times before I hit him."

"I had been driving my car for 40 years when I fell asleep at the wheel and had an accident."

"I was having rear-end trouble when my universal joint gave way, causing me to have an accident."

217

This Lesson in Your Life

Peter teaches that "participating in the divine nature is contingent upon behavior. Consider those traits that support the life of faith.

Goodness is the first support of faith. Good people do the right things for the right reasons. They are persons who give their word and keep their word. They don't have to talk about honesty, integrity or decency because they live those characteristics all the time. Good people don't even have to talk about their goodness because it can readily be experience by all those who come into contact with this person. The King James Version calls this trait virtue.

Knowledge is the second support of faith. Each of these traits appears to be built on the previous one. Knowledge implies head and heart. The word used in the Bible means "head knowledge" as well as experience. I know that when my spiritual life seems to be stagnant it is time to go on a personal spiritual retreat. I know this because I have experienced this. You know that if you speed, you might get a ticket. Some of you even know that because you have experienced that. Knowledge of Jesus Christ comes not from intellectual inquiry, but from a personal relationship. People know Jesus because they have spent time with Him. This experiential knowledge comes through prayer, Bible study and living as faithful disciples. The knowledge of our church doctrines, statements of faith and a working knowledge of the Bible are underpinnings that keep our faith strong.

Because we have knowledge we can practice **self-control.** One of my teenage daughter's favorite tricks is to claim ignorance of the parental law. When she has done something wrong, she'll say, "I didn't know I wasn't suppose to do that." In some ways she is correct. When we know what is pleasing to God, we do those things. When we have the knowledge of what is to be avoided, we stay away from those behaviors. Self-control involves an understanding of the consequences of our actions. The Bible is plain when it speaks on the consequences of sin. It is equally bold about listing the blessings of faithful discipleship.

Self control brings about **endurance.** I have often said that endurance is self-control practiced for a long time. The word is the picture of a soldier in battle. This soldier is standing at the point of the battle. He is engaged in the fiercest combat. He is standing and fighting with no end in sight. That is the image the Greek word for endurance evokes. It is the person who never gives up. It is the person who practices integrity and self-control no matter the consequences.

Godliness is the product of endurance. Our God's love for us will endure to the end. Some persons feel it is presumptuous to talk about godliness. After all, isn't it arrogant to say we want to be like God? The whole message of the New Testament is that we are to become Christ-like. We are to be imitators of Jesus.

Godliness is a characteristic that produces mutual affection. If "God is love" then we are more like God when we are loving one another than at any other time.

The mutual affection brings about **love.** The essence of our lives as children of God is to love. We love God. We love each other. Hopefully, we arrive at the point where we love ourselves properly. The world is looking for love. The church has the greatest word of love ever spoken. That word of love came in the life and ministry of Jesus Christ. His act of love on Calvary brought us salvation. He still reaches out to all the world in love.

If we have these characteristics the world will want to share our "secret." That secret is Jesus the Lord.

Seed Thoughts

1. What was the result of God's divine power being shared with the Christians?

They have been given everything needed for life and for godliness.

2. How are God's divine power and His gifts of supply shared with the Christians?

"Through the knowledge of him who called us by his own glory and goodness." That person is Jesus.

3. What were the promises that God would fulfill in the Christians?

That through God's goodness they would escape the corruption that is in the world.

4. What is the corrupting power in the world and how can the Christians avoid this power?

The corrupting power in the world is lust. Christians overcome this power by participating in the divine nature.

5. With what did Simon Peter wish the Christians to support their faith?

Their faith was supported by goodness, knowledge, self-control, endurance, godliness, mutual affection and love.

(Please turn page)

1. What was the result of God's divine power being shared with the Christians?

2. How are God's divine power and His gifts of supply shared with the Christians?

3. What were the promises that God would fulfill in the Christians?

4. What is the corrupting power in the world and how can the Christians avoid this power?

5. With what did Simon Peter wish the Christians to support their faith?

6. What was the result of having these traits in a life?

7. How could the Christians avoid stumbling in their walk?

8. What was the reward of walking faithfully?

9. What did Simon Peter promise these Christians he would do for them?

10. What did Simon Peter reveal about what was going to happen to him?

They have been given everything needed for life and for godliness.

"Through the knowledge of him who called us by his own glory and goodness." That person is Jesus.

That through God's goodness they would escape the corruption that is in the world.

The corrupting power in the world is lust. Christians overcome this power by participating in the divine nature.

Their faith was supported by goodness, knowledge, self-control, endurance, godliness, mutual affection and love.
They kept the Christians from becoming ineffective and unfruitful.

If they were eager to confirm their call and election they would never stumble.

The Christian would gain entry into God's eternal kingdom and be richly provided for.

He was going to keep reminding them of the things he had been writing about to this point.

Peter had been shown by the Lord that his death would soon take place.

6. What was the result of having these traits in a life?

They kept the Christians from becoming ineffective and unfruitful.

7. How could the Christians avoid stumbling in their walk?

If they were eager to confirm their call and election they would never stumble.

8. What was the reward of walking faithfully?

The Christian would gain entry into God's eternal kingdom and be richly provided for.

9. What did Simon Peter promise these Christians he would do for them?

He was going to keep reminding them of the things he had been writing about to this point.

10. What did Simon Peter reveal about what was going to happen to him?

Peter had been shown by the Lord that his death would soon take place.

Rejecting False Teaching

2 Peter 2:1-10, 17-19

1 But there were false prophets also among the people, even as there shall be false teachers among you, who privily shall bring in damnable heresies, even denying the Lord that bought them, and bring upon themselves swift destruction.

2 And many shall follow their pernicious ways; by reason of whom the way of truth shall be evil spoken of.

3 And through covetousness shall they with feigned words make merchandise of you: whose judgment now of a long time lingereth not, and their damnation slumbereth not.

4 For if God spared not the angels that sinned, but cast them down to hell, and delivered them into chains of darkness, to be reserved unto judgment;

5 And spared not the old world, but saved Noah the eighth person, a preacher of righteousness, bringing in the flood upon the world of the ungodly;

6 And turning the cities of Sodom and Gomorrha into ashes condemned them with an overthrow, making them an ensample unto those that after should live ungodly;

7 And delivered just Lot, vexed with the filthy conversation of the wicked:

8 (For that righteous man dwelling among them, in seeing and hearing, vexed his righteous soul from day to day with their unlawful deeds;)

9 The Lord knoweth how to deliver the godly out of temptations, and to reserve the unjust unto the day of judgment to be punished:

10 But chiefly them that walk after the flesh in the lust of uncleanness, and despise government. Presumptuous are they, selfwilled, they are not afraid to speak evil of dignities.

17 These are wells without water, clouds that are carried with a tempest; to whom the mist of darkness is reserved for ever.

18 For when they speak great swelling words of vanity, they allure through the lusts of the flesh through much wantonness, those that were clean escaped from them who live in error.

19 While they promise them liberty, they themselves are the servants of corruption: for of whom a man is overcome, of the same is he brought in bondage.

February 8

Memory Selection
2 Peter 2:1

Devotional Reading
Ephesians 4:7-16

Background Scripture
2 Peter 2

Printed Scripture
2 Peter 2:1-10, 17-19

Teacher's Target

Lesson purpose: *To heighten our awareness of the dangers of false teaching by reflecting on Peter's warning to the early church.*

In modern times, terms such as "heretic" and "unorthodox" have largely lost the impact they had in the Bible. Now such words may even evoke sympathy, and bring people to the defense of "the minority view." It must be admitted that over-sensitivity to heresy has created far too many divisions in the history of the church; and that the practice of "branding" people as false teachers has in the past destroyed the reputation and influence of many genuine Christians.

To appreciate Peter's teaching in this passage we must transport ourselves back to the time when the infant church was perched precariously on the brink of success or failure. False teaching then could destroy the Cause for which Jesus died. This lesson will endeavor to show the nature of that teaching and to show that it is still worth watching for today.

Lesson Introduction

Peter pulls no punches in denouncing heretics in this lesson. Who were these false teachers, and what was the nature of their doctrine? In answering this question, we should recall that Christian doctrine was a "work in progress" when Peter wrote. The fine points of Christian doctrine that would later be debated by Church councils, and sometimes used to brand heretics, were still being formed at this time. They were being revealed "here a little, there a little" through the writings of the authors of our New Testament.

We should recognize, therefore, that the false teachers referred to in this letter were denounced for the most basic heresy of all: denying that Jesus was the Christ (2:1). While the modern Church is called to be just as firm in resisting such error, the endless details of orthodoxy that commonly divide contemporary Christians are not at stake here.

Teaching Outline	Daily Bible Readings
	Mon. God Rescues the Godly *2 Peter 2:1-10a*
I. False Teachers Will Come—1	**Tue.** Teachers Gone Astray *2 Peter 2:10b-16*
II. Fiery Judgment Is Sure—2-10	**Wed.** Slaves of Corruption *2 Peter 2:17-22*
A. Inevitable damage, 2-3	
B. A history of judgment, 4-8	**Thu.** Grow Up in Christ *Ephesians 4:7-16*
C. Lessons learned, 9-10	**Fri.** See No One but Jesus *Matthew 17:1-8*
III. Foolish Beliefs Are Empty —17-19	**Sat.** Be Guileless in Evil *Romans 16:17-21*
A. Empty promises, 17-18	**Sun.** To Love and Obey Means Life *Deuteronomy 30:15-20*
B. The bondage of error, 19	

VERSE BY VERSE

I. False Teachers Will Come—1

1 But there were false prophets also among the people, even as there shall be false teachers among you, who privily shall bring in damnable heresies, even denying the Lord that bought them, and bring upon themselves swift destruction.

From Balaam in Numbers 22 throughout their history, the Israelites had been plagued with false prophets; and Peter predicts the Christian movement will also have to deal with them. The kjv word "privily" means secretly (NIV), indicating the common ploy of false teachers using deception to gain a foothold among the faithful (see Matt. 24:4-5).

The original meaning of "heresy" was "sect," indicating the divisive nature of false teachings. They are "damn- able" or destructive (the same word is used at the end of the verse) for at least three reasons: the prophets are false (Grk. *pseudo*), their teachings are sectarian or divisive, and they deny the authentic nature of Jesus, who redeemed them.

Apparently these false teachers were former Christians who fell away. Since their teaching is said specifically to deny the Lord, we may speculate that it denied the twofold nature of Jesus, which was affirmed as both "very God and very man" in the earliest orthodox creedal statements. Mentioning "the Lord who bought them" may also indicate that the false teaching challenged the "vicarious atonement" of Christ. Perhaps it was similar to humanistic views of Jesus in modern times that consider Him to have been only a man, and His death on the Cross only a murder instead of an act of atonement.

II. Fiery Judgment Is Sure—2-10

A. Inevitable damage, 2-3

2 And many shall follow their pernicious ways; by reason of whom the way of truth shall be evil spoken of.

3 And through covetousness shall they with feigned words make merchandise of you: whose judgment now of a long time lingereth not, and their damnation slumbereth not.

Another likely characteristic of the false teaching was that it led to sexual sin, since that is the implication of the word translated "pernicious" (NIV "shameful"). If Jesus was only a man, and not holy, why should His followers live a holy life? Given human nature, it isn't surprising that Peter predicts that the loose life-style the false prophets endorsed would have wide appeal.

Verse 3 hints that these false teachers had a monetary motive; apparently they were trying to worm their way into the Christian congregations to get positions as paid leaders. Their judgment, said to be "swift" in verse 1, "slumbereth not"—not meaning immediate but sudden and sure, at the day of judgment (vss. 4, 9).

B. A history of judgment, 4-8

4 For if God spared not the angels that sinned, but cast them down to hell, and delivered them into chains of darkness, to be reserved unto judgment;

5 And spared not the old world, but saved Noah the eighth person, a

preacher of righteousness, bringing in the **flood** upon the **world of the** ungodly;

6 And turning the cities of Sodom and Gomorrha into ashes condemned them with an overthrow, making them an ensample unto those that after should live ungodly;

7 And delivered just Lot, vexed with the filthy conversation of the wicked:

8 (For that righteous man dwelling among them, in seeing and hearing, vexed his righteous soul from day to day with their unlawful deeds;)

Peter can confidently predict God's condemnation of the false teachers because He knows His Old Testament. In rapid-fire succession he calls up three examples designed to dispel notions that God is a "softie" who is so tolerant He would never bring anyone into condemnation.

The sins of the people in Noah's day are clearly documented (Gen. 6:5-8), as are those of Sodom and Gomorrha (Gen. 19:1-29). As for the disobedient angels and their fate, Scripture provides only hints (see Jude 6; Gen. 6:2). Peter may be citing a Jewish tradition that elaborated on these biblical clues. Severe though God's judgments can be, we know they are righteous. The best way to take these threats is not to question how a loving God can take such action but to be grateful that a loving God would warn us about self-destructive ways.

C. Lessons learned, 9-10

9 The Lord knoweth how to deliver the godly out of temptations, and to reserve the unjust unto the day of judgment to be punished:

10 But chiefly them that walk after the flesh in the lust of uncleanness, and despise government. Presump- tuous are they, selfwilled, they are not afraid to speak evil of dignities.

The God of judgment is no more real than the God of grace; He redeems those who love Him as certainly as He punishes those who reject Him. The nature of the latter group that Peter has in mind is again related to sexual immo- rality in verse 10a.

Verse 10b emphasizes again the divi- sive nature of false doctrine. The pseudo-prophets were ignoring God's plan for the governance of His people by flaunting "government" (lit. "lord- ship")—not the local civic authorities but church leaders—elders, bishops, or pastors (1 Pet. 5:1-2). God has pro- vided such leaders to watch over the church's teaching for the benefit of the members (Heb. 13:7, 17); but this spiri- tual discipline was being ignored by the false teachers Peter confronts.

These "heretics" were not even afraid to blaspheme "dignities." The original word here meant "glory," then "glori- fied beings," as the reference to angels in verse 11 indicates. Angels were con- sidered to have been the administrators of the Law of Moses (Gal. 3:19). Further- more, they are a part of the ministry God ordained to care for believers (Heb. 1:7, 13-14). The false prophets therefore had the audacity to flaunt their evil doc- trines in the face of these "celestial beings" (NIV).

III. Foolish Beliefs Are Empty—17-19
    A. Empty promises, 17-18

17 These are wells without water, clouds that are carried with a tempest; to whom the mist of darkness is re- served for ever.

18 For when they speak great swelling words of vanity, they al- lure through the lusts of the flesh

224

through much wantonness, those that were clean escaped from them who live in error.

These verses give helpful insight into the nature of false doctrine and those who teach it. Peter chooses vivid metaphors to say first that they promise more than they can deliver. They are like a cistern that looms up before a person crossing a dry and waterless desert, but when the well-cover is removed it turns out to be dry. They are like clouds that form during a drought, promising rain, only to withhold their moisture and dissipate. The images are especially apt because of the sexual nature of the false teaching (vs. 18), as will become even more apparent in the next verse.

B. The bondage of error, 19

19 While they promise them liberty, they themselves are the servants of corruption: for of whom a man is overcome, of the same is he brought in bondage.

Permission to satisfy sexual urges— "the lusts of the flesh" (vs. 18)—seems to be a liberating experience. Pornography is a good example. Some Chris-tians feel at liberty to purchase and fantasize over smut "as long as it doesn't hurt anybody." At first it seems to provide a harmless outlet. Eventually, however, its addictive power asserts itself. Higher and higher "doses" in the form of more and more lurid visual experiences are required to deliver the supposed satisfaction. More than one sex criminal has testified that rape and murder began with "harmless" pornography. Prison provides plenty of time to reflect on whether the freedom to peruse pornography is liberty or enslavement.

AIDS and sexually transmitted diseases are equally instructive. Of course we must recognize that some have inherited the disorder, and others contracted it from blood transfusions. Yet the origin of these blights make it obvious that they have placed in bondage many people who thought that modern timmes had "liberated" them to be promiscuous. False teaching and ungodly living turn out to bring the wrath and judgment Peter describes in this lesson on ourselves, instead of being arbitrary punishment visited on us by an angry God.

225

Evangelistic Emphasis

The greatest number of missionaries in the world are sent to what country? Did you know the answer to that question is the United States of America. In an ironic twist the third world countries are sending missionaries to America at an astounding rate. The reason is simple. There are well over one hundred and seventy-five million Americans who claim no affiliation with any church.

Even more disquieting are the numbers that George Barna is reporting in his book on evangelism. George Barna is to the American church what George Gallup is to American politics. Barna reports that half of all people going to church today have not had a personal experience with Jesus Christ.

There is little wonder that Jesus told us the harvest is plentiful. So many people are thirsting for God's Word. They want to hear messages from the pulpit that are Biblically based. They want Sunday School teachers who teach the word, not the latest pop psychology. These same people are not finding God in the church.

Ironically in an effort to reach more people, we have watered down the truth. It is not that the church is guilty of heresy. We are more guilty of Biblical and theological apathy.

The harvest is plentiful. The call to the church is to train up workers willing to work those fields.

Memory Selection

But there were false prophets also among the people, even as there shall be false teachers among you, who privily shall bring in damnable heresies, even denying the Lord that bought them and bring upon themselves swift destruction.— *2 Peter 2:1*

I once heard a preacher claim he had a new translation for a fairly old Greek verb. His new translation changed completely the meaning of this certain passage of Scripture. Being a bit of a ministerial skeptic, I looked up this Greek verb. Sure enough, one could use the fourth meaning of the verb and translate the way this preacher did. It was not, however, good Greek, good exegesis or good homiletics. But this preacher thrived on being on the cutting edge and finding something new in the Bible.

When you hear a preacher talk about a new revelation that no other preacher has ever had, run. If you stay around I guarantee that preacher will lead you astray. It happens almost every Sunday. The preachers are guilty and church members are culpable. We can't be seduced by false teachers if we know the truth.

That's why preachers take days out of their schedules to write for you. So that you might know the truth and be wise to those who would lead you astray.

Weekday Problems

Charlie was one of the characters in Blue Bayou Church. He had been a member of the church for as long as the longest memory could remember. Charlie was a character because he was strange. He claimed that he had seen Big Foot. He claimed that angels inhabited his garden. He was once known to have covered his entire kitchen floor with flour to capture "pixie footprints." He claimed the pixies were stealing the food from his refrigerator.

Charlie was in Blue Bayou Church each and every Sunday. Each and every Sunday he would capture the preacher for a theological conversation. Charlie didn't believe that any minister was as good as Rev. Swindle. Charlie asked every minister why he didn't do the things that Rev. Swindle did, and why he didn't believe like Rev. Swindle did. Charlie even claimed that a former preacher left the church because he dared to preach a sermon about Rev. Swindle, and "God got him for it."

The current preacher at Blue Bayou tried to talk with Charlie about his faith, but Charlie never would talk about Jesus. His only topic of conversation was the Bible and Big Foot, angels and the devil. Charlie's proudest moment was when he wrestled personally with the Devil. At least, that was the claim he made.

Charlie finally got mad at something at Blue Bayou Church and left the preacher a note stating that the angels had told him to go join Rev. Swindle's church.

*   Are "characters" like Uncle Bubba harmless?
*   How would you present the gospel of Christ to this person?

Asking for It

Q: Where do armies go?
A: Up the sleevies of your jacket.

Q: What's a nun's favorite song?
A: "I Left My Heart with San Franciscans."

Q: Where do fleas go in winter?
A: Search me.

Q: What's the best way to get to the hospital?
A: Just stand there in the middle of the street.

Q: Where does a sick ship go?
A: To the doc.

Q: Where does a whale go when it needs a loan?
A: To a loan shark.

Q: Why do steel workers put in such long hours?
A: Because they find their work so riveting.

This Lesson in Your Life

We live in the most spiritual culture and at the most religious time in history. While book sales will rise about 6 percent a year, the sale of religious books will rise 25 percent a year. People are hungering for spiritual insight and depth. The problem with their hunger is that any spirituality seems to satisfy, at least for awhile. People are paying millions each year to have their palms read and their stars charted. They are seeking out mediums, gurus and spiritual guides in a quest for "the spiritual."

Along with this rush to the spiritual realm is the church's retreat from evangelism. It seems just as the world was looking for God, the church got tired of trying to convince the world it should be looking for God.

Right now in your church, you have persons who have been seduced by the world's spiritualities. They believe in many of the same things that you do. However, these persons have added some things to the mix. Many of them, influenced by Eastern mysticism, believe in reincarnation. Many of the people in your church do not believe in a place called hell. Never mind the fire and brimstone, they simply don't believe that a "loving God could send people to Hell." Many don't really believe in the resurrection of Jesus Christ. You ask them what they believe happened on that first Easter and they will tell you that Jesus appeared to those disciples "spiritually."

When pressed about their beliefs on God, people have many different pictures. Some believe He is non-existent. Others see Him.God as an absentee landlord. Some believe He created everything but has been off doing whatever God does ever since. Still others believe that God is their cosmic errand boy ready at a moment's notice to understand their need and give them what they wish.

Before we blame Eastern mysticism for all the heresy in the church, we must look at ourselves. Someone should have yanked the plug on many of the television evangelists years ago. Now, don't get me wrong. I believe that television is a vehicle for carrying the gospel. I also believe that it is best done as local churches broadcast their services of worship. There is nothing quite like a live congregation of faith to keep a minister honest. The prosperity gospel was brought to us via television. The prosperity gospel says if you want to make a certain amount of money, give God one tenth of what you want to make and God will provide the other 90 percent. It is reversing the flow on tithing. The theology of suffering has been skewed by faith healers. They have alternatively told devout Christians they were sick because they either were "letting the devil get the victory" or "they lacked faith." I wonder what these faith healers would have said about Paul's thorn in the flesh?

It is time for some old-time religion Actually it is time to return to the fundamentals of our faith. It is time to worry less about entertaining congregations and begin teaching them the word of truth. It is time to make the Sunday School hour an emphasis in the life of a church. If you go to class this week, you'll get about 50 percent more time to share the Word than the preacher will get.

Simon Peter warned all of us that there are false teachers in our midst. It is time for the church to wake up. The fox has been in the henhouse too long.

Seed Thoughts

1. What was the warning about false prophets?

They afflicted the people before. They were among the people at that time.

2. What kind of damage did false prophets do to the church?

They secretly brought destructive opinions. They would even deny the deity of the Master.

3. In the end, what would happen to false prophets and those who followed them?

These groups would bring swift destruction on themselves.

4. What were the other dangers of being involved with false prophets?

Many would follow their licentious ways. They would cause the way of truth to be maligned. In their greed they would exploit persons.

5. Why haven't the false prophets and teachers been stopped before?

Peter promised the Christians that their destruction had not been idle, or "asleep."

1. What was the warning about false prophets?

2. What kind of damage did false prophets do to the church?

3. In the end, what would happen to false prophets and those who followed them?

4. What were the other dangers of being involved with false prophets?

5. Why haven't the false prophets and teachers been stopped before?

6. Who were the first group of false teachers and what happened to them?

7. Why was Noah saved through the flood according to this passage?

8. What towns were destroyed because of their ungodly behavior?

9. Why was Lot saved? What had happened to his faith because he lived in Sodom?

10. If the Lord punished evil in the Old Testament, what is the inference about God's abilities today?

(Please turn page)

They afflicted the people before. They were among the people at that time.

They secretly brought destructive opinions. They would even deny the deity of the Master.

These groups would bring swift destruction on themselves.

Many would follow their licentious ways. They would cause the way of truth to be maligned. In their greed they would exploit persons.

Peter promised the Christians that their destruction had not been idle, or "asleep."

The first group were the angels who sinned. God cast them into hell.

Noah was a herald of righteousness in the midst of an evil world.

Sodom and Gomorrah were turned to ashes and made an example of what is coming to the ungodly.

Lot was saved because he was righteous. Living in Sodom tormented his soul.

God knows how to rescue the righteous. He also knows how to keep the unrighteous under punishment until Judgment Day.

6. Who were the first group of false teachers and what happened to them?

The first group were the angels who sinned. God cast them into hell.

7. Why was Noah saved through the flood according to this passage?

Noah was a herald of righteousness in the midst of an evil world.

8. What towns were destroyed because of their ungodly behavior?

Sodom and Gomorrah were turned to ashes and made an example of what is coming to the ungodly.

9. Why was Lot saved? What had happened to his faith because he lived in Sodom?

Lot was saved because he was righteous. Living in Sodom tormented his soul.

10. If the Lord punished all of the evil in the Old Testament what is the inference about God's abilities today?

God knows how to rescue the righteous. He also knows how to keep the unrighteous under punishment until Judgment Day.

230

Lesson 11

Believing in the Promise

---

2 Peter 3:1-13

1 This second epistle, beloved, I now write unto you; in both which I stir up your pure minds by way of remembrance:

2 That ye may be mindful of the words which were spoken before by the holy prophets, and of the commandment of us the apostles of the Lord and Saviour:

3 Knowing this first, that there shall come in the last days scoffers, walking after their own lusts,

4 And saying, Where is the promise of his coming? For since the fathers fell asleep, all things continue as they were from the beginning of the creation.

5 For this they willingly are ignorant of, that by the word of God the heavens were of old, and the earth standing out of the water and in the water:

6 Whereby the world that then was, being overflowed with water, perished:

7 But the heavens and the earth, which are now, by the same word are kept in store, reserved unto fire against the day of judgment and perdition of ungodly men.

8 But, beloved, be not ignorant of this one thing, that one day is with the Lord as a thousand years, and a thousand years as one day.

9 The Lord is not slack concerning his promise, as some men count slackness; but is longsuffering to us-ward, not willing that any should perish, but that all should come to repentance.

10 But the day of the Lord will come as a thief in the night; in the which the heavens shall pass away with a great noise, and the elements shall melt with fervent heat, the earth also and the works that are therein shall be burned up.

11 Seeing then that all these things shall be dissolved, what manner of persons ought ye to be in all holy conversation and godliness,

12 Looking for and hasting unto the coming of the day of God, wherein the heavens being on fire shall be dissolved, and the elements shall melt with fervent heat?

13 Nevertheless we, according to his promise, look for new heavens and a new earth, wherein dwelleth righteousness.

Memory Selection
2 Peter 3:13

Devotional Reading
Jeremiah 17:5-10

Background Scripture
2 Peter 3

Printed Scripture
2 Peter 3:1-13

231

Teacher's Target

Lesson purpose: *To learn the proper attitude toward living in the present in light of the certainty of God's promised Day of Judgment in the future.*

Few topics provoke more arguments among believers than the doctrine of the End-times. There are pre-millenialists, post-millenialists, a-millenialists—and the poor man who gave up trying to sort it all out and said he was a *pan*-millenialist, meaning "It'll all pan out in the end."

Hopefully your class won't get mired in such arguments. Try to focus instead on two main points in Peter's teaching: (1) The *fact* of a Day of Judgment; and (2) How we should live today in the light of this fact.

Interpreters differ on the timing of the events of the Last Days. The words of the old song, however, bear the central message: "There's a Great Day Coming!"

Lesson Introduction

This section of 2 Peter is a part of the biblical teaching on "the last things"—often called "eschatology" after the Greek word *eschatos* for "last" (as in vs. 3). While the present passage focuses on the *very* last day, other Bible teaching indicates that this will be the final event of a whole series of occurences in "the last *days*"—in which we now live.

This period was introduced by the coming of John the Baptist, the new "Elijah" (Mal. 4:5-6; Matt. 11:11-14). It was inaugurated with the pouring out of the Holy Spirit and the proclamation of the gospel (Joel 2:28; Acts 2:16ff.). Great tribulation is predicted toward the end of this period (Mark, 13:24-25), culminating with the Second Coming (vs. 26), the resurrection of the dead (1 Cor. 15:51-52), and, from the present passage, the Last Judgment, the destruction of the earth, and the establishment of new heavens and the new earth; to be followed by the banishment of the wicked and the ushering of the faithful into eternal rest.

Teaching Outline	Daily Bible Readings	
I. Remembering the Past—1-2	**Mon.**	The Day of the Lord Will Come *2 Peter 3:1-10*
II. Preparing for the Future—3-7	**Tue.**	Where Righteousness Is at Home *2 Peter 3:11-18*
A. The scorn of scoffers, 3-4	**Wed.**	Heaven and Earth Created Anew *Isaiah 65:17-25*
B. The working of the Word, 5-7		
III. Appreciating God's Patience—8-9	**Thu.**	God to Live Among Mortals *Revelation 21:1-14*
IV. Looking for the Renewal—10-13	**Fri.**	Year of the Lord's Favor *Isaiah 61:1-8*
A. Being ready for the thief, 10		
B. Seizing the present, 11-12	**Sat.**	Wealth As an Obstacle *Luke 18:18-27*
C. Anticipating the end, 13	**Sun.**	Believe the Promise *Jeremiah 17:5-10*

VERSE BY VERSE

I. Remembering the Past—1-2

1 This second epistle, beloved, I now write unto you; in both which I stir up your pure minds by way of remembrance:

2 That ye may be mindful of the words which were spoken before by the holy prophets, and of the commandment of us the apostles of the Lord and Saviour:

When the biblical authors want to encourage God's people in hard times they recall "salvation history." Beginning with the exodus from Egypt they recount the story of prophets, judges, and kings who served as "saviors" or deliverers (see, for example, Ps. 136). Now Peter reminds us that there is also a biblical history of judgment. He bases his description of a future accounting and Day of judgment not on speculation but on what God has actually done in the past. Since those he addressed knew their Old Testaments, he has but to stir their memories to remind them of the seriousness of forsaking God.

Specifically, Peter points to prophets who predicted doom on the unrighteousness (see Hos. 4:1-5); then to apostolic predictions of judgment and the Day of the Lord (see 1 Thess. 5:1-3); and finally to such teaching from the lips of Jesus Himself (see Luke 21:34-36). It was important for Peter to compare his teaching on the End-time with previous Scripture to show that his teaching was neither novel nor false.

Because he knows of skeptics who doubt this teaching, he also marshals evidence from other sources in the next verses.

II. Preparing for the Future—3-7

A. The scorn of scoffers, 3-4

3 Knowing this first, that there shall come in the last days scoffers, walking after their own lusts,

4 And saying, Where is the promise of his coming? For since the fathers fell asleep, all things continue as they were from the beginning of the creation.

Although all parts of the gospel story have been attacked by scoffers, the teachings about the Day of Judgment are an easy target because they lie in the future. Doubts about the love of God can be dispelled by pointing to the historical Jesus. Questions about the resurrection also have a historical frame of reference—we can point to reliable sources who saw the empty tomb and the risen Lord.

Two parts of the biblical story, however, are less subject to historical verification: the creation of matter from non-matter, and events in the future. Creation occurred before time began, and the Second Coming will occur at the end of time. Although the entire story of salvation requires faith, these two elements of the story require a special measure of faith since they lie outside the framework of time and human observation. We need not be surprised, therefore, when scoffers make the rather foolish statement that "The end has not occurred before, so where is the promise of His coming?"

One answer to the question is, "He came once; why is it far-fetched to believe He will come again?"

In verse 3b, Peter introduces a *moral* factor in some unbelief. Some people do not *want* to believe in judgment to come because they do not want their lustful lives to be examined by the Righteous Judge.

B. The working of the Word, 5-7

5 For this they willingly are ignorant of, that by the word of God the heavens were of old, and the earth standing out of the water and in the water:

6 Whereby the world that then was, being overflowed with water, perished:

7 But the heavens and the earth, which are now, by the same word are kept in store, reserved unto fire against the day of judgment and perdition of ungodly men.

Some people may be persuaded to believe that the earth was created from non-matter by philosophical arguments, such as "Is it more reasonable to believe that matter created mind than that mind created matter? That's like believing a piano could create a person, instead of a person creating a piano!" The most powerful argument, however, is that *God said so in His Word.* That Word affirms the empty tomb; is it any harder to believe in creation from nothing?

Next, Peter argues that this same Word that describes the earth appearing from the waters (Gen. 1:2) also describes God's judgment in the days of Noah, when he consigned evil persons to the waters of the flood (Gen. 6)—again, just as God's Word promised. It is not far-fetched, therefore, to believe that the world is presently preserved from destruction by that same Word, and that the Word about future judgment is also believable. Once more, Peter is arguing from history, not just telling us how he *feels* about future judgment.

III. Appreciating God's Patience–8-9

8 But, beloved, be not ignorant of this one thing, that one day is with the Lord as a thousand years, and a thousand years as one day.

9 The Lord is not slack concerning his promise, as some men count slackness; but is longsuffering to us-ward, not willing that any should perish, but that all should come to repentance.

Now the author introduces another argument in support of the reality of future judgment: *God does not count time like people do.* Time is a property of creation; but God is above and beyond creation. Human days are the result of the earth's rotation on its axis, and years can be counted because of the earth's revolution around the sun. Since God is Spirit, and not subject to such geographical limitations, He is "timeless"—which is to say He is eternal instead of temporal. What is a mere day to Him?

The fact is, the very postponement of judgment that causes some people to scoff is a sign of God's grace: He is giving people time to repent of their sins. How ironic that the very person who scoffs at the idea of future judgment is scoffing also at the grace that he, of all people, so desperately needs. (See also Rom. 2:4.)

IV. Looking for the Renewal—10-13

A. Being ready for the thief, 10

10 But the day of the Lord will come as a thief in the night; in the which the heavens shall pass away with a great noise, and the elements shall melt with fervent heat, the earth also and the works that are therein shall be burned up.

The analogy of the end coming as a thief is designed to teach us to stay prepared—just as we might keep our doors locked since we have no idea when a thief might test them. Whenever that great Day occurs, Peter expects it to include a holocaust (see also vs. 12). The reassuring tone of verse 13, however, indicates that those who "keep their doors locked"—who live with the knowledge that judgment can occur at any moment—have nothing to fear.

B. Seizing the present, 11-12

11 Seeing then that all these things shall be dissolved, what manner of persons ought ye to be in all holy conversation and godliness,

12 Looking for and hasting unto the coming of the day of God, wherein the heavens being on fire shall be dissolved, and the elements shall melt with fervent heat?

We may think that Peter's question is simplistic. In light of the burning, fiery judgment that is to rain down on the unrighteous, does it not make sense to live right? The fact is, many of us live in a state of denial of things we know will occur. A man drinks excessively although a doctor tells him his liver is being eaten away. A woman continues to smoke after losing part of a lung to cancer caused by nicotine. Peter's question would knife through such denial: *ought not our manner of life* ("conversation") *reflect our knowledge of the certainty of a fiery end of the world?*

"Hasting" can mean "speeding" (as the NIV translates); but how can our hurrying on the End bring it sooner? It seems better to give it its other meaning: "be zealous" or "industrious."

C. Anticipating the end, 13

13 Nevertheless we, according to his promise, look for new heavens and a new earth, wherein dwelleth righteousness.

The passage closes with the reassuring note that those whose lives reflect the certainty of judgment need not live in fear, but with hope and anticipation. The flaming judgment pronounced on the unrighteous is balanced by the cre-ation of new heavens and a new earth, outfitted for just the kind of people whose love for righteousness on the old earth prompted them to invest in the new creation.

Evangelistic Emphasis

The great oxymoron of our society is found in the grocery store. The lane marked "express lane" is one of the great deceptions of the marketing industry. Have you noticed that persons in the "express lane" are usually still there after you have finished checking out a whole month's worth of groceries?

Airlines, rental car companies and hospitals have all discovered the popularity of "express service." However, the service expressed in "express service" is seldom fast. In our mania for hurry, we feel more efficient if we are standing in something marked "express."

Our frustration arises when we find out that express lines and lanes don't afford us any time savings. This same frustration is often translated into our spiritual lives. We pray for the help and blessing of God, and we want those things now. Simon Peter, who in his younger days lacked patience, encouraged the Christians in Asia Minor to be patient in waiting for God.

God is never late! He may not do things as we would have them scheduled but He is never late. We don't fully comprehend the plan that God is working in our lives. The good news is that God has not forsaken us or forgotten us. He is working things on His schedule for His glory. You know from remembering God's activities in your life in the past that this is so. It is also very good news.

Memory Selection

Nevertheless we, according to his promise, look for new heavens and a new earth, wherein dwelleth righteousness—*2 Peter 3:13*

The promise of God is that He will make all things new. Simon Peter recorded this promise as did the author of the Revelation. The promise itself is an extension of the new birth granted to all through Jesus Christ.

The promise of the new heaven and earth brings hope. Simon Peter was clear that only righteousness will exist in the new heaven and the new earth. To image that kind of relationship is to imagine the impossible. It is a world of "no more." In this place there will be no more pain, no more suffering, no more death and no more tears.

To give you an earthly picture of divine perfection, we will not lock a door in the new heaven and the new earth. We will not worry about being safe. We will not look with suspicion at our neighbor. We will not worry about who knows us and our deepest secrets. We will be in a place where all is well, and everything is good.

It is hard to imagine such a place, isn't it? This is the place that Jesus has gone to prepare for all who believe in Him and await His coming.

Weekday Problems

Missy had always been frustrated with her faith. She had grown up in First Church. She had never known a time when she was not actively involved in the life of the church. She had married young and raised two children. She and her husband Dale were happy in their marriage. Missy felt as though she were not spiritual enough.

So Missy tried every new thing that came along. She read all the pop spirituality gurus the week after they were on Oprah. She searched the book store looking for new books on religion, natural healing, spirituality and the Bible. She tried alternative means of meditation. She was involved in macrobiotic diets. She refused to eat sugar or consume caffeine.

The one thing that Missy would not do was to confide in the members of her church how she felt. In Sunday School, Missy always seemed to be asking strange questions or taking "weird" positions. She never pressed her point, but members of the class noticed that her positions were often "off the wall."

One Sunday she finally confessed to the class that she was thinking about leaving the church. She had been listening to another one of those gurus and had decided to join her movement. The class listened with rapt attention as Missy catalogued for them her frustration with her spiritual progress.

* Have you ever thought about leaving your church because of spiritual reasons?

* How do you respond to people who try "different" religious experiences in an attempt to connect with God?

As the End Approaches...

For when the One Great Scorer comes/To write against your name,/He marks—not that you won or lost—/but how you played the game. — *Football coach Grantland Rice*

Eternity is not something that begins after you are dead. It is going on all the time. We are in it now.—*Charlotte P. Gilman*

Hell is paved with good intentions, but heaven goes in for something more dependable. Solid gold.—*Joyce Cary*

Down the street his funeral goes,/As sobs and wails diminish./He died from drinking straight shellac,/But he had a lovely finish.—*Anonymous*

This Lesson in Your Life

Today's Scripture passage has several important issues. One is the reality of the end of time. Some persons take great delight in knowing the "signs of the times." Some preachers can describe the events leading up to the cataclysmic ending with such gory detail that your hair stands on end. They are in the genre of the old ghost story tellers around camp fires. It is not that they are not sincere. It is rather that they have not heeded the words of Jesus, who said, "Of that time, no one knows but the Father." The closer we move to the dawning of the 21st century the more of these gloom and doom predictions you will hear. Even if some of them come true, our faith is that our Lord will sustain us no matter what is transpiring in history. So as you hear these dire forecasts, don't worry because Jesus will sustain you. Don't purchase their books and tapes because you will have enough to worry about anyway.

The other issue in this passage deals with false teachers that will arise and lead persons astray. The church must make the true gospel of Jesus available. While we need to preach the "faith of our fathers," we must package the eternal message of Jesus in ways that will appeal to our world. Where the church has failed is in trying to change the message of Jesus. We have slickly packaged a do-good, feel-good gospel that is not related to the message of salvation. This has happened because of something I fondly call the "feline captivity of the church."

I own three dachshunds. (I tell people that it takes three dachshunds to equal one dog.) My three wiener dogs are as friendly as they can be. Anyone can pet them. They like to be petted on their back, necks, stomach and little dachshund heads. They will always stop whatever they are doing and allow you to pet them.

We also own a cat. The cat will only let family members pet him, and only when he is ready. No matter where you are petting him, he wants to be rubbed someplace else. When you rub his back, he turns over. When you scratch his tummy, he stands back up. The cat can't be satisfied because he doesn't know where he itches.

The same problem has arisen in the church. We can't satisfy certain groups in the church because they don't know what itches. You give them Bible study and they want Eastern meditation. You offer Eastern meditation and they want parenting skill classes. The church offers the parenting classes and the people then want Bible study. You see, the real itch they have in their life is for a personal relationship with Jesus Christ. The problem is that they can't admit that, so they try to satisfy the itch in other ways.

The false prophets are successful because of this "feline captivity" of the church. They offer all of the alternatives to meeting and trusting Jesus Christ. They are subtle in that they promise a "deeper spiritual experience." I have wondered why all of these alternative "deeper spiritual experiences" cause people to leave the church. What kind of experiences are they having?

One of the best organized defenses against these false prophets will meet at your church during the Sunday School hour. As you study God's Word and hold each other accountable for your discipleship, you close the door to any who would seek to lead you astray. False prophets can be effective in churches where people don't know the Word of truth. This Sunday as you study God's Word you are fortressing yourself and others against persons who would seek to destroy the faith you have. You didn't know that there was a war being fought every Sunday did you? It is a war for the hearts and minds of God's people.

Seed Thoughts

1. How many letters had Simon Peter written to this group of Christians? Which letter was this one?

Peter had written at least two letters to the Christians in Asia Minor. This was the second letter he'd written.

2. What was Peter's express purpose in writing to these Christians?

Peter wanted to "arouse their sincere intention" to continue to be faithful in their Christian discipleship.

3. How did Peter intend to accomplish the task of "arousing your sincere intention?"

Peter did this by reminding the Christians of the message of Jesus that had been delivered to them.

4. How was the gospel of Jesus Christ presented to the first century church?

The gospel came in the understanding of the Old Testament and the preaching of the apostles.

5. What was one of the challenges faced by the first generation of believers?

Their faith in Jesus was challenged by a group that Peter labeled "scoffers."

1. How many letters had Simon Peter written to this group of Christians? Which letter was this one?

2. What was Peter's express purpose in writing to these Christians?

3. How did Peter intend to accomplish the task of "arousing your sincere intention"?

4. How was the gospel of Jesus Christ presented to the first century church?

5. What was one of the challenges faced by the first generation of believers?

6. What was the question the "scoffers" raised as they confronted Christians?

7. What was the message that Peter wanted the church to express to the "scoffers"?

8. How, according to 2 Peter, would the world be destroyed the next time?

9. How does God count time in relationship to how humans count time?

10. What did God's reckoning of time have to do with confronting those who scoffed at His promise to come again?

(Please turn page)

Peter had written at least two letters to the Christians in Asia Minor. This was the second letter he'd written.

Peter wanted to "arouse their sincere intention" to continue to be faithful in their Christian discipleship.

Peter did this by reminding the Christians of the message of Jesus that had been delivered to them.

The gospel came in the understanding of the Old Testament and the preaching of the apostles.

Their faith in Jesus was challenged by a group that Peter labeled "scoffers."

They claimed that the message of the gospel was false because Jesus had delayed his second coming.

The scoffers did not understand the nature of the second coming or of God's judgment.

The world was destroyed by water in the day of Noah. The next time the world would be destroyed by fire.

With God one day is like a thousand years and a thousand years is like a day.

The delay of judgment showed God's patience. He was giving people more time to repent and believe.

6. What was the question the "scoffers" raised as they confronted Christians?

They claimed that the message of the gospel was false because Jesus had delayed his second coming.

7. What was the message that Peter wanted the church to express to the "scoffers"?

The scoffers did not understand the nature of the second coming. They also did not understand the nature of God's judgment.

8. How, according to 2 Peter, would the world be destroyed the next time?

The world was destroyed by water in the day of Noah. The next time the world would be destroyed by fire.

9. How does God count time in relationship to how humans count time?

With God one day is like a thousand years and a thousand years is like one day.

10. What did God's reckoning of time have to do with confronting the scoffers?

The delay of judgment showed God's patience. He was giving people more time to repent and believe.

Lesson 12

Keeping the Faith

Jude 3-4, 17-25

3 Beloved, when I gave all diligence to write unto you of the common salvation, it was needful for me to write unto you, and exhort you that ye should earnestly contend for the faith which was once delivered unto the saints.

4 For there are certain men crept in unawares, who were before of old ordained to this condemnation, ungodly men, turning the grace of our God into lasciviousness, and denying the only Lord God, and our Lord Jesus Christ.

17 But, beloved, remember ye the words which were spoken before of the apostles of our Lord Jesus Christ;

18 How that they told you there should be mockers in the last time, who should walk after their own ungodly lusts.

19 These be they who separate themselves, sensual, having not the Spirit.

20 But ye, beloved, building up yourselves on your most holy faith, praying in the Holy Ghost,

21 Keep yourselves in the love of God, looking for the mercy of our Lord Jesus Christ unto eternal life.

22 And of some have compassion, making a difference:

23 And others save with fear, pulling them out of the fire; hating even the garment spotted by the flesh.

24 Now unto him that is able to keep you from falling, and to present you faultless before the presence of his glory with exceeding joy,

25 To the only wise God our Saviour, be glory and majesty, dominion and power, both now and ever. Amen.

Memory Selection
Jude 3

Background Scripture
The Book of Jude

Devotional Reading
Isaiah 55:6-13

Printed Scripture
Jude 3-4, 17-25

February 22

241

Teacher's Target

Lesson purpose: *To capture the book of Jude's spirit of urgency as it warns us that we must "walk the talk" and keep the faith.*

Since Christians aren't perfect, there will always be something of a gap between their faith and their practice. As the poet asked, "What's a heaven for?" if not to call us to an ideal that's often beyond our reach.

The book of Jude, however, confronts those who would justify their short-comings instead of repenting of them. Strange teachings that sometimes actually exalted immorality, instead of trying to rise above it, had arisen. Lead your class to distinguish between loving the sinner and hating the sin; and between being judgmental of people with human weakness they try to rise above, and being so tolerant of immorality that we seem to approve of life-styles more akin to the world than to Christ.

Lesson Introduction

This brief, one-chapter letter is a twin to the letter of 2 Peter, containing many similar expressions and topics. The author's name is the same as "Judas," which may be one reason he quickly identifies himself as James' brother, lest he be confused with Judas Iscariot. We are not told *which* James was his brother. He was probably not the Jude who is called an apostle in Luke 6:16, since Jude 17 refers to the apostles as though the author is not counting himself among them. Some scholars believe the author was the brother of James the Lord's brother (Matt. 13:55), and hence brother or half-brother to the Lord Himself.

The purpose of the letter is to warn that the faith must be *practiced* to be *preserved*. Perhaps some of the professed believers were saying they should "continue in sin that grace may abound" (Rom. 6:1). With Paul, Jude answers, "God forbid!"

Teaching Outline	Daily Bible Readings
I. Contend for the Faith—3-4	**Mon.** False Guides Abuse God's Grace *Jude 1-13*
A. A common heritage, 3	**Tue.** Build Yourselves Up in the Faith *Jude 14-25*
B. The uncommon deceivers, 4	**Wed.** Jesus Christ Is Our Foundation *1 Corinthians 3:1-11*
II. Counteract the Ungodly—17-19	**Thu.** A Prayer Without Empty Phrases *Matthew 6:7-13*
A. Apostolic warnings, 17-18	
B. Sinful sectarians, 19	**Fri.** Be Holy as God Is Holy *Leviticus 19:1-2, 9-18*
III. Keep the Faith—20-21	**Sat.** They Desired a Better Country *Hebrews 11:8-16*
IV. Compassionately Save Some—22-23	
V. A Benediction—24-25	**Sun.** Names on God's Hands *Isaiah 49:13-18*

VERSE BY VERSE

I. Contend for the Faith—3-4
A. A common heritage

3 Beloved, when I gave all diligence to write unto you of the common salvation, it was needful for me to write unto you, and exhort you that ye should earnestly contend for the faith which was once delivered unto the saints.

Jude felt a strong urgency to write to these Christians because the faith they share in common has been threatened by unfaithful practices. "Common" is from the same root as the word for "fellowship," and means that which is shared, not that which is "lowly." Jude felt too passionately about the great truths of Christianity to stand by idly while pseudo-believers made light of them by a life-style that reflects badly on both the faith and its Founder.

The author urges his readers to "contend" for the faith in the language of the Greek Olympic games. The same root gives us the term "agony"—indicating the earnest passion of the contestants in the earliest Olympics. Since we are warned elsewhere against being "contentious" (Rom. 2:6-9), we can assume that the offenses Jude urges Christians to contend against are very serious; and that it is possible to contend for the faith without being contentious.

B. The uncommon deceivers

4 For there are certain men crept in unawares, who were before of old ordained to this condemnation, ungodly men, turning the grace of our God into lasciviousness, and denying the only Lord God, and our Lord Jesus Christ.

Since the word for "men" in verse 4 is the general term for "people," women may also have been among those who had "crept in" to the community of faith with their dangerous practices. The KJV "ordained" actually means "written (about) before." Rather than indicating that these evil people were predestined to be so, Jude is setting the stage for his reminder in verses 17-18 about the apostolic predictions written earlier, in the developing body of New Testament documents.

Since "lasciviousness" refers especially to sexual immorality, it is possible that Jude's enemies were "denying the Lord" by their flagrantly immoral lifestyles instead of merely by words. Apparently they were denying the Lord not so much in their teaching as in the practice that made His grace ineffective by insisting on living immorally.

II. Counteract the Ungodly—17-19
A. Apostolic warnings, 17-18

17 But, beloved, remember ye the words which were spoken before of the apostles of our Lord Jesus Christ;

18 How that they told you there should be mockers in the last time, who should walk after their own ungodly lusts.

How could the apostles have known that some people who professed to be Christians would not "walk their talk," but would live lustful lives? Of course they were inspired by the Holy Spirit to give such warnings; but it is also clear that the apostolic message of grace leaves itself open to such abuses by insincere or self-seeking people. This is the very tendency Paul fought in Romans, where he anticipated people saying that if sin is done away with by grace, then let's sin the more so we can have more grace! (Rom. 5:1.)

We have noted earlier that by the second century some "gnostics" taught that since the flesh is evil we should "burn out" the evil by living as fleshly or immoral a life as possible. Although Jude may be fighting an early version of this position, there is no mention of his opponents' belief that matter, and the flesh, are evil, as the later gnostics taught. It is more likely that they are half-converted Christians trying to get away with "cheap grace."

B. Sinful sectarians, 19

19 These be they who separate themselves, sensual, having not the Spirit.

The most obvious meaning here is that the immoral people Jude addressed were creating division in the Body, the Church. They were apparently seized not by a "holier than thou" spirit but a "more liberal than thou," creating their own cliques of people who supposed themselves to be sexually "liberated."

It is also possible, however, that Jude refers to the division such behavior creates between body and soul, flesh and conscience. Perhaps these opponents gloried in a grace they thought applied to their spirits, while giving in to fleshly lusts involving the body. The ideal, of course, is to bring *behavior* in line with *faith*, integrating the whole person—as Paul prayed that our spirit, soul and body would be sanctified (1 Thess. 5:23).

III. Keep the Faith—20-21

20 But ye, beloved, building up yourselves on your most holy faith, praying in the Holy Ghost,

21 Keep yourselves in the love of God, looking for the mercy of our Lord Jesus Christ unto eternal life.

In contrast to the immoral people in the church, true believers were to build on the faith referred to in verse 3—the body of teachings that included such doctrines as "Walk in the Spirit, and ye shall not fulfil the lust of the flesh" (Gal. 5:16). (The KJV term "ghost" is from *pneuma*, spirit, just as in verse 19). They are also reminded that while God offers His love to all, we have the responsibility to respond to it, or "keep" ourselves within its powerful influence that enables us to control lust. Otherwise, love is just "sloppy agape"!

IV. Compassionately Save Some —22-23

22 And of some have compassion, making a difference:

23 And others save with fear, pulling them out of the fire; hating even the garment spotted by the flesh.

Jude is not exhorting the faithful to pick and choose between having compassion on some and saving others. He is writing in parallel form; we are to discriminate between those who *will* to do evil, and those who are simply in error, or in the grasp of habits they cannot immediately break.

The even more difficult judgment to make involves hating the "garment," or sin, while loving the sinner. We do this, however, for ourselves, often maintaining self-esteem while knowing full well our imperfections. Jude urges us to have the same capacity to make this distinction in our attitude to other sinners.

V. A Benediction—24-25

244

24 Now unto him that is able to keep you from falling, and to present you faultless before the presence of his glory with exceeding joy,

25 To the only wise God our Saviour, be glory and majesty, dominion and power, both now and ever. Amen.

Jude wants his final words to be less filled with the tension created by deliberately sinful people in the church. As he pronounces a beautiful benediction on the Christians he addresses, he affirms that the faithful have no grounds for boasting over the unfaithful. If they appear "faultless" before the throne of judgment, it will be because God is "able" to save, through the grace of Christ, not their own righteousness.

The majesty and dominion ascribed to God in verse 25 reminds us that all this counsel not to give in to the lusts of the flesh occurs in the Kingdom of God. We are not to think that God's dominion or kingdom is merely in the future, postponed until Christ returns again. Christians have already, in this life, been "translated into the kingdom of His dear Son" (Col. 1:13). This is why it is so urgent to heed Jude's counsel that we commit ourselves to high moral standards, or a "kingdom ethic." To do otherwise dishonors the King.

Evangelistic Emphasis

We are living in the last days. That is both good news and challenging news. The good news is that God is preparing to bring history to a close. The struggles of humanity, the groaning of the environment and the work of salvation are almost finished. The Christian has nothing to fear as he contemplates the end of this epoch. He is safe in God's hands no matter what cataclysmic events befall the world.

The good news about living in the last days is also challenging news. The most important part of a race is just before the finish line. The same is true of any sporting event. How many baseball games are lost in the bottom of the ninth inning? How many football games are lost in the last two minutes?

You might be able to think of persons who began their faith journey brightly, but faded before the end of life. It is a calamity to watch persons who have been active in the church drop by the wayside.

All of this means that as we live in the "last days" we are called to do so faithfully. The important part of our faith is how we finish our journey. The conclusion is a true indicator of the essence of our belief in Jesus Christ.

God has called you to be faithful in service to Him. These are exciting days to be Christian. The challenge before the church is great. The labor is hard. The rewards of our labor are eternal. Have you heeded the call that God has placed on your heart in these last days?

Memory Selection

Beloved, when I gave all diligence to write unto you of the common salvation, it was needful for me to write unto you, and exhort you that ye should earnestly contend for the faith which was once delivered unto the saints.— *Jude 3*

I have watched shoppers run over each other trying to be first in line when a new check-out lane opened at the local Wal-Mart. I have seen people cut each other off in traffic to get to the head of the line. You might be one of these demolition derby drivers. There is a gene within all of us that compels us to be first and try harder. I wonder why this gene doesn't effect us when we deal with matters of the faith?

The church is hatching a new paradigm for ministry. It is a lay-lead movement. Laity like the idea of taking over. This new movement is not some organized *coup de tat*. Laity and clergy are combining forces to bring a new day of ministry into the church. The new paradigm will mean shared responsibilities in all areas of church life, even those once reserved for clergy.

This new image will only work to the extent that you are willing to "contend for the faith." The church will only be fruitful in ministry to the extent you are willing to put the church first in the ordering of your priorities. It is time for us again boldly to proclaim, there is nothing more important in your life than Jesus Christ.

Weekday Problems

More than one upset soul had been to see Rev. Morgan after having a conversation with Paul Brown. Paul took seriously every mandate and every commandment of Jesus Christ. He was the self-appointed prophet of Littletown. Paul knew everyone in town. Paul knew what everyone in town was doing. He knew the sinners and the sins. He had a harder time naming the saints.

In Paul's mind, there were few saints in Littletown. What Christians there were had perverted the pure gospel of Jesus Christ with lustful and licentious thinking. They refused to believe in the Word of God the way that Paul believed in the Word of God. Paul wasn't even sure that his pastor, Rev. Morgan was a true Christian.

Paul's last confrontation was with Sally Smart. Sally was a new convert and recent transfer to Littletown. Paul caught Sally coming out of the local restaurant and began to question her on the Tribulation. Sally confessed that she didn't know much about the end of time. When Paul heard this admission of theological weakness, he lit into her with a Biblical tirade of eschatological proportions. He left Sally in tears.

After talking a while with Rev. Morgan, Sally felt better about her faith and relationship to Christ. Rev. Morgan, however had become convinced that Paul Brown was a theological disaster that should be stopped.

* What is the difference between a person who "contends for the faith of Jesus Christ" and one who is simply contentious?

* Is it wrong to confront others about their specific beliefs?

* In what ways do you engage persons about their beliefs? Do you have such conversations?

A Way with Words

My grandfather has a wooden leg.
Well, my grandmother has a cedar chest.

Do you like raisin bread?
Don't know; never tried raisin' any.

Did you ever hear the rope joke?
Nope.
Skip it.

Hey! That snake just snapped at me!
Snakes don't snap. They coil and strike.
This one was a garter snake.

Did you hear about the cow that gave buttermilk?
Ridiculous!
No—have you ever heard of a cow giving anything but-her-milk?

This Lesson in Your Life

What you believe about Jesus Christ matters. What you don't know about your faith can hurt you. Jude warned the early Christians about those who would seek to destroy their faith by claiming to have a "deeper version" of the same faith. Early in the church a heresy called gnosticism arose. The gnostics taught that giving one's heart to the Lord meant one was free to give his body to pleasure. All sorts of problems arose as the result of these persons who "pervert the grace of our God into licentiousness" (Jude 4).

We don't have persons called gnostics in the church any longer. However, we have all known persons who were acting out the gnostic belief. Gnosticism taught that the spirit was good and of God. They taught that the body was evil and of the devil. This dichotomy allowed for these persons to express a deep faith and then live the wild life. Their message was appealing for some. They could have eternal life and not miss any of the fun that their world offered.

Without thinking about it, people in your church have decided on the same kind of life-style. For these persons Jesus is a vaccine against eternal doom. They admire His teachings. They look to Him as their Savior. However, they will not trust Him to be the Lord of their lives. They want the church there when they are in a crisis. In the ministry we say that people want the church for hatching, matching and dispatching. (Baptism, marriage and funerals are the three times that people seem to need the church.) With these three exceptions, a few people want a faith that leaves them alone. They especially don't want any pressure to attend the Sunday services of a church. Even faithful Christians are beginning to share a feeling that attending church on Sunday morning is not an absolute for their faith. It almost seems that people believe a religion quota can be met. They have attended church for years and suddenly stop.

Jude warned about people who would be led astray by belief systems that were antithetical to the Christian cause. Our duty as God's children is to be faithful to the central message of Jesus Christ. We are to love Him with all of our heart, mind, soul and strength. Then we are to be obedient to the rest of that calling. We are to love our neighbors as ourselves. There is no time limit stated on how long we are to carry on. We can't reach a point where we can faithfully say that we have served Jesus enough. There is always something left for us to accomplish. There is always one more sinner to lead to Christ. There is always one more wound to bind. This should challenge us to seek the Spirit of God dwelling in us as the source of our strength.

Perhaps that is why people fall away from the faith or never take their faith seriously. They haven't felt God's Spirit energizing them for ministry. The Holy Spirit is promised to the believer as the source of strength and as a beacon guiding the way.

The Spirit helps us as we pray. The Spirit makes it possible for us to love those persons that otherwise are impossible to love. The Spirit helps us look up, when the rest of the world is downcast, and anxiously waiting for tomorrow. The ministry of the Holy Spirit keeps the believer on track. The presence of the Spirit in the church keeps that fellowship alive and dynamic.

The Spirit is the source of power that allows us to minister effectively to those who are wavering in their faith. When persons find the Spirit of God they are not satisfied with a part-time faith. They find themselves spending more and more time with God. Their desire is for the Lord and what He has for them.

The cure for our age is a good dose of God's Spirit poured out on His people. That prescription will sustain us as we face these last days.

Seed Thoughts

1. What was Jude's original intention in writing to the church in his day?

His original intention was to write to the church about the "salvation we share."

2. Was Jude able to carry out his original intention for writing?

He seemed to indicate that while he was thinking about one subject, it became necessary to write about another.

3. What was the subject that Jude addressed in this epistle?

Jude wrote to these Christians encouraging them to "contend for the faith that was once entrusted to all the saints."

4. According to Jude, who were the keepers of the faith?

Jude indicated that the keepers of the faith were "all the saints."

5. The group of scoffers who had infiltrated the church were preaching two things. What were they?

They perverted the grace of God into licentiousness. They denied the Lord, Jesus Christ.

(Please turn page)

1. What was Jude's original intention in writing to the church in his day?

2. Was Jude able to carry out his original intention for writing?

3. What was the subject that Jude addressed in this epistle?

4. According to Jude, who were the keepers of the faith?

5. The group of scoffers who had infiltrated the church were preaching two things. What were they?

6. What was the prediction that the apostles of the Lord Jesus had already made?

7. Who did Jude seem to be echoing in verse seventeen?

8. How should the believers "build themselves up on your most holy faith?"

9. According to Jude what was it that allowed the Christian to have assurance of eternal life?

10. What promise did Jude make to the believers in his Benediction?

His original intention was to write to the church about the "salvation we share."

He seemed to indicate that while he was thinking about one subject, it became necessary to write about another.

Jude wrote to these Christians encouraging them to "contend for the faith that was once entrusted to all the saints."

Jude indicated that the keepers of the faith were "all the saints."

They perverted the grace of God into licentiousness. They denied the Lord, Jesus Christ.

"In the last time there will be scoffers, indulging in their own ungodly lusts" (Jude 17).

Jude and 2 Peter have many things in common. Some have suggested that Jude is a copy of 2 Peter chapter 3.

They should pray in the Holy Spirit, keep themselves in the love of God and have mercy on those who are wavering.

It is the mercy of Jesus Christ that leads to eternal life.

Jesus is able to keep us from falling and to make us stand without blemish in the presence of His glory.

6. What was the prediction that the apostles of the Lord Jesus had already made?

"In the last time there will be scoffers, indulging in their own ungodly lusts" (Jude 17).

7. Who did Jude seem to be echoing in verse seventeen?

Jude and 2 Peter have many things in common. Some have suggested that Jude is a copy of 2 Peter chapter 3.

8. How should the believers "build themselves up on your most holy faith"?

They should pray in the Holy Spirit, keep themselves in the love of God and have mercy on those who are wavering.

9. According to Jude what was it that allowed the Christian to have assurance of eternal life?

It is the mercy of Jesus Christ that leads to eternal life.

10. What was the promise that Jude made to the believers in the Benediction?

Jesus is able to keep us from falling and to make us stand without blemish in the presence of His glory.

Lesson 1

The Beginning of Jesus' Ministry

Mark 1:1-4, 7-20

1 The beginning of the gospel of Jesus Christ, the Son of God;

2 As it is written in the prophets, Behold I send my messenger before thy face, which shall prepare thy way before thee.

3 The voice of one crying in the wilderness, Prepare ye the way of the Lord, make his paths straight.

4 John did baptize in the wilderness, and preach the baptism of repentance for the remission of sins.

7 And preached, saying, There cometh one mightier than I after me, the latchet of whose shoes I am not worthy to stoop down and unloose.

8 I indeed have baptized you with water: but he shall baptize you with the Holy Ghost.

9 And it came to pass in those days, that Jesus came from Nazareth of Galilee, and was baptized of John in Jordan.

10 And straightway coming up out of the water, he saw the heavens opened, and the Spirit like a dove descending upon him:

11 And there came a voice from heaven, saying, Thou art my beloved Son, in whom I am well pleased.

12 And immediately the Spirit driveth him into the wilderness.

13 And he was there in the wilderness forty days, tempted of Satan; and was with the wild beasts; and the angels ministered unto him.

14 Now after that John was put in prison, Jesus came into Galilee, preaching the gospel of the kingdom of God,

15 And saying, The time is fulfilled, and the kingdom of God is at hand: repent ye, and believe the gospel.

16 Now as he walked by the sea of Galilee, he saw Simon and Andrew his brother casting a net into the sea: for they were fishers.

17 And Jesus said unto them, Come ye after me, and I will make you to become fishers of men.

18 And straightway they forsook their nets, and followed him.

19 And when he had gone a little further thence, he saw James the son of Zebedee, and John his brother, who also were in the ship mending their nets.

20 And straightway he called them: and they left their father Zebedee in the ship with the hired servants, and went after him.

Memory Selection
Mark 1:11

Devotional Reading
Acts 10:34-43

Background Scripture
Mark 1:1-20

Printed Scripture
Mark 1:1-4, 7-20

Teacher's Target

Lesson purpose: *To rediscover the impact of the early ministries of John the Baptist and Jesus, and to apply principles in Mark's description of their work to our own lives.*

The challenge in presenting this lesson is to let the themes and the people surrounding John the Baptist's preaching and the early ministry of Jesus come alive for people who have become accustomed to "church language." The teacher can portray John the Baptist with all his rugged and outspoken manner. Encourage the class to try to imagine people streaming out of their own city in large numbers to hear a man dressed in rough clothing who accused his hearers of needing to repent.

As for the early ministry of Jesus, focus on His need for a cadre of spokespersons to assist Him in His work. Note that selecting 12 for this ministry must have rep-resented to His hearers the 12 tribes that had made up their nation. Anticipation and excitement about the coming of the Messiah were high. A new day was dawning!

Lesson Introduction

Mark's compact Gospel may have been written to appeal to the Roman mind. Mark is a Roman name, and early tradition held that he was the apostle Peter's interpreter to Romans. He was also helper on a mission with Paul and Barnabas (Acts 12:25).

As the Gospels open, mighty nations—Egypt, Babylonia, Persia, Assyria, Greece and Rome—had marched across the pages of history, using Palestine as a crossroads. Jewish leaders alternately rebelled agains Rome, the current ruling power, and made political deals.

Faithful Jews lamented the decline of national faithfulness. It had been more than 400 years since God had spoken to the people through the prophets. Many knew the Scripture's promise that the prophet Elijah would precede the Messiah; but what could this mean? Some were burdened by sin. Knowing that the nation needed to turn to God before He would send the long-anticipated Messiah, they prayed for reform. The air was tense with anticipation. Could these be the days when the righteous kingdom called for by the prophets would actually be established?

Teaching Outline	Daily Bible Readings	
	Mon.	One More Powerful *Mark 1:1-11*
I. Announcing the Good News—1-4	Tues.	God's Kingdom Has Come Near *Mark 1:12-20*
A. John's message, 1-3		
B. John's work, 4	Wed.	Revealing God's Glory *Isaiah 40:1-11*
II. Anointing the Messiah—5-15	Thu.	The Anointed One *Psalm 2*
A. Inauguration, 5-11		
B. Temptation, 12-13	Fri.	Ordained by God as Judge *Acts 10:34-43*
C. Proclamation, 14-15	Sat.	Nations Tremble at the Presence *saiah 64:1-7*
III. Appointing Apostles—16-20		
	Sun.	Servant Bringing Justice *Isaiah 42:1-9*

VERSE BY VERSE

I. Announcing the Good News—1-4
  A. John's message, 1-3
  1 The beginning of the gospel of Jesus Christ, the Son of God;

  2 As it is written in the prophets, Behold I send my messenger before thy face, which shall prepare thy way before thee.

  3 The voice of one crying in the wilderness, Prepare ye the way of the Lord, make his paths straight.

According to Mark, the gospel or good news starts not with Jesus but with John the Baptizer. (The word "beginning" gives us our word "archaic," and indicates that Mark is going back to the oldest or earliest point of the gospel story.)

This is important, because Mark wants us to understand that the story of Jesus fulfills a prophecy in Malachi that was one of the Old Testament's last words (see Mal. 3:1). John the Baptist is the messenger Malachi predicted! He is also, in a figurative sense, Elijah reborn (Matt. 11:14).

In verse 3 Mark also weaves in a prophecy from Isaiah 40:3, from a section of Scripture that describes the work of the Messiah to come. From the very start of his story, therefore, Mark affirms that both John the Baptist and Jesus fulfill God's promises made long ago. They do not appear accidentally on the stage of history.

B. John's work, 4
  4 John did baptize in the wilderness, and preach the baptism of repentance for the remission of sins.

Note that Mark is careful to show that John the Baptist's work was in the "wilderness," just as Isaiah 40:3 had predicted. Although baptizings, or washings, had been known among some Jewish sects such as the Essenes, it became more prominent among the followers of Jesus. A baptismal washing was a fitting symbol of the clean page being written in the story of God's interaction with people, for it was part of His call to people to repent (lit. change their minds) of their sins. As Acts 19:1-6 shows, John's baptism was temporary, eventually giving way to baptism in the name of Jesus.

II. Anointing the Messiah—7-15
  A. Inauguration, 7-11
  7 And preached, saying, There cometh one mightier than I after me, the latchet of whose shoes I am not worthy to stoop down and unloose.

  8 I indeed have baptized you with water: but he shall baptize you with the Holy Ghost.

  9 And it came to pass in those days, that Jesus came from Nazareth of Galilee, and was baptized of John in Jordan.

  10 And straightway coming up out of the water, he saw the heavens opened, and the Spirit like a dove descending upon him:

  11 And there came a voice from heaven, saying, Thou art my beloved Son, in whom I am well pleased.

Throughout the Gospels, John defers

of salvation, insisting here that he is not worthy of being Jesus' valet (see also John 1:8, 19-21).

John also describes his baptism as secondary to Jesus' baptism. Although baptism in the name of Jesus also involved water (see Acts 10:47-48), John focuses in verse 8 on the more startling aspect of baptism with the Holy Spirit—which is also illustrated in Acts 10:47-48 and Acts 19:6. John's baptism was no less important for God's intended use merely because it did not confer the miraculous dimension of Holy Spirit baptism.

Verses 9-11 describe Jesus Himself submitting to John's baptism, not because He needed the forgiveness of sins but in order to submit Himself to God's new order, which included baptism (see Matt. 3:13-15).

"Coming up out of the water" indicates the ancient practice of baptism by immersing. As Jesus does so, heaven itself places its stamp of authenticity on what is being acted out on this earthly stage. The Holy Spirit, in the form of a dove, is accompanied by God's own voice testifying to all that Jesus is more than a man; He is the very Son of God. Although the voice seems to quote from Isaiah 42:1—again from the "Messianic" portion of Isaiah—"beloved" and "in whom I am well pleased"—are added. These terms all show Jesus' unique relationship to God. The claim of Sonship was taken by the Jews in John 5:18 as making Jesus equal with God.

B. Temptation, 12-13

12 And immediately the Spirit driveth him into the wilderness.

13 And he was there in the wilderness forty days, tempted of Satan; and was with the wild beasts; and the angels ministered unto him.

The fact that it was the Holy Spirit who drove Jesus into the wilderness for the Great Temptation contains a word for the Christian today who faces similar trials. Although Satan is sometimes the source of our woes, they may also be occasions of loving discipline from God, preparing us for a future mission like that awaiting Jesus.

Matthew's Gospel elaborates on this experience by being more specific about Satan's temptations (see Matt. 4:1-11). These physical, mental and spiritual endurance tests remind us that Jesus was human as well as divine. Just as a runner prepares for a race by punishing exercise, Jesus was building Himself up for the arduous work ahead. His conquering of Satan in the wilderness would become essential background for the many times He would cast out demons during His ministry.

Later Christians who also subjected themselves to living alone in the desert would testify to the anguish of body and soul such an experience can bring. An entire movement of "desert fathers" left a legacy testifying to the way going without food, water and human companionship can be both terrifying and, ultimately, spiritually strengthening.

C. Proclamation, 14-15

14 Now after that John was put in prison, Jesus came into Galilee, preaching the gospel of the kingdom of God,

15 And saying, The time is fulfilled, and the kingdom of God is at hand: repent ye, and believe the gospel.

The Kingdom of God had been a prominent theme among God's people since the days of King David. God had promised that the kingdom that began with David would last "forever" (2 Sam.

7:12-13). This is why the Gospels are so careful to trace Jesus' family tree back to David, showing that He is fully qualified to assume the mantle of a Davidic king.

Now, as Jesus begins His public ministry, He proclaims that a new phase of this eternal reign is about to begin. The imprisonment of John marks stiffening resistance to Jesus' mission; and His response is to begin immediately to affirm that the power of neither the Jews nor the Romans will be able to withstand the impact of the Kingdom of God.

Although today the Kingdom is widely thought of as something still in the future, Jesus said that it actually exists wherever He is enthroned in people's hearts (Luke 17:21). Also, people who are converted from the kingdom of darkness are said to be transferred into Christ's kingdom (Col. 1:13). The appearance of Christ the King at the end of time will be an extension of the Kingdom whose throne Jesus assumed after His ascension (Acts 2:30).

III. Appointing Apostles—16-20

16 Now as he walked by the sea of Galilee, he saw Simon and Andrew his brother casting a net into the sea: for they were fishers.

17 And Jesus said unto them, Come ye after me, and I will make you to become fishers of men.

18 And straightway they forsook their nets, and followed him.

19 And when he had gone a little further thence, he saw James the son of Zebedee, and John his brother, who also were in the ship mending their nets.

20 And straightway he called them: and they left their father Zebedee in the ship with the hired servants, and went after him.

Another important aspect of the early days of Jesus' ministry was calling His apostles. The occupation of those listed here is appropriate, for they will soon cast their nets for people and bring them into the Kingdom. Jesus must have had some personal magnetism, or perhaps some compelling quality of presence and voice, for these fishermen to leave their work immediately to follow him. The group will grow to 12, no doubt corresponding to the original 12 tribes of Israel to show that they are a part of the fulfillment of God's promise to the Jews. (See Mark 3:16-19 for the complete list.)

Evangelistic Emphasis

Another word for the term "gospel" is "good news." To many, the message we call the gospel doesn't sound like good news. "Stop that!" "Give up this!" "You can't do that!" In reality, there are some things we give up and discontinue when we grasp the gospel. Yet, there are many, many more things we gain.

Maggie Gallagher contributed an article entitled "Religion Is Good for Your Health" to the *Dallas Morning News* on Feb. 12, 1996. She cited several positive benefits of religion. Here are some of the findings from a Heritage Foundation study which were cited in her article.

Churchgoers have lower rates of depression, alcohol/drug abuse and criminal activity. Frequent worshipers have longer, happier marriages.

Regular church attendance reduces a person's blood pressure by five millimeters—enough to reduce the mortality rate by 20 percent.

According to one study in 1993, the average income for regular churchgoers is $37,021. The average income for the unchurched was $24,361.

If those results fail to sound like good news, I don't know good news when I hear it! We may have to give up some things when we repent and believe in the gospel, but the benefits far outweigh our sacrifice. Here and now as well as "in the sweet by and by," that is good news.

Memory Selection

And there came a voice from heaven, saying, "Thou art my beloved Son, in whom I am well pleased.—*Mark 1:11*

Have you ever been to a softball game in which one of the children hits a home run and a parent in the stands shouts, "That's my girl!" Have you been to a recital in which a child plays flawlessly and the person next to you whispers loud enough for all to hear, "That's my boy!"

It is natural for us to want others to know who our children are. We claim our kids.

In a sense, that is what God did at the baptism of Jesus Christ. No longer did people think of Jesus as merely "Joseph and Mary's boy." On that day God publicly laid claim on His Son. From that day on, the life of Jesus Christ took on a new dimension in the eyes of the world.

In a very similar fashion, when we recognize God's claim on our lives we are forever different. When we grasp that we have a heavenly Father who loves us and cares for us more than any earthly parent can, our lives are positively transformed.

Isn't it great to be a child of the King?

Weekday Problems

Scott had been feeling uneasy for months. He wasn't quite sure why. Things were going well. His wife and two children were doing fine. There were no particular health problems. His relationship with his wife was solid.

His business was going well. He made more money last year than he ever had before. This year looked even better. It wasn't his job that was the cause for his restlessness.

His spiritual life was great. Scott hated to admit it, but that seemed to be the problem. It seemed that every time he turned around he was reading some scripture that spoke to him about going into full-time Christian ministry. Christian brothers and sisters for whom he had great respect quite often affirmed his gifts as a preacher and teacher. He enjoyed talking to people about the Lord. He had a knack for saying and doing just the right things to bring the presence of the Lord into tough situations.

He often thought about full-time ministry. Just as quickly, he would try to dispel those thoughts. Frankly, he was scared. He knew pastors did not get paid very much. He knew there was unusual stress upon a pastor's spouse and family. He felt torn. He felt uneasy.

* How would you advise Scott about his future?

* Have you ever felt God calling you to a deeper walk that would require great sacrifice on your part? If so, how did you handle it?

Gospel Lights

Our word "gospel" is from the old term "God-spell," meaning good-story or, later, God-story.

One of the earliest uses on record of the Greek word for "gospel" was in a reference to the birthday of the Roman emperor Caesar Augustus as so important it could be called the beginning of a new year, and "good news" for the whole world. How much greater was the news that Jesus, Son of David and Son of God, had come!

Ancient tradition assigned a human or animal figure to each Gospel, perhaps as memory crutches. Matthew was portrayed as a lion, the king of beasts, recalling Matthew's emphasis on the Kingdom of God. Mark was a man, just as his Gospel portrays the humanity of Jesus. The symbol for Luke was an ox, a pastoral symbol reminding us of Luke's sensitive way of dealing with the poor and the forsaken. The symbol for John—"the spiritual Gospel"—was an eagle, reminding us of John's "eagle's eye view" of Jesus as though looking at Him from above.

This Lesson in Your Life

Good News for Today

There is a joke told about a man who had not been feeling well for some time. Finally, he went to the doctor for a battery of tests. Eight days after his doctor's visit his physician calls him.

"Well, John, I have good news and some bad news. Which do you want first?" John said, "Give me the good news first."

"Okay," the doctor replies, "The tests show you only have 24 hours to live." John is floored. "Twenty-four hours to live! Doc that's terrible! If that's the good news, what's the bad news?"

"Well, John," the doctor answers, "I was supposed to call you yesterday."

That is a corny joke that leads me to this point. Sometimes bad news sounds like good news. Sometimes good news sounds like bad news.

For instance, if someone told you that you would have to give up everything you own to be a Christian, would that sound like good news? If someone told you that you would have to give up certain things you liked to be a Christian, would that sound like good news ? If someone told you that to be a disciple of Jesus Christ you would have to be willing to be executed, would that sound like good news to you?

You know, at first glance none of those things sound like good news to me. Yet, if we were to look at the good news of Jesus Christ, the gospel, we would have to admit that all three of those examples have something to do with the message of the gospel.

Jesus told a rich man to go and sell all that he had, give it to the poor and follow Him (Matt. 19). Jesus told a woman to go and sin no more (John 8). Jesus told a crowd that to be his disciple each person would have to take up her/his cross and follow Christ (Mark 8).

These calls to discipleship may sound like bad news. In reality, it is good news. When we give our hearts to Jesus, He blesses us in ways we had only imagined before. When we give ourselves to Christ he gives us back eternal life. When we allow the Holy Spirit to come into our lives God's character begins to form within us. Galatians 5:22-23a calls that character the Fruit of the Spirit, "But the fruit of the Spirit is love, joy, peace, patience, kindness, goodness, faithfulness, gentleness and self-control." The world longs for these character traits. The world seeks after true love, joy that lasts longer than happiness, peace that comes from within, not from pharmaceuticals. The world seeks after these things. They grow in the hearts of the Spirit-filled Christian.

Yet, the good life, the abundant life in Christ comes only after we first give ourselves up to Him. We may be drawn to Christ by what He can do for us. Yet, to be truly a disciple of Christ, to be truly saved, we must come to a point of confession and repentance, thus receiving forgiveness. To be truly a disciple, one must eventually come to the point of dying to self that one may be able to live in and for Christ.

When we have given ourselves to Him and allowed Him to fill our hearts with His Spirit, then He grows within us His character. He bestows upon us eternal life. We learn to live lives that benefit God and benefit our fellow humans.

That is good news for the world today.

Seed Thoughts

1. List two things John was noted for accomplishing in the scripture.

John baptized in the wilderness and he preached the baptism of repentance for the remission of sins.

2. What was John's attitude about himself and his attitude about the One to come after him?

John was humble and felt "the One to come after him" was much greater and mightier than he was.

3. Name the two types of baptisms listed in verse 8. Who performs each baptism?

John baptizes with water, but "the One to come after" will baptize with the Holy Ghost.

4. Name the river where Jesus was baptized and name the person that baptized Him.

John the Baptist baptized Jesus in the Jordan River.

5. Name two significant supernatural things that happened at Jesus's baptism.

The Spirit descended like a dove upon Jesus and a voice from heaven said, "Thou art my beloved Son, in Whom I am well pleased."

(Please turn page)

1. List two things John was noted for accomplishing in the scripture.

2. What was John's attitude about himself and his attitude about the One to come after him?

3. Name the two types of baptisms listed in verse 8. Who performs each baptism?

4. Name the river where Jesus was baptized and name the person that baptized Him.

5. Name two significant supernatural things that happened at Jesus's baptism.

6. Where did Jesus go after his baptism and how long was He there?

7. Who tempted Jesus while He was in the wilderness? Who ministered to Him?

8. What was the prophetic message that Jesus preached in verse 15?

9. Name the four men that Jesus called in these passages of Mark. What was their livelihood?

10. What did Jesus say to these four men to convince them to follow Him and leave their business?

John baptized in the wilderness and he preached the baptism of repentance for the remission of sins.

John was humble and felt "the One to come after him" was much greater and mightier than he was.

John baptizes with water, but "the One to come after" will baptize with the Holy Ghost.

John the Baptist baptized Jesus in the Jordan River.

The Spirit descended like a dove upon Jesus and a voice from heaven said, "Thou art my beloved Son, in Whom I am well pleased."

The Spirit drove Jesus into the wilderness where He stayed for forty days.

Satan tempted Jesus while He was in the wilderness, but the angels ministered to Him.

"The time is fulfilled, and the kingdom of God is at hand: repent ye, and believe the gospel."

Jesus called four fishermen: Simon, Andrew, James, and John.

Jesus told the fishermen to follow Him and He would make them "fishers of men."

6. Where did Jesus go after his baptism and how long was He there?

The Spirit drove Jesus into the wilderness where He stayed for forty days.

7. Who tempted Jesus while He was in the wilderness? Who ministered to Him?

Satan tempted Jesus while He was in the wilderness, but the angels ministered to Him.

8. What was the prophetic message that Jesus preached in verse 15?

"The time is fulfilled, and the kingdom of God is at hand: repent ye, and believe the gospel."

9. Name the four men that Jesus called in these passages of Mark. What was their livelihood?

Jesus called four fishermen: Simon, Andrew, James, and John.

10. What did Jesus say to these four men to convince them to follow Him and leave their business?

Jesus told the fishermen to follow Him and He would make them "fishers of men."

Lesson 2

Jesus' Works and Words

Mark 1:21-27, 32-34, 40-45

21 And they went into Capernaum; and straightway on the sabbath day he entered into the synagogue, and taught.

22 And they were astonished at his doctrine: for he taught them as one that had authority, and not as the scribes.

23 And there was in their synagogue a man with an unclean spirit; and he cried out,

24 Saying, Let us alone; what have we to do with thee, thou Jesus of Nazareth? Art thou come to destroy us? I know thee who thou art, the Holy One of God.

25 And Jesus rebuked him, saying, Hold thy peace, and come out of him.

26 And when the unclean spirit had torn him, and cried with a loud voice, he came out of him.

27 And they were all amazed, insomuch that they questioned among themselves, saying, What thing is this? What new doctrine is this? For with authority commandeth he even the unclean spirits, and they do obey him.

32 And at even when the sun did set, they brought unto him all that were diseased, and them that were possessed with devils.

33 And all the city was gathered together at the door.

34 And he healed many that were sick of divers diseases, and cast out many devils; and suffered not the devils to speak, because they knew him.

40 And there came a leper to him, beseeching him, and kneeling down to him, and saying unto him, If thou wilt, thou canst make me clean.

41 And Jesus, moved with compassion, put forth his hand, and touched him, and saith unto him, I will; be thou clean.

42 And as soon as he had spoken, immediately the leprosy departed from him, and he was cleansed.

43 And he straitly charged him, and forthwith sent him away;

44 And saith unto him, See thou say nothing to any man: but go thy way, shew thyself to the priest, and offer for thy cleansing those things which Moses commanded, for a testimony unto them.

45 But he went out, and began to publish it much, and to blaze abroad the matter, insomuch that Jesus could no more openly enter into the city, but was without in desert places: and they came to him from every quarter.

Memory Selection
Mark 1:41

Devotional Reading
Acts 9:32-42

Background Scripture
Mark 1:21-45

Printed Scripture
Mark 1:21-27, 32-34, 40-45

Teacher's Target

Lesson purpose: *To learn to trust the power of Christ in our lives today by reflecting on early incidents in His teaching and healing ministry.*

Amazing though Christ's life and work were, it can all seem so long ago and far away. How can your class members possibly relate to Jesus as one who can cast out demons and heal the sick with but a word?

One way to narrow the gap between this account and our own times is to note that the passage begins with a portrait of Christ the Master Teacher. Many people can recall a gifted teacher whose towering presence inspired them both to listen and to learn. If we can place our confidence in Jesus as that kind of teacher, it's but a short step to believing this account of His power over infirm bodies and souls. Then faith can build a bridge from that century to this, as the testimony of Scripture leads us to confess the Lordship of Christ in our own lives.

Lesson Introduction

If, as some have held, Mark addressed his Gospel to the Roman mind, we can easily suppose that he places this demonstration of Jesus' divine power near the opening of His Gospel to appeal to Romans who appreciated power and authority.

Note that this divine power is described on three fronts: in teaching, casting out demons and healing the sick. Mark is telling us that Jesus' power extends to the whole person. He treats the mind, the soul, and the body.

The passage also shows that Jesus had a sure sense of timing for the fulfillment of His mission. It would not do to broadcast His identity as God's Son immediately. He has many things to teach His disciples before succumbing to the authorities who will later put Him to death; so He commands the man He heals not tell who He is. Although the man tells the news anyway, the crowds that gather do not yet have murder on their mind.

Teaching Outline	Daily Bible Readings

I. Amazing with Authori ity–21-27
  A. Over petty opinions, 21-22
  B. Over a demon, 23-27
II. Attracting with Power—32-34
  A. Healing and exorcising, 32-33
  B. The Messianic secret, 34
III. Announcing the secret—40-45
  A. A leper healed, 40-42
  B. The secret shared, 43-45
	Mon. Compassion in Action
	Mark 1:21-34
	Tue. Jesus Helped and Healed People
	Mark 1:35-45
	Wed. Laying Hands on the Sick
	Mark 16:14-20
	Thu. Peter Heals the Sick
	Acts 9:32-42
	Fri. Faith to Be Made Well
	Acts 14:8-18
	Sat. Prayer Will Save the Sick
	James 5:13-18
	Sun. Leaves for Healing the Nations
	Revelation 22:1-7

VERSE BY VERSE

I. Amazing with Authority—21-27
A. Over petty opinions, 21-22

21 And they went into Capernaum; and straightway on the sabbath day he entered into the synagogue, and taught.

22 And they were astonished at his doctrine: for he taught them as one that had authority, and not as the scribes.

The town of Capernaum was on the northwest shore of the Sea of Galilee, and only a few miles northeast of Jesus' boyhood home, Nazareth. Jesus did many of His mighty works there during the early months of His ministry. Perhaps this was because the area was known as "Galilee of the Gentiles," and Jesus wanted to give an early signal that His ministry would one day include all nations (see Matt. 4:12-15; Isa. 9:1-2.)

At first, however, He focuses on His own people, the Jews, by teaching in the local synagogue (the remains of which some archeologists believe has been found in the ruins of Capernaum). After all, Jesus was the Messiah promised to the Jews. The apostle Paul would follow this same priority, going "to the Jew first, and also to the Greeks."

Why were Jesus' hearers astonished at his teaching? Perhaps because the Law had become such an object of debate that their previous teachers, the scribes, spent most of their time weighing what one rabbi said against another. With divine insight, Jesus must have knifed through petty arguments and nice distinctions, getting to the heart of the matter—and to the hearts of His hearers.

B. Over a demon, 23-27

23 And there was in their synagogue a man with an unclean spirit; and he cried out,

24 Saying, Let us alone; what have we to do with thee, thou Jesus of Nazareth? Art thou come to destroy us? I know thee who thou art, the Holy One of God.

25 And Jesus rebuked him, saying, Hold thy peace, and come out of him.

26 And when the unclean spirit had torn him, and cried with a loud voice, he came out of him.

27 And they were all amazed, insomuch that they questioned among themselves, saying, What thing is this? What new doctrine is this? For with authority commandeth he even the unclean spirits, and they do obey him.

"Unclean spirit" is another term for "demon." Some modern interpreters believe people thought to have demons were only suffering from mental illness; but it is strange to think of an illness "speaking," as is the case here. It seems likely that they were real spiritual forces loosed on earth to do Satan's will. Perhaps their victims at one time let down their moral or spiritual guard and allowed evil influence to enter their hearts. Eventually the demon took over, or "possessed" the person.

The issue of whether being "demonized" is still possible is too broad to discuss here. Whatever can be said about the possibility of modern demon-possession, it is wise to resist temptation in its early stages in order never to leave Satan an opening.

Despite being evil, the satanic force within the man is from the spiritual realm, and therefore recognizes Jesus as God's Holy One. Jesus, however, commands it to be silent, beginning a systematic attempt in the early chapters of the Gospels to keep His identity from being made known. This is often called "the Messianic secret." Jesus probably commands the spirit to be silent because evil is a poor advertisement of holiness. Another reason will be suggested for the silence commanded in verse 44.

The evil spirit is no match for Jesus' superior spiritual power. It is allowed only a brief protest before Jesus forcefully orders it to leave the poor man's body and soul. And leave it must, although in departing it strikes one more tormenting blow. This amazing miracle has the same result as Jesus' amazing gift of teaching: the people are astonished.

The mention of Jesus' authority or power twice in six verses illustrates why many scholars believe that Mark's Gospel was addressed to Romans, who were quite familiar and perhaps fascinated with the mighty power of the Empire and its Caesars.

II. Attracting with Power—32-34

A. Healing and exorcising, 32-33

32 And at even when the sun did set, they brought unto him all that were diseased, and them that were possessed with devils.

33 And all the city was gathered together at the door.

After healing Simon Peter's mother-in-law (vss. 29-31, Jesus receives at the door of Peter's house the crowds of people who have heard about these miraculous deeds.

B. The Messianic secret, 34

34 And he healed many that were sick of divers diseases, and cast out many devils; and suffered not the devils to speak, because they knew him.

Again we see that being ill is different in Mark's view from having a demon; but neither ailment is a match for Jesus' power. For a second time, Jesus orders the demons He exorcises not to speak His name and acknowledge His divinity.

III. Announcing the secret—40-45

A. A leper healed, 40-42

40 And there came a leper to him, beseeching him, and kneeling down to him, and saying unto him, If thou wilt, thou canst make me clean.

41 And Jesus, moved with compassion, put forth his hand, and touched him, and saith unto him, I will; be thou clean.

42 And as soon as he had spoken, immediately the leprosy departed from him, and he was cleansed.

Leprosy was incurable in Jesus' day. It was an especially cruel task-master, since it both disfigured the body and created a horrible stench. Hence lepers were outcasts, and required to signal their presence by ringing little bells to warn others to avoid them.

Even this disease, however, bows to the divine authority of God's Son. "Moved with compassion" translates a Greek saying that literally referred to a person's entrails or "gut," and was used to describe deep feelings that arose from the heart. Jesus is not an unfeeling teacher, but a compassionate minister.

Mark is careful to note that Jesus healed the leper instantly, closing the door on any attempt for a critic to say the man just got well gradually, as though "nature" or medicine may have cured him.

B. The secret shared, 43-45

43 And he straitly charged him, and forthwith sent him away;

44 And saith unto him, See thou say nothing to any man: but go thy way, shew thyself to the priest, and offer for thy cleansing those things which Moses commanded, for a testimony unto them.

45 But he went out, and began to publish it much, and to blaze abroad the matter, insomuch that Jesus could no more openly enter into the city, but was without in desert places: and they came to him from every quarter.

The man is not to go tell everyone he had been healed, but to go to the priest with an offering and be declared ritually clean. By this command Jesus shows that He honors Moses' Law, illustrating His statement that He came not to destroy the Law, to fulfill it (Matt. 5:17).

We can now note another reason for "the Messianic secret." The large numbers of people Jesus attracted (vss. 28, 33) would not serve Jesus well this early in His mission. He needed time not only to heal but to teach, and to prepare His followers for His coming death. If the occupying forces of Rome were to notice too many people gripped with Messianic fever, it could cut Jesus' ministry short by imposing martial law—or killing Him, as indeed would eventually happen.

The leper Jesus healed, however, is too excited to restrain himself. Sure enough, the crowds attracted by Jesus' growing fame become unmanageable. Jesus has to leave the cities around Galilee and retreat to the country. Still, the crowds stream out to hear this Teacher, and to be rid of their spiritual, mental and physical ailments by His divine touch.

Evangelistic Emphasis

When Jesus healed the man with leprosy, he gave the man this command, "See that you don't tell this to anyone." Jesus probably gave this warning for several reasons: (1) Jesus did not want to be considered just a miracle worker, (2) he did not want his teaching ministry hindered by too much publicity being given to his healing miracles, and (3) he did not want his death to come before he had finished his ministry.

Even after this admonition, what did the man do? He told everyone who would listen about the miraculous change Jesus had made in his life.

Now, brothers and sisters, Jesus has not given us the same warning he gave the man in Mark 2. We are not commanded to keep quiet. In fact, if we read the entire gospel, Jesus tells all of us who follow Him that we are supposed to tell everybody about Him. Yet, many times, we who are supposed to tell others about Jesus do not.

Do you ever wonder why that is? The man healed of leprosy had no trouble telling others about the change Jesus had made in his life. He didn't tell himself, "I don't want to be pushy." He didn't tell himself, "Well, healing is a private matter. I don't want to intrude on others' privacy." Indeed not! The man was excited to tell of the change in his life.

What if each person whose life was changed by Jesus was as willing to tell others today?

Memory Selection

And Jesus, moved with compassion, put forth his hand, and touched him, and saith unto him, "I will; be thou clean.—*Mark 1:41*

Jesus touched a leper. That act was amazing in itself. In those days a leper was considered unclean. He was banished from all contact with humans except for other lepers. The leper was required to shout, "Unclean! Unclean!" everywhere he went, announcing his presence so he could be easily avoided.

In touching this man, Jesus rendered himself ceremonially unclean. Many times we are required to "get our hands dirty" when reaching out to others in compassion. Sometimes it is distaste-ful. Reaching out to others in compassion often forces us out of our comfort zones. Sometimes it requires us to associate with the outcast.

Jesus touched the leper with life-changing results. We may not be healers of bodies as Christ was. Yet, a touch can often be a part of the healing of one's soul.

Weekday Problems

Ken lay in his bed. Just like yesterday and the day before, Ken dreaded getting out of bed. Every day was another day of pain. He had been hurting with this arthritis for so long that he had forgotten how a pain-free day felt. He was only 40 years old. "That's too young to be a physical wreck," Ken thought. Yet, there he was, struggling to get out of bed through the pain and stiffness.

There was another reason Ken dreaded to get out of bed today. His friend Ron had called him last week. It seems there was an evangelist who was going to be at Ron's church who prayed for people and they got well. Ron said the evangelist had "the gift of healing." Ken did not know about all that. Ken was a Christian. He had read the Bible. He knew that folks had been healed by the laying on of hands and prayer in the Bible. He just wasn't so sure those things happened today.

There was another thing. Ken didn't want to look like a fool. He was educated. He was respected in the community. He didn't know exactly what would happen to his social status if word got out he had gone to a faith healer.

Ken dreaded getting out of bed. He lay there with his thoughts and his pain and his stiffness.

* Do you think there is still miraculous healing today? Why or why not?

* What do you think the leper of our scripture passage would say to Ken if they could converse?

It Only Hurts When I Laugh

Doctor: Say—this check you gave me came back.
Patient: So did my arthritis.

Jo: I had an operation, and they left a sponge inside.
Flo: Does it hurt?
Jo: No, but I sure get thirsty.

Dentist: What kind of filling do you want in your tooth?
Boy: Chocolate!

Doc: I have good news and bad news.
Patient: Give me the bad news first.
Doc: We amputated the wrong leg.
Patient: Oh, no! What's the good news?
Doc: Your other leg won't need to be amputated after all.

This Lesson in Your Life

Compassion in Action

In 1947, a young African-American man named Jackie Robinson became the first black man to play baseball in the major leagues. Robinson came up with the old Brooklyn Dodgers. As one might imagine, that first year was not the most pleasant of experiences. He encountered racial prejudice at every turn. He could not eat with the team in many of the restaurants because of his color. He was harassed by fans everywhere the Dodgers played. He was called every derogatory name in the book. There were even some players on other teams that vowed not to be on the same field with him. It was a rough first year.

If I remember the story correctly, on one particular night the fans were getting on him worse than usual. Then, Robinson booted a ground ball. The crowd's racial anger boiled over to a critical point. All of their wrath was focused upon this great baseball player who was black.

Robinson tells the story: "I'll never forget that game. I had never felt so alone. Just then, all-star shortstop PeeWee Reese came over to where I was and put his arm around my shoulders and stood with me looking up into the stands. In just a moment, the fans got quiet and the game resumed. That was the defining moment of my career. I don't think I could have gone on had he not done what he did. His arm around me made all the difference."

Have you ever noticed that compassion, to be of any good, must be combined with action? PeeWee Reese could have stood over at his position thinking, "Gee, I feel for that Robinson kid," and nothing would have been accomplished. Yet, when he was willing to put his care into action, it made a difference in a young man's life. By putting his arm around Robinson's shoulder, Reese was identifying himself with one many white fans thought was an outcast.

In a sense, Jesus did the same thing for the leper in our scripture passage. The leper was an outcast, reviled by society. Yet, Jesus was willing to be identified with this leper. He indicated his compassion initially with a loving touch.

I believe this is one of the most revealing pictures of Jesus. Notice what happened. First, the leper had no right to have spoken to Jesus at all. Yet, Jesus did not drive the man away who had broken the law. Jesus met the desperation of human need with understanding. Then, Jesus reached out and touched the leper. He touched a man who was unclean. To Jesus he was not an untouchable leper, he was simply a human soul in desperate need of a touch from Christ. Finally, after having cleansed the leper, Jesus sent him to fulfill the requirements of his healing according to the Law as a testimony of the power of God.

There is an old saying, "Jesus has no hands but our hands, no feet but our feet, no voice but our voices." There is a wealth of truth in that statement. If we have made up our minds to be Christ-like, then compassionate action must be part of who we are. Jesus reached out to the least, the last and the lost. We must do likewise.

Seed Thoughts

1. Where did Jesus teach and how did the people respond to Him?

Jesus taught in the synagogue in Capernaum. The people were astonished at His doctrine.

2. What was the difference between Jesus's teaching and the scribes' teaching?

The scripture says that Jesus taught the people not as the scribes, but as One who had authority.

3. Who was in the synagogue that day and what did he say to Jesus?

A man with demons. They begged Jesus to leave them alone, asking if He had come to destroy them and proclaiming Him to be the "Holy One of God."

4. How did Jesus respond to the man with the unclean spirit?

Jesus commanded the unclean spirit to be quiet and come out of the man.

5. How did the unclean spirit in the man respond to Jesus's rebuke?

The unclean spirit shook the man, cried out with a loud voice, and then came out of the man.

1. Where did Jesus teach and how did the people respond to Him?

2. What was the difference between Jesus's teaching and the scribes' teaching?

3. Who was in the synagogue that day and what did he say to Jesus?

4. How did Jesus respond to the man with the unclean spirit?

5. How did the unclean spirit in the man respond to Jesus's rebuke?

6. How did the people respond to what had taken place between Jesus and the man with the unclean spirit?

7. Did the people believe that Jesus had the power to heal? How do you know?

8. When Jesus cast out demons, He refused to let them speak. Why?

9. When Jesus healed the leper He gave the man specific instructions. What were these instructions?

10. Did the healed leper obey Jesus's command? Explain your answer.

(Please turn page)

Jesus taught in the synagogue in Capernaum. The people were astonished at His doctrine.

The scripture says that Jesus taught the people not as the scribes, but as One who had authority.

A man with demons. They begged Jesus to leave them alone, asking if He had come to destroy them and proclaiming Him to be the "Holy One of God".

Jesus commanded the unclean spirit to be quiet and come out of the man.

The unclean spirit shook the man, cried out with a loud voice, and then came out of the man.

The people were amazed. They asked questions among themselves and were puzzled that Jesus had such authority.

Yes, because by evening the people were bringing everyone who was sick or demon-possessed to Jesus and the whole city gathered to watch.

The devils all knew who Jesus really was.

He told the healed man not to tell anyone of his healing but to go directly to the priest and offer the necessary sacrifice.

No. The healed man began to tell everyone what Jesus had done for him.

6. How did the people respond to what had taken place between Jesus and the man with the unclean spirit?

The people were amazed. They asked questions among themselves and were puzzled that Jesus had such authority.

7. Did the people believe that Jesus had the power to heal? How do you know?

Yes, because by evening the people were bringing everyone who was sick or demon-possessed to Jesus and the whole city gathered to watch.

8. When Jesus cast out demons, He refused to let them speak. Why?

The devils all knew who Jesus really was.

9. When Jesus healed the leper He gave the man specific instructions. What were these instructions?

He told the healed man not to tell anyone of his healing but to go directly to the priest and offer the necessary sacrifice.

10. Did the healed leper obey Jesus's command? Explain your answer.

No. The healed man began to tell everyone what Jesus had done for him.

So that you may know that the Son of Man has authority... to forgive sins.

Lesson 3

Jesus' Authority Established

Mark 2:3-12; 3:1-5

3 And they come to him, bringing one sick of the palsy, which was borne of four.

4 And when they could not come nigh unto him for the press, they uncovered the roof where he was

5 When Jesus saw their faith, he said unto the sick of the palsy, Son, thy sins be forgiven thee.

6 But there were certain of the scribes sitting there, and reasoning in their hearts,

7 Why doth this man thus speak blasphemies? Who can forgive sins but God only?

8 And immediately when Jesus perceived in his spirit that they so reasoned within themselves, he said unto them, Why reason ye these things in your hearts?

9 Whether is it easier to say to the sick of the palsy, Thy sins be forgiven thee; or to say, Arise, and take up thy bed, and walk?

10 But that ye may know that the Son of man hath power on earth to forgive sins, (he saith to the sick of the palsy,)

11 I say unto thee, Arise, and take up thy bed, and go thy way into thine house.

12 And immediately he arose, took up the bed, and went forth before them all; insomuch that they were all amazed, and glorified God, saying, We never saw it on this fashion.

3:1 And he entered again into the synagogue; and there was a man there which had a withered hand.

2 And they watched him, whether he would heal him on the sabbath day; that they might accuse him.

3 And he saith unto the man which had the withered hand, Stand forth.

4 And he saith unto them, Is it lawful to do good on the sabbath days or to do evil? To save life, or to kill? But they held their peace.

5 And when he had looked round about on them with anger, being grieved for the hardness of their hearts, he saith unto the man, Stretch forth thine hand. And he stretched it out: and his hand was restored whole as the other.

Memory Selection
Mark 2:10—11

Devotional Reading
Acts 2:22-36

Background Scripture
Mark 2:1—3:6

Printed Scripture
Mark 2:3-12; 3:1-5

Teacher's Target

Lesson purpose: *To reflect on the implications of Jesus' demonstrated power over illness, as illustrated in two accounts from His early ministry.*

It is always appropriate to challenge unbelievers with the evidence for Christ's miracle-working power. Believers themselves, however, also need to be challenged to follow up on the implications of that power in their own lives.

This lesson offers three of these important implications. The story of the healing of the man with palsy is also a story of friends who cared about each other. It illustrates a call to modern believers to bring their friends to Christ, too.

Another implication in this story and that of the healing of the paralyzed man is Christ's authority over sin. Finally, there is the lesson of the priority of doing good over legalistic and ritual requirements.

Are we ready to accept these implications of the power over illness that Jesus demonstrates in these two events?

Lesson Introduction

The issue of whether Christ still heals as He did in New Testament times is likely to arise in this lesson. Just as there are differing doctrinal positions on the issue, so people bring different experiences to such a discussion. For example, doctors give up on a woman maimed in an automobile accident—but friends and relatives pray earnestly by her bedside and she recovers. A finely-tuned doctrine that denies modern-day healing isn't likely to weigh much with this woman.

On the other hand, a believer in modern-day healing prays earnestly for a loved one's recovery, only to have him die. This experience can produce unwarranted guilt: "If I were a better person, God would have healed my loved one."

Can opposing viewpoints on this issue be harmonized by affirming that God still heals, whether by medicine and science or by prayer; but that just as rain falls on both the just and the unjust, cures are not always a measure of spiritual health?

Teaching Outline	Daily Bible Readings	
	Mon.	Authority to Help People *Mark 2:1-12*
I. Sin and Sickness vs. Jesus—2:3-12	**Tue.**	Come to Call Sinners *Mark 2:13-22*
A. Authority to forgive, 3-7	**Wed.**	Grieved by Hardness of Heart *Mark 2:23-3:6*
B. Authority to heal, 8-12		
II. Sabbath-keeping vs. Doing Good—3:1-5	**Thu.**	Authority to Judge *John 5:19-29*
A. The test of the sabbath, 1-2	**Fri.**	Authority over all People *John 17:1-11*
B. The priority of doing good, 3-5	**Sat.**	Authority in Heaven and Earth *Matthew 28:160-20*
	Sun.	Named Lord and Messiah *Acts 2:22-36*

VERSE BY VERSE

I. Sin and Sickness vs. Jesus—2:3-12
A. Authority to forgive, 3-7

3 And they come to him, bringing one sick of the palsy, which was borne of four.

4 And when they could not come nigh unto him for the press, they uncovered the roof where he was

5 When Jesus saw their faith, he said unto the sick of the palsy, Son, thy sins be forgiven thee.

6 But there were certain of the scribes sitting there, and reasoning in their hearts,

7 Why doth this man thus speak blasphemies? Who can forgive sins but God only?

The opening verses of this chapter portray Jesus having returned to Capernaum after going "throughout all Galilee" (1:39). Verse 1 has said simply that Jesus was in "the house"— probably indicating the house of Simon Peter, where the events in our last lesson occurred. Wherever they were, it was a modest place, not large enough to accommodate the crowds who were beginning to flock to this miracle worker and authoritative teacher (1:22).

The fact that the place apparently had only one story—since that's the only way the sick man's friends could have let him down through the roof— also indicates that it was far from a mansion. Although Luke's account refers to a tiled roof (Luke 5:19), we are not to picture the cement tiles of modern Mediterranean roofs, but a mud-and-thatch tile that could be dug through—for that is the literal meaning of verse 4 (see the NIV). Imagine both the love for their friend that these four had, and the courage and faith it took to tear up someone else's roof to get their friend to Jesus!

Although "palsy" was the King James term for paralysis, it usually refers to tremors today. We are probably to picture a man so crippled and paralyzed he could not move off the pallet on which he lay.

Surprisingly, Jesus first pronounces the man's sins forgiven instead of healing him. Although priests under the Old Testament could pronounce a per-son's sins forgiven, they had no divine authority to actually remove guilt. We can imagine startled gasps from the crowd— especially the scribes among them (as well as Pharisees and "doctors of the law," Luke 5:17), who are all too ready to charge with blasphemy anyone who dared assume a role that belongs exclusively to God.

The implications of this situation Jesus has deliberately set up are awesome. If He is not divine, he is guilty of blasphemy. If He can actually forgive sins, He is in some way uniquely related to God the Father. To confront His critics with this possibility, Jesus shrewdly takes another step.

B. Authority to heal, 8-12

8 And immediately when Jesus perceived in his spirit that they so reasoned within themselves, he said unto them, Why reason ye these things in your hearts?

9 Whether is it easier to say to the sick of the palsy, Thy sins be forgiven thee; or to say, Arise, and take up thy bed, and walk?

10 But that ye may know that the Son of man hath power on earth to forgive sins, (he saith to the sick of the palsy,)

11 I say unto thee, Arise, and take up thy bed, and go thy way into thine house.

12 And immediately he arose, took up the bed, and went forth before them all; insomuch that they were all amazed, and glorified God, saying, We never saw it on this fashion.

"They" refers to the scribes and Pharisees, Jesus' ever-present critics. With insight as divine as His authority to forgive sins and to heal, He knows that they have charged Him with blasphemy in their hearts. As proof of His power to perform the inner miracle of removing guilt and sin, He then performs the external miracle of restoring the damaged nerves and wasted muscles of paralysis. The crippled man takes up the very bed by which his friends had let him down through the roof and walks out with it!

In passing, we may note that many modern Christians who believe that Christ performed a physical miracle here doubt, like the scribes, that He can "cure" sin as well. Some withhold a forgiving spirit from sinful but penitent people, indicating they doubt they have been forgiven (see vss. 15-17). Others struggle all their lives under a burden of guilt, believing their sins are too grievous for Jesus to forgive.

II. Sabbath-keeping vs. Doing Good —3:1-5

A. The test of the sabbath, 1-2

3:1 And he entered again into the synagogue; and there was a man there which had a withered hand.

2 And they watched him, whether he would heal him on the sabbath day; that they might accuse him.

Jesus is at the synagogue now, rather than in a private home, showing again that He is no rebel against Jewish religious practice. It is the sabbath; and Jesus' critics have followed Him to "church." They watch closely to see if He would heal (literally "do therapy") a man with a crippled hand, in violation of their views of keeping the sabbath.

It must be realized that Jewish tradition had gone far beyond God's original law against working on Saturday (remember that Sunday isn't really "the Christian sabbath"; the sabbath is still the seventh day). Long and torturous debates had resulted in rules against anything that might even appear to be work. If it was wrong for a man to plow on the sabbath, some rabbis taught that it was wrong for a boy to drag a stick in the sand—for the track it makes is only a smaller version of a plow's furrow!

Probably because of Jesus' shocking claim to have the authority to forgive sin, His critics aren't just observing Him now; they are searching for something like breaking such sabbath laws so they will have a good case against Him before the religious courts.

B. The priority of doing good, 3-5

3 And he saith unto the man which had the withered hand, Stand forth.

4 And he saith unto them, Is it lawful to do good on the sabbath days or to do evil? To save life, or to kill? But they

held their peace.

5 And when he had looked round about on them with anger, being grieved for the hardness of their hearts, he saith unto the man, Stretch forth thine hand. And he stretched it out: and his hand was restored whole as the other.

Again Jesus sees into the hearts of His critics—and what He finds there angers Him. He has the man stand, so all can see, and boldly challenges the sabbath tradition by healing the man's hand. He had already served notice of His position when He defended His disciples for plucking grain on the sabbath when they were hungry (2:23-28). (He had also challenged the ritual of fasting in 2:18-20.)

Jesus' defense here is in the form of a question (vs. 4). Later writings show that the rabbis taught that it was permissible to treat a person on the sabbath if his life were at stake. If that tradition extends back to the time of Christ, Jesus' second question may indicate both that

He knew about it, and that He knew His opponents did as well. Building on something they had to agree with, He expands the principle. The net effect of His teaching is that human need must have priority over religious ritual.

The last verse of chapter 2, however, indicates an even more important reason for Mark's having recorded these conflicts over sabbath-keeping. Jesus is showing that He is Lord of the sabbath (2:28). Since sabbath-keeping had been elevated to the point that it was virtually the sign of being a faithful Jew, Jesus chooses it to illustrate His very nature as Lord, and the very reason He came. In order to fulfill the Old Covenant (Matt. 5:17), and institute the New, He had to show His high-priestly authority not only to forgive sin, but to interpret the Law as well.

The next verse following our text (vs. 6) shows the way Jesus' opponents reacted to these bold claims. They began the plot that would eventually result in His death.

Evangelistic Emphasis

I love this account of four men who brought their paralyzed friend to Jesus. The four men knew the help the paralyzed man needed could be found in Jesus. It seems they were determined. Nothing could discourage them from their mission. They brought

the man to the house but could not even get in the door because of the crowd. They climbed to the roof and somehow hoisted this paralyzed man up with them. Then they tore a hole in the roof of the house big enough that a man could be lowered through it. Next, by sheer strength they lowered the man into the house, into the presence of Christ. There the paralyzed man received the things he needed most—forgiveness for his sins and healing for his body.

What a great bunch of friends those four men must have been! They were willing to go to almost any length to see that their friend made it into the presence of Jesus. Folks, we have friends that need to experience the presence of Christ. It is just as important that they come in contact with Jesus as it was for this paralyzed man.

Are we the same type of friends as these four men were? Four friends carried a man to the place where Jesus was, hauled the man up on a roof, tore a hole in the roof and lowered that man to Jesus. They went through all that simply to insure that their friend came in contact with Christ. May we be as loving toward our friends who need to meet Jesus.

Memory Selection

But that ye may know that the Son of man hath power on earth to forgive sins, (he saith to the sick of the palsy,) I say unto thee, Arise, and take up thy bed, and go thy way into thine house.—*Mark 2:10-11*

If you are like me, when you first read this you asked yourself, "How are the power to forgive and healing connected in this passage?" I think it is like this. Jesus could say the man was forgiven of his sins and no one would know if the man was actually forgiven or not. Why? Because forgiveness is an inner action offered to us by God. A forgiven person probably does not look any different from an unforgiven one.

Now, healing, on the other hand, can be seen. Healing is a visible action. This man could prove his healing by taking up his bed and walking right out. Thus, Jesus proved His power to forgive sins (an invisible action) by healing the man (a visible action).

The connection, you see, is not necessarily in the actions of Jesus. The focus is on the authority of Jesus.

Weekday Problems

It was a beautiful Saturday morning. Sharon hummed as she drove to Claire's house. She was going to keep Claire's three children while Claire goes to the mall with her mother. Claire has been having a rough time since Tom left. His leaving devastated her and the kids. She was thrown back into the work force. Her minimum salary barely allowed her and the kids to survive. Every now and then Tom would send some money, but never as much as he was supposed to send.

Claire was gamely holding on. She still tried to get the kids to dance, soccer, basketball and all the other activities they were in. She never had time for herself. She never had time to go to church either.

That is where Claire's friend Sharon comes in. Sharon is a Christian. She knows that Claire needs Christ more than anything else in the whole world. Regrettably, every time Sharon brings up Jesus, Claire cuts her off. Sharon decided what Claire needed first is a friend. Then, maybe one day Claire will allow Sharon to share Christ with her.

Sharon hums as she drives to Claire's house.

* How would you try to introduce Christ to Claire?

* Have you ever had an occasion where it was hard to help someone meet Jesus?

Out of the Mouths of Boys

Son: Dad, did you go to Sunday School when you were a kid?
Dad: Yep. Never missed.
Son: Bet it won't do me any good, either.

The Sunday School teacher asked her class to draw pictures of the birth of Jesus, but in a modern setting. One little boy drew Mary, Joseph, the Babe and several animals with their head sticking out of the windows of an airplane.

"But who is this?" she asked, not recognizing another figure at the front of the plane.

Oh that's Pontius the Pilot," the boy replied.

Miss Gill: What does the story of Jonah teach us?
Little Bill: You can't keep a good man down.

This Lesson in Your Life

Authorized to Help

In our passage we see two incidents of miraculous healing: one in which four men bring a paralyzed man to Jesus, and the other in which Jesus heals a man on the Sabbath. Both healings are significant.

In the first case, apparently the four men were convinced that Jesus offered what the fifth man needed. As you remember from the account, they went to great lengths to get the man to Christ. The first way was blocked, they could not get into the house through the door. Yet, they were not discouraged. They found another way to get the man to Jesus. This other way cost them additional time and effort.

We sing a song, "Jesus is the answer for the world today. Above Him there's no other. Jesus is the way." There are other songs such as, "No one ever cared for me like Jesus." There is a chorus about Jesus that says, "You are my strength when I am weak. You are the treasure that I seek. You are my all in all." We believe those words, don't we? We are convinced that knowing Jesus is the most important thing in all eternity. We are convinced that Jesus is worth giving up everything for. He is that pearl of great price, worthy of our lives. We are also convinced that "my God shall supply all your need according to His riches in glory by Christ Jesus" (Phil. 4:19, NKJV).

Since we are convinced of all these things, shouldn't we be like the four men who brought their friend to Jesus? They went through all obstacles to get their friend to Christ. Too often when I meet an obstacle I say, "Well, it must not have been God's will," and I give up. I wonder what our churches, our communities and our nation would be like if each of us were as determined as those four men about bringing folks to Jesus.

The men saw that Jesus was what the paralyzed man needed and they allowed nothing to distract them from their goal.

In the second account in our passage, we see Jesus healing a man's withered hand on the Sabbath. Now, we know that the Law stated that no work could be done on the Sabbath. The Jews then had to interpret exactly what constitutes work, so they would know what not to do. That is where Jesus got into trouble when he healed the man. According to Jewish tradition, medical attention could only be given on the Sabbath if a life was in danger. This was not a life-threatening condition. Therefore, the healing went against Jewish tradition. The folks in the synagogue thought the most important thing was to keep Jewish tradition. Jesus saw the most important thing as helping to relieve human suffering.

The Pharisees saw only tradition. Jesus, saw a man in need. Jesus decided people were more important.

We saw two encounters with Jesus. We saw two healings. The common things about these two accounts were these: both men had their needs met when they came in contact with Jesus; and both were healed in a fashion that broke convention.

That might be the lesson here. Sometimes we Christians get locked into thinking that we have Jesus figured out. About the time we think we have Christ in our box, we discover someone dropping through the roof or a man getting healed in a manner we think inappropriate.

May we bring our friends to Christ, regardless of the obstacles. May we expect Jesus to act, even if it goes against how we think he should act. May we always rely on His ability and authority.

Seed Thoughts

1. In this passage, what was the matter with the man who was sick?

He was "sick of the palsy," or rather the man was paralyzed.

2. What clue is given that this man had friends who were concerned for his welfare?

Four friends were trying to get the sick man to Jesus so that the sick man could be healed.

3. What drastic measures did these four men take to get the sick man to Jesus?

The men uncovered the roof of the house where Jesus was and lowered the sick man's bed into the room.

4. What was the first thing Jesus said to the sick man that caused a reaction in the crowd?

Jesus said, "Son, thy sins be forgiven thee."

5. What was the scribes' reaction to Jesus's radical statement to the sick man?

The scribes felt Jesus was guilty of blasphemy because they were sure only God could forgive sins.

1. In this passage, what was the matter with the man who was sick?

2. What clue is given that this man had friends who were concerned for his welfare?

3. What drastic measures did these four men take to get the sick man to Jesus?

4. What was the first thing Jesus said to the sick man that caused a reaction in the crowd?

5. What was the scribes' reaction to Jesus's radical statement to the sick man?

6. Why did Jesus publicly forgive the sick man of his sins?

7. What was the crowd's response to the paralyzed man's healing?

8. Where did Jesus meet the man with the withered hand? What day was it?

9. What questions did Jesus ask the crowd that Sabbath day?

10. What was Jesus' command to the man with the withered hand? What was the result?

(Please turn page)

He was "sick of the palsy," or rather the man was paralyzed.

Four friends were trying to get the sick man to Jesus so that the sick man could be healed.

The men uncovered the roof of the house where Jesus was and lowered the sick man's bed into the room.

Jesus said, "Son, thy sins be forgiven thee."

The scribes felt Jesus was guilty of blasphemy because they were sure only God could forgive sins.

Jesus wanted the scribes and the others to know that He, the Son of man, had the power to forgive sins.

They were all amazed, glorified God and exclaimed that they had never seen anything like that before now.

Jesus went to the synagogue on the Sabbath day and met a man there with a withered hand.

Jesus asked, "Is it lawful to do good on the Sabbath day, or to do evil? to save life, or to kill?

Jesus told the man to "Stretch forth thine hand." The man obeyed, and his hand was miraculously healed.

6. Why did Jesus publicly forgive the sick man of his sins?

Jesus wanted the scribes and the others to know that He, the Son of man, had the power to forgive sins.

7. What was the crowd's response to the paralyzed man's healing?

They were all amazed, glorified God and exclaimed that they had never seen anything like that before now.

8. Where did Jesus meet the man with the withered hand? What day was it?

Jesus went to the synagogue on the Sabbath day and met a man there with a withered hand.

9. What questions did Jesus ask the crowd that Sabbath day?

Jesus asked, "Is it lawful to do good on the Sabbath day, or to do evil? to save life, or to kill?"

10. What was Jesus' command to the man with the withered hand? What was the result?

Jesus told the man to "Stretch forth thine hand." The man obeyed, and his hand was miraculously healed.

Lesson 4

Jesus' Power Demonstrated

Mark 5:21-24, 35-43

21 And when Jesus was passed over again by ship unto the other side, much people gathered unto him: and he was nigh unto the sea.

22 And, behold, there cometh one of the rulers of the synagogue, Jairus by name; and when he saw him, he fell at his feet,

23 And besought him greatly, saying, My little daughter lieth at the point of death: I pray thee, come and lay thy hands on her, that she may be healed; and she shall live.

24 And Jesus went with him; and much people followed him, and thronged him.

35 While he yet spake, there came from the ruler of the synagogue's house certain which said, Thy daughter is dead: why troublest thou the Master any further.

36 As soon as Jesus heard the word that was spoken, he saith unto the ruler of the synagogue, Be not afraid, only believe.

37 And he suffered no man to follow him, save Peter, and James, and John the brother of James.

38 And he cometh to the house of the ruler of the synagogue, and seeth the tumult, and them that wept and wailed greatly.

39 And when he was come in, he saith unto them, Why make ye this ado, and weep? the damsel is not dead, but sleepeth.

40 And they laughed him to scorn. But when he had put them all out, he taketh the father and the mother of the damsel, and them that were with him, and entereth in where the damsel was lying.

41 And he took the damsel by the hand, and said unto her, Talitha cumi; which is, being interpreted, Damsel, I say unto thee, arise.

42 And straightway the damsel arose, and walked; for she was of the age of twelve years. And they were astonished with a great astonishment.

43 And he charged them straitly that no man should know it; and commanded that something should be given her to eat.

Memory Selection
Mark 5:36

Devotional Reading
1 Corinthians 1:18-31

Background Scripture
Mark 5:21-43

Printed Scripture
Mark 5:21-24, 35-43

Teacher's Target

Lesson Purpose: *To deepen our faith in Christ as Lord over death, and over our sense of loss when loved ones die, through the story of Jairus' daughter.*

Previous lessons have dwelt on Jesus' power to cast out demons, to heal, and to forgive sin. As astounding as these miracles are, this lesson takes us even farther into faith. The moving story of the death of Jairus' daughter, and of Jesus' restoring her to life, is a monument to Christ's power over death itself. Here is evidence that through Him, we can connect even in this life with the power that overcomes "the last enemy" (1 Cor. 15:26).

Be aware as you present this lesson of any in the class who may have lost a child in death. In cases where such a loss isn't too recent, it may be appropriate to encourage sharing of how the parents dealt with it; but be respectful of any hesitance to do so.

Lesson Introduction

Be sure to read the Background Scripture for this lesson (Mark 5:21-43), because the setting and placement of the story of the raising of Jairus' daughter is significant. Note that this incident is interrupted by another miracle—the healing of the woman with a hemorrhage (vss. 25-34).

At first glance, the two events seem to have little in common. When we look more closely, however, we are reminded of the Jewish knowledge that "the life is in the blood " (Lev. 17:11). Both stories demonstrate Jesus' sovereign power over the life-blood on which our existence depends. The life of both the woman with the hemorrhage and of Jairus' daughter depended on being touched by this One through whom the relationship between life and blood was created in the beginning.

We can also celebrate the link between these stories and the blood of Christ, which conquers spiritual death as well.

Teaching Outline	Daily Bible Readings
I. A Parent's Cry—21-23	**Mon.** A Twelve-year Illness *Mark 5:21-34*
A. A prominent man's loss, 21-22	**Tue.** Dealing with Death *Mark 5:35-43*
B. A heartfelt plea, 23	**Wed.** God's Power to Save *1 Corinthians 1:26-31*
II. A Prompt Response—24	
III. Premature Despair—35-39	**Thu.** Mighty in Deed and Word *Luke 24:13-27*
A. One perspective on death, 35	**Fri.** Power over the Enemy *Luke 10:16-24*
B. The perspective of faith, 36-40	**Sat.** Power Made Perfect in Weakness *2 Corinthians 12:1-10*
IV. Proof of Power—41-43	**Sun.** Power at Work Within *Ephesians 3:14-21*

VERSE BY VERSE

I. A Parent's Cry—21-23

A. A prominent man's loss, 21-22

21 And when Jesus was passed over again by ship unto the other side, much people gathered unto him: and he was nigh unto the sea.

22 And, behold, there cometh one of the rulers of the synagogue, Jairus by name; and when he saw him, he fell at his feet,

As 5:1 and 21 both indicate, Jesus is cris-crossing the Sea of Galilee during this period in His ministry. The raising of Jairus' daughter and the healing of the woman with the issue of blood occur opposite the "Decapolis " (vs. 20), or "Ten Cities." They were given the name because they were an ancient confederation or coalition put together by their Greek citizens, perhaps in the name of common defense, to preserve the Greek culture in an area of mixed ethnic groups. Since Jesus "passed over again " from the Ten Cities, the setting here may be back in Capernaum, to the northwest. Once again, crowds throng about Him because of His growing acclaim.

Jairus, whose office was something like that of a modern minister, was apparently among those who had heard of Jesus' miracles. He was not, however, among those Jewish leaders who attacked this wonder-worker. Any parent who has had a seriously ill child can identify with the way Jairus abandoned all polite conventions and threw himself at Jesus' feet. This was a common way of approaching someone in authority with an urgent plea (see 7:25).

B. A heartfelt plea, 23

23 And besought him greatly, saying, My little daughter lieth at the point of death: I pray thee, come and lay thy hands on her, that she may be healed; and she shall live.

Jairus has heard enough about Jesus to believe that He could make a difference in his daughter's condition. Perhaps the synagogue he led was the very one where Jesus had first preached (1:21). As this account was told and retold, one version had it that the little girl had already died; and this is the way it appears in Matthew's account (Matt. 9:18). This puts Jairus' faith in Jesus' power in an even brighter light.

II. A Prompt Response—24

24 And Jesus went with him; and much people followed him, and thronged him.

Usually Scripture describes people following Jesus. Here we are treated to the unusual scene of the very Son of God following a person. Yet it is not so unusual after all when we think of the Incarnation, when God became man, following us into every area of need, just as Jesus follows Jairus in his grief and anxiety. In our own times of anxiety, can we summon the faith to assure ourselves that Jesus still responds promptly when we call on Him, even when we do not see as dramatic an answer to prayer as we are about to see here?

III. Premature Despair—35-39

A. One perspective on death, 35

35 While he yet spake, there came from the ruler of the synagogue's house certain which said, Thy daughter is dead: why troublest thou the Master any further.

Other family members or servants came while Jesus was on the way to Jairus' home to tell him that since the little girl had already died, Jesus should be spared the trip. Those who have lost loved ones can understand their sense that there is nothing more to be done. Yet the rest of the story reminds us that even when our prayers do not seem to "work " and our loved ones die, Jesus—not death—will have the last word.

B. The perspective of faith, 36-40

36 As soon as Jesus heard the word that was spoken, he saith unto the ruler of the synagogue, Be not afraid, only believe.

37 And he suffered no man to follow him, save Peter, and James, and John the brother of James.

38 And he cometh to the house of the ruler of the synagogue, and seeth the tumult, and them that wept and wailed greatly.

39 And when he was come in, he saith unto them, Why make ye this ado, and weep? the damsel is not dead, but sleepeth.

40 And they laughed him to scorn. But when he had put them all out, he taketh the father and the mother of the damsel, and them that were with him, and entereth in where the damsel was lying.

Although Jairus' faith is stronger than those who come with the news that his daughter has died, Jesus quickly offers His reassurance. Doubt and despair are contagious, and it was important that Jairus be encouraged to persevere with his original instinct in coming to Jesus for help.

Peter, James, and John are often brought into an especially close relationship with their Teacher. Although we are never told why, we know that while we may have many close friends, a special "chemistry" often distinguishes our closest relationships. This is taking nothing away from the other nine apostles, and we never read of this causing jealousy among the Twelve. Even now it's a sign of insecurity when we become jealous when a friend has a closer relationship with someone else.

Some scholars say Jewish custom at this time was to have at least two flute players and one female "wailer" to help set an appropriate tone of sadness when someone died. We can also imagine neighbors joining in the mourning and creating a "tumult."

Jesus does not mean that the girl was mistakenly diagnosed as dead, but that in God's eyes death is only the separation of the body from the soul. Hence we are as much in God's hands when we die as when we are alive. Lacking Jesus' true view of death, the mourners laugh. Undaunted, Jesus asks them to leave the room. We can hardly imagine a more under-stated scene for a "resurrection" as He takes only Peter, James, John and the child's mother and father with him into her room. Thankfully, Jesus lacked a sense of showmanship; there is no public "healing service" here.

IV. Proof of Power—41-43

41 And he took the damsel by the

hand, and said unto her, Talitha cumi; which is, being interpreted, Damsel, I say unto thee, arise.

42 And straightway the damsel arose, and walked; for she was of the age of twelve years. And they were astonished with a great astonishment.

43 And he charged them straitly that no man should know it; and commanded that something should be given her to eat.

Talitha cumi is one of several expressions in the Aramaic language, a dialect of Hebrew, that survive in the Bible. They indicate the native language Jesus spoke. Writing in Greek, Mark helpfully translates the term for his Gentile readers. Gently taking the little girl by the hand, Jesus proves that, indeed, she was merely "asleep"—in the sense of not being permanently dead. This is our own faith when we gather at a funeral and sing the old song "Asleep in Jesus."

Imagine the excitement of the girl's family—and the embarrassment of those who had so confidently pronounced their sentence of doom and despair on the girl's condition.

The curtain falls on this astounding but under-stated scene with Jesus issuing two final commands with very practical implications. First, as excited as they are about the raising of Jairus' daughter, the people are not to tell anyone. The Messianic secret mentioned in a previous lesson is still to be kept because Jesus does not want His fame to alarm Rome, or the Jewish authorities, and bring His ministry to a premature end. ("Straitly" means narrowly or strictly.)

Second, in yet another remarkably low-keyed touch, Jesus gives the very human word that after the high drama of dying and being raised from the dead, the little girl just might enjoy a snack!

Evangelistic Emphasis

"That's not my job. Somebody else will do it!" Have you ever heard those words or statements very similar to those on the lips of Christians? "Let somebody else do it." We hear those words in our churches. Sometimes we hear those words concerning evangelism. "Evangelism is not my gift. Get someone else to do it." Jesus told us in Matthew 28:19-20 that evangelism is everybody's job. Too often, however, a job that is every-body's gets done by nobody.

Jairus' daughter was sick and about to die. Jairus knew that Jesus could somehow remedy the situation. Jairus went to find Jesus and bring Him to his dying daughter. When Jesus met the daughter, she was given life. Now, I wonder if Jairus thought, "Somebody else ought to go get Jesus. I am too busy." Or, "My business comes first." Or, "I don't want to be too pushy." I wonder if Jairus thought any of those things. I expect not. Jairus' primary concern was to see that his dying daughter came in contact with Jesus.

Today, there are millions of people in this world who are dying without Christ. If we leave the job of evangelism to somebody else, chances are nobody will do it. It is up to each Christian. May we have the same love for a lost and dying world as Jairus did for his dying daughter.

✳ ✳ ✳

Memory Selection

As soon as Jesus heard the word that was spoken, he saith unto the ruler of the synagogue, "Be not afraid, only believe."—*Mark 5:36*

Jesus said, "Be not afraid, only believe." That is often easier said than done, isn't it? When our world is falling apart around us, when we feel like we have to reach up just to touch bottom, when we are up to our elbows in alligators, Jesus says, "Be not afraid, only believe." It really is rather difficult to avoid being caught up in negative circumstances. Yet, when circumstances are at their worst, that is exactly the time it is most important to walk by faith.

When times are at their worst, it is more important to believe our Savior than our eyes. Paul reminds us in 2 Corinthians 5:7, "We live by faith, not by sight." When times get bad, don't look around and focus on the circumstances. Look up and focus on Jesus, "the author and perfecter of our faith." (Heb. 12:2)

Weekday Problems

Sean said a silent prayer as he sat in the hall before the meeting. He was to appear before the Board to present his plan for feeding needy families in the community. Sean believed this plan was of God. He had discovered a source for grocery items that could be purchased for only pennies on the dollar. He had secured a van to pick up the groceries. He had found a spare room in the church in which he could store the groceries. What he needed now was funding.

Old Wilson Memorial Church had been on the decline for years. It was an aging congregation. The young families had long since moved out of the area. The new families that were coming in all seemed to be poor. None of the new families were coming to Wilson Memorial. Plus, it seemed Wilson Memorial Church always had money problems. They hardly had enough cash to meet the church's needs. Now Sean was going to ask them to help meet needs of others outside the church.

Sean was confident the food program had been given to him by God. He had not especially wanted to pursue the ministry of feeding the hungry. Yet, God seemed constantly to confront him with the need in the community.

The door opened and Sean was invited into the meeting.

* Can God make a way where there is no way?

* Describe a situation you have been in where God asked you to believe before you saw results.

Living Words About Death

Death is as the foreshadowing of life. We die that we may die no more. —*Herman Hooker*

This world is the land of the dying; the next is the land of the living. — *Tryon Edwards*

Men fear death, as if unquestionably the greatest evil, and yet no man knows that it may not be the greatest good.—*W. Mitford*

We picture death as coming to destroy; let us rather picture Christ as coming to save . . . . We think of losing; let us think of gaining. We think of parting; let us think of meeting. We think of going away; let us think of arriving. And as the voice of death whispers "You must go from earth," let us hear the voice of Christ saying, "You are but coming to Me!"—*N. Macleod*

This Lesson in Your Life

Hope in the Face of Death

A little girl is dying. A desperate father seeks Jesus. How many times do you think this drama has been played out in the centuries since Jairus, his wife and his daughter were alive? As a pastor, I see the drama periodically. A child is critically ill or injured. The parents turn to Jesus in time of need, seeking His help in behalf of their child.

People often turn to Jesus in a crisis. We have even coined a phrase, "foxhole religion," for instances in which a life is in peril and the endangered one turns to God. I believe that folks turn to Christ in a crisis because, deep down, most folks know that Jesus can help. And He can.

Jairus turned to Christ to help his child. Jairus was a ruler of the synagogue. He knew that he could be censured by the Jews and possibly lose his position of prominence if he sought Jesus. Apparently he did not care. Jairus' main concern was the well-being of his child. He was willing to do anything for her.

Like Jairus, we are concerned for the well-being of our children. We will do almost anything to improve our children's lives. We see to it that they get the best education possible. We send them to school even when they whine. We see to it that they eat right. They have to taste that broccoli, at least. We make sure they get plenty of rest. They have to go to bed by 8:00 p.m. on school nights if they are elementary age. We must see to it that their souls are nurtured as well. If we are determined to care for the whole child, then we must take care of body, mind and spirit.

Jairus knew where to turn in crisis. He turned to Jesus. He sought Jesus for the healing of his daughter. We do the same. There may be no other time in which we are more fervent or sincere than when we are praying for a son or daughter. We may be casual about prayer during good times, but when an illness or accident strikes a child we get intensely serious about prayer. We seek Jesus above all else. Our faith in Christ is well-founded.

We know that Jesus can heal miraculously. We read of instance upon instance in the Bible. Many of you have witnessed miraculous healing. Knowing and following Jesus also brings better health. Recent studies have shown that churchgoers have lower rates of depression and alcohol/drug abuse. Regular church attendance reduces a person's blood pressure by 5 millimeters (5 points). Convalescents who are prayed for have significantly fewer complications and less need for antibiotics. ("Religion Is Good for Your Health" by Maggie Gallagher, *Dallas Morning News*, Feb. 12, 1996.) Not only does Jesus miraculously heal, He also enables us to enjoy better health every day. Jesus takes care of the whole person.

Yet, Jairus' daughter died. Notice, the care of Christ did not end with her death. She was brought back to life. Now, not many of us will witness the raising of the dead in such a spectacular fashion as with Jairus's daughter. Yet, everyone who is in Christ will live again with Him after death. That is one of the most beautiful things about knowing Christ. He gives us a better life, a more healthy life, on this earth. He also gives us a marvelous life after death with Him in heaven.

Jesus gives us abundant life . . . on both sides of the grave. No wonder Jairus turned to Christ in a crisis. We can, too.

Seed Thoughts

1. Who was Jairus? Where was Jesus when Jairus came to meet Him?

Jairus was ruler of the synagogue. He and many others met Jesus by the sea.

2. What request did Jairus ask of Jesus? What was his attitude?

Jairus desperately, yet humbly, fell at Jesus's feet, asking Him come lay hands on her that she would be healed.

3. Was Jesus willing to comply with Jairus' request? Who accompanied Jairus back home?

Yes. Jesus and a whole crowd started back to Jairus' house with him.

4. Before Jairus reached home, what message did he receive?

Before Jairus and Jesus reached home, a message was sent from his house that his daughter was already dead.

5. What was Jesus' reaction to the message received from Jairus' house?

Jesus turned to Jairus and said, "Be not afraid, only believe."

1. Who was Jairus? Where was Jesus when Jairus came to meet Him?

2. What request did Jairus ask of Jesus? What was his attitude?

3. Was Jesus willing to comply with Jairus' request? Who accompanied Jairus back home?

4. Before Jairus reached home, what message did he receive?

5. What was Jesus' reaction to the message received from Jairus' house?

6. Who was allowed to keep going with Jesus and Jairus to Jairus' house after the message was received?

7. When Jesus reached the house, what was the crowd's mood?

8. What did Jesus say to the crowd? How did they react to His statements?

9. Recount the facts of the healing. Who was allowed to witness this miracle?

10. What two commands did Jesus give the little girl's parents in verse 43?

(Please turn page)

Jairus was ruler of the synagogue. He and many others met Jesus by the sea.

Jairus desperately, yet humbly, fell at Jesus's feet, asking Him come lay hands on her that she would be healed.

Yes. Jesus and a whole crowd started back to Jairus' house with him.

Before Jairus and Jesus reached home, a message was sent from his house that his daughter was already dead.

Jesus turned to Jairus and said, "Be not afraid, only believe."

Only Peter, James, and John the brother of James were allowed to follow Jesus to the house.

The crowd was grieving when Jesus reached the house. Many wept and wailed and there was great tumult.

Jesus asked them why they were crying. He said the girl was not dead, only asleep. The crowd laughed and scorned Him.
Jesus put the crowd out. He, the parents, and the three disciples went into the girl's room. Jesus took her hand and commanded her to rise.

He told them to give the little girl something to eat and commanded them to tell no one what they had seen.

6. Who was allowed to keep going with Jesus and Jairus to Jairus' house after the message was received?

Only Peter, James, and John the brother of James were allowed to follow Jesus to the house.

7. When Jesus reached the house, what was the crowd's mood?

The crowd was grieving when Jesus reached the house. Many wept and wailed and there was great tumult.

8. What did Jesus say to the crowd? How did they react to His statements?

Jesus asked them why they were crying. He said the girl was not dead, only asleep. The crowd laughed and scorned Him.

9. Recount the facts of the healing. Who was allowed to witness this miracle?

Jesus put the crowd out. He, the parents, and the three disciples went into the girl's room. Jesus took her hand and commanded her to rise.

10. What two commands did Jesus give the little girl's parents in verse 43?

He told them to give the little girl something to eat and commanded them to tell no one what they had seen.

Lesson 5

Jesus' Identity and Mission

Mark 8:27–9:1

27 And Jesus went out, and his disciples, into the towns of Caesarea Philippi: and by the way he asked his disciples, saying unto the, Whom do men say that I am?

28 And they answered, John the Baptist: but some say, Elias; and others, One of the prophets.

29 And he saith unto them, But whom say ye that I am? And Peter answereth and saith unto him, Thou art the Christ.

30 And he charged them that they should tell no man of him.

31 And he began to teach them, that the Son of man must suffer many things, and be rejected of the elders, and of the chief priests, and scribes, and be killed, and after three days rise again.

32 And he spake that saying openly. And Peter took him, and began to rebuke him.

33 But when he had turned about and looked on his disciples, he rebuked Peter, saying, Get thee behind me, Satan: for thou savourest not the things that be of God, but the things that be of men.

34 And when he had called the people unto him with his disciples also, he said unto them, Whosoever will come after me, let him deny himself, and take up his cross, and follow me.

35 For whosoever will save his life shall lose it; but whosoever shall lose his life for my sake and the gospel's, the same shall save it.

36 For what shall it profit a man, if he shall gain the whole world, and lose his own soul?

37 Or what shall a man give in exchange for his soul?

38 Whosoever therefore shall be ashamed of me and of my words in this adulterous and sinful generation; of him also shall the Son of man be ashamed, when he cometh in the glory of his Father with the holy angels.

9:1 And he said unto them, Verily I say unto you, That there be some of them that stand here, which shall not taste of death, till they have seen the kingdom of God come with power.

Memory Selection
Mark 8:34

Devotional Reading
Isaiah 43:10-21

Background Scripture
Mark 8:27–9:13

Printed Scripture
Mark 8:27–9:1

291

Teacher's Target

Lesson purpose: *To highlight Jesus' teaching, and promise, about the cost and rewards of complete commitment to Him.*

Picture the faces of those in the class you teach Sunday after Sunday. In many groups, the predominant expression may be neither agony nor ecstasy, but boredom.

Certainly Jesus warns in this passage that following Him involves a cross. This emphasis needs to knife throughour self-centeredness and love of luxury, replacing them with a willingness to serve others.

Yet this uncompromising call to discipleship includes a promise, too. The cross-bearing offers exciting purpose, meaning and fulfillment to human existence. In short, taking up our cross daily is more rewarding than costly. After all, what is of more value than our souls?

Lesson Introduction

Jesus' message of the Kingdom was drawing huge crowds (see Mark 8:1-9). Peter and the other disciples seemed to be treated to daily miracles. Anticipation was growing that this Teacher and Miracle-worker would re-establish the "throne of David."

Could it be that the hated legions of Rome would finally be routed? Jesus' disciples even speculated that He would set up a new religious-political system in which they would displace corrupt leaders, and rule in His name (Mark 9:33-34).

In this famous passage, Jesus bluntly corrects such notions. The Kingdom He came to inaugurate has more to do with service than with power. It is more about sacrifice than political advancement. It is more about dying to self and living for others—but, in that life-style, finding, after all, our own souls.

Teaching Outline	Daily Bible Readings
I. The Good Confession—8:27-30	**Mon.** The Messiah Must Suffer
A. Various views of Jesus, 27-28	*Mark 8:27-33*
B. The personal response, 29-30	**Tue.** Disciples Practice Self-Denial
II. The Goal of the Christ—31-33	*Mark 8:34—9:1*
A. The Servant-Son, 31	**Wed.** Seeing Jesus in a New Light
B. Twin rebukes, 32-33	*Mark 9:2-13*
III. The Glory of Commitment	**Thu.** God Is Doing a New Thing
—8:34–9:1	*Isaiah 43:10-21*
A. Bearing our cross, 34	**Fri.** Blessing in the Midst of Earth
B. Finding our lives, 35-37	*Isaiah 19:18-25*
C. Sooner than you think! 38–9:1	**Sat.** Together We Will Be Saved
	Acts 15:6-11
	Sun. Declare His Glory to All People
	Psalm 9:1-13

VERSE BY VERSE

I. The Good Confession—8:27-30

A. Various views of Jesus, 27-28

27 And Jesus went out, and his disciples, into the towns of Caesarea Philippi: and by the way he asked his disciples, saying unto the, Whom do men say that I am?

28 And they answered, John the Baptist: but some say, Elias; and others, One of the prophets.

Jesus' Galilean ministry is winding down, and He is preparing to go to Jerusalem for the last days of His earthly sojourn. Before moving south, he goes to the very northern edge of the Promised Land, to a largely gentile city named for Tiberius Caesar. In choosing this setting to define His true mission, and the nature of true discipleship, perhaps Jesus is sending the message that He is a Messiah for the world, not just for Jews.

Jesus, of course, has divine knowledge of what people were saying about Him, but He asks His followers for a report so their own view of who He is can be clarified against competing claims. It is not surprising that people held differing views of Jesus. Various strands of Messianic expectations were abroad: He would be a human descendant of King David, a divine figure coming in the clouds, a priest to replace the corrupt Jewish priesthood.

The views cited by the disciples are also understandable. John the Baptist had been put to death for defying King Herod (Mark 6:14-28), but the prophet had been so popular that some thought he was re-embodied in Jesus. Others thought Jesus was Elias (Elijah), whom the prophet Malachi had said would precede the Messiah (Mal. 4:5-6). Still others envisioned Him to be the reincarnation of another prophet or a new one, as John the Baptist had been.

B. The personal response, 29-30

29 And he saith unto them, But whom say ye that I am? And Peter answereth and saith unto him, Thou art the Christ.

30 And he charged them that they should tell no man of him.

Reciting what others think about Christ is never enough. Jesus confronts His disciples (and all others) with the real issue of personal belief. It is the outspoken apostle Peter who blurts out the consensus view of the disciples. "Christ" is from the Greek word for "Messiah." As wrong as the disciples were on the role of the Messiah, they at least had His identity correct. (And in Matthew's version of this scene Jesus commends Peter for what was right about his "good confession" [2 Tim. 6:13] before rebuking him for what was wrong—see Matt. 16:16-18.)

Previously, demons and those Jesus healed had been order to keep "the Messianic secret." In verse 30 the disciples themselves are warned that it is too early to broadcast the Good News.

His enemies among the Roman and Jewish rulers must not interrupt Jesus' work; He will work out His own time-table.

II. The Goal of the Christ—31-33

A. The Servant-Son, 31

31 And he began to teach them, that the Son of man must suffer many things, and be rejected of the elders, and of the chief priests, and scribes, and be killed, and after three days rise again.

Having drawn out the correct answer to His identity, Jesus proceeds to teach His disciples what His Messiahship entailed. To do so, He refers to Himself as the "Son of man." This title would have reminded the well-read Jew of the Son of man descriptions in the book of Daniel, connecting with some of the "divine figure" Messianic expectations. For in Daniel, the Son of man is an awesome, powerful figure who rules the world (Dan. 7:13-14).

The name itself, however, lends itself to quite a different interpretation, since it includes the human term "man." Jesus shocks His disciples by choosing that aspect to describe the path of pain He must walk before appearing in any majestic form: He must suffer and die.

It is hard for us to imagine the impact this would have made on Jews expecting the Messiah to be a conquering, warrior-king of David's lineage. For them, the term "suffering Messiah" would have been an oxymoron—a self-contradictory statement like "hot ice." Only the more thoughtful among Jesus' hearers would have recognized that in predicting His suffering and death He was applying to Himself the great Messianic passage Isaiah 53: "He was wounded for our transgressions, he was bruised for our iniquities."

B. Twin rebukes, 32-33

32 And he spake that saying openly. And Peter took him, and began to rebuke him.

33 But when he had turned about and looked on his disciples, he rebuked Peter, saying, Get thee behind me, Satan: for thou savourest not the things that be of God, but the things that be of men.

Again it is Peter who is as quick to rebuke the Lord as He was to confess His Messiahship. The notion of a suffering Messiah is too contradictory for Peter to contain within his mental parameters.

On the other hand, it is not within God's plan to save mankind by a warrior-king; so Jesus returns the rebuke in kind. Only a Son and a Servant willing to give His life for His enemies can reverse the self-defeating pattern of conquering by force, and constitute an adequate sin-offering. Jesus could be a gentle and understanding Friend; but on this point He cannot compromise, and He uses strong language to say so. Since the word "Satan" means "adversary," Christ bluntly applies the name to Peter. Even today, those who think of salvation in terms other than through Christ's death on the Cross mark themselves as adversaries against God's plan.

III. The Glory of Commitment—8:34–9:1

A. Bearing our cross, 34

34 And when he had called the people unto him with his disciples also, he said unto them, Whosoever will come after me, let him deny himself, and take up his cross, and follow me.

The next pill prescribed by the Great Physician is equally difficult to swallow.

Just as Messiah must subject His personal comfort to the needs of others, so must His followers.

It is natural to think of this saying as a call to suffer, since that was the essential meaning of the cross of Christ. Hence Christians often speak of a disobedient child or poor health or an overly talkative mother-in-law as "the cross I must bear." The cross Jesus has in mind, however, is both easier and more burdensome than such problems. It is easier in that there is no way a burden can earn our salvation, as did Jesus' cross. It is heavier in that denying the self requires putting that child or that mother-in-law's needs over our own. Bearing our cross, means the daily "crucifixion" of fleshly self-centeredness, and living for others.

B. Finding our lives, 35-37

35 For whosoever will save his life shall lose it; but whosoever shall lose his life for my sake and the gospel's, the same shall save it.

36 For what shall it profit a man, if he shall gain the whole world, and lose his own soul?

37 Or what shall a man give in exchange for his soul?

Difficult though it is to crucify the self, Christ's next statement shows that it meets our deepest needs. Those who live for self are rarely fulfilled, while those who serve others find purpose and meaning in life—not to mention the salvation of their soul.

C. Sooner than you think! 38–9:1

38 Whosoever therefore shall be ashamed of me and of my words in this adulterous and sinful generation; of him also shall the Son of man be ashamed, when he cometh in the glory of his Father with the holy angels.

9:1 And he said unto them, Verily I say unto you, That there be some of them that stand here, which shall not taste of death, till they have seen the kingdom of God come with power.

Verse 38 seems to be a warning to Peter and the other disciples that if they insist on clinging to a picture of a warrior-Messiah, and are embarrassed by the "weakness" of a servant-Messiah, they will paradoxically be denied the honor of reigning with Him when, after His suffering and death, He returns in the true splendor of a conquering king.

Finally, Jesus says that the coming of this Kingdom will be within the lifetime of some who heard His description of Messiahship and servanthood. This actually occurred in Acts 1–2, when these very disciples saw the Lord who previously suffered and died raised to His throne by God's right hand, and the doors of the Kingdom thrown open. The culmination of that Kingdom is yet to come; but those who are willing to accept the King's ransom and take up their cross are even now "translated" into the dominion of God (Col. 1:13).

Evangelistic Emphasis

What do you talk about when you meet someone? You probably would ask that person what he or she does for a living. You might talk about sports. You might talk about the weather. You might comment on what that person is wearing. You would make all kinds of small talk.

Most of us find it very easy to talk about things that really don't amount to much. Not that children and marital status are not important, but we generally feel more comfortable talking about superficial things when we visit with people. Wouldn't it be great if we could talk to folks about Jesus as naturally and as easily as we talk about the weather?

By and large, most of us are slightly timid about talking about the most important thing in our lives, Jesus Christ. We may not know how to share about Jesus. We may be afraid the other person will think we are weird. We may not want to be pushy. For whatever reasons, most of us have missed opportunities to talk about Jesus. We were hesitant and the opportunity passed.

Think of this. Have you ever seen a grandparent who was embarrassed to show off pictures of grandchildren? May we never miss a chance to talk about our King of Kings and Savior. We must be wise. We must be sensitive. We must also be bold.

Memory Selection

And when he had called the people unto him with his disciples also, he said unto them, "Whosoever will come after me, let him deny himself, and take up his cross, and follow me.—*Mark 8:34*

This is the definitive call to discipleship. People have tried to sugar coat it. People have tried to camouflage it. People have even tried to deny it. Yet, this remains the call to discipleship.

We have heard popular preachers of our day send a message that sounds as if they are calling souls simply to come to Jesus to receive everything their hearts desire. There is much truth in that, as far as it goes. Yet, we must never get the sequence of the call out of order.

First comes the call to self-denial. One can scarcely be filled with Christ if one remains full of oneself. Once we follow Christ, then He will fill us with good things.

Dietrich Bonhoeffer, a great German theologian, was quoted as saying, "When Christ calls a man, He bids him come and die." So it is. Christ calls us to die to self and live for Him.

Weekday Problems

Lynette had been a Christian since she was a little girl. She loved Christ with all her heart. Lynette had a problem, though. She was really, really turned off by people who tried to convince other people to become Christians. "People don't want to be preached at," Lynette figured. "They want to be loved. Christians can do their best witnessing by simply showing the love of Christ in their day-to-day lives."

One day Lynette was sitting in the park, reading her Bible. Her friend Marie plopped down beside her. "Lynette," Marie observed, "you have a certain quality about you. It's ... it's as if you know what's really important. You don't let the silly details of life drag you down. You seem happy, kind of self-assured all the time."

"Aha!" Lynette thought, "my silent witness is working.

"Why, thank you very much, Marie. It's so nice of you to say that," Lynette said aloud.

"No, really," Marie persisted. "It's just like you have something that I don't have. I can't quite put my finger on it. What's your secret?"

Lynette just smiled. She wasn't about to turn Marie off with "Jesus talk" now that Marie was so close to the Lord.

* Can Christians be so afraid of being pushy that they miss opportunities to witness?

* What might you have said to Marie?

Questions, Questions

Can you tell me how you became so rich?
Turn out the lights, and I'll tell you a story.
Never mind. I think I already know.

Is Mrs. Wilson an active member of your sewing club?
No, she never says a word. She just sits there and sews.

How far is it to the next service station?
About two miles, as the crow flies.
How long will it take if the crow has to walk, and roll a flat tire?

Aren't you ashamed to ask for hand-outs in this neighborhood?
Why, no ma'am. I've seen worse.

This Lesson in Your Life

Our passage begins with a question from Jesus, "Who do people say I am?" Who do people of the 20th century say Jesus is? If we ask, let's look to those who are competent to give testimony. Too often we give more credence to the words of an actor or actress who has had an out-of-body experience and gets 15 minutes on Oprah than we do to the careful work of first-class minds who have dedicated their lives to the task. Somehow, many have reached the perverse conclusion that everyone has a right to a verdict on Jesus except those who know most about Him.

Who do people say Jesus is? To whose voice will we listen? Will we listen to John the Baptist? He saw Jesus on the banks of the River Jordan and said, "Behold, the Lamb of God who takes away the sin of the whole world."

Will we listen to Paul? He described Jesus as "the image of the invisible God, the firstborn over all creation . . . and in Him dwells the fullness of the Godhead, bodily" (Col. 1:15. 19)."

We should listen to the voices coming from history books of those who were willing to die at the hands of gladiators or torn apart by lions rather than deny that Jesus Christ is Lord.

We should listen to the voice coming from the circuit riders of the 18th century. We should listen to those who gave their lives, both figuratively and literally, to spread scriptural holiness throughout the colonies and the young nation called the United States of America.

Yet it is not enough just to ask others who Jesus is. Jesus asked, "Who do *you* say that I am?" You see, no amount of historical exploration or general knowledge can be a substitute for a personal verdict. An academic-thesis, "term-paper" attitude which ends, "These are the various views of Jesus" cannot free us from the question, "Who do *you* say that I am?"

Rev. Joe McLain, a Methodist preacher, has often said, "In matters of religion, if you're wrong about God, you're wrong about everything!" There-fore, the question is an important one. Our eternity hangs upon our answer.

Jesus asks us, "But what about you? Who do you say that I am?" Is Jesus a poetic idealist, a baby in a manger, or a sentimental figure who has no relevance for our day?

Is Jesus a dear companion for the home and family, blessing it with intimate love, but no master for business dealings or politics?

The question is asked of us today, "Who do we say this man Jesus is?" Peter gives the right answer, "You are the Christ!" When Jesus asks us, "Who do you say that I am?" can we answer as Peter did, "You are the Christ"? Until we are able to answer that Jesus is the Christ, the Anointed One, the Messiah, to *us*, we have yet to let Him into our hearts. Until we confess Him as our personal Savior, we are lost still.

Who do *you* say Jesus is?

Seed Thoughts

1. What question did Jesus ask His disciples as they traveled into the towns of Caesarea Philippi?

Jesus asked His disciples this question, "Whom do men say that I am?"

2. What was the disciples' response to Jesus's first question?

Some thought Jesus was John the Baptist. Others thought maybe He was Elijah. Still others just said He was one of the prophets.

3. What was Jesus's next question? How did Peter answer?

Jesus then asked, "But whom say ye that I am?" Peter replied, "Thou art the Christ."

4. How did Jesus react to Peter's insightful answer to His second question?

Jesus instructed His disciples not to tell anyone that He was the Christ.

5. What did Jesus begin to teach the disciples that other Jews were unaware of at the time?

Jesus began to teach the disciples that the Son of man must suffer and be rejected and even be killed, but after three days He would rise again.

(Please turn page)

1. What question did Jesus ask His disciples as they traveled into the towns of Caesarea Philippi?

2. What was the disciples' response to Jesus's first question?

3. What was Jesus's next question? How did Peter answer?

4. How did Jesus react to Peter's insightful answer to His second question?

5. What did Jesus begin to teach the disciples that other Jews were unaware of at the time?

6. How did Peter respond to this new teaching of Jesus'?

7. How did Jesus react to Peter's rebuke? What name did He call Peter?

8. What did Jesus indicate was Peter's problem in accepting these new teachings?

9. List the paradoxes and conditions that Jesus gave for discipleship.

10. What was Jesus' prophecy in Mark 9:1?

299

Jesus asked His disciples this question, "Whom do men say that I am?"

Some thought Jesus was John the Baptist. Others thought maybe He was Elijah. Still others just said He was one of the prophets.

Jesus then asked, "But whom say ye that I am?" Peter replied, "Thou art the Christ."

Jesus instructed His disciples not to tell anyone that He was the Christ.

Jesus began to teach the disciples that the Son of man must suffer and be rejected and even be killed, but after three days He would rise again.

This new teaching made Peter uncomfortable. Peter took Jesus and began to rebuke Him.

Jesus called Peter "Satan" and rebuked Peter in front of the other disciples.

Jesus said Peter was looking at things the way man looked at them and not the way God saw them.

He who desires to follow Jesus must deny himself, being willing to lose his life for the gospel's sake and not be ashamed of Jesus.

Jesus prophesied that some hearing the message that day would live to see it fulfilled.

6. How did Peter respond to this new teaching of Jesus'?

This new teaching made Peter uncomfortable. Peter took Jesus and began to rebuke Him.

7. How did Jesus react to Peter's rebuke? What name did He call Peter?

Jesus called Peter "Satan" and rebuked Peter in front of the other disciples.

8. What did Jesus indicate was Peter's problem in accepting these new teachings?

Jesus said Peter was looking at things the way man looked at them and not the way God saw them.

9. List the paradoxes and conditions that Jesus gave for discipleship.

He who desires to follow Jesus must deny himself, being willing to lose his life for the gospel's sake and not be ashamed of Jesus.

10. What was Jesus's prophecy in Mark 9:1?

Jesus prophesied that some hearing the message that day would live to see it fulfilled.

HOSANNA

BLESSED IS THE ONE WHO COMES IN THE NAME OF THE LORD

Lesson 6

Entering Jerusalem

Mark 11:1-10, 15-18

1 And when they came nigh to Jerusalem, unto Bethphage and Bethany, at the mount of Olives, he sendeth forth two of his disciples,

2 And saith unto them, Go your way into the village over against you: and as soon as ye be entered into it, ye shall find a colt tied, whereon never man sat; loose him, and bring him.

3 And if any man say unto you, Why do ye this? Say ye that the Lord hath need of him; and straightway he will send him hither.

4 And they went their way, and found the colt tied by the door without in a place where two ways met; and they loose him.

5 And certain of them that stood there said unto them, What do ye, loosing the colt?

6 And they said unto them even as Jesus had commanded: and they let them go.

7 And they brought the colt to Jesus, and cast their garments on him; and he sat upon him.

8 And many spread their garments in the way: and others cut down branches off the trees, and strawed them in the way.

9 And they that went before and they that followed, cried, saying Hosanna; Blessed is he that cometh in the name of the Lord:

10 Blessed be the kingdom of our father David, that cometh in the name of the Lord: Hosanna in the highest.

15 And they come to Jerusalem: and Jesus went into the temple, and began to cast out them that sold and bought in the temple, and overthrew the tables of the moneychangers, and the seats of them that sold doves;

16 And would not suffer that any man should carry a vessel through the temple.

17 And he taught, saying unto them, Is it not written, My house shall be called of all nations the house of prayer? But ye have made it a den of thieves.

18 And the scribes and chief priests heard it, and sought how they might destroy him: for they feared him, because all the people was astonished at his doctrine.

Memory Selection
Mark 11:9

Devotional Reading
Psalm 118:19-29

Background Scripture
Mark 11:1-33

Printed Scripture
Mark 11:1-10, 15-18

Teacher's Target

Lesson purpose: *To dwell again on the authority of Jesus by focusing on two events that introduce the last week of His life—the Triumphal Entry, and the cleansing of the Temple.*

"Everyone loves a parade." The first "Palm Sunday" celebration draws a tumultuous crowd to welcome the mighty Miracle Worker and Teacher whose fame had preceded Him in Jerusalem. Attempts to squelch their joy would have brought shouts from the stones along the way! (See Luke 19:39-40.) Riding the crest of popularity, Jesus then proceeds to cleanse the Temple, to the further astonishment of the crowds.

A week later, Jesus would be executed. The crowds who hailed Him as King turned angry and called for His death.

The contrast here confronts modern believers who find it easy to follow Jesus when it is popular to do so, but more difficult when it calls for taking unpopular stands in His name. Lead your class to ask themselves how far they are willing for Christ to lead them as their Lord.

Lesson Introduction

Nearly three years of teaching, preaching, and healing lay behind Jesus as He approached the Holy City of Jerusalem in Mark 11. He has spent much of this time around the Sea of Galilee, to the north. Now it is time to go to the center of Jewish authority and to confront those who had often sent informants to investigate Him.

No longer will Christ counsel people not to spread the word about His divine identity. He freely allows the people lining the streets as He enters Jerusalem to give Him a welcome fit for a king. He boldly enters the Temple and physically drives out those who were desecrating it. The soft-spoken carpenter's son begins to show another side of the Son of man, as He called Himself. In doing so He shakes the very foundations of the previous religious order, and positions Himself as having the divine authority to be God's herald of a new day.

Teaching Outline	Daily Bible Readings	
	Mon.	Hosannas Rise to Heaven *Mark 11:1-11*
I. The Authority of a King—1-10	**Tue.**	A Temple for All Nations *Mark 11:12-19*
A. Jesus' instructions, 1-3	**Wed.**	Faith Finds God's Will *Mark 11:20-33*
B. The disciples' obedience, 4-7	**Thu.**	Obedient to the Cross *Philippians 2:1-11*
C. The Triumphal Entry, 8-10	**Fri.**	The Suffering Servant *Isaiah 50:4-11*
II. The Fire of a Reformer—15-18	**Sat.**	He Heals the Brokenhearted *Psalm 147:1-11*
A. Cleansing the Temple, 15-16	**Sun.**	Declare His Glory to All People *Psalm 9:1-13*
B. Challenging teaching, 17-18		

VERSE BY VERSE

I. The Authority of a King—1-10

A. Jesus' instructions, 1-3

1 And when they came nigh to Jerusalem, unto Bethphage and Bethany, at the mount of Olives, he sendeth forth two of his disciples,

2 And saith unto them, Go your way into the village over against you: and as soon as ye be entered into it, ye shall find a colt tied, whereon never man sat; loose him, and bring him.

3 And if any man say unto you, Why do ye this? Say ye that the Lord hath need of him; and straightway he will send him hither.

We last sat at the feet of Jesus on an excursion to the northern part of Palestine, during His Galilean ministry. In 10:1, however, He had turned west, to cross the Jordan, then south toward Jerusalem. Having clearly declared His mission to suffer and die, then rise again (8:31), He is determined to fulfill it in the center of Jewish opposition to His teaching.

Returning to the Mount of Olives, where He had delivered His Sermon on the Mount (Matt. 5–7), Jesus makes plans to have His Messiahship boldly acclaimed. The time for keeping the secret is over. With divine foresight, He knows just where and to whom to send disciples to bring a "colt" ("the foal of an

ass," according to Matthew 21:5, in fulfillment of Zechariah 9:9).

Some authorities hold that riding into Jerusalem on such a humble beast demonstrated Jesus' humility. Others note that the wealth of ancient kings was often gauged by the number of donkeys they possessed. Perhaps the parable Jesus is acting out here cuts both ways: He is indeed the promised King, but He rules by humble service. It is possible to derive the same double symbolism from the term "Son of man" that Jesus chose for Himself, as noted in the preceding lesson.

Equally significant is Mark's note that the colt had not been previously ridden (vs. 2), and that the disciples are simply to say, as servants, that their master needs it. Mark would have us understand that Christ's divinity gives Him power to tame an unbroken animal and to request what He wills, expecting compliance from both man and beast. In a few swift strokes, the Gospel thus paints a picture of impressive authority.

B. The disciples' obedience, 4-7

4 And they went their way, and found the colt tied by the door without in a place where two ways met; and they loose him.

5 And certain of them that stood there said unto them, What do ye, loosing the colt?

6 And they said unto them even as Jesus had commanded: and they let them go.

7 And they brought the colt to Jesus, and cast their garments on him; and he sat upon him.

Christ's authority is again emphasized in the unquestioning response of the disciples. We can well imagine that they had questions. How does Jesus know where the colt will be? How can He expect its owner to lend it on request? Yet they obey. All these elements in the Triumphal Entry story point to the fact that for a few brief moments the veil of mystery is lifted from Jesus in order for His majestic authority as Messiah to be seen.

C. The Triumphal Entry, 8-10

8 And many spread their garments in the way: and others cut down branches off the trees, and strawed them in the way.

9 And they that went before and they that followed, cried, saying Hosanna; Blessed is he that cometh in the name of the Lord:

10 Blessed be the kingdom of our father David, that cometh in the name of the Lord: Hosanna in the highest.

As Luke 19:40 indicates, the joyous praise of the crowds simply cannot be squelched—else "the stones would immediately cry out." Hundreds of years of political oppression and floods of tears for the nation's sins seem pent up within their breasts. In this miracle worker their hopes and dreams seem about to be fulfilled, so their longings burst forth like a flood, and the parade is on!

"Hosannah" translates in one word the Hebrew phrase "Save I (or we) beseech thee" from Psalm 118:25. Along with 118:26, the people shout what they apparently understood to be a Messianic hymn, applying the ancient words to Jesus in acknowledgment of His claims. The fact that many of these same people will only a few days later clamor for Jesus to be crucified indicates the gap between their hope for a conquering, warlike Messiah, and God's plan for

the Messiah to be slain. They must have felt that with Jesus' capture by the Jewish leaders and Roman authorities, He was an imposter. In their limited view, God did not "bless" the One who came down the palm-paved streets; so they turned against Him.

II. The Fire of a Reformer—15-18

A. Cleansing the Temple, 15-16

15 And they come to Jerusalem: and Jesus went into the temple, and began to cast out them that sold and bought in the temple, and overthrew the tables of the moneychangers, and the seats of them that sold doves;

16 And would not suffer that any man should carry a vessel through the temple.

We may recall that Jesus lived in obedience to the Jewish laws. More than once he told those He healed to go offer the required sacrifice (see Mark 1:44, and Lesson 2). He was not prepared, however, to condone abuses of the sacrificial system. One of those abuses was the sale of small animals in the outer court of the Temple.

Verse 11 has noted that Jesus went into the Temple and apparently observed this practice before going out to nearby Bethany to spend the night. It was after that incident that He cursed the non-bearing fig tree; and we may wonder whether He was ventilating His anger over having seen the unfruitful commercialism at the Temple.

Money changers set up booths in the court of the Gentiles to change the pagan coinage brought from Jews throughout the world into Jewish money—perhaps pocketing an unreasonable profit for their services. (This would not be the last time believers would be blighted by the scandal of profiteering religionists.)

It is also possible that Jesus' wrath erupts because these money-making schemes were set up in the outer court, the court of the gentiles, thus slighting His mission to pagans as well as to Jews.

At any rate, He drives the "religion for profit" trade bodily from the Temple grounds, and orders them to stop carrying the vessels containing the animals and their ill-gotten gain through the Temple. (It should go without saying that using this passage to justify physical violence against religious error requires the false assumption that we have the authority and insight of Jesus!)

B. Challenging teaching, 17-18

17 And he taught, saying unto them, Is it not written, My house shall be called of all nations the house of prayer? But ye have made it a den of thieves.

18 And the scribes and chief priests heard it, and sought how they might destroy him: for they feared him, because all the people was astonished at his doctrine.

Quoting Isaiah and Jeremiah, Jesus reminds the offenders that the Temple was a place for faith to be practiced, not questionable business transactions. His insistence that the Temple was "for all nations" is another hint that the commercial enterprises angered him in part because they desecrated the space reserved for gentile worshipers.

Jesus' bold and dramatic action sealed His doom with His opponents. He was already on shaky ground with them since He opposed their legalist doctrines, hypocrisy, and the unreasonable burdens they added to the Law. Upsetting part of the way the scribes and chief priests financed their profession was the last straw. As the modern critic accused the preacher when he preached on giving, Jesus had "quit preachin' and gone to meddlin'"! Furthermore, the popular support of the people Jesus enjoyed threatened their power. The die is cast; the plots that will result in the crucifixion begin to be made.

Evangelistic Emphasis

The day Jesus came into Jerusalem the people gathered on the sides of the road automatically. Their shouts of praise and adoration came spontaneously. They were deliriously happy that the Savior was coming into Jerusalem. The next day Jesus went into the Temple and drove out those who were using the Temple courts for unfair commercial purposes.

If we look closely, we discover the method Jesus follows when He comes into our hearts. When we first invite Jesus into our hearts, we are deliriously happy. We feel all tingly inside. We catch ourselves humming church tunes and thinking about Christ. Jesus will allow us to enjoy the sweetness of salvation without requiring anything of us for a season. However, Jesus has a tendency not to let us stay too long at that point.

Jesus loves us enough to save us. He gave His life for our salvation and made a way for our heavenly reward. Yet, He also loves us so much that He wants us to be like Him, holy and spotless. He does not simply save us. Once He comes into our hearts, He cleans us up by His Holy Spirit. He finds the things within us that do not glorify Him and He throws those things out.

That is what He did in Jerusalem. He does that for us today. He makes us into people more like He is.

Memory Selection

And they that went before, and they that followed, cried, saying, Hosanna; Blessed is he that cometh in the name of the Lord!—*Mark 11:9*

"Hosanna" is a simple transliteration of a Hebrew word which means "save" or "save now." The people thought Christ had come to save them. They saw Him as one of the Davidic line. They expected Him to be a King along the lines of David, a powerful military ruler that would bring freedom to the Jews. They expected an earthly king that would save them from their enemies.

What they got was a King who would save them, and us, from much, much more than just enemies. They were right in that they thought Jesus was the Messiah. They were right in that He had come to "proclaim liberty to the captives . . . to set at liberty those who are oppressed" (Luke 4:18). Their beliefs on how He would do those things were mistaken.

Jesus was the conquering King who would save all who would accept His Kingship. Yet, He did not save by military might. He did it by His death on the Cross.

Weekday Problems

"I didn't think this far ahead," Marcus said to himself. Marcus had just come back from a weekend Christian retreat. During the three days of the retreat, Marcus and the rest of the group were treated to many of the best things Christianity has to offer. There was Bible study, prayer time, joyous fellowship and singing. The volunteer staff at the retreat did everything  possible to make sure the folks attending had a marvelous experience. The folks attending the retreat were showered with blessings and love. That retreat was one of the greatest spiritual events Marcus had ever experienced. His heart was full. His soul was blessed. Now he truly knew what a moun-taintop experience was.

Marcus had considered himself a Christian. He had joined the church when he was twelve. Yet, it seemed his brand of Christianity never made any difference in his life until now.

It was Monday. He was back at work, same as every Monday, but he was a different person than when he left work last Thursday. Today, the overcharges to the clients were not okay.

*   Christian blessing and Christian responsi-bility go hand-in-hand. How might Marcus approach this problem?

*   What might be some of the possible fallout if Marcus "blows the whistle?"

Monkey Business

Harry, Max, and Leo had adjoining shops, with Max's in the middle. One day Harry put up a big sign that said "GOING OUT OF BUSINESS SALE!" Max's other competitor, Leo, retaliated with a larger sign that said "BIG FIRE SALE." Quietly Max put up his own sign in between: "ENTRANCE TO SALE."

A quack was selling a tonic he claimed would make people live 300 years. "Look at me!" he shouted. "You'd never think I was 300 years old!"

"Is he really that old?" a listener asked the quack's youthful-looking assistant.

"Don't know," the assistant replied. "I've only been with him 97 years."

Sign in a hearing-aid shop: "TRUST US. OVER 5,000 EARS OF EXPERI-ENCE."

This Lesson in Your Life

Redefining Leadership

There is great emphasis upon leadership these days. The churches of today are seeking vital, visionary leaders who can hear the call of Christ and communicate that call to others, leaders who have the courage and energy to be the vanguard in the cause of Christ, moving forward in Christ's footsteps.

We need visionary leadership. United Methodist Bishop Reuben P. Job says this about vision, "Vision is a gift from God. It is the reward of disciplined, faithful and patient listening to God. Vision allows us to see beyond the visible, beyond the barriers and obstacles to our mission. Vision 'catches us up,' captivates and compels us to act. Vision is the gift of eyes of faith to see the invisible, to know the unknowable, to think the unthinkable, to experience the not yet. Vision allows us to see signs of the kingdom now, in our midst. Vision gives us focus, energy and the willingness to risk. It is our vision that draws us forward." Visionary leaders draw others forward in the faith, for people will more readily follow someone who knows the way.

Most of us know what it is to submit to leadership. Most of us have a boss in whatever work we do. The boss is saddled with the responsibility of getting the job done. He or she is then required to get that job done through people. That requires leadership. Habakkuk 2:2 tells us, "Then the LORD replied: "Write down the revelation and make it plain on tablets so that a herald may run with it." A leader must be clear about God's direction and communicate that to others. A leader who is not clear about her/his direction will not be confident in leading others. People who are unsure about a leader's vision will be unsure about following. Therefore, it is the leader's task to hear carefully the words of the writer of Hebrews, "Therefore, since we are surrounded by such a great cloud of witnesses, let us throw off everything that hinders and the sin that so easily entangles, and let us run with perseverance the race marked out for us. Let us fix our eyes on Jesus, the author and perfecter of our faith" (Heb. 12:1-2a). As the leader focuses upon Christ she/he can be confident in leading others.

May we never be like the pastor who was supposed to officiate at a funeral for a friend. The friend was a retired military man. The funeral was to be held at the man's home church. The pastor had never been to the church before.

When the pastor got to the church, the funeral director instructed him that there would be a military honor guard. After the service in the church, the pastor was to lead this honor guard to the cemetery out back. When the pastor prayed the closing prayer, he turned around on his heel and, in his best military dignity, marched across the platform, opened the nearest door and led the seven uniformed soldiers into a closet!

It is imperative the leader know where she/he is going! The Christ-like leader follows Christ, confident in the direction, and beckons others to follow.

Seed Thoughts

1. What assignment did Jesus give two of His disciples as they were all traveling to Jerusalem

Jesus sent two of His disciples into the village to find a colt and bring it to Him.

2. How were the disciples to respond if questioned about their actions?

The disciples were simply to say that the Lord had need of the colt.

3. What act of honor did the disciples and other people bestow upon Jesus?

The people spread their garments and leafy branches on the path where Jesus rode the donkey.

4. List some phrases the people used in their celebration.

Hosanna; Blessed is He that comes in the name of the Lord. Blessed be the kingdom of our father David. Hosanna in the highest.

5. By drawing conclusions from the crowd's remarks, why were they celebrating?

They were celebrating the coming of the Lord and the coming of his kingdom.

1. What assignment did Jesus give two of His disciples as they were all traveling to Jerusalem?

2. How were the disciples to respond if questioned about their actions?

3. What act of honor did the disciples and other people bestow upon Jesus?

4. List some phrases the people used in their celebration.

5. By drawing conclusions from the crowd's remarks, why were they celebrating?

6. What was Jesus's mood as He entered the temple that next day? Why?

7. What shocking thing did Jesus do when He entered the temple?

8. How do you think Jesus would react if He came to our churches today? Would He be pleased?

9. What did Jesus want the temple to be called by all nations?

10. How did the scribes and chief priests feel about Jesus?

(Please turn page)

Jesus sent two of His disciples into the village to find a colt and bring it to Him.

The disciples were simply to say that the Lord had need of the colt.

The people spread their garments and leafy branches on the path where Jesus rode the donkey.

Hosanna; Blessed is He that comes in the name of the Lord. Blessed be the kingdom of our father David. Hosanna in the highest.

They were celebrating the coming of the Lord and the coming of his kingdom.

Jesus was angry because people were buying and selling in the temple.

Jesus began casting out those people who were selling and buying in the temple. He turned over the tables and chairs.
Answers will vary. He would not be happy if He saw things going on that were contrary to His Word.

Jesus wanted the temple to be known as a "House of Prayer."

· The scribes and chief priests feared Jesus and sought for a way to destroy Him.

6. What was Jesus's mood as He entered the temple that next day? Why?

Jesus was angry because people were buying and selling in the temple.

7. What shocking thing did Jesus do when He entered the temple

Jesus began casting out those people who were selling and buying in the temple. He turned over the tables and chairs.

8. How do you think Jesus would react if He came to our churches today? Would He be pleased?

Answers will vary. He would not be happy if He saw things going on that were contrary to His Word.

9. What did Jesus want the temple to be called by all nations?

Jesus wanted the temple to be known as a "House of Prayer."

10. How did the scribes and chief priests feel about Jesus?

The scribes and chief priests feared Jesus and sought for a way to destroy Him.

"HE HAS BEEN RAISED"

Lesson 7

Jesus Died and Lives Again!

Mark 15:33-39; 16:1-8

33 And when the sixth hour was come, there was darkness over the whole land until the ninth hour.

34 And at the ninth hour Jesus cried with a loud voice, saying, Eloi, Eloi, lama sabachthani? which is, being interpreted, My God, my God, why hast thou forsaken me?

35 And some of them that stood by, when they heard it, said, Behold, He calleth Elias.

36 And one ran and filled sponge full of vinegar, and put it on a reed, and gave him to drink, saying, Let alone; let us see whether Elias will come to take him down.

37 And Jesus cried with a loud voice, and gave up the ghost.

38 And the veil of the temple was rent in twain from the top to the bottom.

39 And when the centurion, which stood over against him, saw that he so cried out, and gave up the ghost, he said, Truly this man was the Son of God.

16:1 And when the sabbath was past, Mary Magdalene, and Mary the mother of James and Salome, had bought sweet spices, that they might come and anoint him.

2 And very early in the morning the first day of the week, they came unto the sepulchre at the rising of the sun.

3 And they said among themselves, Who shall roll us away the stone from the door of the sepulchre?

4 And when they looked, they saw that the stone was rolled away: for it was very great.

5 And entering into the sepulchre, they saw a young man sitting on the right side, clothed in a long white garment; and they were affrighted.

6 And he saith unto them, Be not affrighted: Ye seek Jesus of Nazareth, which was crucified: he is risen; he is not here: behold the place where they laid him.

7 But go your way, tell his disciples and Peter that he goeth before you into Galilee: there shall ye see him, as he said unto you.

8 And they went out quickly, and fled from the sepulchre; for they trembled and were amazed: neither said they any thing to any; for they were afraid.

Memory Selection
Mark 16:6

Devotional Reading
1 Corinthians 15:19-26

Background Scripture
Mark 15:21–16:8

Printed Scripture
Mark 15:33-39; 16:1-8

311

Teacher's Target

Lesson purpose: *To experience again the joy and hope inherent in the timeless message that Jesus died for our sins, and rose again.*

The Bible contains so many truths that a newcomer to the Christian faith can easily become confused. Use this class to focus on the one defining truth that gives meaning to all the rest. No teaching is as fundamental to the Christian's faith and hope than the angel's announcement, "He is risen; he is not here." That statement is a summary of the gospel message. It is celebrated throughout the world not only when our calendars read "Easter," but every "first day of the week" (Mark 16:2), as Christians gather to commemorate Christ's resurrection.

Why has this ancient story survived centuries of attempts to deny it, and many attempts to stamp out those who believe it? It endures not only because it is the keystone of the Christian story, but because of the hope it ignites in the hearts of believers. Recalling this even enables us to shout Yes! to the age-old question, "If a man die, shall he live again?" (Job 14:14).

Lesson Introduction

For nearly three years, Jesus has taught and healed, preached and prayed, living out His destiny as the Son of God. Now that destiny has brought him to the Cross, just as He predicted (see Mark 8:31; 10:33-34). This was His "destiny" not in the sense of an impersonal fate or inevitable decree, but in the sense that He freely chose to accept His role in God's eternal plan (John 10:17-18).

Part of the mystery of this plan is that Christ's death was the only adequate sacrifice for the sins of the world, supplying what the blood of bulls and goats lacked (Heb. 10:4). Christ's death was "adequate" because He was God in the flesh, meaning that God Himself offered what man could not; and because it is connected with His resurrection. In being raised from the grave, Jesus conquered death—the otherwise inevitable consequence of sin.

The glory of the resurrection is that itshowed Jesus to be the Son of God (Rom.1:3).

Teaching Outline	Daily Bible Reading
	Mon. Crucified Between Two Thieves *Mark 15:21-23*
I. The Darkest Day—15:33-38	**Tue.** Like a Broken Vessel *Psalm 31:9-16*
A. Cry of dereliction, 33-34	**Wed.** An Offering for All Time *Hebrews 10:11-25*
B. Confusion about Elijah, 35-36	
C. Christ dies, 37-39	**Thu.** Body Wrapped in Linen *Mark 15:33-37*
II. The Brightest Hour—16:1-8	**Fri.** Death, the Last Enemy *1 Corinthians 15:21-28*
A. A ministry in mind, 1-3	
B. The great announcement, 4-6	**Sat.** Going Before Them to Galilee *Mark 16:1-8*
C. The charge, 7-8	**Sun.** "I Have Seen the Lord!" *John 20:11-18*

VERSE BY VERSE

I. The Darkest Day—15:33-38
A. Cry of dereliction, 33-34

33 And when the sixth hour was come, there was darkness over the whole land until the ninth hour.

34 And at the ninth hour Jesus cried with a loud voice, saying, Eloi, Eloi, lama sabachthani? which is, being interpreted, My God, my God, why hast thou forsaken me?

Although not without difficulties, the traditional view of the timing of these important events is that Jesus was crucified on a Friday. Verse 25 has said that He was nailed to the Cross at "the third hour"—9 a.m., according to the Jewish conception of the day's beginning at 6 o'clock. It is noon—the "sixth hour"—when nature recoils in horror at the blackest of deeds. Appropriately, the sun is obscured, either by an eclipse or by thick, heavy cloud, as though the heavens cannot tolerate the sight.

Incredibly, the prophet Amos had predicted that God "will cause the sun to go down at noon, and I will darken the earth in the clear day . . . and I will make it as the mourning of an only son" (8:9-10). Just as the heavens had opened at Christ's baptism in glad acknowledgment of His Sonship (Mark 1:10), so they close now as a judgment against His

being put to death.

Three hours later Jesus cries out in what seems to be a reaction to heaven's hiddenness. The words are from Psalm 22:1, showing that even in His death Jesus intends for us to understand He is fulfilling prophecy. Yet the words are also intensely personal. Although He is the divine Son, He is also human; and His soul seems to break under the load of the sins of all mankind, before and since. Did His outcry indicate that He expected God to rescue Him from the Cross, even after choosing it? Or was it in response to the Father's turning His face from the hideous sight? We are not told.

B. Confusion about Elijah, 35-36

35 And some of them that stood by, when they heard it, said, Behold, He calleth Elias.

36 And one ran and filled sponge full of vinegar, and put it on a reed, and gave him to drink, saying, Let alone; let us see whether Elias will come to take him down.

Given the ordeal Jesus had been through, He must have cried out in a voice cracking with hoarseness. It would have been easy to misunderstand "Eli" for "Elijah"—especially since many Jews of the day though that this prophet, who had been wafted to heaven without dying (2 Kings 2:11), was a kind of ministering spirit who sometimes descended to help those in great need. Also, Jesus had been acclaimed as the Messiah, and Elijah was expected to return to prepare His way (Mal. 4:5). As if often the case, people heard what they expected to hear, or had on their minds. The "vinegar" was probably a cheap wine. It was offered Jesus to quench His thirst and perhaps to dull His pain.

C. Christ dies, 37-39

37 And Jesus cried with a loud voice, and gave up the ghost.

38 And the veil of the temple was rent in twain from the top to the bottom.

39 And when the centurion, which stood over against him, saw that he so cried out, and gave up the ghost, he said, Truly this man was the Son of God.

In a final, agonizing outburst, Jesus gives vent both to His excruciating physical pain and to the unfathomable anguish of a soul carrying the world's sins. His cry also signals the departure of His spirit, in what is at once the most sobering but the most potentially glorious event history has ever known. (Although the KJV term "ghost" is often said to be from an old English word for "guest," it is more likely borrowed from the German word for spirit: *Geist*.)

Mark records two significant events resulting from Christ's death. First, the "veil" or wall separating the Most Holy Place from the Holy Place in the nearby Temple was split from top to bottom. This was no doubt a sign of the end of the Jewish system, and a demonstration that Jesus' death brought a new and glorious access to God.

Second, the Roman centurion (captain of 100 men) assigned to keep peace at the scene seems to have been converted by the awesome way nature responded to Christ's death. Matthew adds that the darkness was accompanied by an earthquake, and by the release of spirits from nearby graves (Matt.

27:51-53). This soldier's confession of Jesus' Sonship is the first of millions that will follow.

II. The Brightest Hour—16:1-8

A. A ministry in mind, 1-3

16:1 And when the sabbath was past, Mary Magdalene, and Mary the mother of James and Salome, had bought sweet spices, that they might come and anoint him.

2 And very early in the morning the first day of the week, they came unto the sepulchre at the rising of the sun.

3 And they said among themselves, Who shall roll us away the stone from the door of the sepulchre?

There is yet no way for these women to know the significance of what has happened. They can only have been weighed down by sorrow at the lost of their Master, and by disappointment that He did not seem to have been the Messiah after all (for how could a Deliverer actually suffer death?). Yet they tend to the practical details called for by any set of close friends or family at the death of a friend.

Intending to semi-embalm Jesus' body, as was the Jewish custom, they come to the tomb as soon as they have enough light and can be ritually allowed to work (even embalming would not be allowed on Saturday, or the sabbath). Although their hearts must have been bursting with other questions, the most immediate is how they will be able to get past the heavy stone that had been rolled across the cave-like tomb to protect it from grave-robbers.

B. The great announcement, 4-6

4 And when they looked, they saw that the stone was rolled away: for it was very great.

314

5 And entering into the sepulchre, they saw a young man sitting on the right side, clothed in a long white garment; and they were affrighted.

6 And he saith unto them, Be not affrighted: Ye seek Jesus of Nazareth, which was crucified: he is risen; he is not here: behold the place where they laid him.

Good news! (Gospel!) The One the world thought to do away with has conquered death! The tomb is empty. Matthew records another earthquake as the reason for the stone's displacement. He also says the "young man" of Mark's account was actually an angel. The women could have been frightened from being in the presence of an angel, or because they thought they were seeing Jesus' ghost. Either way, the young man's reassuring words echo down through the centuries. In the light of Jesus' resurrection, we need not be afraid of even the last enemy, death (1 Cor. 15:26).

C. The charge, 7-8

7 But go your way, tell his disciples and Peter that he goeth before you into Galilee: there shall ye see him, as he said unto you.

8 And they went out quickly, and fled from the sepulchre; for they trembled and were amazed: neither said they any thing to any; for they were afraid.

Had the resurrection story merely been invented, its authors would have portrayed men as the first witnesses of the resurrection, since the testimony of women was discounted to the extent that it was not allowed in courts of the day. With uncontrived directness, however, the women here are given the first "great commission." Ironically, they say nothing, apparently afraid they would not be taken seriously. They may also have doubted what their eyes had just seen.

Luke and John describe Jesus also appearing in Jerusalem after His resurrection (Luke 24:34ff.; John 20:11-28). John then devotes an entire chapter (21) to a beautiful homecoming between Jesus and His disciples at Galilee. These appearances became an important part of the core message of early Christian preaching because they demonstrated that Jesus was a real person after His encounter with death (see 1 Cor. 15:3-8). They add a realistic dimension to the ongoing story that must still be broadcast today: He lives!

Evangelistic Emphasis

"O, how He loves you and me. O, how he loves you and me. He gave His life. What more could He give? O, how He loves you and me." That is just a short love song. These words describe the greatest love any human being has had for another.

Those words describe the love God has for His creation. Those describe the love Jesus has for us.

In this day of strife and turmoil, of violence and hatred, of mistrust and greed, folks need to hear that Jesus loves them. We know people need to hear of the holiness of God. We know people need to hear about right-living. We know people need to hear about self-sacrifice. We know people need to hear about helping their fellow human beings. Yet, sometimes folks need to hear first and foremost the story that tells about the astounding, amazing, awesome love of God in Christ Jesus.

All the love of God in Christ was poured into the love demonstrated on the Cross. John 15:13 tells us, "Greater love hath no man than this, that a man lay down his life for his friends." That is awesome love! Tell some folks this week that God loves them. That is good news!

✻ ✻ ✻

Memory Selection

And he saith unto them, Be not affrighted: Ye seek Jesus of Nazareth, which was crucified: He is risen; He is not here: behold the place where they laid Him.
—Mark 16:6

The women were looking for Jesus in the wrong place. It was an honest mistake. Everything natural led them to believe He would be there in that tomb. They saw Him die. They saw His lifeless body taken from the cross. They probably thought, "He's dead. How could He be anything otherwise?" The women were sure they would find the body of Jesus in the tomb.

Jesus said He would rise after three days (Mark 8:31). The women forgot that promise. They were looking for Jesus in the wrong place.

Do we ever make the same mistake the women did? Do we ever give more weight to circumstances than to the word of Christ? Do we ever forget Christ's promises? If we do, we may discover we are looking for Christ in a place where He is not.

May we look for Jesus through the eyes of faith rather than the eyes of circumstances. We may discover a miracle, just as the women at the tomb did.

Weekday Problems

It is March 17, 1996. A lone figure stands on the wind-swept hill. She stares at the slate colored slab of stone. Tears sting her eyes. The last words carved on the headstone read, "Died, March 3, 1996."

The woman speaks aloud, though no one else is present. "I don't know how I can go on without you. There's just so much. It's not the big things. You saw to it that I knew all about that. But I need you with me. I can't get the lid off the pickles. I turn for your help. You're not there. I hear a cute joke and think about how much you would enjoy it before I remember you're not here to share it with me. Drinking coffee in the morning on the back porch is just not the same. I wait for you to say, 'Amen!' in church but there's only silence. I miss you so much."

Then, though no one is there except the woman, she hears a kind voice deep inside her heart say, "For as in Adam all die, so in Christ all will be made alive. We do not want you to be ignorant about those who fall asleep or grieve like the rest of men, who have no hope. God will bring with Jesus those who have fallen asleep in Him."

Though the loneliness remains in her heart, the woman is strangely encouraged by those words.

* What might you say to someone who just lost a loved one?

* Are words always necessary to comfort grief?

Good News/Bad News

Did you hear about the man who fell out of an airplane? The good news is that there was a haystack right below him. The bad news is that a pitchfork was sticking out of the hay, business end first. The good news is that the man missed the pitchfork. The bad news is that he missed the haystack.

Doctor: I have good news and bad news. The bad news is that we have to amputate both your legs. The good news is that there's a woman in the waiting room who wants to buy your shoes.

Agent to author: I have good news and bad news. The good news is that Paramount loved your script—absolutely ate it up.
Author: What's the bad news?
Agent: The bad news is that Paramount is the name of my dog.

This Lesson in Your Life

The Mystery of Death and Resurrection

Death. It could be called the final frontier. In reality, we know very little about death. We know something about near death, but none of us has ever spoken to anyone who was dead and buried and has lived to tell about it. Death is a journey that we all must experience. From the beginning of time all humans, except for a couple, have died. The mortality rate, for all statistical purposes, is 100 percent. All people eventually die.

We will die, too. All who read this will face death unless the Lord hastens and returns to take us home before our bodies wear out. It is said that there are two things that are inevitable, death and taxes. Because death is certain for us all, many folks have great concerns about dying.

A story is told about a little boy with leukemia. He had suffered for so long with treatments and nausea and hair loss. The leukemia entered its final stages and the youngster became weaker and bedridden. One day, the question his mother dreaded came out, "Mom, what's it like to die?"

Unable to answer for the lump in her throat, the mother excused herself, went to the bathroom and with tears streaming down her face, began to pray for wisdom for the answer. Immediately she felt peace. She returned to the boy's bedroom and explained.

"Do you remember on some of those nights when you couldn't sleep because you hurt too badly or were a little scared? You would come in here and go to sleep with Dad and me." She continued, "And every morning you woke up in your own bed?"

"Yes, ma'am," the boy replied.

"Well, sometime during the night, while you were sleeping soundly, your father or your older brother would pick you up from this room and take you to your own." She began to weep again, "And that's how death is. You go to sleep in one place and wake up in heaven."

The youngster was satisfied with that explanation. He closed his eyes to rest. Sure enough, a few days later, the boy went to sleep, then his Big Brother (our Big Brother, too) picked him up from his bed here and took him to his room with his Heavenly Father.

I love that story. As far as I know, it is just a story. Yet a profound truth is illustrated. When the Christian dies he or she has the promise of living forever with God in a place we call Heaven. That promise might have been simply words, had not Jesus Christ been raised from the dead and ascended into heaven in bodily form. The resurrection of Christ verified that all who live in Christ on this earth will live again, even though they may die. Those who walk with Christ, serve Christ, love Christ on this earth and trust Him for salvation have the assurance of living forever with Christ in the world beyond.

Paul wrote in 1 Corinthians 15:19, "If in this life only we have hope in Christ, we are of all men most miserable." This world is not the end. Death is not a period, it is simply a comma. The empty tomb of Jesus proved that statement.

Many folks are concerned about death. That is good. Where there is concern, there is time to turn to Christ. That is the secret—accepting Christ as Savior and living our lives "in Him." As we live with Christ here on this earth, knowing that He has blessed us and guided us and provided for us and loved us all our lives, we can be assured He will do the same in the life to come.

Seed Thoughts

1. What unusual thing is recorded as happening at the sixth hour?

From the sixth to the ninth hour the whole land was covered with darkness.

2. Jesus has been recorded as having cried out at the ninth hour. What did He say?

Jesus cried out saying, "My God, my God, why hast thou forsaken me?"

3. Some people standing close by heard Jesus's cry. What did they mistake Him as saying?

Some misunderstood Jesus's cry and thought He cried out for Elijah.

4. What comfort was offered Jesus when He cried out? How many people offered comfort?

One person ran and filled a sponge full of vinegar, and put it on a reed, and gave Him a drink.

5. What happened at exactly the same time that Jesus died?

The veil of the temple was ripped from top to bottom at the same time that Jesus died.

1. What unusual thing is recorded as happening at the sixth hour?

2. Jesus has been recorded as having cried out at the ninth hour. What did He say?

3. Some people standing close by heard Jesus's cry. What did they mistake Him as saying?

4. What comfort was offered Jesus when He cried out? How many people offered comfort?

5. What happened at exactly the same time that Jesus died?

6. What did the centurion who stood near the cross realize when he saw Jesus die?

7. List the three women who went to anoint Jesus's body the first day of the week?

8. What was one of the women's concerns about anointing the body?

9. Describe the scene the women found when they arrived at the tomb.

10. What instructions were the women given? How did they respond?

(Please turn page)

From the sixth to the ninth hour the whole land was covered with darkness.

Jesus cried out saying, "My God, my God, why hast thou forsaken me?"

Some misunderstood Jesus's cry and thought He cried out for Elijah.

One person ran and filled a sponge full of vinegar, and put it on a reed, and gave Him a drink.

The veil of the temple was ripped from top to bottom at the same time that Jesus died.

The centurion who stood near the cross said, "Truly this man was the Son of God".

Mary Magdalene; Mary, the mother of James; and Salome. These women, who had witnessed the crucifixion, were coming to anoint Jesus's body.

The women worried about rolling the heavy stone away from the door of the sepulcher.

When the women arrived at the tomb, they found a young man dressed in white. He showed them where Jesus had lain and told them that Jesus had risen.

The young man told them to go and tell Peter and the disciples, but the women were too afraid to tell anyone.

6. What did the centurion who stood near the cross realize when he saw Jesus die?

The centurion who stood near the cross said, "Truly this man was the Son of God".

7. List the three women who went to anoint Jesus's body the first day of the week?

Mary Magdalene; Mary, the mother of James; and Salome. These women, who had witnessed the crucifixion were coming to anoint Jesus's body.

8. What was one of the women's concerns about anointing the body?

The women worried about rolling the heavy stone away from the door of the sepulcher.

9. Describe the scene the women found when they arrived at the tomb.

When the women arrived at the tomb, they found a young man dressed in white. He showed them where Jesus had lain and told them that Jesus had risen.

10. What instructions were the women given? How did they respond?

The young man told them to go and tell Peter and the disciples, but the women were too afraid to tell anyone.

Lesson 8

The Son Rejected

April 19

Mark 12:1-12

1 And he began to speak unto them by parables. A certain man planted a vineyard, and set an hedge about it, and digged a place for the winefat, and built a tower, and let it out to husbandmen, and went into a far country.

2 And at the season he sent to the husbandmen a servant, that he might receive from the husbandmen of the fruit of the vineyard.

3 And they caught him, and beat him, and sent him away empty.

4 And again he sent unto them another servant; and at him they cast stones, and wounded him in the head, and sent him away shamefully handled.

5 And again he sent another; and him they killed, and many others; beating some, and killing some.

6 Having yet therefore one son, his well beloved, he sent him also last unto them, saying, They will reverence my son.

7 But those husbandmen said among themselves, This is the heir; come, let us kill him, and the inheritance shall be ours.

8 And they took him, and killed him, and cast him out of the vineyard.

9 What shall therefore the lord of the vineyard do? he will come and destroy the husbandmen, and will give the vineyard unto others.

10 And have ye not read this scripture; The stone which the builders rejected is become the head of the corner;

11 This was the Lord's doing, and it is marvellous in our eyes?

12 And they sought to lay hold on him, but feared the people: for they knew that he had spoken the parable against them: and they left him, and went their way.

Memory Selection
Mark 12:10-11

Devotional Reading
Isaiah 5:1-7

Background Scripture
Mark 12:1-12

Printed Scripture
Mark 12:1-12

Teacher's Target

Lesson purpose: *To emphasize, on the basis of the parable of the vineyard, the importance of "bearing fruit" in the sense of leading productive and responsible lives.*

Be sure to read Isaiah 5:1-7, the Background Scripture for the lesson, in preparation for your class. Isaiah describes Israel's unfaithfulness in terms of an unfruitful vineyard. Jesus seems to build on this passage as He teaches His parable.

Your class will become more relevant, however, if you encourage response to how Jesus' teaching might apply to our own situation. Do we use our gifts and talents responsibly? Do we accept accountability gracefully? Are we growing spiritually, using our gifts to bless others? Or do we buy in to the widespread practice of blaming others for our inadequate performance?

Lesson Introduction

A word about the purpose of parables is appropriate background for this lesson and several to follow. Although it is well known that Jesus used such "teaching stories," it is often assumed that He did so to illustrate truths so plainly that no one could misunderstand. When Jesus' own disciples asked Him why he taught in parables, He gave quite a different answer (see Matt. 13:10-17).

Jesus' parables required people to enter into the story and see themselves as participants. If their hearts were attuned to the truth, Christ wanted them to have an "Aha!" experience and gain enlightenment from the story. If, however, their hearts were hard, He taught in parables to confuse and confound them further. An open heart and pure motives are more essential than intellectual prowess for understanding the parables of Jesus.

Teaching Outline	Daily Bible Readings

I. Great Expectations—1-2
  A. Investing in hope, 1
  B. Collecting the rent, 2
II. Irresponsible Responses—3-8
  A. Three servants abused, 3-5
  B. The son slain, 6-8
III. Pay-back Time—9-12
  A. Judgment on the unfaithful, 9
  B. Alternative success, 10-11
  C. A point driven home, 12
	Mon. Wild Grapes in God's Vineyard
	Isaiah 5:1-7
	Tue. Rejected One Becomes Cornerstone
	Mark 12:1-2
	Wed. Forsaken by Everyone
	Psalm 22:1-15
	Thu. Prophets and Sages Rejected
	Matthew 23:34-39
	Fri. He Knows Our Weaknesses
	Hebrews 4:12-16
	Sat. Obedient though Suffering
	Hebrews 5:5-10
	Sun. Struck Down for Our Sins
	Isaiah 52:13–53:12

VERSE BY VERSE

I. Great Expectations—1-2
A. Investing in hope, 1
1 And he began to speak unto them by parables. A Certain man planted a vineyard, and set an hedge about it, and digged a place for the winefat, and built a tower, and let it out to husbandmen, and went into a far country.

A parable is a story about something that represents something else. Although this makes the parable a kind of comparison or metaphor, a parable is more subtle and indirect than a straightforward comparison. It has the advantage of inviting the reader to participate in its meaning, and thus applying the point to himself.

The word comes straight from the Greek *parabole*, which meant literally a "throw-alongside." That is, a primary element in the story is "thrown" or placed alongside its counterpart. In this parable, for example, the husbandmen or vineyard-keepers are the primary element. They are to be compared with the "others" of verse 9.

Parables are one of the earliest forms of "rhetoric" or formal oral communication. No one, however, is known to have used them as extensively as Jesus (see Mark 4:34). As mentioned in the Introduction, Jesus used parables as a test of the sincerity of His hearers. Usually He would explain them clearly to His closest followers (4:34), and leave others to work them out on their own.

A parable is best understood if one or two main elements are identified, with lesser elements allowed merely to carry the story instead of the point. To insist on a double meaning for every item in the story burdens them beyond their intent and prevents our seeing the main point clearly. As we shall see, for example, the identity of the vineyard, its owner and the husbandmen will be clear; but to struggle to assign a meaning to the "winefat" and tower could result in profitless speculation.

We must jump ahead of the story to keep up with the meaning of the primary elements. We know from Isaiah 5:1-7 that the vineyard is "the house of Israel." The "man" or owner of the vineyard must stand for God; and the husbandmen for the Chosen People, the Jews, who were expected to tend the vineyard so it would bear fruit.

Vineyards were often surrounded by thornbush hedges to keep out predators and thieves. No doubt Jesus meant for the hedge here to stand for the protection He had given the Jewish nation—although they often forfeited it by disobedience.

B. Collecting the rent, 2
2 And at the season he sent to the husbandmen a servant, that he might receive from the husbandmen of the fruit of the vineyard.

"The season" would have been the time of year when the grapes were ripe. Since the vineyard did not belong to the husbandmen, they were bound to return to the owner a profit from his investment. The form of payment was sometimes the fruit itself; perhaps the farmers were working "on shares."

II. Irresponsible Responses—3-8

A. Three servants abused, 2-5

3 And they caught him, and beat him, and sent him away empty.

4 And again he sent unto them another servant; and at him they cast stones, and wounded him in the head, and sent him away shamefully handled.

5 And again he sent another; and him they killed, and many others; beating some, and killing some.

In keeping with sticking to the parable's main points, it is not necessary to assign personal identities to the three servants sent in succession to collect on the owner's investment. We know from the way Israel so often treated her prophets that Jesus is speaking of them. They were God's messengers sent to urge His people to accept responsibility for earning a good return on the investment God had made in them. Yet prophets such as Elijah and Elisha were hounded by the leaders of God's people. Tradition has it that Isaiah was sawn in two with a wooden saw. Jeremiah was thrown into a well. Jesus accused "Jerusalem," standing for the nation as a whole, of killing the prophets sent to tell them of God's love and to warn them of His judgment (Matt. 23:37).

Imagine the patience and forbearance of God, the vineyard's owner. He could have relieved the husbandmen of their duties upon their first rejection. When the reception they gave succeeding representatives became more violent, He could have had them arrested and put to death. Just as the books of Judges, Samuel, Kings, and Chronicles record, however, He sent "saviors" (anointed rescuers) to them again and again, in vain looking for responsible servants who would bear fruit in His vineyard.

B. The son slain, 6-8

6 Having yet therefore one son, his wellbeloved, he sent him also last unto them, saying, They will reverence my son.

7 But those husbandmen said among themselves, This is the heir; come, let us kill him, and the inheritance shall be ours.

8 And they took him, and killed him, and cast him out of the vineyard.

Finally, the owner of the vineyard sent his one beloved son. Jesus chooses His words carefully here, so it will be clear that He himself is the Son referred to. He echoes the voice that came from heaven at His baptism: "Thou art my beloved Son" (Mark 1:11). Yet instead of responding with respect and giving honor to their master's own son, the wicked husbandmen kill him, too—in an obvious prediction of the Crucifixion.

III. Pay-back Time—9-12

A. Judgment on the unfaithful, 9

9 What shall therefore the lord of the vineyard do? he will come and destroy the husbandmen, and will give the vineyard unto others.

The destruction of the husbandmen refers not only to the last judgment, but to the judgment against Judaism as God's Chosen People. Since its leaders rejected the Son, the Owner of the vineyard gave it to "others"—to Gentiles. The apostle Paul acted out the meaning of this verse when the Jews he always approached first on his early mission trips rejected his message once too often. Their defiance wrung from Paul the anguished decision, "From henceforth I will go unto the Gentiles" (Acts 18:6).

B. Alternative success, 10-11

10 And have ye not read this scripture; The stone which the builders rejected is become the head of the corner; 11 This was the Lord's doing, and it is marvellous in our eyes?

The passage Jesus quotes from Psalm 118:22 was probably thought by the Jewish leaders to refer to Israel. Were not they the nation chosen to be built into the Temple of God? Jesus must have shocked them by applying the passage to Himself. The Jewish leaders were supposed to be the builders of the Kingdom. Ironically, however, they rejected the very cornerstone of the structure. Since that Stone was rejected, it became a stumbling-stone for the builders (Isa. 8:14).

C. A point driven home, 12

12 And they sought to lay hold on him, but feared the people: for they knew that he had spoken the parable against them: and they left him, and went their way.

There was no need for Jesus to draw His disciples apart and explain this parable to them. The comparison between the wicked husbandmen and the Jewish leaders was so clear that they were cut to the heart with conviction.

This state of mind is necessary for conversion; but when the convicted heart is also proud, resentful, or bitter, the result is rejection instead. Seeing themselves so clearly mirrored in Jesus' parable, His enemies withdrew. No doubt they redoubled their efforts to put to death this man who dared speak of their history so disparagingly and charge them with having been irresponsible husbandmen of God's vineyard.

Evangelistic Emphasis

Have you ever wondered what the servants said when they went to the tenants to collect the owner's fruit? Did they threaten the tenants? Did they plead? Did they try to offer some kind of deal? How did they present the message from the master?

However the servants presented the message, it was never well received. The tenants beat or killed and otherwise treated shamefully each one of the servants who was sent with the master's message. I would expect the servants became rather hesitant to go after the first three or four messengers were treated badly. I expect the enthusiasm for their mission waned dramatically as more and more were beaten. Yet, apparently they continued to go on their master's request.

This is a parable, a story Jesus told to make a point to the leaders of Israel. It makes a point for us, too. We have been given a message from our Master. We are to tell everyone the message, which is the good news of Jesus Christ. When we tell the story, we may be mistreated. We may be ridiculed. We may even be beaten or killed. Yet, the story must still be told. The story must be told in whatever manner necessary to get folks to listen.

Folks must hear the message for one day the Owner of the vineyard will return.

Memory Selection

And have ye not read this scripture; The stone which the builders rejected is become the head of the corner: This was the Lord's doing, and it is marvelous in our eyes?—*Mark 12:10-11*

Some folks just don't get it. These days folks are trying to build things that last, things with permanence and significance. I am not speaking of houses, bridges or skyscrapers. People are trying to build relationships that are meaningful and lasting.

Too often, folks try to build something permanent without the most important piece . . . the cornerstone. There is a piece without which the structure will be forever unstable. There is a piece without which a relationship will be shaky. There is a piece without which a personal commitment will be subject to collapse at any time.

That piece is Jesus. All our relationships, whether with our boss, our spouse, our parents or children or simply with friends and neighbors, will be stronger with Jesus as the chief ingredient. He is the sure foundation.

Weekday Problems

Charles had been friends with Bobby all his life. They had worked at the mill together since they got out of high school. They rode to work together. They were best friends.

Charles had always seemed to do the right thing. He came to work on time. He worked hard. He was honest almost to a fault. He never even took a long lunch or coffee break.

Bobby was a different story. Often he would miss his ride with Charles and come in to work late. Bobby was great at his job, but he always seemed to work harder at getting out of work. It seemed he was always in the foreman's office getting a good talking to about his work habits.

Charles tried talking to him, "Man, the foreman's going to let you go. He'll only put up with that for so long!" The talk never helped.

One day the foreman called Charles in. "Charles, I've talked to Bobby until I'm blue in the face. You're his best friend. I want you to see if you can get through to him. He needs to know that one more time late and he's through."

Charles relayed the message to Bobby, pleading with him to straighten up. Two weeks later, Bobby missed his ride and was late for work. The foreman called him into his office.

* Would Bobby's firing be justified?

* Do people expect consequences when they fail to follow God's rules? Explain your answer.

No More Excuses

To take care of all the excuses for not attending church, one congregation posted this notice:

1. Beds will be placed in the fellowship hall for those who say, "Sunday is my only day to rest."

2. Eye drops will be provided for those with tired eyes from watching TV too late Saturday night.

3. Steel helmets will be given those who say, "The roof would fall in if I ever went to church."

4. Blankets will be furnished those who think the church is too cold, and fans for those who say it's too hot.

5. TV dinners will be available for those who can't go to church because they have to cook the noon meal for the family.

6. We will have a selection of trees and shrubs for those who say they like to see God in nature.

7. Ear-plugs will be given those who say they don't like the pastor's sermons.

This Lesson in Your Life

The Cost of Irresponsibility

One of Isaac Newton's laws of physics states, "For every action there is an equal and opposite reaction." That physical law has been proven over and over through the centuries. Almost every area of our lives is affected in some way in our reliance upon the truth of that law.

There is a similar spiritual law that is equally true. Paul stated it in Galatians 6:7-8, "Be not deceived; God is not mocked: for whatsoever a man soweth, that shall he also reap. For he that soweth to his flesh shall of the flesh reap corruption; but he that soweth to the Spirit shall of the Spirit reap life everlasting."

In our secular lives, that law of sowing and reaping is generally true. We expect a return on our investment. We put our money in a bank expecting it to draw interest for us. We plan to withdraw that money, plus interest, at some future date. We would be extremely upset if the day came when we needed our money and we discovered that one of the Vice Presidents of the bank had taken the money as if it were his own and bought himself a mansion in the mountains with it. Our anger would be justified. The banker did not follow the rules and laws set down to regulate and govern banking.

In general, if a person works hard that person gets ahead. In general, we reap what we sow. If we give our boss a good day's work, we receive a good day's pay. If we do our jobs well over a period of time, we put ourselves in line for a raise or promotion. If we treat people right, if we are honest, if we give people a quality service or product at a fair price and take care of our business in a fiscally responsible manner, we will succeed. As I said before, in the secular world Newton's law and God's law of action and reaction, reaping and sowing, are generally true.

In the spiritual realm, God's law of reaping and sowing is *always* true. As Galatians 6:7-8 reminds us, if we plant good spiritual seeds we will produce a good harvest. If we cultivate our own selfish desires, willful ways and negative actions we will reap a destructive harvest. Therefore, we must take care to sow good seed for sooner or later the harvest will come. It may come in this life or our eternal one, but the harvest will come.

Our scripture addresses still another dimension. God has made a tremendous investment in us. In fact, He paid for us by sending His only Son. Jesus literally invested His life for us. Now we are the tenants from the passage. God has set us up in the "business" of being His children and disciples. He expects a return on His investment. He expects us to bear fruit.

We are to bear fruit by producing more of our own kind. He told us to go and make other disciples. We are also to bear fruit within. That is, our changed character which reflects love, joy, peace, patience, kindness, goodness, faithfulness, gentleness and self-control. These are called the fruit of the Spirit according to Galatians 5:22-23.

One day, the vineyard owner Himself will return. Jesus will return, but this time He will come not as the Son of the vineyard owner who was beaten and killed. This time He will come in all power and all authority.

Will He find He has made a good investment in you?

Seed Thoughts

1. What popular form of teaching did Jesus use to teach the disciples and others?

Jesus often taught by using parables or stories to illustrate a point or truth.

2. List some things the man in the story did to set up his business.

He planted a vineyard and put a protective hedge around it. He dug a place for the wine vat. He built a tower. He hired workers to tend the vineyard.

3. Why did the owner of the vineyard send a servant to the tenant of the vineyard?

The owner sent a servant to the worker of the vineyard to collect the owner's profit from the vineyard.

4. How was the servant received by the workers of the vineyard?

The workers caught him, beat him and sent the servant away without anything.

5. What action did the owner take when his servant returned? What was the result?

He sent other servants. The workers treated them harshly also. Some servants were even killed.

(Please turn page)

---

1. What popular form of teaching did Jesus use to teach the disciples and others?

2. List some things the man in the story did to set up his business.

3. Why did the owner of the vineyard send a servant to the tenant of the vineyard?

4. How was the servant received by the workers of the vineyard?

5. What action did the owner take when his servant returned? What was the result?

6. Finally, the owner was desperate. Whom did he send? What was his reason?

7. What was the result of the owner's last attempt? Was it what he expected?

8. What action did Jesus expect the owner of the vineyard to take against the workers?

9. Jesus related this parable to scripture. Which scripture did he refer to?

10. How did Jesus's enemies react to His story? What action did they take?

Jesus often taught by using parables or stories to illustrate a point or truth.

He planted a vineyard and put a protective hedge around it. He dug a place for the wine vat. He built a tower. He hired workers to tend the vineyard.

The owner sent a servant to the worker of the vineyard to collect the owner's profit from the vineyard.

The workers caught him, beat him and sent the servant away without anything.

He sent other servants. The workers treated them harshly also. Some servants were even killed.

The owner sent his only son because he was sure the tenants would respect him.

The workers killed the owner's only son. They reasoned that if the son were dead the workers would be in line for the inheritance.

Jesus said the owner would come and destroy the tenants and give the vineyard to others.

"The stone which the builders rejected is become the head of the corner" (Ps. 118:22).

They wanted to grab Jesus but were afraid of the crowd's reaction. They understood the parable was spoken against them, and they went their way.

6. Finally, the owner was desperate. Whom did he send? What was his reason?

The owner sent his only son because he was sure the tenants would respect him.

7. What was the result of the owner's last attempt? Was it what he expected?

The workers killed the owner's only son. They reasoned that if the son were dead the workers would be in line for the inheritance.

8. What action did Jesus expect the owner of the vineyard to take against the workers?

Jesus said the owner would come and destroy the tenants and give the vineyard to others.

9. Jesus related this parable to scripture. Which scripture did he refer to?

"The stone which the builders rejected is become the head of the corner" (Ps. 118:22).

10. How did Jesus's enemies react to His story? What action did they take?

They wanted to grab Jesus but were afraid of the crowd's reaction. They understood the parable was spoken against them, and they went their way.

Lesson 9

The New Covenant

Mark 14:12-25

12 And the first day of unleavened bread, when they killed the passover, his disciples said unto him, Where wilt thou that we go and prepare that thou mayest eat the passover?

13 And he sendeth forth two of his disciples, and saith unto them, Go ye into the city, and there shall meet you a man bearing a pitcher of water: follow him.

14 And wheresoever he shall go in, say ye to the goodman of the house, The Master saith, Where is the guestchamber, where I shall eat the passover with my disciples?

15 And he will shew you a large upper room furnished and prepared: there make ready for us.

16 And his disciples went forth, and came into the city, and found as he had said unto them: and they made ready the passover.

17 And in the evening he cometh with the twelve.

18 And as they sat and did eat, Jesus said,

Verily I say unto you, One of you which eateth with me shall betray me.

19 And they began to be sorrowful, and to say unto him one by one, Is it I? and another said, Is it I?

20 And he answered and said unto them, It is one of the twelve, that dippeth with me in the dish.

21 The Son of man indeed goeth, as it is written of him: but woe to that man by whom the Son of man is betrayed! good were it for that man if he had never been born.

22 And as they did eat, Jesus took bread, and blessed, and brake it, and gave to them, and said, Take, eat: this is my body.

23 And he took the cup, and when he had given thanks, he gave it to them: and they all drank of it.

24 And he said unto them, This is my blood of the new testament, which is shed for many.

25 Verily I say unto you, I will drink no more of the fruit of the vine, until that day that I drink it new in the kingdom of God.

Memory Selection
Mark 14:22-24

Devotional Reading
1 Corinthians 11:17-26

Background Scripture
Mark 14:12-25

Printed Scripture
Mark 14:12-25

Teacher's Target

Lesson purpose: *To revisit, through Mark's account, the scene of the Last Supper, dwelling on its relationship to the New Covenant.*

From time immemorial, sharing a meal has been a sign of good will and friendship. Old Abraham's first reaction to the Lord's appearance in Genesis 18 was to cook Him a meal. There is something both friendly and festive about dining together —especially when there is a special event to commemorate.

For Christians, there is no more special event than the offering of Christ on the Cross for the sins of the world. The Supper commemorating this event tempers festivity with pathos because of the death that it recalls. In addition to showing how this Meal commemorates the New Covenant, encourage members of your class to share ways to make its observance partake of both the sober reality of the Cross and the joyful promise of the Covenant.

Lesson Introduction

Some scholars find the background of the Lord's Supper not only in the Jewish Passover but in much older ceremonial meals among Bedouin tribes in the Middle East.

Picture a desert king whose forces have swept through the land bringing order out of the chaos of warring tribes. He brings lesser princes together, helping them settle their differences. The former enemies sit down together in the tent of the great king. He promises to protect the interests of each one. They promise not to take up arms against each other, and to serve only the king.

To seal their agreement the desert nobles sit opposite the king to share a meal. A goat roasts on a spit between them. The king solemnly slices off a generous portion of the meat to symbolize the "cutting" of the covenant. All partake, sharing a cup of wine with the meat offered by the king.

The "covenant meal" they have shared symbolizes a new relationship. Just as the meat and wine will nourish their bodies, a new spirit will nourish this relationship. They will live together now, each committed to keeping the covenant.

Teaching Outline	Daily Bible Readings
I. Preparation—12-16 　A. The background, 12 　B. The room prepared, 13-16 II. Prediction—17-21 　A. Christ's foreknowledge, 17-19 　B. Judas' complicity, 20-21 III. Proclamation—22-25 　A. The body, 22 　B. The blood, 23-24 　C. The banquet, 25	**Mon.** Keep the Passover as a Sign 　　*Exodus 12:1-14* **Tue.** Lift Up the Cup of Salvation 　　*Psalm 116:12-19* **Wed.** Blood Poured Out for Many 　　*Mark 14:12-25* **Thu.** New Covenant with God's People 　　*Jeremiah 31:27-34* **Fri.** Sharing in the Blood and Body 　　*1 Corinthians 10:14-22* **Sat.** Love as Christ Loved 　　*John 13:3-15* **Sun.** New Covenant in Christ's Blood 　　*1 Corinthians 11:17-26*

VERSE BY VERSE

I. Preparation—12-16

A. The background, 12

12 And the first day of unleavened bread, when they killed the passover, his disciples said unto him, Where wilt thou that we go and prepare that thou mayest eat the passover?

As a faithful Jew, Jesus kept the annual feast commemorating the exodus from Egypt, when the angel of death "passed over" the houses of the Hebrews that were marked with the blood of the Passover lamb (Exod. 12:3-30). This festival was a family rite (vss. 24-26); and it is a sad commentary on our times that such rituals have lost much of their meaning in both families and churches.

B. The room prepared, 13-16

13 And he sendeth forth two of his disciples, and saith unto them, Go ye into the city, and there shall meet you a man bearing a pitcher of water: follow him.

14 And wheresoever he shall go in, say ye to the goodman of the house, The Master saith, Where is the guest-chamber, where I shall eat the passover with my disciples?

15 And he will shew you a large upper room furnished and prepared: there make ready for us.

16 And his disciples went forth, and came into the city, and found as he had said unto them: and they made ready the passover.

Only Mark records the twin miracles of Jesus' foreknowledge that the disciples would find the man bearing a pitcher of water, and that the "goodman" (lit. "house-master") would so quickly consent to allowing his second-story room to be used by this stranger and His followers. Jerusalem was packed with visitors for the feast (Acts 2:5). Only by divine insight could Jesus have known His disciples would find this "upper room."

Since the feast required baking unleavened bread, killing and cooking the lamb, and preparing bitter herbs, Jesus and His disciples needed to find a house where these elaborate preparations could be made.

II. Prediction—17-21

A. Christ's foreknowledge, 17-19

17 And in the evening he cometh with the twelve.

18 And as they sat and did eat, Jesus said, Verily I say unto you, One of you which eateth with me shall betray me.

19 And they began to be sorrowful, and to say unto him one by one, Is it I? and another said, Is it I?

The Passover was to be eaten at night, since that was the time of day of the original meal at the exodus. It was "evening" in a figurative sense, too: Jesus was nearing the evening of His life, and he foresaw the dark day of Judas' betrayal. Verses 10-11 have told about Judas' plot to deliver Jesus over to His enemies. (Matthew 26:15 specifies that the price of betrayal was 30 pieces of silver.)

Jesus' foreknowledge that Judas would betray Him is one pole—but only one pole—of the twin doctrines of predestination and free will, discussed below, at verse 21.

The admission that Jesus was betrayed by one of the Twelve disciples closest to Him is an indication that the story was not fabricated—a concocted tale would have made the traitor an enemy, not a friend. Jesus' announcement cuts 11 of the men to the heart. Their question "Is it I?" indicates that they wonder if their own faith is about to be tested beyond endurance. Incidentally, the question is parallel to the way Christians are to "examine themselves" when they partake of the Lord's Supper, which is being instituted here (1 Cor. 11:28).

B. Judas' complicity, 20-21

20 And he answered and said unto them, It is one of the twelve, that dippeth with me in the dish.

21 The Son of man indeed goeth, as it is written of him: but woe to that man by whom the Son of man is betrayed! good were it for that man if he had never been born.

Jesus ends the questioning by giving a sign that would identify the traitor. Matthew (26:25) adds in more specific terms that Jesus identifies Judas. In Mark, we do not next hear of Judas and his dark deed until verse 43. John adds that he got up from the supper after being revealed as the betrayer and went to work immediately (John 13:27-30).

Sadly, the Body of Christ has suffered deep divisions between those who emphasize the foreknowledge implied in the first part of verse 21, and those who are attracted by the free-will indicated in the latter part. Jesus did not have a problem holding both facts in tension with each other. It was "written" that Jesus would be betrayed, and God in His foreknowledge may even have known the betrayer would be Judas Iscariot. Yet Jesus' pronouncement of personal woe on "the betrayer" indicates some freedom on Judas' part to choose whether he would play that role. God wrote the script and made the casting call, while Judas decided to take the part.

III. Proclamation—22-25

A. The body, 22

22 And as they did eat, Jesus took bread, and blessed, and brake it, and gave to them, and said, Take, eat: this is my body.

In this solemn moment, the Jewish Passover feast begins to take on the nature of the Christian observance of the Lord's Supper, Communion, or "the Eucharist" (from the Greek *eucharisteo*, "give thanks," in vs. 23). As is well known, the Roman Catholic doctrine of *transubstantiation* takes these words quite literally: the bread becomes the actual body of Christ and the wine His actual blood. Actually, this doctrine was not made official until the 13th century.

In contrast, most Protestants have a *representational* view of the bread and wine, holding that they are merely symbolic of Christ's body and blood. In a similar way, children making the fingerplay, in which they chant, "Here is the church and here is the steeple," mean that their hands stand for the reality. Martin Luther held a mediating position often called *consubstantiation*, in which the literal body and blood are held to exist alongside the bread and wine.

While this long-standing dispute can be neither analyzed adequately nor solved here, the words of Paul as he explained the Lord's Supper can provide some common ground. He said the bread and wine constitute fellowship, participation, or communion (Grk. *koinonia*) with the body and blood of Christ (1 Cor. 10:16). While various groups may differ over fine points of interpretation, we can agree that in the Supper we are actually enjoying "table fellowship" with Jesus. We can agree that the Supper offers a unique measure of intimacy with the slain but soon-to-risen Lord.

B. The blood, 23-24

23 And he took the cup, and when he had given thanks, he gave it to them: and they all drank of it.

24 And he said unto them, This is my blood of the new testament, which is shed for many.

The words of institution for the wine are the same as those for the bread, except for the important description that the cup stands for the "blood of the new testament" (or "covenant," NIV). This phrase reminds us that the real "New Testament" is the promise that our sins are forgiven by the sacrifice of Christ's blood. Matthew through Revelation are the *Scriptures* of the New Covenant. It is a popular but short-hand practice to speak of the Scriptures of the New Covenant as the New Testament itself.

C. The banquet, 25

25 Verily I say unto you, I will drink no more of the fruit of the vine, until that day that I drink it new in the kingdom of God.

Some interpreters take this as evidence that Jesus and His disciples expected the Kingdom of God to be set up as a literal political entity within the lifetime of His hearers, but were disappointed. Actually, Jesus began to rule over His Kingdom when He Ascended to the Father. Ever since, the saved have been placed in His Kingdom (Col. 1:13). He did not share the Supper with His followers only during the brief time between His death and Ascension. Jesus' rule exists now, and Christians enjoy "table fellowship" with Him each time they partake of the Supper.

Evangelistic Emphasis

When we were kids there were times when we wanted to insure that we were telling the truth or that a promise made was guaranteed to be kept. In times like those, we might have said, "Cross my heart and hope to die." This was supposed to mean that the statements made were gospel and the promise made was inviolate. We outgrew those times. When we began to study God's Word, we discovered that we were not supposed to do that anyway. Our word was to be our bond, not an oath upon some outside entity.

In this passage of scripture, Jesus speaks of a new covenant He is making with people. He makes the Covenant then seals it with His life.

In His covenant we have promises. All who believe in Jesus have the promise of eternal life (John 3:16). Disciples of Jesus have the promise that wherever we go in His name, He is always with us (Matthew 28:20). We have the promise from Jesus Himself that He is preparing a place for us to live forever with Him in heaven and one day He will return to bring us to that place (John 14:1-4). Those are just a few of His promises.

The New Testament is filled with promises that we have through the New Covenant Jesus established. We have promises that serve to make our lives richer, fuller, more meaningful and rewarding. Won't you accept His promises with a promise of your own? Follow Jesus.

Memory Selection

And as they did eat, Jesus took bread, and blessed, and brake it, and gave to them, and said, "Take, eat: this is my body." And he took the cup, and when he had given thanks, he gave it to them: and they all drank of it. And he said unto them,"This is my blood of the new testament, which is shed for many.—*Mark 14:22-24*

More than once in the past prophets of Israel resorted to symbolic, dramatic actions when they felt that words were not enough. That is what Jeremiah did when he made bonds and yokes and wore them in token of the coming servitude of Israel (Jeremiah 27). That is what the prophet Hananiah did when he broke the yokes that Jeremiah wore (Jeremiah 28:10-11). It was as if words were easily forgotten, but a dramatic action would print itself on the memory.

That is what Jesus did. He said, "Look! Just as this bread is broken my body will be broken for you. Just as this cup of wine is poured out my blood will be shed for you."

Thus, the bread and wine became more than bread and wine to the disciples and to us. They became reminders of the sacrifice Christ made to save us from our sins. We eat the bread and drink the wine and remember.

Weekday Problems

Jon and Margie had decided to put their Christmas tree up the first weekend of December. Jon had found a magnificent tree. It was full and green and it had the room filled with pine scent.

Jon had pulled the boxes of decorations from the attic. Margie was unpacking ornaments while Jon and the kids were heating up a batch of hot chocolate.

She came to one brown, flat box. She opened it with love. Inside were wooden ornaments which had been hand-painted. "Dad and Mom," Margie said to herself. Her father had cut out each ornament with his scroll saw. Mom had painted each one with loving care.

Margie took out two ornaments. As the gazed at those two flat, wooden images, memories flooded over her. She remembered Christmases past, times of love and laughter. She remembered her parents and how they were always helping others, quietly and unnoticed, all year long. She thought about things her parents had instilled in her. She remembered things she learned from them, not because they taught them to her, but because they modeled them.

"Hmmph!" she said to herself with a tear in her eye. "Isn't it funny what a box full of painted figures can do for my soul."

   *   What are some symbols in your life that cause you to remember good things?

   *   What are some of the symbols the church has that remind us of what Christ has done?

Beneath the Forms of Outward Rite

Beneath the forms of outward rite
Thy supper, Lord, is spread
In every quiet upper room
Where fainting souls are fed.

The bread is always consecrate
Which men divide with men;
And every act of brotherhood
Repeats thy feast again.

The blessed cup is only passed
True memory of thee,
When life anew pours out its wine
With rich sufficiency.

O Master, through these symbols shared,
Thine own dear self impart,
That in our daily life may flame
The passion of thy heart.

—*James A. Blaisdell*

This Lesson in Your Life

Sadness in the Midst of Celebration

Our study finds Jesus celebrating Passover with His disciples. Passover was one of the most significant events in the life of a Jew. The celebration reminded the Jew of the night in Egypt when the angel of death "passed over" the houses which had the door frame marked with the blood of a lamb. The angel of death took the firstborn son of all those Egyptian homes unmarked by the blood. As a consequence, Pharaoh let the people of Israel have their freedom. We can read that story in Exodus chapter 12.

The Passover was to be a joyous celebration. Yet, on the night we read about in Mark 14, the occasion was less than joyful. There was sadness mixed with joy.

Many of our holidays are like that. They are days of joy mixed with sadness. At Thanksgiving we get together and thank God for the blessings of the year. Yet many families lost loved ones in the past twelve months and their loss is magnified by their absence during a holiday in which families traditionally get together. We wish the loved one was still with us and our joy is mixed with sadness.

We look forward to Christmas for months. Yet during the season of good cheer, gifts and peace on earth, there is still pain and suffering and poverty. The pain and suffering and poverty stand in stark contrast to the bounty of the holiday season. We have read that depression and suicide seem to increase during the Christmas season.

The announcement of Jesus' betrayal and death at the Passover celebration took some of the joy out of the occasion for the moment. All joy was restored after His resurrection. Jesus has a way of doing that. He has a way of bringing joy into situations. We must remember that. Christ brings joy. When we allow Him to be a part of our lives, he brings joy in the midst of depression and pain.

One of the most joyful occasions in our church is the day we celebrate Holy Communion. Remember, Holy Communion is the commemoration of this very time that is recorded in Mark chapter 14. We remember that Christ's body was broken for us. We remember that His blood was poured out for us. Jesus died for us.

When we think only about His death Holy Communion is a sad occasion. If we consider only His suffering and pain, Communion can only be a time of grief for us, and rightly so. Yet, Communion is a celebration, for we remember what His death means to us. Through His death, Jesus gave us eternal life. Through His broken body and poured out blood, Jesus made a way for us to live forever with Him in heaven. Through His sacrificial death on the cross, Jesus became the full, perfect and sufficient sacrifice for the forgiveness of any sin for which we could ever ask forgiveness.

In a sense, Jesus' death was like a Christmas present that cost too much. As we open the present, we may say to that person, "You shouldn't have done this. You can't afford this." We know that the person gave us that expensive gift because of that person's love. That is what Jesus did. He gave us a most costly gift, His life. He did it because He loves us.

Thus, the celebration of Holy Communion is the most joyful/sad occasion of the Christian faith. Holy Communion reminds us of the gift Jesus gives to each one of us AND the great price He paid to purchase that gift.

Seed Thoughts

1. What important holy event were the disciples and Jesus going to observe?

The disciples and Jesus were preparing to celebrate the Passover, or the Feast of Unleavened Bread.

2. What was the significance of the Passover lamb? See Exodus 12:1-11.

The Passover lamb was the one killed whose blood was used to mark the door posts so the angel of death would "passover."

3. Jesus gave the disciples specific instructions for finding a place to eat. What were these instructions?

Two disciples were to go into the city, follow a man carrying water and tell him that the Master needed the guest chamber. He would show them the room.

4. What was the result of the disciples' obedience to Jesus' instructions?

The disciples found everything just as Jesus had said. There they prepared the Passover.

5. What shocking thing did Jesus reveal to the disciples during the Passover meal?

Jesus revealed that one of the disciples that was sitting in the room sharing the meal with Him would betray Him.

(Please turn page)

1. What important holy event were the disciples and Jesus going to observe?

2. What was the significance of the Passover lamb? See Exodus 12:1-11.

3. Jesus gave the disciples specific instructions for finding a place to eat. What were these instructions?

4. What was the result of the disciples' obedience to Jesus' instructions?

5. What shocking thing did Jesus reveal to the disciples during the Passover meal?

6. How did the disciples react to such a statement? What was the mood?

7. What did Jesus have to say about the man who would betray Him?

8. What did Jesus do before they ate the bread that night? What words did He say over the bread?

9. What similar statements did Jesus make over the wine that night?

10. What indication do you have that Jesus knew His death was very near?

The disciples and Jesus were preparing to celebrate the Passover, or the Feast of Unleavened Bread.

The Passover lamb was the one killed whose blood was used to mark the door posts so the angel of death would "passover."

Two disciples were to go into the city, follow a man carrying water and tell him that the Master needed the guest chamber. He would show them the room.

The disciples found everything just as Jesus had said. There they prepared the Passover.

Jesus revealed that one of the disciples that was sitting in the room sharing the meal with Him would betray Him.

The disciples began to be sorrowful and some even asked Jesus, "Is it I?" The mood was one of shock and sadness.

Jesus said it would have been better if that man had never been born.

Jesus blessed the bread, broke it, and then said, "Take, eat: this is my body."

"This is my blood of the new testament, which is shed for many."

Jesus told the disciples that He would drink no more wine until the day that He drank new wine in the kingdom of God.

6. How did the disciples react to such a statement? What was the mood?

The disciples began to be sorrowful and some even asked Jesus, "Is it I?" The mood was one of shock and sadness.

7. What did Jesus have to say about the man who would betray Him?

Jesus said it would have been better if that man had never been born.

8. What did Jesus do before they ate the bread that night? What words did He say over the bread?

Jesus blessed the bread, broke it, and then said, "Take, eat: this is my body."

9. What similar statements did Jesus make over the wine that night?

"This is my blood of the new testament, which is shed for many."

10. What indication do you have that Jesus knew His death was very near?

Jesus told the disciples that He would drink no more wine until the day that He drank new wine in the kingdom of God.

Lesson 10

Teaching in Parables

Mark 4:1-9, 26-32

1 And he began to teach by the sea side: and there was gathered unto him a great multitude, so that he entered into a ship, and sat in the sea; and the whole multitude was by the sea on the land.

2 And he taught them many things by parables, and said unto them in his doctrine,

3 Hearken; Behold, there went out a sower to sow:

4 And it came to pass, as he sowed some fell by the way side, and the fowls of the air came and devoured it up.

5 And some fell on stony ground, where it had not much earth; and immediately it sprang up, because it had no depth of earth:

6 But when the sun was up, it was scorched; and because it had no root, it withered away.

7 And some fell among thorns, and the thorns grew up, and choked it, and it yielded no fruit.

8 And other fell on good ground, and did yield fruit that sprang up and increased; and brought forth, some thirty, and some sixty, and some an hundred.

9 And he said unto them, He that hath ears to hear, let him hear.

26 And he said, So is the kingdom of God, as if a man should cast seed into the ground;

27 And should sleep, and rise night and day, and the seed should spring and grow up, he knoweth not how.

28 For the earth bringeth forth fruit of herself; first the blade, then the ear, after that the full corn in the ear.

29 But when the fruit is brought forth, immediately he putteth in the sickle, because the harvest is come.

30 And he said, Whereunto shall we liken the kingdom of God? or with what comparison shall we compare it?

31 It is like a grain of mustard seed, which, when it is sown in the earth, is less than all the seeds that be in the earth:

32 But when it is sown, it groweth up, and becometh greater than all herbs, and shooteth out great branches; so that the fowls of the air may lodge under the shadow of it.

May 3

Memory Selection
Mark 4:33

Devotional Reading
2 Corinthians 5:6-17

Background Scripture
Mark 4:1-34

Printed Scripture
Mark 4:1-9, 26-32

Teacher's Target

Lesson purpose: *To learn more about the nature of the Kingdom of God, and the kind of people we must be as subjects in it.*

We return here to the Christ of the parables whom we met in Lesson 8. Remember that Jesus used this form of teaching to invite hearers to participate in the story, and to decide how it might apply to them. Such opportunities are best created by the teacher with persistent questions.

In connection with the first parable, in Mark 4:1-9, you might ask such questions: Has there been a time in your life when you felt like a beaten-down pathway? Can a thorny plot of soil ever change? Can you always tell right away what kind of soil a person's heart is made of?

For the second parable, ask: What does the seed growing secretly say about human judgments? Why does Jesus use such a tiny seed as an example? Can a person be too quiet about the faith? What "tiny" seeds do you have the opportunity to plant?

Lesson Introduction

In Lesson 8 we noticed that Jesus used parables not merely to make profound truth simple, but to veil it from those who did not have a heart to understand it (see Matt. 13:10-15). For example, in the Parable of the Soils, a hard-hearted person might be so resentful of being compared with a beaten-down pathway that he refuses to change.

Most of Jesus' parables were designed to illustrate a truth about the Kingdom of God for those with "willing ears"—as indicated in Mark 4:30. The Kingdom of God is an important thread running through both Testaments. As noted in the preceding lesson, the Kingdom is a present reality, having more than merely future significance.

Note that these two stories are both "growth parables," using plant metaphors to communicate truths about the Kingdom of God. This shows the dynamic, living nature of living under God's rule, as opposed to the Kingdom's being a static place to dwell, sheltered from the risks and trials of life.

Teaching Outline	Daily Bible Readings
I. The Setting—1-2	**Mon.** Learning from Sowing Seeds *Mark 4:1-9*
II. The Parable of the Soils—3-9	**Tue.** Secrets of God's Kingdom *Mark 4:10-20*
A. The pathway, 3-4	**Wed.** Heed What You Hear *Mark 4:21-34*
B. Rocky ground, 5-6	**Thu.** Live for the Risen One *2 Corinthians 5:6-15*
C. Thorny soil, 7	**Fri.** Sowing and Reaping Bountifully *2 Corinthians 9:6-15*
D. Good soil, 8-9	**Sat.** Sow the Spirit and Reap Eternity *Galatians 6:1-10*
III. The Parable of the Secret Kingdom—26-32	**Sun.** Reap with Shouts of Joy! *Psalm 126:1-6*
A. In God's good time, 26-29	
B. Seed-sized faith, 30-32	

VERSE BY VERSE

I. The Setting—1-2

1 And he began to teach by the sea side: and there was gathered unto him a great multitude, so that he entered into a ship, and sat in the sea; and the whole multitude was by the sea on the land.

2 And he taught them many things by parables, and said unto them in his doctrine,

In our times, many people think of faith as a warm feeling—and certainly it warms the heart to believe in Christ. The emphasis in these two verses, however, reminds us that Christianity is also *taught*, not just *caught*. It is a continuing challenge to maintain a healthy balance between the rational and the emotional components of faith. Jesus came as the Master Teacher—not just to help people feel better about themselves but to teach them "many things." The crowds that made it necessary for him to enter a boat and push out a few yards from shore in order to have an outdoor "pulpit" attest to the drawing power of His teaching.

To us it may seem somewhat casual for an important teacher to sit down to teach. Sitting, however, was the customary position assumed by rabbis in Jesus' day, and by doing so Jesus signals that His message is authoritative.

II. The Parable of the Soils—3-9
A. The pathway, 3-4

3 Hearken; Behold, there went out a sower to sow:

4 And it came to pass, as he sowed some fell by the way side, and the fowls of the air came and devoured it up.

Jesus bids for our attention with the opening word, "Listen!" or "Pay attention!" As with all His parables, He chooses a story that is both close to people's life, and easily applied to the point He wants to make. Everyone understands how soil conditions determine whether seeds grow or languish; and it is a short step from there to perceiving that the human heart or mind has a similar capacity to accept or reject what we hear.

As Lesson 8 emphasized, Jesus intends for His hearers to wrestle with parables themselves as a test of their receptivity to them (vs. 12). Only to His disciples does He draw out the meaning in explicit detail (vss. 14-20). He explains that the sower is sowing "the word," and that the various soils represent the human heart or mind (vss. 14-15). Although we often use the term "the Word" today to refer to the entire Bible, Jesus probably uses it here to refer to His own message about Himself as the Son of man, bringing God's love in fulfillment of Old Testament prophecy.

A constantly-pounded and sun-baked footpath is hardly ideal for growing anything. Lacking a soft or open surface, the seed can only lie there as an easy target for birds. Although Satan has a part in scooping up seed that falls on such surfaces (vs. 15), Jesus clearly means for us to take responsibility for having plowed or cultivated hearts that are more receptive to the truth.

B. Rocky ground, 5-6

5 And some fell on stony ground, where it had not much earth; and immediately it sprang up, because it had no depth of earth:

6 But when the sun was up, it was scorched; and because it had no root, it withered away.

An example of people who are like thin soil are those who are so eager to please that they agree with everything anyone says. "Immediately they receive (the Word) with gladness" (vs. 16); but they have no commitment and perseverance. Notice that having "no depth of earth" in verse 5 is parallel to having "no root" in verse 17.

Jesus warned more than once that we should look before we leap to accept His teaching. We are to count the cost (Luke 14:28), realizing that to follow Jesus might involve a "baptism" of suffering (Mark 10:38). In this parable Jesus is calling for followers who won't turn back at the first blush of criticism, suffering, or difficult questions.

C. Thorny soil, 7

7 And some fell among thorns, and the thorns grew up, and choked it, and it yielded no fruit.

Unfortunately, the same nutrients in soil that can grow good crops also nourish weeds. People represented by thorny soil are unable to set priorities and cull out the many things in life other than following Jesus that clamor for our attention. The specific examples Jesus gives are worldly cares, riches and improper desires or lusts (vs. 19).

Again, Jesus was very clear in warning that His followers would be challenged to keep Him first in their lives. In radical overstatement He calls for such "thorns" as the lustful eye to be cut out and the thieving hand to be cut off (Matt. 5:29-30). "Lust" does not refer to sexual desire alone. Loving the praise of men more than the praise of God, and loving "this present world" are also improper desires that often choke the growth of faith.

D. Good soil, 8-9

8 And other fell on good ground, and did yield fruit that sprang up and increased; and brought forth, some thirty, and some sixty, and some an hundred.

9 And he said unto them, He that hath ears to hear, let him hear.

After three examples of woefully inadequate soils, or hearts, Jesus finally describes the kind of person who will be fruitful in His Kingdom. Unlike the hard heart, this person's heart is receptive to the Word. Unlike the stony ground, such persons have souls too deep to give up easily under pressure. Unlike the thorn-infested soil, good-soil people are willing to weed out elements of life that do not contribute to their being fruit-bearing disciples.

Note, however, that the amount of fruit they produce varies widely. This is a reminder not to compare ourselves with other Christians, neither despising ourselves for not being as productive as someone more gifted, nor belittling others who are less visibly productive in the Kingdom.

The closing line of the parable calls attention to a fact that is commonly observed, especially by parents when they ask their children to do something! Not everyone who has ears really hears.

In the Bible, true hearing equals obeying. The parable isn't difficult to understand; but we show we really hear it only by seeing that the soil of our hearts and minds is receptive to the Word.

III. The Parable of the Secret Kingdom—26-34

A. In God's good time, 26-29

26 And he said, So is the kingdom of God, as if a man should cast seed into the ground;

27 And should sleep, and rise night and day, and the seed should spring and grow up, he knoweth not how.

28 For the earth bringeth forth fruit of herself; first the blade, then the ear, after that the full corn in the ear.

29 But when the fruit is brought forth, immediately he putteth in the sickle, because the harvest is come.

Many people in Jesus' day expected the Messiah to come in the war-like trappings of King David to reassert the prominence of Israel as a world power. These next two parables correct that concept. In the first, Jesus affirms that His rule would assert itself gradually as people grow in faith and obedience. The "harvest" will not be the violent overthrow of the Roman and Jewish establishment, but the result of individual spiritual growth.

B. Seed-sized faith, 30-32

30 And he said, Whereunto shall we liken the kingdom of God? or with what comparison shall we compare it?

31 It is like a grain of mustard seed, which, when it is sown in the earth, is less than all the seeds that be in the earth:

32 But when it is sown, it groweth up, and becometh greater than all herbs, and shooteth out great branches; so that the fowls of the air may lodge under the shadow of it.

In the Palestine of Jesus' day, the tiny mustard seed grew into a tree-like bush. This parable tells us that the Kingdom of God is best seen not in showy claims of Christian triumphalism, but in the cups of cold water given in Jesus' name, the ill person who suffers without complaint, the unadvertised visit to the hospital—"seed-sized" acts of faith that at the day of Judgment will be seen to be the most towering "trees" of all.

Evangelistic Emphasis

If you have ever planted a garden you are aware of a valuable truth. The truth of gardens is exactly like one of the truths of evangelism in the Kingdom of God. If we want to harvest tomatoes we must set out some tomato plants. If we want to harvest corn we must plant some kernels. If we want to harvest souls we must sow the gospel, the Word of God.

This parable reminds us that not all of that which is sown will produce a good crop. That is so in our gardens as well as the Kingdom. Sometimes outside forces stop our plants from growing and producing fruit. Rabbits and birds may eat them up. Disease may destroy the plants. In the same sense, outside forces sometimes thwart our efforts to spread the Good News. Yet we must spread the News anyway.

Sometimes we fail to prepare the soil properly in our gardens. We fail to get rid of the rocks. We neglect the weeds. That failure diminishes our harvest. In the same sense, failure to do the groundwork, cultivating the "soil" of the lives of others, will diminish the harvest of souls.

We who love Jesus are compelled to cultivate the soil and spread the Good News of Jesus. We are not guaranteed a harvest in every case. Yet, we can be sure of this. There will be no harvest if no seed is planted.

✳ ✳ ✳

Memory Selection

And with many such parables space He the word unto them, as they were able to hear it.—*Mark 4:33*

Radio has been around a long time. Radios can still teach us a truth about God's Word and Christ's teaching. There are radio waves coursing through the air 24 hours a day, but we can neither see nor hear them. For us to enjoy (or endure, depending on your viewpoint of what is on the air these days) the radio waves, we must have something that will receive those waves and turn them into audible sound.

We must have a radio in good working order. The radio must have a proper power source. The radio must be turned on. The radio must be tuned in. When those things happen we hear the sound.

God is speaking to His people daily. We must have our spiritual radios plugged into the Power Source, turned on and tuned in to Him. Then will we hear from God.

Turn your radio on.

Weekday Problems

Keith opened the letter and read in his wife's handwriting: "Keith, let me tell you a story. Once upon a time there was a boy who wanted a dog more than anything in the world. 'If I had a dog my life would be perfect,' he often thought. One day a neighbor's dog had puppies. When they were old enough, the neighbor gave one of the puppies to the boy.

"The boy was so happy. He cared for the pup. He built the puppy a dog house himself. He bought the puppy all kinds of toys. The boy played with the puppy constantly. They romped and ran and they tussled and tumbled. They were inseparable. At least, they were inseparable at first.

"Slowly as the months went by, the boy seemed to lose interest in the puppy. He began to spend more time with his friends while leaving the puppy at home. The boy would come home and lock himself in his room while the puppy longed to get in. He quit playing with the puppy. He quit caring for the puppy. Sometimes days went by before the boy thought about tending to the puppy's basic needs.

"One day the boy went looking for his puppy but the puppy had gone. Goodbye, Keith.

"Sincerely, Kylie."

* Do you think Keith got the message from Kylie's story? Why or Why not?

* Sometimes stories (parables) are more effective in communicating truth and sometimes less effective. Explain your viewpoint.

I Wish I'd Said That

A fat man said to his skinny friend, "From the looks of you, there must have been a famine."
Retorted the thin man, "Yep, and from the looks of you, you caused it."

The speaker was being heckled by a man in the audience who finally shouted, "Tell 'em all you know. It'll only take a minute."
"I'll tell 'em all we both know," the speaker shot back. "It won't take any longer."

Envious of the author's new book, a rival writer tried the put-down, "I loved your new book. Who wrote it for you?"
"Glad you liked it," the author said. "Who read it to you?"

"Oh, darling," said the snob. "I completely forgot about your little party last night."
"Oh?" was the reply. "Weren't you there?"

This Lesson in Your Life

Open to Truth

Storytelling has been around as long as there has been speech, I suppose. From the days when the mighty hunter recounted the events of the day's kill around a campfire to our day of E-mail on the Internet, humans have told stories.

Sometimes the stories are purely for our enjoyment, such as a John Grisham novel or a Harlequin romance. Sometimes the stories communicate facts, such as when we tell about the big fire down at the fertilizer plant or the hair-raising events that occurred the night we had to rush the baby to the hospital. Sometimes the stories make a point, such as Aesop's Fables and the parables of Jesus.

It is upon these pointed stories that we want to focus, specifically the parables of Jesus. Parables communicate truth. A parable may not be true in itself, yet it tells the truth. Let's take the story Jesus told about a sower as an example. Jesus could have approached his topic head-on. It may have sounded something like this: "If you are a shallow person the Word of God may find root in your heart, but when the heat is on you will shrivel. If you hang out with a bad crowd, they will keep the Word of God from producing its proper effect in you. If your heart is properly prepared, when you hear and receive the Word of God it will produce its proper effect many times over."

Now, wasn't the parable more interesting? Jesus used word pictures common to His people. They could visualize what He was saying, for they had seen these things occur. Most had planted crops and could relate to the agricultural situations. When He applied those stories to spiritual truths, His listeners were required to chew on them awhile. Parables are like that. The truth is not always right on the surface. Sometimes we have to dig. When we discover the truth after digging, it tends to stick with us longer.

Parables and stories are effective vehicles for the truth when the listener is not open to hearing the truth. A parable tells a story seemingly unrelated to the point at hand. What does a mustard seed have to do with the Kingdom of God anyway? When the unreceptive person hears the story he or she may study on it awhile. Then the person may discover the truth contained in the parable. Discovering the truth for ourselves or having the truth "sneak up" on us is a powerful tool for teaching.

The three parables contained in our scripture passage convey timeless truths. In the first we understand how the gospel brings powerful and long-lasting results when it is received by those who have the faith to understand and respond. The second tells how the gospel message grows and multiplies with power of its own. In the third we see how the Kingdom of God, with seemingly insignificant beginnings, will grow until its power is seen by all the world.

The story tells the truth.

Seed Thoughts

1. Was Jesus accustomed to teaching in the synagogue? Explain your answer.

No. In this passage He was teaching by the seaside and then from a boat. Jesus went where the people were.

2. What method did Jesus use for teaching? Did He use the language of the priests or that of the people?

Jesus used parables to teach in story form for the common, uneducated people.

3. Name the first hindrance to the seed or the plant in the parable of the sower.

Some of the seed fell by the way side and the fowls of the air came and ate it.

4. What was the second hindrance to the seed or the plant in the parable of the sower?

Some seed fell on stony ground. It immediately grew, but did not have a deep root. The sun scorched the shallow root and the plant withered.

5. What was the last hindrance mentioned in the parable of the sower.

Some seed fell among thorns. The thorns choked the plant and it yielded no fruit.

(Please turn page)

1. Was Jesus accustomed to teaching in the synagogue? Explain your answer.

2. What method did Jesus use for teaching? Did He use the language of the priests or that of the people?

3. Name the first hindrance to the seed or the plant in the parable of the sower.

4. What was the second hindrance to the seed or the plant in the parable of the sower?

5. What was the last hindrance mentioned in the parable of the sower.

6. How much fruit did the seed yield that fell on good ground?

7. To what does Jesus compare the Kingdom of God in verse 26?

8. According to this comparison, does the sower understand and see exactly how the seed develops?

9. What second comparison of the Kingdom of God does Jesus make in verses 30-32?

10. When Jesus was alone with His disciples, what did He do?

No. In this passage He was teaching by the seaside and then from a boat. Jesus went where the people were.

Jesus used parables to teach in story form for the common, uneducated people.

Some of the seed fell by the way side and the fowls of the air came and ate it.

Some seed fell on stony ground. It immediately grew, but did not have a deep root. The sun scorched the shallow root and the plant withered.

Some seed fell among thorns. The thorns choked the plant and it yielded no fruit.

Some seed brought forth thirty, some sixty and some a hundred times more.

Jesus compares the kingdom of God to a man casting seed onto the ground.

The sower doesn't know how the seed grows, but does knows when the harvest time comes.

He compares the Kingdom of God to a tiny mustard seed that, when full grown, grows bigger than other herbs.

When Jesus was alone with the disciples, He explained the parables to them.

6. How much fruit did the seed yield that fell on good ground?

Some seed brought forth thirty, some sixty and some a hundred times more.

7. To what does Jesus compare the Kingdom of God in verse 26?

Jesus compares the kingdom of God to a man casting seed onto the ground.

8. According to this comparison, does the sower understand and see exactly how the seed develops?

The sower doesn't know how the seed grows, but does knows when the harvest time comes.

9. What second comparison of the Kingdom of God does Jesus make in verses 30-32?

He compares the Kingdom of God to a tiny mustard seed that, when full grown, grows bigger than other herbs.

10. When Jesus was alone with His disciples, what did He do?

When Jesus was alone with the disciples, He explained the parables to them.

DO NOT WORSHIP GOD WITH WORDS WHEN YOUR HEART IS FAR FROM GOD

Lesson 11

Traditions or God?

Mark 7:1-15

1 Then came together unto him the Pharisees, and certain of the scribes, which came from Jerusalem.

2 And when they saw some of his disciples eat bread with defiled, that is to say, with unwashen, hands, they found fault.

3 For the Pharisees, and all the Jews, except they wash their hands oft, eat not, holding the tradition of the elders.

4 And when they come from the market, except they wash, they eat not. And many other things there be, which they have received to hold, as the washing of cups, and pots, brasen vessels, and of tables.

5 Then the Pharisees and scribes asked him, Why walk not thy disciples according to the tradition of the elders, but eat bread with unwashen hands?

6 He answered and said unto them, Well hath Esaias prophesied of you hypocrites, as it is written, This people honoureth me with their lips, but their heart is far from me.

7 Howbeit in vain do they worship me, teaching for doctrines the commandments of men.

8 As for laying aside the commandment of God, ye hold the tradition of men, as the washing of pots and cups: and many other such like things ye do.

9 And he said unto them, Full well ye reject the commandment of God, that ye may keep your own tradition.

10 For Moses said, Honour thy father and thy mother; and, Whoso curseth father or mother, let him die the death:

11 But ye say, If a man shall say to his father or mother, It is Corban, that is to say, a gift, by whatsoever thou mightest be profited by me; he shall be free.

12 And ye suffer him no more to do ought for his father or his mother;

13 Making the word of God of none effect through your tradition, which ye have delivered: and many such like things do ye.

14 And when he had called all the people unto him, he said unto them, Hearken unto me every one of you, and understand:

15 There is nothing from within a man, that entering into him, can defile him: but the things which come out of him, those are they that defile the man.

May 10

Memory Selection
Mark 7:8

Devotional Reading
Ephesians 6:10-20

Background Scripture
Mark 7:1-23

Printed Scripture
Mark 7:1-15

Teacher's Target

Lesson purpose: *To examine our faith and practice in light of Jesus' challenge to serve Him with the heart, instead of developing ways to appear religious while avoiding His will.*

Jesus "gets under our skin." That is, He expects heart-felt obedience, not just lip-service. This can be inconvenient. At such times, it's tempting to fashion a way to appear to be obedient, while going our own way.

One way to introduce Jesus' teaching on the subject is to brainstorm with your class some of the ways the call of Christ can be uncomfortable. Are we sometimes called to take an unpopular stand? Can following Christ interfere with what "feels good"? Does caring for others seem to intrude on tending to our own desires? Lead class members to face squarely the temptation to devise ways to protect ourselves from obedience.

Lesson Introduction

Scripture does not claim to offer a "Thus saith the Lord" for every minute means of doing God's will. Thus, every community of faith has its own ways of handling its incidentals—"traditions" as opposed to the core of God's will.

Such commonly accepted practices and procedures have their place. They facilitate the work of the church, and avoid wasting time re-inventing procedural matters. They provide a comfort zone that enables one to feel at home away from home. No one likes the furniture in their spiritual home to be rearranged every day.

In this lesson, however, Jesus warns against using tradition to avoid "weightier matters" of God's will, and to appear to be a faithful Christian while inwardly having a disobedient heart. That elevates tradition over the work and will of God.

Teaching Outline	Daily Bible Readings
	Mon. Testing Traditions *Mark 7:1-13*
I. Details Observed—1-5	**Tue.** Soiled by the Human Heart *Mark 7:14-23*
A. Ritual cleanliness, 1-4	**Wed.** Preserve the Ancient Landmark *Proverbs 23:6-11*
B. Carping criticism, 5	**Thu.** The Old Has Passed Away *2 Corinthians 5:16-21*
II. Duty Dodged—6-13	**Fri.** Put on the New Nature *Ephesians 4:17-24*
A. The trouble with tradition, 6-7	**Sat.** Know Christ's Resurrection *Philippians 3:1-11*
B. A weightier matter, 8-13	**Sun.** Stand Strong in the Spirit *Ephesians 6:10-20*
III. Defilement Defined—14-15	

VERSE BY VERSE

I. Details Observed—1-5

A. Ritual cleanliness, 1-4

1 Then came together unto him the Pharisees, and certain of the scribes, which came from Jerusalem.

2 And when they saw some of his disciples eat bread with defiled, that is to say, with unwashen, hands, they found fault.

3 For the Pharisees, and all the Jews, except they wash their hands oft, eat not, holding the tradition of the elders.

4 And when they come from the market, except they wash, they eat not. And many other things there be, which they have received to hold, as the washing of cups, and pots, brasen vessels, and of tables.

The setting here is back in Galilee. The Jewish authorities in Jerusalem have sent a delegation to investigate this upstart prophet in the north country, to be sure His teachings conform with those of the ruling authorities.

At stake was a tradition that had developed out of a sincere desire to obey the Law. God had decreed, apparently for both religious and hygienic reasons, that touching many potentially infectious things rendered one "unclean"— (see Lev. 15 and 25). Scrupulous keepers of the Law had gone one better and ruled that to avoid any possibility of breaking this commandment, people should observe a host of washings. After all, in a busy marketplace, how could one know if he had brushed against a woman who was having her menstrual cycle?

These additions to the law are called "traditions," which comes from a word that literally meant "hand-alongs." That is, they were handed down from the Jewish leaders ("elders") from one generation to the next. Mark explains to his Roman audience that these traditions, added to the law, had grown to include not only washing hands but many religious objects as well.

B. Carping criticism, 5

5 Then the Pharisees and scribes asked him, Why walk not thy disciples according to the tradition of the elders, but eat bread with unwashen hands?

The fact that Jesus' disciples had relaxed their conformity to the tradition of washings (vs. 2) is seen as a threat to the investigators. Note that they are not upset that Christ and His disciples have disobeyed the Law, but the *traditions* that had been collected to keep the Law from even a hint of violation.

The Jewish rabbis had meant for tradition to be "a hedge about the Law." If worshipers avoided breaking through the "hedge," they surely would be safe from breaking the Law. It was perhaps inevitable that the tradition would become more sacred than the Law, since it was the Law's first line of defense.

II. Duty Dodged—6-13

A. The trouble with tradition, 6-7

6 He answered and said unto them, Well hath Esaias prophesied of you hypocrites, as it is written, This people honoureth me with their lips, but their heart is far from me.

7 Howbeit in vain do they worship me, teaching for doctrines the commandments of men.

Jesus confounds His questioners by quoting Isaiah, one of their prophets with greater authority than "the elders." Isaiah had pled with the southern kingdom to obey from the heart (29:13). Instead, the people had given only lip-service to God, going through the motions of religiosity while cheating each other, abusing human rights, and engaging in idolatry. Their hypocrisy had become so great that God finally called on them even to stop such rituals as fasting, because it only underlined how far away from Him their hearts really were (Isa. 58). Jesus sees the same kind of hypocrisy in His critics: over-scrupulous attention to ritual correctness without corresponding sincerity in right living. Any tradition kept merely for appearance's sake voids our worship, Jesus says.

B. A weightier matter, 8-13

8 As for laying aside the commandment of God, ye hold the tradition of men, as the washing of pots and cups: and many other such like things ye do.

9 And he said unto them, Full well ye reject the commandment of God, that ye may keep your own tradition.

10 For Moses said, Honour thy father and thy mother; and, Whoso curseth father or mother, let him die the death:

11 But ye say, If a man shall say to his father or mother, It is Corban, that is to say, a gift, by whatsoever thou mightest be profited by me; he shall be free.

12 And ye suffer him no more to do ought for his father or his mother;

13 Making the word of God of none effect through your tradition, which ye have delivered: and many such like things do ye.

In these verses, the Lord weighs in against another problem with tradition: it easily supersedes the core of God's commandments. Shrewdly turning the tables on His critics again, Jesus shows that their fastidious attention to tradition had actually led them to violate the fifth Commandment, "Honor thy father any thy mother" (Exod. 20:12)—which ordinarily would have incurred the death penalty (21:17).

Corban is a Hebrew word for "gift." Apparently the rabbis had allowed exasperated adult children with difficult parents, or greedy children who did not want to the financial burden of aged parents, to give a gift to the synagogue or Temple commensurate with the expense of caring for their parents—thus buying freedom from their responsibility. Some scholars hold that verse 12 indicates that the gift was not retrievable even if a person changed his mind and decided to care for his aging parents. (Remember that "suffer" in the kjv means "allow.")

How does this distinction between tradition and sincerely keeping the core of God's will apply to Christians today? Perhaps one example is the fact that traditions have created the myriad of denominations today. Most agree on core New Covenant doctrine, such as the death, burial, and resurrection of Christ—the outline of the gospel Paul supplies in 1 Corinthians 15:1-6. Many sectarian walls have been erected with the good intention of protecting or furthering this "core curriculum." Is the validity of our worship threatened, however, when these traditions assume a position equal with or superior to Scripture—as when they cause us to break the plain teaching that "there is one body" (Eph. 4:4)?

III. Defilement Defined—14-15

14 And when he had called all the people unto him, he said unto them, Hearken unto me every one of you, and understand:

15 There is nothing from within a man, that entering into him, can defile him: but the things which come out of him, those are they that defile the man.

Now Jesus probes to the heart of the tradition about ritual washing before eating, and the ceremonial cleansing of utensils. Obviously such washings might prevent physical disease. Jesus, however, says that such practices have no relationship to spiritual "defilement." In fact, His opponents have just provided a powerful illustration of spiritual uncleanness by their neglect of such humane aspects of the Law as caring for their aged parents; yet their devotion to ritual cleansing was without fault.

If what defiles us comes from the heart, then what, in summary, can we say came from the hearts of Jesus' enemies? (1) Carping criticism of those who fail to observe the "correct" rituals; (2) devotion to tradition over the core of the faith; (3) placing more emphasis on religious rules than ministering to the needs of people; and (4) a desire to escape personal responsibility.

Are such defilements limited to the critics of Jesus?

Evangelistic Emphasis

Have you noticed that many of the rapidly expanding congregations in the United States are non-traditional? For most mainline Protestant denominations a worship service consists of announcements, prayer, three hymns (over fifty years old and sung from hymnals), an offering  and a sermon. These may vary, but they are traditionally present. In non-traditional congregations one might see drama presented. There may be a band with guitars, a keyboard and drums, but no organ. Worship hymns and choruses are sung from images projected on a screen.

The traditional folk think the "new-fangled" folk ought to be more reverent. The new-fangled folk think the traditional folk ought to be more lively. Now, the traditional folk do not look at the non-traditional folk askance because they think the new styles are ungodly. Most do not like the new ways simply because they are unfamiliar. "We've never done it like that before!"

Sometimes we hang on to our tradition and miss God. Sometimes we fail to recognize that God can move in a new way. Sometimes we are hesitant to believe God can reach others in a way unfamiliar to us.

God can move and act in old, traditional ways. God can also move in new ways. Neither tradition nor progress has any merit in itself. The merit comes when God is in it. If it is God, it is good.

✳ ✳ ✳

Memory Selection

For laying aside the commandment of God, ye hold the tradition of men.—*Mark 7:8*

We folks in the U.S.A. know what Jesus was talking about when he chastised the Pharisees with this phrase. We have seen how racism, a tradition of men, has divided our people and damaged our country. We all, "red and yellow, black and white," can read the scriptures in which Jesus teaches us to love one another. Jesus puts neither conditions nor disclaimers on that love. Yet we too often do as others around us do. Too often we act toward those of races different from our own in a manner that we have seen our parents or grandparents act. Too often we react according to the traditions of men rather than the command-ments of our Savior and Lord.

He commanded us to love one another. We must rise above what we might have been taught. We must rise above what others in our culture might try to shape us into doing. We must hold to Christ's commands above all.

Weekday Problems

David was relatively new in the church. He hesitated to speak up. "Still," he thought, "it's just not right."

It seems that Old Memorial Church had a huge fall carnival every year. People came from all over that part of the country to attend Old Memorial's Fall Carnival. It was a great time. They had rides and game booths and a pie eating contest and a bake-off that was to die for.

There was one problem David had with the whole thing. They had a raffle for a hand-sewn quilt. People bought raffle tickets for a dollar a chance to win a beautiful quilt.

David told the committee, "That's not right. That's gambling!" The arguments came back, "It's really not gambling. It's all in fun." Another said, "But David, we raise over a thousand dollars just on the quilt alone!" Still another argued, "We do a lot of good with that money. The people we help don't care where the money comes from." The committee stiffened their backs and snarled, "We've had this Carnival and this raffle since before the war. It's become a tradition of Old Memorial."

"I know," David replied softly, "but it's just not right."

* Was David right in calling a raffle gambling?

* How would you have handled the arguments of the committee?

You Know You're a Hypocrite When . . .

You stay away from church because "there are too many hypocrites there." (There's always room for one more.)

You can't help a stranded motorist because you might be late to church.

Reputation becomes more important to you than character.

You lie to yourself in order to ease a guilty conscience.

You want so much to show someone you care that you wipe your eyes with a handkerchief containing an onion.

You find it easier to fall on your knees than to rise to serve.

You think a lie is only something you tell instead of some way you live.

You think it's more important to keep a smile on your face than in your heart.

You search for a Bible verse to uphold an ungodly practice.

This Lesson in Your Life

Barriers to Truth

Do you remember a movie called "A Few Good Men?" It is a lawyer/military movie. It was quite entertaining if one could overlook the bad words in it. Still, in one scene a Navy lawyer has a Marine colonel on the witness stand. The lawyer shouts at the colonel, "I want the truth!" The colonel thunders back, "You can't handle the truth!"

I have thought of that since then. I think the colonel was right in some instances. We can't handle the truth. At least, the truth would be uncomfortable for us because truth sometimes goes against what we have allowed ourselves to believe. Truth sometimes rocks traditional thinking.

Do you remember reading in history books that people believed the world was flat? From the days of recorded history until the time Christopher Columbus sailed in 1492 people believed the world was flat. That is ridiculous to us now, for we have seen photograph upon photograph taken from space that shows without a doubt our planet is not flat. Yet, for hundreds of years people believed the world was flat.

Why might that be? Well, some wise person put forth the theory that the world was flat. The theory seemed logical. No one wanted to argue with the wise person. No one could think of any way to prove the world was anything but flat. Therefore, humanity believed the world was flat for hundreds and hundreds of years. All of this was based on someone's opinion. This hypothesis stayed around so long that people began to accept it as fact.

As a matter of fact, some people still believed the world was flat years after the theory was proven wrong by sailors circumventing the globe. People continued to believe what seemed logical. People continued to hold on to tradition.

That sometimes happens in the Christian walk. We hear about things that contradict our tradition and we refuse to believe. We see things that violate what our denomination tells us and we refuse to believe. Sometimes we even read in the scripture things that are astounding, too astounding for our logic, and we refuse to believe.

Did you know that at the birth of Jesus Christ, the shepherds and the wise men were not at the manger at the same time? Now, we do not want to go around tearing down manger scenes all over town this Christmas, but when we see Mary, Joseph, Baby Jesus, shepherds and wise men all in the scene, it is incorrect. Yet, it is traditional.

I have discovered many things in my own life that I had been taught as tradition that are not necessarily true. When I discover the truth in God's Word I must walk in that. I must keep the letter and the spirit of God's commands.

We don't ever want to be accused of holding on to human tradition and abandoning God's Word.

Seed Thoughts

1. What criticism did the scribes and Pharisees have of Jesus' disciples?

The scribes and Pharisees were shocked that Jesus' disciples ate without washing first. That was against Jewish ceremonial customs.

2. Why did the Pharisees and other Jews always wash their hands in a special way?

The Pharisees and the Jews were following the traditions of the elders.

3. Name two more washing rituals that were common to Jews.

Jews were expected to wash when they came from the marketplace. They also washed their table and dishes.

4. Why did the Pharisees ask Jesus about the conduct of the disciples? What did Jesus call the Pharisees?

He called the Pharisees "hypocrites" because they questioned the disciples' conduct while breaking the law themselves.

5. Whose commandment did Jesus accuse the Pharisees of breaking?

Jesus said the Pharisees were breaking the commandment of God, yet they kept the tradition of man.

(Please turn page)

---

1. What criticism did the scribes and Pharisees have of Jesus' disciples?

2. Why did the Pharisees and other Jews always wash their hands in a special way?

3. Name two more washing rituals that were common to Jews.

4. Why did the Pharisees ask Jesus about the conduct of the disciples? What did Jesus call the Pharisees?

5. Whose commandment did Jesus accuse the Pharisees of breaking?

6. What prophet did Jesus quote in order to rebuke the Pharisees?

7. What had Isaiah prophesied long years before regarding the Pharisees and the laws they followed?

8. What specific commandment of Moses did Jesus say the Pharisees were breaking?

9. Specifically, how were the Pharisees breaking one of the ten commandments?

10. Could we ever be accused of honoring God with our lips but not our hearts? Give an example.

The scribes and Pharisees were shocked that Jesus' disciples ate without washing first. That was against Jewish ceremonial customs.

The Pharisees and the Jews were following the traditions of the elders.

Jews were expected to wash when they came from the marketplace. They also washed their table and dishes.

He called the Pharisees "hypocrites" because they questioned the disciples' conduct while breaking the law themselves.
Jesus said the Pharisees were breaking the commandment of God, yet they kept the tradition of man.

Jesus quoted from Isaiah 29:13.

Isaiah said they would honor God with their lips, but their hearts would be far from God.

"Honor your father and your mother."

They were depriving their parents of needed support in the guise of giving a gift to God.

Answers will vary according to experiences among class members.

6. What prophet did Jesus quote in order to rebuke the Pharisees?

Jesus quoted from Isaiah 29:13.

7. What had Isaiah prophesied long years before regarding the Pharisees and the laws they followed?

Isaiah said they would honor God with their lips, but their hearts would be far from God.

8. What specific commandment of Moses did Jesus say the Pharisees were breaking?

"Honor your father and your mother."

9. Specifically, how were the Pharisees breaking one of the ten commandments?

They were depriving their parents of needed support in the guise of giving a gift to God.

10. Could we ever be accused of honoring God with our lips but not our hearts? Give an example.

Answers will vary according to experiences among class members.

Lesson 12

Marriage and Divorce

Mark 10:1-12

1 And he arose from thence, and cometh into the coasts of Judæa by the farther side of Jordan: and the people resort unto him again; and, as he was wont, he taught them again.

2 And the Pharisees came to him, and asked him, Is it lawful for a man to put away his wife? tempting him.

3 And he answered and said unto them, What did Moses command you?

4 And they said, Moses suffered to write a bill of divorcement, and to put her away.

5 And Jesus answered and said unto them, For the hardness of your heart he wrote you this precept.

6 But from the beginning of the creation God made them male and female.

7 For this cause shall a man leave his father and mother, and cleave to his wife;

8 And they twain shall be one flesh: so then they are no more twain, but one flesh.

9 What therefore God hath joined together, let not man put asunder.

10 And in the house his disciples asked him again of the same matter.

11 And he saith unto them, Whosoever shall put away his wife, and marry another, committeth adultery against her.

12 And if a woman shall put away her husband, and be married to another, she committeth adultery.

May 17

Memory Selection
Mark 10:9

Devotional Reading
Genesis 2:18-24

Background Scripture
Mark 10:1-12

Printed Scripture
Mark 10:1-12

Teacher's Target

Lesson purpose: *To reemphasize God's ideal that marriages last "'til death do us part."*

Almost every Bible study group these days will include people whose lives have been touched by divorce and remarriage. This lesson's purpose is not to pronounce judgment on those whose marriages have been less than perfect. God's ideal for our hearts is that we do not hate or have impure thoughts; but we do. His ideal for families is that members show love to each other; but the best families have quarrels. God's ideal is that we maintain our health; but we sometimes bring illness on ourselves. Yet we do not usually condemn ourselves or others for not attaining perfection in these areas.

On the other hand, the teacher need not apologize for presenting God's original intent for marriage. Even divorced Christians would be glad to spare others the heartache usually involved in the breakup of a marriage. Indeed, the whole enterprise of Bible study is to remind imperfect people of a better Way.

Lesson Introduction

God's ideal for marriage—monogamy without divorce—has rarely been the norm. God's own chosen people, Israel, practiced polygamy, and many men who could afford it even added concubines to their harem.

As Jesus teaches in this passage, however, God's original plan was one man and one wife, for life (see Prov. 5:18-29). This ideal was even a model for God's relationship with His people (Hosea 3; 1 Cor. 11:2). Even in the Greek and Roman societies of Jesus' day, although divorce was legal, monogamy was the rule.

In modern times, most non-Christian religions have moved toward God's ideal of one man and one wife, for life. Ironically, divorce is becoming more common in "Christian" nations than in societies that are predominantly Hindu, Buddhist, and Islamic. However strict Jesus' teaching may sound, there is a special need in our own land to take His teaching seriously.

Teaching Outline	Daily Bible Readings
	Mon. Facing the Fact of Divorce *Mark 10:1-12*
	Tue. Two Become One *Genesis 2:18-24*
I. The Teaching Messiah—1	
II. The Test—2-4	**Wed.** Hold Marriage in Honor *Hebrews 13:1-6*
A. The ticklish question, 2	**Thu.** Love as Christ Loves You *Ephesians 5:21-33*
B. Moses' answer, 3-4	
III. The Truth—5-12	**Fri.** Our Bodies Are Members of Christ *1 Corinthians 6:19-20*
A. God's original plan, 5-9	
B. Consequences of disobedience, 10-12	**Sat.** Facing Distress in Marriage *1 Corinthians 7:25-38*
	Sun. God Has Called You to Peace *1 Corinthians 7:10-16*

362

VERSE BY VERSE

I. The Teaching Messiah—1

1 And he arose from thence, and cometh into the coasts of Judæa by the farther side of Jordan: and the people resort unto him again; and, as he was wont, he taught them again.

Again Mark emphasizes the work of Jesus as a teacher. "As he was wont" (NIV "As was his custom") translates a word implying that teaching was Christ's "habitual" style of communication. He is intent not on mere short-term treatment of human emotions, but on instructing their minds so they can bring their lives into long-term harmony with God's will. This will become an especially important aspect of Jesus' purpose as the Messiah as we consider His strict teaching on divorce, to follow.

II. The Test—2-4

A. The ticklish question, 2

2 And the Pharisees came to him, and asked him, Is it lawful for a man to put away his wife? tempting him.

Again Jesus faces enemies who are trying to trap Him, not honest questioners who want to know the truth about divorce (lit. "loosing from" a spouse). His reply, therefore, is not in the pastoral tone of a concerned counselor, but in the challenging voice needed to address not only their question but their attitude.

The fact that they chose this particular question indicates that it was a topic of considerable current interest. As a matter of fact, the opinions on the subject of two leading rabbis, from about the time of Christ, have survived. Rabbi Hillel held that a man could divorce his wife for almost any reason, however trivial. (Among the Greeks and Romans, women also had some rights of divorce, but not among the Jews of this period.) On the other hand, Rabbi Shammai taught a more conservative view, holding that divorce was to be permitted only for a serious offense such as adultery. The Pharisees who confronted Jesus may have been trying to force Him into taking sides, with the intent of dividing His followers.

B. Moses' answer, 3-4

3 And he answered and said unto them, What did Moses command you?

4 And they said, Moses suffered to write a bill of divorcement, and to put her away.

Instead of answering immediately, Jesus pulls His questioners into the argument by asking them to cite Moses' position on the issue. As we shall see, He does so not in order to side with Moses against Rabbis Shammai or Hillel, but to show that Moses' ruling was only a concession to human weakness. It was not God's ideal will.

The Pharisees answer correctly, knowing that in Deuteronomy 24:1-2 the Law of Moses gives permission for divorce.

The conditions for such action are not clear. In verse 1 it seems to require something like adultery to qualify as sexual "uncleanness"; but verse 2 implies that divorce was allowed when a man merely hated his wife. At any rate, the Pharisees' correct answer only gives Jesus the opportunity to make a point about God's ideal.

III. The Truth—5-12

A. God's original plan, 5-9

5 And Jesus answered and said unto them, For the hardness of your heart he wrote you this precept.

6 But from the beginning of the creation God made them male and female.

7 For this cause shall a man leave his father and mother, and cleave to his wife;

8 And they twain shall be one flesh: so then they are no more twain, but one flesh.

9 What therefore God hath joined together, let not man put asunder.

Putting together two passages from Genesis (1:27 with 2:20-23), Jesus teaches that God's original intention was that marriage be between one man and one wife, for life. The concession authorized by Moses was granted because of people's resistance to God's ideal. Some authorities believe that because God allowed the concessions Moses made, He still does so today; but if so, we must also confess that the same reason—hardness of heart—is also at work.

Verse 9 actually contains the heart of Jesus' teaching on divorce, in the form of what is often called a "dominical" statement—one that seems to carry with it the authority of a King, which indeed it does. (It must be admitted, however, that His ruling is no more regal or authoritative than His teaching against murder or any other practice which, while against God's ideal will, is not the unforgivable sin.)

B. Consequences of disobedience, 10-12

10 And in the house his disciples asked him again of the same matter.

11 And he saith unto them, Whosoever shall put away his wife, and marry another, committeth adultery against her.

12 And if a woman shall put away her husband, and be married to another, she committeth adultery.

Jesus' position on divorce is so conservative—and apparently so at variance with contemporary prac-tice—that His disciples pursue the matter further in private. In Matthew's version of the incident, they are so taken aback at the strictness of Jesus' teaching that they suggest it might be better not to marry in the first place (Matt. 19:10). Jesus' answer implies that celibacy may well be best; but that it isn't for everyone (vss. 11-12).

Matthew also records the famous "exception clause," qualifying Jesus' statement in Mark by saying that divorce is allowable in cases of sexual unfaithfulness (Matt. 19:9; see also 5:31-32). Most scholars agree that Mark's Gospel was written before Matthew, who is also assumed to have had Mark before him as he wrote. Some believe that Matthew, or a later copyist, found Jesus' teaching in Mark so strict as to be unbelievable, and inserted the "exception clause" as a more likely reflection of Jesus' true position on the subject. This view, however, is also open to the possibility that later copyists merely "doctored" the text to reflect current practice.

Even if Jesus did allow divorce in cases of adultery, with Mark for some reason omitting the exception, His position is still much more strict than divorce laws in most cultures. In some Christian fellowships, attempts are made to return to Jesus' high standard by requiring people divorced and remarried for reasons other than adultery to end their new marriage. Others say that such separation is required only if the remarriage occurred after the persons involved became Christians. Still others note that we have no record of such separations being required in New Testament times, when divorce was relatively frequent, and that grace covers cases of divorce and remarriage that do not meet God's ideal.

This issue of grace is at the core of the many contemporary positions and debates on the question of marriage and divorce. Do those who have divorced and remarried for reasons other than adultery have access to the same grace as a murderer? Or does the impossibility of making restitution in the case of murder put the two cases on different grounds? Does grace apply even when divorce and remarriage occur after people become Christians?

Such questions may remain with us as long as we are earth-bound creatures in a fallen world, since only in heaven will there be "neither marrying nor giving in marriage."

Evangelistic Emphasis

Notice in our scripture passage the Pharisees came to Jesus with a question about divorce. Verse two informs us that their purpose was not to gain knowledge, but to test Jesus. They tell Jesus that Moses allowed divorce. Then Jesus reminds them that divorce is not God's way. God's way is a lifelong commitment between a man and woman. Therein lies the good news of this passage. Marriage is for a lifetime.

Marriages don't have to slide into a state of misery. A couple can nurture dedication for a lifetime. Research shows that dedicated mates make their marriages a high priority, are happier and experience fewer conflicts.

Marriage is also good for us, at least it's good for the men. According to an article by Joyce Price in Insight magazine in February of 1996, divorced men are twice as likely to die from hypertension. Divorced men are four times more likely to die from throat cancer and seven times more likely to die from pneumonia. Divorced men also have significantly higher rates of depression, substance abuse, auto accidents and suicide.

We can get out of marriages. It is lawful. In some cases where life and limb are threatened, getting out of a marriage can save our lives. Yet, a good marriage is good for you. Work at it. It will pay great dividends.

Memory Selection

What therefore God hath joined together, let not man put asunder.—*Mark 10:9*

This verse illustrates the high ideal God has for the joining of a man and a woman in marriage. A wedding is not simply an occasion in which a man and woman find a preacher who will speak the right words over them that they may be legally married. A wedding is not simply a beautiful time in which the bride looks radiant in her white dress and the groom handsome in his dark tuxedo. It is not simply an occasion for hundreds of friends and family to get together to eat too much cake and have a good time.

A wedding is a spiritual occasion in which a man and a woman become one. It is a spiritual event in which God joins two individuals to become one unit. It is a holy event which God ordained from the beginning of time.

We must never take that lightly. God is involved.

Weekday Problems

Ron and Sharon drove home from the church in silence. They just left the pastor's office after their third session of marriage counseling.

Ron was lost in his thoughts. His mind gravitated to Gina, a fellow partner in his firm. "Gina has it all together," he reasons. "She is attractive. She is competent. She understands me. If only I weren't tied to Sharon. Gina would be the perfect partner. What if I were married to Gina instead?"

Sharon was deep in thought, too. "What's the use of going to a marriage counselor? We've now wasted the pastor's time and ours for three weeks in a row. Every time Ron and I have words he brings up the idea of a divorce. Why in the world do I keep investing in this marriage when he may have already decided to quit? Maybe a divorce would be better. At least it would be quieter."

Then they both began to think about the good times they had experienced together. Their pastor had reminded them that love never fails. They remembered how Jesus said all things were possible with God. They drove on in silence.

* If one of these folks were your friend and came to you for advice, what might you say?

* Is a bad marriage better than a "good" divorce?

Marriage This Side of Heaven

Did you hear about the man who met his wife at a travel agency? She was looking for a vacation, and he was the last resort.

The best way for a man to remember his wife's birthday is to forget it just once.

You can tell when a marriage is shaky. The husband and wife even watch TV commercials to avoid talking to each other.

Marriage is like a midnight phone call. You get a ring and then you wake up.

It's been proved that married life is healthy. Statistics show that single people die sooner than married folks. So if you're looking for a slow death, get married!

This Lesson in Your Life

Struggling with Marriage and Divorce

"Till death us do part." That phrase has been uttered by millions of men and women through the years as they stood at the altar of their church and took the vows of marriage. Alas, the words, though heartfelt at the time, have proven not to be pro-phetic for many couples in a time when divorce is at epidemic proportions in the U.S.

One of the problems that fuels the fire of divorce is that couples enter the union with the idea that it is only temporary. Oh, they would never say that exactly, but they go into the relationship with the notion that if it doesn't work out, we'll just split up. We leave the back door unlocked, so to speak. We leave ourselves a way out. Then, when the bills pile up or "He/she is not paying enough attention to me" or "I want to find myself" or things just get tough in general (pick one or more), we begin to look at that back door. Too often it is easier to run than it is to work at a marriage. Many couples take the easy way out.

Yet, there is always pain in divorce. And the children pay a price. An article entitled "Divorce's Toll on Children" in *American Enterprise* magazine, May/June 1996 notes that adults wishing to justify divorce often claim that conflict in a marriage hurts children more than divorce. Kids don't buy it, and evidence doesn't support it. Children want both parents, and studies show that the misery in an unhappy marriage is usually less significant than the changes after a divorce. Most marital breakups are driven not by high levels of conflict, but by a "quest for greener grass." Parents tend to badly underestimate the damage divorce will inflict on their children.

It's commonly believed that children eventually adjust, though they're initially traumatized by divorce. Psychologist John Guidubaldi notes that people in prisons and mental institutions make adjustments, too. But, he asks, are those adjustments healthy? Guidubaldi coordinated a large study documenting the longer-term effects of divorce and concludes that "the old argument of staying together for the sake of the kids is still the best argument." Couples, he maintains, simply aren't working hard enough at saving their marriages.

Specific behavior changes in children of divorce include greater withdrawal, dependency, inattention and unhappiness. Kids tend to put forth less effort to achieve and are more likely to abuse drugs and commit violent acts, including suicide. There are higher rates of delinquency, out-of-wedlock pregnancy and abortions. More than 80 per cent of teens in mental hospitals and 60 per cent of children in psychiatric clinics have experienced divorce. In school, these children are twice as likely to repeat a grade and five times as likely to be expelled or suspended.

The Council of Families in America said in a 1995 report entitled Marriage in America: A Report to the Nation, "Divorce has created terrible hardships for children, incurred insupportable social costs and failed to deliver on its promise of greater adult happiness. The time has come to shift the focus of national attention from divorce to marriage and to rebuild a family culture based on enduring marital relationships."

Indeed, that's what Jesus said all along.

Seed Thoughts

1. What was Jesus doing when the Pharisees approached Him?

Jesus was teaching the multitudes in Judea.

2. What question did the Pharisees ask Jesus? What was their motive?

The Pharisees asked, "Is it lawful for a man to put away his wife?" They were testing Jesus.

3. How did Jesus respond to the Pharisees' trick question?

He answered their question with a question of his own, "What did Moses command you?"

4. Did Moses allow for divorce? How did Jesus explain Moses's action?

Yes. Moses permitted a written a bill of divorcement because the people's hearts were hard.

5. What did Jesus say was God's plan for men and women from the beginning?

Jesus said a man shall leave his parents and cleave to his wife. Marriage was to be a lifelong relationship.

1. What was Jesus doing when the Pharisees approached Him?

2. What question did the Pharisees ask Jesus? What was their motive?

3. How did Jesus respond to the Pharisees' trick question?

4. Did Moses allow for divorce? How did Jesus explain Moses's action?

5. What did Jesus say was God's plan for men and women from the beginning?

6. According to Jesus's words, what mystery takes place at a marriage?

7. Who joins the man and woman in marriage? Who should separate them?

8. Who else asked Jesus about divorce? Were they trying to trick Jesus also?

9. What sin did Jesus say a divorced person would commit if he/she married again?

10. Why do you think divorce is so prevalent in our society today?

(Please turn page)

Jesus was teaching the multitudes in Judea.

The Pharisees asked, "Is it lawful for a man to put away his wife?" They were testing Jesus.

He answered their question with a question of his own, "What did Moses command you?"

Yes. Moses permitted a written a bill of divorcement because the people's hearts were hard.

Jesus said a man shall leave his parents and cleave to his wife. Marriage was to be a lifelong relationship.

The two people become one flesh. They will be two no more, but will be one flesh.

God joins them together, it is a spiritual matter. No human being should ever separate them.

The disciples asked Jesus about this issue later. They genuinely desired to know and wanted Him to explain more about the matter.

He said the divorced person would be guilty of committing adultery.

There are a variety of reasons. Divorce is too easy. We lack the commitment to make a marriage work. Could it be that we too have a hardness of heart?

6. According to Jesus's words, what mystery takes place at a marriage?

The two people become one flesh. They will be two no more, but will be one flesh.

7. Who joins the man and woman in marriage? Who should separate them?

God joins them together, it is a spiritual matter. No human being should ever separate them.

8. Who else asked Jesus about divorce? Were they trying to trick Jesus also?

The disciples asked Jesus about this issue later. They genuinely desired to know and wanted Him to explain more about the matter.

9. What sin did Jesus say a divorced person would commit if he/she married again?

He said the divorced person would be guilty of committing adultery.

10. Why do you think divorce is so prevalent in our society today?

There are a variety of reasons. Divorce is too easy. We lack the commitment to make a marriage work. Could it be that we too have a hardness of heart?

True Greatness

Mark 9:33-37; 10:35-45

9:33 And he came to Capernaum: and being in the house he asked them, What was it that ye disputed among yourselves by the way?

34 But they held their peace: for by the way they had disputed among themselves, who should be the greatest.

35 And he sat down, and called the twelve, and saith unto them, If any man desire to be first, the same shall be last of all, and servant of all.

36 And he took a child, and set him in the midst of them: and when he had taken him in his arms, he said unto them,

37 Whosoever shall receive one of such children in my name, receiveth me: and whosoever shall receive me, receiveth not me, but him that sent me.

10:35 And James and John, the sons of Zebedee, come unto him, saying, Master, we would that thou shouldest do for us whatsoever we shall desire.

36 And he said unto them, What would ye that I should do for you?

37 They said unto him, Grant unto us that we may sit, one on thy right hand, and the other on thy left hand, in thy glory.

38 But Jesus said unto them, Ye know not what ye ask: can ye drink of the cup that I drink of? and be baptized with the baptism that I am baptized with?

39 And they said unto him, We can. And Jesus said unto them, Ye shall indeed drink of the cup that I drink of; and with the baptism that I am baptized withal shall ye be baptized:

40 But to sit on my right hand and on my left hand is not mine to give; but it shall be given to them for whom it is prepared.

41 And when the ten heard it, they began to be much displeased with James and John.

42 But Jesus called them to him, and saith unto them, Ye know that they which are accounted to rule over the gentiles exercise lordship over them; and their great ones exercise authority upon them.

43 But so shall it not be among you: but whosoever will be great among you, shall be your minister:

44 And whosoever of you will be the chiefest, shall be servant of all.

45 For even the Son of man came not to be ministered unto, but to minister, and to give his life a ransom for many.

Memory Selection
Mark 10:45

Devotional Reading
John 13:3-17

Background Scripture
Mark 9:33-37; 10:35-45

Printed Scripture
Mark 9:33-37; 10:35-45

May 24

Teacher's Target

Lesson purpose: *To examine the concept of servant leadership taught by Jesus, with a view to applying it especially in the life of the Church.*

This lesson sets a good example for you, the teacher, to take stock of the kind of leadership you exert as a teacher. As we have seen, Jesus came as a teacher. As the Messiah promised through the lineage of King David, He also came as a King. Yet, although He had "all authority in heaven and in earth," He also came as a gentle Shepherd.

The effective teacher seeks to blend these elements. Because the material a Bible class teacher presents is Scripture, it carries with it divine authority. Yet it can be presented in such a domineering way that this authority is subtly transferred to the teacher—and usually resented by the learners. Effective teachers allow questions and discussion, with the goal of helping learners internalize for themselves the authority of the Word in their own lives.

Lesson Introduction

Many churches struggle over issues of "Who's in charge around here?" In others, the issue of authority rarely comes up. What makes the difference? Often, churches that have the issue settled are led by "servant leaders." They do not need to throw their weight around because their style of leadership is to minister to others. Instead of being threatened by others with leadership skills, they actually seek to empower others, for individual and corporate health.

Servant leadership does not mean abandoning responsibility, or being so "humble" that no real leadership is exerted. It means fulfilling the responsibility of leading by setting examples of serving. To borrow the words of one early Christian leader, it means becoming "a servant of the servants of God."

Teaching Outline	Daily Bible Reading	
I. Leadership as Being Last—9:33-37	**Mon.**	True Greatness *Mark 9:33-37*
A. Competing for power, 33-34	**Tue.**	Greatness Through Service *Mark 10:35-45*
B. Childlikeness as leadership, 35-37	**Wed.**	Righteousness Produces Peace *James 3:13-18*
II. Lust for Being First—10:35-37	**Thu.**	True Treasure in Clay Jars *2 Corinthians 4:1-5*
A. Misunderstanding the Kingdom, 35-37	**Fri.**	Serving Christ by Serving Others *Matthew 25:31-40*
B. Leadership as Suffering—38-41	**Sat.**	The Humble Will Be Exalted *Luke 14:7-14*
III. Leadership as Service—42-45	**Sun.**	Christ Exalted in His Ascension *Ephesians 1:15-23*
A. The example of the Gentiles, 42		
B. The example of Christ, 43-45		

VERSE BY VERSE

I. Leadership as Being Last—9:33-37
  A. Competing for power, 33-34
  33 And he came to Capernaum: and being in the house he asked them, What was it that ye disputed among yourselves by the way?
  34 But they held their peace: for by the way they had disputed among themselves, who should be the greatest.

As we noted in Lesson 2, Capernaum was the town on the northwest shore of the Sea of Galilee where Jesus did so much of His early work. "The house" is referred to without explanation, Mark perhaps assuming that readers will know that Jesus is still using the house of Peter, Andrew, James and John that has already figured so prominently as a ministry base for Jesus (see Mark 1:29-30; 2:1-5).

We are not told whether Jesus overheard the disciples' dispute along the way through the region around Galilee toward the house, or perceived it by supernatural power. The important thing is that He wanted them to state openly what they thought they had discussed in secret. The topic of their argument was embarrassingly self-centered; and they may have suspected that it violated something Jesus had already taught. In Matthew 18:1 Christ gives the same or similar teaching about childlikeness in response to the question, "Who is the greatest in the kingdom of heaven?" The disciples therefore sadly misunderstand the kingdom to be an earthly domain in which Christ as King would dole out powerful positions as rewards for those who had been His closest advisors.

  B. Childlikeness as leadership, 35-37
  35 And he sat down, and called the twelve, and saith unto them, If any man desire to be first, the same shall be last of all, and servant of all.
  36 And he took a child, and set him in the midst of them: and when he had taken him in his arms, he said unto them,
  37 Whosoever shall receive one of such children in my name, receiveth me: and whosoever shall receive me, receiveth not me, but him that sent me.

Although Jesus' answer turns all human measures of power topsy-turvy, it is plain enough: the way up is down. The Gospel of John depicts Christ giving a visual aid to this lesson at the Last Supper, by taking a basin and towel and washing His disciples feet. Here is the King stooping to serve His subjects— a very surprising definition of royal power. Yet it is this very definition of "servant leadership" that Christ expects to be at work among His followers.

The visual aid here involves a child— the most powerless person at hand. It's as though Jesus says, "Here is how a great person in the Kingdom acts. He hugs a child, accepting as another great person those who have the least power to wield."

As we shall see in the next passage, the disciples apparently miss the point. They even fail to understand the lesson from the little child; for in 10:13-16 they try to dismiss those who brought little children for Jesus to bless! There Jesus goes a step further from defining greatness as being a lover of children, saying even that the Kingdom is barred to those who cannot become "as a little child" (10:13-16).

II. Lust for Being First—10:35-37

A. Misunderstanding the Kingdom, 35-37

35 And James and John, the sons of Zebedee, come unto him, saying, Master, we would that thou shouldest do for us whatsoever we shall desire.

36 And he said unto them, What would ye that I should do for you?

37 They said unto him, Grant unto us that we may sit, one on thy right hand, and the other on thy left hand, in thy glory.

These verses pick up again the same theme of misunderstanding the kind of power Jesus exerted, and the nature of the Kingdom. Matthew's account portrays the disciples asking for prominent positions through their mother (20:20). To be seated on the right and the left hand of a king was a special honor (see 1 Kings 2:19). "In thy glory" is equivalent to "in thy Kingdom" in Matthew 20:21, showing again that the disciples expected Jesus to exert His Messianic power by inaugurating a temporal rule that would turn the tables on Rome, the ruling power, and subject them to the rule of God's people.

The same mistake is made in our day by modern proponents of "dominion theology," who expect, and in some cases maneuver to obtain, positions of power in government in order to install God's rule over unbelievers in an earthly, political sense. The fact is that Jesus had begun in Mark 8:30-31 to define His version of Kingdom power as self-sacrificing. Just before our present passage, He had said again that the King would demonstrate His power by being killed! Then he would rise the third day (10:31-32). Still the disciples do not understand. The mistake of James and John here is that of Peter in Mark 8, when he rebuked Christ for such self-effacing tactics. It will not be until Christ's resurrection that they understand that "my kingdom is not of this world" (John 18:36).

B. Leadership as Suffering—38-41

38 But Jesus said unto them, Ye know not what ye ask: can ye drink of the cup that I drink of? and be baptized with the baptism that I am baptized with?

39 And they said unto him, We can. And Jesus said unto them, Ye shall indeed drink of the cup that I drink of; and with the baptism that I am baptized withal shall ye be baptized:

40 But to sit on my right hand and on my left hand is not mine to give; but it shall be given to them for whom it is prepared.

41 And when the ten heard it, they began to be much displeased with James and John.

Again referring to His approaching suffering, Jesus chooses the veiled symbols of a cup, and "baptism" or washing. These images might be taken in one of several ways. The cup might stand for the wine offered an earthly king by his cup-bearer—or a cup of hemlock such as that given to put Socrates to death! A baptism might be a symbolic bath initiating one into royalty—or a watery grave in which a criminal is drowned! Of course the disciples choose the positive images, agreeing quickly that a cup of honor would be their cup of tea.

We might think Jesus would have every right to be exasperated at these slow learners; but He answers them gently. The cup they will drink will indeed be like His own cup of suffering, and their baptism will be in fire, as it were (see Luke 12:50). Tradition has it that all the apostles died the death of martyrs.

To whom does Jesus refer when He says positions of honor in His Kingdom are reserved for those "for whom it is prepared"? Remembering how little children play such a prominent role in His teaching on Kingdom-power, we may conclude that He refers to those who become "as a little child"—those who give up their lust for power in favor of humble obedience to their Father.

As often happens when peers struggle for prominence, the other disciples are miffed that James and John would beat them to the punch!

III. Leadership as Service—42-45

A. The example of the Gentiles, 42

42 But Jesus called them to him, and saith unto them, Ye know that they which are accounted to rule over the gentiles exercise lordship over them; and their great ones exercise authority upon them.

Here Jesus charges that the model of power the disciples are following is actually of "gentile" origin. That is, "lording it over" people is the way an unbeliever would act. Leadership in the Kingdom is totally opposite (see 1 Pet. 5:1-3). While such worldly leaders grasp at counterfeit authority, Jesus says "all authority is given to me" (Matt. 28: 18, niv). How much does that leave for human leaders of God's people?

B. The example of Christ, 43-45

43 But so shall it not be among you: but whosoever will be great among you, shall be your minister:

44 And whosoever of you will be the chiefest, shall be servant of all.

45 For even the Son of man came not to be ministered unto, but to minister, and to give his life a ransom for many.

Finally, Jesus grounds His daring redefinition of leadership and power in the "Suffering Servant" passages of Isaiah, the great Messianic prophet. Isaiah 53 especially foretells the coming of the Servant who would give His life for the redemption of many. If even "the Son of man" exerted leadership by sacrificial service, the leaders among His followers can be expected to lead the same way.

Evangelistic Emphasis

When asked the question, "What is evangelism?" D.T. Niles answered, "Evangelism is one beggar telling another beggar where to find bread." That answer is very close to the whole truth. When Jesus was on this earth he reached out especially to those who were suffering. They were suffering from poverty, rejection and the consequences of sin. How did Jesus reach out? He became a servant.

Serving others is a marvelous way to reach out in Jesus' name today. When we take small steps to lighten people's pain, it gets their attention and makes them receptive to hear more of the gospel story.

Evangelism is a process that takes planting, watering and reaping. A significant harvest comes from diligent sowing and watering. This is where the servanthood comes in. The Apostle Paul wrote, "It is the kindness of God that leads to repentance" (Rom. 2:4). Deeds of kindness give us entrance into people's hearts.

The beauty of servanthood evangelism is that even the most timid person can participate. It doesn't take much talent or money or boldness to be a servant. It just takes low-risk deeds accompanied by a high amount of God's grace.

Memory Selection

For even the Son of man came not to be ministered unto, but to minister, and to give His life a ransom for many.—*Mark 10:4*

We Christians must regularly remind ourselves of these words of Christ. We are in a day when self-sufficiency has been elevated to a virtue, when folks are drawn to the spectacular as moths to a flame and when being powerful is venerated.

Christ shunned all three of these. He became a servant. Chuck Swindoll writes that the Christian's job consists of being a faithful servant in whatever ministry to which one is called.

This requires that we:
* Do more with others. "Ministry is not a solo, it's a chorus."
* Emphasize quality over quantity. "Excellence is our goal, not expansion."
* Stay accountable.
* Keep a level head. It will protect one from both criticism and excessive admiration.
* Model the Master. Most importantly, leaders need to live out Jesus' "servant-hearted attitude and grace-oriented style."

Weekday Problems

Cary has been praying for a ministry in his community. His prayers have sounded something like this, "Lord, show me what you want me to do. I am ready to be used by you. Make your will known to me so that I can do it."

Cary is a marvelous musician. He plays the keyboard. He has a beautiful singing voice. Time and time again after attending worship services, Cary has thought, "You know, I would good at leading worship. I could get folks involved. I could pick the proper hymns and choruses. I wish Pastor would ask me to lead worship on Sunday mornings." Often Cary day-dreams of himself upon the platform before hundreds of worshipers singing and playing the keyboard.

Last Sunday Pastor came up to Cary. "Cary, I've noticed how well you sing and play. We've been praying about a special ministry in our church and the elders believe you are the one God would have do it. Would you consider leading worship at the Nursing Home every Saturday evening? We believe God wants our congregation to begin an outreach there."

"Nursing home!" Cary exclaimed in his head. "Why, there probably won't be more than 40 old people there who can't sing."

* What might be some things Cary needs to learn about servanthood?

* Have you ever felt that a particular task was "too small" for you?

This 'n' That

Do you believe in the survival of the fittest?
I don't believe in the survival of anyone. I'm the undertaker.

First actor: Why is the leading lady upset?
Second actor: She only got nine bouquets of roses.
First actor: Good grief! Isn't that enough?
Second actor: Nope. She paid for 10.

Slick: My hometown is dead, man.
Mick: How dead is it?
Slick: Ever see a cemetery with traffic lights?

Woman: What size ski pants do you have?
Sales lady: Small, medium, and don't bend over.

Man at the florist's: Ouch! A bee in your shop stung me. I want you to do something about it.
Florist: Certainly, sir. Just show me which bee it was and I'll see that it's punished.

This Lesson in Your Life

What Is True Greatness?

Jesus said, "Whoever desires to become great among you shall be your servant" (Mark 10:43b). True greatness in God's eyes is in servanthood. Just what is servanthood?

Serving means sacrifice. It requires us to give what we have (time, money, energy) so others will have more. Some of us find it easier to give of our money than to give of our abilities, our compassion or ourselves. We come to believe that exceptionally gifted people have a good excuse for not serving and sacrificing themselves for others. We are aghast at the idea that the very talented should neglect their abilities in order to do what any ordinary person could do.

We are dumbfounded by the teenager who passes up a prestigious university in order to stay near the group of inner-city kids she has been coaching. We are shocked when the bright executive passes up a promotion in order to spend more time with his children. Stories like that of Henri Nouwen, a world-renowned author, lecturer and professor, who left academia to serve the mentally handicapped. Yet, we cannot distance ourselves from the fact that serving means sacrifice.

Serving is personal. We cannot let institutions do our serving for us. Second-hand servanthood loses something. The most effective service is face-to-face.

Serving others begins within us. Paul wrote in Philippians 2:5-7a (NIV), "Your attitude should be the same as that of Christ Jesus: Who, being in very nature God, did not consider equality with God something to be grasped, but made himself nothing, taking the very nature of a servant . . . ." The King James Version begins, "Let this mind be in you . . . ." Servanthood begins within us. We must make up our minds and set our hearts to be servants.

It is customary in this country to give a bride-to-be a wedding shower. The bride goes to a fine store and picks out a beautiful china pattern. She picks out a pattern for her silver. She registers those patterns at the store and folks go by and purchase a piece of the china or silverware for a wedding gift.

After the wedding the fine china is carefully packed away in a china hutch so that it will not become cracked or chipped. The silver is carefully placed in a special drawer. Now and again, on very special occasions, the fine china and silverware are brought out and actually used. Between those special occasions we use stainless steel utensils and cheaper dishes. We call those our "everyday" place settings.

Let me ask you. Are you fine china and silver...or are you "everyday?" Do you say to God, "I want to be used, Lord, but just on special occasions. If the event is big enough or spectacular enough, count me in." Or, are your words more like the Wesleyan prayer, "Lord, Put me to what thou wilt, rank me with whom thou wilt. Put me to doing, put me to suffering. Let me be employed by thee or laid aside for thee, exalted for thee or brought low by thee. Let me be full, let me be empty. Let me have all things, let me have nothing. I freely and heartily yield all things to thy pleasure and disposal."

When we can pray that prayer, we have discovered a servant's heart. When we can pray that prayer from the heart, we have discovered true greatness.

Seed Thoughts

1. What were the disciples arguing about on the way to Capernaum?

They were arguing about who should be the greatest among them.

2. How did they react when Jesus asked them what they had been talking about.

They were quiet. They were probably embarrassed and ashamed.

3. What lesson did Jesus teach the disciples upon learning the issue they had been discussing?

Those who desire to be first shall be last. To be first is to be a servant to all.

4. Why did Jesus pick up a little child? What did He say?

He used the child as an example saying, "Whoever receives one of such children in my name, receiveth me."

5. According to the end of verse 37, what happens to us when we receive Jesus?

Jesus says that whoever receives Him, shall actually receive the One who sent Him, meaning God Himself.

(Please turn page)

1. What were the disciples arguing about on the way to Capernaum?

2. How did they react when Jesus asked them what they had been talking about.

3. What lesson did Jesus teach the disciples upon learning the issue they had been discussing?

4. Why did Jesus pick up a little child? What did He say?

5. According to the end of verse 37, what happens to us when we receive Jesus?

6. Did Jesus's lesson at Capernaum end all discussion of who would be the greatest?

7. What two questions did Jesus ask them at their request?

8. Did Jesus grant their request to sit by His side? Why or why not?

9. How did the others respond to James and John's request? How did Jesus temper them?

10. What was the Son of man's job on this earth? Was it a glorious position?

They were arguing about who should be the greatest among them.

They were quiet. They were probably embarrassed and ashamed.

Those who desire to be first shall be last. To be first is to be a servant to all.

He used the child as an example saying, "Whoever receives one of such children in my name, receiveth me."

Jesus says that whoever receives Him, shall actually receive the One who sent Him, meaning God Himself.

No. James and John came to Jesus later and asked Him if one could sit on His left hand and one on His right hand when He came into His glory.

Can you drink of the cup I am to drink of and be baptized with the baptism that I am baptized with?

No. Jesus said it was not up to Him who would have those places of honor.

They were angry. Jesus called them together and again told them that the greatest of them must be the servant of all.

No. He came, not to be ministered to but to minister, and to give His life as a ransom for many.

6. Did Jesus's lesson at Capernaum end all discussion of who would be the greatest?

No. James and John came to Jesus later and asked Him if one could sit on His left hand and one on His right hand when He came into His glory.

7. What two questions did Jesus ask them at their request?

Can you drink of the cup I am to drink of and be baptized with the baptism that I am baptized with?

8. Did Jesus grant their request to sit by His side? Why or why not?

No. Jesus said it was not up to Him who would have those places of honor.

9. How did the others respond to James and John's request? How did Jesus temper them?

They were angry. Jesus called them together and again told them that the greatest of them must be the servant of all.

10. What was the Son of man's job on this earth? Was it a glorious position?

No. He came, not to be ministered to but to minister, and to give His life as a ransom for many.

Lesson 14

Help for the Future

Mark 13:1-7, 24, 27, 32-35

1 And as he went out of the temple, one of his disciples saith unto him, Master, see what manner of stones and what buildings are here?

2 And Jesus answering said unto him, Seest thou these great buildings? there shall not be left one stone upon another, that shall not be thrown down.

3 And as he sat upon the mount of Olives over against the temple, Peter and James and John and Andrew asked him privately,

4 Tell us, when shall these things be? and what shall be the sign when all these things shall be fulfilled?

5 And Jesus answering them began to say, Take heed lest any man deceive you:

6 For many shall come in my name, saying, I am Christ; and shall deceive many.

7 And when ye shall hear of wars and rumours of wars, be ye not troubled: for such things must needs be; but the end shall not be yet.

24 But in those days, after that tribulation, the sun shall be darkened, and the moon shall not give her light,

27 And then shall he send his angels, and shall gather together his elect from the four winds, from the uttermost part of the earth to the uttermost part of heaven.

32 But of that day and that hour knoweth no man, no, not the angels which are in heaven, neither the Son, but the Father.

33 Take heed, watch and pray: for ye know not when the time is.

34 For the Son of man is as a man taking a far journey, who left his house, and gave authority to his servants, and to every man his work, and commanded the porter to watch.

35 Watch ye therefore: for ye know not when the master of the house cometh, at even, or at midnight, or at the cockcrowing, or in the morning:

Memory Selection
Mark 13:31

Devotional Reading
Joel 2:28-32

Background Scripture
Mark 13

Printed Scripture
Mark 13:1-7, 24, 27, 32-35

May 31

Teacher's Target

Lesson purpose: *To gain insight into Jesus' prediction of the destruction of the Temple in Jerusalem, and of the End of Time which it prefigured.*

Many people find biblical prophecy like that in this lesson the most fascinating of all Bible topics. Yet few topics find a wider variety of views. In this class, try to emphasize three primary points from biblical teaching about the End.

First, some language of the End refers to the End of the Jewish system, not the end of the world. Second, God promises that the willfully wicked will be punished in the End—that right, not might, will win out. And third, the faithful will be delivered through all the tribulations and struggles preceding the End.

For God's people, the future is spelled H-O-P-E!

Lesson Introduction

The language of much of Mark 13 (and its parallels in Matthew 24 and Luke 21) is often called "apocalyptic," from a Greek word referring to a "revelation." Since sincere Christians disagree so widely on how to interpret this material, some of the author's presuppositions are in order.

(1) Much apocalyptic language is symbolic, and cannot be interpreted literally. (2) The "church phase" of the Kingdom of God began with the opening of its doors by Peter in Acts 2; we do not await the End of Time for the coming of the Kingdom. (3) Some of Mark 13 refers to the end of the Jewish age, some to the end of time, and the difference is often obscure. (4) The essential message here is not about signs of the End, but about the urgency of living in constant readiness for Christ's return, whenever it occurs. Christ's main point is, in a word, *"Watch!"*

Teaching Outline	Daily Bible Readings	
	Mon.	Test of Our Faith *Mark 13:1-13*
I. The End of Judaism—1-7		
A. The magnificent Temple, 1	**Tue.**	Christ Will Come in Power *Mark 13:14-27*
B. Its destruction predicted, 2		
C. Signs of the times, 3-7	**Wed.**	Day and Hour Are Unknown *Mark 13:28-37*
II. The End of Time—24, 27		
A. Cosmic signs, 24	**Thu.**	Jesus Will Come for Us *John 14:22-29*
B. The great gathering, 27		
III. Living in View of the End—32-35	**Fri.**	Look for the City to Come *Hebrews 13:7-16*
A. At an unknown time, 32		
B. Watch! 33-35	**Sat.**	Jesus Is Coming Soon! *Revelation 22:12-31*
	Sun.	An Outpouring of the Spirit *Joel 2:28-32*

VERSE BY VERSE

I. The End of Judaism—1-7

A. The magnificent Temple, 1

1 And as he went out of the temple, one of his disciples saith unto him, Master, see what manner of stones and what buildings are here?

The original Temple built by Solomon. had been destroyed in 586 B.C. Jews returning from Babylonian captivity some 70 years later began to rebuild it into "the second Temple." This version, however, was desecrated and ruined by various waves of Greek and Roman invasion. Then, about 4 B.C., King Herod the Great envisioned the grandest Temple restoration project yet—not because he was religious but for political purposes. It was this "third Temple" that awed Jesus' disciples. Some of its stones were 40 feet long and weighed 100 tons. It, too, was destroyed before it reached the gold-plated splendor Herod envisioned; but this third Temple was considered an "eighth wonder" of the ancient world.

B. Its destruction predicted, 2

2 And Jesus answering said unto him, Seest thou these great buildings? there shall not be left one stone upon another, that shall not be thrown down.

Jesus is less interested in material Temples than in people, the new Temple of the Holy Spirit (1 Cor. 3:16-17). Besides—He knows that the political unrest in the city and its anti-Roman forces will soon bring the armed might of the Empire down on the Jewish nation, the Holy City, and Herod's stunningly beautiful Temple. In Luke 19:41-44, He wept over the city's sad destiny.

C. Signs of the times, 3-7

3 And as he sat upon the mount of Olives over against the temple, Peter and James and John and Andrew asked him privately,

4 Tell us, when shall these things be? and what shall be the sign when all these things shall be fulfilled?

5 And Jesus answering them began to say, Take heed lest any man deceive you:

6 For many shall come in my name, saying, I am Christ; and shall deceive many.

7 And when ye shall hear of wars and rumours of wars, be ye not troubled: for such things must needs be; but the end shall not be yet.

The very atmosphere in Jerusalem was electric with Messianic hopes, as well as with fears. If Rome did fulfill its frequent threats to destroy the Temple, it would mean the end of the world as the Jews knew it. Naturally, such a catastrophe would be of concern; but Jesus disciples are more interested in how to read world events and construct a timetable for the future than they are about the inner and spiritual significance of what Jesus is saying.

In Matthew's version of this conversation, the disciples seem to separate the question about when the Temple would be destroyed from that of when Christ would return (Matt. 24:3). It is therefore tempting to read some of the verses to follow as an answer to when the Temple would be destroyed, and make others apply to the Second Coming or the End of Time. One useful feature of apocalyptic language, however, is that its symbols can stand for more than one event. Unfortunately this usefulness is balanced by the fact that moderns have lost the "code" to understanding the precise meaning of the symbols. Many of the signs in the rest of the chapter may therefore refer to both events.

Despite this difficulty, verses 5-7 seem to refer to the need for calm, courage, and perception during the days preceding the Temple's destruction. Messianic-style leaders tried to deceive people even as the early Church was spreading (see Acts 5:36-37; 21:38). The Jewish historian Josephus, a Roman sympathizer, describes another case of a false Messiah who called 6,000 Jews to their death when the Temple was destroyed in A.D. 70.

"The end" that "is not yet" (vs. 7) would therefore seem to refer primarily to the end of the Jewish system. The Roman general Vespasian invaded Jerusalem in A.D. 66, and his son Titus finished its destruction four years later. In the verses to follow (8-23), other signs are given that also seem to have primary application not to the End of Time but to the destruction of Jerusalem—although it should be emphasized again that some of these signs may be duplicated in both events. For example, the "abomination of desolation" or Temple desecration in verse 13, first predicted in Daniel, 9:27, occurred when Antiochus Epiphanes set up an idol to Zeus in the Temple in 168 B.C. Apparently Jesus foretells an-

other similar event before the Temple's final ruin. This is the nature of apocalyptic language: what appears to be a present event may prove to be a window on the future as well. The language may have "double fulfillment."

II. The End of Time—24, 27

A. Cosmic signs, 24

24 But in those days, after that tribulation, the sun shall be darkened, and the moon shall not give her light,

Again, the principle of double fulfillment may mean we should apply this verse symbolically to the horribly dark days of tribulation that accompanied the destruction of the Temple. Partly because of the verses to follow, however, it seems more likely that the primary application of these towering cosmic pictures is to Christ's Second Coming and the End of the World. Although "tribulations" or troubles will precede that great day, theories of who will endure them and who will be caught up in a "rapture" to escape them are more highly developed in modern writings than in Scripture.

B. The great gathering, 27

27 And then shall he send his angels, and shall gather together his elect from the four winds, from the uttermost part of the earth to the uttermost part of heaven.

There is more comfort than fear in Christ's picture of the End. It will be, He says, a time of Homecoming and reunion. Although the Old Covenant Scriptures speak of Jacob (Israel) and his descendants, the Jews, as the "elect," Colossians 3:12 and other passages clearly broaden the elect to include Christians. The Second Coming of Christ, therefore, will apparently not involve a literal re-gathering of the Jews to

Jerusalem, but a great cosmic "church service" attended by all people, Jew and gentile alike, who are followers of the Jewish Messiah, Jesus Christ. (See also 1 Thess. 4:16-17.)

III. Living in View of the End—32-35

A. At an unknown time, 32

32 But of that day and that hour knoweth no man, no, not the angels which are in heaven, neither the Son, but the Father.

Despite some modern claims to the contrary, God alone knows the time-table for all these events. People who have concluded from painstaking math processes that the Second Coming will be in this or that year claim to know more than Jesus.

Another issue arises from this verse: How can Jesus be divine if He was ignorant of something God knew? The answer lies in the historic confession that Jesus is "very God and very man." In His humanity there were perhaps many things—for example, the science of genetics—that He did not know. Yet this limited human aspect of His nature is as precious as the divine aspect; for it was in His humanity that He died for our sins.

B. Watch! 33-35

33 Take heed, watch and pray: for ye know not when the time is.

34 For the Son of man is as a man taking a far journey, who left his house, and gave authority to his servants, and to every man his work, and commanded the porter to watch.

35 Watch ye therefore: for ye know not when the master of the house cometh, at even, or at midnight, or at the cockcrowing, or in the morning:

Here Jesus is clearly referring to His Second Coming, since He compares it to a householder who goes away on a journeys and leaves his servants to care for his property. Since they do not know when the master will return, and thus when they will have to give an account, they are simply to *live* accountably, and watchfully.

This saying would correct the modern tendency to spend so much time and energy trying to discern in current events signs of the future, and to consider this world so transitory in view of the "soon return of Christ," that we neglect urgent problems of the present.

Evangelistic Emphasis

There is a story about the devil and his demons having a discussion concerning ways to thwart soul-winning on earth. It was decided the most effective way would be to sidetrack the hearer with lies.

"What would be the best lie?" Satan asked his demons.

"How about, 'There is no God', for an effective lie?" one demon asked.

"Pretty good," replied Satan. "But if someone takes a good look at creation he could be convinced there is a God."

"How about, 'There is no hell?'" another asked.

"Good," replied Satan. "But some folks will get into such a big mess on earth that they won't have any trouble believing there is a hell."

"I've got it!" another replied. "The most effective lie to keep people from ever coming to God is . . . 'There is no hurry.'"

And so it is. Those words, "There is no hurry," have kept many people from coming to Christ at the time the Holy Spirit convicts them. There are those who never got another chance.

The end will come for us all. We don't know when. Therefore, now is the time of salvation.

Memory Selection

Heaven and earth shall pass away: but my words shall not pass away.—*Mark 13:31*

I have seen a bumper sticker that says, "God said it. I believe it. That settles it." At first I thought that was very clever. At first I thought it was a good testimony. After thinking about it further, I decided the writer wasted some words.

To be correct the bumper sticker should have read, "God said it. That settles it." The truth of God's words does not rest on whether or not we believe them. God's Word is truth. We can count on the Word of God. We can count on the words of God as spoken by Christ Jesus.

All that we enjoy on this earth, all that we hold dear will pass away, including friends, family and possessions. But the Word will endure.

We can stand upon the words of Jesus. We can stake our lives on the words of Jesus. We can rest assured that the words of Jesus will sustain us. Cling to the Word.

Ed was concerned. He had been teaching the class on the book of Revelation for seven weeks now. More people were showing up each week. Ed was more than a little flattered. He had worked hard on the study. He had read extensively in preparation for teaching the class. He spent hours and hours cross-referencing sources. He had searched the Bible prophecies. He had consulted the minds of great scholars as he scoured the seminary library shelves for works concerning the end times. He had developed detailed charts and timetables chronicling the events leading up to and including the Second Coming of Christ. He was ready.

The people seemed to appreciate his preparation. He made it clear. The crowd swelled from week to week.

None of those things concerned Ed. What troubled Ed was that, as far as he could tell, almost everyone was viewing the study as an intellectual exercise designed to help them gain special knowledge that others may not know. It seemed no one was listening to the warnings issued by Jesus to be ready for that time. All seemed more concerned with knowing the time of Christ's return than with living for Him right now.

* How important is it to try to figure out when Christ will return? Explain.

* Why do you think some people are so intrigued about knowing the time of the Second Coming?

Now and Forever, Amen

We are born for a higher destiny than that of earth. There is a realm where the rainbow never fades, where the stars will be spread before us like islands that slumber on the ocean, and where the beings that now pass over before us like shadows, will stay in our presence forever.

—*Edward Bulwer.*

To me there is something thrilling and exalting in the thought that we are drifting forward into a splendid mysteryinto something that no mortal eye hath yet seen, and no intelligence has yet declared.

—*E. H. Chapin*

The grand difficulty is to feel the reality of both worlds, so as to give each its due place in our thoughts and feelings: to keep our mind's eye and our heart's eye ever fixed on the land of promise, without looking away from the road along which we are to travel toward it.

—*August W. Hare*

This Lesson in Your Life

Faith for Uncertain Times

Jesus said that no one would know the exact time of His return to earth. Still, the approach of the year 2,000 has stimulated an upsurge in doomsday prophecies. An article by Jeffery Sheler in *U.S. News & World Report*, reported that some 1,100 groups or individuals (Christian and non-Christian) that see the dawn of the new millennium as having cosmic significance. We have seen what distorted views of the end times prophecies can produce. We remember the disaster in Waco, Texas, involving David Koresh and the Branch Davidian cult.

Belief in the apocalypse is not limited to religious fanatics, however. It has been reported that six out of 10 Americans think the world will come to an end, and two of the six expect it to happen within a few decades. More than 61 percent profess to believe that Jesus is coming to earth again.

The rising concern over the end times is not new to this age, either. There was a great deal of apocalyptic speculation surrounding the year 1,000, even to the point that artistic and cultural activity practically ceased in Europe's monasteries. Belief in the approaching return of Christ filled early Christian writings, just as it does today. St. Augustine warned against date-setting and detailed speculation about the Second Coming over 1,500 years ago. His warnings were not heeded. Throughout church history there have been those who thought they had figured out biblical symbolism enough to construct elaborate timetables. At different periods in history people have quit their jobs, sold their homes, cashed in their life insurance, etc., anticipating the Second Coming of Christ on a certain date or at a certain location. So far, all attempts at pinpointing a time and place have been wrong. We should not be surprised that our efforts to spotlight a date have been frustrated, however, for Jesus said , "but of that day and hour no one knows . . . ."

We are not comfortable with not knowing. We read about the terrible things that will occur before Christ comes again. We read about the great disasters that will precede the end. We shudder at the opening of the seven seals and the sounding of the seven trumpets and the bowls of wrath John describes in the Revelation. We want to know what these things are and when they will occur. When we see a great disaster on the earth we ask ourselves, "Is this it?" We see the morality and ethical behavior of our nation declining and we ask ourselves, "Is this it?" We see leaders who seem to be leading us further and further from the precepts of God and we ask ourselves, "Is this it? Are we near the end?" We want to know because we sometimes wonder if things can get much worse.

Yet, our primary concern should not be the time of Christ's return, but being faithful until His return. The Scripture is clear that God will reward His faithful. Revelation 2 and 3 remind us that God will richly bless those who overcome.

Some time ago I was discussing the time of the Second Coming of Christ with a Christian friend of mine. He had these words of wisdom: "Deciding the time for Christ to come again is a policy decision. That decision should be made by management. God is in management. I'm in sales. I'll let God make that decision. In the meantime I'm going to try to do my job the best I can." That sounds good to me!

Seed Thoughts

1. What building was the disciple talking about being so beautiful and full of grandeur?

The disciple was exclaiming about how beautiful the temple was.

2. What did Jesus prophesy about the temple when the disciple was commenting on it?

Jesus prophesied the temple's total destruction. In fact, the destruction would be so complete there would not be one stone left on top of the other.

3. After Jesus's prophecy about the temple, what did some of the disciples ask Jesus?

They asked Jesus to tell them of other signs to look for.

4. What serious warning did Jesus have for the disciples?

Jesus warned them about false prophets. He said many would come and say "I am the Christ," deceiving many.

5. What did Jesus say about wars? Should the disciple be alarmed at the rumor of war?

Jesus said not to be troubled over rumors of wars. This would happen, but this was not an indication of the end.

(Please turn page)

1. What building was the disciple talking about being so beautiful and full of grandeur?

2. What did Jesus prophesy about the temple when the disciple was commenting on it?

3. After Jesus's prophecy about the temple, what did some of the disciples ask Jesus?

4. What serious warning did Jesus have for the disciples?

5. What did Jesus say about wars? Should the disciple be alarmed at the rumor of war?

6. What will happen to the sun and the moon at the time of tribulation?

7. God will send His angels on a mission. What will be their job?

8. Name everyone who will know the day and the hour that the end will come.

9. What should we as Christians do in preparation of that day?

10. To whom is the Son of man compared in verses 34 and 35?

The disciple was exclaiming about how beautiful the temple was.

Jesus prophesied the temple's total destruction. In fact, the destruction would be so complete there would not be one stone left on top of the other.

They asked Jesus to tell them of other signs to look for.

Jesus warned them about false prophets. He said many would come and say "I am the Christ," deceiving many.

Jesus said not to be troubled over rumors of wars. This would happen, but this was not an indication of the end.

The sun will be darkened and the moon will not give light.

The angels will gather together God's elect from all the earth.

No one will know except the Father - not the angels, not the Son nor any human will know.

We should watch and pray because we will not know the time and we will want to be ready.

He is as a man on a journey. He also is compared to the master of the house.

6. What will happen to the sun and the moon at the time of tribulation?

The sun will be darkened and the moon will not give light.

7. God will send His angels on a mission. What will be their job?

The angels will gather together God's elect from all the earth.

8. Name everyone who will know the day and the hour that the end will come?

No one will know except the Father - not the angels, not the Son nor any human will know.

9. What should we as Christians do in preparation of that day?

We should watch and pray because we will not know the time and we will want to be ready.

10. To whom is the Son of man compared in verses 34 and 35?

He is as a man on a journey. He also is compared to the master of the house.

Lesson 1

More Questions Than Answers

Ecclesiastes 1:1-3; 2:1-2, 10-13; 4:1-3; 12:1, 13-14

1 The words of the Preacher, the son of David, king in Jerusalem.

2 Vanity of vanities, saith the Preacher, vanity of vanities; all is vanity.

3 What profit hath a man of all his labour which he taketh under the sun?

2:1 I said in mine heart, Go to now, I will prove thee with mirth, therefore enjoy pleasure: and, behold, this also is vanity.

2 I said of laughter, It is mad: and of mirth, What doeth it?

10 And whatsoever mine eyes desired I kept not from them, I withheld not my heart from any joy; for my heart rejoiced in all my labour: and this was my portion of all my labour.

11 Then I looked on all the works that my hands had wrought, and on the labour that I had laboured to do: and, behold, all was vanity and vexation of spirit, and there was no profit under the sun.

12 And I turned myself to behold wisdom, and madness, and folly: for what can the man do that cometh after the king? even that which hath been already done.

13 Then I saw that wisdom excelleth folly, as far as light excelleth darkness.

4:1 So I returned, and considered all the oppressions that are done under the sun: and behold the tears of such as were oppressed, and they had no comforter; and on the side of their oppressors there was power; but they had no comforter.

2 Wherefore I praised the dead which are already dead more than the living which are yet alive.

3 Yea, better is he than both they, which hath not yet been, who hath not seen the evil work that is done under the sun.

12:1 Remember now thy Creator in the days of thy youth, while the evil days come not, nor the years draw nigh, when thou shalt say, I have no pleasure in them;

13 Let us hear the conclusion of the whole matter: Fear God, and keep his commandments: for this is the whole duty of man.

14 For God shall bring every work into judgment, with every secret thing, whether it be good, or whether it be bad.

Memory Selection
Ecclesiastes 12:13-14

Devotional Reading
1 Corinthians 13:1-13

Background Scripture
Ecclesiastes 1:1-3; 2:1-4, 10-15; 4:1-3; 12:1, 13-14

Printed Scripture
Ecclesiastes 1:1-3; 2:1-2, 10-13; 4:1-3; 12:1, 13-14

Teacher's Target

Lesson purpose: *To explore some of the book of Ecclesiastes' ques-tions about the seemingly meaning-less aspects of life "under the sun."*

People assemble for Bible study scrubbed and neat and smiling. Often, however, troubles, unanswered questions, and pessimism simmer beneath the surface. Usually all this goes unvoiced. We don't want to be "negative." We suspect some of our questions have no answers. We don't want to feed our doubts.

The author of Ecclesiastes had no such inhibitions. He probed the times when life seems meaningless with unblinking and even bitter realism. Although his musings lack the perspective of a future life that would be painted by Christ many years later, they have the advantage of calling us to make the best we can of this life.

This lesson is a good time to allow class members to voice their own tough questions about life—with the reminder that Ecclesiastes can only probe life "under the sun" (1:3b), while Christians deal with life in the light of the Son.

Lesson Introduction

We can see the English word "ecclesiastical" in this book's title. The term is related to the Greek word *ekklesia,* "church." The Hebrew title, *qohelet,* means "preacher," the spokesman of a "church" or assembly; "teacher"; or "collector of wise sayings." Traditionally the teacher here has been viewed as Solomon, famed for his wisdom. It is therefore appropriate that the book is in a section of the Old Testament called "Wisdom Literature," which also includes Job, Psalms, Proverbs, and The Song of Solomon.

Although the author of Ecclesiastes had neither the advantage of the "positive thinking" movement nor the good news about the resurrection of Christ, his often bleak observations speak to our need to face life as it is, rather than how we might wish it to be. He is to be listened to not only because he is wise, but because he has tried so many routes to happiness—and discovered that all but godly joy left him unfulfilled.

Teaching Outline	Daily Bible Readings
I. Life Under the Sun—1:1-3	**Mon.** Solomon Prays for Understanding 1 Kings 3:5-15
II. Living Without Limits—2:1-2, 10-13	**Tue.** Nothing New Under the Sun Ecclesiastes 1:1-11
A. The pursuit of pleasure, 2:1-2	**Wed.** Chasing After Wind Ecclesiastes 1:12-2:5
B. The vanity of things, 10-11	
C. The limits of worldly wisdom, 12-13	**Thu.** Our Days Are Full of Pain Ecclesiastes 2:9-23
III. Life Without a Comforter—4:1-3	**Fri.** Life Isn't Fair Ecclesiastes 4:1-6
IV. Living with God in Mind—12:1, 13-14	**Sat.** Don't Wait to Know God Ecclesiastes 12:1-8
A. The God-habit in youth, 12:1	**Sun.** Keep God's Commandments Ecclesiastes 12:9-14
B. The conclusion of the quest, 13-14	

VERSE BY VERSE

I. Life Under the Sun—1:1-3

1 The words of the Preacher, the son of David, king in Jerusalem.

2 Vanity of vanities, saith the Preacher, vanity of vanities; all is vanity.

3 What profit hath a man of all his labour which he taketh under the sun?

The traditional view that Solomon wrote this book is shaped by the author's position as king in Jerusalem and David's son, combined with what is known elsewhere of Solomon's wisdom (1 Kings 3:5-28; 4:29-34).

The word for "vanity" can also refer to a "vapor" or wisp, indicating the author's feeling that so much of life is insubstantial and transitory. He has lived long enough to notice that "history repeats itself," and concludes that "there is no new thing under the sun" (vs. 9). As the old folk song goes, sometimes we feel that:

The sun comes up, and the sun goes
  down,
The hands on the clock keep goin'
  round,
I jus' git up, and it's time to lay
  down.
Life gits tejious, don't it?

II. Living Without Limits—2:1-2, 10-13

A. The pursuit of pleasure, 2:1-2

1 I said in mine heart, Go to now, I will prove thee with mirth, therefore enjoy pleasure: and, behold, this also is vanity.

2 I said of laughter, It is mad: and of mirth, What doeth it?

In 1:16 the author began a "dialogue" with his own heart, testing or "proving" it to see what might satisfy its yearnings. Neither wisdom nor knowledge had done so (1:18); perhaps their opposite—acting the fool, or a life of hedonism (pleasure)—would bring satisfaction. So, like many people in our own times, the author next tries to abandon himself to merry-making. Perhaps life is a joke, and can best be dealt with by laughing away our questions. Unfortunately, the author discovers that while funny stories may provide comic relief, seeking long-term fulfillment in them is "vanity." After the laughter dies away, life's deepest questions remain.

B. The vanity of things, 10-11

10 And whatsoever mine eyes desired I kept not from them, I withheld not my heart from any joy; for my heart rejoiced in all my labour: and this was my portion of all my labour.

11 Then I looked on all the works that my hands had wrought, and on the labour that I had laboured to do: and, behold, all was vanity and vexation of spirit, and there was no profit under the sun.

If laughter does not answer the heart's hunger for meaning, perhaps a career, or the material pleasures wealth can buy, will do so. Solomon's works and wealth were legendary even in his own time. The queen of Sheba, visiting to marvel at them, reported that "the half was not told me" (1 Kings 10:7). "King Solomon's mines" and the stables with 4,000 stalls (2 Chron. 9:25) are still storied evidence of his material success—but also of the fact they did not satisfy his soul's quest for meaning.

The adage in our own times that "everyone will have 15 minutes of fame" is a cynical insight into the fleeting nature of the prominence Solomon sought, and achieved. He could ride only so many horses, eat only so much rich food, and occupy only a few rooms even in a huge castle. After the queen of Sheba paid her plaudits and returned home, the rooms echoed with the hollow, mocking question: Is this all there is?

C. The limits of worldly wisdom, 12-13

12 And I turned myself to behold wisdom, and madness, and folly: for what can the man do that cometh after the king? even that which hath been already done.

13 Then I saw that wisdom excelleth folly, as far as light excelleth darkness.

Now the author makes a summary statement about the pursuits he has followed up to now—wisdom, madness and fun. All this seems to be empty because of the question of time: God has "set eternity" in our hearts (3:11, NIV). However enjoyable all this is for the moment, we will die; and our heirs will be faced with the same quest for fulfillment and the same perception that life consists of cycles of sameness instead of being a journey toward a goal. Here is

one place the Christian doctrine of the resurrection functions: the present is given meaning in light of an eternal future with Christ.

Still, while wisdom did not provide answers to all his questions, the wise man is able to see that its relative value over folly is like the difference between sunlight and darkness.

III. Life Without a Comforter—4:1-3

1 So I returned, and considered all the oppressions that are done under the sun: and behold the tears of such as were oppressed, and they had no comforter; and on the side of their oppressors there was power; but they had no comforter.

2 Wherefore I praised the dead which are already dead more than the living which are yet alive.

3 Yea, better is he than both they, which hath not yet been, who hath not seen the evil work that is done under the sun.

Up to now, the author's quest for fulfillment has been self-centered. We are often advised to "get out of ourselves" and find fulfillment in others; but when the author does so, his deep pessimism enables him to see only their plight, not their happiness. The masses are oppressed, and have no one in power to take up their cause. Ironically, Solomon was one of the world's greatest slave-owners. Apparently his inability to solve world oppression paralyzed him and prevented his lighting a candle of freedom where he lived, instead of cursing the larger darkness.

Verses 2-3 are in the same despairing mood expressed by the classic sufferer Job: "Let the day perish wherein I was born" (see Job 3:1-13). The complaint has been felt by many who are in the grips of deep depression. Perhaps one of the reasons life can seem meaningless is the inability to answer the basic question, Why was I born? The author will give a tentative answer at the close of his book.

IV. Living with God in Mind—12:1, 13-14

A. The God-habit in youth, 12:1

1 Remember now thy Creator in the days of thy youth, while the evil days come not, nor the years draw nigh, when thou shalt say, I have no pleasure in them;

Notice the implied difference between old age and youth: the young do not typically ask the kind of questions about the meaning of life that the author has been asking. One reason many people have difficulty identifying with the bleak and pessimistic questions and answers in Ecclesiastes is that they have been schooled from their youth to reverence God. People who grew up with the sense that their tiny hand is in God's great hands, and that they can entrust life's unanswerable questions to Him, have built-in stability.

It has been suggested that the first seven verses of this chapter describe the aging process—with the fading lights of verse 3 representing failing eyesight; the "grinders" the teeth; and shorter or lighter sleep hours described in verse 4. The wise man's point is that regardless of our questions, we should live fully in the present.

B. The conclusion of the quest, 13-14

13 Let us hear the conclusion of the whole matter: Fear God, and keep his commandments: for this is the whole duty of man.

14 For God shall bring every work into judgment, with every secret thing, whether it be good, or whether it be evil.

After his failed experiments in the laboratory of life "under the sun," the wise man can only conclude that God's call to obedience must have priority over all restlessness and anxiety about unanswered—and unanswerable—questions.

This is not to recommend the life of a Polyanna, an invitation to join a positive thinking cult or a call to stop asking tough questions. It is, however, to draw a boundary marking off an arena in which we can rise above navel-gazing and act on life. It is a call to trust that God will judge us on whether we walk faithfully in the light that we have, even as we confess that, a little way beyond, is a darkness only He can fathom.

Evangelistic Emphasis

What is your labor worth? We measure work's value in terms of dollars —our paychecks. In this world we must buy our food, pay the rent and meet all the other costs of living. The Preacher (Solomon) asks the same question, worded only slightly differently: "What profit hath a man of all his labor . . . ?" (Eccles. 1:3). It is a question which demands our serious thought. While this life is important, it is not the "main event," but rather our opportunity to prepare for the hereafter.

Jesus asked a slightly different question, "For what is a man profited, if he shall gain the whole world, and lose his own soul?" (Matt. 16:26). This contrast between the importance of seeking worldly gain and the saving of souls graphically reflects the life of Christ. He did not seek worldly wealth, did not have a place to lay His head (Luke 9:58), but when we look at His life, we see that His priority was soul-saving. His declaration just before He was crucified makes that clear: "The Son of man is come to seek and to save that which was lost." (Luke 19:10)

If Jesus was committed to saving souls, even to costing Him His own life, how deeply should we care about the saving of our own souls and the souls of others? Jesus truly understood that our secular "work" is meaningless unless we also concentrate on the preservation of our most precious possession—our souls.

Memory Selection

 Let us hear the conclusion of the whole matter: Fear God, and keep His commandments: for this is the whole duty of man. For God shall bring every work into judgment, with every secret thing, whether it be good, or whether it be evil.—*Ecclesiastes 12:13-14*

In the book of Ecclesiastes, Solomon has explored numerous theories of life and possible answers to man's questions about existence. Having looked at all the possibilities, he draws the only conclusion which his divine wisdom could permit: "Fear God, and keep His commandments." He offers two basic reasons for this conclusion: first, it is man's duty; and second, the consequences of disobedience are fearful.

By explaining that our duty is to fear God and obey Him, Solomon answers the age-old question, "Why am I here?" The answer: "To do God's will."

All our sins will be remembered at the Judgment. Even the sins we thought were secret are seen by God and will be exposed at the Last Day. Though Solomon gave good advice, he failed in later years to live uprightly, actually following other gods (1 Kings 11:4). How important it is that we seek God's kingdom and His righteousness before it is too late.

Weekday Problems

Jason is a Christian young man with a lot of ability. He has been active in the church since his childhood. He was very successful in school, graduating in the top quarter of his class. After completing his education, he landed a good job with one of the biggest companies in his region. He seems to be on his way to a successful career.

Not long after getting his first good job, Jason began hearing about the famous weekend parties that the owner of the company throws twice a year. Called "company retreats," these parties are really excuses for over-indulgence in drinking and other behaviors he considers evil. However, the owner of the company has made it clear that attendance is required for budding young employees who want to advance in the company. As he asks around, he finds that all the employees above him have been regulars at these events. He has visited with a leader in the church and asked his advice.

*   Is this a business issue or a spiritual one?

*   How does Solomon's search for answers to life's meaning bear on Jason's dilemma?

*   If Jason were to ask your advice, how would you try to direct him? (Discuss the consequences of whatever decision he might make.)

✛   ✛   ✛

Doubting Our Doubts

The doubter's great dissatisfaction with his doubts is evidence of hope that he will one day doubt his doubts, and believe.—*Anon.*

Doubt, indulged and cherished, is in danger of becoming denial; but if honest, and bent on thorough investigation, it may soon lead to full establishment in the truth.—*Tryon Edwards*

The doubts of an honest man contain more moral truth than the profession of faith of people under a worldly yoke.—*Xavier Doudan*

When we are in doubt and puzzle out the truth by our own exertions, we have gained something that will stay by us and will serve us again. But if to avoid the trouble of the search we avail ourselves of the superior knowledge of a friend, such knowledge will not remain with us; we have not bought, but borrowed it.
—*Caleb Colton*

This Lesson in Your Life

The story of Ecclesiastes may not differ greatly from the story of our own lives. In a way, Solomon did the same thing most of us have done—sought the answer to life's meaning through "trial and error." It seems that most of us learn best through our own experiences, even though many of these experiences may be damaging to our souls.

Solomon speculated that hard work would bring comfort and satisfaction , but it did not. He pronounced such effort as "Vanity of vanities," meaning that it was insignificant, of little value or meaningless.

He also investigated the benefits of following the fads, whatever is "new." But he discovered that nothing is truly "new." If you look closely at fads, you can see their roots in the past.

The "Preacher" wondered about the benefits of knowledge and wisdom. Since he was the wisest man who ever lived, it would seem that he could achieve satisfaction through that wonderful quality. Yet, he pronounces that "in much wisdom there is much grief " (Eccles. 1:18).

Gaining wealth was another experiment in seeking life's meaning. Solomon became the richest man in the world. He could buy anything he wanted. He bought countless flocks and herds, acquired hundreds of slaves, lived in sumptuous surroundings and dressed in the finest clothes. That life-style would surely appeal to most people in our society. Most of us might say that being able to buy whatever we want would be the ultimate in satisfaction. But listen to what Solomon said about that experiment: "Behold all was vanity and vexation of spirit, and there was no profit under the sun" (Eccles. 2:11). And again in chapter 5, verse 10, he says, "He that loveth silver shall not be satisfied with silver; nor he that loveth abundance with increase: this is also vanity."

The pursuit of fame was another route to happiness which Solomon explored. He was certainly famous, known throughout the world for his wisdom and his wealth. But he concluded that even fame, intoxicating though it may be, is fleeting and "... in the days to come shall all be forgotten" (Eccles. 2:16).

In his frustration with finding no real satisfaction in life, he declared that it would be better never to have been born.(Eccles. 4:3) At least the unborn have not experienced the evil of this life.

If neither hard work, finding and adopting new ways, seeking knowledge and wisdom, becoming wealthy nor becoming famous could assure happiness, then what could possibly bring joy to one's heart? The answer Solomon found is the same one repeated throughout Scripture. At the end of his treatise on the meaning of life, he writes his conclusion, "Fear God, and keep His commandments: for this is the whole duty of man" (Eccles. 12:13).

Why does Solomon conclude that "to fear and obey God" is the best answer to the question, "Why am I here?" Perhaps it is because he came to realize that God had a purpose in mind for human beings before He even created the first man and woman. As the apostle Paul says in Eph. 2:10, "we are His workmanship, created in Christ Jesus unto good works, which God hath before ordained that we should walk in them." What an exciting thought that God has had us in mind from before the beginning! And He has had a purpose for us, a place where we could fit into His marvelous universe. Knowing that His thoughts are higher than our thoughts and His ways higher than our ways, we know we can achieve divine joy in doing His will (Isa. 55:9).

Seed Thoughts

1. Of what value is human benevolence without love (charity)?

It is of no value (1 Cor. 13:3).

2. Who was the "Preacher" who wrote Ecclesiastes?

Solomon (Eccles. 1:1, 1:16; 1 Kings 4:29-31).

3. What does the Preacher mean by the statement, "Vanity of vanities; all is vanity."?

The word "vanity" carries the meaning of "insignificant," "of little value," "meaningless."

4. Name some of the ways by which Solomon sought the meaning of life.

He tried hard work, adopting new ways, achieving knowledge and wisdom, gaining wealth and pursuit of fame.

5. What was the result of gaining great wealth?

All was vanity and vexation of spirit, and there was no profit under the sun (Eccles. 2:11).

1. Of what value is human benevolence without love (charity)?

2. Who was the "Preacher" who wrote Ecclesiastes?

3. What does the Preacher mean by the statement, "Vanity of vanities; all is vanity."?

4. Name some of the ways by which Solomon sought the meaning of life.

5. What was the result of gaining great wealth?

6. Why does the Preacher say the unborn are better off than those who have lived?

7. What deeds will be brought into judgment by God?

8. When does the Preacher urge that people remember God?

9. According to the writer of Ecclesiastes, what is the "whole duty of man?"

10. Did Solomon live by his own advice?

(Please turn page)

It is of no value (1 Cor. 13:3).

Solomon (Eccles. 1:1, 1:16; 1 Kings 4:29-31).

The word "vanity" carries the meaning of "insignificant," "of little value," "meaningless."

He tried hard work, adopting new ways, achieving knowledge and wisdom, gaining wealth and pursuit of fame.

All was vanity and vexation of spirit, and there was no profit under the sun (Eccles. 2:11).

The unborn have not experienced the evil of this world (Eccles. 4:3).

"He will bring every work into judgment, with every secret thing, whether it be good, or whether it be evil" (Eccles. 12:14).

"Remember now thy Creator in the days of thy youth " (Eccles. 12:1).

To fear God, and keep His commandments (Eccles. 12:13).

When Solomon was old, ... his heart was not perfect with the Lord his God, as was the heart of David his father (1 Kings 11:4).

6. Why does the Preacher say the unborn are better off than those who have lived?

The unborn have not experienced the evil of this world (Eccles. 4:3).

7. What deeds will be brought into judgment by God?

"He will bring every work into judgment, with every secret thing, whether it be good, or whether it be evil" (Eccles. 12:14).

8. When does the Preacher urge that people remember God?

"Remember now thy Creator in the days of thy youth " (Eccles. 12:1).

9. According to the writer of Ecclesiastes, what is the "whole duty of man?"

To fear God, and keep His commandments (Eccles. 12:13).

10. Did Solomon live by his own advice?

When Solomon was old, ... his heart was not perfect with the Lord his God, as was the heart of David his father (1 Kings 11:4).

"...BLESSED BE THE NAME OF THE LORD"

Lesson 2

Job's Questions

Job 1:1-3, 8-11; 2:3-6; 3:1-3

1 There was a man in the land of Uz, whose name was Job; and that man was perfect and upright, and one that feared God, and eschewed evil.

2 And there were born unto him seven sons and three daughters.

3 His substance also was seven thousand sheep, and three thousand camels, and five hundred yoke of oxen, and five hundred she asses, and a very great household; so that this man was the greatest of all the men of the east.

8 And the Lord said unto Satan, Hast thou considered my servant Job, that there is none like him in the earth, a perfect and an upright man, one that feareth God, and escheweth evil?

9 Then Satan answered the Lord, and said, Doth Job fear God for nought?

10 Hast not thou made an hedge about him, and about his house, and about all that he hath on every side? thou hast blessed the work of his hands, and his substance is increased in the land.

11 But put forth thine hand now, and touch all that he hath, and he will curse thee to thy face.

2:3 And the Lord said unto Satan, Hast thou considered my servant Job, that there is none like him in the earth, a perfect and an upright man, one that feareth God, and escheweth evil? and still he holdeth fast his integrity, although thou movedst me against him, to destroy him without cause.

4 And Satan answered the Lord, and said, Skin for skin, yea, all that a man hath will he give for his life.

5 But put forth thine hand now, and touch his bone and his flesh, and he will curse thee to thy face.

6 And the Lord said unto Satan, Behold, he is in thine hand; but save his life.

3:1 After this opened Job his mouth, and cursed his day.

2 And Job spake, and said,

3 Let the day perish wherein I was born, and the night in which it was said, There is a man child conceived.

Memory Selection
Job 2:3

Devotional Reading
Job 3:11-26

Background Scripture
Job 1:1-4, 8-11; 2:3-8;
3:1-4, 20-26

Printed Scripture
Job 1:1-3, 8-11; 2:3-6; 3:1-3

Teacher's Target

Lesson purpose: *To come to grips with the kind of test Job faced, in order to ask whether we serve God only for the blessings He bestows.*

No biblical character other than Christ is more famous than Job. The New Testament book of James assumes that everyone has heard of "the patience of Job" (Jas. 5:11). Even modern playwrights retell the story, as in the drama "J.B."

Allow this lesson to raise the question in Job 1:9 for each member of your class: *Do I serve God for nothing, or for the blessings He bestows?* Be sensitive to people in the group whose faith, like Job's, has been tested by devastating losses. Some may have experienced the death of loved ones, investment losses, or being thrown out of work. In their anguish they may have questioned the goodness or even the existence of God.

While accepting such questions non-judgmentally (with the patience of Job!), remind the class that this lesson doesn't tell "the rest of the story"—just as the losses of this life are not the last word. That Word is reserved for the life to come.

Lesson Introduction

The book of Job is part of a category of ancient writings some scholars call "The Test," since it portrays God allowing Satan to test the strength of a believer's faith. When and by whom it was written are unknown.

Sometimes it is said that the book was written to answer the question of why good people suffer, and as a "theodicy"—an attempt to justify the ways of God to man. If these were true descriptions, we would have to say that Job is a very unsuccessful book, since it accomplishes neither goal! As a book about "The Test," however, it is very successful, calling believers to remain faithful even when we *cannot* explain why people suffer, or fathom God's reasons for allowing it.

In this, the first of four lessons on Job, the stage is set for the problem with which the entire book grapples. Like the parables of Christ, the book invites the hearer into the story. It challenges us to ask how well our own faith holds up under the pressure of undeserved suffering.

Teaching Outline	Daily Bible Readings	
I. When Life Was Good—1:1-3	**Mon.**	The Limits of Righteousness *Ezekiel 14:12-23*
A. Job the just, 1:1	**Tue.**	Believing When Things Go Right *Job 1:1-12*
B. His wealth and happiness, 2-3	**Wed.**	Believing When Things Go Wrong *Job 1:13-22*
II. When Loss Occurs—8-11	**Thu.**	Blameless but on Trial *Job 2:1-8*
III. When Life Is Threatened—2:3-6	**Fri.**	Job Didn't Sin in Word *Job 2:9-13*
IV. "Why Was I Born?"—3:1-3	**Sat.**	Cursing the Day of His Birth *Job 3:1-10*
	Sun.	When "Why" Has No Answer

VERSE BY VERSE

I. When Life Was Good—1:1-3
A. Job the just, 1:1

1 There was a man in the land of Uz, whose name was Job; and that man was perfect and upright, and one that feared God, and eschewed evil.

The name "Job" means "sorrowful" or "he who weeps." The name so neatly fits the man's story that some have wondered if he was a historical person, or the main character of a parable on human suffering. At least by the time the book of Ezekiel was written, however (some 600 years before Christ), Job was considered an actual person (Ezek. 14:14ff.).

Uz is generally considered to have been in the area of Edom, southeast of the Dead Sea, an area populated by the descendants of Esau. Genesis 46:13 says that one "Job" was a descendant of Jacob's son Issachar, but it cannot be determined whether this is the same person who is named in this book.

The main point here is that the main character of the book, who will suffer so greatly, did not deserve it. If he had been anything but a righteous, God-fearing person, the ancient and universal tendency to assume that suffering results from unrighteousness would not be questioned, as it is in this book.

B. His wealth and happiness, 2-3

2 And there were born unto him seven sons and three daughters.

3 His substance also was seven thousand sheep, and three thousand camels, and five hundred yoke of oxen, and five hundred she asses, and a very great household; so that this man was the greatest of all the men of the east.

Readers who took very literally God's Old Covenant promise to bless the righteous and curse the wicked would not be surprised to learn of Job's large family and great wealth. The Covenant promise to the righteous was "Blessed shall be the fruit of thy body, and the fruit of thy ground, and the fruit of thy cattle . . . ." (Deut. 28:4). On the other hand, many assumed that lacking such wealth indicated God's retribution for wickedness (28:15ff.). The author is boldly setting up the great question of the ages in general and of the Covenant in particular: *Are the Covenant blessings and cursings to be taken literally and universally, and as having a direct relationship to our actions, good or bad?*

II. When Loss Occurs—8-11

8 And the Lord said unto Satan, Hast thou considered my servant Job, that there is none like him in the earth, a perfect and an upright man, one that feareth God, and escheweth evil?

9 Then Satan answered the Lord, and said, Doth Job fear God for nought?

10 Hast not thou made an hedge about him, and about his house, and about all that he hath on every side?

thou hast blessed the work of his hands, and his substance is increased in the land.

11 But put forth thine hand now, and touch all that he hath, and he will curse thee to thy face.

We may be shocked by the portrayal of God and Satan carrying on a conversation as though they are sitting on the front porch surveying, and boasting about, their separate kingdoms. The reader is not, however, to imagine that they are "on the same side," but only that they both inhabit the same spiritual realm, and both have those who serve them.

Satan is the Great Accuser; and here he accuses Job of serving God for gain. He has no more depth of commitment, Satan accuses, than the businessman who wants to be a member of the largest church in town because of the business contacts it affords. He supposes that "godliness is gain" (see 1 Tim. 6:5).

Satan's prediction that if God took away Job's blessings the man would "curse thee to thy face" is the central temptation of the book. While Job will curse his fate and his birth, the "test" is whether he will curse God. When a person fails to pass this test, it is an indication that he wrongly thinks that the good life really is defined by "the abundance of the things which he possesseth" (Luke 12:15).

III. When Life Is Threatened—2:3-6

3 And the Lord said unto Satan, Hast thou considered my servant Job, that there is none like him in the earth, a perfect and an upright man, one that feareth God, and escheweth evil? and still he holdeth fast his integrity, although thou movedst me against him, to destroy him without cause.

4 And Satan answered the Lord, and said, Skin for skin, yea, all that a man hath will he give for his life.

5 But put forth thine hand now, and touch his bone and his flesh, and he will curse thee to thy face.

6 And the Lord said unto Satan, Behold, he is in thine hand; but save his life.

Verse 3 repeats God's praise of Job from 1:8, since Job has passed the first test. As 1:13-22 has described, God allowed Satan to take away all of Job's family and possessions, stopping short only of visiting bodily affliction on him. (Throughout, the book of Job pictures God as "allowing" Job to suffer, rather than sending suffering Himself.)

Satan sees an opening to press Job's test further, arguing that it is one thing for a person to lose his loved ones and possessions, and quite another to lose his health, strength, and vitality. As though to prove Job's character, God consents for Satan to afflict him—but not to take his life. Actually, Job will prove the strength of his faith even in the face of death. The ringing victory of the entire story is expressed in Job's affirmation that "Though he slay me, yet will I trust him" (13:15).

In the meantime, however, Satan strikes Job with painful boils (NIV "sores"; see 2:7-10). Some have suggested that he had leprosy, others smallpox. Whatever the disease, it apparently created great itching, for Job takes refuge in ashes and abrading, or scraping his skin.

Job's wife is not helpful. She has the same naive notion about suffering that Job's friends express in the next lesson: it is the immediate result of wrong-doing. Therefore, she suggests that her husband commit the ultimate wrong of cursing God in order to be struck dead and put of his misery.

IV. 'Why Was I Born?'—3:1-3

1 After this opened Job his mouth, and cursed his day.

2 And Job spake, and said,

3 Let the day perish wherein I was born, and the night in which it was said, There is a man child conceived.

After Job's three friends sit with him sympathetically for the customary seven days of mourning, as though someone had died (2:11-13), he finally gives vent to his anguish. Because of his lament that he had been born in verse 3, we can assume that verse 1 means that he cursed his birthday (see also 1:4, where Job's sons apparently celebrated their birthdays with feasting).

Such a cry is hardly rare. Most people have the sense that they have been put here for a purpose; and we tend to ask what that purpose can possibly be if all we can do is hurt. If intense pain were not so all-consuming, perhaps we could remember the inspiration we have drawn from other people who endure pain bravely, and affirm such a purpose for our own suffering.

Note that despite wishing he had not been born, Job apparently does not consider taking his own life. This reflects the biblical view of the sacredness of life. Since man did not give himself life, he does not have the prerogative to take it. As Job said in 1:21, it is the Lord who gives life, and who alone has the right to take it away.

Evangelistic Emphasis

When things are going our way, we seldom pause to think about the meaning of life. We get on with getting more. When tragedy strikes, we often reassess our life. We examine where we have come so far. Sometimes we realize we drifted far from what we meant to be and do. We come finally to discern what is of lasting importance. We sometimes see how conflicts that consumed us were really not important. Relationships with friends and family have been too long neglected. In a time of trial we discover how shallow is our relationship with God, how feeble is our faith.

That same adversity, by God's grace, may cause us to reorder our priorities. With a new commitment we seek first the kingdom of God. We find a new peace from anxiously striving after things which perish.

What happens to us may happen to others. When illness, sorrow or tragedy strikes others we may need to be present with them. Our role is not to speak as did Job's friends, "What did you do to deserve this suffering?" Indeed it is not our role glibly to speak about the suffering. In standing by our friends and by standing with them, we can share our faith when they ask us. The crisis may bring a new beginning. The suffering may lead to a turning around, to a new birth. Our love, concern and presence may be like the service of a mid- wife in bringing to birth a new creature in Christ whom God is creating.

Memory Selection

And the Lord said to Satan, Hast thou considered my servant Job, that there is none like him in the earth, a perfect and upright man, one that feareth God, and escheweth evil: and still he holdeth fast his integrity, although thou movedst me against him, to destroy him without cause.—*Job 2:3*

The story of the testing of Job brings into focus the question of the motivation for serving God. In the ancient folk tale with which the book of Job begins, Satan insists that Job's loyalty and piety is because God has "put a fence around him." His wealth, his family, his health are the rewards of loyalty. Take these away, Satan argues, and Job will curse God.

It raises for us the question of the deepest motivation of our going to church, saying our prayers, giving to others. Is it done because we expect to be rewarded? Is it because we are afraid of God's judgment if we do not? In the story in chapters 1 & 2 Job responds to his wife's urging "Curse God and die" with an expression of faith: "Shall we receive the good at the hand of God and not receive the bad?" In the New Testament we find more explicitly that all of our Christian behavior is a response to a love already given by God, through Jesus Christ. "We love because He first loved us." (1 John 4:19)

Weekday Problems

On television we see the terrible suffering of refugees driven from their homes by war. We have seen the mass graves of the people of whole villages killed in ethnic purges. We read of the continued conflict of Protestant and Catholic in Northern Ireland. We read of the senseless bombings of air planes and public buildings. We see the effects of the ravages of AIDS. We wait helplessly as we see Alzheimer's wasting the minds and bodies of those we love. We see young children denied a chance at fullness of life because of cancer. We wonder what we can do to reach out to those who suffer.

When we consider the scope of human suffering in the world and our limited ability to offer a healing response, we can become overwhelmed. It is important that we respond to the suffering at hand in ways that are available to us. Otherwise we can be paralyzed with feelings of impotence and guilt. That will lead to despair, and we will become a part of the problem rather than a part of the solution. Let us be caring about all the suffering in the world, and let us be responsive to that which is within our reach and the scope of our ability.

* How is your church reaching out to those who suffer? Are there other ways you think it should help?

* How can Christians deal with the temptation of "paralysis"—to think that since we can't help everyone, we will do nothing?

Insights on Suffering

Suffering is a form of gratitude to experience or an opportunity to experience evil and change it into good.—*Saul Bellow,* in *Herzog.*

When I consider my crosses, tribulations, and temptations, I shame myself almost to death, thinking what are they in comparison of the sufferings of my blessed Savior Christ Jesus?—*Martin Luther*

Is it so, O Christ in heaven,
that the highest suffer most?
That the strongest wander farthest,
and more hopelessly are lost?
That the mark of rank in nature
is capacity for pain?
That the anguish of the singer
makes the sweetness of the strain?

—*Sarah Williams,* in *Is It So, O Christ in Heaven?*

407

This Lesson in Your Life

The book of Job raises the question of the reason for suffering. It questions the traditional, orthodox interpretation that suffering is punishment for sin. Through their many words, Job's friends provide no other interpretation of Job's misery than as a just punishment for his misdeeds. But Job knows he has done nothing to deserve such punishment, for he was "blameless and upright, one who feared God and turned away from evil" (Job 1:1). The author of the dialogues between Job and his friends, and between Job and God, demonstrates the inadequacy of the traditional, orthodox interpretation that suffering is punishment for sin. The book of Job does not offer a simple explanation.

As the Biblical story unfolds we see that sometimes suffering can be made to serve a good purpose. Paul writes: "We know that in everything God works for good with those who love him, who are called according to his purpose" (Rom. 8:28). Paul does not share the view that all suffering is sent as a punishment from God. He suffered much persecution because of his loyalty to Christ (2 Cor. 11:24-28). Paul learned and testified that even a "thorn in the flesh," while not sent as punishment for sin, could be made by the Lord into a source of blessing. God promised: "My grace is sufficient for you, for power is made perfect in weakness'" (2 Cor. 12: 7-9).

In the story of Jesus' suffering and death we learn that suffering can be redemptive. The very love of God is revealed in the offering of His Son. Jesus, through His death on the cross, lives out the words of the prophet Isaiah: "But he was wounded for our transgressions, crushed for our iniquities; upon him was the punishment that made us whole, and by his bruises we are healed" (Isa. 53:4-5).

The New Testament suggests that God can use suffering to strengthen us. It testifies that God can work through the suffering caused by evil and even bring good out of evil. It gives witness that the suffering of the innocent can be redemptive. Yet it nowhere offers a neat, simple explanation of the suffering of the innocent. What the New Testament offers is more important than an explanation of the mystery of suffering. In the presence of God with us in the midst of suffering, the gospel points us to a power greater than ourselves that enables us to master the suffering. It is not solving the mystery of suffering which is our greatest need. We may never find the answer to our anguished cry "Why" in the face of tragic accident, illness, war, flood and famine. The Scriptures do not solve the mystery. They point us to the One who enables us to continue, to survive, to master it, to become more than conquerors. It is this mastery that causes the apostle Paul to rejoice, "I have learned to be content with whatever I have. I know what it is to have little, and I know what it is to have plenty. In any and all circumstances I have learned the secret of being well-fed and of going hungry, of having plenty and of being in need. I can do all things through him who strengthens me" (Phil. 4: 11-13).

Seed Thoughts

1. Where does Job live?

Job lives in the land of Uz. (Job 1:1)

2. What kind of man is Job?

"That man was blameless and upright, one who feared God and turned away from evil? (Job 1:1) "He was the greatest of all the people of the east." (Job 1:3)

3. What did Job do after his sons held feasts in one another's houses?

Job would sanctify them, rising early in the morning and offering burnt offerings, in case they had sinned and cursed God in their hearts. (Job 1:5)

4. In the testing of Job, what did Job lose?

Five hundred yoke of oxen, seven thousand sheep, three thousand camels, his many servants, his seven sons and three daughters.

5. What was Job's wife's advice to him?

"Curse God and die." (Job 2:9)

---

1. Where does Job live?

2. What kind of man is Job?

3. What did Job do after his sons held feasts in one another's houses?

4. In the testing of Job, what did Job lose?

5. What was Job's wife's advice to him?

6. What response might you expect if you sang "Happy Birthday" to Job?

7. What Old Testament prophet cursed his birthday?

8. In Jesus' view, were the Galileans killed by Pilate worse sinners than all other Galileans? (Luke 13:2)

9. In Jesus' view were the eighteen killed when the tower of Siloam fell on them worse sinners than others?

10. Does Jesus, like Job, ever raise the question "why" concerning his suffering?

(Please turn page)

Job lives in the land of Uz. (Job 1:1)

"That man was blameless and upright, one who feared God and turned away from evil? (Job 1:1) "He was the greatest of all the people of the east" (Job 1:3).

Job would sanctify them, rising early in the morning and offering burnt offerings, in case they had sinned and cursed God in their hearts (Job 1:5).

Five hundred yoke of oxen, seven thousand sheep, three thousand camels, his many servants, his seven sons and three daughters.

"Curse God and die" (Job 2:9).

Job cursed the day of his birth: "Let the day perish in which I was born, and the night that said, 'A man-child is conceived'" (Job 3:1-3).

Jeremiah. "Cursed be the day on which I was born! The day when my mother bore me, let it not be blessed." (Jer. 20:14)

"No, I tell you, but unless you repent, you will all perish as they did." (Luke

"No, I tell you; but unless you repent, you will all perish just as they did." (Luke 13:5)

Yes. On the cross Jesus cries out with a loud voice "My God, my God, why have you forsaken me?" (Mark 15:34)

6. What response might you expect if you sang "Happy Birthday" to Job?

"Job cursed the day of his birth: "Let the day perish in which I was born, and the night that said, 'A man-child is conceived.'" (Job 3:1-3)

7. What Old Testament prophet cursed his birthday?

Jeremiah. "Cursed be the day on which I was born! The day when my mother bore me, let it not be blessed." (Jer. 20:14)

8. In Jesus' view, were the Galileans killed by Pilate worse sinners than all other Galileans? (Luke 13:2)

"No, I tell you, but unless you repent, you will all perish as they did." (Luke 13:3)

9. In Jesus' view were the eighteen killed when the tower of Siloam fell on them worse sinners than others?

"No, I tell you; but unless you repent, you will all perish just as they did." (Luke 13:5)

10. Does Jesus, like Job, ever raise the question "why" concerning his suffering?

Yes. On the cross Jesus cries out with a loud voice "My God, my God, why have you forsaken me?" (Mark 15:34)

410

Job's Unhelpful Friends

Job 2:11; 4:1, 6-7; 8:1-6; 13:1-4

2:11 Now when Job's three friends heard of all this evil that was come upon him they came every one from his place; Eliphaz the Temanite, and Bildad the Shuhite, and Zophar the Naamathite: for they had made an appointment together to come to mourn with him and comfort him.

4:1 Then Eliphaz the Temanite answered and said, ...

6 Is not this thy fear, thy confidence, thy hope, and the uprightness of thy ways?

7 Remember, I pray thee, who ever perished, being innocent? or where were the righteous cut off?

8:1 Then answered Bildad the Shuhite, and said,

2 How long wilt thou speak these things? and how long shall the words of thy mouth be like a strong wind?

3 Doth God pervert judgment? or doth the Almighty pervert justice?

4 If thy children have sinned against him, and he have cast them away for their transgressions;

5 If thou wouldest seek unto God betimes, and make thy supplication to the Almighty;

6 If thou wert pure and upright; surely now he would awake for thee, and make the habitation of thy righteousness prosperous.

13:1 Lo, mine eye hath seen all this, mine ear hath heard and understood it.

2 What ye know, the same do I know also: I am not inferior unto you.

3 Surely I would speak to the Almighty, and I desire to reason with God.

4 But ye are forgers of lies, ye are all physicians of no value.

Memory Seclection
Job 13:3

Devotional Reading
Job 7:1-11

Background Scripture
Job 2:11; 4:1-7; 8:1-7;
11:1-6; 13:1-4; 23:1-7

Printed Scripture
Job 2:11; 4:1, 6-7; 8:1-6;
13:1-4

Teacher's Target

Lesson purpose: *To challenge, through the story of Job and his friends, the assumption that all suffering is the result of wrong-doing.*

A missionary returned to the States and described the horrible living conditions of poor people in a foreign land. A Christian responded: "No wonder they aren't better off—they're not Christians."

Unfortunately, some people think that unbelief and sin always bring suffering, and that good fortune is the result of good works—as in the otherwise beautiful song from "The Sound of Music":

Nothing comes from nothing, / Nothing ever could,
So somewhere in my youth or childhood / I must have done something good.

In this class, correct this "tit-for-tat" theology. Encourage those who think "God got me for that" when they suffer. Challenge those who look down on sufferers as wrong-doers, and remind those who think their good fortune is the result of good works that God sends rain on both the just and the unjust" (Matt. 5:45).

Lesson Introduction

As Lesson 2 noted, God's Covenant with Israel included His promise of blessings for obedience and hardship for disobedience (see Deut. 28:1-6, 15-19; Joshua 24:20.) As a general rule, this kind of reciprocal arrangement is even the way the world works. We "sin" against the environment, and breathe foul air as a consequence. We are friendly to others, and they are friendly to us.

As everyone knows, however, there are important exceptions to the way the world generally works. We can break cycles of environmental harm by filtering factory smoke. Occasionally people to whom we are friendly do not reciprocate with friendliness.

The book of Job deals with this kind of exception to the rule. Although sin *sometimes* results in suffering, it must not be made a rule that over-rules God's sovereignty. "Reciprocal" theology that attaches inevitable blessing to doing right and suffering to doing wrong is closer to the Hindu concept of "karma" than it is to Christianity.

Teaching Outline	Daily Bible Readings
	Mon. Man Isn't Better Than His Maker *Job 4:1-11*
I. The Wisdom of Silence—2:11	
A. Job's friends, 11a	**Tue.** Job's Anguish in Spirit *Job 7:1-11*
B. The comfort of silence, 11b	
II. The Worst Advice—4:1, 6-7; 8:1-6	**Wed.** Bildad: God is Just *Job 8:1-10*
A. Errors by Eliphaz, 4:1, 6-7	
B. Blunders by Bildad, 8:1-6	**Thu.** Zophar: God Knows More *Job 11:1-12*
III. The Wish to Argue with God—13:1-4	
A. Equal to others in the audience, 1-2	**Fri.** Job: Laughingstock to His Friends *Job 12:1-12*
B. Appeal for an audience with God, 3-4	
	Sat. God Even Destroys Great Nations *Job 12:13-25*
	Sun. Arguing with God *Job 13:1-12*

VERSE BY VERSE

I. The Wisdom of Silence—2:11

A. Job's friends, 11a

11a Now when Job's three friends heard of all this evil that was come upon him they came everyone from his place; Eliphaz the Temanite, and Bildad the Shuhite, and Zophar the Naamathite:

Although Job's friends' view of suffering will anger God and fail to bless Job, they cannot be faulted for remaining aloof. They come to his side in his suffering. Many modern sufferers in our own isolationist and individualistic times have no such friends. In many communities such "ministries of visitation" are a vital way for Christians to serve.

The kingdoms and areas where Job's friends lived seem to have been close to his home in the "land of Uz" south of the Dead Sea.

B. The comfort of silence, 2:11b

11b for they had made an appointment together to come to mourn with him and comfort him.

Job's friends had another praiseworthy trait: they did not at first overwhelm him with conversation or explanations. Although they will not stick to this ministry of silence, they at least pay him the courtesy of not rushing to say "I know how you feel" and offering other

platitudes. Instead, they oberve a seven-day ritual of silence, similar to funeral customs in some lands.

Ironically, Job's three friends do their best comforting at this point—not later in the book when they attempt to explain why Job was suffering. The riddle of undeserved suffering has occupied the entire lives of many brilliant thinkers. Scripture raises the issue frequently, but we are not given many specifics beyond the invitation to trust in Christ's triumph over suffering in the resurrection. It is far better just to sit in silence with a suffering friend than to presume to provide answers.

II. The Worst Advice—4:1, 6-7; 8:1-6

A. Errors by Eliphaz, 4:1, 6-7

1 Then Eliphaz the Temanite answered and said . . . . .

6 Is not this thy fear, thy confidence, thy hope, and the uprightness of thy ways?

7 Remember, I pray thee, who ever perished, being innocent? or where were the righteous cut off?

Job's friend Eliphaz can keep silent no longer. His name possibly means "God is fine gold," and he wants to defend God as having the character of pure gold. Job has not yet accused God of injustice, but his complaints against life (chapter 3) might be taken as an indirect accusation, since God is the author of life. Eliphaz' view of why we suffer is better understood from the rendering in the NIV:

Should not your piety be your confidence and your blameless ways your hope? Consider now: Who, being innocent, has ever perished? Where were the upright ever destroyed? (vss. 6-7).

Eliphaz' naive but common view is that Job has done some evil to deserve the loss of his property and family, and the horrible disease that covered his body. Here is the tit-for-tat view mentioned above. It is also akin to salvation by works, which the apostle Paul will oppose hundreds of years later.

Job will correctly protest that he *is* a pious man. He is not perfect (7:20), but he has not sinned in proportion to the tragedies that have befallen him. Our own reply to Eliphaz' glib point of view might well be "Yes, the innocent *do* perish." The death of Christ on the Cross, and the martyrdom of thousands of His followers through the ages, are cases in point.

B. Blunders by Bildad, 8:1-6

1 Then answered Bildad the Shuhite, and said,

2 How long wilt thou speak these things? and how long shall the words of thy mouth be like a strong wind?

3 Doth God pervert judgment? or doth the Almighty pervert justice?

4 If thy children have sinned against him, and he have cast them away for their transgressions;

5 If thou wouldest seek unto God betimes, and make thy supplication to the Almighty;

6 If thou wert pure and upright; surely now he would awake for thee, and make the habitation of thy righteousness prosperous.

In chapters 6 and 7, after Job's first friend, Eliphaz, spoke, the classic sufferer had complained long and loud about his fate. His misery would outweigh the sand of the sea (6:3). True friends would offer more dependable counsel (6:14-15). He insists on continuing to complain "in the bitterness of my soul" (7:11). While he admits to being less than perfect, he wonders why God apparently will not forgive (7:20-22).

Now it is the second friend, Bildad's, turn. Some scholars think his name means "son of contention" or "debater." Verse 6 makes it clear that he agrees with Eliphaz' view that Job's suffering is the result of his sin; if he were righteous, God would be moved either to lift Job's burdens or give a reason for them.

To this argument Bildad adds the counsel that man is not made of the stuff required to probe into the mysteries of God: "We are but of yesterday, and know nothing, because our days upon earth are a shadow" (vs. 9). Apparently an older friend, Bildad urges Job to accept the long-standing, traditional views that he and Eliphaz have expressed.

Imagine standing by the bedside of a suffering friend and assuring him that unless he confesses the sin that brought on his sickness, God will not help him! This is Bildad's position (vs. 20).

III. The Wish to Argue with God—13:1-4

A. Equal to others in the audience, 1-2

1 Lo, mine eye hath seen all this, mine ear hath heard and understood it.

2 What ye know, the same do I know also: I am not inferior unto you.

Job has grown up with the traditional view that suffering is evidence of sin, and blessings proves one's righteousness. Ironically, his faith in God as a just and good God is why he protests so intensely. In the absence of grievous sin, it seems out of character for God to allow him to suffer so. He knows he is not perfect, but he at least is a believer; and he can see no difference in the way God treats him and unbelievers (9:20-22). Job is offended that his friends have presumed to answer his complaint with old arguments with which he has long been familiar. Like many others who suffer, traditional answers no longer seem to fit the question.

B. Appeal for an audience with God, 3-4

3 Surely I would speak to the Almighty, and I desire to reason with God.

4 But ye are forgers of lies, ye are all physicians of no value.

Job's desire to "reason with God" is surely understandable. God does not ask us to put our brains and reasoning power in neutral when we become Christians. Yet anyone who dares enter into a debate with God should remember that He has warned that "My thoughts are not your thoughts, neither are your ways my ways" (Isa. 55:8). As the next lesson will show, God reminds Job of this in forceful and eloquent terms. Of course if the mind of God were not greater than ours, we could hardly worship Him. Yet when we suffer, we often want to argue with Him as though we were on equal ground.

We can also understand Job's dissatisfaction with the adequacy of the views expressed by his friends. While half-agreeing with their point of view, and the system of suffering in retaliation for sin, the fact that he is not aware of such sin wrings from him the charge that they have lied. They have pulled from their philosophical medicine kit bromides that do not ease his pain.

Evangelistic Emphasis

In seeking to share our faith, it is often better to be silent than to speak. It is to the credit of the friends of Job that they went to him when they heard of his tragedies. It speaks well of them that they sat with him seven days and seven nights. They were more helpful  when they sat with him in silence than when they spoke. It was when they started trying to lay on him their traditional and trite answers that they proved less helpful.

In our commissioned task of sharing the gospel, we sometimes must earn the right to be heard. It is only when others know we care that they care to know.

We sometimes turn others off from the richness of the gospel when we have our views too neatly packaged. When our witness falls too glibly from our lips, like a canned or memorized speech. God's mystery and majesty is beyond our comprehension. When we begin to shout dogmatically that there is no other way to express the way God works than the way we say, we may be guilty of a greater arrogance than that of Job in demanding that God hear his case. When we glibly trot out our pat answers to every religious problem, we may do more harm than good. A silent presence, and empathetic listening, a love incarnate in deeds of service and acts of mercy may better communicate the love of God than many words of pompous pronouncements.

Memory Selection

Surely I would speak to the Almighty, and I desire to reason with God.—*Job 13:3*

Job gives expression to his desire to be in communion with God. It is a universal desire. The desire to know that God hears and understands us, to know God's will for us and to simply be in God's presence is deep in the heart of every person. We were created for this relationship with God, a relationship of trust, obedience and love.

Nothing else can finally satisfy this deep yearning to know and be known of God. We try to satisfy this deep desire to be in communion with God by success in work, recognition for our achievements, accumulation of things, new experiences and exotic pleasures. Back in the twelfth century Bernard of Clairvaux wrote: " From the best bliss that earth imparts, we turn unfilled to thee again."

Henri Nouwen writes: "God has given us a heart that will remain restless until it has found full communion. Jesus came to proclaim that our desire for communion is not in vain, but will be fulfilled by the One who gave that desire" (*Here and Now*, pp. 43,44).

Weekday Problems

Carole was weeping. She was a single parent. Her only son, John, age 15, had been killed in an automobile accident. He had been drinking, and driving too fast. He lost control of the car. Miraculously his date escaped unharmed. John was on the school football team, an honor roll student, popular with students and with his teachers. Why John?

Her friends came to visit. Susan said, "That's what he gets for drinking. You're lucky the girl wasn't killed also. Drinking and driving don't mix. You and your ex always had liquor in the house. It's no wonder he follows your example. If you and your husband had stayed together, his dad would have kept him under control. This would never have happened."

Her pastor called. "It's the will of God. We can't always see the reason for these things. Don't cry. John had accepted Jesus when he was six. We know he is better off with God. God took him from us to be with Him in heaven. We can be sure there's a blessing in it for us all. Maybe other teenagers will realize the evils of drinking and become total abstainers. The Lord gives. The Lord takes away. Praise the Lord."

Amy dropped by with a casserole. She sat quietly while Carole wept. She listened while Carole talked about her anger at John for drinking, her anger at God for John's death. She held her hand while Carole wondered what she should have done differently. Then Amy offered a simple prayer that God would be with her to comfort her.

* Which of the three do you think was most helpful to Carole?

* What would you say to Carole?

Riddled with Religion

Q: Who was the smallest man in the Bible?
A: Some say it was Ne-high-miah, or Bildad the Shu-hite. Actually, though it was Christ's disciple Peter. He slept on his watch.

Q: Where is deviled ham mentioned in the Bible?
A: Luke 8, where the evil spirits entered the swine.

Q: Where is high finance first mentioned in Scripture?
A: In Genesis, when Pharaoh's daughter took a little prophet from the bulrushes.

Q: Who was Round John Virgin?
A: One of the 12 Opossums.

Q: Who was the most popular actor in Scripture?
A: Samson. He brought the house down.

This Lesson in Your Life

The story of Job is the story of one struggling for a new way of thinking, a new perspective. For Job's friends, there was only one way to interpret suffering. It was punishment from God. If you suffered, you must have sinned. Disease, loss of livestock, even loss of family was a sure sign that you had sinned against God. It was the only way they had to look at the suffering of others.

Job knew that he had done nothing to deserve such tragedy. He steadfastly professes his innocence. He persistently asks for a chance to talk with God, to present his case. In the faith perspectives of his day, there was no other way to view human suffering. Job was breaking new ground with his persistent challenge to God.

In Job's speeches there is anger, despair, sometimes even arrogance. Yet somehow there seems to be even in his accusations against God an underlying faith which is lacking in his friends who simply repeat over and over again the single, narrow, inappropriate explanation of suffering. The poet Tennyson wrote: "There's more faith in honest doubt, believe me, than in half the creeds."

In his speeches there are momentary break-throughs, a wishing, a hoping, even a believing that there is another side of God. "There is no umpire between us who might lay his hand on us" (Job. 9:25). A human being cannot bridge the gap between an almighty and all righteous God. Ceremonies, rituals, and deeds are no avail. If only there were an umpire, a daysman, a mediator who could bring God and a human face to face! If only that great gap between Creator and creature could be bridged! Much later, in Christian thought Christ is described as that mediator, reconciler. "In Christ God was reconciling the world to himself" (2 Cor. 5:19).

Job insists "Even now, in fact, my witness is in heaven, and he that vouches for me is on high" (Job 16:19). The witness, an angelic being, or God's better self, is pleading his case. In the midst of the chorus of his friends insisting he repent, Job anticipates there is more to God than the One in their neat little formulas. Job will die but this will not mean the closing of his case. The witness will not bring a restoration of his worldly fortunes but will vindicate him. Centuries later in Christian thought the role of Christ is described as advocate. "But if anyone does sin, we have an advocate with the Father, Jesus Christ the righteous" (1 John 2:1).

Job is discontent with neatly packaged, simple but flawed solutions. He breaks ground for a new way of thinking, a new way of seeing. Even when he seems to have no hope that he will live, no hope that he will receive vindication in his lifetime, he voices a hope that ultimately vindication will come. "For I know that my Redeemer lives and that at the last he will stand upon the earth" (Job 19:25). The Hebrew word for "redeemer" denotes the duty of a relative to protect and defend the rights of a member of his family who was in trouble. His innocence will be vindicated. This redeemer will live beyond Job's death and usher him into God's presence. But now Job expects neither reward or clearance. The vision of God is enough. "Then in my flesh I shall see God, whom I shall see on my side and my eyes shall behold and not another" (Job 19:26-27). In the New Testament "Redeemer" takes on a richer connotation of redemption from sin. Paul writes of Christ: "In him we have redemption through his blood, the forgiveness of our trespasses according to the riches of his grace" (Eph. 1:7).

Job, in daring to challenge God, in claiming a hearing in the divine court, prepares the way for a new way of understanding suffering and anticipates the necessity of a Christ.

Seed Thoughts

Eliphaz the Temanite, Bildad the Shuhite, and Zophar the Naamathite (Job 2:11)

2. How long did Job's friends sit in silence with him?

"They sat with him on the ground seven days and seven nights, and no one spoke a word to him" (Job 2:13).

3. What images of the brevity of life does Job use?

a) A weaver's shuttle 7:6; b) a runner 9:25; c) skiffs of reed 9:26; d) an eagle swooping on the prey 9:26

4. What passages in Job express his hope of some final vindication before God?

His wish for a mediator (9:33); "My witness is in heaven and vouches for me" (16:19); "I know that my redeemer lives . . . I shall see God" (19:25).

5. For Eliphaz what is the basis of confidence and hope?

4:5 Fear of God is your confidence, and the integrity of your ways is your hope.

(Please turn page)

1. What are the names of Job's friends?

2. How long did Job's friends sit in silence with him?

3. What images of the brevity of life does Job use?

4. What passages in Job express his hope of some final vindication before God?

5. For Eliphaz what is the basis of confidence and hope?

6. For Bildad what are the conditions of restoration for Job?

7. What question does Zophar ask to remind Job of the limits of his wisdom?

8. What is Job's chief desire?

9. If Job could find God what would he do?

10. What does Job believe the ultimate outcome of such a meeting with God would

Eliphaz the Temanite, Bildad the Shuhite, and Zophar the Naamathite (Job 2:11)

"They sat with him on the ground seven days and seven nights, and no one spoke a word to him" (Job 2:13).

a) A weaver's shuttle 7:6; b) a runner 9:25; c) skiffs of reed 9:26; d) an eagle swooping on the prey 9:26

His wish for a mediator (9:33); "My witness is in heaven and vouches for me" (16:19); "I know that my redeemer lives . . . I shall see God" (19:25).

4:5 Fear of God is your confidence, and the integrity of your ways is your hope.

"If you will seek God and make supplication to the Almighty, if you are pure and upright, surely then he will restore to you your rightful place" (Job 8:5-6).

"Can you find out the deep things of God? Can you find out the limit of the Almighty?" (Job 11:7).

"I would speak to the Almighty, and I desire to argue my case with God" (Job 12:3).

"I would lay my case before him. I would learn what he would answer me" (Job 23:4-5).

"I should be acquitted forever by my judge" (Job 23:7).

6. For Bildad what are the conditions of restoration for Job?

"If you will seek God and make supplication to the Almighty, if you are pure and upright, surely then he will restore to you your rightful place" (Job 8:5-6).

7. What question does Zophar ask to remind Job of the limits of his wisdom?

"Can you find out the deep things of God? Can you find out the limit of the Almighty?" (Job 11:7).

8. What is Job's chief desire?

"I would speak to the Almighty, and I desire to argue my case with God" (Job 12:3).

9. If Job could find God what would he do?

"I would lay my case before him. I would learn what he would answer me" (Job 23:4-5).

10. What does Job believe the ultimate outcome of such a meeting with God would accomplish?

"I should be acquitted forever by my judge" (Job 23:7).

God's Questions and Job's Response

Job 38:1-7; 42:1-6, 10

1 Then the Lord answered Job out of the whirlwind, and said,

2 Who is this that darkeneth counsel by words without knowledge?

3 Gird up now thy loins like a man; for I will demand of thee, and answer thou me.

4 Where wast thou when I laid the foundations of the earth? declare, if thou hast understanding.

5 Who hath laid the measures thereof, if thou knowest? or who hath stretched the line upon it?

6 Whereupon are the foundations thereof fastened? or who laid the corner stone thereof;

7 When the morning stars sang together, and all the sons of God shouted for joy?

42:1 Then Job answered the Lord, and said,

2 I know that thou canst do every thing, and that no thought can be withholden from thee.

3 Who is he that hideth counsel without knowledge? therefore have I uttered that I understood not; things too wonderful for me, which I knew not.

4 Hear, I beseech thee, and I will speak: I will demand of thee, and declare thou unto me.

5 I have heard by the hearing of the ear: but now mine eye seeth thee.

6 Wherefore I abhor myself, and repent in dust and ashes.

10 And the Lord turned the captivity of Job, when he prayed for his friends: also the Lord gave Job twice as much as he had before.

Memory Selection
Job 42:1-2

Devotional Reading
Job 28:20-28

Background Scripture
Job 38:1-7; 42:1-6, 10

Printed Scripture
Job 38:1-7; 42:1-6, 10

Teacher's Target

Lesson purpose: *To use Job's encounter with God to reflect on His majesty, and the limits of our capacity to understand His ways.*

The surprise ending of the story of Job, in which "the Lord blessed the latter end of Job more than his beginning" (42:12), reassures us that we can trust and serve God despite our questions about His ways. Yet it does not *answer* those questions.

In presenting the lesson, the teacher should note two precautions. First, the happy ending does not "compensate" for Job's earlier tragedies. His ultimately happy state illustrates the creative power of God to wrest good from evil; but to treat it as a "reason" for Job's previous suffering—so he would wind up with more than he had before—is to trivialize his previous suffering, not to mention that of his first family.

Second, the blessings God showers on Job at the end should not be allowed to obscure Job's heroic faith during the dark days. The triumph of Job is not in receiving riches for enduring, but in affirming his faith even when they were taken away.

Lesson Introduction

In the chapters between our last lesson and this one, Job's third friend Zophar has his turn at speaking on why we suffer, continuing the argument that suffering is the result of sin. Job continues to protest that his pain is out of all proportion to whatever sins he has committed. A fourth counselor, Elihu, argues that suffering's purpose is to point man to God (see 33:29-30).

In a general sense, suffering *is* the result of sin, since suffering entered the world as a result of the Fall of man in Genesis 3, . It may also result from sins that bring woes on ourselves—as in living a life of crime and being shot by a fellow gangster. What Job cannot accept is the notion that God always sends punishment for *specific* sins. As we have noted, Jesus upheld this view when He said that God "sendeth rain on the just and on the unjust" (Matt. 5:45).

Teaching Outline	Daily Bible Readings

I. The Majesty of God—38:1-7
  A. Words without knowledge, 1-2
  B. Where were you?, 3-7
II. The Meager Resources of Man—42:1-6
  A. Confession, 1-3
  B. Petition, 4
  C. Worship, 5-6
III. The Ministry of Suffering—10
  A. Grace for Anger, 10a
  B. Gifts for loss, 10b
	Mon. Larger Mystery of Creation
	 Job 38:1-7
	Tue. Job Has Heard and Seen
	 Job 42:1-10
	Wed. Stand in Awe Before God
	 Ecclesiastes 3:9-17
	Thu. Fear of God Is Wisdom
	 Job 28:20-28
	Fri. Full of the Knowledge of God
	 ' *Isaiah 11:1-9*
	Sat. God Gives Us Dignity
	 Psalm 8:1-9
	Sun. God's Way
	 John 14:1-7

VERSE BY VERSE

I. The Majesty of God—38:1-7

A. Words without knowledge, 1-2

1 Then the Lord answered Job out of the whirlwind, and said,

2 Who is this that darkeneth counsel by words without knowledge?

God has heard enough. He breaks into the attempts to explain His ways with four chapters challenging the debaters' competence even to discuss the topic of innocent suffering. God's question, "Who is this that darkeneth counsel by words without knowledge?" can apply both to Job and his four counselors. Job has dared question the justice of God, and his counselors have presumed to know the mind of God. Theirs is the greater sin.

The first remarkable thing to notice is that God finally speaks with Job. He condescends to answer Job's plea in 13:3—"I desire to reason with God." Although God rebukes everyone involved in the dialogue for speaking of matters that are beyond them, He does not join the chorus that has accused Job of sin. Perhaps we are to learn from this that it is no sin to argue with God! Sincere and earnest questions can bring us into His presence better when pretending to know more about Him than He has told us.

God's speaking face to face with Job prompts the elegant profession of faith made famous in Handel's "Messiah"— "I know that my redeemer liveth, and that he shall stand at the latter day upon the earth: And though after my skin worms destroy this body, yet in my flesh shall I see God" (19:25).

It is possible, but doubtful, that this is a prophecy of the Messiah. Since there is no other evidence that Job knew of the concept, it is more likely a generalized expectation that he will somehow "see" an explanation for his suffering.

B. Where were you?, 3-7

3 Gird up now thy loins like a man; for I will demand of thee, and answer thou me.

4 Where wast thou when I laid the foundations of the earth? declare, if thou hast understanding.

5 Who hath laid the measures thereof, if thou knowest? or who hath stretched the line upon it?

6 Whereupon are the foundations thereof fastened? or who laid the corner stone thereof;

7 When the morning stars sang together, and all the sons of God shouted for joy?

How ironic for the creature to put his Creator on trial! God properly reverses the process by challenging Job to "gird up his loins," or tuck the long robe of the Middle Easterner into his waistband after the manner of wrestlers squaring off against each other. Then God proceeds to question man instead of feeling obligated to answer man's questions. Man has not "stretched the line" or measured the earth. He did not lay its foundations or create the starry heavens. (See the rest of the chapter for similar contrasts between divinity and humanity.)

Someone has carelessly charged that while Job asks for an answer to suffering in terms of justice, God only answers in terms of size. This shallow view misses the point. God is drawing out the eternal difference between divinity and humanity in order to show that He is fully worthy to receive man's worship, even when He does not answer all our questions. He states His superiority not to humiliate man, but to make the point that divinity cannot be weighed in humanity's balance scales. God *invented* the scales of justice and ethics; it is ludicrous to envision Him climbing down from His throne and lying on them himself.

The references to creation remind us that God's main work is the cosmic task of holding reality together. Like a man going to work over the protest of his four-year-old, who isn't through asking the endless question, "Why?", it is more important for God to be God than to pause to answer our own endless questions.

II. The Meager Resources of Man — 42:1-6

A. Confession, 1-3

1 Then Job answered the Lord, and said,

2 I know that thou canst do every thing, and that no thought can be withholden from thee.

3 Who is he that hideth counsel without knowledge? therefore have I uttered that I understood not; things too wonderful for me, which I knew not.

Stunned by God's presence and voice, Job responds first—and appropriately— by confessing that he has spoken out of turn by accusing God of being unjust. Not only can God do all the mighty works of creation and world-maintenance recited in chapters 38-41, He can even probe thoughts. This is important; for Job and His friends have been engaged in the very task of reading God's mind. Here Job finally confesses that only God reads minds.

In asking "Who is he that hideth counsel," Job echoes God's question in 38:3. It's as though he confesses, "*I* did; and I'm sorry."

B. Petition, 4

4 Hear, I beseech thee, and I will speak: I will demand of thee, and declare thou unto me.

Recovering somewhat from his being addressed by God, Job regains enough boldness to ask Him for a hearing. It is not presumptuous to beg for God to listen to our heartfelt pleas for release from suffering, or for Him to hear our intercessory prayers in behalf of others. Job has confessed that he may not be able to understand God, and he is merely doing what Jesus counseled in his parable of the unjust judge: coming to God in persistent prayer. (See Luke 18:1-8.)

C. Worship, 5-6

5 I have heard by the hearing of the ear: but now mine eye seeth thee.

6 Wherefore I abhor myself, and repent in dust and ashes.

God's overall purpose for Job is realized in consenting to be *present* with him, not to answer his questions. Were He to impart to man divine knowledge of the purpose for all suffering, man would be divine, not human. It is best for God to portray Himself in His true might and majesty, as He has done, so man will realize He is worthy of worship.

Note also that finally seeing God's true purpose (not a vision of God with a body) enables Job to worship with a sense of intimacy and warmth. His penitence is so thorough that his worship is heartfelt, not merely resigned and resentful at the lack of an explanation for all he has gone through.

III. The Ministry of Suffering—10

A. Grace for Anger, 10a

10a And the Lord turned the captivity of Job, when he prayed for his friends:

In verses 7-9 God has expressed anger at the counsel Job's three friends, who falsely accused Job of sin great enough to result in the loss of his family, estate, and health. Since Job has finally come into a closer relationship with God, he is told to offer sacrifices and pray for his three friends. His being able to do so is evidence that he has been released from the "captivity" of his anger.

Can you imagine a person who has been so unjustly accused as Job, returning good for evil? Yes, if you have ever reflected extensively on the forgiveness God has extended you. Job has discovered a depth of grace he could not have known apart from his own suffering, and subsequent release. While, as we have said, the book of Job does not give a systematic and thorough reason for innocent suffering, we learn here that one way to wring meaning from it is to allow it to soften our spirits toward those who oppose us to the extent that we can pray for them. This is also the high calling of Jesus (see Matt. 5:43-48); and believing sufferers are privileged to share that ministry with their Lord.

B. Gifts for loss, 10b

10b also the Lord gave Job twice as much as he had before.

We leave Job with a new estate, renewed fellowship with his extended family, and a new family of his own (see vss. 11-13). Yet these surprising gifts are hardly more miraculous than Job's earlier determination to trust God "though he slay me" (13:15); and his gift of being able to intercede for his friends, who had acted more like enemies.

The book of Job's probe of the problem of suffering leaves us not with a philosophical answer to the problem of suffering, but with a call to worship, and to patience—the patience of Job.

Evangelistic Emphasis

After his encounter with the Lord, Job testified: "I had heard of thee by the hearing of the ear, but now my eye sees thee" (Job 42:5). It is one thing to know about God. It is life changing to know God in one's own experience.

In many ways the Church seeks to share the knowledge of God's love with others. The Bible gives witness to God's redemptive love. Faithful teachers of Bible classes help us to understand the Bible stories. Preachers never tire of telling the old, old story of Jesus and his love. What makes our witness effective is when we tell how God has dealt with us. It is through personal experience that we appropriate that truth for ourselves. We know that our sins have been forgiven. We know we stand in the holy presence of God. God becomes not an abstract idea but living reality, a real Person who loves us.

The great transition that Job makes from "hearing of the ear" to seeing for himself is an essential step to our sharing the faith. We can't share what we don't have. It's hard to lead others where we have not been.

Our five-year-old grandson was puzzled by a hump in the rug. His grandmother explained the hump was caused by the connection from the extension cord which ran from the wall plug on one side of the room to the lamp on the other. It was not until this inquisitive lad lifted up the rug, pointed the beam of his flashlight and saw for himself, with his own eyes, that he really understood. May God grant us such persistence until we see God face to face.

Memory Selection

Then Job answered the Lord, and said, I know that Thou canst do everything, and that no thought can be withholden from thee.—*Job 42:1-2*

In the Revised Standard Version, this verse is translated: "I know . . . that no purpose of thine can be thwarted." Years ago a movie was made in which the star, Deborah Kerr played the role of a Christian martyr in Rome during the persecution of Christians. The character she played was to be thrown to the lions. A reporter asked Miss Kerr if that experience of being in the arena with all those lions frightened her. She replied: "Oh no, I've read the script through to the end." Christians are those who live each day as those who have read the script through to the end.

What God has purposed, God will accomplish. What God has started, God will finish. "No purpose of thine can be thwarted" (Job 42:2). So we pray, "Thy kingdom come, thy will be done."

Weekday Problems

John was a bright boy six years of age. He was fascinated by butterflies, creeping bugs, pretty flowers and agile squirrels. Everything about life seemed to fascinate him. Viewing the world through his eyes was like seeing the world for the first time. He took joy in life. Each new day brought new opportunities to explore.

Then he was struck with a fatal disease. In a matter of weeks he died. All that joy and love seemed suddenly snuffed out. His young life, so full of promise, seemed wasted.

Yet that tragic death was held in a larger context of God's love. This precious one was made in God's image. This little boy was created to love God, and to receive God's love, to give love to others and to receive love from others. His parents were sustained by a faith that allowed them to entrust their precious child to God's love, in whose love he still lives. All that was promised would find fulfillment. All that was potential, in God's time and way, would be realized. God's will would not be thwarted. God's plan would not be defeated. Nothing could separate that child from God's love, neither death nor life.

By God's grace, in time of grief and sorrow, in times of unexplainable suffering, we are enabled to affirm with Job: "I know that thou canst do all things, and that no purpose of thine can be thwarted" (Job 42:2).

Human Reason—Pro and Con

The authority of reason is far more imperious than that of a teacher; for he who disobeys the one is unhappy, but he who disobeys the other is a fool. —*Pascal*

"Theirs is not to make reply, theirs not to reason why," may be a good enough motto for men who are on their way to be shot. But from such men expect no empires to be builded, no inventions made, no great discoveries brought to light.—*Bruce Barton*

How can (the) finite grasp infinity?—*Dryden*

The heart has reasons that reason does not understand.—*Bossuet*

Reason is our intellectual eye, and like the bodily eye it needs light to see; and to see clearly and far it needs the light of heaven.—*Anon.*

This Lesson in Your Life

Job concludes: "I know that no purpose of thine can be thwarted" (Job 42:2). The ultimate end of God's creation is not uncertain, hanging in the balance, up for grabs. We may not be on earth to see God's final victory. Job's affirmation "no purpose of thine can be thwarted" is reinforced throughout the Bible. The perspective of faith sees a divinely appointed destiny toward which all human history moves. The poet celebrates it: "Though the wrong seems oft so strong, God is the ruler yet." We pray each day: "Thine is the kingdom and the power and the glory."

We view the cross in different, even conflicting ways, both providing a partial glimpse of the truth. In one view, it is the free act of Jesus, voluntarily taking up the cross, to fulfill his Messianic role through suffering. He is no helpless victim. He set his face steadfastly to go to Jerusalem. He is obedient even unto death. At the same time the Church sees the crucifixion of Christ in a cosmic setting. So Paul asserts: "We are redeemed through Jesus Christ whom God put forward." John declares: "God so loved the world that he gave his only son." This cosmic drama of redemption is not only the free choice of Jesus but was a part of God's redemptive plan from the beginning. Job comes to see "No purpose of thine can be thwarted."

There are mysteries in life. Mark Trotter observes: "Some mysteries clear up as we grow older. A little boy wonders who would ever want to kiss a girl. But one day he will understand. There are also mysteries which are enhanced by knowledge. The more you know, the greater the mystery. Immature scientists talk about the laws of the universe. Mature scientists talk about the mystery of the world. More knowledge in science does not erase the mystery from the world, it heightens it. God is not a mystery that more knowledge will explain. The more God reveals to us, the more wonderful God is to us. The more God reveals to us, the more mysterious God becomes. More knowledge about God does not lead to more information about God. It leads to worship. 'God's judgments are unsearchable and God's ways are inscrutable' (Rom 11:33)" (*Grace All the Way Home*).

Any morning newspaper, any evening telecast, any visit to a hospital, any visit to the inner city of any city can confront us with suffering, pain, infirmity, disease, hunger, homelessness and violence. Good people suffer. The book of Job does not provide a reason why.

Job and Biblical witnesses after him point us to resources to sustain our hearts. The apostle Paul does not promise an escape from tribulation, nor an explanation for the dark mystery of suffering. Rather it is Paul's testimony that "If God be for us, who is against us? Who will separate us from the love of Christ. No, in all these things we are more than conquerors through him who loves us" (Rom. 8:31, 35, 37). In Job's words: "No purpose of thine can be thwarted" (Job 42:2).

Seed Thoughts

1. What parts of God's creation are mentioned in the Lord's first speech to Job (Job:38)?

Foundations of the earth, the sea, morning, springs, earth, light, darkness, lightning, snow, hail, wind, rain, constellations, and clouds.

2. What animals are mentioned (Job 39)?

Mountain goats, wild ass, wild ox, ostrich, horse, hawk, eagle.

3. What great monsters are mentioned in chapters 40–41?

Behemoth (hippopotamus) and Leviathan (crocodile).

4. What hymn reflect Job's faith that the purposes of God cannot be thwarted?

"Fairest Lord Jesus": "Though the wrong seems oft so strong, God is the ruler yet."

5. What New Testament writer expresses an awe, similar to Job's, before the mystery of God's will and rule?

Paul in Romans 11:33: "O the depth of the riches and wisdom and knowledge of God! How unsearchable are his judgments and how inscrutable his ways."

---

1. What parts of God's creation are mentioned in the Lord's first speech to Job? (Job:38)

2. What animals are mentioned? (Job 39)

3. What great monsters are mentioned in chapters 40–41?

4. What hymn reflect Job's faith that the purposes of God cannot be thwarted?

5. What New Testament writer expresses an awe similar to Job's, before the mystery of God's will and rule?

6. What was the condition for God's restoring the fortunes of Job?

7. How many more years did Job live after being tested by the Lord?

8. How many sons and daughters did Job have after the test?

9. What were the names of the three daughters given to Job after the test?

10. How were Job's daughters described?

(Please turn page)

Foundations of the earth, the sea, morning, springs, earth, light, darkness, lightning, snow, hail, wind, rain, constellations, and clouds.

Mountain goats, wild ass, wild ox, ostrich, horse, hawk, eagle.

Behemoth (hippopotamus) and Leviathan (crocodile).

"This is My Father's World"—"Though the wrong seems oft so strong, God is the ruler yet."

Paul in Romans 11:33: "O the depth of the riches and wisdom and knowledge of God! How unsearchable are his judgments and how inscrutable his ways."

"Now the Lord restored the fortunes of Job *when he had prayed for his friends*" *(Job 42:10).*

"And after this Job lived a hundred and four years" (Job 42:16).

Job had seven sons and three daughters (Job 42:13).

Jemima, Kezia, and Keren-happuch (Job 42:14).

In all the land there were no women so fair as Job's daughters (Job 42:15).

6. What was the condition for God's restoring the fortunes of Job?

"Now the Lord restored the fortunes of Job *when he had prayed for his friends*" *(Job 42:10).*

7. How many more years did Job live after being tested by the Lord?

"And after this Job lived a hundred and four years" (Job 42:16).

8. How many sons and daughters did Job have after the test?

Job had seven sons and three daughters (Job 42:13).

9. What were the names of the three daughters given to Job after the test?

Jemima, Kezia, and Keren-happuch (Job 42:14).

10. How were Job's daughters described?

In all the land there were no women so fair as Job's daughters (Job 42:15).

Lesson 5

Listen to Wisdom

Proverbs 2:1-15

1 My son, if thou wilt receive my words, and hide my commandments with thee;

2 So that thou incline thine ear unto wisdom, and apply thine heart to understanding;

3 Yea, if thou criest after knowledge, and liftest up thy voice for understanding;

4 If thou seekest her as silver, and searchest for her as for hid treasures;

5 Then shalt thou understand the fear of the Lord, and find the knowledge of God.

6 For the Lord giveth wisdom: out of his mouth cometh knowledge and understanding.

7 He layeth up sound wisdom for the righteous: he is a buckler to them that walk uprightly.

8 He keepeth the paths of judgment, and preserveth the way of his saints.

9 Then shalt thou understand righteousness, and judgment, and equity; yea, every good path.

10 When wisdom entereth into thine heart, and knowledge is pleasant unto thy soul;

11 Discretion shall preserve thee, understanding shall keep thee:

12 To deliver thee from the way of the evil man, from the man that speaketh froward things;

13 Who leave the paths of uprightness, to walk in the ways of darkness;

14 Who rejoice to do evil, and delight in the frowardness of the wicked;

15 Whose ways are crooked, and they froward in their paths:

Memory Selection
Proverbs 2:6

Devotional Reading
Psalm 53:1-6

Background Scripture
Proverbs 2:1-15

Printed Scripture
Proverbs 2:1-15

Teacher's Target

Lesson purpose: *To examine the blessings of true wisdom and how to attain it, as described in the book of Proverbs.*

A good way to introduce this lesson is to ask the group to describe how life has become more complicated in their lifetime. Some older people have seen transportation go from horse-drawn buggies to supersonic jets. Whereas a "shade-tree mechanic" could set any old car to running only 20 years ago, computers are needed now just to diagnose a problem. While chewing gum in class was the main discipline issue in schools a generation ago, *guns* in class are now a problem.

Then point out how desperately we need *wisdom* to cope with such changes. Talk about the difference between wisdom and *knowledge*, noting that while the world isn't short on knowledge, how to use it often escapes us. This leads us to the definition of wisdom and how to attain it as outlined in the book of Proverbs.

Lesson Introduction

Most of Proverbs is said to have been written by King Solomon (1:1, 9:1). In English, the word "proverb" literally means a "before-word." It is a brief maxim that equips us with information or wisdom to face life before it "happens" to us. The book of Proverbs collects many of these sayings almost at random, except for the first nine chapters which are more deliberately organized around the topic of true wisdom.

This is Hebrew poetry, in which thoughts, not words, "rhyme." The lines may be in "antithetical parallelism," with the second line contrasting with the first (as in 1:7); or "synonymous parallelism," with the second line repeating the thought in the first (1:8).

The Bible insists that true wisdom comes from believing and obeying God, rather than learning the ways of the world. Fools are not those who lack knowledge, but who say "No" to God.

Teaching Outline	Daily Bible Readings
I. The Road to Wisdom—2:1-6	**Mon.** Wisdom Begins with God *Proverbs 1:1-7*
A. Receiving, 1	**Tue.** Guard Against Sinners *Proverbs 1:18-19*
B. Seeking, 2-4	**Wed.** Seek Wisdom and You'll Find *Proverbs 2:1-15*
C. Locating, 5-6	**Thu.** Wise Persons Look for God *Psalm 53:1-7*
II. The Rewards of Wisdom—7-15	**Fri.** Established in the Word *Psalm 119:129-136*
A. Protection, 7-8	**Sat.** Be Hearers and Doers *James 1:22-27*
B. Understanding, 9-11	**Sun.** Delight in the Law *Psalm 1*
C. Deliverance, 12-15	

VERSE BY VERSE

I. The Road to Wisdom—2:1-6

A. Receiving, 1

1 My son, if thou wilt receive my words, and hide my commandments with thee;

We are probably to understand that the author, the wise man, is speaking here, although in 1:20 "Wisdom" herself speaks. This "personification" of wisdom is common in Proverbs 1–9; but because wisdom is used as a thing to be gained in verse 2, it is more likely that we are to envision a wise teacher addressing a young "apprentice" or learner. "Son" often has that meaning, rather than a male offspring—as the old priest Eli called the young apprentice priest Samuel "my son" (1 Sam. 3:6).

The topic is how to gain wisdom, which is here equated with the wise man's "words" or "utterances." Note that the first qualification for gaining wisdom is *receptivity*. This is particularly appropriate in urging youth to follow the path of wisdom, since youth is a stage during which we are so often non-receptive or even rebellious toward receiving instruction. To hide the wise man's words or commandments in the heart shows their value, and the effort we are to put forth to keep them from slipping away. People who have thus "tucked away" or internalized scripture passages in their youth have a treasure to draw from in all kinds of situations.

B. Seeking, 2-4

2 So that thou incline thine ear unto wisdom, and apply thine heart to understanding;

3 Yea, if thou criest after knowledge, and liftest up thy voice for understanding;

4 If thou seekest her as silver, and searchest for her as for hid treasures;

The process of attaining wisdom is racheted up a notch from the more passive advice to be receptive to the more aggressive postures of *inclining toward, applying, crying after, seeking, and searching*. Such intense desire for wisdom is illustrated in the ancient story of a young man who came to a Greek philosopher, saying he sought wisdom. The philosopher is supposed to have led him to the sea and plunged him under water. Of course the young man fought for air, his flailing arms and violent convulsions finally convincing the philosopher to release him. The philosopher explained that he could not teach the young man wisdom until he wanted it as much as he wanted air while under water. Could it be that much modern confusion and bewilderment comes from simply not putting forth enough effort to gain wisdom?

What is this thing called wisdom? Sometimes we think of it as the possession of a guru atop a faraway mountain. However, the Hebrew word used here for wisdom, *hokmah*, is a word "from the trenches." Sometimes it actually means "skill in warfare" (see Isa. 10:13). It can also mean shrewdness in business dealings, and technical ability like that of a master craftsman. It is sound insight into God-fearing morality, and the way the world should work.

In keeping with the "synonymous parallelism" of Hebrew poetry (see the Lesson Introduction), "my words" and "commandments" in verse 1, and "understanding" and "knowledge" in verses 2-3 mean virtually the same thing.

C. Locating, 5-6

5 Then shalt thou understand the fear of the Lord, and find the knowledge of God.

6 For the Lord giveth wisdom: out of his mouth cometh knowledge and understanding.

Where is wisdom to be found? The book of Proverbs consistently answers that it comes from God, and "the fear of the Lord," which is "the beginning of wisdom" (9:10; see also 1:7). This does not mean that we cannot gain wisdom from sources other than the Bible. Solomon himself was occupied with scientific learning as well as theology (see 1 Kings 4:33). He examined the world, however, in the light of God. For him, creation was another "word" from God akin to the Law. Solomon knew that it is only fools who say "There is no God" (Ps. 53:1).

"The fear of the Lord" in this context does not mean fright at His awesome power, but a reverent and obedient attitude, and the willingness to acknowledge that He is the source of wisdom. In Scripture's value system, a simple person who fears (reverences) God is wiser than a person who knows everything except the importance of faith in God and

obedience to His will.

II. The Rewards of Wisdom—7-15

A. Protection, 7-8

7 He layeth up sound wisdom for the righteous: he is a buckler to them that walk uprightly.

8 He keepeth the paths of judgment, and preserveth the way of his saints.

Imagine walking down a lonely Palestinian road at night with no light to dispel the darkness and no weapon to defend against robbers. Solomon teaches that those who are wise because they fear God need not fear the darkness. Godly wisdom becomes the "buckler" from which hangs our sword of defense (or, see the niv, "shield"). God, the source of wisdom, "keeps" or protects the path down which a believer walks. (Remember that "saints" in biblical use refers to those "set apart for God's service," not perfect people, or the dead that have been elevated to a special position for popular worship.)

B. Understanding, 9-11

9 Then shalt thou understand righteousness, and judgment, and equity; yea, every good path.

10 When wisdom entereth into thine heart, and knowledge is pleasant unto thy soul;

11 Discretion shall preserve thee, understanding shall keep thee:

Which principles by which people live—which laws made by governments— are just and good, and which are harmful? Which direction should we take in life? Answers to such questions escape those who ask them outside the context of obedience to the will of God, or else they are forced to make up their own standards. Those for whom the wisdom and knowledge of God are "pleasant" have the advantage of a solid base for making such decisions. (Incidentally, there is an important implication for parents here regarding the attitude their children have toward school, and toward learning in general. If the conversation and attitudes in the home reflect on learning as "pleasant," children are more likely to have a positive attitude toward getting a good education.)

Note again the words the author piles up to describe the effects or rewards of wisdom: *righteousness, judgment, equity, the good path, knowledge, discretion,* and *understanding.* Solomon remains the model of all this, as exemplified in the famous story of the judgment he rendered in the case of the child whom two women each claimed was her own (1 Kings 3:16-28).

C. Deliverance, 12-15

12 To deliver thee from the way of the evil man, from the man that speaketh froward things;

13 Who leave the paths of upright- ness, to walk in the ways of darkness;

14 Who rejoice to do evil, and delight in the frowardness of the wicked;

15 Whose ways are crooked, and they froward in their paths:

Wisdom is not simply a nice commodity to have around; it also equips believers with philosophical radar, night vision, and other defenses against attacks from fools or the "froward." This word isn't just a King James spelling of "forward." It means a wickedly perverse person, or someone who is opposed to the right (see the NIV). In yet another instance of "parallelism," it is synonymous in verse 12 with "the evil man." The "froward" deliberately rejoice in doing evil and in taking crooked paths—like those that lead to the houses of prostitutes (vss. 16-19). The good are the opposite of the "froward" (vs. 20). Again, the way to avoid such paths is not merely in knowing where they lead, but in fearing, or reverencing, the Lord.

Evangelistic Emphasis

In coming to know God, to gain understanding and wisdom, there is both challenge and promise for the seeker.

Those who would know God must be receptive. They are to "accept (God's) word, and treasure up (God's) commandments, making your ear attentive to wisdom and incline your heart to understanding" (Prov. 2:11-2). Some things no one else can do for you. The one who would know God must place himself before the word.

To share in regular personal study of the Scriptures, to share in group Bible study, to participate in congregational worship regularly is a part of "inclining of the heart."

No less important than these disciplines is the attitude we bring. When we come to the Bible with a sense of expectancy, openness, readiness to hear what God would say to us, we learn.

We are called to seek God with persistence. If we were seeking for silver, if we were searching for precious treasure, we would overcome every obstacle. Nothing could discourage us. In seeking to know God, which is the most important search anyone could have, we must likewise put all other things aside. "Seek ye first the kingdom of God and his righteousness and all these things shall be yours as well" (Matt. 6:33).

With the challenge there comes a promise: If you cry out for insight, if you seek it, then you will find the knowledge of God. Then you will understand, for wisdom will come into your heart.

As Jesus said: "Seek and you will find" (Luke 11:9).

Memory Selection

For the Lord gives wisdom: out of his mouth cometh knowledge and understanding. —*Proverbs 2:6*

We are confronted by mysteries we cannot understand. Our minds cannot comprehend the nature of God. We cannot make sense of what happens to us. Life seems fragile. The good suffer. The innocent bear the brunt of evil. We feel adrift in an indifferent world.

Understanding will not come from our brilliant logic. Ultimate meaning will not be the result of our determined study. A knowledge of God's will does not come from scholarly research.

That knowledge we seek is a gift. That wisdom we want is not under our control. Understanding is more than acquiring facts and information.

What we cannot acquire by our own efforts is given. "The Lord gives wisdom. From his mouth come knowledge and understanding" (Prov. 2:6).

Weekday Problems

The KAIROS ministry is a ministry within the prison. It brings a weekend of witness and renewal, the sharing of the gospel of new beginnings, grace and healing. The core of the making new disciples in the prison is not the enthusiastic singing or heart-warming preaching by those who come into the prison from the outside world. The key to changing lives  is forming the new Christians into small groups that meet each week for prayer, Bible study, and accountability.

What is needed by new Christians inside prisons, is no less needed by new and mature Christians in the outside world. The company we keep shapes us.

Youth often get started on the road to crime, drugs, illicit sex and violence by "hanging around" with the wrong crowd.

No one ever outgrows the need for a supportive fellowship. A prayer and share group reinforces Christian values and attitudes. A Bible study group can help us make right choices.

When we get in with the wrong group, we start to blend in. When others act out of prejudice and fear, or shade the truth to get ahead, it begins to rub off on us.

The writer in Proverbs reminds us of the importance of being centered in God. "When wisdom comes into your heart, discretion will watch over you, understanding will guard you, delivering you from the way of evil, from men of perverted speech, who forsake the paths of uprightness to walk in the paths of darkness" (Prov. 2:10-13).

Modern Proverbs

You can't lose weight just by talking about reducing. You must keep your mouth shut.

The best thing about telling the truth is that you don't have to remember what you said.

Happiness is that peculiar sensation you get when you stay too busy to be miserable.

He who would make his dreams come true must wake up.

He who isn't big enough to stand criticism is too small to be praised.

Courage is hanging in there five minutes longer.

A bright eye indicates healthy curiosity. A black eye indicates too much.

This Lesson in Your Life

The sage suggests some conditions for gaining wisdom. The first is: "If you accept my words, and treasure up my commandments within you . . . ." The writer points us to an old way of praying the Scriptures. There is a place to study the Bible, seeking to know what the writer meant for his day and for his first readers. There is a need to understand when a book in the Bible was written and for whom it was intended.

But these words from Proverbs call for a meditation on the Scriptures. Henri Nouwen suggests we build a little nest in our heart for a single word or phrase and focus on it for maybe 20 minutes. We leave it fixed in our mind all day. The purpose of this discipline is not to deepen our insight in God but to help us experience the awareness of God in our lives. We treasure God's commandments within us.

When we memorize verses of the Bible, then they can move from the mind to the heart by saying them and praying them with as much attention as possible. As you lie in bed, as you wait in a grocery line, as you wait for a traffic light to change, as you wait in the doctor's office, as you take a daily walk you can slowly let the words, as Nouwen writes, "Go through your mind simply trying to listen with your whole being to what they are saying."

A second condition of gaining wisdom is: If you make "your ear attentive to wisdom, and incline your heart to understanding" (Prov. 2:2). There were no textbooks to fall back on. The student would learn what he heard and remembered. He needed an attentive ear.

We are bombarded by words all day long. The radio and television fill the room with words and sounds. As we drive along the streets and highways we are bombarded with signs, a jumble of words, a jungle of images claiming our attention. We have to learn to filter out some words to hear others. Those who seek wisdom need an attentive ear, an inner disposition, an inclination of the heart if they would find God and learn God's ways.

Throughout the book of Proverbs there is a contrast between the wise and the foolish. Fools are so self conceited they think they know it all. "Fools think their own way is right, but the wise listen to advice" (Prov. 12:15).

The wise elder who instructs the young seeker lays out conditions for the quest. If you treasure my words (memorize and meditate), if you make your ear attentive to wisdom (open to learning), if you cry out for insight (with urgency), if you seek it like silver (with persistence), then you will find the knowledge of God (Prov. 2:6), gain sound wisdom (2:7), be equipped with a shield (2:7) and be given a new understanding of justice (2:9).

The writer speaks of "sound wisdom" (v. 7). According to the Scottish Old Testament scholar Kenneth T. Aitken, " 'sound wisdom' is one word in Hebrew. It lays special emphasis on wisdom's effectiveness in getting results, here as resulting in right conduct. The wisdom that leads to knowing God leads to doing right."

God is a buckler or shield to those who walk blamelessly, protecting them from those who speak perversely (Prov.2:12) and loose women with smooth words (v.16). God preserves the saints, those who are devoted to Him and faithful to His covenant.

In walking that path of justice, we come to see the world in a different way. We see it from the viewpoint of the downtrodden and oppressed. We feel their hurt and pain. We taste their anger and frustration. In that experience we come to "understand" justice in a new way. This understanding comes into our heart and seeps into our soul.

Seed Thoughts

1. What comes from God's mouth?

Knowledge and understanding come from God's mouth (Prov. 2:6).

2. What happens when wisdom enters your heart?

Discretion will watch over you, understanding will guard you (Prov. 2:10-11).

3. What happens if you cry for insight and raise your voice for understanding?

You will understand the fear of the Lord and find the knowledge of God (Prov. 2:5).

4. In Jesus' parable (Matt. 13:44) what did the man do when he found the treasure hidden in the field?

He sold all that he had and bought that field.

5. What other words may be used to express what the writer means when he speaks of "the fear of the Lord"?

Awe, respect, reverence suggest what "fear of the Lord" means (Prov. 2:5).

---

1. What comes from God's mouth?

---

2. What happens when wisdom enters your heart?

---

3. What happens if you cry for insight and raise your voice for understanding?

---

4. In Jesus' parable (Matt. 13:44) what did the man do when he found the treasure hidden in the field?

---

5. What other words may be used to express what the writer means when he speaks of "the fear of the Lord?"

---

6. What terms in Proverbs 2:3-5 show the need to actively pursue wisdom?

---

7. What prophet spoke of justice and righteousness?

---

8. Through what prophet does God promise that all shall have "knowledge of God"? (Prov. 2:5).

---

9. How does James describe wisdom? (James 3:17)

---

10. For James what are the signs of wisdom? (James 3:13).

(Please turn page)

Knowledge and understanding come from God's mouth (Prov. 2:6).

Discretion will watch over you, understanding will guard you (Prov. 2:10-11).

You will understand the fear of the Lord and find the knowledge of God (Prov. 2:5).

He goes and sells all that he has and buys that field.

Awe, respect, reverence suggest what "fear of the Lord" means (Prov. 2:5).

Crying after it, lifting up our voice after it, seeking it like silver and other treasure.

The prophet Amos wrote: "But let justice roll down like waters, and righteousness like an ever-flowing stream" (Amos 5:24).

Jeremiah writes: "I will write my law on their hearts. No longer shall they say to each other "Know the Lord" for they shall all know me" (Jer.31:34).

"The wisdom from above is first pure, then peaceable, gentle, willing to yield, full of mercy and good fruits, without a trace of partiality or hypocrisy."

"Who is wise and understanding among you? Show by your good life that your works are done with gentleness born of wisdom."

6. What terms in Proverbs 2:3-5 show the need to actively pursue wisdom?

Crying after it, lifting up our voice after it, seeking it like silver and other treasure.

7. What prophet spoke of justice and righteousness?

The prophet Amos wrote: "But let justice roll down like waters, and righteousness like an ever-flowing stream" (Amos 5:24).

8. Through what prophet does God promise that all shall have "knowledge of God"? (Prov. 2:5).

Jeremiah writes: "I will write my law on their hearts. No longer shall they say to each other "Know the Lord" for they shall all know me" (Jer.31:34).

9. How does James describe wisdom? (James 3:17)

"The wisdom from above is first pure, then peaceable, gentle, willing to yield, full of mercy and good fruits, without a trace of partiality or hypocrisy."

10. For James what are the signs of wisdom? (James 3:13).

"Who is wise and understanding among you? Show by your good life that your works are done with gentleness born of wisdom."

TRUST IN THE LORD....

Lesson 6

Trust God

Proverbs 3:1-15

1 My son, forget not my law; but let thine heart keep my commandments:

2 For length of days, and long life, and peace, shall they add to thee.

3 Let not mercy and truth forsake thee: bind them about thy neck; write them upon the table of thine heart:

4 So shalt thou find favour and good understanding in the sight of God and man.

5 Trust in the Lord with all thine heart; and lean not unto thine own understanding.

6 In all thy ways acknowledge him, and he shall direct thy paths.

7 Be not wise in thine own eyes: fear the Lord, and depart from evil.

8 It shall be health to thy navel, and marrow to thy bones.

9 Honour the Lord with thy substance and with the first-fruits of all thine increase:

10 So shall thy barns be filled with plenty, and thy presses shall burst out with new wine.

11 My son, despise not the chastening of the Lord; neither be weary of his correction:

12 For whom the Lord loveth he correcteth; even as a father the son in whom he delighteth.

13 Happy is the man that findeth wisdom, and the man that getteth understanding.

14 For the merchandise of it is better than the merchandise of silver, and the gain thereof than fine gold.

15 She is more precious than rubies: and all the things thou canst desire are not to be compared unto her.

Memory Selection
Proverbs 3:5-6

Devotional Reading
Psalm 91:1-16

Background Scripture
Proverbs 3:1-20

Printed Scripture
Proverbs 3:1-15

441

Teacher's Target

Lesson purpose: *To reflect, with Solomon, on the practical advantages of developing a higher level of trust and reliance on the wisdom and loving care of God.*

The watchword of Protestantism is "salvation by grace through faith." This lesson emphasizes that faith or trust in God also has some this-worldly, practical aspects.

We often think of the "leap of faith" as risky business. You might introduce this lesson, however, by asking group members whether trusting and obeying God, in their experience, has ever proved the best thing to do in the circumstance.

For example, a doctor told of a patient who had a life-threatening heart ailment. She happened to be a Christian, and entered treatment with a sense of calm instead of anxiety. The doctor later said a more "uptight" person with a racing heart and high blood pressure would have not recovered as she did. What other examples can members of the group share?

Lesson Introduction

Our recent study of Job and of Ecclesiastes taught us that we cannot always gauge the health of our spiritual life by whether life's externals are going smoothly "under the sun." This lesson describes the other side of the coin, reminding us that blessings in this life are the *usual* result of godliness. This is not a "reward" system in which God "pays us off" for right living, but the normal result of the normal life of faith and obedience.

The promises of the proverbs in this lesson build on God's Covenant with Abraham, which was repeated through Moses. It promised blessings on the obedient and curses on the disobedient (see Deut. 28). Since neither the blessings nor the curses are always immediate or in the form we expect, living under the Covenant (or, in Proverbs, living by wisdom) requires a great deal of faith.

Teaching Outline	Daily Bible Readings
	Mon. Rely on God *Proverbs 3:1-10*
I. The Power of Obedience—3:1-4	**Tue.** Wisdom Is a Tree of Life *Proverbs 3:11-20*
A. Length of days, 1-2	
B. Favor with God and man, 3-4	**Wed.** Angels Come to Guard Us *Psalm 91:1-16*
II. The Potential of Trust—3:5-8	**Thu.** God Will Ransom Us *Psalm 49:1-15*
A. God knows best, 5-7	
B. The body can tell!, 8	**Fri.** Trust and Be Like Mount Zion *Psalm 125:1-5*
III. The Potency of Sacrifice—3:9-10	**Sat.** Giving God Credit *Deuteronomy 8:11-18*
IV. The Possibilities in Discipline—3:11-12	
V. The Pricelessness of Wisdom—3:13-15	**Sun.** God Will Bring Us Home *Zephaniah 3:12-20*

VERSE BY VERSE

I. The Power of Obedience—1-4

A. Length of days, 1-2

1 My son, forget not my law; but let thine heart keep my commandments:

2 For length of days, and long life, and peace, shall they add to thee.

These proverbs echo the Ten Commandments, and provide a kind of commentary on the practical advantages of living in harmony with God's moral and theological system. The promise of "length of days" recalls the Fifth Commandment, which promises long life to Covenant people who "Honour thy father and thy mother" (Exod. 20:12).

Length of days is not necessarily a "supernatural" gift or reward for keeping God's commandments. The same God who gave the commandments created life and designed the "natural processes" that sustain it. It therefore comes as no surprise that keeping His commandments makes man the creature more compatible with those aspects of creation that deliver good health and long life. For example, a Sabbath was not only a ritual to be observed; it provided life-extending rest.

B. Favor with God and man, 3-4

3 Let not mercy and truth forsake thee: bind them about thy neck; write them upon the table of thine heart:

4 So shalt thou find favour and good understanding in the sight of God and man.

In this proverb we hear something of the commandment against bearing false witness. Again it is easy to see how living in harmony with the moral order brings harmony to relationships. Treating others with mercy, and not spreading falsehoods about them, would ordinarily result in being treated mercifully. Jesus' "Golden Rule" has the same power: doing to others as we would have them do to us usually creates a cycle of healthy relationships.

II. The Potential of Trust—5-8

A. God knows best, 5-7

5 Trust in the Lord with all thine heart; and lean not unto thine own understanding.

6 In all thy ways acknowledge him, and he shall direct thy paths.

7 Be not wise in thine own eyes: fear the Lord, and depart from evil.

Lest we fall prey to the notion that we should do right merely because it benefits us, the wise man now gives the basic reason for following God's way: He knows best. In some exceptional situations, as when God allowed Satan to strike Job, a person who is merciful and truthful may be cut off in the prime of life. Acting truthfully and with mercy toward some enemies might occasionally result in death instead of "favor." Shall we then forsake God's ways because they do not work like an automatic pitching machine that spits out blessings like baseballs—one in, one out? No; that is where trust comes in. Reverting to our own "understanding," or inventing our own rules for living, would separate us from the intimate connection between the moral/spiritual life and nature, which was created by the same God.

B. The body can tell!, 8

8 It shall be health to thy navel, and marrow to thy bones.

Now the wise man returns to the usual pattern of obedience resulting in blessing. In doing so he shows remarkable insight into modern scientific truth that has taught us that the life of an unborn infant is sustained through the umbilical cord, and that bone marrow contains life-giving "factories" for red blood cells. We have but to notice the widespread incidence of alcohol and drug abuse to be reminded of the intimate connection between health and right living.

III. The Potency of Sacrifice—9-10

9 Honour the Lord with thy substance, and with the first-fruits of all thine increase:

10 So shall thy barns be filled with plenty, and thy presses shall burst out with new wine.

Can it be that there are physical blessings even in returning to God a part of our material wealth? The tithe was as much a part of God's commandments to His people as was the law of the Sabbath. In more than one instance, refusing to give of their means robbed Israelites of the "plenty" with which God would otherwise have blessed them. For example, He told the people through the prophet Malachi that their poor crops and bare cupboards were the direct result of having withheld their tithes and offerings: "Ye are cursed with a curse: for ye have robbed me," He said (Mal. 3:9). Even under the New Covenant, God promises to bless those who give to His work liberally (2 Cor. 9:6-9).

IV. The Possibilities in Discipline—11-12

11 My son, despise not the chastening of the Lord; neither be weary of his correction:

12 For whom the Lord loveth he correcteth; even as a father the son in whom he delighteth.

All these connections between doing right and being blessed may raise questions, so the author weaves back and forth between promising that the connections are true and dealing with the exceptions to the rule. Promised a good crop if he will but tithe, we can hear an Israelite protest, "But I did tithe, so why was my grain blasted with drought?"

The wise man's answer is, once more, that God never intended for His usual policy to limit His sovereignty or reduce Him to an automatic blessing machine. If the believer really follows the admonition to trust God, and to rely on His wisdom rather than the wisdom that quits the game in a huff when exceptions arise, he can treat a ruined crop as discipline from the hand of the same God who gives other kinds of blessings. As Job asked valiantly: "Shall we receive good at the hand of God, and not evil?" (see Job 2:10). This important principle is also cited by the author of the book of Hebrews (Heb. 12:5-11).

Unbelievers are often exasperated by this two-fold argument that (a) God usually blesses the righteous, but (b) when He doesn't (in the way we expect) we can view it as the blessing of discipline. It is a philosophy of life that forms an impregnable wall of faith about the true believer.

V. The Pricelessness of Wisdom—13-15

13 Happy is the man that findeth wisdom, and the man that getteth understanding.

14 For the merchandise of it is better than the merchandise of silver, and the gain thereof than fine gold.

15 She is more precious than rubies: and all the things thou canst desire are not to be compared unto her.

The wise man now adds a "beatitude" to the more famous beatitudes of Jesus: true wisdom and understanding make a person more blessed than does material gain. (Note that when wisdom is "personified" the feminine pronoun "she" is used. In both Hebrew and Greek the most common word for wisdom is feminine. In fact, the female name "Sophia" is the Greek word for wisdom.)

A few years ago, a remarkable family in California vividly illustrated this principle. The father had been thrown out of work, and the family was living on the streets. One day they made their way to a cafeteria in a mall to scavenge leftover food from the plates of diners before the tables were cleared. Suddenly their 10-year-old son spotted a wallet that had fallen out of some diner's pocket. It contained twenty-three $100 bills.

Instead of keeping the money, the family took it, cash and all, to a police sub-station in the mall. Authorities soon found the owner, who thanked the family—and left without offering any reward.

For months, the media carried the story of the family's commitment to a higher principle than material gain. When asked why they turned in the money, the mother would always reply: "Teaching our son honesty is more important to us than food."

Of course thousands of dollars poured in from a public hungry to reward this kind of principled behavior. Like the story of Job, the family's "latter end (was) more than the beginning." However, even when believers must wait until a future life to realize such a blessing, the Way recommended by the wise man is "more precious than rubies."

Evangelistic Emphasis

When we gather week by week to study the Bible, we are being trained to be God's witnesses where we live and work during the week. To be a disciple of Jesus is to be included in His commission to His disciples: "Go and make disciples" (Matt 28:19). Today's lesson from Proverbs reminds us that we must not forget the teaching, the commandments, the story of God's way. We return day by day, week after week, year after year in a never-finished study of God's teaching. There is always more to know than we know. But what we know is enough to know. We serve a God of love.

The sage, instructing younger persons in the faith, also reminds us it is not enough to know the commandments; we must keep them. If we would make disciples we need not only to know our story but to show the fruits of God's saving acts in lives that have been changed.

"My child do not forget my teaching, but let your heart keep my commandments" (Prov. 3:1).

✳ ✳ ✳

Memory Selection

 **Trust in the Lord with all thine heart; and lean not unto thine own understanding. In all thy ways acknowledge Him, and He shall direct thy paths.—** *Proverbs. 3:5-6*

Here is expressed the essence of religious faith: "Trust in the Lord with all thine heart. In all thy ways acknowledge Him."

The memory verse provides a corrective to every attempt at self salvation by good works. To be sure we respond to the good news of God's grace with lives of joyful gratitude and obedient service. But our trust is not in what we have done or what we can do. Our assurance is not in our knowledge or understanding. Our confidence is not in government, nor technology nor wealth. The only source of ultimate salvation is the Lord God who made us.

"In all thy ways acknowledge Him." No area is outside God's sovereignty. God is not limited to special seasons or sacred places. God's rule is to be acknowledged as much in the mall as at the altar, at the office as at the communion table, in the bedroom as in the prayer closet. We praise God when we sing hymns on Sunday morning and when we go to work throughout the week. "In all thy ways acknowledge Him."

Weekday Problems

A young couple was having a difficult time making ends meet. When the paychecks were spent they had too much month left over. They could hardly pay the interest on their credit cards. With car payments and house payments, debt on last summer's vacation and last year's Christmas bills, they simply didn't have enough money to go around. Both were already working. If one of them took a second job, they would never see each other, and their children would be raised by sitters.

One Sunday an older couple in the church gave their stewardship testimony. They had decided from their first pay check to set aside a portion for the Lord. To set it aside first and live on on what was left rather than meet all their other obligations first and share with the church out of what was left over. They were not a wealthy couple but they testified they had never been in want, or lacked anything they really needed.

For the Israelites, who were mostly farmers, the land was among God's greatest gifts and the harvest was the sign of God's providential care. There was always the risk they would view the harvest as the result of their hard work and cleverness. The offering of the first fruits was important to them and to us as an acknowledgment that all we have is owed to the goodness of God.

"Honor the Lord with your substance and with the first fruits of all your produce" (Prov. 3:9).

Signs of the Times*

At a shoe-shine stand: "FREE! FREE! One shoe shined absolutely free!"

At a pawn shop: "BE SURE TO SEE US AT YOUR EARLIEST INCONVE-NIENCE."

At the office: "THE BEST WAY TO MAKE ENDS MEET IS TO GET OFF YOUR OWN."

At the butcher shop: "HONEST SCALES—NO TWO WEIGHS ABOUT IT."

At the sporting goods store, near a mounted fish: "IF I'D KEPT MY MOUTH SHUT I WOULDN'T BE HERE."

At the travel agency: "PLEASE GO AWAY!"

At the undertaker's: "PLEASE DRIVE CAREFULLY. WE CAN WAIT."

*From Bob Phillips, *The All-New Clean Joke Book* (Eugene, Ore.: 1990). Used by permission.

This Lesson in Your Life

In relating today's passage from Proverbs to everyday living there are two emphases that need the balance of the whole Biblical witness to avoid a distortion of the truth.

We are exhorted "Trust in the Lord with all your heart, do not rely on your own insight." This is a needed corrective to those who trust their own wisdom too much, who think the coming of God's kingdom rests only on their shoulders. It is a needed corrective to the secular humanist who sees no transcendent purpose or divine help in human affairs. It is needed judgment on rampant self reliance, as expressed in the poem of William Ernest Henley: "I am the master of my fate / I am the captain of my soul."

The other extreme is to abdicate our God-given responsibility for life and for our community. It is the temptation of a pious escape, to pray "Thy will be done," then to opt out of social responsibilities. In all things we acknowledge the lordship of God. This acknowledgement does not relieve us of responsibility but sends us forth as God's servant. "Whom shall I send?" and we answer "Here am I."

We go forth confident that the final outcome is not in our hands. We are called to be faithful. God will fulfil God's purposes in God's own time. As Luther taught us to sing: "Were not the right man on our side / our striving would be losing. / Dost ask who that may be? / Christ Jesus it is he. / And he shall win the battle."

The other place in today's Scripture passage, and throughout the book of Proverbs, that needs the balance of the whole Bible to prevent distortion is on the simple equation of faithful obedience with the reward of long life and prosperity.

"Let your heart keep my commandments for the length of days and years of life and abundant welfare they will give you (Prov. 3:1-2)." "Bind loyalty and faith-fulness around your neck . . . so you will find favor and good repute in the sight of God and of people" (Prov. 3:4). "Honor the Lord with the first fruits of all your produce; then your barns will be filled with plenty" (Prov. 3:9-10).

Everyone can recall good persons whose lives were cut short. Everyone can name innocent persons whose lives were filled with suffering. Faithful stewards can lose jobs. The tradition that viewed sickness and suffering as a punishment from God was the view being challenged in the book of Job. It was the very challenge put to Jesus by his tormentors: "He trusts in God; let God deliver him now" (Matt. 27:43).

Such rewards as wisdom, prosperity, long life, peace *may* follow right living, but not *inevitably*. Perhaps that is good. It would make our best actions only enlightened self interest, trying to gain the rewards of heaven or avoid the flames of hell. Rather we are called to love and responsibility because first we are loved (1 John 4:19). Our service is not in order to win the love of God. Love is freely given and grace is undeserved. Rather we help, serve and give out of gratitude for a grace already bestowed.

The sage does suggest another meaning to suffering. It is not a final explanation for the mystery of suffering or evil in the world. His words, repeated and expanded in the letter to the Hebrews, suggest that suffering can be God's means of disciplining us, helping us to grow, as a loving father disciplines his son.

"My son, do not despise the Lord's discipline or be weary of his reproof, for the Lord reproves him whom he loves, as a father the son in whom he delights" (Prov. 3:11-12).

Seed Thoughts

1. To what does the word "law" (King James) or "teaching" (RSV) refer (Prov. 3:1)?

It is a translation of the Hebrew word "torah," which includes the first five books of the Old Testament. It is the instruction given to guide God's people.

2. To what does the word "peace" (King James) or "abundant welfare" (RSV) refer (Prov. 3:2)?

It is a translation of the Hebrew word "shalom" which means wholeness, salvation, destiny and everything which makes life complete and worth living.

3. What is the value or pain or suffering according to Proverbs 3:11-12?

Suffering is viewed as the disciplinary action of God, not as punishment but as a means to correct and direct.

4. What writer in the New Testament quotes from Proverbs 3:11-12?

The writer of the letter to the Hebrews.

5. According to Hebrews 3:11 what is the value of discipline?

"Now discipline . . . yields the peaceful fruit of righteousness to those who have been trained by it" (Heb. 3:11).

1. To what does the word "law" (King James) or "teaching" (RSV) refer (Prov. 3:1)?

2. To what does the word "peace" (King James) or "abundant welfare" (RSV) refer (Prov. 3:2)?

3. What is the value of pain or suffering according to Proverbs 3:11-12?

4. What writer in the New Testament quotes from Proverbs 3:11-12?

5. According to Hebrews 3:11 what is the value of discipline?

6. What New Testament writer echoes Prov. 3:7: "Do not be wise in your own eyes"?

7. How does the writer of Proverbs describe one who is "wise in his own eyes"?

8. How else does the sage in Proverbs characterize a fool?

9. Is there a connection between a right relationship with God and one's physical health and well-being?

10. In what area of your life do you have the greatest difficulty acknowledging God as Lord (Prov. 3:6)?

(Please turn page)

It is a translation of the Hebrew word "torah," which includes the first five books of the Old Testament. It is the instruction given to guide God's people.

It is a translation of the Hebrew word "shalom" which means wholeness, salvation, destiny and everything which makes life complete and worth living.

Suffering is viewed as the disciplinary action of God, not as punishment but as a means to correct and direct.

The writer of the letter to the Hebrews.

"Now discipline . . . yields the peaceful fruit of righteousness to those who have been trained by it" (Heb. 3:11).

Paul, writing to the Romans: "do not claim to be wiser than you are" (Rom. 12:17).

"The way of a fool is right in his own eyes, but a wise man listens to advice" (Prov. 12:15).

"A fool takes not pleasure in understanding but only in expressing his opinion" (Prov. 18:2).

"Fear the Lord and turn away from evil. It will be a healing for your flesh and refreshment for your body" (Prov. 3:8).

Choose an area and tell why it is most difficult for you: finances, time, fairness with persons of other races, relationship with competitors, forgiveness.

6. What New Testament writer echoes Prov. 3:7: "Do not be wise in your own eyes"?

Paul, writing to the Romans: "do not claim to be wiser than you are" (Rom. 12:17).

7. How does the writer of Proverbs describe one who is "wise in his own eyes?"

"The way of a fool is right in his own eyes, but a wise man listens to advice" (Prov. 12:15).

8. How else does the sage in Proverbs characterize a fool?

"A fool takes not pleasure in understanding but only in expressing his opinion" (Prov. 18:2).

9. Is there a connection between a right relationship with God and one's physical health and well being?

"Fear the Lord and turn away from evil. It will be a healing for your flesh and refreshment for your body" (Prov. 3:8).

10. In what area of your life do you have the greatest difficulty acknowledging God as Lord (Prov. 3:6)?

Choose an area and tell why it is most difficult for you: finances, time, fairness with persons of other races, relationship with competitors, forgiveness.

Lesson 7

Be a Good Neighbor

Proverbs 3:27-32; 11:9-13

27 Withhold not good from them to whom it is due, when it is in the power of thine hand to do it.

28 Say not unto thy neighbour, Go, and come again, and to morrow I will give; when thou hast it by thee.

29 Devise not evil against thy neighbour, seeing he dwelleth securely by thee.

30 Strive not with a man without cause, if he have done thee no harm.

31 Envy thou not the oppressor, and choose none of his ways.

32 For the froward is abomination to the Lord: but his secret is with the righteous.

11:9 An hypocrite with his mouth destroyeth his neighbour: but through knowledge shall the just be delivered.

10 When it goeth well with the righteous, the city rejoiceth: and when the wicked perish, there is shouting.

11 By the blessing of the upright the city is exalted: but it is overthrown by the mouth of the wicked.

12 He that is void of wisdom despiseth his neighbor: but a man of understanding holdeth his peace.

13 A talebearer revealeth secrets: but he that is of a faithful spirit concealeth the matter.

July 19

Devotional Reading
James 2:1-13

Memory Selection
Proverbs 3:27

Background Scripture
Proverbs 3:27-35; 11:9-13

Printed Scripture
Proverbs 3:27-32; 11:9-13

Teacher's Target

Lesson purpose: *To glean from Proverbs principles that enhance living together in a spirit of community and neighborliness.*

The word "neighbor" is a blend of two old terms that mean "near-dweller." The word certainly describes an increasing fact of life. Better communication has made the world our neighbor. Population increases mean that more than ever we "dwell near" each other. The reason occasional stories of people living in an isolated mountain shack make the news is because they are becoming so rare.

This means that we are challenged as never before to learn to live near each other in ways that enhance the lives of all concerned. Invite your class to discover from Solomon the wisdom required for building neighborliness.

Lesson Introduction

Christians first began to be accepted in the ancient world not because of their doctrine, but because of their neighborliness. Twice in the days immediately following the establishment of the Church in Acts 2, Scripture records that those who were wealthy sold their property in order to meet the needs of those who were poor (see Acts 2:44-45; 4:34).

This concern for others was a natural fulfillment of Jesus' life and teachings. In his parable of "the good Samaritan," He not only taught the importance of tending to the needs of others; He redefined "neighbor" as anyone in need. Ever since, Christianity has been more outward-turned than many other world religions. Its Founder did not establish a philosophy or school of thought so much as a way of living in which people are to love their neighbors as themselves.

Teaching Outline	Daily Bible Readings	
I. Be a Good Neighbor—3:27-30	**Mon.**	Be a Good Neighbor *Proverbs 3:27-35*
A. Be generous to the poor, 27-28	**Tue.**	Be Kind to the Poor *Proverbs 14:18-22*
B. Don't plan evil, 29-30	**Wed.**	Wisdom Better than Weapons *Ecclesiastes 9:3-18*
II. Don't Envy Evil Neighbors—31-32	**Thu.**	Live Together in Unity *Psalm 133:1–134:3*
III. Don't Be a Hypocrite—11:9	**Fri.**	Love One Another *John 13:31-35*
IV. Be a Good Influence on the City —10-11	**Sat.**	Seek the Welfare of Babylon *Jeremiah 29:1-14*
V. Don't Disrespect Your Neighbor —12-13	**Sun.**	Show Respect for the Poor *James 2:1-13*

VERSE BY VERSE

I. Be a Good Neighbor—3:27-30
A. Be generous to the poor, 27-28

27 Withhold not good from them to whom it is due, when it is in the power of thine hand to do it.

28 Say not unto thy neighbour, Go, and come again, and to morrow I will give; when thou hast it by thee.

Verses 27 and 28 state neighborliness in positive terms. A poor neighbor is envisioned, and the wise man assumes he is addressing a person with enough means to help. We may recall that Jesus defined a neighbor not simply as someone who lives nearby, but anyone who is in need (see Luke 10:29-37).

The Hebrew word for "due" in verse 27 is *baal*, the same word that is used for the Canaanite god. The essence of the word refers to power; so it is also used something like the word "lord" in the New Testament, a title showing honor or respect to someone in authority. In that sense it sometimes even refers to the true God. But what is the word doing in this passage? In what sense can it refer to the poor? Aren't they in fact powerless? Only when we assume that wealth belongs exclusively to the people who own it.

In the Bible, "the cattle on a thousand hills" and "all the gold of Ophir" belong to God. It is He who empowers certain stewards to tend to these possessions; and one important part of this stewardship is to share it with others of God's children. It is their "baal"—their power or due—simply by merit of being created in His image.

Jesus' concept of "importunity" is similar to this principle. The man who was already in bed when his friend came asking to borrow bread in order to feed unexpected company exerted enough moral obligation or "due" to cause the man to get up and supply the needs of his neighbor (see Luke 8:1-8).

This, of course, is no call for any particular social program, or even less an excuse for someone who can work remaining poor to take advantage of this "due." It is, however, a clear declaration that those who have are to share with those who have not.

B. Don't plan evil, 29-30

29 Devise not evil against thy neighbour, seeing he dwelleth securely by thee.

30 Strive not with a man without cause, if he have done thee no harm.

These verses state neighborliness from the standpoint of what *not* to do. We can envision two families in Palestine who settle down near each other with their herds of goats and flocks of sheep. They are to look out for each other's interest instead of, for example, plotting with thieves to steal each other's possessions. An example of such unneighborliness was Shechem, who lived near a parcel of land purchased by Jacob. Instead of allowing Jacob and his family to dwell securely nearby,

Shechem raped Dinah, Jacob's daughter (Gen. 33:18–34:2).

While verse 30 forbids "striving" with a neighbor who has done us no harm, it suggests that we might well strive with one who wrongs us. Jesus, however, elevated the principle of neighborliness to doing good to those who would do us harm. One modern neighbor, for example, lived next to a real grouch—but won him over one summer by regularly mowing the lawn between their two houses.

II. Don't Envy Evil Neighbors—31-32

31 Envy thou not the oppressor, and choose none of his ways.

32 For the froward is abomination to the Lord: but his secret is with the righteous.

The word for "oppressor" means one who oppresses by violence ("Do not envy a violent man," NIV). As "neighbors" have come to live closer and closer to each other in our cities, violence has become a way of life for many. As believers see the violent getting their own way by intimidating the community, it is tempting to adopt violent ways because they seem to "work."

Note here, however, that they would not only join the "froward"—perverse and deliberately wicked people who are an "abomination" to the Lord; they would also forfeit intimacy with God, and the privilege of sharing His secret. Probably this secret is the hidden power of turning the other cheek and other peaceful methods of solving problems, which the violent do not know. What an urgent need our cities have for people (neighbors) who are willing to break the cycle created by returning violence for violence.

III. Don't Be a Hypocrite—11:9

9 An hypocrite with his mouth destroyeth his neighbour: but through knowledge shall the just be delivered.

The word for "hypocrite" also means profane or polluted. The idea is that neighborliness is impossible when one or the other hypocritically pretends to like the other while bearing false tales of otherwise dealing underhandedly. This kind of unneighborliness pollutes the relationship. On the other hand, the neighbor to whom hypocrisy is displayed, or who is the victim of gossip, is made secure or "delivered" by her understanding that the hypocrite's words are not true.

IV. Be a Good Influence on the City—10-11

10 When it goeth well with the righteous, the city rejoiceth: and when the wicked perish, there is shouting.

11 By the blessing of the upright the city is exalted: but it is overthrown by the mouth of the wicked.

The "antithetical parallelism" in these two verses places the first lines in stark contrast with the second, in both cases. The sense of both statements is the important truth that when neighbors band together for just and right causes, entire cities are blessed. We see something of the tug of war between such people and "the wicked" in the latter part of these verses in the contemporary problem of gangs in so many American cities. The movement to "take back our streets"—to return to the old-fashioned practice of neighbors sitting out on their front porches in the evening to keep an eye on the neighborhood, to have "block parties" that show good people united for good, to report cases of drug dealing—are illustrations of what the author of Proverbs had in mind so long ago.

A leader in the early Church expanded this principle to the entire Roman Empire during a period when Rome was persecuting Christians. He pointed out that it was foolish for Rome to put to death people who worked for justice and even prayed for the very rulers who persecuted them. In fact, he said, Christians were actually "the soul of the nation."

V. Don't Disrespect Your Neighbor— 12-13

12 He that is void of wisdom despiseth his neighbor: but a man of understanding holdeth his peace.

13 A talebearer revealeth secrets: but he that is of a faithful spirit concealeth the matter.

Being neighbors isn't always easy. Occupying space close to each other can raise all kinds of difficulties because of different lifestyles and practices. When such differences arise, neighbors can choose to live and let live, or to despise (NIV "deride") each other, and allow being neighbors to degenerate into a relational war.

Verse 13 gets more specific, describing the familiar temptation for some neighbors to gossip about each other. While "faithful" is a term we usually think of as describing one's relationship to God, or to his or her spouse, it probably refers here to the person who is faithful to the true spirit of neighborliness, keeping shameful talk "secret" instead of spreading it through the neighborhood.

Evangelistic Emphasis

To a company of believers commissioned to make disciples of all nations, the words of the ancient sage come as clear marching orders. If we would win others as followers of Jesus, what we do is as important as what we say. The good news we would share as witnesses of our Lord is communicated by who we are as new creatures in Christ Jesus. It is essential that we witness to God's love made known in Jesus Christ, through his life, death and resurrection. Yet the love to which we witness must also be made incarnate in deeds of mercy and acts of justice.

James reminds us of the importance of expressing our faith through our works. "What good is it my brothers and sisters, if you say you have faith but do not have works? If a brother or sister is naked and lacks daily food, and one of you says to them, 'Go, in peace; keep warm and eat your fill,' and yet you do not supply their bodily needs, what is the good of that?" (James 2:14-16).

So this part of Proverbs could be read as instructions for those who would be witness to our Lord: Do not plan harm against your neighbor; do not quarrel with anyone; do not withhold good from those to whom it is due; do not say to your neighbor go and come again tomorrow, when you have it with you.

Memory Selection

Withhold not good from them to whom it is due, when it is in the power of thine hand to do it.—*Proverbs 3:27*

The literal Hebrew reads: "Do not withhold good from its owners." Who are these owners of "the good"? Some suggest the poor. Others suggest any one in need. Probably the sage intends his words to be general and inclusive of many situations, wherever our neighbor may be in need. The emphasis in this verse is that the neighbor has a right to it (to whom it is due) rather than that he has need of it.

In response to the lawyer's question "Who is my neighbor?" Jesus tells a parable (Luke 10:30-37). Jesus suggests that neighbor is any person in need or that the one who helps proves he is neighbor. The neighbor's need becomes our obligation to help. In Jesus' story the priest and the Levite "passed by on the other side." Jesus' Jewish hearers were surprised that the Samaritan helped. There was enmity and hate between Jews and Samaritans. The need of the man robbed, stripped and beaten was obligation enough.

"Do not withhold good from those to whom it is due, when it is in your power to do it" (Prov. 3:27).

Weekday Problems

Do not say to your neighbor "tomorrow" when you have it with you today.

Rebecca called an older, trusted friend to ask if she could come by to talk. The older friend, busy and preoccupied, missed the urgency in her young friend's voice. She suggested they get together next week. That evening Rebecca took her life. Tomorrow came too late.

The pastor called a young couple to ask if they would serve as youth counselors. It was not a good time in their lives to take on extra work. They had a young child, a new job, a new church. They said they would be willing, but at some later time. It was five years before they found the time to help to get the youth group up and going. In the meantime one of the church youth got in with the wrong crowd, started using drugs, and was caught stealing to support his addiction. He's serving time in a juvenile detention center. Tomorrow came too late.

Joe and Mary, his pregnant wife, came to an Inn in a crowded city. The Inn was already full. Perhaps, the Innkeeper said, he could make room tomorrow. They found a stable on that cold night in Bethlehem. Mary laid her infant son in a manger. Tomorrow came too late.

"Just as you did it not to one of the least of these, you did not do it to me" (Matt. 25:45).

Neighbor to Neighbor

Repairman: Here's your lawnmower, Mr. Wilson. We fixed it good as new. It's in such good shape, though, that we should give you just one word of precaution. Don't lend it to your neighbor.

Customer: Er, that's just the trouble. I am the neighbor.

Mom: I don't the think the man in the apartment upstairs likes for Mike to play his drums.

Dad: How's that?

Mom: Well, this afternoon he gave Mike a knife and asked him if he knew what was inside the drum.

Frank: Well, neighbor, we enjoyed our visit but we'd better go now. Hope we didn't keep you up too late.

Hank (yawning): Not at all. We would have been getting up soon anyway.

She (doing a puzzle): What's a good definition of a necessity?

He: Anything you see that the neighbors have and we don't.

This Lesson in Your Life

Some suggest the wise sayings collected in the Book of Proverbs represent the instruction given by an elder statesman in the king's court to aspiring civil servants just entering the king's service. From his vantage point of years the respected elder points out ways to get along with others, to get ahead. Much of his practical advice seems to fit those working their way up in any institution.

Do not refrain from helping a co-worker when you are in a position to help. You build relationships by doing favors. It never hurts to go out of your way to help.

Do not procrastinate, put off, delay. If you can do it now, don't make your friend come back and ask your help another day. There is an old saying, "Help which is long on the road is no help at all."

Don't plan harm against your neighbor. If another trusts you, prove worthy of that confidence. Don't do them in to gain advantage for yourself.

Don't quarrel with anyone without cause. Some conflicts you can't avoid. Some differences have to be faced up front and dealt with. But a lot of energy can be wasted and much good will dissipated when we get involved in pointless arguments. If you don't have a dog in that fight, stay clear.

Don't envy the violent or imitate their ways. Sometimes it may seem that they are gaining an advantage. They run roughshod over any in their way. You are to live by a higher standard. You are concerned about other's welfare.

The guidance of the elder statesman sounds like a mild version of Jesus' rule for getting along with others: "In everything do to others as you would have them do to you" (Matt. 7:12). Such day-to-day relationships with others shape one's relationship with God. Those who are upright are in God's confidence. They are able to discern God's will. They are made aware of God's presence in their midst. They enjoy God's friendship.

In the long run all will see God's curse on the wicked, and His blessing on the righteous. The house of the one will fall, and the house of the other will stand. It may not be apparent now. In the end, there is a final accountability. The wise are clothed with honor, while the foolish wear the coat of disgrace.

What seems to begin as simple rules for getting along with others ends by a sobering distinction between the wise and the foolish. It is not unlike the parable with which Jesus concludes what we know as the Sermon on the Mount. "Everyone who hears these words of mine and acts on them will be like a wise man who built his house on rock. And everyone who hears these words of mine and does not act on them will be like a foolish man who built his house on the sand."

Jesus summarizes the law and prophets in two commandments: "You shall love the Lord your God with all your heart, and with all your soul, and with all your strength. You shall love your neighbor as yourself" (Mark 12:30-31). The sage teaches us that our love of God is expressed in and through our love for neighbor.

"Those who despise their neighbors are sinners, but happy are those who are kind to the poor" (Prov. 14:21).

Seed Thoughts

1. What is Jesus' rule for getting along with others?

"Whatever ye would that men should do to you, do ye even so to them" (Matt 7:12).

2. According to James, what is the "royal law?"

"You do well if you really fulfill the royal law according to the Scriptures, 'You shall love your neighbor as yourself'" (James 2:8).

3. How did Moses summarize the rules for living with neighbors?

The Ten Commandments (Exod. 20:1-17; Deut. 5:6-21).

4. Which commandments deal with relationships with others?

Honor your father and mother, do not murder, do not commit adultery, do not steal, do not bear false witness, do not covet what is your neighbor's.

5. Do children have a right to health care or is it a privilege reserved for those who can afford it?

Proverbs 3:27 suggests that God's good gifts are to be shared with all. It is due them.

(Please turn page)

---

1. What is Jesus' rule for getting along with others?

2. According to James, what is the "royal law?"

3. How did Moses summarize the rules for living with neighbors?

4. Which commandments deal with relationships with others?

5. Do children have a right to health care or is it a privilege reserved for those who can afford it?

6. According to 1 John 4:19, what is the chief motive of love?

7. What proverb is similar to 1 John 4:21: "those who love God must love their brothers also"?

8. Proverbs often distinguishes between the wise and the foolish. What parables of Jesus make this distinction?

9. To what teaching of Jesus is the proverb, "Do not withhold good from those to whom it is due" similar?

10. What actions could your church take to convince unbelievers of the power of God's love?

"Whatever ye would that men should do to you, do ye even so to them" (Matt 7:12).

"You do well if you really fulfill the royal law according to the Scriptures, 'You shall love your neighbor as yourself' " (James 2:8).

The Ten Commandments (Exod. 20:1-17; Deut. 5:6-21).

Honor your father and mother, do not murder, do not commit adultery, do not steal, do not bear false witness, do not covet what is your neighbor's.

Proverbs 3:27 suggests that God's good gifts are to be shared with all. It is due them.

"We love because he first loved us" (1 John 4:17). Our service and help to others is first a response to God's love for us.

Proverbs 14:21: "Those who despise their neighbors are sinners."

Parables of the wise and foolish brides-maids (Matt. 25:1-13), and of the wise and foolish builders (Matt. 7:24-27).

"Give to everyone who begs from you, and do not refuse anyone who wants to borrow from you" (Matt. 5:42).

Feed the hungry, house the homeless, heal the sick, visit those in prison, welcome all who come.

6. According to 1 John 4:19, what is the chief motive of love?

"We love because he first loved us" (1 John 4:17). Our service and help to others is first a response to God's love for us.

7. What proverb is similar to 1 John 4:21: "those who love God must love their brothers also"?

Proverbs 14:21: "Those who despise their neighbors are sinners."

8. Proverbs often distinguish between the wise and the foolish. What parables of Jesus make this distinction?

Parables of the wise and foolish brides-maids (Matt. 25:1-13), and of the wise and foolish builders (Matt. 7:24-27).

9. To what teaching of Jesus is the proverb, "Do not withhold good from those to whom it is due" similar?

"Give to everyone who begs from you, and do not refuse anyone who wants to borrow from you" (Matt. 5:42).

10. What actions could your church take to convince unbelievers of the power of God's love?

Feed the hungry, house the homeless, heal the sick, visit those in prison, welcome all who come.

Lesson 8

Obey God's Law

Proverbs 28:1-13

1 The wicked flee when no man pursueth: but the righteous are bold as a lion.

2 For the transgression of a land many are the princes thereof: but by a man of understanding and knowledge the state thereof shall be prolonged.

3 A poor man that oppresseth the poor is like a sweeping rain which leaveth no food.

4 They that forsake the law praise the wicked: but such as keep the law contend with them.

5 Evil men understand not judgment: but they that seek the Lord understand all things.

6 Better is the poor that walketh in his uprightness, than he that is perverse in his ways, though he be rich.

7 Whoso keepeth the law is a wise son: but he that is a companion of riotous men shameth his father.

8 He that by usury and unjust gain increaseth his substance, he shall gather it for him that will pity the poor.

9 He that turneth away his ear from hearing the law, even his prayer shall be abomination.

10 Whoso causeth the righteous to go astray in an evil way, he shall fall himself into his own pit: but the upright shall have good things in possession.

11 The rich man is wise in his own conceit; but the poor that hath understanding searcheth him out.

12 When righteous men do rejoice, there is great glory: but when the wicked rise, a man is hidden.

13 He that covereth his sins shall not prosper: but whoso confesseth and forsaketh them shall have mercy.

Memory Selection
Proverbs 28:5

Devotional Reading
Matthew 7:15-27

Background Scripture
Proverbs 28:1-13

Printed Scripture
Proverbs 28:1-13

461

Teacher's Target

Lesson purpose: *To elaborate on the importance of personal, financial, and civic integrity, as taught in the book of Proverbs.*

Some recent polls have indicated that many Americans no longer place personal integrity high on their list of qualifications for public office. Is this a reflection of a lowering of the public's own moral standards? Does it merely indicate the expectation that the opposition will manage to lead the media to distort what we know about the integrity of our leaders? Or does it reflect a certain fatigue in expectations —a hopelessness that leaders of high moral standards can be found any more?

Use this lesson to affirm that integrity is evaluated in a court higher than public opinion. Emphasize the wise man's view that wickedness in personal dealings or affairs of state cannot long be hidden, and that its consequences are sure.

Lesson Introduction

While few people are either wholly righteous or altogether wicked, the author of Proverbs wants to draw the distinction between integrity and immorality as sharply as possible. One way this is accomplished is by "antithetical parallelism." As 28:1 illustrates, the first part of a verse states a truth, while the second part states its opposite. This style is also easily seen by counting the times the word *but*, the conjunction of contrast, is used to introduce the second line of a verse.

Another feature of the wise man's moral teaching is that the punishment or "come-uppance" for doing evil is portrayed as occurring in this life. Of course the wise man knew some wicked people seem to get away with their wickedness; but his faith in God's eventual judgment is so strong that he brings it into the present.

Teaching Outline	Daily Bible Readings
I. Public Ethics—1-4	**Mon.** Keep the Law Like Wise Children *Proverbs 28:1-7*
A. The courage of integrity, 1	**Tue.** Turn from Sin and Get Mercy *Proverbs 28:8-13*
B. The effects of transgression, 2-4	**Wed.** Happy Are Those Who Keep the Law *Proverbs 29:14-18*
II. Private Morality—5-9	**Thu.** Spiritual Wisdom for the Good Life *Colossians 1:9-14*
A. Seeking the Lord, 5-6	**Fri.** Learn Inner Wisdom and Be Clean *Psalm 51:1-14*
B. Effects of unrighteousness, 7-9	**Sat.** Happy to Keep God's Decrees *Psalm 119:1-7*
III. Personal Influence—10-13	**Sun.** Wise Builders Choose the Rock *Matthew 7:15-27*
A. Self-made destruction, 10-11	
B. Effects of righteousness, 12-13	

VERSE BY VERSE

I. Public Ethics—1-4

A. The courage of integrity, 1

1 The wicked flee when no man pursueth: but the righteous are bold as a lion.

A child with his hand in the cookie jar jumps when he hears the dog enter the room, thinking the noise signals his mother's angry entrance. If the tot is up to mischief, both mom and dad can enter the room without startling him. So it is with adults whose deeds are subject to public scrutiny. Those who have nothing to hide can proceed with courage and boldness, while those with "skeletons in the closet" are so fearful of being found out that they must devise elaborate diversions and cover-ups. God said through Moses that those who reject His laws will be subject to "terror," and will "flee when none pursueth" (Lev. 26:17).

B. The effects of transgression, 2-4

2 For the transgression of a land many are the princes thereof: but by a man of understanding and knowledge the state thereof shall be prolonged.

3 A poor man that oppresseth the poor is like a sweeping rain which leaveth no food.

4 They that forsake the law praise the wicked: but such as keep the law contend with them.

Three kinds of civic evil-doers are described here—a multitude of rulers who take advantage of a lawless society (vs. 2), a poor man who oppresses others like him (vs. 3), and those who are so depraved they redefine good and evil (vs. 4).

The NIV makes verse 2 more understandable: "When a country is rebellious, it has many rulers, but a man of understanding and knowledge maintains good order." A land in which "every man (does) that which is right in his own eyes" (Judges 17:6) often falls prey to unscrupulous petty "princes" at many levels of government. In contrast, order is encouraged when the land has at the top a strong leader with integrity.

Verse 3 portrays the irony of a poor person taking advantage of others like him. Would a parallel be an immigrant who finds wealth in this country, only to oppose allowing other immigrants to enter? We are also reminded of Jesus' parable in which a servant was forgiven a large debt by his master, only to demand repayment of a small amount owed him by a fellow debtor (Matt. 18:23-30).

Verse 4 describes the sorry state of affairs when those in influential places try to cover their unjust deeds by standing moral standards on their head, calling "evil good, and good evil" (Isa. 5:20).

II. Private Morality—5-9

A. Seeking the Lord, 5-6

5 Evil men understand not judgment: but they that seek the Lord understand all things.

6 Better is the poor that walketh in his uprightness, than he that is perverse in his ways, though he be rich.

People who will not take personal responsibility for wrong-doing are among those who fail to understand judgment (or "justice," NIV). Instead, they blame their behavior on social circumstances, God, or other persons. On the other hand, those who seek the Lord understand that the basis of judgment rests on accepting responsibility for their actions. Even when living by their convictions renders them poor, they are to be praised more than the unjust.

B. Effects of unrighteousness, 7-9

7 Whoso keepeth the law is a wise son: but he that is a companion of riotous men shameth his father.

8 He that by usury and unjust gain increaseth his substance, he shall gather it for him that will pity the poor.

9 He that turneth away his ear from hearing the law, even his prayer shall be abomination.

In keeping with the theme of responsibility in verses 5 and 6, the three kinds of unrighteous people described here have in common the fact that their behavior has consequences. Eastern and Middle Eastern cultures have traditionally placed a premium on honoring one's parents; so the son who keeps "riotous" (or "gluttonous," NIV) company not only disgraces himself but his father.

The consequence of over-charging for money lent to another (usury) is said to come home when the usurer dies, and his estate is inherited by a more righteous person who will actually share the ill-gotten gain with the poor. The consequence of turning one's back on God and His commandments is that God will turn His back when the person prays to

be rescued (taking for granted that the prayer is not the sincere petition for forgiveness, but the short-lived wish for immediate relief).

III. Personal Influence—10-13

A. Self-made destruction, 10-11

10 Whoso causeth the righteous to go astray in an evil way, he shall fall himself into his own pit: but the upright shall have good things in possession.

11 The rich man is wise in his own conceit; but the poor that hath understanding searcheth him out.

What more grievous sins are there than those of the person who is not content to go astray himself, but must find an otherwise innocent person to lead astray? Is the motivation that guilt, like misery, "loves company"? A contemporary example is the person who must find companionship in a drug habit by hooking a friend. As noted in the Lesson Introduction, the author is so convinced that such a person will receive double judgment that he paints a picture of immediate recompense. Whether the "pit" he digs for himself is being caught and jailed by the authorities, or judged in an after-life by the Supreme Authority, he will pay a high price for leading someone else down his own path.

Verse 11 observes that it is better to be wise and poor, than wealthy and deluded that wealth makes a person righteous. Jesus' commentary on the poor widow who gave a small sum of money—but all she had—illustrates the point. While the wealthy might make a great show of their own gifts, casting gold coins into the metal coffer with just the right twist of the wrist to produce a loud "clang," the poor widow's gift in effect "searches out" (NIV "sees through") the others with its own sort of wisdom—sincerity.

B. Effects of righteousness, 12-13

12 When righteous men do rejoice, there is great glory: but when the wicked rise, a man is hidden.

13 He that covereth his sins shall not prosper: but whoso confesseth and forsaketh them shall have mercy.

Again, verse 12 is better understood by the reading in the NIV: "When the righteous triumph, there is great elation; but when the wicked rise to power, men go into hiding." We have only to think of historical events in recent times to illustrate this obvious truth. When Adolph Hitler came into power in Germany in the 1930s, his demonic racism drove thousands of Jews into hiding.

The passage closes on a more encouraging note. The author has condemned many kinds of wickedness by many kinds of sinners. However, there is hope—as long as there is the capacity for confession and repentance. Only those who are too hard of heart to admit their wrong will find that God withholds His mercy from them. As the apostle Paul discovered, even his murderous days as Saul, the persecutor of Christians, were not beyond redemption when he was able to turn to God and forsake his former ways.

Evangelistic Emphasis

The key to evangelistic outreach, the sharing of the gospel with those who do not know Christ is prayer: effectual, fervent prayer. The sage who speaks in Proverbs puts his finger on the ineffectual praying of many congregations.

"If one turns away his ear from hearing the law, even his prayer is an abomination" (Prov. 28:9). All through the Scriptures the close connection between doing justice and appropriate worship is stressed. The prophet Isaiah tells the people their fasting and praying were not well received by the Lord. "Is not this the fast I choose: to loose the bonds of injustice, to let the oppressed go free; to share your bread with the hungry and bring the homeless poor into your house; . . . Then shall you call and the Lord will answer; you shall cry for help, and he will say Here I am" (Isa. 58:6-7,9).

We shall be more effective evangelists for the Lord when we give more attention to inviting others in than keeping others out. We shall find the power of the Lord moving through our witness when we give less attention to the proper wording of our prayers and more effort in the proper housing of God's children.

Through Amos the Lord spoke: "I hate, I despise your festivals, and I take no delight in your solemn assemblies. But let justice roll down like waters, and righteousness like an ever-flowing stream" (Amos 5:21, 24).

Memory Selection

Evil men understand not judgement: but they that seek the Lord understand all things.—*Prov. 28:5*

The person who is evil, who is turned away from God, cannot understand the judgement or decisions of the Lord. The justice which is God's will is beyond his ability to comprehend.

The knowing of God and of God's will is more than gaining information. To really know God requires a relationship of trust, respect, commitment.

Those who seek God are questing for a relationship. When one seeks the Lord first, above all else, one's will is changed. We come to will what God wills, we want what God wants. We come to see others not as competitors, threats or things to be used. We come to see them as God's children, persons made in God's image, persons in whom Christ dwells.

When we come to think like God, to see like God, to love like God, then we come to understand in fuller measure justice and mercy.

It is as though we are given new glasses that enable us to see reality in a new way, God's way.

Weekday Problems

George was depressed. He was unable to focus on his work. He couldn't settle down on any task. It was as though he was being eaten up within. No matter what he did, no matter how hard he tried, he was unable to forget what he had done. He was consumed by guilt. He could not undo the past.  His best efforts could not atone for it. He lived in fear of being revealed for who he really was. No façade of goodness or respectability could make George feel right about himself.

Finally he shared his deepest self with a trusted friend. He confessed his sin. He could not believe the great relief that came to him. It was like a flood of peace sweeping over him. A burden was lifted from his soul.

The sage in Proverbs shares this warning and this hope: "No one who conceals transgressions will prosper, but one who confesses and forsakes them will obtain mercy" (Prov. 18:13).

It was the discovery of the psalmist: "While I kept silence, my body wasted away through my groaning all day long. Then I acknowledged my sin to you..and you forgave the guilt of my sin" (Ps. 32:3, 5).

This is the good news of the gospel: "But if anyone does sin, we have an advocate with the Father, Jesus Christ the righteous; and he is the atoning sacrifice for our sins, and not for ours only but also for the sins of the whole world" (1 John 1:1-2).

Suffering the Consequences

Immigrant just learning English: What is this word, "spanking"?
Tutor: Stern punishment.

Son: Dad, you wouldn't spank me for something I didn't do, would you?
Dad: Why, of course not.
Son: Good! I didn't do my homework.

Dad: Now remember, son, I'm spanking you because I love you.
Son: I sure wish I was big enough to return your love.

Cop, walking up to a hunter's car: Nice buck you have there on top of your car.
Hunter's son: That's nothing, officer. You should see the one we've got in the trunk!

This Lesson in Your Life

A recurring theme in the Proverbs is the contrast between the righteous and the wicked. From the wisdom accumulated across the years the sage repeatedly urges those who would learn from him to choose the path of righteousness.

"The wicked flee when no one pursues" (Prov. 28:1). They are so full of fear they see danger when none exists. They think everyone is out to get them, because they take delight in hurting others. In contrast, "the righteous are as bold as a lion" (Prov. 28:1). Their hearts are good and pure. They assume others are as they. They do not fear shadows or imagine threats.

In disobeying the Law, in ignoring the heritage of their people, in taking expedient short cuts, the wicked turn values upside down. They praise what is wicked (Prov. 28:4) and scoff at what is good. They lose all sense of right and wrong, calling evil good, and good evil. The end of that road is destruction.

"The evil do not understand justice" (Prov. 28:3). They lose the capacity to feel compassion, to recognize the truth, to acknowledge the rightness of God's decisions. "Those who seek the Lord," who meditate on the law, who continually quest to know God's will come to "understand it completely" (Prov. 28:6).

The wicked may flourish for the moment. In their crooked and devious ways they may make a profit. But in the larger scale, by God's judgment it's "better to be poor and walk in integrity than to be crooked in one's ways even though rich" (Prov. 28:6). Wealth, earthly possessions, stocks and bonds are fleeting. The "one who augments wealth by exorbitant interest gathers it for another who is kind to the poor" (Prov. 28:8). You can't take it with you.

The consequences of these two different roads, wickedness and righteousness are vastly different: "Those who mislead the upright into evil ways will fall into pits of their own making, but the blameless will have a goodly inheritance." In every way possible the ancient sage seeks to draw the contrast between the way of righteousness and the way of wickedness, the way of obedience to the law and the way of disobedience, the way of good and the way of evil.

The consequences outlined by the sage are not limited to the individual called to choose between the good and evil way. The whole community suffers when evil persons come into authority and power. "When a land rebels it has many rulers; but with an intelligent ruler there is lasting order" (Prov. 28:2). With leaders who seek public office for private gain and not to serve, there is corruption and crime. It leads to instability in government. All are the worse for it. "When the righteous triumph, there is great glory, but when the wicked prevail people go into hiding" (Prov. 28:12). In many places in the world, we have seen the breakdown of law and order. Evil men, petty rulers, little tyrants terrorize the country side and people go into hiding.

The sage writes down his wisdom, drawn from a lifetime of observation and experience, that the young might learn, might profit. We read his words today, not as an interesting bit of ancient folk lore, but as a word through which the Lord may speak to us today, calling us to choose which way we shall go. We can be wise or foolish. Which way do you choose?

Seed Thoughts

1. What other proverbs reflect the connection between obeying the law and effective prayer as Proverbs 28:9?

Proverbs 15:8, 21:27, 21:3, 15:29

2. Where in Jesus' teaching did He make plain the connection between relationship to others and worship?

Matt. 5:23-24: "When you are offering your gift at the altar, if you remember your brother or sister has something against you . . . first be reconciled."

3. In Prov. 28:8 the sage warns about the impermanence of wealth. Where does Jesus teach a similar message?

Matthew 7:19-21: "Do not lay up for yourselves treasures on earth where moth and rust consume and where thieves break in and steal."

4. In what other proverbs is the way of the wicked and the way of the righteous contrasted?

Proverbs 10:24; 10:28; 10:30; 11:5; 11:19; 11:23; 12:2; 12:7; 12:26; 12:28.

5. According to Proverbs 28:7, who shame their parents?

Companions of gluttons shame their parents (Prov. 28:7).

(Please turn page)

---

1. What other proverbs reflect the connection between obeying the law and effective prayer as Proverbs 28:9?

2. Where in Jesus' teaching did He make plain the connection between relationship to others and worship?

3. In Prov. 28:8 the sage warns about the impermanence of wealth. Where does Jesus teach a similar message?

4. In what other proverbs is the way of the wicked and the way of the righteous contrasted?

5. According to Proverbs 28:7, who shame their parents?

6. When are one's prayers an abomination (Prov. 28:9)?

7. Who finds mercy (Prov. 28:13)?

8. Who are bold as a lion (Prov. 28:1)?

9. Who understands justice fully?

10. What happens to wealth increased by exorbitant interest (Prov. 28:8)?

Proverbs 15:8, 21:27, 21:3, 15:29

Matt. 5:23-24: "When you are offering your gift at the altar, if you remember your brother or sister has something against you, ..first be reconciled."

Matthew 7:19-21: "Do not lay up for yourselves treasures on earth where moth and rust consume and where thieves break in and steal."

Proverbs 10:24; 10:28; 10:30; 11:5; 11:19; 11:23; 12:2; 12:7; 12:26; 12:28.

Companions of gluttons shame their parents. (Prov. 28:7)

"When one will not listen to the law, even one's prayers are an abomination" (Prov. 28:9).

"One who confesses and forsakes (transgressions) will obtain mercy" (Prov. 28:13).

"The righteous are as bold as a lion" (Prov. 28:1).

"Those who seek the Lord understand (justice) completely" (Prov. 28:5).

That wealth, gained through exorbitant interest, is gathered for another who is kind to the poor (Prov. 28:8).

6. When are one's prayers an abomination (Prov. 28:9)?

"When one will not listen to the law, even one's prayers are an abomination" (Prov. 28:9).

7. Who finds mercy? (Prov. 28:13)

"One who confesses and forsakes (transgressions) will obtain mercy" (Prov. 28:13).

8. Who are bold as a lion (Prov. 28:1)?

"..the righteous are as bold as a lion" (Prov. 28:1).

9. Who understand justice fully?

"Those who seek the Lord understand (justice) completely" (Prov. 28:5).

10. What happens to wealth increased by exorbitant interest (Prov. 28:8)?

That wealth, gained through exorbitant interest, is gathered for another who is kind to the poor (Prov. 28:8).

Lesson 9

Wisdom or Foolishness

Proverbs 8:1-11, 33-36

1 Doth not wisdom cry? and understanding put forth her voice?

2 She standeth in the top of high places, by the way in the places of the paths.

3 She crieth at the gates, at the entry of the city, at the coming in at the doors.

4 Unto you, O men, I call; and my voice is to the sons of man.

5 O ye simple, understand wisdom: and, ye fools, be ye of an understanding heart.

6 Hear; for I will speak of excellent things; and the opening of my lips shall be right things.

7 For my mouth shall speak truth; and wickedness is an abomination to my lips.

8 All the words of my mouth are in righteousness; there is nothing froward or perverse in them.

9 They are plain to him that understandeth, and right to them that find knowledge.

10 Receive my instruction, and not silver; and knowledge rather than choice gold.

11 For wisdom is better than rubies; and all the things that may be desired are not to be compared to it.

33 Hear instruction, and be wise, and refuse it not.

34 Blessed is the man that heareth me, watching daily at my gates, waiting at the posts of my doors.

35 For whoso findeth me findeth life, and shall obtain favour of the Lord.

36 But he that sinneth against me wrongeth his own soul: all they that hate me love death.

August 2

Memory Selection
Proverbs 8:11

Devotional Reading
Psalm 1:1-6

Background Scripture
Proverbs 8

Printed Scripture
Proverbs 8:1-11, 33-36

Teacher's Target

Lesson purpose: *To reinforce the importance and the advantages of choosing the kind of wisdom defined in Scripture.*

Some choices in life are of minor consequence. We may argue over the advantage of choosing General Motors vehicles over Fords, but we attach little eternal importance over the choice. A strong Democrat may even forgive relatives, friends and fellow Christians for voting Republican!

In today's lesson, however, choosing "wisdom" is placed on a more serious level. It is said to mean the difference between being wrong-headed or right, blessed or cursed, oriented toward death or life.

In this lesson, stress the urgency of identifying and choosing biblical wisdom. What *is* this commodity or quality of life that is said to be so important? Once we identify it, how can we obtain it? What are the consequence of choosing otherwise?

Lesson Introduction

As in other passages in Proverbs 1–9, wisdom is "personified" here—given a human voice. As the verse-by-verse section will discuss more extensively, this raises an interesting question about the possible connection between "wisdom" in the book of Proverbs and the New Testament's declaration that Christ Himself is "the wisdom of God." As we read the statements of "wisdom personified" in Proverbs 1–9, are we hearing, at a deeper level, the voice of Jesus? How did those who originally heard or read these statements perceive the personal quality of the language?

Despite the profound implications of the question, another issue is perhaps more basic. The wise man asserts that embracing biblical wisdom, whether as a principle or a Person, involves adopting a point of view and a mind-set that can make a practical difference in this life, and an eternal difference in the life to come. What does it really mean to adopt this viewpoint?

Teaching Outline	Daily Bible Readings
I. Wisdom's Appeal—1-5	**Mon.** Wisdom Is Better than Jewels *Proverbs 8:1-11*
A. The personification of wisdom, 1	
B. The positioning of wisdom, 2-3	**Tue.** Wealth for Lovers of Wisdom *Proverbs 8:12-21*
C. The plea of wisdom, 4-5	
II. Wisdom's Attraction—6-9	**Wed.** God Created Wisdom *Proverbs 8:22-31*
A. Truth, 6-7	**Thu.** Choose Life! *Proverbs 8:32-36*
B. Righteousness, 8-9	
III. Wisdom's Benefits—10-11	**Fri.** Fools Deny the Reality of God *Psalm 14:1-7*
IV. Wisdom's Blessings—33-36	**Sat.** Obedience Is Better than Sacrifice *1 Sam. 15:22-31*
A. The advantage of instruction, 33-35	
B. A warning, 36	**Sun.** Enter by the Narrow Gate *Matthew 7:1-14*

VERSE BY VERSE

I. Wisdom's Appeal—1-5

A. The personification of wisdom, 1

1 Doth not wisdom cry? and understanding put forth her voice?

The first nine chapters of Proverbs have an intriguing way of allowing wisdom to speak as a person. It is also fascinating that wisdom is described as having existed with God before the creation of the world (8:22-31). Wisdom is even said to have functioned as an agent of creation: "The Lord by wisdom hath founded the earth" (3:19).

The Christian often hears echoes of the doctrine of Christ in these descriptions. Because Christ is also described as pre-existent, and the agent of creation (see John 1:1-3, 14), it has been suggested that Proverbs 1–9 are prophetic references to Him. To add to this possibility, we may recall that the apostle Paul calls Jesus "the wisdom of God" (1 Cor. 1:24). At least it can be said that wisdom here is a figure of speech that functions parallel to the pre-existent Word (logos) of God. Both the logos and wisdom are creative powers beckoning the wise to march in step with them.

B. The positioning of wisdom, 2-3

2 She standeth in the top of high places, by the way in the places of the paths.

3 She crieth at the gates, at the entry of the city, at the coming in at the doors.

Recall that wisdom is perhaps portrayed as a woman because the most common words for wisdom in the biblical languages are feminine (Heb. *hochmah*, Grk. *sophia*). She is pictured as standing at prominent places (see also 1:20; 9:3) and crying out to sell her wares, perhaps to compete with the "strange woman" or prostitute (2:16; 5:3). In contrast to what those women have to "sell," wisdom's wares are "good doctrine" (4:2). She positions herself at the entrance of every city and every home, reminding us that the right paths are there for the taking if we will respond to her call.

C. The plea of wisdom, 4-5

4 Unto you, O men, I call; and my voice is to the sons of man.

5 O ye simple, understand wisdom: and, ye fools, be ye of an understanding heart.

We have no excuse for remaining ignorant of the way of righteousness, since wisdom does not simply sit passively by, awaiting our search for her. Instead, she aggressively calls to us all, offering understanding for the taking.

There is a poignancy to wisdom's call here, as though she knows many will reject her. The imagery is similar to the plaintive plea of Christ, who, like a child trying to entice other children to play, offered to play happy games or "funeral," but to no avail (see Matt. 11:16-19).

II. Wisdom's Attraction—6-9

473

A. Truth, 6-7

6 Hear; for I will speak of excellent things; and the opening of my lips shall be right things.

7 For my mouth shall speak truth; and wickedness is an abomination to my lips.

Wisdom is to be desired above rubies, riches, and honor, in part because what she teaches is "excellent" and "right." The word for "excellent" here refers to "ruling principles"—ways of living that both undergird all of life and are noble enough to guide a righteous ruler.

From verse 7 we can infer that those who despise truth will not be attracted by what wisdom has to offer. As verse 9 will note again, wisdom has some conditions attached. If we love lies and wickedness more than truth or righteousness, we will obviously turn our back on the kind of wisdom spoken of here.

B. Righteousness, 8-9

8 All the words of my mouth are in righteousness; there is nothing froward or perverse in them.

9 They are plain to him that understandeth, and right to them that find knowledge.

While foolishness leads to wickedness, choosing wisdom as a guide will lead us to righteousness. There is nothing "froward" (NIV "crooked") or "perverse" in behaving in the light of the wisdom offered by God—nothing "cantankerous" or insistently opposed to doing right. Remember that all this is not said of a human being but of wisdom, a divine quality. Although no one can boast that all their words and thoughts are righteous, wisdom is that totally righteous goal toward which we journey.

Moreover, wisdom affirms here that her way is plain, or well-marked, so that almost anyone can find it. It is remarkable, for example, how right-thinking and wise people from many cultures and times have agreed on broad moral principles such as telling the truth, sexual purity, the superiority of wisdom over material goods, honoring the aged. The universal aspects of wisdom are evidence of the close association she claims here with creation. All created beings have access to her.

Why, then, don't more people follow wisdom? Verse 9 suggests one reason: wisdom is plain only to those with understanding. This is almost circular reasoning, like saying that if we have wisdom we shall find it. The author is speaking of an attitude that welcomes wisdom when it is found—a principle Christ also taught. He said the wisdom of the Kingdom is for those "who hath hears to hear," and that those who had really rather not hear, will not understand (see Mat. 13:9-15).

III. Wisdom's Benefits—10-11

10 Receive my instruction, and not silver; and knowledge rather than choice gold.

11 For wisdom is better than rubies; and all the things that may be desired are not to be compared to it.

It is important to remember that the basis of wisdom in Proverbs is not intellectual knowledge but "the fear of the Lord"—a heart that reverences Him and desires the right way. Defined thus, the author again affirms that wisdom is more valuable than any material good. In a nice touch of irony, he affirms the superiority of wisdom over the stuff of jewelry—silver, gold, and rubies—yet pictures the adornment of wisdom as a true "ornament of grace unto thy head, and chains about thy neck" (1:9).

IV. Wisdom's Blessings—33-36

A. The advantage of instruction, 33-35

33 Hear instruction, and be wise, and refuse it not.

34 Blessed is the man that heareth me, watching daily at my gates, waiting at the posts of my doors.

35 For whoso findeth me findeth life, and shall obtain favour of the Lord.

The imagery here recalls that wisdom positions herself at the doors and gates (vs. 3)—the places where people walk in and out of the homes and cities, busy in the commerce of everyday life. She is like a vendor selling food that will nourish us on our journey, walking sticks to make it easy to climb the hills, or hats to shield us from the sun. In keeping with the practical nature of Proverbs, "buying" wisdom's wares is not a theoretical program but a way of walking and working. We are counseled to "Buy the truth, and sell it not" (23:23), because since God created the world, His wisdom fits the way it works, ministering life to the obedient.

B. A warning, 36

36 But he that sinneth against me wrongeth his own soul: all they that hate me love death.

From the positive advantages and blessings living wisely has to offer, the author turns to the negative side of the coin. Note that the primary negative in sinning against wisdom, or behaving in ways that do not acknowledge (fear) God, is that we ourselves are harmed. We wrong our own soul, and deliberately choose death over life.

Evangelistic Emphasis

The message of "Lady Wisdom" as described in Proverbs 8 is addressed to all the sons of men, to all who live. It is not alone to the sons and daughters of Abraham that she is sent. The wisdom she would share is for all persons. Its appeal is universal.

Persons of every age and station stand in need of the grace of our Lord Jesus Christ. No one is so good and righteous that he does not need the saving mercy of God. No one is so lost in sin that he is beyond the reach of God's grace. "My cry is to all that live" (Prov. 8:4).

"Lady Wisdom" goes everywhere with her message: "on the heights, beside the way, at the cross roads, besides the gates." She takes her message where the people are.

The disciples of Christ can be no less diligent in sharing God's word. We need to move beyond the cozy walls of the church, talking to each other about God's love. Henri Nouwen reminds us of some of these persons to whom we need show compassion right are where we are. There is the teenager who does not feel secure. There is the husband or wife who feel there is no longer love between them. There is the wealthy executive who thinks people are more interested in his money than in him. There is the gay man or woman who feels isolated from family and friends. There are millions who are lonely and wonder if life is worth living.

Memory Selection

For wisdom is better than rubies; and all the things that may be desired are not to be compared to it. — *Proverbs 8:11*

Wisdom, personified as a woman, describes the value of what she can teach. In the ancient world, jewels were among the most treasured possessions. A rare and perfect ruby could be passed on from generation to generation. Its value only increased with the passing of the ages. It was a precious treasure to be cherished.

Its worth pales in comparison with the value of wisdom. An understanding of the ways of God is more important than wealth. A knowledge of God's love makes all the difference in this life and in the life to come. A relation to God of trust and obedience leads to life eternal.

All the things you might desire, houses or cars, stocks or bonds, honors or titles, reputation or popularity last only for a moment. They all pass away. A knowledge of God, an understanding of God's way, the wisdom imparted by God is better than rubies.

Weekday Problems

Susan grew increasingly concerned about the build up of waste in her community. Old tires provided a breeding ground for mosquitoes. The beautiful lake was littered with beer cans and foam cups. The evening news reminded her of the low quality of air. But more than the pollution outside was the poison inside. She seemed harried, burned out. She was filled with angers and resentments, anxieties and fears. There seemed no peace in her heart.

She finally took a day off. She allowed herself to feel the gentle breeze. She stopped to smell the flowers. Her eye followed the graceful flight of a hawk high in the sky. She marveled at the intricate design of a tiny wild flower. She felt the varied textures of the rough bark as she caressed the tree. Her bare feet snuggled in the cool smooth grass. It is as though all her senses came alive. She rejoiced in the world around her. She delighted in God's good creation. She remembered good friends, helpful neighbors, loving family, courageous leaders.

She understood in a new way "Lady Wisdom's" words about God and God's creation: "then I was beside him as a little child, and I was his daily delight, rejoicing before him always, rejoicing in his inhabited world and delighting in the human race" (Prov. 8:30-31). The day apart, playing in God's presence, brought renewal. Her discouragement changed to new hope as she resolved to do what she could to keep the earth a place where all could rejoice with God in God's good creation.

Windows on Wisdom

The good Lord set definite limits on man's wisdom, but set no limits on his stupidity—and that's just not fair!—*Konrad Adenauer*

The intellect of the wise is like glass; it admits the light of heaven and reflects it.—*Augustus William and Julius Charles Hare*

For never, never, wicked man was wise.—*Homer*

The wise man does not lay up treasure.—*Lao-tze*

He who provides for this life, but takes no care for eternity, is wise for a moment, but a fool forever.—*John Tillotson*

The wise man is also the just, the pious, the upright, the man who walks in the way of truth. The fear of the Lord, which is the beginning of wisdom, consists in a complete devotion to God.—*Otto Zockler*

This Lesson in Your Life

There is a strangeness to "Lady Wisdom's" claim: "All the words of my mouth are righteous; there is nothing twisted or crooked in them. They are straight (plain) to the one who understands and right to those who find knowledge" (Prov. 8:8-9).

Like other propositions of faith, the truth is discovered only when we trust them, act on them, believe them. The truth is not self evident. The evidence is not overwhelming. There is always room for doubt and disbelief. If we wait until every question is answered, every doubt dispelled, we will never act at all.

Peter and Andrew, James and John were called to follow Jesus. They came to believe he was the Christ, even God's son. But they followed him first, then came to understand who He really was.

The truth about God comes to us not in abstract propositions that can be proved beyond all doubt. It is as we trust in God that we find God to be trustworthy, and faithful to God's promises.

In John's Gospel we read of the Word that was with God. "He was in the world, and the world came into being through him; yet the world did not know him. He came to what was his own, and his own people did not accept him. But to all who received him, who believed in his name, he gave power to become children of God" (John 1:10-13). The fuller knowledge of God was a relationship like a child trusting in her father. The trust comes first and then the knowledge.

An exercise in trust-building in groups involves blindfolding a volunteer. He is placed in the center of the group. He is instructed to fall backward, trusting the group to catch him. He can know a lot about the group, their names, where they are from, even their academic degrees. But when he fully trusts himself to them, to catch him, he knows them in a different and fuller way.

"Lady Wisdom" implies that her words will not be plain to all, but those who trust her will find her words to be true. The rightness of her teaching will be convincing only to those who already know God in trust and obedience.

On the one hand we read how "Lady Wisdom" goes to cross roads and gates to call " all that live"; on the other hand we are reminded that "those who seek me diligently find me" (Prov. 8:17).

There is more about God that we do not know than we know. What we know is enough to know. "In this is love, not that we love God but that he loved us and sent his Son to be the atoning sacrifice for our sins" (1 John 4:10).

God does not compel our faith. God does not force His way upon us. But when we respond, when we come to glimpse truth, it is as though our hearts have been prepared before hand. There is a readiness as though One has gone before that we may say "yes," that we *may* believe.

This fuller knowledge of God's love comes only as we trust in Christ and Christ alone for our salvation.

Seed Thoughts

1. Where does "Lady Wisdom" go to proclaim her message?

"The top of high places," "by the way in places of the paths," "at the gates, at the entry of the city, and the coming in at the doors" (Prov. 8:2).

2. To whom is "Lady Wisdom's" message addressed?

"To the sons of men "to all that live" (NRSV).

3. How does she (Wisdom) describe her words?

"All the words of my mouth are righteous; there is nothing twisted or crooked in them" (Prov. 8:8).

4. What is the fear of the Lord?

The fear of the Lord is hatred of evil (Prov. 8:13).

5. To whom does "Lady Wisdom" give counsel?

Kings, princes, nobles, judges of the earth (Prov. 8:15-16).

---

1. Where does "Lady Wisdom" go to proclaim her message?

2. To whom is "Lady Wisdom's" message addressed?

3. How does she (Wisdom) describe her words?

4. What is the fear of the Lord?

5. To whom does "Lady Wisdom" give counsel?

6. What are the rewards of those who love Wisdom?

7. How is the relation of "Wisdom" to God described in Prov. 8:30 according to different translations?

8. What happens to him who finds Wisdom?

9. What happens to those who miss "Wisdom?"

10. When was Wisdom created?

(Please turn page)

"The top of high places," "by the way in places of the paths," "at the gates, at the entry of the city, and the coming in at the doors" (Prov. 8:2).

"To the sons of men "to all that live" (NRSV).

"All the words of my mouth are righteous; there is nothing twisted or crooked in them" (Prov. 8:8).

The fear of the Lord is hatred of evil (Prov. 8:13).

Kings, princes, nobles, judges of the earth (Prov. 8:15-16).

They will be endowed with wealth, and their treasuries shall be filled. (Prov. 8:21)

KJV: as one brought up with him; RSV: like a master workman; New English Bible: at his side each day; other ancient manuscripts: like a little child.

"Whoever finds me finds life and obtains favor from the Lord" (Prov. 8:35).

"He who misses me injures himself (Prov. 8:36).

"The Lord created me at the beginning of his work, ages ago I was set up, at the first, before the beginning of the earth" (Prov. 8:22, 23).

(Seed Thoughts, continued)

6. What are the rewards of those who love Wisdom?

They will be endowed with wealth, and their treasuries shall be filled. (Prov. 8:21)

7. How is the relation of "Wisdom" to God described in Prov. 8:30 according to different translations?

KJV: as one brought up with him; RSV: like a master workman; New English Bible: at his side each day; other ancient manuscripts: like a little child.

8. What happens to him who finds Wisdom?

"Whoever finds me finds life and obtains favor from the Lord" (Prov. 8:35).

9. What happens to those who miss "Wisdom?"

"He who misses me injures himself (Prov. 8:36).

10. When was Wisdom created?

"The Lord created me at the beginning of his work, ages ago I was set up, at the first, before the beginning of the earth" (Prov. 8:22, 23).

Lesson 10

Hard Work and Laziness

Proverbs 6:6-8; 10:4-5; 13:4; 15:19; 18:9; 20:4; 24:30-34

6 Go to the ant, thou sluggard; consider her ways, and be wise:

7 Which having no guide, overseer, or ruler,

8 Provideth her meat in the summer, and gathereth her food in the harvest.

10:4 He becometh poor that dealeth with a slack hand: but the hand of the diligent maketh right.

5 He that gathereth in summer is a wise son: but he that sleepeth in harvest is a son that causeth shame.

13:4 The soul of the sluggard desireth, and hath nothing: but the soul of the diligent shall be made fat.

15:19 The way of the slothful man is as an hedge of thorns: but the way of the righteous is made plain.

18:9 He also that is slothful in his work is brother to him that is a great waster.

20:4 The sluggard will not plow by reason of the cold; therefore shall he beg in harvest, and have nothing.

24:30 I went by the field of the slothful, and by the vineyard of the man void of understanding;

31 And, lo, it was all grown over with thorns, and nettles had covered the face thereof, and the stone wall thereof was broken down.

32 Then I saw, and considered it well: I looked upon it, and received instruction.

33 Yet a little sleep, a little slumber, a little folding of the hands to sleep:

34 So shall thy poverty come as one that travelleth; and thy want as an armed man.

August 9

Memory Selection
Proverbs 15:9

Devotional Reading
1 Corinthians 13:1-13

Background Scripture
Proverbs 6:6-8; 10:4-5; 13:4; 15:19; 18:9; 20:4; 24:30-34

Printed Scripture
Proverbs 6:6-8; 10:4-5; 13:4; 15:19; 18:9; 20:4; 24:30-34

Teacher's Target

Lesson purpose: *To glean from Proverbs insights into its view of hard work as a virtue and material gain as a fitting reward.*

The view that material wealth is a just reward for hard work contributed to the growth of early America—and still does, to some extent. Although this philsophy is often called "the Protestant (or Puritan) ethic," it is actually much older—going back at least to the book of Proverbs.

Discuss with your class their view of wealth, and the wealthy. It is likely that some notions of resentment toward the rich, or of guilt for having wealth, will arise. Often such views stem from religious warnings about the abuse of wealth, rather than about wealth itself. Use the biblical material to work toward a balanced view that is not embarrassed by the material rewards of hard work, but which accepts some responsibility on the part of the "haves" to share with the "have-nots."

Lesson Introduction

The book of Proverbs' teaching on the value of work and the place of material gain is rooted in Genesis 1. Since God was at work in creation, and since He made man in His image, it is good for man to work and to be created. In some cultures and philosophies, material gain is an embarrassment. In the Bible, since the material world God created is "very good" material gain is not evil.

The passages to follow add another dimension to these views: industry and hard work are virtues that often lead to wealth, while slothfulness (which would later become one of the "seven deadly sins") is evil.

What is absent here is the view that not having wealth is always a sign of laziness, or unrighteousness—views which are opposed, as we have seen, in such writings as the book of Job.

Teaching Outline	Daily Bible Readings
I. Lessons from an Ant—6:6-8	**Mon.** Hear This, Lazybones! *Proverbs 6:6-11*
II. The Way to Riches—or Poverty —10:4-5	**Tue.** Slackers vs. Workers *Proverbs 10:4-5; 13:4; 15:19; 18:9*
III. Warnings Against Sloth—13:4; 15:19; 18:9; 20:4	**Wed.** Lazy Ones Lose Control *Proverbs 12:24-28*
A. The lazy vs. the industrious, 13:4; 15:19	**Thu.** Children Are Known by Their Acts *Proverbs 20:4-11*
B. Traits of the slothful, 18:9; 20:4	**Fri.** An Overgrown Vineyard *Proverbs 24:20-34*
IV. An Object Lesson—24:30-34	**Sat.** Warning Against Idleness *2 Thessalonians 3:6-13*
	Sun. Laborers with God Work with Care *1 Corinthians 3:12-20*

VERSE BY VERSE

I. Lessons from an Ant—6:6-8

6 Go to the ant, thou sluggard; consider her ways, and be wise:

7 Which having no guide, overseer, or ruler,

8 Provideth her meat in the summer, and gathereth her food in the harvest.

Solomon was not only a philosopher and a keen observer of human nature; "he spake also of beasts, and of fowl, and of creeping things, and of fishes" (1 Kings 4:33). Even the lowly ant did not escape his observation, and from it he drew this lesson on independent industry. Ants need no "bosses" to instruct them to scurry about collecting seeds and other food for their underground storehouses, in order to have it available in the "off season."

A "sluggard" is a person who moves as slowly as a "slug," or shell-less snail—hence a lazy person. "Meat" is from the Hebrew word *lechem*, which refers not just to animal flesh but food in general.

The point is not just a lesson on the value of hard work, but on being self-motivated.

II. The Way to Riches–or Poverty — 10:4-5

10:4 He becometh poor that dealeth with a slack hand: but the hand of the diligent maketh right.

5 He that gathereth in summer is a wise son: but he that sleepeth in harvest is a son that causeth shame.

For the "parallelism" to work in verse 4, the word "right" at the end of the line is better translated "wealth" (as in the NIV). The idea is that a diligent hand "makes right" or corrects the poverty brought on by slack or lazy behavior. The passage does not say that all poor people are lazy, but that laziness is a sure means of becoming poor.

Verse 5 applies the same principle to the father-son relationship, building again on traditional Eastern and Middle Eastern respect for older people in general and one's parents in particular. No farmer, having raised a son to know farming ways, would be proud to have others see that he turned out too lazy to bring in a good crop. Late summer is harvest time in Palestine to this day.

III. Warnings Against Sloth—13:4; 15:19; 18:9; 20:4

A. The lazy vs. the industrious, 13:4, 15:9

13:4 The soul of the sluggard desireth, and hath nothing: but the soul of the diligent shall be made fat.

15:19 The way of the slothful man is as an hedge of thorns: but the way of the righteous is made plain.

It is instructive to gather everything commendable these verses say against being slothful, lazy or a "sluggard" into one list; and everything commending industry in another, matching up the parallel elements. It would look like this:

The Sluggard	The Industrious
13:4 Desires much but gets nothing.	Grows sleek and "fat" (healthy).
15:9 Treads a treacherous path of thorns.	Walks a path free of obstacles.

The author perceives that a strange shift in proportions may happen in the mind of the slothful: their desires may increase with their laziness. This explains the intense resentment and envy many have-nots have toward the haves. The poor therefore often have a double burden. They must guard against bitterness toward the rich, as well as learning to live on less. (Of course the opposite often happens, too: the more we have, the more we may want.)

The imagery of a field bordered by a hedge is used in 15:9. Many such hedges were deliberately planted in thorns to discourage thieves and wild animals. The hard path of the lazy person is compared to that of someone losing his way at night and wandering into such a hedge, in contrast to the easier path the diligent have to walk.

B. Traits of the slothful, 18:9, 20:4

18:9 He also that is slothful in his work is brother to him that is a great waster.

20:4 The sluggard will not plow by reason of the cold; therefore shall he beg in harvest, and have nothing.

The author leaves for a moment the strict parallel writing he has been using, to give two specific examples or descriptions of the slothful or lazy person. First he is akin to a careless and wasteful person. A sluggard wastes one of the most valuable resources we have: time.

Time as we count it is a part of the created order. It did not exist until there were suns, moons, and planets whose regular rotating relationships mark off the years and seasons, months and days. Time is therefore a part of the creation God gave us to "subdue" in Genesis 1:28. A sluggard who habitually wastes huge amounts of time is like a desert-dweller who pours large amounts of precious water into the sand, only to die of thirst. Instead of making creation do their bidding, both become victims of the very order God told them to subdue.

(The same failure to subdue creation is also seen in those who allow their schedules to "subdue" them by becoming "workaholics," or always being "too busy" for quality and intentional use of time.)

IV. An Object Lesson—24:30-34

24:30 I went by the field of the slothful, and by the vineyard of the man void of understanding;

31 And, lo, it was all grown over with thorns, and nettles had covered the face thereof, and the stone wall thereof was broken down.

32 Then I saw, and considered it well: I looked upon it, and received instruction.

33 Yet a little sleep, a little slumber, a little folding of the hands to sleep:

34 So shall thy poverty come as one that travelleth; and thy want as an armed man.

Obviously the wise man is not warning against getting enough sleep to maintain health, but against sleeping virtually all of the time. His warning is couched in a vivid word picture or parable too plain to misunderstand. We are invited to imagine the scene unfolding in the following sequence.

A man walks along the road and observes a field overgrown with thorns, and with the wall—originally built to keep out intruders and predators—in a shambles. He knows the owner hasn't been ill, so he concludes correctly that he is slothful. Regardless of how much he may know or understand about other aspects of life, he obviously doesn't understand the wise use of time.

Proceeding down the way, the wise observer meditates on what he has just seen. His conclusion is that the owner of the field is so lazy he sleeps his life away. He may think he is "doing nothing"; but in fact he is actively inviting poverty to descend on him with steps as sure as those of a traveler, and rob him of his wealth as surely as though the assailant were an armed robber.

Because the work ethic praised in the book of Proverbs ordinarily produces wealth, the book supplements these reflections with certain other guidelines on gaining and using money. First, those with wealth are to share with the poor: "He that hath a bountiful eye shall be blessed; for he giveth of his bread to the poor" (22:9). Second, wealth is never to be gained wrongfully: "Better is a little with righteousness than great revenues without right" (16:8).

Third, riches are never to be the primary goal in life, as though we trust in them instead of God: "He that trusteth in his riches shall fall: but the righteous shall flourish as a branch" (11:28); "riches are not for ever" (27:24). Fourth, wealth is hardly the supreme value: "How much better is it to get wisdom than gold!" (16:16); "A good name is rather to be chosen than great riches, and loving favour rather than silver or gold" (22:1).

Evangelistic Emphasis

The selected proverbs for this lesson remind us of the importance of hard work and thorough preparation for the evangelistic outreach of the church. We rightly honor the visiting evangelists, the well known preachers, the gifted musicians who are up front in evangelistic crusades and revival meetings. Behind any effective evangelistic outreach there are many hours of preparation and follow up. Lists of prospects are prepared, letters sent, telephone calls made, rides arranged. The building must be prepared with adequate sound system, provision for music, worship center, greeters and ushers. Persons are recruited and trained as counselors.

After the outreach, follow up is planned carefully so every person making a new or renewed profession of faith is contacted by a church in the community, welcomed to Bible classes or prayer groups, nurtured in the faith, assimilated into the congregation. Materials are prepared or ordered in advance so new Christians have guidance for next steps. Apart from careful preparation and diligent invitation, only the faithful come. Apart from thorough follow up, the seeds are sown but there is no harvest in changed lives, no fruits in new disciples of Christ.

"The soul of the sluggard craves, and gets nothing." Good intentions are not enough. "The soul of the diligent is richly supplied." Preparation in prayer and hard work bring the rich harvest of souls.

Memory Selection

The way of a slothful man is as a hedge of thorns: but the way of the righteous is made plain.—*Proverbs 15:18*

While the context of the sage's advice is material prosperity, the admonition to work fits as well growth in the spiritual life. Undisciplined habits, no time for regular Bible study, irregular quiet times for prayer, infrequent sharing in public worship and the sacrament allow weeds to grow up. Resentments, anger, greed and jealousy choke out the fruits of the Spirit. While growth in grace is a gift of God, there is work for us to do.

We need to cultivate the space in our hearts as the dwelling place of God. We need to learn to keep silent so God can speak. We need to remove those obstacles to growth in the spirit. Such obstacles might include an overly busy schedule, feeding our mind on trash, cultivating a critical attitude toward others, becoming calloused towards others' needs, growing overly anxious about what others think of us. As with God's help we work at removing these thorns and weeds, the way we walk is level and plain.

Weekday Problems

Sally has a problem. She and her husband Jim have two teenage sons, a comfortable suburban home, two late model cars, a boat, a TV for each bedroom, and a computer for each of the boys. As a big sister she has always tried to look out for her younger sister, Betsy.

Betsy is married to Herb. They have two small girls. Herb is an insurance agent. He has changed companies frequently. He is always complaining that the boss expects too much, the work is too hard, the hours are too long. He works on commission. He only goes to work three or four days a week with plenty of time for golf at least twice a week. Their bills are often unmet. Betsy comes time and again to Sally for financial help, to pay for unexpected car repairs, high medical expenses and just last month for help with the rent. Sally believes if Herb worked at his job six days a week, or if Betsy went to work, they could handle their obligations.

Sally's husband Jim is a hard worker. In fact he works all the time. It's been six years since they have had a vacation. He doesn't take Saturdays off. He has not time to play ball or go camping with their sons. The boat stays unused in the car port.

Surely somewhere between Jim's addiction to work and Herb's aversion to work is a right balance.

* Should Sally keep bailing out Betsy's family financially?

* If Jim were less conscientious, had a job with lesser responsibility and smaller salary, a nine to five job, would Sally be willing to adjust to a simpler standard of living?

More Wisdom on Work

The only time some people work like a horse is when the boss rides them.

Bo: Why do you always wear dark glasses?
Joe: Because I can't bear to see my wife work so hard.

Dan: I'm so near-sighted I'm about to work myself to death.
Stan: What do your eyes have to do with it?
Dan: Why, I can't tell whether the boss is watching me or not, so I have to work all the time.

Sign at work: NEW POLICY. Effective immediately, in and around coffee breaks, lunch breaks, rest periods, joke-telling, ticket-selling, questions to the personnel office, personal phone calls, collecting for the United Way and rehashing the ball game, each employee is urged, sometime during the day, to take a work break.

This Lesson in Your Life

For the author of Proverbs, there is a positive value in work. He has disdain for the lazy person. Too much sleep, taking it easy, neglecting one's responsibility will lead to poverty (Prov. 6:10-11). The vineyard of the sluggard is overgrown with weeds, and he has only his own laziness to blame (Prov. 20:4). To neglect doing your share when you are able is close to robbing your brother. "One who is slack in work is close kin to a vandal" (Prov. 18:9). According to the sage, hard work is rewarded with plenty and laziness leads to poverty.

Paul echoes the call to work in his letter to the church at Thessalonica. Many were so expectant of the second coming of Christ in the immediate future that they gave up their regular jobs. He writes: "Anyone unwilling to work should not eat. For we hear that some of you are living in idleness, mere busybodies, not doing any work. Now such persons we command and exhort in the Lord Jesus Christ to do their work quietly and to earn their own living" (2 Thess.3:10-13).

For the wise sage of Proverbs, prosperity was sufficient motivation for hard work. Later, the Protestant Reformation, brought new motivation, and new dignity was conferred on common labor. Every person was called of God. For some that calling was fulfilled through the ordained priesthood. For others the calling (vocation) was answered as farmer, cook, teacher or parent. Through one's daily work the calling of God was being fulfilled. While work still had the purpose of providing for oneself and one's family, it was also seen as a means of working with God in the ongoing task of caring for God's creation and providing for God's children.

In our time discussion of work relates to welfare and to unemployment. In trying to break the "welfare cycle" some proposals would make payments to mothers with dependent children contingent on those mothers taking training and finding work. Another issue complicating the sage's simple warnings about "laziness" is that of massive displacement of workers, due to military bases closing down, plants shutting down or relocating. As industries shift to more automated processes, the need for workers is reduced, in the short run. Many drawing unemployment compensation or forced into early retirement would prefer to work. Age or lack of marketable skills leave them unemployed. They feel humiliated. Reared on a simple ethic that if you work hard, your work will be rewarded with prosperity, they find that their years of experience seem no longer needed, wanted, or appreciated.

While some in our society need to hear the admonition of the sage about the rewards of work and the consequences of laziness, others have made an idol of work. They are "workaholics." They seem never to take any time off, time for themselves, time for their families. In their drive to succeed they sacrifice family and health. In the natural desire for security, that goal of what is sufficient seems always to exceed what they accumulate. More and more is needed. They discover too late that their life has been all work. They have neglected some greater values. They have been absent, "working at providing for the family" during crucial years of growth.

For most in America, one's self-identity is bound up with his work. That's who they are.. a teacher, engineer, doctor, pastor. When that office ends, they are at loose ends. It is as though they have no meaning or purpose in life apart from their job, their company, their title.

Seed Thoughts

1. What can be learned from considering the ant?

Without official leaders, she prepares her food in summer and gathers her food in the harvest (Prov. 6:6-8).

2. What did the apostle Paul say about work in his letter to the Thessalonians?

Anyone unwilling to work should not eat (2 Thes. 3:10).

3. Do you think the sage giving advice to younger men was an "morning person" or a "night person"?

Likely a morning person, according to Proverbs 6:9: "How long will you lie there, A sluggard? When will you rise from your sleep?"

4. Of what saying of Ben Franklin do these proverbs about hard work and laziness remind you?

"Early to bed, early to rise, makes a man healthy, wealthy and wise."

5. What other well known adage provides contrary advice?

"All work and no play makes Jack a dull boy today."

1. What can be learned from considering the ant?

2. What did the apostle Paul say about work in his letter to the Thessalonians?

3. Do you think the sage giving advice to younger men was an "morning person" or a "night person"?

4. Of what saying of Ben Franklin do these proverbs about hard work and laziness remind you?

5. What other well known adage provides contrary advise?

6. What is the fruit of the spirit we should diligently cultivate?

7. What happens to those who are lazy or sleep on the job (Prov. 24:33-34)?

8. What happens to a lazy person who does not plow in season (Prov. 20:4)?

9. To whom does the sage compare one who is slack in his work (Prov. 18:9)?

10. What old hymn reflects the sage's view of work?

(Please turn page)

Without official leaders, she prepares her food in summer and gathers her food in the harvest (Prov. 6:6-8).

Anyone unwilling to work should not eat (2 Thes. 3:10).

Likely a morning person, according to Proverbs 6:9: "How long will you lie there, A sluggard? When will you rise from your sleep?"

"Early to bed, early to rise, makes a man healthy, wealthy and wise."

"All work and no play makes Jack a dull boy today."

"The fruit of the Spirit is love, joy, peace, patience, kindness, generosity, faithfulness, gentleness, and self control" (Gal. 5:22-23).

Poverty will come upon them (Prov. 24:33-34).

The harvest comes and there is nothing to be found (Prov. 20:4).

One who is slack in work is close kin to a vandal (or "brother to him who is a great waster," Prov. 18:9).

"Work for the night is coming, work through the morning hours / work for the night is coming, when man's work is done."

6. What is the fruit of the spirit we should diligently cultivate?

"The fruit of the Spirit is love, joy, peace, patience, kindness, generosity, faithfulness, gentleness, and self control" (Gal. 5:22-23).

7. What happens to those who are lazy or sleep on the job (Prov. 24:33-34)?

Poverty will come upon them (Prov. 24:33-34).

8. What happens to a lazy person who does not plow in season (Prov. 20:4)?

The harvest comes and there is nothing to be found (Prov. 20:4).

9. To whom does the sage compare one who is slack in his work (Prov. 18:9)?

One who is slack in work is close kin to a vandal (or "brother to him who is a great waster," Prov. 18:9).

10. What old hymn reflects the sage's view of work?

"Work for the night is coming, work through the morning hours / work for the night is coming, when man's work is done."

Helpful and Harmful Speech

Proverbs 11:12-13; 12:18; 13:3; 15:1-2, 23, 28; 16:24; 17:27; 21:23; 26:21, 28

11:12 He that is void of wisdom despiseth his neighbour: but a man of understanding holdeth his peace.

13 A talebearer revealeth secrets: but he that is of a faithful spirit concealeth the matter.

12:18 There is that speaketh like the piercings of a sword: but the tongue of the wise is health.

13:3 He that keepeth his mouth keepeth his life: but he that openeth wide his lips shall have destruction.

15:1 A soft answer turneth away wrath: but grievous words stir up anger.

2 The tongue of the wise useth knowledge aright: but the mouth of fools poureth out foolishness.

23 A man hath joy by the answer of his mouth: and a word spoken in due season, how good is it!

28 The heart of the righteous studieth to answer: but the mouth of the wicked poureth out evil things.

16:24 Pleasant words are as an honeycomb, sweet to the soul, and health to the bones.

17:27 He that hath knowledge spareth his words: and a man of understanding is of an excellent spirit.

21:23 Whoso keepeth his mouth and his tongue keepeth his soul from troubles.

26:21 As coals are to burning coals, and wood to fire; so is a contentious man to kindle strife.

28 A lying tongue hateth those that are afflicted by it; and a flattering mouth worketh ruin.

Memory Selection
Proverbs 15:1

17:27; 21:23; 26:21, 28

Devotional Reading
James 3:1-12

Background Scripture
Proverbs 11:12-13; 12:18;
13:3; 15:1-2, 23, 28; 16:24;

Printed Scripture
Proverbs 11:12-13; 12:18;
13:3; 15:1-2, 23, 28; 16:24;
17:27; 21:23; 26:21, 28

Teacher's Target

Lesson purpose: *To sample the book of Proverbs' teaching on the importance of speech, to urge its positive use, and to warn against its misuse.*

This lesson lends itself to discussion as group members recall examples from real life that illustrate the various kinds of speech mentioned. For 12:18, a group member may be able to share a verbal exchange from work in which someone was "pierced." Everyone should have a vivid illustration of gossip. You may even want to introduce the class by playing the old game of "Gossip." One person whispers a sentence quickly to another, then another, with each person required to pass along the whisper whether they understood it or not. Repeating or clarifying it is not allowed. By the time the whisper makes it around the group, it has little resemblance to what was originally said.

Children chant, "Sticks and stones may break my bones, but words can never hurt me." Of course this is whistling in the dark. Words both hurt and heal. Use this time to raise the consciousness of group members to the right use of the mighty tongue.

Lesson Introduction

In our last lesson we noted that the teaching of Proverbs on work echoes Genesis 1, when God worked to create the universe. Proverbs' teaching on the power of speech in this lesson is also grounded in the doctrine of creation. God *spoke* worlds into existence. Furthermore, the Jews' very lives were governed by the "ten words," or the Ten Commandments. God's word is living, active, and powerful (Heb. 5:12).

Because God's Word is powerful, and because people are created in His image, the book of Proverbs reminds us that our words have power, too. Its teachings on the good and bad use of the tongue are scattered throughout the book. Several of these passages are brought together in this lesson, organized under two categories— their power to hurt or heal, and the wisdom of not using too many words.

Teaching Outline	Daily Bible Readings
I. Words that Hurt or Heal 　A. Softness vs. strife, 12:18; 15:1-2; 　　27:21, 28 　B. Joy instead of sorrow, 15:23 　C. Sweets for the soul, 16:24 　D. Gossip vs. keeping confidences, 　　11:13 　E. Lying and flattering, 12:28; 26:28 II. Words that Are Left Unsaid 　A. Showing wisdom, 11:12; 17:27 　B. Preserving life, 13:3; 21:23 　C. Showing care, 15:28	**Mon.** An Apt Answer Is Good 　　*Proverbs 11:12-13; 12:18; 13:3;* 　　*15:1-2; 23, 28* **Tue.** Pleasant Words Like Honeycomb 　　*Proverbs 16:24; 17:27-28;* 　　*21:23; 26:20-21, 28* **Wed.** Let Yea Be Yea, Let Nay Be Nay 　　*Matthew 5:33-37* **Thu.** Words from an Abundant Heart 　　*Matthew 12:33-37* **Fri.** Speech Seasoned with Salt 　　*Colossians 4:2-6* **Sat.** Words Acceptable to God 　　*Psalm 19:7-14* **Sun.** Fire and Evil Words Spread 　　*James 3:1-12*

VERSE BY VERSE

I. Words that Hurt or Heal

A. Softness vs. strife, 12:18; 15:1-2; 26:21

12:18 There is that speaketh like the piercings of a sword: but the tongue of the wise is health.

15:1 A soft answer turneth away wrath: but grievous words stir up anger.

2 The tongue of the wise useth knowledge aright: but the mouth of fools poureth out foolishness.

26:21 As coals are to burning coals, and wood to fire; so is a contentious man to kindle strife.

For 12:18 to flow more smoothly in modern English we would need to say: "There is speaking that is like. . ." This verse and 15:1-2 are additional examples of "antithetical parallelism," with the thought in the first part of the sentence balanced by a second and opposite thought. Perhaps everyone has felt the sharp pain of words that pierce to the heart like a sword. It is easy for spouses and co-workers to lapse into careless communication habits that deliver such barbs. In sharp contrast are words that bring health and healing.

In 15:1-2 is a famous maxim that is easy to put to the test. The difficult part about turning away anger with a "soft answer" is maintaining the state of mind required to think about our words before they escape our lips. Unfortunately, the motivation in arguments is often to win, not to make peace.

The strife of 26:21 calls out a word picture of the power of glowing embers to catch anything it touches on fire. We use similar imagery when we speak of our words or temper being "hot." Nothing is more combustible or contagious than strife.

B. Joy instead of sorrow, 15:23

23 A man hath joy by the answer of his mouth: and a word spoken in due season, how good is it!

Here there is no parallelism; only the simple and pleasing reminder of the happiness someone's timely speech can bring. A young singer and guitar player—amateur, but highly accomplished— anted very much to perform for friends and family and other groups, but was too shy. It was the encouraging word of a minister's wife "in due season" that led him into a lifetime of making others joyful with his music.

C. Sweets for the soul, 16:24

16:24 Pleasant words are as an honeycomb, sweet to the soul, and health to the bones.

The thought of pleasing, nourishing words is continued by describing their effect in terms of tasty, healthful food. We are reminded of the *Chicken Soup for the Soul* series of books, filled with anecdotes that deliver positive words instead of negative. As for honey, it is not only sweet, but smooth going down—recalling the difference between the way compliments go down so much more smoothly than criticism. It should be noted, however, that compliments can be addictive, and constructive criticism, which is far better than flattery (see below), is often an opportunity for growth.

D. Gossip vs. keeping confidences, 11:13

13 A talebearer revealeth secrets: but he that is of a faithful spirit concealeth the matter.

Gossiping is one of the wise man's favorite targets. Some talebearing is malicious, repeated for the sole purpose of putting someone in a bad light. Although it is a little more innocent here, it is equally damaging. The verse describes the person who betrays a friend's confidence—a use of the tongue that is as destructive as gossiping. This warning is to be taken especially seriously when people share their problems with us. Even if repeating the conversation is to solicit additional help, we should not share the information without the person's permission.

E. Lying and flattering, 26:28

28 A lying tongue hateth those that are afflicted by it; and a flattering mouth worketh ruin.

Of all the sins of the tongue, lying is the most universally condemned—yet is strangely prevalent even among some believers. One common motive is to place oneself in a light more favorable than the truth. A minister who was scandalized at "large lies" once confessed that he had lapsed into the habit of telling "small" ones to his wife, usually to save face. When she asked "Did you mail that letter I gave you?" he would assure her that he had—even if it was still in his pocket. Then he would hurry to the post office!

It is interesting that flattery is condemned in the same breath as lying. The word used in the Greek translation of the Old Testament literally means "unroofed" or "homeless," referring to words that gush so far beyond reality that they know no bounds, and are strangers to the truth.

II. Words that Are Left Unsaid

A. Showing wisdom, 11:12; 17:27

11:12 He that is void of wisdom despiseth his neighbour: but a man of understanding holdeth his peace.

17:27 He that hath knowledge spareth his words: and a man of understanding is of an excellent spirit.

The tone now changes from warnings about using words wrongly to warnings against using them too freely. The "talkers" referred to here are those who are more glib than articulate, and who speak when they should be listening. The first half of 11:12 must refer to not knowing when to stop talking, since the second half poses speaking little as an opposite. Committing the offense of talking too much and thus "despising" the poor neighbor who must listen recalls Dennis the Menace, and the way he accosts his neighbor, Mr. Wilson, with more conversation than the poor man can bear.

In contrast to the person who reveals his ignorance by talking about how much he knows, the truly knowledgeable man is said in 17:27 to speak sparingly. The equally vivid verse 28, "Even a fool, when he holdeth his peace, is counted wise," was illustrated in the old movie "Being There." In the film, accidental events propel a not-quite-bright gardener into the limelight in Washington, D.C. He says almost nothing; when he says anything at all, it's about what is required to grow a garden. His reticence is taken for wisdom, and his talk of gardening for how to grow a nation—and the poor half-wit is elected president!

B. Preserving life, 13:3;21:23

13:3 He that keepeth his mouth keepeth his life: but he that openeth wide his lips shall have destruction.

21:23 Whoso keepeth his mouth and his tongue keepeth his soul from troubles.

Older adults can remember the poster from World War II: LOOSE TALK COSTS LIVES!—with a picture of a U.S. ship torpedoed and sunk by careless civilian talk about its destination. Gossip, flattery, lying, nagging, and carping criticism can also cost lives. On the other hand, a well-disciplined tongue refrains from destroying others, building them up instead.

While 13:3 promises destruction for those who maliciously injure others by their speech, those who "hold their tongue" save themselves from troubles. This is not just a promise of future punishment—vicious verbal attacks have a way of returning to destroy the attacker in this life: "A fool's mouth is his destruction, and his lips are the snare of his soul" (18:7).

C. Showing care, 15:28

15:28 The heart of the righteous studieth to answer: but the mouth of the wicked poureth out evil things.

None of the foregoing warnings about "stirring up strife" with our words are to be taken as a prohibition against disagreement. Honest disagreement over important issues must often be voiced. People who are too "nice" to disagree openly often bury their feelings, only to have them erupt more violently later.

This verse shows the balance that must be sought: we are to "study" — consider, weigh, think about—our words to each other, in contrast to allowing them to "pour out" with unchecked venom. How many family arguments eventually find the combatants saying, "I didn't mean what I said!" Yet what was said has floated out on the unforgiving air waves of communication, and cannot be called back. Basic respect for each other can help us to think before we speak.

Evangelistic Emphasis

No one is argued into the kingdom. As we seek to witness to our faith we can use too many words. Through these ancient proverbs we may hear a needed word from the Lord concerning our task to lead others to Christ.

If we would share the gospel, we must learn to listen. We need to know the concerns of others, their needs, their hurts and dreams. Only when we have listened can we relate the good news to them (Prov. 18:13).

We will not get far if we begin by belittling their faith, scorning their beliefs or trying to prove them wrong. Keeping silent and listening is more fruitful (Prov. 11:12).

We do a disservice when we fail to understand other people and what is important to them. Too often we turn them off from the very Christ we would share by spouting off our own opinions dogmatically (Prov. 18:20).

Too many words make the witness seem glib. It makes the witness seem more like a used car salesman eager to close the deal before the buyer discovers the defects of the car than a beggar telling another beggar where there is bread (Prov. 10:19; 16:24).

When we truly listen to another then we can present the good news in a way that speaks to his real need and concerns. "To make an apt answer is a joy to anyone, and a word in season, how good it is!" (Prov. 15:23).

Memory Selection

A soft answer turneth away wrath: but grievous words stir up anger.—*Proverbs 15:1*

When hard words come, words of criticism or words of anger, we are free to choose how we will respond. We tend to respond in kind. Another's angry words provoke our bitter response. Our bitter response is met with still harsher language. The conflict escalates.

There is another way. When we are controlled by a different Spirit within, we are not driven to hurt another as we have been hurt. Rather we see the person's anger as expressing a deeper hurt, sometimes having little to do with us at all. The angry insult may be a disguised cry for help. When we refuse to let ourselves be drawn into a futile exchange of angry taunts, other possibilities can emerge. A gentle word absorbs the hurt without response in kind. We can acknowledge the anger we hear in the words. That acknowledgment may free the person to deal at a deeper level with hurt, fear, resentment or grief. The loving response may open the way to a healthy dialogue where feelings too long hidden can be explored. The "soft answer" may start the process of healing.

Weekday Problems

Miss Jones was viewed as cranky both by the children and by the teachers. She never had a kind word for anyone. Her clothes were old and out of fashion. She worked well past the usual time of retirement. The other teachers avoided her. The students were afraid of her. When the principal retired and Miss Jones was appointed principal, matters grew even worse. A group of teachers complained to the school superintendent. When Mrs. Jones heard of their complaint, she was livid. She berated them in front of the students in the cafeteria.

One of the younger teachers, Phyllis, started praying for Miss Jones. It helped her see her in a new light—a lonely old woman in need of friends. Phyllis invited other teachers to pray for Miss Jones. They began to remember her birthday and other special days with cards and gifts. They went out of their way to include her at their table during lunch.

They learned that Miss Jones had gone into debt to help pay for critical surgery for a young niece. That explained why she continued to work and why she lived so frugally. As the teachers were kind to her, she opened up to them. A new atmosphere pervaded the school. The young teachers found a helpful mentor, a capable principal, a new friend.

"A soft anger turns away wrath but a harsh word stirs up anger" (Prov. 15:1).

Speaking of Speaking

The best way to save face is to keep the bottom part of it closed.

Trying to get a word in edgewise with some people is like trying to thread a sewing machine with the thing running.

There's nothing wrong with having nothing to say, unless you insist on saying it.

Cled: What is better than speaking several languages?
Fred: Keeping your mouth shut in one.

History repeats itself—just like that speaker.

Old Stewart speaks straight from the shoulder. Too bad his words don't start from higher up.

Flattery is like perfume. It's to be sniffed, not swallowed.

This Lesson in Your Life

"Rash words are like sword thrusts, but the tongue of the wise brings healing" (Prov. 12:18). Words have a great power, power to hurt or to heal, to cure or to bless, to destroy or to build up, to affirm or demean, to deal death or to bring life.

We see the destructive power of words in gossip. The character of persons is undermined. "For lack of wood the fire goes out and where there is no whisperer, quarreling ceases" (Prov. 26:20). According to the sage, to listen to the whisperer is every bit as bad as being one. "A gossip reveals secrets; therefore do not associate with a babbler" (Prov. 20:19). "An evil doer listens to wicked lips; and a liar gives heed to a mischievous tongue" (Prov. 17:4). The rabbis said gossiping slays three persons: the speaker, the spoken to, and the spoken of.

The words of parents have great effect upon their children. Some spend their lives trying to earn the blessing of a parent. Some parents may bless one but not another of their offspring. Children need the affirmation of those significant to them. When they feel only correction, reproof, condemnation those bad feelings are taken within. They come to believe they are "no good." The most effective teachers are those who draw out the best possibilities in each of their students. Genuine words of praise, frequent affirmations can make the difference. There is a great power in words to heal, and bring new life.

Persons in authority have influence on others they never realize. A word of praise can make the day. An angry word of reproof can send a person into depression. Persons who care especially for each other are vulnerable. They know where a person is most sensitive. Wounds inflicted by words can take a long time healing. Timely expressions of affirmation, appreciation and love can be more important than material gifts.

A preacher in the slums has children chant, "I am somebody." The words help create a new identity. Thomas Edison was expelled from school. School officials thought him too addled to learn. His mother believed in him. She persuaded him he had great gifts to share. Jesus saw in an impetuous, volatile, unstable Simon, son of John, a person capable of great strength. He called him Peter, the rock. Simon Peter then lived up to his name. Such is the power of words. Persons who have the privilege of preaching, of teaching children and youth, of sharing their faith with others are reminded by the ancient sage of the power of their words. What a tragedy if our friends come for help and we only pass on gossip about a mutual "friend"! What a tragedy if we have a chance to guide youth and we poison their minds with our fears and prejudices! What a tragedy if persons come to church seeking to find God and we try to impress them with our cleverness!

What a joy when healing comes through what is said! What a miracle when new life comes through what is spoken! What a glory when sinners are reconciled to God through the story of the cross, proclaimed in human words!

The renewing, life-giving Word of God has been passed on through human words, imperfect words. Our journey in discipleship is testimony to that. For our day and generation we are commissioned to tell and retell the story of the Bible, of the God who comes to save, of the God whose name is love. Sometimes through our stammering tongues, halting lips and inadequate words God's Word is heard. "A word in season, how apt it is" (Prov. 15:23). Thanks be to God.

Seed Thoughts

1. To what does James compare the tongue?

James compares the tongue to the very small rudder of a ship, which allows the pilot to direct the ship (James 3:4).

2. According to Proverbs 11:12, what is the mark of an intelligent person?

"An intelligent person remains silent."

3. What are the advantages of watching what you say and the risks of speaking too much (Prov. 13:3)?

"Those who guard their mouths preserve their lives; those who open wide their lips come to ruin" (Prov. 13:3).

4. What is the difference between the speech of the wise and the foolish (Prov. 15:2)?

"The tongue of the wise dispenses knowledge, but the mouths of fools pour out folly" (Prov. 15:2).

5. What brings joy to a man?

"To make an apt answer is a joy to anyone" (Prov. 15:23).

1. To what does James compare the tongue?

2. According to Proverbs 11:12, what is the mark of an intelligent person?

3. What are the advantages of watching what you say and the risks of speaking too much (Prov. 13:3)?

4. What is the difference between the speech of the wise and the foolish (Prov. 15:2)?

5. What brings joy to a man?

6. What is the difference in the speech of the righteous and the wicked (Prov. 15:28)?

7. What is like a honey comb (Prov. 16:24)?

8. What is like wood to fire (Prov. 26:21)?

9. Can flattery be overdone?

10. Is a word of rebuke ever in order?

(Please turn page)

James compares the tongue to the very small rudder of a ship, which allows the pilot to direct the ship (James 3:4).

"An intelligent person remains silent."

"Those who guard their mouths preserve their lives; those who open wide their lips come to ruin" (Prov. 13:3).

"The tongue of the wise dispenses knowledge, but the mouths of fools pour out folly" (Prov. 15:2).

"To make an apt answer is a joy to anyone" (Prov. 15:23).

"The mind of the righteous ponders how to answer but the mouth of the wicked pours out evil" (Prov. 15:28).

"Pleasant words are like a honeycomb, sweetness to the soul and health to the body" (Prov. 16:24).

"As charcoal is to hot embers and wood to fire, so is a quarrelsome person for kindling strife." (Prov. 26:21)

Yes. "It is not good to each much honey, so be sparing of complimentary words" (Prov. 25:27).

Yes. "He who rebukes a man will afterward find more favor than he who flatters with his tongue" (28:23). "Like a gold ring...is a wise reprover (25:12).

6. What is the difference in the speech of the righteous and the wicked (Prov. 15:28)?

"The mind of the righteous ponders how to answer but the mouth of the wicked pours out evil" (Prov. 15:28).

7. What is like a honey comb (Prov. 16:24)?

"Pleasant words are like a honeycomb, sweetness to the soul and health to the body" (Prov. 16:24).

8. What is like wood to fire (Prov. 26:21)?

"As charcoal is to hot embers and wood to fire, so is a quarrelsome person for kindling strife" (Prov. 26:21).

9. Can flattery be overdone?

Yes. "It is not good to each much honey, so be sparing of complimentary words" (Prov. 25:27).

10. Is a word of rebuke ever in order?

Yes. "He who rebukes a man will afterward find more favor than he who flatters with his tongue" (28:23). "Like a gold ring.. is a wise reprover (25:12).

Lesson 12

Slow to Anger

Proverbs 12:16; 14:17, 29; 15:18; 16:32; 19:11; 22:24-25; 25:28; 27:4; 29:20, 22

12:16 A fool's wrath is presently known: but a prudent man covereth shame.

14:17 He that is soon angry dealeth foolishly: and a man of wicked devices is hated.

29 He that is slow to wrath is of great understanding: but he that is hasty of spirit exalteth folly.

15:18 A wrathful man stirreth up strife: but he that is slow to anger appeaseth strife.

16:32 He that is slow to anger is better than the mighty; and he that ruleth his spirit than he that taketh a city.

19:11 The discretion of a man deferreth his anger; and it is his glory to pass over a transgression.

22:24 Make no friendship with an angry man; and with a furious man thou shalt not go:

25 Lest thou learn his ways, and get a snare to thy soul.

25:28 He that hath no rule over his own spirit is like a city that is broken down, and without walls.

27:4 Wrath is cruel, and anger is outrageous; but who is able to stand before envy?

29:20 Seest thou a man that is hasty in his words? there is more hope of a fool than of him.

22 An angry man stirreth up strife, and a furious man aboundeth in transgression.

Memory Selection
Proverbs 19:11

Devotional Reading
Matthew 5:21-26

Background Scripture
Proverbs 12:16; 14:17, 29;
15:18; 16:32; 19:11; 22:24-25;
25:28; 27:4; 29:20, 22

Printed Scripture
Proverbs 12:16; 14:17, 29;
15:18; 16:32; 19:11; 22:24-25;
25:28; 27:4; 29:20, 22

August 23

Teacher's Target

Lesson purpose: *To examine Proverbs' counsel on self-control, paying special attention to the importance of controlling anger.*

One Friday morning on a construction job, a bricklayer approached his foreman and asked for his weekly paycheck. "Too early in the day," the foreman replied gruffly. Exploding with rage, the bricklayer picked up a three-foot level and leveled the foreman with a swinging blow. Although other workmen stopped the fight, the foreman was left with an ugly gash in his head. The bricklayer got his check, but it was his last one.

You may want to introduce this lesson by asking group members to share similar incidents from their personal experience or reading—or incidents when such outbursts were avoided when someone was able to turn away wrath with a "soft answer." Supplement the discussion throughout the lesson with practical ways to implement the counsel to control our anger.

Lesson Introduction

The tone of the book of Proverbs' wise sayings on anger and self-control strikes a strange note among some people today. Many seem to believe that human emotions are "natural" forces that are largely uncontrollable. Sexual appetite, anger, envy, the spirit of vengeance, violence—such urges can only be dealt with defensively, not controlled, according to some conventional wisdom.

Powerful though these emotions are, Proverbs insists that they can be "ruled" or controlled. The primary emphasis here is on the "horizontal" or human effects of un-controlled passion. Yet the degree of choice and personal responsibility indicated in these passages also links our behavior with God's approval, not just human consequences.

The New Testament teaching in Ephesians 4:26 must be added. To say "be ye angry" indicates that not all anger is wrong. To add "and sin not" indicates both the possibility and the importance of controlling even justified wrath.

Teaching Outline	Daily Bible Readings
I. The Wisdom of Self-Control—12:16; 14:17, 29	**Mon.** Hot Tempers Stir Up Strife *Prov. 12:16; 14:17, 29; 15:28;16:32*
A. A window to the soul, 12:16	**Tue.** Don't Mingle with Hotheads *Prov. 19:11; 22:24-25; 25:28; 27:4; 29:20, 22*
B. A fool's folly, 14:17, 29	**Wed.** Shun Anger and Forsake Wrath *Psalm 37:1-9*
II. The Effects of Non-Control—15:18; 16:32; 19:11; 22:24-25; 25:28; 27:4; 29:20,22	**Thu.** Anger Can Lead to Murder *Matthew 5:21-26*
A. Stirring up trouble, 15:18,	**Fri.** Put Away Bitterness and Anger *Ephesians 4:25-32*
B. Loss of power and dignity, 16:32, 19:11, 22:24-25; 25:28	**Sat.** Be Clothed in Love, not Wrath *Colossians 3:5-17*
C. Loss of hope, 27:4; 29:20, 22	**Sun.** Be Quick to Hear, Slow to Anger *James 1:12-21*

VERSE BY VERSE

I. The Wisdom of Self-Control—12:16; 14:17, 29

A. A window to the soul, 12:16; 14:17

12:16 A fool's wrath is presently known: but a prudent man covereth shame.

14:17 He that is soon angry dealeth foolishly: and a man of wicked devices is hated.

The wise man says the thoughtless, immediate expression of rage is a window to the soul, and reveals its content to be foolish. In the Old Testament, a "fool" is first a person who rejects God (see Ps. 14:1). He is for that reason—not a lack of brain-power—someone who lacks good sense.

The Hebrew word used here for "fool" is pronounced *avil* or *evil*. Although this may be just a coincidence, some scholars think the term lies behind our word "evil" because of the connection in Scripture between morality and the rejection of God.

On the other hand, the wise restrain their anger and express it appropriately. The word translated "presently" means literally "in the day." That is, a fool reacts with rage at the very moment of a potentially upsetting occurrence. In contrast, a prudent or wise person is able to "cover the shame" of irrational wrath by taking time to "cool off."

Notice that the last part of verse 14 warns that the result of unrestrained anger is that people hate us. This focus on the down side of foolish behavior in this life, not just the threat of hell, is typical of the practical, this-worldly emphasis of Proverbs.

A youth of 17, seeking friendship, was attracted to a group of older hoodlums. At first, a kind of "honor among thieves" seemed to deliver the acceptance he needed. Soon, however, he was caught up in their criminal behavior. Instead of standing up for him as he expected, his new "friends" were only too quick to turn him in, to protect themselves.

B. A fool's folly, 29

29 He that is slow to wrath is of great understanding: but he that is hasty of spirit exalteth folly.

Now the wise man says that quickly exploding in rage is not only foolish but actually exalts (NIV "displays") folly. The fact is that those who give measured response to enraging situations instead of "flying off the handle" are more likely to be able to correct the situation—as 15:18 will now illustrate.

II. The Effects of Non-Control—15:18; 16:32; 19:11; 22:24, 25; 25:28; 27:4; 29:20,22

A. Stirring up trouble, 15:18

15:18 A wrathful man stirreth up strife: but he that is slow to anger appeaseth strife.

Just as James says (3:5-6), the tongue has the power to set huge fires; and angry words are a prime example. Uncontrolled anger is often the cause of riots, with one person's rage igniting the capacity for rage that lies just beneath the surface of so many. In contrast, those who are "slow to anger" have the ability to "pour oil on the water" (NIV "calm a quarrel").

B. Loss of power and dignity, 16:32, 19:11, 22:24-25; 25:28

16:32 He that is slow to anger is better than the mighty; and he that ruleth his spirit than he that taketh a city.

19:11 The discretion of a man deferreth his anger; and it is his glory to pass over a transgression.

22:24 Make no friendship with an angry man; and with a furious man thou shalt not go:

25 Lest thou learn his ways, and get a snare to thy soul.

25:28 He that hath no rule over his own spirit is like a city that is broken down, and without walls.

Notice the way that the illustration of walled cities in the ancient world provides a link between 16:32 and 25:28. Ironically, the word for "rule" in 16:32 also means "proverb," and in the plural is the name of the book of Proverbs. The connection is that a wise saying provides a single "ruling principle" for entering the many and varied life situations we face. Here, the "ruling principle" is that those who practice self-control or rule over their spirits are stronger than the violent who can invade a city by breaking down its walls. This is one of the greatest challenges of parents and teachers in our day: to model restrained and controlled behavior in ways that empower children to see that the strength required to control anger is more heroic and admirable than giving way to violence. Countless young people have been hurt and even killed for small wrongs that are responded to with flashing rage that indicates the failure to rule one's spirit.

This is the thrust of 19:11. The immediate and irrational venting of rage is a quality that is no higher than the animals. In contrast, the capacity to use discretion and defer anger is a distinguishing and even glorifying attribute of mankind. It is this capacity that gave rise to the advice to "count to 10" before saying anything when we're angry.

Again, 22:24-25 brings a very practical lesson on anger home to our everyday lives. We are admonished not to make friends with those who habitually display unrestrained anger, lest we pick up their habits. This is an illustration of a New Testament proverb: "Bad company corrupts good character" (1 Cor. 15:33, NIV).

Returning to issues confronting youth and today's society, many a young person has been caught up in gangs for quite understandable reasons, such as the sense of family and acceptance they have not felt at home, the need to belong. In many cases, they did not join a gang to participate in crimes and violence. Yet the companionship in the gang is so strong an evil influence that the best of young people are corrupted.

C. Loss of hope, 27:4; 29:20, 22

27:4 Wrath is cruel, and anger is outrageous; but who is able to stand before envy?

29:20 Seest thou a man that is hasty

in his words? there is more hope of a fool than of him.

22 An angry man stirreth up strife, and a furious man aboundeth in transgression.

Although 27:4 admits that "envy" can be an even more powerful force, wrath and anger are said to be "cruel" and "outrageous." As a matter of fact, some Bible words link both anger and envy with the idea of "burning." Just as dry grass cannot stand before a wind-whipped fire, what hope do ordinary people have of resisting explosive rage, which, like envy, burns out of control?

Again comparing these proverbs with James, the New Testament "book of Proverbs"—"behold how great a matter a little fire kindleth" (Jas. 3:5b).

In 29:20, 27, doubt is cast on the possibility of changing those whose anger is expressed hastily. Perhaps this is because they lack the mental/moral "equipment" to be receptive to change. When someone approaches them suggesting that they need to give more measured response to life's confrontations, they can only respond with haste—the very apparatus that is consuming them and others.

Evangelistic Emphasis

For one afflicted with an uncontrollable temper, the advice of the sages of Proverbs sounds impossible.

"Do you see someone who is hasty in speech? There is more hope for a fool than for anyone like that" (Prov. 29:20). "A fool gives full vent to anger but the wise quietly holds it back" (Prov. 29:11). "Like a city breached, without walls is one who lacks self control" (Prov. 25:28). To one who is enslaved by this habit the directives of Proverbs simply increase his frustration. No one knows better than he the destruction brought about by his short fuse. His hot temper keeps him in hot water. His angry words have caused him to hurt people he deeply loves. His uncontrolled temper tantrums have cost him his job. But how can he change? He needs more than someone to show him the way. He needs a Savior to change his heart, enabling him to walk in a new way.

The good news of the gospel is that we can be "new creatures in Christ." There is a power greater than our anger, hurt, and fear. There is a grace to make us whole. The message to one whose best years are being wasted with uncontrollable anger, fits of temper, continual strife is the good news of a new birth. The love of God made known in Christ has to do not only with life after death but also with the death of the old self and the creation of a new being. The blind are given sight; the oppressed are set free; the sick are made well; wild passions can be controlled, and harnessed to God's purposes.

Memory Selection

The discretion of a man deferreth his anger; and it is his glory to pass over a transgression. —*Proverbs 19:11*

"The discretion of a man defers anger." One modern translation reads, "Those with good sense are slow to anger.." A person's greatest fulfillment lies not in getting even. Rather true glory is to reflect the image of God, and like God be "slow to anger and plenteous in mercy (Ps. 103:8). Humans are at their highest when they are able to forgive, as God forgives. "Be merciful just as your Father is merciful" (Luke 7:36).

The capacity to control response is a sign of strength, not of weakness. When persons are consumed with the desire to get even, they waste their lives away. It is a far greater gift to be able "to pass over a transgression." We are made in the image of God (Gen. 1:26). We reflect this divine glory when we do not allow momentary impulses to control us. Rather, through the Spirit of God dwelling in us, we find the grace to overlook and to forgive. God enables us to overcome the enmity and to be reconciled.

Weekday Problems

J. Wallace Hamilton relates the story of the gifted Afro-American tenor Roland Hayes. As a boy he heard an old, illiterate preacher tell of Jesus before Pilate. "No matter how angry the crowd got, Jesus never said a mumberlin' word, not a word." Years later the famous Roland Hayes stood before a Nazi audience in Berlin's Beethoven Hall. The audience was hostile, ugly, scornful of a black man daring to sing at the center of Aryan culture. He was greeted with a chorus of Nazi hisses, growing louder and louder.

For ten minutes Hayes stood there in silence at the piano, resentment swelling up in him like an irresistible tide. Then he remembered the sermon long ago—"He never said a mumberlin' word, not a word." He shouted back no words born in anger; he kept his head. He stood there and prayed, silently, and the quiet dignity of his courage conquered the savage spirits in his audience. In a hushed pianissimo he began to sing a song from Schubert. He won, without so much as a "mumberlin word."

"He that is slow to anger is better than the mighty, and he that ruleth his spirit than he that taketh a city.'

Good and Mad

Tired of being billed for a book he didn't buy, a customer angrily wrote the book dealer: "I never ordered this book. If I did, you didn't send it. If you did, I didn't receive it. If I got it, I paid for it. If I didn't, I won't."

The irate tourist pounded on the door of the motel manager's apartment at midnight. "This room's too small!" he said, fuming. "First, when I stuck the key in the lock I broke the window. Then when I closed the door, the doorknob was in bed with me."

My wife stays mad at me all the time. For my birthday she gave me two ties. I wore one of them the next day and she hollered, "What's the matter? You don't like that other tie?"

Ma: Pa, why did you spank little Billy?
Pa: Because I'm mad about the report cards he brings home.
Ma: But he doesn't get his report card until tomorrow.
Pa: I know, but I'll be out of town then.

This Lesson in Your Life

Often our anger is uncontrolled. Anger in a baby is a normal sign. When hungry, frustrated, unable to instantly have what he wants, the infant gets angry. Some children learn to get their way by throwing temper tantrums. Some carry this habit into adulthood, flying into a rage at the slightest provocation. J. Wallace Hamilton recalls the story of Winston Churchill. He once listened to a hot-tempered, raving, ranting tirade directed against him by an opponent whose mouth worked faster than his mind. At the end of it Churchill rose and said: "Our honorable colleague should, by now, have trained himself not to generate more indignation than he has the capacity to withhold." The colleague could profit by the sage's advice: "Whoever is slow to anger has great understanding, but one who has a hasty temper exalts folly." (Prov. 14:29)

There is, however, a constructive and important role for anger, spiritually dedicated. We see Jesus in the temple, angry that his Father's house, intended to be a house of prayer for all people, had been made into a den of thieves. He drove out the merchants and the money changers. It is no virtue not to feel deeply about anything. It is a waste of a God given capacity of anger when all that stirs us up is some petty inconvenience, or something which threatens our comfort. An old saying puts it: "You can tell the size of a man by the size of the thing that makes him mad." J. Wallace Hamilton insists that stormy emo-tions are divinely planted; they are nature's way of mobilizing our forces for the fight. They must not be destroyed nor suppressed but harnessed, put to use, consecrated to the work of the kingdom of God.

Anger is not always the opposite of love; often it is love's clearest expression. When we see systems destroying God's children, when we see other profiting by exploiting the weaknesses of others, when we see the tragic waste of human life, when we see children hungry when there is food enough for all, we ought to get angry. That anger can be focused to correcting evil and harnessed to bringing justice. Moses was angry with the mistreatment of the Hebrew slaves; Jesus was angry as he stood in the Temple Court. Lincoln was angry that day in New Orleans when he saw a slave woman being sold at auction. Lincoln stood there, tall and gaunt and furious. He vowed, "That's wrong, and if I ever get a chance to hit it, I'll hit it hard."

Hamilton recalls an incident in the life of Robert E. Lee. After the Civil War, Lee was approached by advocates of the infamous Louisiana Lottery. He sat in his rocking-chair, listening to their proposition. They said they wanted no money from him, only the use of his name—and for that they would make him rich. Lee straightened up in his chair, buttoned his old gray tunic and thundered, "Gentlemen, I lost my home in the war, I lost my fortune in the war. I lost everything in the war except my name. My name is not for sale, and if you fellows don't get out of here I'll break this crutch over your heads."

Seed Thoughts

1. Who is better than the mighty, than one who captures a city (Prov. 16:32)?

"One who is slow to anger is better than the mighty, and one whose temper is controlled than one who captures a city."

2. Where lies the glory of a human being (Prov. 19:11)?

It is the glory (of those with good sense) to overlook an offense, to pass over a transgression.

3. Who is like a city broken into, left without walls (Prov. 25:28)?

One who lacks self-control is like a city breached, without walls.

4. Why should you not make friends with those given to anger or associate with hotheads (Prov. 22:23)?

Because you may learn their ways and entangle yourself in a snare (Prov. 22:24).

5. How do fools respond to an insult?

They show their anger at once (Ps. 12:16).

---

1. Who is better than the mighty, than one who captures a city (Prov. 16:32)?

2. Where lies the glory of a human being (Prov. 19:11)?

3. Who is like a city broken into, left without walls (Prov. 25:28)?

4. Why should you not make friends with those given to anger or associate with hotheads (Prov. 22:23)?

5. How do fools respond to an insult?

6. How do the prudent respond to an insult?

7. In ancient times it was said: "You shall not murder." How does Jesus go beyond the old law (Matt. 5:21-22)?

8. What is Paul's advice about anger (Eph. 4:26)?

9. When and how did Jesus express his anger?

10. When and how did Jesus control his anger?

(Please turn page)

"One who is slow to anger is better than the mighty, and one whose temper is controlled than one who captures a city."

It is the glory (of those with good sense) to overlook an offense, to pass over a transgression.

One who lacks self-control is like a city breached, without walls.

Because you may learn their ways and entangle yourself in a snare (Prov. 22:24).

They show their anger at once (Ps. 12:16).

They ignore an insult (Ps. 12:16).

"But I say to you if you are angry ... you will be liable to judgment; and if you insult a brother or sister, you will be liable to the council."

"Be angry but do not sin; do not let the sun go down on your anger."

When he saw how the merchants and money-changers had profaned the temple, He overturned their tables and drove them out (Matt 21:12-13).

On the cross he prayed for those who taunted and persecuted him. "Father, forgive them, for they know not what they do" (Luke 23:34).

6. How do the prudent respond to an insult?

They ignore an insult (Ps. 12:16).

7. In ancient times it was said: "You shall not murder." How does Jesus go beyond the old law (Matt. 5:21-22)?

"But I say to you if you are angry with a brother or sister you will be liable to judgment; and if you insult a brother or sister, you will be liable to the council."

8. What is Paul's advice about anger (Eph. 4:26)?

"Be angry but do not sin; do not let the sun go down on your anger."

9. When and how did Jesus express his anger?

When he saw how the merchants and money-changers had profaned the temple, He overturned their tables and drove them out (Matt 21:12-13).

10. When and how did Jesus control his anger?

On the cross he prayed for those who taunted and persecuted him. "Father, forgive them, for they know not what they do" (Luke 23:34).

Wisdom for Family Relationships

Proverbs 4:1-5; 6:20; 10:1; 15:27; 18:22; 19:18; 22:6; 31:26-28

4:1 Hear, ye children, the instruction of a father, and attend to know understanding.

2 For I give you good doctrine, forsake ye not my law.

3 For I was my father's son, tender and only beloved in the sight of my mother.

4 He taught me also, and said unto me, Let thine heart retain my words: keep my commandments, and live.

5 Get wisdom, get understanding: forget it not; neither decline from the words of my mouth.

6:20 My son, keep thy father's commandment, and forsake not the law of thy mother:

10:1 The proverbs of Solomon. A wise son maketh a glad father: but a foolish son is the heaviness of his mother.

15:27 He that is greedy of gain troubleth his own house; but he that hateth gifts shall live.

18:22 Whoso findeth a wife findeth a good thing, and obtaineth favour of the Lord.

19:18 Chasten thy son while there is hope, and let not thy soul spare for his crying.

22:6 Train up a child in the way he should go: and when he is old, he will not depart from it.

31:26 She openeth her mouth with wisdom; and in her tongue is the law of kindness.

27 She looketh well to the ways of her household, and eateth not the bread of idleness.

28 Her children arise up, and call her blessed; her husband also, and he praiseth her.

Memory Selection
Proverbs 22:6

Devotional Reading
Psalm 128:1-6

Background Scripture
Proverbs 4:1-5; 6:20; 10:1; 15:27; 18:22; 19:18; 22:6; 31:26-28

Printed Scripture
Proverbs 4:1-5; 6:20; 10:1; 15:27; 18:22; 19:18; 22:6; 31:26-28

August 30

Teacher's Target

Lesson purpose: *To explore, and encourage the application of, the book of Proverbs' advice on family relationships.*

One of the most frequent comments on life in America is that the traditional family structure has broken down. The thoughtful teacher will not merely join this chorus, but will be aware of members of the group whose own families have been disrupted by divorce, abandonment, and abuse. Care will also need to be exercised to include any singles in the discussion. After all, all Christians are part of God's family, through Christ (see Matt. 12:46-50).

The counsel on family relationships in this lesson represents some of God's teaching on ideal family relationships. As long as we live in a world that is less than ideal, there will be a gap between goals and practice in the family. Everyone can benefit from this encouragement to work toward the ideal, regardless of his family situation.

Lesson Introduction

The Bible's teachings on family relationships are rooted in God's Covenant with Father Abraham. God promised, "I will establish my covenant between me and thee and thy seed after thee in their generations" (Gen. 17:7). Later, God expressed confidence that Abraham would "command his children and his household after him, and they shall keep the way of the Lord" (18:19). Thus, parents were to teach God's Law to their children, keeping it before them by posting some version of it on the gates and door posts of the house (Deut. 11:19).

It is important to keep this larger framework in mind as specific relationships are discussed in this lesson. Instead of the often radical independence and solitary status of many family members in today's society, families of faith have a covenant with each other and a commitment to God to carry on the faith. Of course this covenant includes singles and the elderly—not just parents with children.

Teaching Outline	Daily Bible Readings

I. Responsibility of Children—4:1-5; 6:20; 10:1
  A. Hearing and obeying, 4:1-2; 6:20
  B. Acting like a son, 4:3-5; 10:1
II. Role of Parents—15:27; 18:22; 19:18; 22:6
  A. Family matters, 15:27
  B. The advantages of marriage, 18:22
  C. On the discipline of children, 19:18; 22:6
III. Reliable Mothers—31:26-28
  A. Wise love, 26
  B. Industriousness, 27
  C. Reward, 28
	Mon. Pass Along Wisdom
	    Proverbs 4:1-5; 6:20
	Tue. Train Children in the Right Way
	    Proverbs 10:1; 22:6; 30:17; 31:26-29
	Wed. Home and Family, Gifts of God
	    Psalm 128:1-6
	Thu. Rituals of a Family in Nazareth
	    Luke 2:39-52
	Fri. Grandchildren Crown the Aged
	    Proverbs 17:1-6
	Sat. Family Members in the Church
	    1 Timothy 5:1-8
	Sun. The True Family of Jesus
	    Matthew 12:46-50

VERSE BY VERSE

I. Responsibility of Children—4:1-5; 6:20; 10:1

A. Hearing and obeying, 4:1-2; 6:20

1 Hear, ye children, the instruction of a father, and attend to know understanding.

2 For I give you good doctrine, forsake ye not my law.

6:20 My son, keep thy father's commandment, and forsake not the law of thy mother:

In our society we generally think of sending our children to school to learn. Among the ancient Hebrews, imparting learning was first the responsibility of the home. Also in our time, we tend to blame the school when our children do not learn. Here the responsibility is on the children.

Note the words in these verses that imply this arrangement: instruction and understanding (4:1); doctrine and law (4:2); commandment and, again, law (6:20). The word for "law" in these verses is torah—the same word used for the Ten Commandments, and for the first five books of the Old Testament. This indicates both that a large part of what the parents were to teach their children was of a religious nature, and that the children were expected to take their parents' teaching seriously, as the words of God to them through their father and mother.

It is also important to note the emphasis here on the role of the father in imparting wisdom and instruction to the children. Far from leaving the instruction of the children to his wife, he was to be the "lead teacher" in the family.

B. Acting like a son, 4:3-5; 10:1

3 For I was my father's son, tender and only beloved in the sight of my mother.

4 He taught me also, and said unto me, Let thine heart retain my words: keep my commandments, and live.

5 Get wisdom, get understanding: forget it not; neither decline from the words of my mouth.

10:1 The proverbs of Solomon. A wise son maketh a glad father: but a foolish son is the heaviness of his mother.

The personal pronouns "I" and "me" in verses 2-4 reminds us that "Wisdom" is often personified in Proverbs 1–9 (see Lesson Introduction, Lesson 9). Here, "Wisdom" (or, possibly, Solomon) backs up the commandment for children to listen to parental instruction by saying that was true when Wisdom was a child as well. It is the way the generations are supposed to work. It is the way for a "tender" or young child to grow in understanding.

In 10:1, carrying on the tradition of accepting instruction from one's parents is said to make them glad. Any parent who has had this experience knows the feeling of pride in their

513

children's accomplishments—just as those whose children have strayed struggle with a sense of disappointment.

II. Role of Parents—15:27; 18:22; 19:18; 22:6

A. Family matters, 15:27

15:27 He that is greedy of gain troubleth his own house; but he that hateth gifts shall live.

In the ancient Jewish family structure, just as it is in most families today, it was the father's responsibility to be the family's primary bread-winner. Here, however, is a warning that his role is far broader as well. He is not to be so greedy that he accepts bribes (as the NIV translates "gifts"), thus bringing the family into disrepute. In our day we might expand the principle even more, noting that "workaholic" and other "absentee" fathers also bring trouble to the family. It betrays a skewed sense of values when such men respond that they are absent from their families in order to get gain for them. They need far more than financial support.

B. The advantages of marriage, 18:22

18:22 Whoso findeth a wife findeth a good thing, and obtaineth favour of the Lord.

Since, as has been noted, God's Covenant was administered through the family unit in the Old Testament, the normal expectation was for a man and a woman to marry and have children. Now, all people, not just members of Jewish families, may be a part of "the Israel of God" (Gal. 6:16). The New Covenant therefore takes on a more individualistic tone, and we find the apostle Paul not only remaining unmarried, but counseling others to consider staying single themselves (1 Cor. 7:8, 38).

Even so, couples who have experienced the joys of the most intimate of human relationships can say a resounding "Amen!" to the wise man's observation that finding a good spouse is "a good thing." Of course marriage is also capable of producing more strife than any other relationship. In the very next chapter, Solomon will preface the sentiment in 18:22 with a warning (from a male's point of view!): "The contentions of a wife are a continual dropping . . . (but) a prudent wife is from the Lord" (19:13, 14).

C. On the discipline of children, 19:18; 22:6

19:18 Chasten thy son while there is hope, and let not thy soul spare for his crying.

22:6 Train up a child in the way he should go: and when he is old, he will not depart from it.

"Chastening," in the biblical view, included occasional doses of "hickory tea"—hence the reference to crying in 19:18. As many a parent has told the child, spanking "hurts me more than it does you"; so Solomon encourages them not to let the child's crying keep them from doing what might save his life while he is young enough to benefit from it.

A more famous passage is 23:13-14, from which another proverb, "spare the rod and spoil the child," was created. When the wise man says such children "will not die," he obviously has in mind the rational, measured punishment of a loving parent—not the horror stories we sometimes hear today in which beatings harm or even kill a child.

The promise in 22:6 that a child will not depart from "the way he should go" if he is trained right is a powerful incentive for parents to do their best. Unfortunately, the passage has also caused some guilt in parents who did their best, only to have children depart from "the way." It is a general rule—one that is subject to adjustment by societal forces, the child's own will, and other influences over which parents have little or no control.

III. Reliable Mothers—31:26-28

A. Wise love, 26

26 She openeth her mouth with wisdom; and in her tongue is the law of kindness.

Although Proverbs 31 was written by one "King Lemuel," instead of Solomon, it has always been accepted as a part of Scripture. Its famous description of a "virtuous woman" (vs. 10) has caused not a little guilt among women who don't sew and aren't very good cooks! Actually, the passage is about "a wife of noble character" (NIV), which may be shown today by means that may differ from the household duties of most women in Solomon's day.

The essential requirement is that she be wise and loving. Despite earlier references to the importance of disciplining children, this verse shows a remarkable sensitivity for children's self-concept. The ideal mother is to allow kindness to be typical of what comes from her mouth, resisting the temptation to allow her tongue to lay down a "law" of constant criticism that can tear down self-esteem.

B. Industriousness, 27

27 She looketh well to the ways of her household, and eateth not the bread of idleness.

The modern woman may not bake bread, but she is still to be characterized by industry instead of laziness. The fact that her domain is said to be the "household" indicates the high value the Bible places on a woman's skills in that arena. It must also be noted that the skills of this "ideal mother" also extend to real estate transactions! (See vs. 16.) Yet it is now documented that the modern tendency—and in many cases the necessity—of women working outside the home when their children are still young does not provide the ideal environment for child-rearing.

C. Reward, 28

28 Her children arise up, and call her blessed; her husband also, and he praiseth her.

This reliable woman knows also the sense of accomplishment and justifiable pride when her home-making skills are appreciated by the entire family. The failure of husbands and other family members to express such appreciation has been at the root of more than one mother's feelings of "burn-out."

Evangelistic Emphasis

Parents have a great responsibility for making disciples. In the early years there is no greater influence than parents on shaping the faith of their children. Through the fragile bridge of their love and care the love of God moves. In their own imperfect lives, God's love is made incarnate. That love is not an indulgent love. Discipline may at times be the most appropriate expression of love. Discipline is not to relieve the anger of the parent but to help the child improve. Even more important are words of encouragement, expressions of affirmation, ways of showing love.

There is no more important task in the congregation than the task of teaching children and youth. In many denominations the primary source of persons making a profession of faith is from the Sunday School. When Sunday School attendance and enrollment declines, then church decline cannot be far behind.

Seen in this light, teaching is not a burden, assumed out of duty, or guilt, or because no one else will do it. It is a sacred privilege to help to shape young, pliable lives. It is worthy of the best we can give to it.

No matter how well we are prepared, how creatively we plan, what children recall from Sunday School is most often not the lesson, but the teacher, the teacher who cared enough to be there every Sunday, who cared enough to expect good things of them, one who even cared enough to discipline.

Memory Selection

Train up a child in the way he should go: and when he is old, he will not depart from it.—*Proverbs 22:5*

Not many recognize the name of Sarah Cannon. But "Minnie Pearl" is well known as a star of the Grand Ole Opry. She and her husband were life long and active members of their church in Nashville, TN. She reflects on her childhood. "For me going to church was as normal as going to school. If we stayed home from school, we took castor oil. If we stayed home from church, we took castor oil. In my home it was just as important to go to church as to go to school."

While not many would recommend castor oil, it might in fact double Sunday School attendance. But young Sarah Canon was taught that learning to read and write was no more important than learning of God through Jesus. Her parents were concerned that she not only know how to walk but were concerned about where she was walking to. What she became as a faithful member of the church and a gracious witness to Christ gladdening the hearts of America began back in her home where Sunday School and church were a regular part of every Sunday.

Weekday Problems

A college boy, home from a distant campus for the summer, was asked by his pastor what impressed him most during his year away at school. Instead of describing his classes and professors, the boy said, "Last weekend, when my parents came to drive me home."

The college student went on to describe how his father and mother and driven a great distance and had taken a motel room some distance from the campus for the night. After a late dinner, the boy and his parents had returned to the motel room to visit and watch television. The boy became engrossed in the late movie, the parents stretched out on one double bed and the boy on the other. After the program they noticed how late it was and commented on how far it was for the boy to return to his dormitory. The boy thought to himself how easy it would be to crawl under the covers of that big double bed. How would anyone in the motel ever know?

To the boy's surprise, the father got up, put on his shoes and coat, picked up his wallet , then walked down to the motel office to pay the extra three dollars. The boy settled into bed wiser for having seen how his father lived out the honesty and integrity he talked about. The father resisted the subtle temptation, even though the family could have used the three dollars. The college student concluded, "That's what impressed me most during the entire time I was away." (Adapted from Frank Meade.)

Training up a child in the way he should go involves the way we live every day.

All in the Family

Children are nuts these days. I have a child who will be 10 next year . . . if I let him.

The growing rate of juvenile delinquency indicates that many parents aren't getting to the seat of the problem.

Dad to daughter: What's wrong, honey? You usually tie up the phone for hours, but this time you only talked 30 minutes. How come?
Daughter: I got the wrong number.

(This one really happened:)
Daughter, sitting on Dad's lap while playing with a mirror: Dad, did God make you?
Dad: Of course he did. And He made you, too.
Daughter: Well, He seems to be doing much better work lately.

Jed: Your sister is spoiled, isn't she?
Ted: Nah, that's the perfume she's wearing.

517

This Lesson in Your Life

John Westerhoff stresses the crucial role of the family as the chief agency by which the Christian faith is transmitted. "Whatever the church does is only a supplement to what parents live and share with their children."

The primary teachers of the Bible are the parents. The stories need to be told and retold. The stories of the Bible can be a part of that rich deposit you place in your childhood memory bank.

Do you have Bibles in your home? Are they dusty? Are they often read? Are they well marked? Do you read the Bible when you are by yourself? Do you read it aloud with other members of your family?

Westerhoff writes that we should not focus on how we can make children Christians but how we can be Christians with our children. If we really want our children to grow in Christian faith, we need to spend more time working at our own growth in the faith. Faith cannot be given to a child; it can only be shared with him or her.

Our teaching is most effective by example. It is well if you can recite the ten commandments. It will be even more effective if you keep them. All a father's preaching on telling the truth is nullified when he tells his child, "Just tell them I'm not home." All the literature on drug abuse is not as effective as a parent who lives a drug free life.

Robert Fulghum advises his son, now a new father: "Don't worry that they never listen to you; worry that they are always watching you."

Josh Billings modifies the proverb just a bit: "Train up a child in the way he should go . . . and walk there yourself once in a while."

Character is not so much taught as caught.

Children are nurtured through prayer and celebration in the home. Every common meal is a time to give thanks. Major events of life, birthdays, first driver's license, graduation, weddings, births and deaths are times for a family to pray together.

Traditions and rituals help a family to mark the church seasons. Many families use the Advent wreath during the weeks before Christmas. Each child can participate in that activity. The action of the lighting of the candles may well precede an understanding of it. Later the tradition and its meaning may help link that holy season with the coming of the Savior. Times of prayer, planned, regular or spontaneous, help provide that occasion for the family to look together in the same direction toward God.

Stanley Hauerwas writes that it isn't enough to welcome children into our families and societies; we must also be willing to initiate them into what we think is true and good about human existence. For example, we should not admire religious or non-religious parents who fail to educate their children in the parents' convictions. It is a false and bad-faith position to think we can or should raise our children to make up their own minds when they grow up. Children are not without values today. All parents are charged with forming their children's lives according to what they know best.

"Train up a child in the way he should go and when he is old he will not depart from it."

Seed Thoughts

1. What makes a glad father (Prov. 10:1)?

A wise son makes a glad father.

2. Who is a sorrow to his mother (Prov. 10:1)?

A foolish son is a sorrow to his mother.

3. What is the result of "training up a child in the way he should go" (Prov. 22:6)?

"When he is old he will not depart from it."

4. What is the attitude of the sage toward parental discipline of children?

The sage believes discipline is an expression of love. "He who spares the rod hates his son, but he who loves him is diligent to discipline him" (Prov. 13:24).

5. What other proverbs speak of discipline?

Proverbs 29:15; 20:30; 22:15; 19:18; 29:17; 23:13; 23:14.

---

1. What makes a glad father (Prov. 10:1)?

2. Who is a sorrow to his mother (Prov. 10:1)?

3. What is the result of "training up a child in the way he should go" (Prov. 22:6)?

4. What is the attitude of the sage toward parental discipline of children?

5. What other proverbs speak of discipline?

6. What brings shame upon a father (Prov. 28:7)?

7. Who is more precious than jewels (Prov. 31:10)?

8. What does a "good wife" do, according to Proverbs 31:10-31?

9. Who calls her blessed (Prov. 31:28)?

10. What is her attitude toward the poor and needy (Prov. 31:20)?

(Please turn page)

A wise son makes a glad father.

A foolish son is a sorrow to his mother.

"When he is old he will not depart from it."

The sage believes discipline is an expression of love. "He who spares the rod hates his son, but he who loves him is diligent to discipline him" (Prov. 13:24).

Proverbs 29:15; 20:30; 22:15; 19:18; 29:17; 23:13; 23:14.

"He who keeps the law is a wise son, but a companion of gluttons shames his father."

"A good wife who can find? She is far more precious than jewels."

She buys a field and plants it (v.16), she prepares the meals (v. 15), she shops around in the market (v.14), she makes her clothes and sells them (v. 22, 24).

Her children and her husband.

"She opens her hand to the poor, and reaches out her hands to the needy."

6. What brings shame upon a father? (Prov. 28:7).

"He who keeps the law is a wise son, but a companion of gluttons shames his father."

7. Who is more precious than jewels? (Prov. 31:10).

"A good wife who can find? She is far more precious than jewels."

8. What does a "good wife" do, according to Proverbs 31:10-31?

She buys a field and plants it (v.16), she prepares the meals (v. 15), she shops around in the market (v.14), she makes her clothes and sells them (v. 22, 24).

9. Who calls her blessed? (Prov. 31:28)

Her children and her husband.

10. What is her attitude toward the poor and needy? (Prov. 31:20).

"She opens her hand to the poor, and reaches out her hands to the needy."